ROCK CLIMBING
SMITH ROCK STATE PARK

A Comprehensive Guide to More Than 1,800 Routes

Second Edition

Alan Watts

FALCONGUIDES

GUILFORD, CONNECTICUT
HELENA, MONTANA
AN IMPRINT OF THE GLOBE PEQUOT PRESS

FALCONGUIDES®

Copyright © 1992, 2010 by Alan Watts

All interior photos, topos, and maps by Alan Watts unless otherwise indicated.
Text design: Casey Shain
Layout: Sue Murray
Project editor: John Burbidge

Library of Congress Cataloging-in-Publication data
Watts, Alan.
  Rock climbing Smith Rock State Park : a comprehensive guide to more than 1,700 routes
/ Alan Watts. — 2nd ed.
       p. cm.
  Rev. ed. of: Climber's guide to Smith Rock. 1992.
  Includes index.
  ISBN 978-0-7627-4124-3
  1. Rock climbing—Oregon—Smith Rock State Park. 2. Smith Rock State Park (Or.)—
Guidebooks. I. Watts, Alan. Climber's guide to Smith Rock. II. Title.
  GV199.42.O72S769 2009
  796.522309795'87—dc22

                                                                                    2009022537

Printed in China
10 9 8 7 6 5 4 3 2 1

WARNING:

Climbing is a sport where you may be seriously injured or die. Read this before you use this book.

This guidebook is a compilation of unverified information gathered from many different climbers. The author cannot assure the accuracy of any of the information in this book, including the topos and route descriptions, the difficulty ratings, and the protection ratings. These may be incorrect or misleading, as ratings of climbing difficulty and danger are always subjective and depend on the physical characteristics (for example, height), experience, technical ability, confidence, and physical fitness of the climber who supplied the rating. Additionally, climbers who achieve first ascents sometimes underrate the difficulty or danger of the climbing route. Therefore, be warned that you must exercise your own judgment on where a climbing route goes, its difficulty, and your ability to safely protect yourself from the risks of rock climbing. Examples of some of these risks are: falling due to technical difficulty or due to natural hazards such as holds breaking, falling rock, climbing equipment dropped by other climbers, hazards of weather and lightning, your own equipment failure, and failure or absence of fixed protection.

You should not depend on any information gleaned from this book for your personal safety; your safety depends on your own good judgment, based on experience and a realistic assessment of your climbing ability. If you have any doubt as to your ability to safely climb a route described in this book, do not attempt it.

The following are some ways to make your use of this book safer:

1. Consultation: You should consult with other climbers about the difficulty and danger of a particular climb prior to attempting it. Most local climbers are glad to give advice on routes in their area; we suggest that you contact locals to confirm ratings and safety of particular routes and to obtain first-hand information about a route chosen from this book.

2. Instruction: Most climbing areas have local climbing instructors and guides available. We recommend that you engage an instructor or guide to learn safety techniques and to become familiar with the routes and hazards of the areas described in this book. Even after you are proficient in climbing safely, occasional use of a guide is a safe way to raise your climbing standard and learn advanced techniques.

3. Fixed Protection: Some of the routes in this book may use bolts and pitons that are permanently placed in the rock. Because of variances in the manner of placement, weathering, metal fatigue, the quality of the metal used, and many other factors, these fixed protection pieces should always be considered suspect and should always be backed up by equipment that you place yourself. Never depend on a single piece of fixed protection for your safety, because you never can tell whether it will hold weight. In some cases, fixed protection may have been removed or is now missing. However, climbers should not always add new pieces of protection unless existing protection is faulty. Existing protection can be tested by an experienced climber and its strength determined. Climbers are strongly encouraged not to add bolts and drilled pitons to a route. They need to climb the route in the style of the first ascent party (or better) or choose a route within their ability—a route to which they do not have to add additional fixed anchors.

Be aware of the following specific potential hazards that could arise in using this book:

1. Incorrect Descriptions of Routes: If you climb a route and you have a doubt as to where it goes, you should not continue unless you are sure that you can go that way safely. Route descriptions and topos in this book could be inaccurate or misleading.

2. Incorrect Difficulty Rating: A route might be more difficult than the rating indicates. Do not be lulled into a false sense of security by the difficulty rating.

3. Incorrect Protection Rating: If you climb a route and you are unable to arrange adequate protection from the risk of falling through the use of fixed pitons or bolts and by placing your own protection devices, do not assume that there is adequate protection available higher just because the route protection rating indicates the route does not have an X or an R rating. Every route is potentially an X (a fall may be deadly), due to the inherent hazards of climbing—including, for example, failure or absence of fixed protection, your own equipment's failure, or improper use of climbing equipment.

There are no warranties, whether expressed or implied, that this guidebook is accurate or that the information contained in it is reliable. There are no warranties of fitness for a particular purpose or that this guide is merchantable. Your use of this book indicates your assumption of the risk that it may contain errors and is an acknowledgment of your own sole responsibility for your climbing safety.

DEDICATION

This book is dedicated to Mike Puddy. Mike played a vital role in the development of Smith Rock sport climbing. He was a great friend, a favorite climbing partner, and an inspiring personality. He will be forever remembered and missed by all of us who were lucky enough to climb with him.

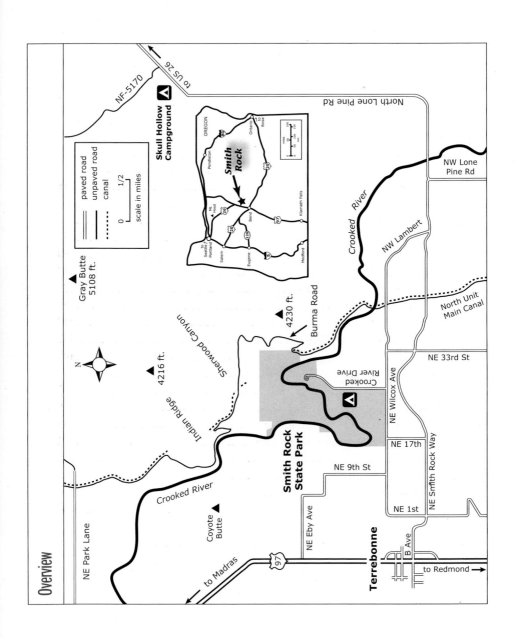

CONTENTS

FOREWORD

Holding this remarkable document, it is easy enough to remember back fifty years to the times when my brother and I were alone in the canyon on Sunday afternoons, and even the discovery of another climber's footprint was an event that was noted and discussed. When we repeated Vivian and Gil Staender's routes on the ridge that bears their name, and found their names and addresses on the summits, the beginnings of the first guide were set in place. Looking at the tiny guide, first published in the 1962 *Mazama,* it's hard to believe that that article/guide and this definitive work could have the same origins.

For us so-called "pioneer climbers," observing and experiencing the incredible evolution of traditional and sport climbing at Smith has been gratifying and astonishing. Equally satisfying has been the non-climbing public's devotion to the park. It has truly become an Oregon icon, and no one has contributed more to this status than Alan Watts, both as a climber and a writer. Alan's name will always be synonymous with Smith Rock. Make no mistake, this is not just another climber's guide. It is also a testament to one man's devotion and passion for his sport and for one of the special places on Earth.

Jim Ramsey

ACKNOWLEDGMENTS

Although my name appears on the cover, I didn't write this book alone. Good guidebooks are never the work of a single person. Solo ascents might be widely respected in the climbing world, but only the most bullheaded climbers go it alone writing a guide. A climbing guide combines thousands of obscure details, biased opinions, and historical tidbits, in a setting changing with every new bolt and every snapped hold. I like to think of this guidebook as a collaboration between myself and everyone who climbs at Smith Rock.

I am grateful to the hundreds of people who steered me back on course when I stumbled in the wrong direction. I thank everyone who grumbled when I missed a grade by several notches, or corrected me I when I wrote "move left" when the route actually cut right. I appreciate those who set me straight when I warned about a loose block that fell off fifteen years ago, or asked why I gave a great route a single, lonely star. One way or another, this feedback gets back to me and I've considered all of it in writing this new edition.

Although I've redone much of my original book, I borrowed heavily from the past. I'm especially indebted to those who wrote Smith guidebooks. Only after writing a guide do you realize how much you borrow from others. In no small way, the thoroughness of my book is because of their efforts. Jeff Thomas, in particular, deserves credit for his encyclopedic knowledge of the early years of Smith climbing.

There are several individuals who went out of their way to help me with this book. Smith pioneer Jim Ramsey graciously wrote the foreword, while Ryan Lawson patiently answered countless questions, providing details on dozens of new lines. Ben Moon provided brilliant action shots of Smith Rock, including the cover photo. Paul Marshall's input on the enigmatic Upper Gorge breathed new life into a section of the book that I knew little about. Kevin Pogue contributed the geology section, while Chris Jones provided me with a detailed lists of his boulder problems from the late 1970s. Mike Volk's Web site, www.smithrock.com, was an invaluable reference. Last but not least, a special thanks goes to my wife, JoAnn, and my children, Ben and Morgan.

I've received help from so many others that it's impossible to thank everyone. Jim Ablao, Tyler Adams, Wayne Arrington, Jack Barrar, Tom Bauman, Joe Brooks, Chuck Buzzard, Ian Caldwell, Ted Davis, Mark Deffenbaugh, Thomas Emde, Jeff Frizzell, Paul Fry, Greg Garretson, Bruce Hahn, Brian Holcomb, Rod Jacobson, Dave Jensen, Jon Marshall, Brent McGregor, John Rich, Tom Rogers, Kim Schmitz, Michael Stöger, Steve Strauch, David Tvedt, Erik Wolfe, and Jim Yoder all made valuable contributions. Curiously, this edition might still be a work in progress if Dave Pegg and Jonathon Thesenga hadn't released an excellent mini-guide in 2006. Seeing their book in print provided the motivation I needed to finally complete this volume. I apologize to anyone I've overlooked—hopefully seeing your comment used in the book will serve as a thank you.

To the best of my abilities, the information in this book is correct and fully up-to-date as of May 2009. I learned from my previous edition how quickly things change. I've made every effort to make this book a complete guide to Smith, ignoring no routes—no matter how bad or insignificant. But by the time this book first hits the shelf, it will already provide an incomplete picture. If you've climbed a new route, spotted an error, or simply want to voice your opinion, please contact me through the publisher at editorial@GlobePequot.com.

PREFACE

As the youngest of three children, I never found my place in the world until I fell under the spell cast by Smith Rock's soaring walls. I might have lived in nearby Madras, but Smith was where I really grew up. From my earliest visits as an intimidated fourteen-year-old, I sensed a connection that would last a lifetime. I taught myself how to climb, miraculously survived my epic early days, and slowly gained a confidence I'd never known before. Smith Rock taught me commitment, determination, patience, and self-discipline. I experienced uplifting highs and crushing lows, inspired successes and haunting failures.

Some days I loved everything about Smith—the kaleidoscope of colors in the early morning sun, the texture of the stone on my chalked fingertips, and especially the people who shared my passion and energy. Other days weren't so easy, as the heat, the cold, or the sheer difficulty of the routes got the best of me. But every visit to the park made me stronger, and moved me closer to achieving a new goal on my never-ending tick list. After thousands of days spent high above the Crooked River, I felt more at home on these crags than anywhere else. While the world changed, Smith Rock was always there—timeless—welcoming me home again.

After eighteen years my abused finger joints slowly snuffed out any hopes of remaining at the higher levels of the sport. Frustration and pain replaced the passion and vigor of my younger years. As a postscript to my Smith climbing career, I finished my first guidebook in 1992. With the birth of my children, Ben and Morgan, my focus shifted away from the park. In many respects my work seemed finished, and I felt ready to leave Smith Rock behind. But I soon discovered that letting go wasn't so easy. I pursued other interests, but Smith was always there on the horizon, beckoning, luring me back.

In 1999 I dug out my rock shoes, bought a larger harness, and started working through the hundreds of new routes in hopes of updating my Smith book. I originally planned a select guide, but I couldn't muster any enthusiasm for the project. These condensed guides are useful for anyone with limited interests, but they often ignore the history and worsen over-crowding on routes that are already too popular. I briefly considered the tempting option of cramming the new lines into the existing book, but I realized the finished product would be a jumbled mess.

In the end I followed the path of most resistance by completely redoing the original guide. Much to the frustration of everyone waiting on the book, I worked at my own pace—ignoring any deadlines. I methodically redrew every drawing again and again, until I was happy with the finished product. I patiently rewrote the text, trying my best to capture the essence of both new routes and old. I spent hours visiting with many of Smith's pioneering climbers, hoping to put a fresh perspective on the history of the area.

Each year the scope of the project grew as new routes sprouted everywhere. With increased family responsibilities, my available working time dwindled to where I was barely treading water. I'd work feverishly for several months before entering a long period of hibernation, waiting for the next spark of inspiration. By then there would be so many new lines I'd have to redo major sections. The months stretched into years, and the book still wasn't finished. And too soon, the trickle of when-will-the-book-be-done questions turned into a torrent. I spent the better part of a decade coming up with shuck-and-jive answers, never having a clue when (or if) the book would make it to press. Yet against all odds, that moment has finally arrived.

Writing a guidebook is a bad business proposition—there's a very limited market, and creating a first-rate book instead of a mediocre one only marginally increases sales. The only way to make good money is to spend minimal time, while getting things right takes a colossal effort. I've chosen the latter approach, treating the project more like a hobby than a business. But despite my efforts, I realize there's no such thing as a completely accurate guide. This book is no exception, though I feel satisfied in knowing I've given it my very best.

At times it seems hard to believe I'm the same person who spent the better part of two decades devoted to Smith Rock. My life today bears little resemblance to the years I spent living in the dirt. In this respect I'm not alone. People change. Some lose interest, others move away, and tragically, some die far too young. The routes remain, but most of my climbing buddies now pursue other interests. Today Smith is home to an entirely new generation of passionate youngsters, pursuing their own dreams on the vertical faces. The cast of characters change, but Smith Rock remains the same. Apart from chalked holds and terraced trails, it looks the same as it did on my first visit.

Trips to Smith are no longer part of my daily ritual. But whenever I step into the canyon, I feel like I'm entering a sacred place, full of the triumphs and struggles of countless climbers. Everywhere I look, memories are piled on top of memories. At times I'll sit and gaze at the cliffs, leafing through my past like turning the pages of a scrapbook. With sadness I realize that the Smith Rock chapter of my life is nearly complete. But at the same time, I feel tremendous gratitude to have been lucky enough to grow up during the golden age of Smith climbing. As the years pass, my memories of the routes slowly fade, but my recollections of the incredible people with whom I shared my journey stay fresh in my mind.

Alan Watts
August 2009

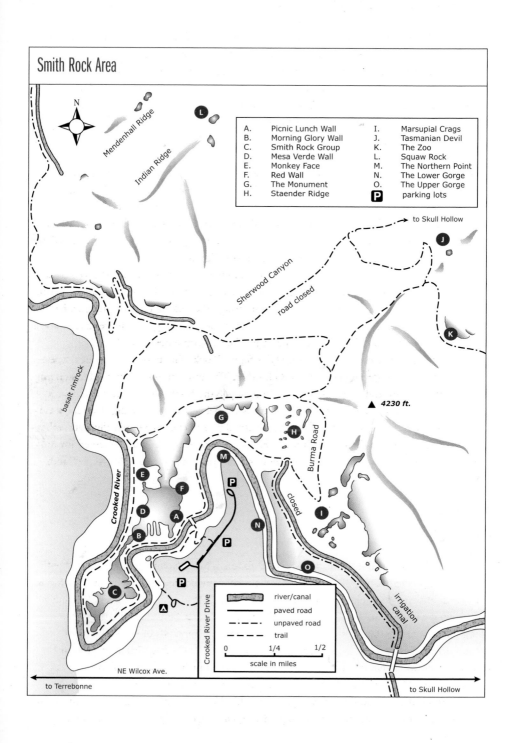

Smith Rock Area

A.	Picnic Lunch Wall	I.	Marsupial Crags
B.	Morning Glory Wall	J.	Tasmanian Devil
C.	Smith Rock Group	K.	The Zoo
D.	Mesa Verde Wall	L.	Squaw Rock
E.	Monkey Face	M.	The Northern Point
F.	Red Wall	N.	The Lower Gorge
G.	The Monument	O.	The Upper Gorge
H.	Staender Ridge	**P**	parking lots

Mendenhall Ridge

Indian Ridge

to Skull Hollow

Sherwood Canyon

road closed

▲ 4230 ft.

basalt rimrock

Crooked River

Burma Road

closed

Irrigation canal

	river/canal
	paved road
	unpaved road
	trail

0   1/4   1/2
scale in miles

Crooked River Drive

NE Wilcox Ave.

to Terrebonne

to Skull Hollow

INTRODUCTION

Smith Rock holds a warm place in the hearts of climbers throughout the world. While every world-class destination offers high-level routes, somehow the big numbers seem secondary to what really makes Smith special. It's one of those magical places that transcends climbing. Gaze at the fiery hues of the massive walls towering against the crispness of a sapphire morning; marvel at a falcon riding the updrafts spiraling high above the serrated spires; experience the stillness of a winter's morning after a freshly fallen snow. You'll understand why there's so much more to Smith Rock than hard routes.

Over a few months in 1986, Smith rose to fame in the climbing world. What for decades had been a closely held secret became the hottest real estate in American climbing. Everyone came to the three-ring circus at Smith Rock—elite climbers, photographers, TV crews, reporters, and groupies. While the level of the routes fueled much of the excitement, the unorthodox techniques used to develop Smith climbing fell under scrutiny. Some saw these local tactics as the wave of the future, while others saw nothing but an ethical travesty. Within a few years, everyone had the same name for it—sport climbing.

Like a rebellious child coming of age, Smith climbing has matured and mellowed over the years. The circus moved on, leaving behind some of the most influential routes on Earth. Climbers still come from around the world, even though the cutting edge of the sport has moved elsewhere—likely never to return. But today, Smith climbing is far more diverse and appealing than ever before. Like a fine wine, it just keeps getting better with time.

Few climbing areas offer as much variety as Smith Rock. The two different rock types—basalt and tuff—bear little resemblance to each other. The tuff features knobby slabs, stunning arêtes, pocketed faces, and overhanging testpieces, while the basalt offers perfect cracks and baffling corners. Given the variety, it's hard putting a label on Smith climbing. Despite mindblowing sport routes, it's not just a sport crag—naturally protected routes actually outnumber bolted climbs. And while there are dozens of high-end testpieces, it's hardly reserved for top-level climbers. The growth of easy to moderate routes over the last decade has made Smith attractive to climbers of all levels.

OVERVIEW

Topography

The most welcome surprise for many first-time visitors is Smith's unique beauty. Lined with juniper trees, ponderosa pine, and sagebrush, the aptly named Crooked River cuts a tortuous path through the basalt columns and towering cliffs of tuff. It eventually joins the Deschutes River, which merges with the Columbia on its path to the Pacific Ocean. To the east are rolling hills leading to the forested Ochoco Mountains and hundreds of miles of eastern Oregon desert. To the west the snowcapped volcanoes of the Cascade Range stand guard along the horizon, above the flat checkerboard of irrigated plains. These distinctive peaks separate Central Oregon from the more densely populated parts of the state.

The Smith Rock region covers an area of roughly 10 square miles along the southwest base of several rounded buttes at the western edge of Central Oregon's high desert. The highest of these peaks is Gray Butte (5,108 feet), rising 4 miles northeast of the parking area (2,850 feet). Dominating the view to the east are the Marsupial Crags (4,230 feet), with the unmistakable Burma Road slashing across the hillside. Although the singular name applies to a large grouping of individual crags, Smith Rock itself rises atop a narrow peninsula of land, almost completely encircled by the winding river, at the southern end of the park.

Climate

With an average of 8.5 inches of rain per year, the desert setting of Smith Rock proves ideal for climbing, as the Cascade Range provides a natural barrier against Pacific storms. Western Oregon soaks in endless winter rains, while Smith Rock benefits from minimal rainfall and mostly sunny weather. The four distinct seasons bring refreshingly different weather patterns, with rain and high humidity rarely part of the equation.

The best seasons to visit Smith are spring and fall. Smith would have a viable year-round climbing season if not for occasional temperature extremes. High temperatures in midsummer often crack 100 degrees, while the winter mercury plunges below freezing for weeks at a time. The spring season (March through May) usually offers ideal conditions for high-level ascents, though the most dependable season is fall, extending from mid-September through the middle of November. The clear cold nights, sunny days, and very low humidity sometimes extend for a good portion of the fall.

Local climbers enjoy acceptable conditions during the off-season as well, though anyone visiting during the winter might be completely shut out, as the days are short and the nights bitterly cold. Locals relish the frequent sunny winter days, as any south-facing cliff warms rapidly in the sun, though the temperature plummets instantly once the sun disappears. Summer conditions are harsh but far more predictable. Despite intolerable conditions in the midday sun, the humidity is usually very low, and the ample shade makes mornings very pleasant. After baking in the sun all day, the canyon cools minimally on a summer evening.

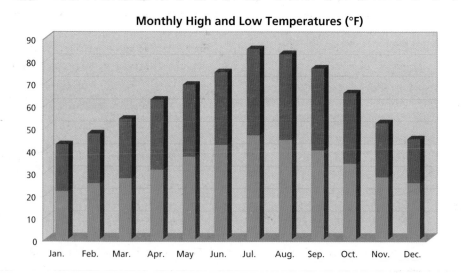

Monthly High and Low Temperatures (°F)

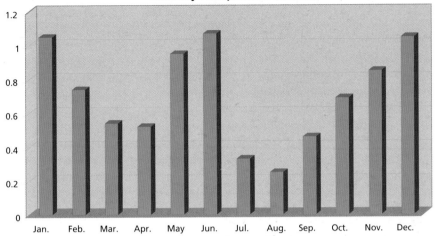

Monthly Precipitation (inches)

The graphs detail the average monthly highs, lows, and precipitation for the Redmond area just 10 miles south. Conditions at Smith are similar, though the highs will average at least 5 degrees warmer in the canyon.

Geology

Smith's most famous routes ascend the multicolored crags of tuff. The Smith Rock tuff is one of several volcanic rock types comprising the Gray Butte Complex. The tuff originated in early Miocene time, between 17 to 19 million years ago, when gaseous, silica-rich magma found its way to the surface near today's park. Relieved of the pressure of overlying rocks, the gas trapped within the magma expanded, producing explosive eruptions that shattered the magma into small fragments. Erupted into the air, the molten rock solidified into volcanic ash and formed incandescent clouds. The hot ash and rock fragments from the explosions accumulated as thick deposits near the site of the eruptions.

Silica-rich magma later intruded the tuff deposits, feeding additional explosive eruptions. These intrusions cooled to form the shattered rhyolite dikes that make up Shiprock and parts of the Smith Rock Group. As the tuff cooled, shrinkage and lithification produced parallel sets of joints that weathered to form the crack systems in the Dihedrals and other areas. Over time, chemical reactions slowly altered the Smith Rock tuff, converting the original glassy volcanic ash into the clay minerals that make up the rock today.

Much of the tuff at Smith Rock contains angular fragments of rhyolite or pumice called xenoliths—a word that literally means "stranger rocks." Incorporated into the tuff during the explosive eruptions, the xenoliths consist of stray fragments of older rocks. Typically finer-grained and less altered than the tuff, they weather less readily. This differential weathering causes them to jut out in relief, producing the nubbins that delight and torment Smith climbers. The pockets, called vesicles, are the remnants of bubbles of trapped gas that accumulated in the tuff immediately after its eruption. They range from bathtub-size buckets to one-finger pockets.

The quality of Smith Rock tuff varies dramatically throughout the park. The darker rock is generally more solid due to a greater concentration of cementing mineral oxides in the outer layers. The process that forms this tough outer crust, called case hardening, distinguishes the best of the rock from the softer junk. The red-brown color is primarily the result of the oxidation of iron.

Besides the tuff, the basalt of the Gorge holds the most interest among climbers. Erupted 1.2 million years ago from the Newberry volcano south of Bend, the highly fluid lava flowed down the valley of the ancestral Crooked River. This basalt flow filled the canyon previously excavated between the Smith Rock tuff and the 4.5-million-year-old Deschutes Formation basalt. The Crooked River slowly eroded the Newberry basalt, producing the present-day canyon. Typical of many basalt climbing areas, the routes generally follow vertical columnar cooling joints.

SMITH ROCK STATE PARK

Most of the climbing lies within the boundaries of Smith Rock State Park, one of the most visited parks in the state (www.oregonstateparks.org; 541-548-7501). This 651-acre wonderland is maintained by a park manager, a full-time ranger, and two seasonal rangers. The positive relationship between the climbing community and Oregon State Parks is the envy of climbers around the country; the mutual trust and respect fostered over decades of cooperation is a big part of why Smith climbing rose to such heights. There are no formal regulations governing bolting, first ascents, and other climbing activities—instead, these issues are left to the consensus of local climbers. This self-governing policy has proven remarkably effective over the years, with the few conflicts between climbers quickly and quietly resolved.

Oregon State Parks places a top priority on protecting the fragile environment of Smith Rock. The hillsides below the cliffs and the riparian zones are very delicate. Fortunately, despite the rising popularity of the park, the setting remains relatively unspoiled. Everyone who climbs at Smith Rock puts a strain on the environment, whether they leave chalk marks, bolts, or boot rubber. Yet it takes only common sense and minimal time to help preserve the natural beauty. The cumulative effort of every climber staying on the trails and picking up their trash makes a huge impact.

In August 1996 a fire swept through Smith Rock. Inadvertently started by a state park employee using a welder to repair a vandalized fee box, the blaze raced through the canyon within minutes. The fire left Smith charred, but in some ways the park benefited in the long run—with the hillsides closed for many months, the vegetation grew back thicker than before, eliminating many wildcat trails. Because of the blaze, the park service is very sensitive about fire risk, placing restrictions on anything that might start a fire (cigarettes, lanterns, gas stoves, and welders).

Smith Rock State Park

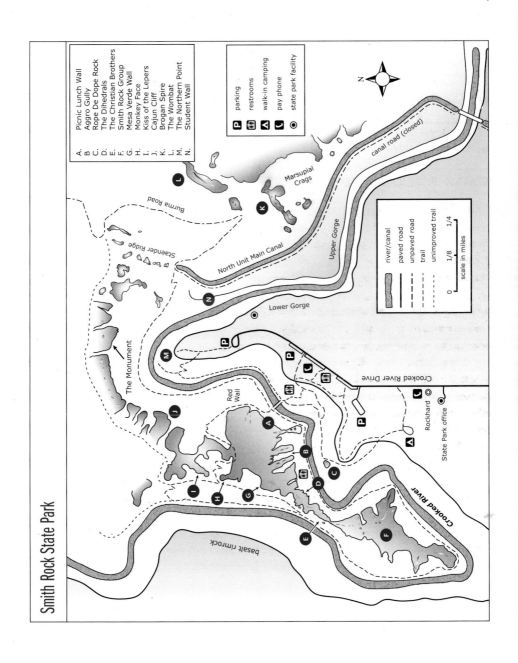

A. Picnic Lunch Wall
B. Aggro Gully
C. Rope De Dope Rock
D. The Dihedrals
E. The Christian Brothers
F. Smith Rock Group
G. Mesa Verde Wall
H. Monkey Face
I. Kiss of the Lepers
J. Cajun Cliff
K. Brogan Spire
L. The Wombat
M. The Northern Point
N. Student Wall

parking
restrooms
walk-in camping
pay phone
state park facility

river/canal
paved road
unpaved road
trail
unimproved trail

scale in miles
0   1/8   1/4

N

Marsupial Crags
canal road (closed)
Burma Road
Staender Ridge
North Unit Main Canal
Upper Gorge
Lower Gorge
The Monument
Red Wall
Crooked River Drive
basalt rimrock
Crooked River
Rockhard
State Park office

How to Get There

Smith Rock State Park sits 2 miles east of U.S. Highway 97, about 25 miles north of Bend, near the geographic center of Oregon. The usual access to Smith Rock is through the small community of Terrebonne. A sign marks the turn east onto B Avenue (which turns into Northeast Smith Rock Way) at the only light in town. With the towering rocks visible to the northeast, and signs clearly marking the way, you'll have no problem arriving at the state park.

Smith Rock is a 2.5-hour drive over a mountain pass from the population centers of the state, including Portland, Salem, and Eugene. These passes can be treacherous in the winter, so be prepared for snowy roads. US 97 stretches from Northern California to the Canadian border. Depending on your direction of travel, you'll likely join this north–south thoroughfare somewhere on your journey. From Portland, follow U.S. Highway 26 east past Mount Hood, joining US 97 south at Madras. Continue 20 miles to Terrebonne. For other starting points, refer to a road map, or enter Smith Rock State Park as your destination on the Internet or your GPS.

If you're traveling a great distance, you should consider flying into the Redmond Airport, just 8 miles south of the park. Flights into Redmond are sometimes no more expensive than flying into Portland International Airport, 2.5 hours to the northwest. After renting a car, turn right after exiting the airport and drive about a mile before turning right onto US 97 north.

Parking Fee

Oregon State Parks requires a permit for any parked vehicle at Smith Rock. There are two self-service kiosks (cash only). Anyone planning to visit the park more than eight days a year should purchase an annual pass (good at any state park in Oregon). The best deal is a two-year pass. You'll pay a steep price if you refuse to participate—a parking ticket costs several times more than a yearly pass. Passes can be purchased at the park headquarters (turn left off Crooked River Drive, just before an abandoned tennis court), or from the camp hosts. For more information go to www.oregon.gov.

Dogs

If you'd like to bring your dog into the park, beware! Smith has one of the most peculiar anti-dog restrictions of any climbing area in the country. Not only must dogs be leashed at all times (6-foot leash maximum), but it's also illegal to tie up your dog at the base of a route. This restriction entered the books after pea-brained climbers abandoned their barking dogs for hours at a time, but the practical implications were never considered. Just try catching a long leader fall with a dog attached to you—both you and your hound will get launched into space. The state park doesn't just pay lip service to these rules—they've handed out count-less expensive citations over the years. The rules apply not just to dogs, but pets of any kind, including cats, iguanas, and parakeets. Fortunately, there's reason to believe these restrictions might ease in the near future.

Wildlife

Protecting the habitat of Smith's diverse wildlife is a primary mission of Oregon State Parks. Mule deer, muskrats, beavers, river otters, cottontail rabbits, and porcupines make Smith Rock their home. Reptiles such as sagebrush lizards and bull snakes are common, though rattlesnakes prefer the less-traveled stretches of the park—sightings in the main climbing areas are fortunately rare. Bird-watchers will find much to catch their eye—Canada geese and great blue herons make their homes near the water, while golden eagles, osprey, prairie falcons, and red-tailed hawks nest on the cliffs, high above the river.

Oregon State Parks closes active nesting sites and all nearby routes a few months each year—usually from February 1 to August 1. Adult birds of prey scare easily, putting their eggs and newly hatched offspring in danger of death from hypothermia. The Endangered Species Act of 1973 and the Federal Eagle Act of 1978 make it a crime to disturb the nesting sites of these rare birds. Anyone threatening active nest sites by attempting nearby routes during nesting season places the future of Smith climbing in jeopardy. Signs at the campground, parking area, overlook, bridge, and at the base of the closed crags detail all current restrictions.

Erosion

The hillsides above the river are deceptively fragile. Nothing detracts more from the beauty of Smith than indiscriminate trail scars. Since Oregon State Parks built a network of staircased trails, many areas are in far better shape today than they were in the 1970s. Aided greatly by the work of the annual volunteer work party (the Spring Thing), the trail system at Smith Rock improves each year. With each newly developed crag, however, the risk of erosion returns. You can help by traversing along the base of the crag to reach an established trail, rather than careening directly down the hillside.

Smoking

Smoking is prohibited during fire season. Please respect other people's right to breathe clean air. And, of course, pick up your cigarette butts.

Water

There is safe drinking water year-round at the day-use parking area and the campground. During the summer months there's also drinking water available in the canyon itself at the bridge. No matter how thirsty you might be, don't drink from the Crooked River, or you'll become well acquainted with the composting toilets described below.

Toilets

The toilet situation within the canyon at Smith Rock has improved greatly from the inadequate facilities prior to the early 1990s. The massive composting toilets at the bridge and below Morning Glory Wall are state-of-the-art, stink-free facilities.

Land Ownership

Private land surrounds much of Smith Rock State Park, and many people make their homes nearby. Please respect their right to privacy by staying off their land and keeping down the noise. An impromptu rock concert in the parking lot during the 1970s damaged relations between climbers and locals for years. Several residents resent Smith's popularity—they have a valid complaint when drunken climbers wander into their backyards at night.

Emergency Services

In case of a medical emergency, dial 911 from your cell phone or from the pay phone at the center day-use parking lot. Cell phone service is spotty at Smith Rock—you'll likely get no signal in the Gorge and at other sheltered crags, though you can always just hike to higher ground. The nearest hospital is St. Charles, in Redmond (541-548-8131), on the north side of town. They have emergency room doctors on staff twenty-four hours a day (US 97 south, continue past Redmond downtown exit, and turn right onto Northwest Larch Avenue).

CAMPING

There are two camping options at Smith Rock—the state park campground at the southern boundary of the park, and Skull Hollow Campground located several miles northeast of the park itself.

Smith Rock State Park Bivouac Area

If you want to stay overnight within the boundaries of the state park, the walk-in campground is your only option. With a pleasant setting amid the junipers atop the rim southwest of the day-use parking area, this campground offers many conveniences. You can enter the canyon directly from your campsite and enjoy a shower at the end of the day. The view of the crags bathed in the early morning sun and the eerie glow of the cliffs during a full moon only add to the charm.

There are a few downsides to the official campground. First, there's absolutely no car or RV camping allowed. You'll need to park and walk a couple hundred feet to your campsite. Open campfires and gas lanterns are prohibited, and you can't even cook your meals at your campsite—instead, you'll need to use the picnic tables at the designated area in the middle of the parking lot. Another consideration is the proximity to nearby residences. Late-night parties are an especially bad idea, as you'll anger other campers and swiftly get booted from the campground.

The clearly marked entrance to the campground turns left off Crooked River Drive, just before the day-use parking lot. After signing in at the self-registration booth and checking the bulletin board for current regulations, you can find a campsite in the trees. Campsites are first come, first served, and the nightly charge includes the use of showers. A state park rule limits your stay to two weeks, but they usually enforce this only to get rid of troublemakers.

Skull Hollow Campground

The unofficial climbers' campground sits in the middle of nowhere, 7 miles northeast of Smith Rock. Managed by the Forest Service, Skull Hollow Campground offers few amenities, but it's usually packed with climbers during peak season, despite the drive from the state park. Car camping, campsite cooking, campfires, and reading at night under the light of a gas lantern are a few of the freedoms here that many climbers find appealing. Unfortunately, the days of free camping at Skull Hollow are over. In the summer of 2009, the Forest Service started charging a nightly camping fee for the use of the Spartan facilities.

Campgrounds don't get more rustic than Skull Hollow. The setting doesn't match the majesty of Smith Rock, but there's a peacefulness that comes from the isolation—especially late in the day as the last rays of sun shine on nearby Grizzly Mountain, the highest of the desert hills. Apart from pit toilets and picnic tables, there's nothing here—you'll even need to bring your own water. Apparently, the eerie name comes from an 1867 Indian massacre. Many human skulls were unearthed near the site of today's campground, a fact that might keep skittish campers awake. At night, the wind blowing through the juniper trees mimics the sounds of a woman's anguished cries—or so the legend goes.

To approach Skull Hollow from the day-use parking lot, exit the park via Crooked River Drive and turn left onto Northeast Wilcox Avenue, which turns into Northwest Lambert Road. After 2 miles, take a left at a stop sign, then a second left onto Northwest Lone Pine Road. Cross a bridge and drive north along the straight road for several miles. Just after the farmer's fields give way to juniper and sagebrush, search for a Skull Hollow Campground sign. Turn left onto an easily missed dirt road and drive 100 yards to the camping spots. If you're starting from Terrebonne, simply stay on Northwest Smith Rock Way for 4 miles and take a left onto Northwest Lone Pine Road.

OTHER ACTIVITIES

While the climbing at Smith receives all the acclaim, most visitors to the park never tie into a rope. The scenic trails, tranquil river, and picturesque cliffs attract sightseers, bird-watchers, photographers, hikers, trail runners, kayakers, mountain bikers, and anyone needing to revitalize their spirit.

The Smith Rock region is well known among Central Oregon mountain bikers. The best rides follow miles of trails east and north of the park. The approach turns right at the bridge and ascends a difficult draw leading to the arduous Burma Road. An alternate access is from the east side of the park, beginning at the Skull Hollow Campground. If you're interested in exploring the mountain biking trails, there are detailed guides available at local bike/outdoor shops. Bikes aren't allowed on Misery Ridge, or any of the climbing access trails.

The Crooked River offers few recreational options as it passes through the state park. High water conditions (usually present in the spring for only a few weeks) give expert kayakers and whitewater rafters a chance to navigate fourth-class rapids, while frustrated anglers along the banks compete for a small population of scrawny fish. Unfortunately, the river makes a poor choice as a swimming spot—it's fast moving in some places and stagnant in others. Miles downstream, the Crooked River eventually joins the Deschutes River at Cove Palisades State Park, located about 30 minutes north of the park. This man-made reservoir offers the best choice for anyone looking for a refreshing dip after climbing in the hot sun.

Smith Rock is a wonderful hiking or trail running destination. Much like the climbing season, it's best to avoid the depths of winter and the oppressive heat of summer. But while much of the Central Oregon high country is buried in snow eight months a year, Smith trails are in fine condition. The distances of the following round-trip hikes assume a starting point from the parking lot (between the center and north lots, at a gated access road). If you choose to start from the east side of the bridge instead of the parking lot, deduct 0.5 mile from the round-trip distance. Hiking to the bridge via the switchbacked access road rather than the normal trail adds 0.3 mile to the round-trip distance. Starting from the entrance sign at the Bivy Area adds 0.9 mile. All wheel-measured distances are accurate enough to please even the most hard-core trail runners.

Misery Ridge Loop Trail (3.5 miles)

The most popular loop trail at Smith follows the river downstream from the bridge, looping around to the west side of the park. Leave the river trail behind just past Asterisk Pass and hike uphill to a path skirting the West Side Crags. Follow a switchbacked trail leading uphill northeast of Monkey Face, before finishing with a descent of the Misery Ridge Trail. You can add a little length (about 4 miles) by ignoring the uphill trail beyond Asterisk Pass, continuing along the river for 0.5 mile until a well-maintained trail switchbacks uphill and back south to Monkey Face, joining the regular loop. Reversing the direction shifts all the uphill hiking to the start of the journey.

Asterisk Loop Trail (2.5 miles)

You can avoid the southern reaches of the Misery Ridge Loop Trail by scrambling over Asterisk Pass, after branching off the river trail below the Christian Brothers. Non-climbers might want to avoid this easy but exposed option.

West Side Trail (5 miles)

You can minimize uphill walking by following the river downstream from the bridge, around the Southern Tip to the west side. Hike uphill to the cliff line just beyond Asterisk Pass and continue beyond Monkey Face, along the base of the Kiss of the Lepers Area, before descending to the river and hiking back upstream to the bridge. The least strenuous option stays along the river all the way on the west side, turning around at a junction past the massive Monkey Boulder north of Monkey Face (4.8 miles).

Staender Ridge Loop Trail (6.1 miles)

An especially strenuous loop trail encircles the entire Smith Rock State Park. Follow the river upstream from the bridge, around the northern bend in the river. As the trail heads uphill below Staender Ridge, take the switchbacked left fork and continue to the base of the Burma Road. Walk far uphill past the big switchback to the crest of the road and take a trail branching left. Hike downhill just north of the ridge crest, behind Staender Ridge and the Monument, and continue as the rim trail heads uphill again. As soon as the top of Monkey Face comes into view, you'll see a junction. Don't hike up the hill; instead traverse across the hillside to the right. Hike down an unimproved trail in a gully (with a short section of unexposed 2nd class scrambling) all the way to the river on the west side. Hike upstream along the Crooked River around the Southern Tip to your starting point. Trail runners won't want to reverse the direction of the loop—it's far easier running up the Burma Road than the scree slope north of Monkey Face. You can avoid the southern reaches of the park by passing over Asterisk Pass (5.3 miles).

Smith Rock Loop Trail (6.7 miles)

The complete loop is the best running trail, with minimal rough terrain. The direction of travel matters little, though it's easier staying on the proper path if you begin moving downstream. From the bridge, hike around the Southern Tip and continue far beyond Monkey Face, traversing the hillside below New World Buttress. Just after the crest of the hill, the trail merges with a dirt road. Follow the road and turn right at a T junction just below the canal. Immediately take another right and follow a long uphill path that eventually switchbacks to the top of the Burma Road. Hike down the road to the river and follow a pleasant trail leading downstream to the bridge. A shorter version of the same loop bypasses the Southern Tip by scrambling over Asterisk Pass (5.9 miles).

CENTRAL OREGON CASCADES

If your fingertips have holes worn in them from too much climbing, you might want to spend a rest day taking in some of Central Oregon's beautiful scenery. The entire region is one of the most sought-after recreational areas in the country, and many world-class outdoor athletes call Central Oregon home.

Anyone enjoying Smith Rock on a sunny day can't help but notice the snow-covered Cascade volcanoes on the western horizon. If you're looking for an escape from the midsummer heat, you might enjoy scaling one of these peaks. The season extends from June through October. During the winter these same pleasant climbs turn into risky adventures with difficult access. In summer most of the volcanoes are nothing more than long hikes, though steep snowfields require alpine gear, and the weather can turn nasty with little warning. The rock quality leaves much to be desired, but the veteran climber will find many adventurous routes. Mount Washington, in particular, features long (up to 1,000 feet) climbs on rock of mixed quality. About 20 miles west of Bend, Mount Bachelor (9,065 feet) dominates the winter sports scene. It's the best snowboard resort in Oregon, with 3,365 vertical feet and more than 370 inches of annual snowfall. It attracts hundreds of thousands of riders each year. Skiers are also allowed on the slopes. The season typically begins before Thanksgiving and ends in May. You can ride the Pine Marten lift throughout the summer to get an effortless view of the spectacular Central Oregon scenery. Oregon's highest mountain, Mount Hood (11,235 feet), is about ninety minutes northwest of Smith. Here you'll find the longest snow season in North America, usually lasting until Labor Day.

SURROUNDING TOWNS

The local campgrounds are fine places to sleep, but most climbers eventually grow weary of hanging out in the dirt and venture out to sample the charms of Central Oregon. Within 30 miles are the towns of Bend, Redmond, Terrebonne, Sisters, Madras, and Prineville. Over the last twenty years, Central Oregon has transformed itself from bucolic communities dominated by agriculture and wood products into some of the trendiest, highest-priced real estate in the state.

Terrebonne

This small community is the gateway to Smith Rock. Home to 1,469 people, Terrebonne (literally "the good earth") has flourished over the past few years, reaping the economic benefits of its proximity to Smith. After decades of decay, new construction is booming. If you're content with the basics, you'll find everything you need nearby, including a grocery store, gas station, ATM, bank, post office, Internet access, coffee shop, and restaurants. Since it's only 3 miles from the campground, you'll stand a good chance of hitching a ride to Terrebonne if you're staying at Smith without a car.

There are a few landmarks worth paying homage to on your visit to Terrebonne. To date, none of these fine establishments has received a National Historic Landmark designation, though it's just a matter of time. Ferguson's Market began business in 1970 and has been the convenience store of choice for decades—almost every climber in Smith history has set foot on these hallowed vinyl floors. At the south end of town is the Sunspot Drive-In, the chief supplier of fast food to climbers for over twenty-five years. They've expanded their offerings over the years—you might want to sample their bargain-priced breakfast. Finally, next to True Value Hardware is the Smith Rock Restaurant. Today the dining is family-oriented, but long ago the building housed a notorious tavern called Terrebonne Jacks, likely the most redneck watering hole in all of Central Oregon. Here lycra-clad Smith pioneers routinely risked their lives (or at least a good ass-kicking) by celebrating first ascents among drunken locals sporting cowboy hats.

By far the best eating and gathering spot is the Terrebonne Depot. Owned and operated by Ian and Kristin Yurdin (the first woman to redpoint *White Wedding*), this restored one hundred-year-old railroad depot is the best thing to happen to Terrebonne since the opening of Ferguson's Market. The food is excellent, and eating dinner on the deck with a view of Smith Rock can't be matched. Where else can you enjoy dinner and a microbrew while getting beta on the crux of almost every hard route in the park?

Redmond

Ten minutes south of Smith Rock is the rapidly growing city of Redmond (www.redmond.or.us; 541-923-5191). With a population of 21,109, Redmond might not match the diversity of

Bend, but it features every amenity you'll need on your visit to Smith. The fast growth has benefited the town greatly—today Redmond is a pleasant community bustling with good-natured, hard-working people. It's also the most convenient place to stay if you'd rather have your bed made for you while you're out climbing.

Bend

As the recreational and economic hub of Central Oregon, Bend (www.bendchamber.org; 541-382-3221) rests in the shadows of the Cascades, between the semiarid desert to the east and the forested foothills to the west. Located 25 miles south of Smith Rock, with a population of 70,238, Bend has boomed more than any other city in the state. The scenic beauty, recreational opportunities, and pleasant climate attract anyone who can afford the prices of the skyrocketing real estate.

Bend is the home base for most of Central Oregon's climbers. Two local climbing companies, Metolius and Entre Prises, provide jobs for roughly one hundred otherwise out-of-work climbers. Redmond might be closer to Smith, but climbers living in Bend benefit from the finest bouldering in the region. Several of the best areas are off-limits, including Awbrey Meadows, the birthplace of Bend bouldering. There aren't any guidebooks, but Bend's so-called "secret bouldering areas" aren't much of a secret anymore.

Since Bend relies heavily on tourism, there's far more restaurants, stores, and nightspots than you'll ever visit. With the influx of people comes both good and bad, but anyone visiting Bend will mostly notice the benefits, including far more cultural opportunities than anyone could have imagined twenty years ago. Bordering the Deschutes River, the revitalized downtown and Old Mill District are the nicest parts of the city. The eating spots recommended in the first edition of this guide almost all went out of business shortly after the book went to press—to avoid a similar curse, you're on your own this time around.

AMENITIES

Redpoint Climbing Supply in Terrebonne offers free Internet access, but if you didn't pack your laptop, you can always head to the Redmond Public Library (541-548-3141; US 97 south past first Redmond exit, right on West Antler Avenue, left on Northwest Sixth, right on Southwest Deschutes, 0.1 mile on the right).

The nearest swimming pool to Smith is Cascade Swim Center (www.raprd.org; 541-548-7275; US 97 south past first Redmond exit, right on West Antler Avenue, left on Northwest Sixth (one block), right on Black Butte Boulevard, left on Southwest Rimrock Drive, 0.25 mile on the right).

If you're looking for a skatepark, the renowned Redmond skatepark is located on the way to the pool. The park is a must-stop if carving concrete bowls is your idea of unwinding on a rest day.

You can catch the latest blockbuster at Redmond Cinemas on the south end of town (541-548-1244; US 97 south beyond all Redmond exits, right on Odem Medo Road, at the Wagner Mall, 50 yards on the right). It has only four screens, so you'll need to venture into Bend if you want to see the latest independent flick.

Inclimb Rock Gym (www.inclimb.com; 541-388-6764) is a must-visit on any poor weather day at Smith. Inclimb features 8,000 square feet of terrain, including freestanding boulders, a steep lead climbing wall, weights, and many other amenities. They moved to a new location in 2009, and they're open from noon to 9:00 p.m. weekdays and noon to 6:00 p.m. on weekends. Take US 97 south into Bend to exit 139 and turn left onto Southeast Reed Market Road. After 0.8 mile, go left on Southeast Paiute Way and then right on Southeast Centennial Court. Inclimb occupies the slanted roof building at the end of the cul-du-sac.

Guide Services

Most experienced climbers won't hire a guide when visiting Smith, but beginners will benefit greatly from instruction. Proper training won't merely speed your progression—it'll provide some of the skills needed to keep you alive. The following four guide services, listed in alphabetical order, are AMGA accredited, and they employ local climbers with a thorough knowledge of Smith climbing.

Chockstone Guide Service
Founded in 2006 by Smith veteran Jim Ablao, Chockstone employs guides that are active in the development of Smith climbing. They operate year-round and specialize in intermediate/advanced instruction and multi-pitch guiding. They also offer AMGA SPI training and certification. Visit www.chockstoneclimbing.com or call (541) 318-7170.

First Ascent Guide Service
Run by Carol Simpson, owner of Redpoint Climbers Supply, First Ascent has served Smith Rock since 1993. It's one of the only female-owned guide services in the country, specializing in camps and clinics for women. Visit www.goclimbing.com or call 800-325-5462.

Smith Rock Climbing Guides
The newest Smith guide service operates out of Rockhard, at the entrance to the park. Operated by owner and lead guide David Potter, Smith Rock Climbing Guides employs some of the most accomplished climbers in the region, with dozens of Smith first ascents to their credit. Visit www.smithrockclimbingguides.com or call (541) 548-4786.

Timberline Mountain Guides
Operating since 1983, the original Smith guide service has a far broader offering of guided ventures, including alpine ascents and international adventures. Guided ascents of Mount Hood provide a sizable chunk of their business, but their guides are Smith veterans led by owner Pete Keane. Visit www.timberlinemtguides.com or call (541) 312-9242.

Climbing Stores

The following stores, listed in alphabetical order, serve the Central Oregon climbing community.

Bend's Mountain Supply (www.mtnsupply.com; 541-388-0688) has sold climbing gear longer than anyone else in Central Oregon. They're open seven days a week, and they stock rental gear for both rock and alpine climbing (US 97 south into Bend, Exit 138, right on Northwest Colorado Avenue, then 0.5 mile on the right).

The arrival of R.E.I. (www.rei.com; 541-385-0594) in Bend's upscale Old Mill District struck fear in the hearts of owners of Central Oregon's smaller outdoor retailers. So far the concerns are mostly unfounded, and the entire region benefits from the presence of the outdoor giant—the corporation and its employees are generous with both time and money for local causes. Their store in the iconic Powerhouse building from the early sawmill days of Bend features three 200-foot silver smokestacks (US 97 south into Bend, Exit 138, right on Northwest Colorado Avenue, left on Northwest Wall Street, left on Southwest Industrial Way veering right on Southwest Bond Street, right on Southwest Powerhouse Drive, 0.25 mile on the left).

Located in the heart of downtown Terrebonne, Redpoint Climbing Supply (www .redpointclimbing.com; 541-923-6207) offers the most extensive selection of rock climbing gear in all of Central Oregon. Their claustrophobic original building is mercifully gone, replaced with a modern facility on the same site. More than any other shop, the staff are intimately familiar with Smith climbing. They're open part-time during the winter months and extended hours during peak season.

At the entrance to Smith Rock State Park is Rockhard (541-548-4786), a climbing shop and ice cream store rolled into one. Originally named Juniper Junction, it started as a gift shop in 1967. The rustic storefront of Kate's Saloon was built as a set for *Rooster Cogburn,* a 1975 movie starring John Wayne and Katharine Hepburn. In the 1980s, climbing gear replaced the knickknacks, and the name changed to Rockhard. Ice cream remains the one constant—they've surely made a small fortune selling countless scoops of their trademark huckleberry ice cream.

Web Sites

The best Smith Web sites are www.smithclimbing.com and www.smithrock.com. The author maintains smithclimbing.com with the intent of providing current information directly related to this guide. New routes, corrections, and other anecdotes will help keep this guide current, without having to wait a decade or more for a new edition. Smithrock.com is the oldest and most extensive site on Smith Rock, and serves a broader purpose with video clips, an online guide, and information on current events.

SMITH ROCK HISTORY

There's far more to Smith history than the often-told tales of the rise of American sport climbing. The annals of Smith Rock extend over seventy-five years with nearly 1,800 routes pioneered by hundreds of climbers. Each of these lines tells a unique story—some are famous throughout the climbing world, while others are unknown to all but the most seasoned Smith veterans. But even the most amazing climbs are just lifeless hunks of stone—it's the people behind the routes that bring them to life.

In researching this chapter, I talked to dozens of climbers, including some who visited Smith before I was born. They told colorful stories and shared vivid memories; their experiences make the history of Smith Rock worth telling. The main focus of my account here are the climbs and characters of the sixties and seventies, followed by my personal perspective on the formative years of the sport climbing era. A significant chunk of this chapter details the years prior to 1993, with the past decade receiving less than its fair share of attention. Hopefully, future historians will right this wrong. I believe that the entire Smith Rock story deserves a book of its own, though out of necessity this condensed version leaves some gaping holes. I apologize for leaving out so many key characters in the development of Smith, but this is a guidebook first and a history book second.

The Pre-Climbing Years

Millennia before the arrival of the first climbers, native Americans passed through the Smith Rock region. Archaeologist Luther Cressman discovered hand-woven sandals at nearby Fort Rock in 1938—radiocarbon testing dated the sandals to roughly 8,000 B.C. The only remnants of Smith's original locals are rare discoveries of perfect arrowheads, meticulously crafted from obsidian. In 1813 John Reed and Alfred Seton, trappers from John Jacob Astor's Pacific Fur Company, were the first white men to travel through Central Oregon. A group of settlers led by Stephen Meeks passed by Smith Rock in 1845 during an ill-fated search for a shortcut on the Oregon Trail. At least twenty-three people died along the trail as disease took its toll. In 1858 Andrew McClure led a group of miners on a search for the mythical Blue Bucket Mine. On his unsuccessful search he explored what is now called Smith Rock, referring in his journal to "the noted bluffs of the followers of Meek."

No one knows exactly why these magnificent crags received such a bland name. A fanciful tale of a soldier named Smith, who leaped from the crags instead of suffering at the hands of Indians, was long thought to be a myth. Surprisingly, parts of this story are true. In the late 1800s state senator J. N. Williamson of Prineville spoke about a company of soldiers who camped along the Crooked River during a clash with local Indian tribes in 1863. Voke Smith, a U.S. Cavalry private, fell to his death after dislodging a boulder while scaling a spire to scout out the battlefront. The crags may well have been named in his memory, though confusion arose in 1867 when a group from the Willamette Valley visited the region. In a letter to the *Albany States Right Democrat* newspaper, they described Smith Rock and attributed the name to future state legislator John Smith: "We came to the main valley of Crooked River—having first arrived at Smith's Rock, a high promontory of marl and sandstone being washed by the waters of Crooked River. The rock is named for the sheriff of Linn Country who discovered it, and is an object of curiosity worthy of any one's admiration." Given that no one will ever know exactly where the name orginated, perhaps John Smith and Voke Smith deserve equal credit for inspiring the name Smith Rock.

A further mystery is why an area of so many cliffs and pinnacles received a singular name. Almost without exception, both local residents and early climbers called the region Smith Rocks, with Smith Rock describing only the southernmost escarpment. The third edition of McArthur's *Oregon Geographic Names* confirmed this, attributing the singular name for the entire region to the creation of the state park. Even today many lifelong residents prefer the plural version.

By the early 1900s the plains surrounding Smith Rock attracted the first permanent settlers. With the hardships of settling a new land there was little interest in exploring the rocky summits. Early in the century an optimistic homesteader built a shack in the pines below the Monument. Irrigated by canals from the nearby Crooked River, he raised crops with little success. Fortunately his experiment failed—otherwise, home sites along the river might today be some of the priciest real estate in all of Central Oregon.

The North Unit Main Canal, a 65-mile irrigation channel built in the 1940s to move water from Wickiup Reservoir to the plains surrounding Madras, provided access to the earliest climbers. At a time when environmental considerations mattered little, the canal cut a path directly through Smith Rock. Workers bore two tunnels, with a combined length of 1.3 miles, under Staender Ridge and Indian Ridge to the north. A 772-foot bridge spanned the canyon upstream from the Upper Gorge, supporting a closed concrete box flume that carried water across the canyon. Forty years later a new pumping station drew excess water out of the Crooked River, moving it uphill to the canal. The most visible by-product of the original construction project is the switchbacked Burma Road, cutting across the hillside north of the Marsupial Crags.

The Early Climbing Years: 1935 to 1959

With the growing population in the region, Smith Rock appealed to those with a taste for adventure. The 1920s saw unrecorded exploration by young locals, including relatives of the author. The first recorded ascent at Smith Rock took place in 1935, when Johnny Bissell spied Squaw Rock on the horizon on a trip to climb the South Sister. He trekked cross-country and soloed the spire while partner Colin Chisholm took pictures. The next year a group of progressive climbers from Portland, the Wyeast Mountaineers, made the first Smith Rock road trip. There's no record of what they climbed, but they surely scaled spires now attributed to others.

There's little doubt that Ross Petrie and Dave Pearson climbed untouched spires when they visited Smith in 1946. With experience gained from the rock spire of Mount Washington in the Oregon Cascades, they managed a remarkable ascent of Shiprock's *West Chimney* (5.7)—a towering rhyolite plug feared by generations of Smith climbers. Petrie returned three years later, making the first ascent of the Poplar on Mendenhall Ridge. In the late 1940s Don Comer climbed the Monument. There's little question that someone had climbed this prominent tower earlier, but he left a record of his ascent on the summit in a pipe with threaded screw caps. In the early years, summit registers provided much of the limited information on Smith climbing—whoever first left proof usually received credit for the first ascent.

Apart from some insignificant climbs early in the decade, the fifties saw no recorded development until the wife/husband team of Vivian and Gil Staender started visiting Smith in 1955. They pioneered several spires on the ridge that today bears their name. Vivian was the stronger and more confident climber of the pair, and she led most of the routes. Jim Ramsey recalls her as "athletic, fearless, and really good." None of their routes were technically difficult, but they soon attracted the attention of others, as they left a record in 35mm film cans on each summit.

Growing up 20 miles north in Madras, with Squaw Rock visible on the horizon from their home, Jim and Jerry Ramsey played a key role in the early history of Smith climbing. With no guidebook they simply climbed the easiest spires, not knowing if they did a first ascent until they reached the summit. Jerry eventually left Central Oregon to become an English professor at Rochester University, and an acclaimed author. Older brother Jim, a University of Oregon alumnus, stayed in Madras, farming and raising his children while visiting the crags he grew up with.

The Sixties

By the end of the 1950s, Smith climbing was very much in its infancy. There were fewer than twenty named climbs, none harder than 5.7. By the end of the sixties, there were over one hundred routes, and standards weren't significantly lower than at more famous climbing areas around the country. Three events early in the decade spearheaded the rapid growth of climbing at Smith—the first ascent of Monkey Face, the creation of Smith Rock State Park, and the publication of the first climbing guide to the area.

Nothing at Smith captures the imagination more than the towering, sharp-edged pinnacle of Monkey Face. In late 1959 Dave Bohn, Jim Fraser, and Vivian Staender teamed to remove it from the list of unclimbed spires. Using siege tactics more commonly seen in the Himalayas, they spent days drilling holes, fixing ropes, and retreating over Misery Ridge each night to their campsite below Staender Ridge. After spending a frigid night in the mouth cave, they reached the summit on the first day of the new decade. Their ascent didn't break new ground in terms of difficulty—they aided and bolted even the easiest stretches. But an account of their ascent of the *Pioneer Route* in the 1960 *Mazama,* published by the Portland-based mountaineering club, put Smith Rock on the map among Oregon climbers.

In 1960 the Oregon State Highway Division created Smith Rock State Park. They constructed parking, picnicking, and sanitation facilities, and soon Smith became a popular scenic stop for anyone driving along US 97. The next year the Ramsey brothers, along with Vivian Staender, wrote a ten-page guide detailing thirty routes at Smith Rock for the 1962 *Mazama.* The Mazamas reprinted the guide as a separate volume, now about as rare as a Gutenberg Bible. In the days before climbing magazines, the Ramsey/Staender guide was the only source of information on Smith, and it caught the attention of Northwest climbers.

Despite the glaring eyesore of the Burma Road, the canyon itself was essentially a wilderness area during the early part of the decade. The hiking bridge spanning the Crooked River wasn't built until 1975, so today's main areas required either a long approach or a dangerous river crossing. Staender Ridge and the Marsupial Crags saw considerable activity, while the rest of Smith was undeveloped. At the start of the decade, it was rare for more than one group of climbers to visit, even on prime weekends. Early pioneer Dave Jensen recalls: "After climbing there several times, I finally saw two other climbers. At the time, it seemed like the oddest of coincidences—what were the chances of there being two groups of climbers at Smith on the same weekend?"

The early days of Smith climbing were a magical time, as Jon Marshall eloquently remembers: "Those were the good old days when climbing at Smith Rocks (we never called it Smith Rock) was an experience in nature, before the houses, the crowds, the rules, etc. It was not a gymnasium for world class super climbers, it was first most a beautiful phenomenon of volcanic nature with wildlife and adventure for us nature worshipping high school and early college kids who loved being there, camping and watching the starry sky at night around a campfire of close friends, learning from a few older experienced climbers and working up the courage to attempt unclimbed strange rocks."

In Smith's early years the focus was on reaching the summit, not on free climbing or pioneering harder lines. Aid, shoulder stands, lassoing the top—it didn't matter, as long as it ended atop a peak. The concept of free climbing wasn't well defined, and climbers rarely sought more difficult routes to the top. Climbing a wall without reaching a summit was equally as foreign. But around the country, free-thinkers like John Gill quietly put their own signature on the sport, in pursuit of pure gymnastic difficulty.

On a single day in 1961, Jim Ramsey invented Smith free climbing. After aiding the first ascent of the Awl, a small spire with a smooth-sided starting dihedral, Ramsey left two soft iron pegs behind. "I don't know why it occurred to me, but at the time I figured it might go free," Jim remembers. A month later, wearing gummy-soled deck shoes, he somehow finessed his way to a good ledge above all difficulties. "It was hard, but not the hardest thing I could imagine doing," he recalled forty-five years later. Partner Bruce Hahn recollects: "Jim scampered right up the corner. It didn't look too hard until I tried to follow, but I couldn't even get started."

Jim Ramsey.

Curiously, Ramsey's breakthrough ascent received no recognition for nearly two decades. Kim Schmitz, a talented teenager from Portland, earned credit for the first free ascent of the spire three years later. Using the same pins Ramsey left behind for protection, Schmitz's effort was no less outstanding, confirming that in the days before pin scars, the Awl was possible. "It was the hardest thing I'd ever climbed," Schmitz recalls. Long graded 5.9, the grade eventually settled at 5.10c.

In 1963 Ramsey and Hahn teamed again on the first ascent of *Bruce's Traverse* (5.8). At a time when most free climbs were short and insignificant, their route was over 300 feet long, with considerable exposure, bad rock, and sketchy protection. Hahn led the run-out opening pitch, while Ramsey led the upper pitches. Much like the Awl, their ascent didn't even warrant a footnote in early Smith histories. Hahn remembers nothing but the good times. "Jim had me laughing the whole time—he was always such a hoot."

Despite these inspired efforts, free climbing was still an anomaly at Smith. The most acclaimed routes of the era were aid ascents, especially on Monkey Face, where almost every new line warranted a feature article in the *Mazama*. In January 1963 Bob Martin and Dave Jensen aided an exposed seam left of the *Pioneer Route* into the West Face Cave. Long regarded as a landmark ascent in the history of Smith aid climbing, the reality removes some of the luster. Jensen recalls the ascent clearly: "We were planning on repeating Dave Bohn's route on Monkey Face, but Bob had other plans." Martin used a hand-cranked eggbeater drill and inch-long homemade dowels, along with shaky pins, to forge a new line. Despite the holes, Martin's ascent was far more dangerous than any other Smith aid route. As Jensen followed, several of the dowels popped out just from the tension of the rope.

Kim Schmitz. BOB MARTIN PHOTO

Without rival, Kim Schmitz emerged as the top all-around Smith climber during the first half of the sixties. Along with Bill Cummins, he repeated Martin's *Bohn Street West Face Cave,* using nothing but pins, while pulling Martin's dowels out of their holes. He recalls: "We had just come back from Yosemite and were pretty full of ourselves, thinking we could do the route better than it had been done before." That's exactly what they did. His 1964 ascent of Monkey Face's *East Face,* with Gerald Bjorkman, was the best aid climb of the era. After two pitches of overhanging nailing with minimal bolts, they bivouacked in a shallow cave just below the top, reaching the summit the next morning.

With ascents of the five spires of the Christian Brothers in 1965, and the free climbing era a few years away, the best ascents of the second half of the decade tackled Smith's largest unclimbed walls—usually combining difficult aid climbing with easy free moves. Some of these routes were unbelievably bad, such as Ted Davis's ascent of the *Southeast Face* of the Monument. Others, such as the *Northwest Corner* of Monkey Face, were nothing short of brilliant.

Nick Dodge's classic *A Climber's Guide to Oregon,* published in 1968, detailed sixty-four routes at Smith, and was the first widely distributed source of information on Smith climbing. There wasn't exactly a tidal wave of new climbers, but eventually a social scene developed in the Old Climbers' Camp near the river below Staender Ridge. There were rarely more than a dozen climbers camped on any given weekend, but the growing camaraderie (and competition) played a key role in the new route expansion.

With Kim Schmitz graduating to hardman status in Yosemite, the most influential Oregon climber of the second half of the sixties was Tom Bauman. By the time Bauman started climbing at Smith in 1965, he had already earned a reputation for his bold alpine ascents. Along with his older brother, Bob, he pioneered routes on the crumbling volcanic rock of the Oregon Cascades that made even the worst Smith tuff seem solid. Bauman's climbs at Smith ranged from classic easy lines, such as the *West Face Variation* (5.8) to an impressive solo first ascent of the *Southwest Corner* of Monkey Face. Bauman also led *Peking* (5.9) on Red Wall, the hardest free climb at Smith apart from the Awl.

The two top Smith climbers of the 1960s teamed together at the end of the decade to climb Smith's mini-version of El Cap. What Picnic Lunch Wall (550 feet tall) lacked in length, it made up for with a level of seriousness rivaling anything in Yosemite at the time. Schmitz had already made a name for himself with fast ascents of Yosemite's biggest walls, and Bauman had recently done the first solo ascent of The Nose of El Capitan. They spent two

Tom Bauman. GARY KIRK PHOTO

full days on the route, with a subfreezing hammock bivouac, made miserable after Schmitz dropped his sleeping bag. The nailing was consistently difficult and rotten, and their quarter-inch bolts were a joke. Schmitz admits, "At the time we weren't very knowledgeable about bolts."

At the end of the second day they faced a choice—either continue farther up a crumbling, dead-end dihedral (facing a second frigid bivy with a single sleeping bag) or traverse right by drilling a short line of bolts to easy terrain. Common sense won out, though Schmitz laments, "We took the chicken way." Their route was clearly A5 at the time of the first ascent. The anchors originally sported three ⅜-inch bolts, but there wasn't much to stop a fall on entire pitches of the route. Repeat ascents and many new bolts lowered the grade and seriousness greatly, but it remains the most respected Smith wall from the sixties.

By the end of the decade, no free routes even approached the level of Ramsey's ascent of the Awl. But one attractive new line hinted at the future. Dave Jensen's *Sky Ridge* (5.8) was far too run-out to qualify as a sport climb, but it was Smith's first rappel-bolted route. "It was something that just had to be climbed, and it seemed to me that the only sensible way to do it was to rappel from the top and drill the bolts," Jensen recalls. More than a decade would pass before his tactic became commonplace. But the shift to free climbing occurred swiftly in the early 1970s as a new cast of characters arrived, intent on finally pushing free standards higher.

The Seventies

With most of the major walls and spires already scaled, the 1970s saw a fundamental shift in Smith climbing. For the first time, the style of the ascent (free versus aid) began to matter more than the ascent itself. The shift to free climbing would have a profound impact on the future. Smith Rock's eventual move onto a world stage was due, in no small part, to the foundation laid by the free climbing pioneers of the '70s.

Apart from Jim Ramsey's free ascent of the Awl, it's hard to identify the exact origins of modern Smith free climbing. Two Portland area climbers—Steve Strauch and Danny Gates—deserve partial credit for starting the movement. Their hardest routes didn't raise the standards, but they were among the first to commit themselves to free ascents. Strauch was likely the first climber at Smith to leave his rack of pitons behind. While climbing in England during the late sixties, he acquired a rack of Peck Crackers and Clog nuts (among the earliest commercially available wedged protection devices) and used them at Smith on routes such as *Spiderman, King Kong,* and *Godzilla.*

Del Young was Smith's first free climbing specialist. With skills honed on granite thin cracks, he freed several routes far beyond the level of the day at Smith. His crack skills rivaled the very best in the country. Although clearly ahead of his time, his best ascents went unrecognized for many years as early guidebooks excluded all basalt routes. In 1971, on the basalt of

Clay Cox on *Last Gasp*. TOM ROGERS PHOTO

the Student Wall, he freed *Minotaur* (5.11a). This short tips crack matched Young's skill set perfectly—there were no face holds to contend with, just straight-in jams for both fingers and feet. *Minotaur* was Smith's first 5.11, at a time when very few cracks of the grade existed anywhere in the United States. Young also climbed nearby *Theseus* (5.10c) on basalt, as well as *Delirium Tremens* and *Sunjammer* (both 5.10b) on the tuff.

The early 1970s would be the final days of camping at the Old Climbers' Camp, before locked gates and NO TRESPASSING signs blocked the canal road access. Tom Rogers remembers: "Camping at the mouth of the Gorge was a blast. You could build a fire, there was some great bouldering, and the calming noise of the stream. We'd cart down all sorts of camping amenities, including food, alcohol, perception enhancement aids, as well as climbing gear. The Eugene and Corvallis climbing crowds also mixed here and we became friends."

As a student at the University of Oregon in Eugene, Tom Rogers perfected his climbing skills on the basalt columns of Skinners Butte. His early new routes at Smith were right in line with everything else from the 1960s—aid ascents of eventual free classics such as *Sunshine Dihedral, Wartley's Revenge,* and *Trezlar*. But his 1972 ascent of a horrifying off-width, *Last Gasp* (5.9), was anything but typical. In the days before wide crack protection, it was run-out, rotten, and dangerous. The next year he climbed *As You Like It* (5.10b) in the Lower Gorge. Despite his efforts, Rogers considers his tutelage of Wayne Arrington to be his biggest contribution to Smith climbing.

Like Rogers, Arrington developed his crack climbing skills in Eugene, where he pioneered testpieces into the 5.11 range and routinely soloed hard 5.10. With a grace under pressure developed as a helicopter pilot in Vietnam, Arrington became a legend in Oregon climbing. His soft-spoken disposition belied a fiery intensity and calm presence in the most tense situations. Tom Rogers remembers, "He was fearless—once he decided to do something, he went for it wholeheartedly and never backed off."

Arrington devoted himself to the columnar basalt of the Gorge at Smith Rock, and he quickly became consumed with the clean, strenuous cracks. He never kept track of his routes, naming only a few, so most of his efforts went unrecorded. But over a three-year period, by his own estimates, he pioneered about sixty basalt routes in the 5.8 to 5.10 range. His most infamous efforts were off-widths, done with minimal protection. *Titus* (5.10b) was feared for more than a decade until wide crack protection eliminated the 40-foot run-out at the top.

Wayne Arrington, 1972.
TOM ROGERS PHOTO

Although best known at Smith for his exploits in the Gorge, Arrington was a formidable all-around climber, mixing big walls and alpine epics. He did the first solo ascent of Bauman and Schmitz's *Picnic Lunch Wall,* in the days when it was still a death route, along with the 1975 first free ascent of *Tombstone Wall,* a 5.10d crack with exposure like no other Smith free route at the time.

With the Old Climbers' Camp at the entrance to the Gorge, the basalt columns soon became the most developed section of rock at Smith. At the time almost the entire Gorge was privately owned, and at least one landowner wasn't too happy about the new uninvited visitors. He responded the only way a Central Oregon redneck knew how—by letting his rifle do the talking. Early explorer Steve Strauch remembers: "I was climbing a crack, not knowing if it had been done before. I wasn't having an easy time with it, and all of a sudden things got a whole lot worse. I heard a gunshot, and a split second later, a bullet bounced off the rock about 10 feet away. Before it even sunk in what was going on, another bullet ricocheted even closer. I climbed down as fast as I could and hid until the shooter figured he'd made his point and left." With stories like this making the rounds, it's understandable why the Gorge developed in a hush-hush environment. Early guidebook authors wisely pretended it didn't exist. But the few named routes soon gained a following among climbers in the know—Todd Rentchler's *Badfinger* (5.10b), Jeff Thomas's *Original Sin* (5.10c), Paul Landrum's *Morning Star* (5.10c), and Mike Seeley's *Cruel Sister* (5.10a) were some of the most respected efforts. By the end of 1975, the Gorge had the highest concentration of hard routes anywhere at Smith Rock.

With Arrington focusing mainly on the basalt, it was left to Dean Fry and Jeff Thomas to change the course of Smith history on the tuff. Fry was a native of nearby Corvallis, while Thomas spent his childhood in California before moving to New York. He learned to climb at the Gunks and moved back west to attend Oregon State University. Jack Barrar recalls: "Dean loved climbing more than anyone else. He was laid back and a lot of fun to be around. Jeff was more straight-laced and conservative, but together they made a great team." Fry and Thomas quickly became best friends, and they immediately made an impact on Smith climbing.

Thomas's 1972 ascent of *Desert Solitaire* (5.10a) on Koala Rock was typical of his ground-up, high-risk style, boldly climbing an overhanging wall of jugs while drilling bolts hanging off hooks. "It was just like climbing in the Gunks—I really didn't think it was anything

Dean Fry and Jeff Thomas, 1972.
USED WITH PERMISSION OF MAZAMAS.

special," Thomas remembers. Dean Fry, wearing his trademark tattered jeans and blue stocking cap, was equally skilled at run-out free routes and difficult aid climbs. Thomas recalls: "The second pitch of *Catfight Cracks* (5.10a) was the best lead of Dean's I ever saw. He wasn't able to put in any decent protection—if he had fallen he would have hit the ground (from 150 feet up). The rock was so bad I was scared just following."

Dean Fry's career at Smith lasted a little over a year. His younger brother, Paul, remembers him as "incredibly driven and talented in everything he did." His first ascents at Smith proved this true, as he quickly staked his claim as the best free climber on Smith tuff. He did the long-awaited third ascent of the Awl and free ascents of *Zebra* and *New Testament,* along with multi-pitch, crumbling horror shows such as *Smith Summit–East Wall.* His most visionary line was *Methuselah's Column,* the first of the Dihedrals' face routes. Ignoring easier cracks on either side, Fry pioneered an unusually bold line up the wall of crumbling stone, drilling widely spaced quarter-inch bolts on lead. This was the first 5.10 face climb anywhere at Smith; even with new bolts, it still warrants an "R" rating.

October 7, 1973, was one of Dean's finest days at Smith Rock. He led the first free ascent of *Math Test* (combining both *Karate Crack* and *Peapod Cave*)—Smith's only route with two pitches of 5.10. On the late-night return trip to Corvallis, Fry sat in the passenger seat of a yellow Triumph as it passed a car on a blind curve on a narrow stretch of U.S. Highway 20. Near milepost 59 the car left the road and was split in half after hitting a tree. The driver survived, but Dean died before reaching the hospital. Smith history would have been completely rewritten had he lived. Today a small plaque on a boulder at the bridge spanning the Crooked River honors his memory.

With Fry's death the development on Smith tuff stagnated for a couple years. Thomas and others pioneered many new lines, but almost everything was below 5.10. Decades later Thomas remembers: "With Dean gone, I suppose I went through a couple years where I didn't work as hard. We always had a friendly, competitive thing going—we pushed each other to do harder routes. He was so focused, I'm sure that if he had lived, he would have succeeded on 5.11 at Smith earlier than I did."

Over the next five years, Thomas matured into the undisputed leader of the Smith free climbing movement. Thomas's calm nature stood in contrast to his fierce determination on the rock. Although not the most physically talented climber of his generation, he countered with refined technique and a willingness to push himself far above protection. Somehow he possessed an intuitive sense for what knobs he could trust—nubbins popped on everyone else, but not on J.T.—they wouldn't dare. By the middle of the decade, Thomas had already racked up a longer list of first ascents on Smith tuff than anyone else. But he never pushed the standards until 1976, when he freed a remote, quirky wide crack splitting a wall of perfect stone. Thomas remembers: "Day after day I kept getting to the base of the off-width, but I couldn't figure out what to do next. It was really committing and I never hung on the rope to figure it out. Finally I discovered a crucial edge and I managed to pull through." *Brain Salad Surgery* (5.11a) became the first 5.11 on Smith tuff.

Despite the barrage of new routes, the biggest impact on Smith Rock during the mid-1970s had nothing to do with climbing. In 1974 Oregon State Parks announced plans to construct a footbridge across the river below Picnic Lunch Wall. Many of Smith's hardcore climbers—Thomas included—opposed the idea, fearing it would bring masses of people onto the fragile hillsides. The critics were right, but in February 1975 the bridge opened to the public, bringing a new level of convenience to Smith climbing.

With full access to the park and skills honed over years of effort, Jeff Thomas dominated the second half of the decade. During the spring of 1977, he freed several pitches of 5.11, including *Shoes of the Fisherman,* his hardest Smith route, and the third pitch of Monkey Face's *Southwest Corner* (later called *Astro Monkey*). His boldest 5.11, *Lion's Chair,* fit Thomas's skill set perfectly. The first pitch of this old aid route was a high-tech stemming corner with an unnerving run-out leading to an old fixed peg. Any pin at Smith is a shaky proposition, but this one was critical, coming right past the crux—15 feet above the last solid piece of gear. Insecure climbing, poor pro, high risk—it suited Thomas perfectly, and he finessed his way to the anchor with the outcome never in doubt.

Thomas's style of free climbing was a tough act to follow on the crumbling tuff. His rules were stringent—no rappel inspection, no cleaning, bolts placed only on lead, no pre-placed gear, and no yo-yos. A free ascent required what many years later became known as a "redpoint"—no falls, with all gear placed on lead. But the one chink in Thomas's armor of impeccable style—rare uses of hangdogging—opened the door to the future of Smith free climbing. In 1978, after getting shut down day after day on the final move of *Wartley's Revenge* (5.11a), he finally relented, hung on the rope, and worked out the crux sequence. The tactic paid off—he breezed through the crux with hardly a pump on his next redpoint go. From that moment on, hangdogging became an accepted tactic at Smith, at least among the impressionable youth.

Thomas's impact on the next generation of climbers was far larger than he remembers. "I don't see how I had anything to do with what eventually happened at Smith Rock," Thomas says thirty year later. But in reality the sport climbing movement during the 1980s might never have occurred if Jeff Thomas hadn't visited Smith Rock. His *Oregon Rock* guidebook, published in 1983, detailed 281 climbs (all on tuff) and was the only source of information on Smith routes throughout the 1980s. Within a few years the standards he established would be left far behind, but to this day there's never been another Smith climber half as skilled at pioneering knobby face routes from the ground up.

Following Thomas's successful lead of *Wartley's* was Chris Jones, an extraordinary talent from Eugene. In many respects Jones was the flipside of Thomas. While Jeff did his best climbing above protection, Chris preferred a toprope. Jeff developed exquisite footwork to succeed on high-level routes, while Chris was so strong he hardly needed his feet at all, often letting them dangle while cranking overhanging boulder problems. Years later John Sherman, author of *Stone Crusade* and creator of the V-grade system, called Jones "the most powerful boulderer in America." Introspective and meticulous, Jones was brilliant (and quirky) both on and off the rock. With his rare power, obliterating Smith standards wouldn't have been much of a problem, but after surviving a 150-foot

Chris Jones, 1979.

ground fall in Yosemite (with little more than a mild concussion and bruised heel), he had little interest in lead climbing. He spent most of his time on the boulders, creating problems that no one else at Smith could touch. During the summer of 1979, Jones pioneered nearly one hundred boulder problems—up to V9 in difficulty. Jones ended Thomas's reign as the dominant force in Smith free climbing, though within a year he moved on, never again climbing a new route.

By the late 1970s, with the 5.11 grade well established, the most obvious prize was a free ascent of Monkey Face. Bob McGown was the first to seriously contemplate freeing the spire, via a line of holds leading into the West Face Cave. McGown made his mark in Smith history by reinventing aid climbing in the late seventies, with ascents of preposterous routes like *Soft Shoe Ballet* and *Journey to Ixtlan*. He was a skilled free climber, but his definition of a "free ascent" was broader than others of the era—enough so that many of his efforts weren't accepted. Nonetheless, he deserves some credit for the eventual free ascent of Monkey Face. He placed a couple bolts swinging over from *Bohn Street West Face Cave* to the right, hanging off hooks while drilling 5-inch-deep holes. He never succeeded, but his bolts were an open invitation to anyone with enough courage to try.

The two leading free climbers of the seventies, Jeff Thomas and Chris Jones, teamed together for the first attempt. Thomas made it to McGown's final bolt but couldn't let go to clip in, flying off the rock with a monstrous pendulum fall. Jones retraced the traverse, easily finding the power to make the clip. But now there were no more bolts, and Jones was out of his element on the sharp end of the rope. After hanging to haul up the bolt kit, he fought off his demons and cranked through the 5.11- crux moves, stepping left to a delicate perch.

Dangling off hooks he anxiously drilled a bolt and jammed an easy crack into the West Face Cave. After Thomas followed, they surveyed the possibilities out of the cave. The normal exit aided a brief line of bolts on a steep wall. Frightfully exposed a few feet left was a bouldering sequence of pockets and edges. The moves were near Thomas's physical limits, but they gave Jones little trouble. Now all that remained was a redpoint ascent.

Jones returned a few weeks later with Bill Ramsey, the son of the Smith pioneer. Bill possessed the same natural free climbing talent as his dad and was one of the few climbers whose physical skills were nearly as impressive as Jones's. Together they succeeded, with Jones leading both pitches to the top while Ramsey followed cleanly. In typical Jones fashion he downplayed his efforts, attributing success to the earlier efforts of McGown and Thomas, saying, "Bill and I merely contributed enough strength-to-weight ratio to succeed." With two pitches of 5.11, *Monkey Space* was

Chris Jones on *Monkey Space* (5.11b).
DALE ALLYN PHOTO

unlike anything seen before at Smith Rock. Jones says, "It more or less marked the beginning of lead bouldering on bolted faces at Smith."

Motivated by his success, Jones soon returned to Monkey Face to free an overhanging thin crack leading to Bohn Street. It took him three days before he stuck the final moves, cranking much harder slopers directly instead of liebacking the final moves like everyone else. *Rising Expectations* (5.11d) was easily the hardest lead anywhere at Smith, but it marked the end of Jones's new routes. "It was just too much work and not much fun," he remembers. Before he relocated to Colorado, he saw one last opportunity to leave a mark in his own quirky way. He returned to *Monkey Space* a final time, leading the crux pitch out of the West Face Cave using no feet. He stopped midpitch, dangling from one hand while clipping the crux bolt, legs hanging limply in the air, and then powered through to the finishing jugs. This contrived exercise in roped bouldering was discounted as a silly stunt at the time, but it showed just what he was truly capable of. Jones's V8 no-feet ascent was roughly equivalent to a midlevel 5.13.

As the 1970s came to a close, with 450 routes (including the basalt) many veteran climbers felt that Smith climbing had peaked. Most of the classic cracks went free—those that remained were either very difficult, unpleasant, or both. The pioneers of the '70s, including Thomas and Jones, moved on to other pursuits, leaving Smith in the hands of an untested generation of youngsters. There seemed little reason to believe that Smith climbing stood at the cusp of moving onto a world stage.

The Emergence of Sport Climbing: 1980 to 1986

It seems hard to believe, but the origins of American sport climbing can be traced in no small way to a small outcrop of basalt—Skinners Butte Columns—located near the center of the second-largest city in Oregon. In September 1978 I arrived in Eugene just out of high school to attend the University of Oregon. My roommate and best friend was Bill Ramsey. Unlike most freshman who were unsure of their course of study, I knew exactly what I wanted to pursue. Ironically, it had nothing to do with school and everything to do with the basalt columns no more than 2 miles from our dorm. I came to Eugene to get good at climbing—it was just that simple.

Alan Watts, 1983.
DEB SCHNELL PHOTO

Growing up 20 miles north of Smith in Madras, stories of climbing were part of my childhood. My dad climbed, and Smith was a frequent hiking destination. After scaling all the Oregon Cascades with my family, I started climbing at Smith when I was fourteen. Along with high school buddies Pat Carr and Randy Hagen, I taught myself how to climb by working through all the easy routes—both the classics and the death traps. I watched Jeff Thomas on the first free ascent of *Shoes of the Fisherman,* memorized the guidebook, and dreamed about climbing every night.

I suppose I possessed more than an average level of talent physically. I was 145 pounds and blessed with fingers that could hold onto just about anything—even if I had minimal upper-body power. But with little desire to push myself, I was an underachiever until I started climbing with Bill Ramsey as a high-school junior. Chiseled out of stone, Bill was self-assured and aggressive on the rock. Years later, after becoming a professor of philosophy at Notre Dame, he developed into the best over-forty sport climber in the country. I soaked up his enthusiasm, and for the first time I felt a hint of competition in my climbing. As high school came to an end, I followed Bill to the University of Oregon, believing every word he said about how good we would get with a daily diet of perfect thin cracks.

As it turned out, Bill knew exactly what he was talking about. Skinners Butte, no more than 45 feet high and 150 feet from end to end, was the perfect venue for developing technical skills. A couple weeks after we arrived, we watched in awe as local expert Chris Jones demonstrated his mastery of low-angle cracks. The three of us became great friends, along with Alan Lester, a fellow freshman who struggled at first but possessed a stronger desire to succeed on the rock than anyone else. With Jones the clear leader of the pack, the four of us pushed each other to levels none of us would have reached alone.

My interest in the Columns quickly grew into an obsession, and I dropped out of most of my classes. I sought out the hardest way of doing every route, eliminating holds on either side of the crack or ignoring the crack completely, using only face holds. I climbed almost every crack and column one-handed. After a year and a half, I went from barely toproping 5.10 to leading 5.12 thin cracks. By the time my parents cut off my school funding (despite the "A" I earned in bowling my final term), I was ready to devote myself to developing the potential I hoped might exist at Smith Rock.

Despite my newfound technical skills, success came slowly. After repeating all of the 5.11s, I focused on freeing aid climbs and any unclimbed cracks. With little confidence on the vertical faces, routes like *Sunshine Dihedral* (5.12a), *Minas Morgul* (5.11d), and the first pitch of Monkey Face's *West Face* (5.12a A0) fit my skill set perfectly. *Karot Tots* (5.11c) didn't match the standards of the hardest routes, but it was the first line in the Dihedrals to venture onto the smooth, vertical faces. With only a single bolt and a rack of gear, it hardly qualified as a sport climb, but it hinted at the future. At the time I didn't take the hint and immediately went back to work on the cracks. Early in 1981 I managed a free ascent of *Smut* (5.12d), a roof crack high on Staender Ridge. It was plenty hard, but despite a couple nut placements it was just a boulder problem. It barely attracted any curiosity, let alone any efforts at a repeat. But for me it was a psychological breakthrough. I started believing in my talent and soon developed a single-minded focus that become my trademark. I was living near Smith Rock, climbing every day, and getting better quickly.

I put most of my energy into freeing old aid routes on the tuff, but I also found success on the basalt of the Lower Gorge. In the pre-sticky-rubber days, my ascents of *Dark Star* and *Neutron Star* were both 5.12. Apart from nuts at the start, *Neutron Star* came very close to meeting the criteria for the first sport climb—fixed gear placed on rappel, with moves carefully rehearsed with the intent of creating a difficult route. In 1982 my momentum slowed, as I managed just two high-level routes. First came *Unfinished Symphony* (5.12b), an old aid climb on Picnic Lunch Wall. It wasn't one of Smith's finer routes, but at least it was hard. Next up was *Midnight Snack* (5.12b), an unclimbed arch to the left. The bolted underclings and smears were a notch harder wearing the clunky, hard-rubber shoes of the era. The awkward moves on pigeon-crap-smeared rock weren't pleasant, but for nearly a year it was Smith's hardest lead.

These routes continued the progression of difficulty at Smith, but they pointed to an uncertain future. Looking at increasingly unpleasant cracks and free ascents of pegged-out aid routes, I feared that Smith might soon be climbed out. I either had to design a new plan or move elsewhere—like most of my friends had already done. I slowly rethought my approach to Smith climbing, broadening my focus beyond freeing old aid routes. For the first time I opened my eyes and carefully studied the untouched walls.

I realized that any potential held by the blank-looking crags wouldn't be revealed by standing on the ground. So I started rappelling everything that looked promising, and I soon found a quiet pleasure in exploring beautiful sections of virgin stone. It didn't take long to discover that the seemingly featureless walls of Smith Rock held a hidden secret—they weren't blank at all. They were studded with edges and pockets, large and small, and the stone was often perfect. I was looking at a gold mine of gorgeous lines; for the first time I saw that Smith might grow beyond my personal obsession into a world-class destination. I faced a choice—either get serious, work my ass off, and realize this potential, or let someone else make the same breakthrough.

Beginning in the Dihedrals with an attractive face right of *Tator Tots,* I used all the tools at my disposal in pursuit of pure difficulty. I studied and bolted the wall on rappel, cleaning any loose rock. I worked out the sequences after hanging on the rope, lowering down to link sections. I mapped out the moves in meticulous drawings in my journal. I didn't invent any of these tactics, but I used them to my advantage. Others had discreetly rap-bolted routes at Smith, hanging their heads in shame. But I turned the art of cleaning, preplacing bolts, hang-dogging, and memorizing sequences into a fully choreographed art form. I developed confidence in my approach and moved ahead as fast as hand-drilling would allow. I wasn't good enough to succeed on *Watts Tots* in 1982, but I was finally heading in the right direction.

At the start of 1983, funded by my parents, I moved to Bend under the guise of returning to school—this time at Central Oregon Community College. On many fronts this was the best move I could have made. As long as I did well in my classes, I had the green light to climb whenever I wanted. With creative scheduling, this meant every day. The best part of moving to Bend was my network of friends. Since leaving the U of O in 1980, I had experienced limited success and much frustration pursuing my dreams alone. But with like-minded allies, the quest to bring Smith to a national stage turned into a great adventure. In the early eighties a close-knit community of active climbers evolved at Smith Rock. Several got better every year, establishing 5.13 routes by the end of the decade, while others played more of a supporting role. But only through the collective energy of everyone did the pieces of the Smith puzzle finally fit together.

In many ways, Chris Grover and I were opposites. Chris grew up just outside Philadelphia in the affluent New Jersey suburb of Cherry Hill. And I was from Madras—a small town even by Central Oregon standards. Chris was outgoing, street-wise, and cool. I was introverted, naive, and a bit of a geek. The last thing I wanted to do in developing Smith climbing was ruffle anyone's feathers—especially those of my heroes. But

Chris Grover.

my style of climbing did just that. Chris, on the other hand, was a rebel who loved stirring up the old guard. Somehow, over countless conversations, his confidence became mine, and I started to believe in the outlandish things we talked about. Chris was far more than a climbing partner—he was a mentor, motivator, friend, and coach. During the 1980s he had as great an influence on the direction of my life—and Smith climbing—as anyone else.

When Chris wasn't holding the rope, more often than not it was Mike Puddy. Mike was an adventurous thrill-seeker who lived his life with more passion than anyone I've ever known, balancing family, career, and his many sports. Better than anyone else, he seemed to understand my personality quirks and soon became one of my best friends and favorite partners.

Brooke Sandahl.

Brooke Sandahl moved to Bend in 1984 and quickly fit into the local scene with his all-around athletic ability, great sense of humor, and fun-loving personality. He possessed as much natural climbing talent as anyone. As a pioneer at Smith and the creative force behind Metolius, Brooke became a well-known figure in the American climbing scene. He teamed with Lynn Hill in 1994 on the first free ascent of The Nose of El Capitan.

Jim Anglin worked as an EMT in Albany and spent his free time climbing at Smith in the early 1980s, pioneering several free routes in the traditional style, while earning his reputation as the dominant aid climber of the time. He repeated almost every aid line—often solo—and added *Air to Spare,* originally rated A5. Jim squeezed more into his day than just about anyone else, but he always had time to mentor the upcoming generation of climbers.

Kent Benesch grew up in Corvallis and started visiting Smith as a teenager in the late seventies along with his older brother, Craig. Good-humored and ageless, he pioneered hard routes throughout the eighties and still makes appearances on the tuff. Sean Olmstead, a likeable Bend youngster with a strict Mormon upbringing, was both inspired and corrupted by the Smith regulars. A natural athlete, he freed difficult routes for nearly a decade.

Chuck Buzzard, Alan Lester, Jim Davis, John Rich, and Tom Blust climbed many new routes on the tuff and basalt—aid and free. Mike Volk became an integral part of the scene when he purchased ten acres behind the main parking lot. His home became an informal headquarters and the scene of the now legendary Smith Rock parties. His backyard of juniper trees and sagebrush became the campground of choice for visiting superstars later in the decade. And Doug Phillips, an inventor and Smith pioneer, started Metolius out of his Camp Sherman garage, eventually providing jobs for scores of unemployed climbers.

The rest of the American climbing community had no way of knowing it, but sport climbing arrived at Smith Rock in February 1983. For those of us who were a part of it, there was no mistaking the shift as two landmark routes went free in the Dihedrals. I had tried *Watts Tots* the previous summer, but a bouldery crux shut me down. After a month in Bend, I was already lighter, stronger, and more confident. Puffing on his Camel straight, Chris Grover held the rope as I succeeded on an icy day, wearing edging shoes as stiff as alpine boots. Two decades later this appealing face became widely recognized as America's first sport route.

Watts Tots was a good effort, but it created far less of a buzz in the local scene than my ongoing attempts on an improbable knife-edged arête 100 feet to the left. I spent a miserable day drilling five bolts by hand and immediately went to work unlocking the route's secrets. Never a master at spotting the best sequence, I pinched the arête with both hands, missing face holds around the corner. I only gave it one go a day, working through the moves and lowering off. After failing at the start of day seven, I tried a different tactic for the first time at Smith. I pulled the draws, waited thirty minutes, and tried again—and again. Soon enough my hand wrapped around the finishing jug and I cranked over the lip with a hoot that echoed through the canyon. For lack of a real name, I called it *Corner Number One* for the better part of a year, before finally settling on *Chain Reaction* (5.12c).

Alan Watts on *Watts Tots* (5.12b). ALAN WATTS COLLECTION

With that one ascent all the pieces fell into place, and it became obvious what we had to do. If something as outrageous as *Chain Reaction* went free, then almost everything would go. All the elements were there—featured rock, rappel bolting, cleaning, hangdogging, lots of free time, sufficient technical skills, and no opposition. The final point was key. I wasn't pursuing my style to revolt against the established norms in climbing. All I was trying to do was tick another route off my list. And I was using the most efficient process that I could devise to do that. I might not have been a rebel, but I didn't give a damn about doing things exactly how they'd been done before. I truly believed that I had found a better way to push the limits of difficulty.

My self-imposed rules were strict in the old days—the primary focus was creating a difficult line, but run-outs and sketchy protection were sometimes part of the equation. All Smith routes done prior to 1987 were drilled by hand. It took about an hour drilling each hole; it wasn't a pleasant way to spend a day, swinging a hammer and twisting a drill until my hands cramped. Minimizing bolts meant less suffering—at least until it came time for the redpoint. I saw no reason to avoid natural protection, so the early routes often combined bolts and trad gear. Before rappelling a route, I'd boulder as high off the ground as my courage allowed, deciding where to place the first bolt—the higher the better. Stick-clips and crash pads disqualified an ascent—so did preplacing any gear, including quickdraws. On some routes attempted prior to 1986, this restriction alone was the difference between success and failure.

After the success of early 1983, the next two years were a single-minded quest to fulfill the promise of Smith climbing before the rest of the world found out about the place. For me, these years were my most memorable at Smith; alongside my best friends in the world, I was following a dream I'd pursued for years. Every day—success or failure—took me closer to what I wanted to achieve. Routes like *Last Waltz, Heinous Cling, Karate Wall, Split Image, Latest Rage,* and *Boy Prophet* fell one after another. Climbing in the Gorge boomed as well, with routes such as *Masquerade* going free.

By 1984 I'd progressed to where 5.13 was within my limits. In a throwback to the old days, the earliest routes of the grade at Smith weren't sport climbs but traditional routes with physically difficult nut placements. While other routes garnered far more attention, an unheralded pin-scarred seam named *Double Stain* quietly became Smith's first 5.13. The pin scars were tough enough, but the real challenge came from placing gear in the middle of hard moves. Despite the appealing grade, it never garnered much interest. With the rise of bolted sport routes, freeing old aid routes quickly fell out of fashion. But there was still one remaining aid line that simply couldn't go unnoticed.

For the free climber no aid line at Smith compared to the strikingly beautiful *East Face* of Monkey Face. I freed the first pitch in 1983, though this gently overhanging crack was just a warm-up for the awe-inspiring bulging wall above the anchors. I set my sights on the improbable second pitch during the summer of 1984. Leaving a rope fixed at the hanging station, I bribed partners to jumar the line to set a belay. The upper pitch was an intense gear-placement exercise, with a technical start followed by locking pin scar jams, ending with a pumping traverse to the finishing arête. I quickly discovered that the real difficulties revolved around placing gear—I had no choice but to whittle down the placements to just four RPs. Late in the summer of 1984, I finally succeeded placing all gear on lead in a redpoint ascent. I considered this pitch alone (with no preplaced gear) to be more difficult than *Grand Illusion*. Although no one else knew it, Smith Rock—from a sheer numbers perspective—now stood atop U.S. free climbing standards.

My New Year's resolution was to climb every day in 1985—all 365 of them. This wasn't easy in the pre–climbing gym days. I climbed in snowstorms and even by headlamp, just to keep the streak alive. For a couple months I was stronger than ever before—doing the hardest boulder problems of my life. Although still better at cracks, my face climbing skills steadily improved. *Darkness at Noon* soon became Smith's first 5.13 face route, and I spent several days working out moves on a futuristic wall left of *Sunshine Dihedral*. I bolted a direct start to *Boy Prophet* and concocted an absurd sequence, bumping the level high into the 5.13 grade. Spotting the easiest way to do a route was never my strong point, and I never succeeded using the original line of holds. Perhaps it had something to do with my upbringing at the Columns, where the objective was to find the hardest (not the easiest) way to do any given route.

Unrestrained obsession is never healthy, as I learned the hard way. I made it until the end of May before it became clear that all was not well. I was getting weak, irritable, and sick. And I was struggling on routes that seemed simple earlier in the year. It was a classic case of overtraining—eventually my body simply couldn't adapt to the constant stress. I developed chronic problems with my fingers—not just pain, but severe inflammation. One rest day extended into a rest week, and then another, before the discomfort faded away. But the damage was already done—some years would be better than others, but I would face joint problems for the remainder of my climbing career.

My injury-forced layoff coincided with the social event of the season at Smith—the first visit by foreign dignitaries—Kim Carrigan and Geoff Weigand from Australia, and Jonny Woodward from England. They climbed most of the classic sport routes in the Dihedrals, with Weigand repeating *Darkness at Noon,* and Woodward on-sighting the second ascent of the entire *Heinous Cling,* placing gear the whole way. We spent hours hanging out and listening to their stories of climbing around the world. For the first time we learned that the budding techniques of sport climbing were evolving independently around the world. Their visit validated what was becoming obvious to those of us who climbed here every day—Smith Rock was a world-class climbing area.

The summer of 1985 was a turning point for my climbing. The inflammation in my fingers eventually went away, and my strength and confidence returned. I spent the months of July and August at Smith, squeaking by on income earned from guiding for Mike Volk's Timberline Mountain Guides. I lived in a massive canvas tent called the "Sun Cottage," large enough that I hauled in furniture. It was one of the best times of my life—climbing every day—first thing in the morning or late in the afternoon. When I couldn't find a partner, I'd either prepare new lines or solo thousands of vertical feet a day. At night I'd light my lantern and visit our secret training facility hidden in the trees.

As anyone who has visited Smith during the summer knows, August is not the best month to climb hard routes. With the Dihedrals roasting in the sun, I turned my attention to Monkey Face. I climbed the beautiful lower arête of *Spank the Monkey* (5.12a) and free climbed into the Mouth Cave via *Young Pioneers* (5.12d). With Mike Puddy holding the rope, I led *Close Shave* (5.12d), an outrageously exposed arête with one of the more intense bouldering cruxes at Smith. To ease my fears of the rope slicing on the sharp arête, I used double 11mm ropes.

My final Smith goal of the summer was eliminating the hanging belay in the middle of the *East Face.* I imagined this would only minimally increase the level of the route, and in many respects this was true—I had done the first pitch so many times it no longer generated a pump. I soon discovered that a significant problem with the single-pitch version was the weight of the rope snaking through gear from the ground. In 1985 few climbers used anything other than 11mm ropes, and I was no exception. More than once I placed all the nuts before getting stopped trying to clip into bolts on the final traversing crux. I used long quickdraws so I wouldn't have to pull up so much slack, but these would swing in the breeze, making them hard to clip.

Always looking for a better way, I had the clever idea of preclipping a long draw into the rope before leaving the ground. I could clip the draw into the bolt, and the rope would already be clipped in—without pulling up any slack at all. My plan worked to perfection, and for the first time I stuck a barn-door deadpoint to a finger jam. I matched, reached right to the arête, and suddenly couldn't move. To my horror I saw that the preclipped carabiner had somehow slipped over my figure-eight knot and was jammed tight. I was stuck and couldn't go farther. I tried wrestling the jammed biner through the knot, but I was too pumped and flew off the rock with an outburst that echoed throughout the park. I lowered to the ground—still fuming. I was leaving soon on a Yosemite trip, so I decided to compromise my standards and settle for a yo-yo ascent. I'd learned from Kim Carrigan that this was the tactic used on the hardest routes around the world at the time—including Wolfgang Gullich's *Punks in the Gym*—the first 5.14. So I yo-yoed back to my highpoint, clipped one more bolt, and finally reached the anchor. A little deflated I lowered off for the last time, pulling all the gear, never to return.

Sometimes the biggest changes arise from the most unexpected circumstances. Late in the summer a scruffy-looking Austrian climber approached me in the parking lot, saying he wanted to take photos of me. I explained that I had no interest in posing for pictures, but he sweetened the deal by offering a free (used) rope. The next morning, long before the sun rose above the horizon, we hiked into the canyon for a first-light photo shoot on *Chain Reaction*. We spent the entire day, moving from one hard route to the next—*Darkness At Noon, Split Image, Close Shave,* and the *East Face* of Monkey Face.

I doubted if I would ever hear from Heinz again, but a few months later he called from Austria to tell me that a shot of me on *Chain Reaction* would be on the cover of *Mountain Magazine,* the most influential climbing magazine in the world at the time. An interview in *Rock & Ice* and articles in almost every foreign language climbing magazine in the world soon followed, along with a feature article in *Outside.* The brilliance and magnitude of Smith Rock was no longer a secret.

In 1986 I found myself back in school full time, living in Eugene. I had fallen in love with the woman I would marry two years later—for the first time as an adult there was something in my life that mattered more than my time on the rock. Smith Rock was finally on the world climbing map, and from that point on, the efforts of others, more than my own, would keep it there. Ironically, at the same time my passion started to fade, the passion of the climbing world for Smith burned brighter than ever.

I spent the summer of 1986 traveling in Europe—climbing occasionally but mainly just enjoying myself. A year of schooling had done nothing positive for my fitness. I met

Jean-Baptiste Tribout, 1986.

Jean-Baptiste Tribout at a climbing competition in the Pyrenees in September 1986. There might have been more gifted climbers in the world at the time, but no one worked harder than Tribout. He possessed a determination and level of endurance far beyond anyone in the United States. He was good, and he knew it. Much to my surprise he had already booked airline tickets to Smith Rock the next month. I returned to school and wasn't around much when Tribout arrived, accompanied by Jean-Marc Troussier and Corrine Labrune.

Tribout quickly disposed of all the established testpieces, including a repeat of the *East Face* of Monkey Face, with key nuts preplaced. Rather than leave early he set his sights on pushing the standards higher. First he succeeded on *Rude Boys,* instantly decoding the sequences I had failed to see. Next he turned to the wall left of *Sunshine Dihedral,* a route I had worked extensively the previous year. I had done all the moves, along with some link-ups of major sections, but the redpoint seemed prohibitively difficult. No one thought he had any real chance for success except Tribout himself. For two weeks he worked on nothing else—somehow keeping his fingertips from wearing out while piecing together hard move after hard move. For the first time a gleaming row of fixed quickdraws adorned a face at Smith Rock. Wearing E.B. Passions—clunky sticky-rubber shoes that only made the climbing more difficult—Tribout succeeded on November 7, 1986. *To Bolt or Not to Be* (5.14a) matched the highest level in the world. The 5.14 grade had arrived in the United States, and even the harshest critics of Smith climbing had no choice but to take notice.

Not everyone was impressed. A surprising number of climbers simply dismissed *To Bolt* as just another route where the end didn't justify the means. They reasoned that the tactics used (preplaced gear and hangdogging) negated any advancement in standards. Kurt Smith, an early sport climbing critic (and later convert) told me, ". . . it's cheating—even my grandma could climb it that way." Others tried to fit *To Bolt* into the context of what had already been done, applying such reasoning as "It's not as powerful as Jim Holloway's problems" or "It's not as serious as John Bachar's routes." And they were right. But what they didn't recognize was that *To Bolt or Not to Be* christened an entirely new branch of climbing's evolutionary tree. It took nothing away from the other disciplines (bouldering and trad climbing) that it borrowed so heavily from—it merely bridged the gap between the two.

The World Comes to Smith: 1987 to 1992

For years I dreamed of the day when climbers from around the world would visit Smith Rock. When it finally happened, everyone showed up at the same time—not just a few curious climbers but dozens, many staying for months. Never before was there such a collection of smoke-belching jalopies in the parking lot, owned by itinerant dirtbags. On many days foreigners outnumbered English-speaking climbers. Smith wasn't just on the map—it was suddenly the coolest destination in the U.S. climbing scene.

As is so often the case, the dream—at least from my perspective—was more pleasant than the reality. The close-knit group of locals diversified into a more competitive scene, where the world's finest showed up to add to their resumes, while aspiring youngsters hoped for a breakthrough to jump-start their climbing careers. An intensity never before felt at Smith Rock changed the ambience at the base of the crags. There were still countless great times, but for me it started feeling less like innocent fun and more like a job.

After graduating from the University of Oregon with a B.S. in finance, I returned to Bend, working for Metolius. The Smith I returned to was different from the one I had left behind. The biggest difference was the caliber of climbers. I was no longer the leader of the push to new levels of difficulty. My two-year hiatus set my climbing back a few notches, and I worked hard to regain my previous levels.

While I was away at school, Chris Grover brought the first Bosch power drill into the canyon. We'd talked about it before, but it took a rebel like Chris to bring the plan to life. Remarkably, rangers didn't hand out a citation when the hum of the drill first broke the calm of a Smith morning. Instantly, placing a bolt shifted from an hour-long ordeal to a couple minutes of empowering fun. With a new toy at his disposal, along with Sean Olmstead, he engineered a Smith classic—*Churning in the Wake* (5.13a). They worked the route together, before Sean came away with the first ascent in March 1987. Smith climbing was now poised for a new route boom like nothing seen before. Power drills did not play a role in the arrival of sport climbing at Smith Rock, but the drill, more than any other factor, led to the explosive growth of the new way of climbing around the country. Hand-drilling Smith tuff was difficult, but drilling half-inch bolts on harder rock was all but impossible.

I had just done the second ascent of *Churning in the Wake* when a powerfully built youngster walked up to the base and introduced himself as Scott Franklin. A Gunks local, Franklin brought a reputation as the most promising East Coast climber. He seemed supremely confident, but I had seen countless climbers arrive at Smith confident and leave with their tails between their legs. I figured Scott would be another victim, but it didn't take long to realize he was a whole different breed. Growing up in Manhattan, Scott brought a new energy to Smith Rock. He was intense, brash—and damn good. He made quick work of *Churning in the Wake* and moved over to *Rude Boys,* doing the second ascent without hardly breaking a sweat. But no one saw what was coming next. For good reason, *To Bolt or Not to Be* had gained a mythical reputation over the last year, and we all wondered which superstar would do the second ascent. Scott was obviously physically gifted, but I doubted if he possessed the finesse to succeed on this hyper-technical wall. But he refused to be intimidated, and after a month of work he succeeded on Thanksgiving Day 1987.

Scott's repeats might have been the biggest news of the year, but he wasn't the only story. New routes sprang up everywhere as the impact of the power drill became clear. Brooke Sandahl broke through with several new sport routes, including *Da Kine Corner* (5.12c) and *Kings of Rap* (5.12d). He also bolted easier lines that became immensely popular. Darius Azin visited Smith and decided to stay. Now a renowned vascular surgeon, Darius was the classic dirtbag of the era. From what I could tell, he owned a single pair of tattered pants that he wore his entire Smith career. Meticulous, supple, and brilliant, he was well suited to the technical nature of Smith climbing. *Oxygen* (5.13b) was his first of many hard routes. He became one of Smith's elite climbers, until medical school shifted his focus.

Much like hippies drawn to San Francisco during the sixties, climbers from around the country flocked to Smith to be part of the rebellious dawn of U.S. sport climbing. A few die-hard trad climbers came just to shake their heads in disgust, but most climbers arrived with an open mind. Some just wanted to be part of the scene, though a surprising number added their own new routes. Many returned home with a fresh perspective on what might be possible at their local crags. With sport climbing still a highly volatile issue in established areas, climbers sought out entirely new crags. On these new cliffs scattered throughout the country, sport climbing took root and flourished.

With so many people focused on getting better and climbing new routes, 1988 was the finest year in the history of Smith climbing. Scott Franklin bolted the sweeping overhanging wall left of *Rude Boys* and started work on what he hoped would be the hardest route at Smith. By now no one doubted Franklin's ability, so it was no surprise when he succeeded on *Scarface* (5.14a), the first route of the grade ever established by an American climber. J. B. Tribout returned to Smith, freeing *White Wedding*—rated 5.14a until new pockets mysteriously appeared at the crux. After struggling to regain my form throughout 1987, things finally clicked for me. I managed five 5.13 first ascents, including *Vicious Fish* (5.13c), and did the second ascent of *Scarface*. Geoff Weigand returned to the scene of his landmark 1985 visit, adding three 5.13 routes of his own. As the most productive decade in the history of Smith climbing came to a close, the whirlwind pace finally slowed. Brooke Sandahl muscled his way up *Power* (5.13b), and sport climbing convert Ron Kauk freed *The Backbone* (5.13a), but by now there were so many hard lines most climbers merely repeated what was already done. With the bar raised so high, it became harder for anyone, apart from international superstars, to make a real impact. The same ascents that would have made headlines five years earlier now went unnoticed. Rather than jumping through the hoops of redpointing hard new routes, many climbers used Smith as a training ground, engaging in marathon toprope sessions. *Churning in the Wake* was the most popular hang, and climbers congregated at the base for hours, taking turns on moves so well memorized that the sessions often continued into the night. Everyone got tremendously fit, but the progression of Smith climbing stalled.

As the growth on the tuff slowed, the massive potential of the Upper Gorge attracted Jeff Frizzell and Tom Egan. Far upstream from the traditional cracks of the Lower Gorge, these beautiful columns received no attention until the power drill opened vast amounts of untouched stone. Frizzell's single-minded focus blended with Egan's upbeat, optimistic energy, and together they bolted dozens of lines. After pioneering *Controlled Hysteria* (5.13a), Egan turned his attention to the tuff, establishing testpieces like *The Product* (5.13a). Frizzell's obsession never wavered, and the Upper Gorge became his personal showpiece. He climbed many 5.13s, including the remarkable column of *Big Tuna* (5.13c)—still Smith's hardest basalt route.

I didn't realize it at the time, but by the end of the decade the days of my Smith career were numbered. After years of abuse I developed significant finger joint problems—not just chronic inflammation but sharp, stabbing pain in my distal IP joints. Undeterred I continued climbing with a rest day after each session on the rock. I managed the fifth ascent of *To Bolt or Not to Be* (after Jerry Moffatt and Ron Kauk) and took pride in redpointing 5.14 in the 1980s. But any hopes I had of returning to the top were far-fetched. Still, I could dream—which is exactly what I was doing when I bolted an outrageous line left of the *East Face* of Monkey Face. I worked through the moves, but my declining endurance forced me to admit that I was in over my head. I gave everyone else the green light to have at it.

With my productivity headed in the wrong direction, other locals had more success. Geoff Weigand pioneered *Villain* (5.14a), an endurance problem interrupted by a horrendous crux. Originally 5.13d, the grade rose a notch after a pocket broke away. Brooke Sandahl got better each year, pioneering routes like *Livin' Large* (5.13a) and *Bum Rush the Show* (5.13b). Sean Olmstead prepared and succeeded on *Scene of the Crime* (5.13b), not realizing that J. B. Tribout had no-so-quietly pilfered his route a few days before. Fortunately, Sean avoided a similar fate with *Kill the Hate* (5.13a).

The east wall of Monkey Face was the natural extension of everything we had worked on since the earliest days of sport climbing. It didn't matter who did it, but I really wanted someone to succeed—if for no other reason than to put an exclamation mark on the golden age of Smith free climbing. Scott Franklin was the only local with the strength, work ethic, and desire to succeed, but the climbing was right at his limit. He worked the route extensively, doing major sections before getting stopped high on the wall with a crank off a one-finger pocket.

J. B. Tribout saw a chance to stake his claim as the best climber in the world, and he worked furiously during an extended visit in 1991. But even he came up short. In the best shape of his life, Scott returned only to discover new edges crafted from epoxy and the mono mysteriously transformed into a two-digit pocket. Disillusioned with Tribout's tactics, Franklin reluctantly focused his energy elsewhere. Didier Rabotou, a French climber with tremendous natural skills, quickly worked out the sequences and was very near success before severely spraining his ankle on the approach hike. In the end the unmatched work ethic of Jean-Baptiste Tribout wouldn't be denied. After a winter of specific training, he finally clipped the anchors on April 6, 1992. *Just Do It* (5.14c) was a reality, and Smith climbing again stood near the top of world standards.

Despite Tribout's tactics, most local climbers—myself included—took pride in the sheer difficulty of the route. But not everyone was pleased. Franklin felt that the route he first attempted would have been possible without Tribout's modifications, perhaps even the world's first 5.15. The questions about what was acceptable and what went over the line became a big issue among the next generation of sport climbers in the United States.

The Post-Golden Years: 1993 to 2008

As 1992 came to a close, with *Just Do It* as the crowning achievement, Smith standards stood far above everything else in the United States. With dozens of dedicated local climbers, international visitors, and more than a decade of unabated growth, there was every reason to believe that Smith would dominate for years—with an eye-popping flood of world-class routes. Everyone assumed that 5.15 was just around the corner. Instead, momentum just stopped—the golden age of Smith free climbing ended as abruptly as it began. After decades where new routes defined each era, it's difficult to characterize the post-boom years at Smith. Smith Rock was more popular than ever, but the focus among leading climbers changed—pioneering ever harder new routes was no longer the name of the game.

Pursuing first ascents at Smith was never a task for the lazy. The highest quality lines were the first to fall, and even they required some cleaning. As the potential thinned out, the hardest new routes required more work than ever before. Bolting, scrubbing, gluing loose flakes—it was messy work, and the ensuing fight to keep others from nabbing the first ascent got even messier. To increase the sky-high standards, you needed to be one of the best in the world. Given all this, it's understandable why climbers ignored first ascents, instead focusing on getting better on the wealth of difficult routes.

Jim Karn epitomized this approach. Karn was one of the first visitors to Smith in 1986, but at the time he was his own worst enemy. With his ranting tirades becoming the stuff of legends, he didn't enjoy the instant success realized by friend and rival, Scott Franklin. While everyone else blew him off as a loose cannon, Karn kept getting better, eventually focusing his emotional energy in a positive direction. By the early 1990s he matured into the most successful male competition climber the United States had ever seen. He flashed 5.13 routes at Smith, and his training days were legendary—he'd routinely climb *White Wedding, Bad Man,* and *Scarface,* along with several easier 5.13s, in a single day. Karn saw Smith as a training ground, not a place to polish his resume with high-level first ascents. "My main focus was getting as good as I could," recalls Karn. "When I was trying to do high-level projects, I spent more time resting than actually climbing. Once I shifted my focus, I finally climbed enough to get really fit. I loved being in total command of a hard route. If I did it once, I felt that maybe I was just lucky. But if I kept going back, I'd eventually get solid enough that I completely owned it."

Fortunately, the pioneers of the 1980s left many unfinished projects—otherwise the progression of new routes would have ground to a halt. After two dead years French legend Marc LeMenestral visited Smith in 1995 and gave the scene a jump-start it desperately needed. He succeeded on an old Darius Azin project on Picnic Lunch Wall—*The Big R* (5.14a)—and an easier line in the Cocaine Gully called *Runt* (5.13d). The bouldery *Runt* never attracted much attention, but *The Big R* became one of the most respected high-level routes at Smith. Easy new lines flourished throughout Smith the next year, but apart from Scott Franklin's *Evil Sister* (5.13b) and Mark Huth's *The Heathen* (5.13a) on basalt, nothing significant happened. Even these routes were less-than-stellar leftovers from the old days.

Joe Brooks visited Smith in 1994 and immediately fell under its spell. Brooks would have fit in perfectly a decade earlier, but he was an anomaly in the 1990s. While almost every other top climber focused on training and repeats, Brooks pioneered original routes on the tuff. Powerful and motivated, Brooks excelled on the overhanging routes of the Aggro Wall, climbing *Repeat Offender* (5.14a), *Mama Docus* (5.13c), and *Disposable Heroes* (5.13c). Like pioneers from the 1980s, he wasn't afraid to dream a little—he equipped three high-level link-ups on the Aggro Wall, all high in the 5.14 grade, and a futuristic route left of *Scarface* that will likely sit undone for decades. His finest efforts came on Picnic Lunch Wall. After nabbing the third ascent of *The Big R* (after local whiz-kid Will Nazarian), he added *Starvation Fruit* (5.14b), a heavily engineered route just a notch easier than *Just Do It*.

Brooks clearly made an impact, but he attracted few imitators. Others, including Larry Brumwell and Adam Grosowsky, would dabble, but no one took up where Joe Brooks left off—preparing and succeeding on standard-pushing routes. Brooks recalls: "At the time, Smith was the only sport climbing area that had any sense of history. It's where it all began—everything spread from there to other crags around the country. For me it was a privilege to be able to climb new lines and be part of that history."

With dozens of climbing gyms throughout the United States, the talent pool was far deeper than ever before. A new generation of teenage superstars soon arrived at Smith.

Chris Sharma spent a week at Smith in April 1997, and nothing slowed him down. Sharma possessed the raw power of Chris Jones, with levels of endurance and talent never seen before in American climbing. He climbed *Just Do It* with minimal effort over three days, flubbing sequences the whole way. Two years later David Hume repeated the route in just four tries. Other young superstars including David Graham, Sonnie Trotter, and Tommy Caldwell traveled to Smith and made astonishingly fast ascents of Smith 5.14s. By the end of the decade, despite the success of the young elite, Smith had grown into an intimidating place for local youngsters. Climbing 5.14, it seemed, was a prerequisite for anyone hoping to earn a place in modern Smith history.

Ryan Lawson, a teenager out of the Portland area, fell in love with Smith Rock in the late 1990s. In an age of young prodigies, Ryan was a blue-collar climber with average talent at best. He didn't possess the strength or desire to succeed on the harder routes, but much in the spirit of the Smith pioneers, he was an impassioned innovator. He saw huge amounts of untouched stone and focused on opening this acreage to the masses. Over the next several years, he pioneered more than one hundred routes—almost all easy sport climbs—and he drilled more holes in the stone than anyone in the history of Smith climbing.

None of his new lines were hard; in fact he never succeeded on a 5.12 first ascent.

Lawson explains: "I worked on so many moderate routes because I liked to climb. Moderates are fun, so most of my first ascents I was able to climb first try." Standing alone, not one of his routes made a blip on the radar screen, but his collective effort ranks with the most productive careers at Smith. He wasn't accepted by many hard-core locals—partly because he never paid his dues by working through existing testpieces. No one knew exactly what to think of his one-of-a-kind, public-service approach to Smith climbing. But his routes helped spread out the crowds and gave Smith one of the finest collections of easy sport climbs in the country.

While Lawson dominated the lower grades, others made news the traditional way—by climbing hard routes. Michael Orr added another 5.14 to the growing list at Smith in 1999 with his ascent of an old Kent Benesch project—*Mr. Yuk* (5.14a). After a seven-year break, Jeff Frizzell returned to the Upper Gorge to work through any remaining lines. Teaming with Paul Marshall, he pioneered three more 5.13 routes and added to the amazing concentration of 5.12s. He didn't bump the basalt standards any higher, but he succeeded in his quest to make the Upper Gorge one of the most impressive basalt climbing areas anywhere. Ten years after Tribout's ascent of *Just Do It,* Scott Milton finally pushed Smith standards higher with his ascent of *Shock and Awe* (5.14c) on the Aggro Wall. His breakthrough route followed the line of a Joe Brooks link-up, combining *Repeat Offender* and *Villain* in a single pitch. With *Just Do It* clinging to the lowest rung of the 5.14c grade, Milton's route is arguably the hardest at Smith. He also finished a Larry Brumwell project named *Chemical Ali* (5.14a).

With its emphasis on technique, endurance, and creativity—not just raw power—Smith climbing appealed to the most talented female climbers in the world. Lynn Hill, already a legend in the sport, made the first female ascent of *To Bolt or Not to Be* in 1998 and *Scarface* the following year. In 1999 eighteen-year-old Beth Rodden did the second female ascent of *To Bolt.* Several women climbed at the lower end of the 5.13 range at Smith—including Bobbi Bensman, Jeanne Young, and Brittany Griffith—but few broke through to the upper levels. Kristin Yurdin did just that with her ascent of *White Wedding* in 2003.

In the fall of 2003, Tommy Caldwell and Beth Rodden visited Smith Rock. Caldwell's resume included *Flex Luther,* arguably the first 5.15 in America, while Rodden was already one of the brightest female stars in the sport. Both strong crack climbers, they set their sights on Smith's last great crack problem—a free ascent of the opening pitch of *The Great Roof* (5.14b). Rodden worked the route for weeks, eventually succeeding on what may well have been the most impressive ascent at Smith in the post–*Just Do It* era. Much like Lynn Hill's free ascent of The Nose a decade earlier, Rodden's effort was a true breakthrough—and not just because it was the hardest route ever established by a woman. With only one repeat (by crack genius Sonnie Trotter), it's one of the hardest crack climbs in the world.

Although Caldwell played only a supporting role on *The Great Roof,* he made his own contribution on Monkey Face. He succeeded on the most visually stunning leftover from the old days, a continuation of *Spank the Monkey* (5.13d R). A modern horror show—technical, exposed, pumping, and run-out—Caldwell wisely used double ropes as he wandered from side to side on the razor-sharp arête.

The last half decade at Smith saw dozens of new lines, mostly in the lower half of the grading scale. With rare exceptions the pursuit of difficulty seemed a thing of the past. Instead the most significant additions were long free routes. Multi-pitch adventures are nothing new at Smith—climbs like *Astro Monkey, Northwest Passage,* and the *Backbone* were all products of the 1980s, but despite unrivaled quality they were more of an anomaly than a trend in Smith climbing—the focus at the time was pushing the standards rather than establishing long routes. Now the opposite seems true.

Ryan Lawson deserves credit for inspiring the shift in focus. His routes, as always, were high quality but rarely difficult—sport-bolted lines like *Wherever I May Roam* (5.9) and *First Kiss* (5.8) were so easy and well protected that everyone could enjoy them. But his insatiable quest for new lines eventually led him to the massive untouched walls of the Northeast Face of the Smith Rock Group, where he bolted a route on the east face of Smith Summit. Teaming with his mentor and frequent partner, Thomas Emde, he succeeded on *The Struggle Within* (5.12a).

Lawson got things moving, but Emde ultimately made the biggest contribution toward the long, free movement at Smith. With alpine rock skills developed in the Dolomites, he found himself at home on Smith's biggest walls. Emde says, "I wanted to bring the alpine experience to Smith Rock, where you need to deal with exposure, commitment, sections of bad rock, and uncertain protection." He pioneered three original lines—*Freedom's Just Another Name for Nothing Left to Lose* (5.12b), *The Good Ol' Days* (5.11c), and *European Vacation* (5.11a)—and also freed *Abraxas* (5.12a) on the Monument. All of these lines blend varying degrees of sport and traditional climbing with a sense of adventure impossible to find in the Dihedrals. They hardly broke

Ryan Lawson and Thomas Emde.
RYAN LAWSON COLLECTION

new ground in terms of difficulty, but many sport climbers running effortless laps on *Churning* will find themselves gripped silly on any of Emde's testpieces.

Several other climbers caught the new route bug over the past fifteen years, contributing dozens of new routes between them. In particular Jim Ablao, Mark Deffenbaugh, Ben Moon, Ted Stahl, and Erik Kirsch deserve credit. Most of these lines are top notch, though only a few broke into the 5.12 grade. But with the help of Michael Stöger and Ian Caldwell, the quest for big numbers isn't completely dead. Much like every other high-level ascent of the last decade, their best efforts finished projects left behind from long ago. Powerfully built Stöger, with over 1,000 worldwide first ascents on his resume, freed *Climb Like A Bomb* (5.13a) at the base of the Mudpile and *100% Beef* (5.13c), a Brooke Sandahl project dating back to the early 1990s. He also added more new 5.12s than everyone else combined over the past five years. Ian Caldwell, state park employee and longtime Smith local, saved the best for last. In October 2007 he linked *Shotgun Wedding* (5.14b), the hardest route ever established by a local climber at Smith. He followed this success with his 2009 ascent of *Little Miss Sunshine* (5.14a), a long-standing project dating back to 1990.

With few old projects left, it remains to be seen where future high-end development will come from—if it will come at all. Ian Caldwell feels that Smith better lends itself to new lines appealing to lower-level climbers. "New routes at the upper 5.13 and 5.14 grade are a ton of work," Caldwell says. "There are still overhanging walls that can yield good routes, but the

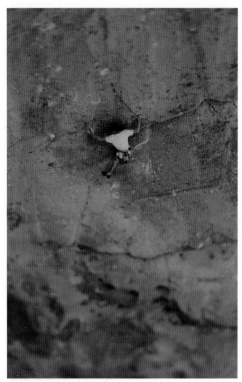

cleaning involved is very intense. If the pre-parer doesn't do a good job at cleaning then the route will be labeled as 'dirty' compared to the established routes." With massive work required and criticism almost a certainty, the returns no longer justify the effort.

One thing is certain—climbers from around the world will continue to visit Smith, to pay respect to the rich history and test themselves on an endless supply of difficult routes. Countless milestones still await new generations—the first on-sight 5.14, the first female ascent of *Just Do It,* and, don't hold your breath, Smith Rock's first 5.15—the same grade that seemed so close, so long ago.

Postscript

Those of us who were part of Smith history won't forget our days spent high above the Crooked River. I started climbing at Smith Rock as a boy and emerged many years later as a man; my experiences shaped me into the person I am today. I feel content

Ian Caldwell on *Shotgun Wedding* (5.14b).
CHRIS CHRISTIE PHOTO

with what I accomplished, though my greatest contribution had nothing to do with the routes I climbed or the tactics I used. Instead, I sense that my passion helped Smith climbing touch the lives of others in a positive way. But any single person played only a limited role, and I was no different. The success of Smith climbing resulted from the collective energy of each generation opening the door for the breakthroughs of the next. I learned from those who came before me, and young climbers throughout the country are still influenced by what happened here.

Will Smith Rock ever rise to the top of American standards again, or will it remain a place where climbers enjoy and challenge themselves on testpieces from long ago? I believe that the golden years of Smith free climbing were a rare phenomenon—a serendipitous convergence of all the right elements needed for change. So many people played a key role, and we all fed off the energy of each other. If a single key player hadn't responded to the calling of Smith Rock, the end result might have been very different.

It'll take more than one person for Smith climbing to regain its luster. It'll take a similar alliance of coincidences and a group of kids with the courage and conviction to do things their own way. Climbers might like to think of themselves as a rebellious lot, but they really aren't—they tend to follow what others have done before, often with such fervent devotion they rarely think for themselves. Original thinkers in rock climbing, as in all walks of life, are rare. Warren Harding, John Gill, Ray Jardine, Tony Yaniro, Todd Skinner, and Wolfgang

Gullich are individuals who created their own path. They are my climbing heroes because they weren't content to follow the herd. For Smith climbing to rise again, a new generation will need to not merely follow in the footsteps of those who came before—but blaze their own trails up the golden walls of tuff.

SMITH ROCK ETHICS

In the mid-1980s Smith Rock magically transformed from a sleepy backwater crag to one of the best-known climbing areas in the country. It wasn't just the high-level routes drawing attention—the tactics used to pioneer these testpieces shook the traditional foundations of the U.S. climbing scene. As the first crag in the country to embrace the sport climbing ethic, Smith was the birthplace of a new branch in the evolution of the sport. Only after a long and bitter struggle did the new way of climbing gain widespread acceptance, yet today it's hard to imagine American rock climbing without it. Looking back twenty years, the entire controversy seems like a colossal waste of energy, putting U.S. free climbing so far behind the game it took more than a decade to catch up. While climbers in Europe focused all their attention on getting better, many U.S. climbers focused on resisting change.

In the first edition of my guide, I went into great detail defending sport climbing methods—now they're so well accepted they need no justification. Debating climbing ethics is a bit like discussing politics. Some people are so certain they possess the correct view of the world, they have trouble accepting the validity of an alternate perspective. The sport climbing ethic developed at Smith isn't the only way; even within the local community there are differing views. It played a critical role in the progression of Smith free climbing, but anyone believing in the intrinsic superiority of traditional climbing might find offense in these tactics. In this section I'm not trying to win any converts; instead, I'm just providing some background and sharing my opinions.

Redpointing

A decade before the term "redpoint" entered the climbing vernacular, all Smith free ascents employed an unusually restrictive version of this same style. Climbers carried their entire rack of gear on each attempt, and they'd remove every piece (including quickdraws) after each try. With the influx of visiting climbers these restrictions eased—now any no-falls, single-push lead qualifies as a redpoint, with or without preplaced gear. Preplacing gear on any traditional crack typically reduces the difficulty of a redpoint ascent by roughly one letter grade—sometimes more. Very few climbers preplace gear on lower-level trad routes, but this is a common practice on harder lines. All traditional grades in this book assume the placement of all gear on lead.

Hangdogging

It might seem hard to believe, but the practice of working out moves after hanging on a bolt was once a source of great controversy throughout the national climbing community. If you'd like to work out moves after falling off, good for you. If you'd like to close your eyes and lower off immediately, more power to you. We don't discriminate here—neither tactic is considered better style than the other at Smith Rock. After all, if style is the issue, you blew it the moment you let go of the stone on your on-sight attempt, didn't you?

Retro-Bolting

Hand-drilled routes at Smith almost always had fewer bolts than today's sport climbs. When it took an hour to drill a single hole, minimizing the number of bolts was a top priority. Without the benefit of a toprope wiring, the most impressive routes were difficult and frightening. With the arrival of the power drill, there was a mad dash to retro-bolt these routes, eliminating any degree of danger. Fortunately, the practice died off before the final bold routes from the old days completely disappeared. Routes like *Close Shave, Spank the Monkey,* and *Low Profile* are still in their original state, and they tantalize anyone looking for a thrill. Since retro-bolting erases a part of Smith history, any historically significant route should remain untouched. If you're unsure of what routes meet this criteria, you shouldn't even contemplate adding bolts to an existing line.

Route Removal

Smith sport routes range from amazing to amazingly bad. At the lower end of the spectrum are climbs that simply don't measure up. Anyone pioneering new routes has a lemon or two on their resume—it's just part of the game. On rare occasions these inferior routes infuriate someone so much they act alone and remove the bolts. This ego-stroking practice could wreak havoc if it ever got out of control. If you chop someone else's piece of crap, they'll likely eliminate one of yours—this is how a chopping war begins. If you have an issue with someone's new route, be courageous and have a direct conversation with them; they'll probably even share your concerns. It's conceivable that someone might put up a route so offensive that everyone agrees it should disappear, but this still hasn't happened in Smith's seventy-five-year history. The only exception to this rule is if Oregon State Parks makes the decision to remove a route. In this case the route should never be rebolted or toproped.

Taking Turns

If you're heading to the main area on a busy weekend, you can almost rest assured that someone will be on the route you're wanting to do. If you somehow got there first, please refrain from extended toprope sessions; recognize that others behind you want their turn as well. If you're leading a weekend class, don't bring twenty students to *Five Gallon Buckets* for an all-day session. Monopolizing a popular route for an entire day during peak season won't just piss people off, it'll give the organization you represent a very bad name.

Chalk

Prior to 1980 almost no one used chalk at Smith Rock. Now the opposite is true. The amount of chalk on the most popular routes varies greatly with the season, but it's unlikely to ever completely wash away. Fortunately, in twenty-five years of chalked cliffs, the state park has never made an issue of it. Some climbers try to minimize the impact by using colored chalk, but it rarely matches the many shades of Smith tuff and gums up holds worse than the white stuff. I'm not advocating restricting the use of chalk—personally, I'd never climb another day without my trusty chalk bag at my side. But carrying a toothbrush helps. Brushing chalk-caked holds not only reduces the visual impact, but it also makes a noticeable difference in the difficulty of higher-level routes.

First Ascent Considerations

For good reason, only a very small percentage of Smith climbers have any interest in pioneering new routes. If you're truly committed to becoming the best climber possible, I'd recommend never preparing a new line at Smith Rock. The large amount of time spent cleaning and bolting takes time away from real climbing; you'd be better off repeating the almost endless supply of challenging routes. Fortunately, there will always be climbers who find pleasure in first ascents. There's something about the thrill of discovering a hidden line of holds that makes it worth all the effort. Smith Rock holds the attention of so many climbers today because of the massive amount of work put in by generations of pioneers.

This section is for climbers interested in putting up new routes at Smith. It's a thankless job, and there's no way to get good at it without making mistakes. Often these mistakes will bring a barrage of criticism. But first ascents are important—without them Smith climbing stagnates. Difficult new routes made Smith famous, and only through more hard climbs will it stay relevant in the climbing world.

Not every unclimbed face at Smith warrants a line of bolts. With the large amounts of unsuitable stone, it's important to search carefully before unleashing the drill. Smith can always use another classic route, but the last thing it needs is another row of bolts on a poorly cleaned, crumbling wall. Before entering the realm of new routes, there's good reason to work through hundreds of existing routes and develop your skills to a high level. You'll find that your first ascents are far more accepted in the local community if you first pay your dues.

First Ascent Etiquette

Climbers preparing new routes at Smith Rock earn the right to make the first ascent of their project. The complete preparation might take days of work; when others don't respect this right, it takes away much of the motivation for doing new lines in the first place. High-level routes sometimes require dozens of attempts, spread over several months, before a redpoint ascent. As long as you're actively pursuing a project, it should remain yours to finish. This might seem like a purely ego-based restriction, but the reality goes beyond this. Most climbers simply lose interest in preparing lines when others are waiting in the shadows to nab the free ascent. This was a huge issue in the early 1990s—route thievery became so rampant that the most prolific climbers simply stopped preparing new lines. As much as any other factor, this marked the end of Smith's reign as America's dominant sport crag.

Cleaning

The style of climbing practiced at Smith developed in response to the environment. We were merely trying to make the best out of what we had. At first glance we didn't have much—at least from a climbing standpoint, as the crumbling walls required a whole new way of looking at things. First ascents on Smith tuff present unusual challenges. The few sections of naturally perfect stone are either fully developed or isolated far off the ground—everything else requires cleaning. Because of this, the top-down approach makes the most sense. You won't face criticism if you establish a climb from the ground up, unless you leave it dirty. Unfortunately, this is almost always the case.

Placing Bolts

From the early days to modern times, bolts played a significant role in the development of Smith climbing. First used atop pinnacles and on multi-pitch aid lines, bolts assumed a new role with the beginning of Smith's free climbing movement. These precursors of today's routes followed terrifying walls of exploding knobs, almost always bolted on lead without any cleaning. The earliest sport climbs at Smith typically avoided drilling by using pieces of natural gear between widely spaced bolts. The introduction of the power drill changed everything—in good ways and bad.

Power drills are the ultimate convenience tool for sport climbers, but they create potential problems. With thirty-second holes, there's a tendency to drill first and think later. For the first time, hard-to-clip bolts, over-bolting, and needless routes became an issue. You face a huge responsibility when you place bolts—others literally put their lives on the line, blindly trusting your work. No matter how many bolts you've drilled, mistakes happen. A bolt might not tighten properly, or it might stick out too far. When this happens, pull the bolt, patch the hole, and drill a good one. Sometimes it's a pain in the ass, but if you're not willing to get it right, you shouldn't be pioneering routes in the first place.

Bolt spacing depends on factors such as route difficulty, rock quality, and the attitude of the person doing the drilling. There's no set formula, but you don't need to take out a tape measure and space bolts equally. For instance, the 5.6 slab at the top of a 5.11 would require far fewer bolts than the crux below. A toprope ascent can help you decide where to place easy-to-clip bolts. But the practice of wiring every move on toprope and placing minimal bolts makes little sense. If you'd like to put up a truly bold climb, don't bother with the toprope and take the whippers like everyone else.

Gluing

Tearing off loose edges can leave big scars and wreck a great sequence; you're better off reinforcing them with a small smear of glue. Glue works well for edges, but it's totally inappropriate for dangerous larger features; no amount of glue can make a teetering flake safe. Working with glue is easier said than done—you'll likely make a mess the first time you try. Be sure to first seek the advice of those who know what they're doing.

Plastic Holds

Plastic holds are not an acceptable means of preparing new routes. Several plastic routes established in the late 1980s were the most brazen ever at Smith; fortunately these holds disappeared long ago. Today anyone pioneering a route with artificial holds should be banned from the park.

Chipping

Everyone putting up high-level routes at Smith knows how fine a line separates cleaning from chipping. Often you can brush away the worst of the tuff with a toothbrush. For the sake of clarification, I define chipping as the deliberate alteration of the rock with the intent of making a climb easier. The cleaning process at Smith sometimes makes a climb easier, though it often bumps the grade higher as edges and knobs break away. The intent, however, is to make the rock clean—not reduce the grade. Yes, there are chipped routes, by anyone's standards, at Smith Rock. But fortunately these are rare. As I've defined it, chipping at Smith Rock is not an acceptable practice. If you feel that the route you're working on needs a chipped (not just cleaned) hold, then perhaps you aren't the right person to do the first ascent.

Everyone criticizes chipping, but a substantial number of the most difficult routes in the world feature at least one suspicious hold. Are the rules at the cutting edge of the sport different than for everyone else? Given the history of high-level routes over the past two decades, it's hard to argue that this isn't true. Everyone denies chipping routes, but everyone can't be telling the truth. Is chipping truly unacceptable in all situations? Might it be justified to chip a single hold in the middle of a blank section to make a 5.15 route possible? Or is chipping an absolute evil? I don't have the answers—but questions like these will be some of the most significant ethical issues facing future generations.

HOW TO USE THIS BOOK

The primary purpose of this guide is to help climbers make satisfying route selections. With 1,809 total routes (1,043 on tuff, 444 on basalt, and 322 boulder problems), the sheer volume can overwhelm anyone trying to pick a line. Smith routes range from easy scrambles to world-class testpieces; some are horrible, and others are brilliant. This section will help climbers find exactly what they're looking for—and stay away from climbs best avoided.

Please don't confuse this guide with a how-to-climb manual. I'm assuming that the reader has a solid understanding of climbing techniques and vocabulary. You should consider buying an introductory book, if terms like redpoint, arête, and quickdraw aren't familiar. Of course, no book is a substitute for the real thing. Anyone wanting to learn the sport should seek qualified instruction.

Route Information

With Smith Rock set in a semi-desert, there's only sparse vegetation below the cliffs. With a clear view of the crag, you shouldn't have any trouble finding your way. Overview maps make it clear where each cliff sits relative to other features. Basalt climbs rely almost totally on photos, while tuff routes use a combination of photos and topos.

I've usually described the routes in order, as you're hiking along the base of the cliff. Confusion arises when a crag has multiple approaches, like the Dihedrals. Regardless of the chosen order, everything will be backward if you approach from the opposite end. An access trail leading to the center of a cliff creates a further dilemma. If there's no clear break in the cliff line, I'd need to pick an arbitrary starting point and describe routes in one direction and then the other. Some climbers prefer this, but I've always disliked thumbing back and forth several pages to find routes only a few feet apart. I believe I've chosen the lesser of two evils, describing the routes on these cliffs from right to left. In describing routes and features, I'll sometimes use compass directions (east, west, south, north). This can confuse those who are unfamiliar with the orientation of Smith Rock. It helps to remember that the snowcapped volcanoes of the Cascade Range on the horizon are lined up perfectly from north to south, while the unmistakable Burma Road cutting across the hillside is at the east end of the park.

I've started each chapter with a short narrative highlighting the characteristics of the crags. These introductions provide details about the type of climbing, history, best times to visit, and other relevant issues. With route descriptions in many guides reduced to arcane symbols, I've chosen the old-fashioned approach—words. Each route has a unique personality and history—I believe that written descriptions convey this better than anything else.

Ratings

There are three types of ratings used in this book—difficulty, seriousness, and quality. These are familiar to all climbers, but I'll explain exactly how I've used them.

Difficulty Grades

This guide uses the familiar Yosemite Decimal System, with the upper levels subdivided into letter grades. Unlike the previous edition, I'm not using split grades (e.g. 5.12b/c). I've also opted for the V-scale for all boulder problems. These systems aren't perfect, but they're well understood and used by all U.S. climbers. As much as possible, I've chosen a consensus grade after feedback from countless climbers. The difficulty of a route sometimes varies from person to person. Someone tall might glide through a reachy crux, only to flail on a rock-over move that shorter climbers cruise. To further complicate matters, ratings can change over time—especially on Smith tuff. Broken holds and rounding edges can increase the grade, while overzealous brushing can reduce the level.

The decimal grade indicates the difficulty of linking a pitch on a redpoint ascent; only rarely will it reveal the rating of the hardest move. A relentless route with lots of 5.12 might rate 5.13, even without any 5.13 sections. Only on routes where endurance doesn't enter into the equation will the rating of the hardest single move equal the overall grade. Preplaced gear typically knocks a letter grade off the difficulty of any traditional route.

Seriousness Grades

The familiar R and X grades warn climbers of high-risk routes. Seriousness has no impact on the decimal grade, but the opposite isn't always true. A 20-foot 5.9 run-out at the top of a 5.13 won't get mentioned, while the same run-out on a 5.9 route will receive at least an R grade.

Thirteen percent of Smith's routes have an R grade. You'll get scared, but probably not seriously injured falling off an R route (although the possibility of injury always exists). Long fall potential, difficult clips, and challenging natural protection are hallmarks of R-rated climbs.

Four percent of the routes at Smith have an X grade. These routes are unusually dangerous, with a very real chance of injury or worse. If you fall off at the wrong place on an X-rated climb, you'll probably be carried out on a stretcher. Climbs with fatally large loose flakes might also receive an X grade, even if they protect easily.

Quality Grades

I've used a zero-through-four-star system in this guide. These grades are purely subjective and reflect the personal opinion of the author. As such, my biases enter into the equation (apologies to all aid climbers and off-width artists). Even more than the difficulty grades, the quality of the tuff can change over time. Smith routes usually improve as the crumbling surface brushes clean, exposing solid stone. The bad routes stand to improve the most—many one-star piles of rubble are now popular three-star gems.

The number of stars does not ensure a negative or positive experience. Adventure climbers might find great joy in a no-star piece of crap, while a difficult four-star classic can be a miserable experience for anyone over their heads. The list below describes the criteria I've used in assigning these grades.

Zero stars means an awful route (3 percent of Smith routes get zero stars). These climbs scrape the bottom of the barrel. Given the nature of tuff, the bottom of the Smith barrel is deeper than most areas. At a minimum you can expect terrible rock, and usually a complete lack of aesthetic qualities.

One star means a below average route (22 percent). One-star routes suffer from an obvious flaw, whether it be bad rock, unpleasant climbing, or an unappealing setting. Despite the shortcoming, they're usually worth doing.

Two stars mean an average route (37 percent). Neither exceptionally good nor bad, these are Smith's run-of-the-mill routes. They aren't unpleasant, but they lack either the great rock or superior moves found on better climbs.

Three stars mean an above average route (31 percent). This rating includes routes with average moves on flawless rock, and those with brilliant climbing on imperfect rock. They are all highly recommended.

Four stars are reserved for the truly classic routes (7 percent). These lines are Smith's cream-of-the-crop. At a minimum classics feature excellent rock and superior moves. Most have tremendous aesthetic appeal as well. Some of these routes are undisputed classics, while others are the subject of never-ending debate among climbers with too much free time on their hands.

Equipment

With Smith rising to fame as a sport climbing haven, you'll be surprised to learn that trad and mixed routes outnumber sport climbs. Bringing a rack of gear into the park opens the door to some amazing lines. Standard rope lengths keep getting longer with each generation. Today it's recommended that anyone visiting Smith should use nothing less than a 60-meter rope. Many sport climbers prefer an even longer length. I'll mention whenever a descent requires two ropes, or a cord longer than 60 meters. If you're using a 50-meter line, expect to come up short at the most inopportune times.

While non-camming, low-tech devices suffice for easier routes, you should carry state-of-the-art gear for the harder lines. If you don't, the difficulty and seriousness grades might be radically higher. The following designations will tell you what to expect from each route:

Removable protection is required on 36 percent of Smith routes. These routes are **trad climbs** with no protection bolts. I've listed the size of the biggest piece of gear required. I won't go into detail about exactly what to bring, preserving an element of adventure.

About 12 percent of the routes at Smith qualify as **mixed routes**. These hybrids are a combination of sport and trad routes. At a minimum there's a single bolt protecting a move on a trad route, or one piece of gear required on a sport route.

About 41 percent of the routes at Smith are fully bolted **sport climbs**. With all bolted sport climbs, you'll need nothing but a rack of quickdraws. I've tried my best to list the exact number of bolts (excluding the anchor) for each fully bolted pitch, but I've surely made errors (probably lots of them).

Aid routes (3 percent of the routes at Smith) requiring a rack of pins and the latest aid gizmos receive this designation. Aid routes that don't require a hammer are designated as **clean routes**.

Some routes (less than 1 percent) lack any protection options and must be **free soloed** (or toproped). Bring a spotter, a stack of bouldering pads, and a good luck charm.

About 2 percent of the climbs at Smith are **toprope problems** only. Also included in this category are chopped sport routes.

I've listed all uncompleted routes as **projects** (about 5 percent). These lines are in varying states of readiness, ranging from minimal preparation to a one-hang ascent. I've made an estimate of the likely grade, using the minus/plus system (5.12-, 5.12, 5.12+), followed by a question mark. I've reserved star grades for completed routes, though I'll list the number of bolts for any fully prepared sport project.

Topos

Since topos provide information that a photo or text can't easily convey, I've drawn nearly one hundred of them. A good topo strikes a balance between too little and too much detail. Some guidebook topos are nothing more than lines and Xs scrawled onto a vague outline of the cliff. Others are beautifully drawn with such detail they completely overwhelm the route information. I've tried hard to strike a balance between the two. My topos are pleasant to look at, but the route details are clear—after all, the purpose of the drawings is to inform, not to dazzle the art world.

The grades of each pitch aren't haphazardly placed on a topo—instead they show the location of the technical crux. I'll sometimes make an estimate of the level of individual sections. Since grading short segments of a pitch is far more prone to error than rating an entire climb, I've deviated from letter grades, using the less specific minus/plus system. On any route with sectional grades, you can glean information about the continuity of the climbing by noticing whether the level on the topo matches the actual grade. On an endurance problem, each section rates lower than the overall level—the difficulty comes from linking the entire pitch together.

Each topo includes a scale showing the approximate height and an estimate of when the cliff goes into the shade. Because of the complexity of Smith's topography, shade varies by season. The same crag might be shaded by midmorning in the winter, and roast in the sun until 3:00 p.m. during the summer. For this reason I've avoided specific times, instead using descriptions like "afternoon shade."

Topo Legend

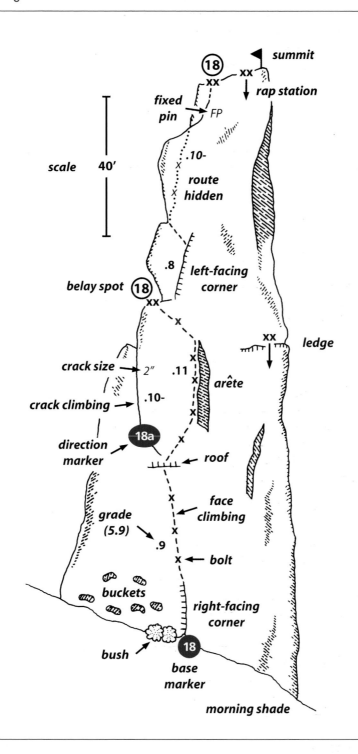

summit

(18)   **xx**   rap station
        xx

fixed
pin   FP

        .10-
     X
        route
     X   hidden

       .8   *left-facing*
            corner

belay spot (18)
        xx
            x

                        xx   *ledge*

crack size → 2"   .11   x
                         x   *arête*
crack climbing → .10- x

                         x
direction (18a)
marker

              ⊢ ← *roof*

                   x   *face*
                       climbing

grade
(5.9) → .9   x

                x ← *bolt*

buckets

              right-facing
              corner

bush → (18)
        base
        marker

              morning shade

scale **40'**

In most cases the topos show a distant view of the cliff, instead of the appearance from the base. A foreshortened view helps in locating a route, but it badly distorts the scale—the first 25 feet takes up half the drawing, while the final 100 feet might be condensed into an inch. With minimal vegetation and distinctive crags, Smith climbs aren't hard to find.

SAFETY CONSIDERATIONS

The gym-like convenience of Smith's sport routes lures inexperienced climbers into a false sense of security. Bad rock, worn anchors, and loose bolts are commonplace, even on Smith's most popular crags. Judging the quality of fixed gear requires experience, and a knowledge of what lies under the surface.

Bolts

Most modern Smith bolts are excellent—the popular ½-inch by 3¾-inch Rawl Bolts are far stronger than the hangers attached to them. Recognized by their distinctive hex heads, these bolts revolutionized Smith sport climbing. Today there are other bombproof options (including glue-ins) that are equally reliable in both tuff and basalt. Unfortunately, you can't say the same thing about every Smith bolt. By learning about the history of the area, you can develop a discerning eye.

Prior to the mid-1970s, the most common Smith bolt was a ¼-inch by 1½-inch split-shaft Rawl. These outdated relics were suicide on Smith tuff—they'd snap off (or pull out) with alarming ease. Fortunately, you won't find any on the most popular routes, but they're not uncommon in more obscure locations. In the 1970s the ⅜-inch bolt added a new degree of safety to Smith climbing. Usually hand-drilled on lead, these bolts weren't likely to sheer off in a fall, but they lacked a suitable expansion system for soft rock. They still protect some routes set as recent as 1986—look for the trademark older hangers (usually SMC) with a fully threaded shaft. The earliest Smith sport routes of the 1980s relied on a full-sleeve bolt with a foolproof expansion system. They required a ⅜-inch hole, but the threaded shaft itself was only ⁵⁄₁₆-inch in diameter—far weaker than today's bolts. Most of these were replaced years ago, but some still remain.

The power drill was the best thing that ever happened to bolting safety at Smith. But no matter how solid a placement, nothing lasts forever. The first sign of age is a spinning hanger, followed by wobbling in the hole—usually a crank with a wrench solves this problem. If a bolt won't tighten properly, it needs to be replaced. Poor placement can severely compromise strength; be especially wary of any bolt sticking out of the hole—this creates a dangerous lever force.

Fixed Pins

Fixed pins were once a common method of protection at Smith. It's been more than twenty years since any new free route relied on a fixed peg, but they're still in place on older climbs. Many of these will pull out in the fingers of the next climber passing by. Fixed pins are far more reliable in basalt, but still use them with caution. They're no longer acceptable on any new free route.

Anchors

Almost all Smith anchors feature a minimum of two bolts. Never rappel off a single bolt, no matter how bombproof it might appear. The days of faded webbing and flimsy rings are fortunately over; almost all modern anchors feature reliable chain links. The best of these are extraordinarily strong, but after years of use they can develop alarming grooves. To preserve these rings, refrain from threading them directly on extended toprope sessions; instead use your own biners.

Rockfall

Few climbers at Smith wear hard hats. Natural stonefall is rare, but we've all experienced the bone-chilling whistle of a rock plummeting to earth from hundreds of feet above. Safety-conscious climbers might prefer wearing a helmet, especially on lower-quality multi-pitch routes. Although scorned by most high-level free climbers, helmets are a personal choice. Wear one if you'd like, and don't concern yourself with any idiot giving you a hard time.

SUGGESTED ROUTES

The following table should help anyone interested in sampling only the finest climbs. The easier routes (below 5.4) aren't nearly as good as the more difficult lines, and they protect sparsely. Distinguishing between the lowest grades at Smith is nothing more than a guessing game. There's almost no discernible difference between a 5.0 and a 5.3.

Grade	Sport Routes	Trad/Mixed Routes
1st	N/A	Misery Ridge Trail, River Trail, Burma Road
2nd	N/A	Aggro Gully, Monument Gully
3rd	N/A	Little Three Fingered Jack, Koala Rock
4th	N/A	The Wombat, Buffalo Practice Rock, Asterisk Pass
5.0	N/A	Chockstone Chimney
5.1	N/A	West Ledges, North Ridge (the Monument)
5.2	N/A	Spiral (Squaw Rock), The Platform, Arrowpoint
5.3	N/A	South Face (Squaw Rock), Limestone Chimney
5.4	Round River (first pitch)	Left Slab Crack, First Ascent Crack, Western Chimney
5.5	Night Flight, My Little Pony, Lollypop League	South Buttress (Brogan Spire), Bowling Alley
5.6	Easy Reader, Round Here, Lounger, 9999	Super Slab, Moscow, Cinnamon Slab
5.7	Dancer, Bunny Face, Round There	Spiderman, Sky Chimney, Bookworm
5.8	Lusty Lady, Five Gallon Buckets, Scary Llamas	West Face Variation, Lion's Jaw, Out of Harm's Way
5.9	Wherever I May Roam, Sunset Slab, Revelations	Moonshine, White Satin, Chouinard's Crack

5.10a	Light on the Path, Phoenix, Suck My Kiss, Cosmos	Zion, Karate Crack, Trezlar, Cruel Sister, Gruff
5.10b	Thin Air, Screaming Yellow Zonkers, J.T.'s Route, Naxis	Hesitation Blues, Pack Animal Direct, Badfinger
5.10c	Lion Zion, Planet Luxury, Orgasmagoria, Buffalo Power	Calamity Jam, Kunza Korner, Morning Star
5.10d	Moon's of Pluto, Headless Horseman, Bay of Pigs	Explosive Energy Child, Much Ado About Nothing
5.11a	Magic Light, Blue Light Special, Pure Palm	Wartley's Revenge, Cry of the Poor, Lion's Chair
5.11b	Toxic, Vomit Launch, Monkey Space, Holier than Thou	Karot Tots, Crack-a-n-go, The Pearl, Windfall
5.11c	Bloodshot, Kevin's Arête, License to Bolt, Drilling Zona	Good Ol' Days, The Sheepgate
5.11d	Ring of Fire, Gulag Archipelago, Northern Lights	Rising Expectations, Sunshine Dihedral, Dark Star
5.12a	Heinous Cling start, Dreamin', Freebase, White Trash	Astro Monkey, Northwest Corner, Neutron Star
5.12b	Latest Rage, Watts Tots, Boy Prophet, Freedom's ...	Northwest Passage, Crossfire, Masquerade
5.12c	Last Waltz, Chain Reaction, Karate Wall, Resuscitation	East Face start, Sheer Trickery
5.12d	King's of Rap, Split Image, The Urge	Smut
5.13a	Churning, Darkness at Noon, The Backbone, Feminazis, Taco Chips,	Double Stain
5.13b	Aggro Monkey, Rude Boys, Waste Case, Hot Lava	none
5.13c	Vicious Fish, Rude Femmes, The Burl Master, Big Tuna	East Face finish
5.13d	White Wedding, Spank the Monkey finish	East Face
5.14a	Scarface, To Bolt or Not to Be, Badman, The Big R	none
5.14b	The Optimist, Starvation Fruit, Shotgun Wedding	none
5.14c	Just Do It, Shock and Awe	none

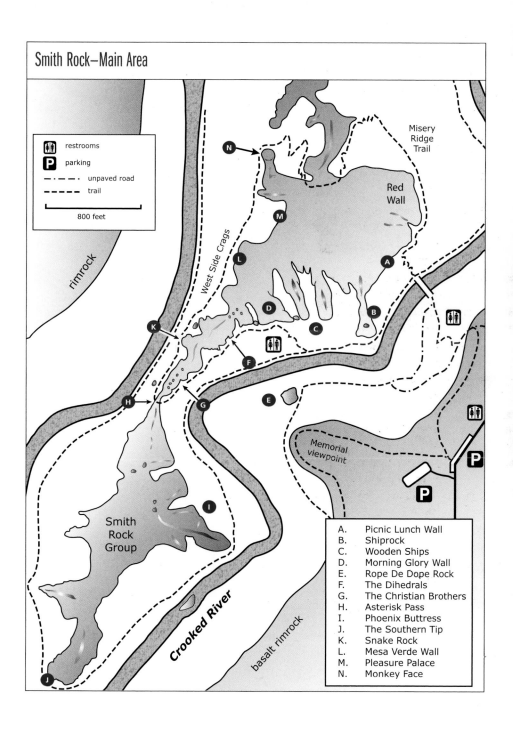

Smith Rock—Main Area

restrooms
P parking
— · — · — unpaved road
— — — trail

800 feet

Misery
Ridge
Trail

Red
Wall

West Side Crags

rimrock

N

M

L

A

D

B

C

K

F

E

Memorial
viewpoint

H

G

Smith
Rock
Group

I

Crooked River

basalt rimrock

J

P

P

A. Picnic Lunch Wall
B. Shiprock
C. Wooden Ships
D. Morning Glory Wall
E. Rope De Dope Rock
F. The Dihedrals
G. The Christian Brothers
H. Asterisk Pass
I. Phoenix Buttress
J. The Southern Tip
K. Snake Rock
L. Mesa Verde Wall
M. Pleasure Palace
N. Monkey Face

Picnic Lunch Wall Area

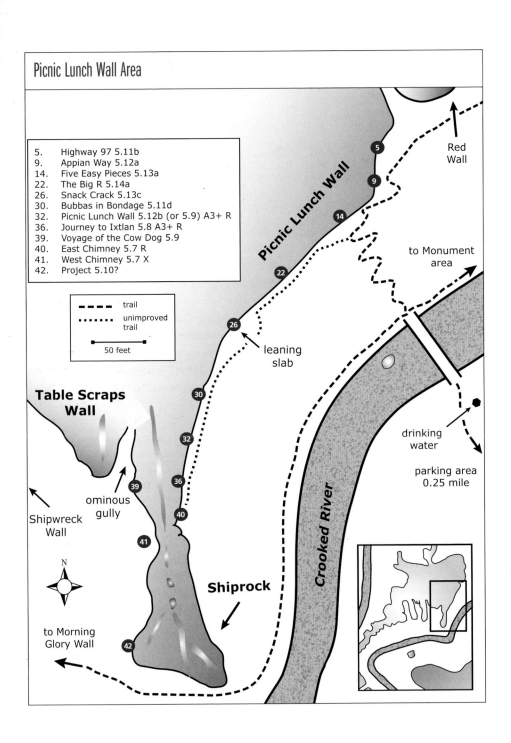

5. Highway 97 5.11b
9. Appian Way 5.12a
14. Five Easy Pieces 5.13a
22. The Big R 5.14a
26. Snack Crack 5.13c
30. Bubbas in Bondage 5.11d
32. Picnic Lunch Wall 5.12b (or 5.9) A3+ R
36. Journey to Ixtlan 5.8 A3+ R
39. Voyage of the Cow Dog 5.9
40. East Chimney 5.7 R
41. West Chimney 5.7 X
42. Project 5.10?

- - - - trail
.... unimproved trail

50 feet

Picnic Lunch Wall

Red Wall

to Monument area

leaning slab

Table Scraps Wall

ominous gully

Shipwreck Wall

Shiprock

Crooked River

drinking water

parking area 0.25 mile

N

to Morning Glory Wall

*The rock was so bad the bolts were falling out
behind me. I kept reaching down, trying to hammer them back into their holes. Of course, by
then the quarter-inch bolt I was hanging from
was already shifting in its hole. We didn't place
many bolts because they were worse than most of
the pins.*

Tom Bauman, describing the first ascent
of the Picnic Lunch Wall in 1969

Welcoming every visitor to the park, Smith's
mini-version of El Cap rises high above the
footbridge spanning the Crooked River.
Picnic Lunch Wall doesn't fare well in
comparison with its more famous rival. El
Capitan towers over 3,000 feet, with flawless
expanses of granite, perfect cracks, and routes
famous throughout the world. Picnic Lunch
Wall, on the other hand, is only 550 feet tall,
composed of disintegrating tuff, and littered
with tons of delicately perched rubble. The
multi-pitch routes to the top aren't world
famous; in fact, few Smith veterans ever scale
the entire cliff. But somehow Picnic Lunch
instills the same sense of awe among tourists
gazing across the canyon as El Cap itself.

Climbers aren't so easily fooled. After
spending a trying day scaling the entire cliff,
big wall fanatics leave covered in grit and
pigeon crap. Fortunately, sport climbers fare
better—the many single-pitch base routes,
ranging from 5.9 to 5.14, are surprisingly
good. In general, the harder the free route
the better the rock, though there's a reason

why there aren't any four-star routes. No
amount of scrubbing and gluing can make a
Picnic Lunch Wall route completely solid.
But diligent cleaning makes all the difference—the many quality routes bear witness
to these efforts. For the beginner, Picnic
Lunch Wall offers little except major-league
trouble; for the higher-level climber, it features a short approach, afternoon shade, and
upper-end difficulties.

Climbers first visited the area in 1946,
as Ross Petrie and Dave Pearson tempted
fate by scaling Shiprock. Their ascent of this
shattered rhyolite pillar was a noteworthy
effort; even today it's Smith's most serious
5.7. Thirty-three years passed before Tom
Bauman and Kim Schmitz scaled Picnic
Lunch Wall, the most difficult aid route
in Oregon for nearly a decade. While free
climbing dominated Smith during the 1970s,
the best ascent on Picnic Lunch Wall was an
improbable aid line called *Soft Shoe Ballet* by
Bill Antel and Bob McGown. Today these
nail-ups are relics of a long-past era, though
they still attract the occasional oddball.

The 1980s brought single-pitch free
routes to Picnic Lunch Wall. Free ascents
of the first pitch of *Unfinished Symphony* and
Midnight Snack (both 5.12b) in 1982 vaulted
the wall to the forefront of Smith free climbing. These lines set the standard for nearly
a year until new routes in the Dihedrals
blew past them. The 1988 ascent of *Snack
Crack* (5.13c) raised the level a full number

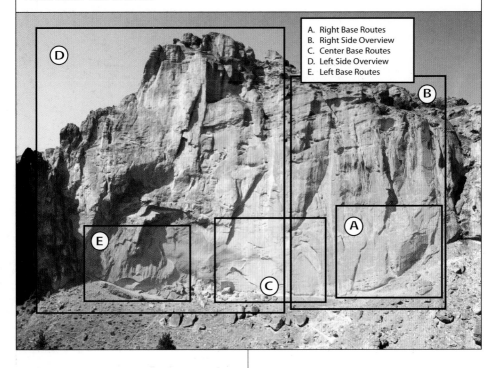

A. Right Base Routes
B. Right Side Overview
C. Center Base Routes
D. Left Side Overview
E. Left Base Routes

grade, but it wasn't until the nineties that the wall returned to the highest levels of Smith climbing. Marc Lemenestral's ascent of *The Big R* (5.14a) in 1995 and Joe Brooks's *Starvation Fruit* (5.14b) two years later were two of the most significant Smith free climbs of the entire decade. Even more difficult lines on the blank faces in the center of the wall hold promise for upcoming generations of super climbers.

The name Picnic Lunch Wall is more commonly used today, but early local climbers called the monolith Parking Lot Wall. Confusion arose after Bauman and Schmitz named their multi-pitch route *Picnic Lunch Wall*. Early Smith guidebooks used the original name, while more recent guides adopted the new name. Many long-time Smith climbers flip-flop back and forth between the two names.

PICNIC LUNCH WALL

Finding the crags: The quick approach ascends the staircase rising directly above the bridge. A deep, black-streaked gully marks the right boundary of Picnic Lunch Wall, separating the cliff from Red Wall to the north. The first several routes start behind a slabby boulder, about 50 feet left of the base of this gully. **Descent:** To hike off from the top of the cliff, walk up and right, joining the Misery Ridge Trail. This switchbacked, well-constructed path ulti-mately leads back to the base. An alternate descent for those familiar with the area veers left to the Aggro Gully.

1. Pisces (5.10b) ★ Mixed to 1.5 inches. An unlikely two-pitch route blazes a path

Picnic Lunch Wall

Shiprock

Red Wall

3.	Scorpio 5.8 X	22.	The Big R 5.14a
4.	Fool's Overture 5.9 R	27.	Soft Shoe Ballet 5.10a A4+ X
9.	Appian Way 5.12a	30.	Bubbas in Bondage 5.11d
10.	No Picnic 5.10c R	32.	Picnic Lunch Wall 5.12b (or 5.9) A3+ R
13.	Free Lunch 5.10a R	36.	Journey to Ixtlan 5.8 A3+ R
19.	Coleslaw and Chemicals 5.13a	40.	East Chimney 5.7 R

up the far right side of the monolith. It might someday finish to the top—the upper headwall looks far better than the lackluster approach. **Pitch 1:** (5.10a) Follow a slab past three bolts and traverse right to natural protection in a finishing crack. **Pitch 2:** (5.10b) 5 bolts. Climb disappointing rock, crossing over the second pitch of *I Lost My Lunch* to a crux rib. Veer right to rappel bolts.

2. I Lost My Lunch (5.9 X) Mixed to 3 inches. Far off the ground on the right side of Picnic Lunch Wall lurks a deep inside corner, guarded by loose flakes. Likely the only ascent of this death trap occurred when climbers got lost on neighboring *Scorpio*. Start atop a low-angle boulder. **Pitch 1:** (5.8) Climb a poorly protected, right-leaning thin crack to a sage-covered ledge. Step right

to belay bolts. **Pitch 2:** (5.9) Clip the first bolt on *Pisces* and step right to an obvious crack system. Jam to a terrifying minefield of rubble, followed by stems in a tight dihedral. More teetering blocks guard the exit. You can belay midpitch at the *Pisces* anchor, but it'll make it harder dodging the inevitable rockfall.

3. Scorpio (5.8 X) Gear to 3 inches. During the eighties, epics and accidents were a common occurrence on this dangerous line. The bad rock, poor protection, and unaesthetic climbing make it a more serious venture than the grade suggests. **Pitch 1:** (5.8) Climb the starting corner of *I Lost My Lunch,* but continue past the ledge via an unprotected direct line or better holds to the right. Belay beneath an unmistakable flatiron. **Pitch 2:**

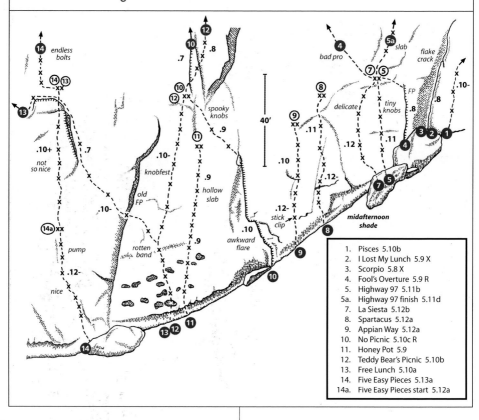

1. Pisces 5.10b
2. I Lost My Lunch 5.9 X
3. Scorpio 5.8 X
4. Fool's Overture 5.9 R
5. Highway 97 5.11b
5a. Highway 97 finish 5.11d
7. La Siesta 5.12b
8. Spartacus 5.12a
9. Appian Way 5.12a
10. No Picnic 5.10c R
11. Honey Pot 5.9
12. Teddy Bear's Picnic 5.10b
13. Free Lunch 5.10a
14. Five Easy Pieces 5.13a
14a. Five Easy Pieces start 5.12a

(5.8) More crumbly face climbing leads into an ominous corner. Follow this pitiful dihedral to the top.

4. Fool's Overture (5.9 R) ★ Mixed to 2.5 inches. Adventurous climbers unafraid of bad rock might enjoy this mediocre route to the top of the wall; budding 5.9 climbers should stay away. The upper portion follows the obvious parallel inside corners just left of the flatiron of *Driveway Gravel*. Start atop a slab below a short dihedral. **Pitch 1:** (5.8) Stem a corner past a fixed pin and foot-shuffle left past an anchor. An easy unprotected slab leads to a short ramp and a bolt belay. **Pitch 2:** (5.9) Tackle a crumbly seam to a shelf and face climb into a left-facing corner. Climb the solid dihedral to a sloping belay ledge. **Pitch 3:** (5.9) Drop down to the left and cut across an unnerving face into the finishing gully.

5. Highway 97 (5.11b) ★★★ 4 bolts. This short route routinely spits off climbers hoping for a straightforward warm-up for the nearby desperates. Begin by motoring up classic pockets, then shift gears, edging on miniature knobs to a ledge.

5a. Highway 97 finish (5.11d) ★ 10 bolts. The upper part of *Highway 97* isn't much fun and rarely sees traffic. Technical, crumbling edges lead past many bolts, ending with a hand traverse right to an anchor. Most ascents combine both pitches into one.

Picnic Lunch Wall–Right Side Routes

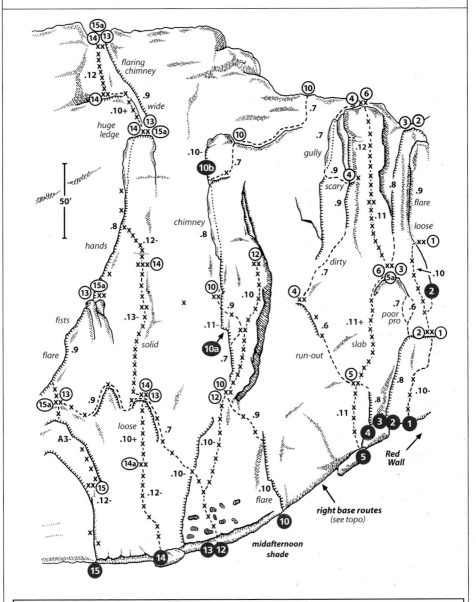

1.	Pisces 5.10b	10a.	Bob's World 5.11a R
2.	I Lost My Lunch 5.9 X	10b.	Farmer's Variation 5.10a R
3.	Scorpio 5.8 X	12.	Teddy Bear's Picnic 5.10b
4.	Fool's Overture 5.9 R	13.	Free Lunch 5.10a R
5.	Highway 97 5.11b	14.	Five Easy Pieces 5.13a
5a.	Highway 97 finish 5.11d	14a.	Five Easy Pieces start 5.12a
6.	Driveway Gravel 5.12c	15.	Unfinished Symphony 5.12b
10.	No Picnic 5.10c R	15a.	Unfinished Symphony finish 5.9 A3-

6. Driveway Gravel (5.12c) ★★ 16 bolts. An attractive, eye-catching flatiron dominates the upper right side of Picnic Lunch Wall. With tedious, unrelenting moves on friable edges, those who succeed rarely have any desire to return. The easiest start follows the first two pitches of *Scorpio,* but *Highway 97* provides a higher-quality alternative.

7. La Siesta (5.12b) ★★ 5 bolts. Just left of the pocketed first pitch of *Highway 97* sits a similar sport route. A strenuous crank on a shallow two-finger pocket at the start was originally the only hard move; the grade rose considerably as nearly every knob snapped off the finishing slab.

8. Spartacus (5.12a) ★★ 6 bolts. A faint, right-leaning seam rises downhill from *La Siesta.* The hardest moves on the right-hand route pull around a dinky roof at the start. Finish with easier but more technical edges.

9. Appian Way (5.12a) ★★ 6 bolts. Downhill from *Spartacus* sits a short route with a physical start. Almost everyone stick-clips the first bolt, toproping through the crux. Easier knobs and pockets finish to the anchor.

10. No Picnic (5.10c R) ★ Mixed to 3 inches. This homely route is one of the better moderate lines to the top of Picnic Lunch Wall. Considering the alternatives, this isn't saying much—there's enough bad rock to make it a serious undertaking. Start below a short, clean alcove. **Pitch 1:** (5.10c) An awkward crux on great rock enters a flaring slot leading to a shallow dihedral. Run-out face moves on dicey knobs lead past two scary bolts to an anchor. **Pitch 2:** (5.9) Grovel up a dirty crack, escaping trouble by moving right onto solid rock. Clip the midpitch anchor chain on *Teddy Bear's Picnic* and traverse back past a bolt to the base of a shallow, foreboding chimney. **Pitch 3:** (5.8)

Ascend the disappointing chimney and cut right onto a ledge when the rock turns to kitty litter. Walk right and climb a short face to a larger ledge. **Pitch 4:** (5.7) Hike right along a ledge and wander up moderate rock to the top.

10a. Bob's World (5.11a R) Gear to 3 inches. Confront trouble on the second pitch of *No Picnic* by struggling directly up the abysmal crack system to the base of the obvious chimney.

10b. Farmer's Variation (5.10a R) Gear to 3 inches. On an early ascent of *No Picnic,* the leader mistakenly stumbled upon this wretched variant. If you care to relive his misfortune, don't step right out of the third-pitch chimney. Instead, plow through miserable rock to the large ledge just below the top.

11. Honey Pot (5.9) ★★★ 11 bolts. The most popular route on the wall begins with massive potholes leading to a knobby slab. The convenient location and the low grade are the biggest draws, along with a starting bolt right off the deck. The entire finishing slab sounds eerily hollow.

12. Teddy Bear's Picnic (5.10b) ★★★ Bolts. Cleaned by hundreds of ascents, this two-pitch face route is solid and worth doing. Many climbers rappel after the knobs of the first pitch, but the best climbing lies above on an attractive, airy face. Start below giant potholes. **Pitch 1:** (5.10a) 11 bolts. Romp up the potholes and climb knobs to the anchors below the obvious clean face. **Pitch 2:** (5.10b) 12 bolts. Step right and enjoy good rock past optional belay bolts to the highest anchor. Descend using two ropes.

13. Free Lunch (5.10a R) ★★ Mixed to 3.5 inches. The original free route to the top of Picnic Lunch Wall isn't a classic, but the spacious ledges, excellent position, and captivating fourth pitch make up for brief stints of nastiness. The retro-bolted starting pitch is now far safer (and cleaner) than on early ascents. Start at the base of the same huge potholes as *Teddy Bear's Picnic*. **Pitch 1:** (5.10a) 9 bolts. Veer left above the potholes to a small right-facing corner. Clip a new bolt and traverse left on crux knobs to a shallow corner ending at a ledge. **Pitch 2:** (5.9) 4 bolts. Climb up and over a pinnacle, stepping left past a couple bolts to a big ledge. It's safer to lead this pitch. **Pitch 3:** (5.9) Jam the obvious flaring crack, stemming out of an awkward alcove to a fist crack and a small ledge. **Pitch 4:** (5.8) Scamper up the long crack on solid rock to a large shelf. **Pitch 5:** (5.9) Grunt up an awkward crack and flared chimney to an anchor at the top.

14. Five Easy Pieces (5.13a) ★★★ Bolts.

This long sport route ranks among the most impressive in the park. Far and away the best free route to the top, *Five Easy Pieces* ascends mostly good rock, with the amazing second pitch highlighting the experience. Start behind a small boulder left of the huge potholes. **Pitch 1:** (5.12a) 13 bolts. High-quality pockets and edges lead past an anchor to a mediocre slab ending at a belay platform. **Pitch 2:** (5.13a) 14 bolts. Face climb past an endless line of bolts on sublime rock to a hanging belay below a roof. Belaying at double bolts in the middle of the pitch drops the grade a notch. **Pitch 3:** (5.12a) 9 bolts. Clear the roof and traverse far left, joining the fourth pitch of *Free Lunch*. Hand jam past a couple bolts to a big ledge. **Pitch 4:** (5.10d) 4 bolts. Follow a subpar left-leaning crack past a few bolts and step left to a big ledge. **Pitch 5:** (5.12b) 7 bolts. Pull over a bulge on chiseled pockets to a finishing slab.

14a. Five Easy Pieces start (5.12a) ★★★ 7

bolts. For good reason, the lower half of *Five Easy Pieces'* first pitch is one of the most popular routes on the crag. Solid rock, plentiful bolts, pumping moves, and a short approach provide all the necessary ingredients.

15. Unfinished Symphony (5.12b) ★★ Mixed

to 1 inch. The original start to *Free Lunch* nailed two pitches up massive arches. The pin-scarred first pitch went free in 1982, briefly holding the title of Smith's hardest route. Few modern climbers attempt the challenging liebacks, jams, and stems. Physical wire placements only add to the difficulty, with the crux coming just below the anchor.

15a. Unfinished Symphony finish (5.9 A3-)

★ Aid rack to 1.5 inches. Above the free pitch looms a menacing aid arch leading into the prominent crack system on *Free Lunch*. The dirty, awkward nailing attracts only the most perverse aid climbers.

16. High Noon (5.12d) ★★ 6 bolts. The ver-

tical crimpfest left of *Unfinished Symphony* will torment anyone who prefers steeper lines. The holds get smaller the higher you go, with a depressing crux near the top. At the start, either traverse left or follow a 5.12 direct line. The direct variant adds little to the overall grade, since there's a good shake at midheight.

17. Project–Rainy Day Diversion (5.13?)

The impressive bolted arch branching left above the anchor of *High Noon* will someday yield a demanding free route.

18. Project (5.13?) 7 bolts. Just left of *High*

Noon rises another line of bolts on a vertical, scarred face. The moves go free, but linkage awaits. If crimping isn't your thing, you might want to look elsewhere.

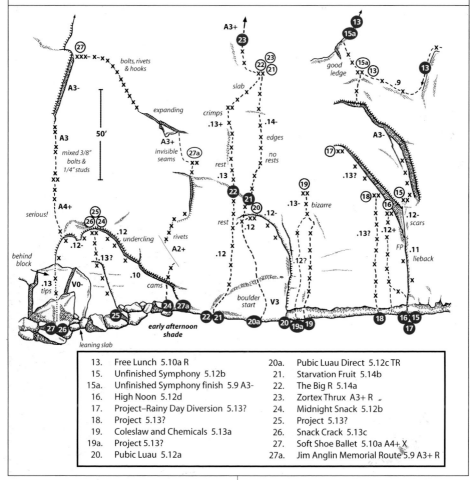

A3+

bolts, rivets & hooks

A3-

expanding

50'

A3

mixed 3/8" bolts & 1/4" studs

A4+

serious!

A3+

invisible seams

27a

slab

crimps

.13+

rest

.13

expanding

.14-

edges

no rests

good ledge

.9

A3-

.13?

A3-

behind block

.12

.13?

.10

cams

.13 tips

V0-

underclining

rivets

A2+

.12

.12-

rest

.12

.12-

.12

boulder start

V3

.13- bizarre

12?

.13?

.13?

.12+

.12-

scars

.12+

FP

.11

lieback

early afternoon shade

leaning slab

13.	Free Lunch 5.10a R	20a.	Pubic Luau Direct 5.12c TR
15.	Unfinished Symphony 5.12b	21.	Starvation Fruit 5.14b
15a.	Unfinished Symphony finish 5.9 A3-	22.	The Big R 5.14a
16.	High Noon 5.12d	23.	Zortex Thrux A3+ R
17.	Project–Rainy Day Diversion 5.13?	24.	Midnight Snack 5.12b
18.	Project 5.13?	25.	Project 5.13?
19.	Coleslaw and Chemicals 5.13a	26.	Snack Crack 5.13c
19a.	Project 5.13?	27.	Soft Shoe Ballet 5.10a A4+ X
20.	Pubic Luau 5.12a	27a.	Jim Anglin Memorial Route 5.9 A3+ R

19. Coleslaw and Chemicals (5.13a) ★★ 7 bolts. This unlikely route scales a rotten-looking wall held together by epoxy. Surprisingly, the climbing is good, with an escalating series of technical moves capped by a baffling crux just below the anchors. Crumbling holds slowly push the grade higher from year to year.

19a. Project (5.13?) An alternate start to the left will someday provide a more challenging approach to the same crux as the regular route.

20. Pubic Luau (5.12a) ★★ Mixed to 2 inches. The right side of this obvious arch contains a forgotten route. With the old webbing anchor replaced with chain links, those who once lunged for the slings now must crank the crux underclings.

20a. Pubic Luau Direct (5.12c) ★★ TR. A rarely attempted toprope problem climbs left of the regular line, starting with a tricky boulder problem. The original route lunged from face holds to defunct anchor slings. A more refined finish veers left before cutting right on underclings.

21. Starvation Fruit (5.14b) ★★ 14 bolts. This rarely repeated endurance problem on a blank-looking wall ranks in the top five of Smith's hardest routes. Apart from a no-hands rest just above the start, the gently overhanging face is unrelenting. With your forearms screaming, the crux comes high on the wall— a throw to a thumb-catch undercling.

22. The Big R (5.14a) ★★★ 15 bolts. The first 5.14 on Picnic Lunch Wall sees many attempts and few ascents. After sharing the same start with *Starvation Fruit,* veer up and left on moderate incuts on a blank-looking wall to a powerful sequence entering a shallow corner. A good rest allows a recovery before the final sequence—a technical arête followed by a horrendous crux, pulling onto the final slab on micro-crimps.

23. Zortex Thrux (A3+ R) ★ Aid rack to 1 inch. Originally, *Pubic Luau* was the start of an uncompleted aid route. *Zortex Thrux* aided the arch and nailed an invisible seam (now part of *Starvation Fruit*) to an anchor. A long section of aid stopped one pitch below the top, where hard aid gave way to moderate free climbing. Nailing the lower part now would do irreparable harm to the free climbs, but the whole route might go free using either of the 5.14s as a first pitch.

24. Midnight Snack (5.12b) ★★ Mixed to 3.5 inches. Before the advent of sticky rubber, this

forgotten relic of the old days was one of Smith's hardest routes. You can't avoid a disgusting smear of bird poop at midheight, though the final moves—thin underclings protected by bolts—are high quality.

25. Project (5.13?) 5 bolts. Directly below the anchors on *Midnight Snack* is a short line of bolts. The finger jams at the start won't be a problem, but pulling onto the holdless face above will be.

26. Snack Crack (5.13c) ★★ 5 bolts. One of Smith's most technical thin cracks splits the wall behind a gigantic leaning slab. After

Alan Watts on the first ascent of *Midnight Snack*.

Picnic Lunch Wall—Left Side Overview

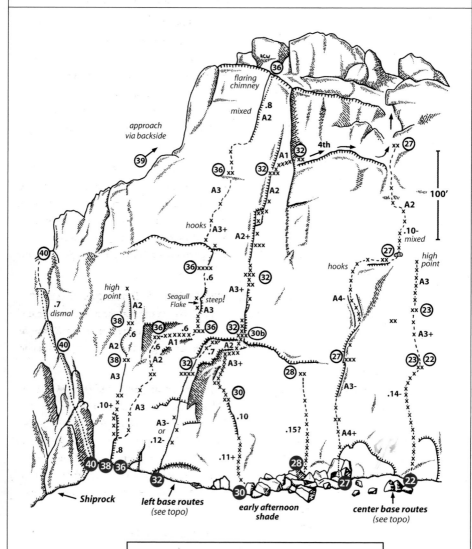

22. The Big R 5.14a
23. Zortex Thrux A3+ R
27. Soft Shoe Ballet 5.10a A4+ X
28. Project 5.15?
30. Bubbas in Bondage 5.11d
30b. Bubbas in Bondage finish A3+
32. Picnic Lunch Wall 5.12b (or 5.9) A3+ R
36. Journey to Ixtlan 5.8 A3+ R
38. Ryan's World 5.10d A3
39. Voyage of the Cow Dog 5.9
40. East Chimney 5.7 R

stick-clipping the first bolt, jam horrid pin scars into an arch and undercling right to an anchor. The grade varies depending on finger size—anyone with plump fingers barely gets off the ground.

27. Soft Shoe Ballet (5.10a A4+ X) ★★
Aid rack to 2 inches. Among Smith's most serious aid routes, this imposing line sees very few ascents. The first pitch is especially dangerous, with a life-extinguishing impact onto the slab below a real possibility. Expect better-than-average rock for a Picnic Lunch Wall aid rõute. **Pitch 1:** (A4+) Aid *Snack Crack* using good nuts, exiting the arch to the left on poor pins. Mind-tweaking nailing past questionable bolts ends at a hanging belay. **Pitch 2:** (A4-) Exit a shallow leaning corner via seams on the left. Hard nailing gives way to a traverse right on hooks and bolts, ending at an idyllic belay ledge. **Pitch 3:** (5.10a A2) Mixed free and aid moves lead past scattered bolts to the top.

27a. Jim Anglin Memorial Route (5.9 A3+ R) ★★
Aid rack to 1.5 inches. A less intense variation to *Soft Shoe Ballet* bypasses the serious first pitch. Expect solid rock and a mixture of bolt ladders, hairline seams, expanding flakes, and hook moves. Shares the same start as *Midnight Snack*. **Pitch 1:** (5.9 A2+). Free moves off the deck lead to rivets clearing a small roof. Nail a seam, clip more bolts, and finish in a left-facing corner to a hanging belay. **Pitch 2:** (A3+) Follow invisible seams and traverse far left on expanding flakes. Bolts, rivets, and hooks lead to the first anchor on *Soft Shoe Ballet*. Rappel with two ropes or continue to the top.

28. Project (5.15?)
About 30 feet left of *Snack Crack* rises a futuristic wall with few features other than an offset at one-third height. The lower half would be 5.15 by

itself, while the upper part looks like a stiff version of *To Bolt or Not to Be*.

29. Ancient Bolt Line (A4+ X) ★
Aid rack to 0.5 inch. A bolt ladder from Smith's early days leads 100 feet up a blank wall. Most of the original quarter-inch bolts disappeared long ago, leaving behind a challenging endeavor for today's aid specialists. Begin atop a stack of blocks, below a short right-facing corner.

30. Bubbas in Bondage (5.11d) ★★★
Mixed to 1 inch. The first pitch of this old aid route is now a varied free climb, mixing sport and traditional climbing. The sport climbing crux comes low on the route, though the naturally protected finishing corner provides the best memories.

30a. Masochistic Tendencies (5.11d) ★★
9 bolts. This sport variant cuts right for no good reason below the corner on *Bubbas in Bondage,* ending at an anchor in the middle of nowhere.

30b. Bubbas In Bondage finish (A3+) ★★
Aid rack to 1 inch. The second pitch of *Bubbas in Bondage* provides the best-quality access to the upper section of Picnic Lunch Wall. Mixed bolts and nailing lead over intimidating roofs to a hanging belay. Either rappel off with two ropes or continue to the top.

31. Out to Lunch (5.12c) ★★
13 bolts. An unmistakable low-level roof arches along the left base of Picnic Lunch Wall. An exceedingly well-bolted sport route leads over the roof, highlighted by a crux undercling/lieback pulling over the lip. It makes a good choice on rainy days.

32. Picnic Lunch Wall (5.12b [or 5.9] A3+ R) ★★
Aid rack to 3.5 inches. For anyone hoping to master the art of Smith aid

Picnic Lunch Wall—Left Base Routes

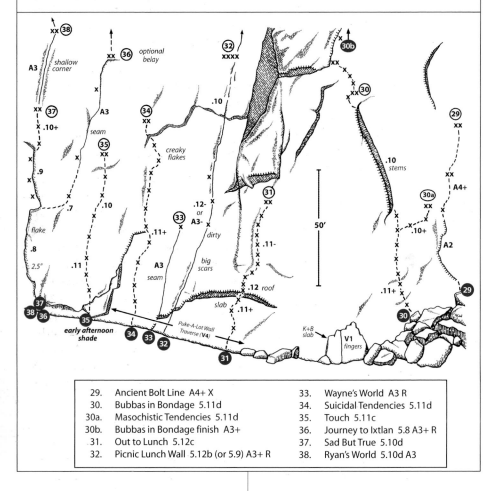

29.	Ancient Bolt Line A4+ X		33.	Wayne's World A3 R
30.	Bubbas in Bondage 5.11d		34.	Suicidal Tendencies 5.11d
30a.	Masochistic Tendencies 5.11d		35.	Touch 5.11c
30b.	Bubbas in Bondage finish A3+		36.	Journey to Ixtlan 5.8 A3+ R
31.	Out to Lunch 5.12c		37.	Sad But True 5.10d
32.	Picnic Lunch Wall 5.12b (or 5.9) A3+ R		38.	Ryan's World 5.10d A3

climbing, the original route to the top of the wall is a rite of passage. Early ascents faced the chilling prospect of zippering entire pitches; repeated nailings and many new bolts lowered the grade and risk. The pegged-out crack systems are a bit of an eyesore now, though the entire route might go free as a result. **Pitch 1:** (5.12b A3-) Gigantic dusty pin scars lead past a few bolts to a hanging belay. If freeing dirty 5.12 isn't part of your repertoire, don't despair—no one actually frees this pitch. **Pitch 2:** (5.7

A2) Aid to the huge roof and face traverse right until bolts lead over the ceiling to a bolt-studded hanging belay. **Pitch 3:** (A3+) Expanding nailing in a scarred left-facing dihedral ends at the first set of anchors. **Pitch 4:** (5.9 A2+) Pound a long right-facing corner past an anchor and around a roof to optional free moves. **Pitch 5:** (A1) Traverse right on shaky bolts to a large ledge. Scramble to the top.

33. Wayne's World (A3 R) ★ Aid rack to 0.5 inch. You'll know you're an aid-addict if you find yourself racking up for this puny seam. Begin a few feet left of the first pitch of *Picnic Lunch Wall* and nail 30 feet to a single-bolt anchor.

34. Suicidal Tendencies (5.11d) ** 10 bolts. Just right of a leaning flake sits this mediocre face route. Crimpy pockets at the start lead to a crux dash around a mini-roof. The climbing eases and the quality deteriorates as creaky flakes lead to an anchor.

35. Touch (5.11c) *** 7 bolts. The better of two parallel sport climbs begins with an undercling flake, leading to technical moves on small holds. The rock remains solid the rest of the way, proving that anything at Smith will clean up after enough ascents.

36. Journey to Ixtlan (5.8 A3+ R) * Aid rack to 3 inches. This intimidating line is the only route up the highest section of Picnic Lunch Wall, topping-out over 100 feet above its more famous neighbor to the right. Once a contender for the title of Smith's worst route, this overhanging wall of rubble isn't nearly as horrible as it looks. If you're a collector of Smith's garbage routes (there really is such a breed), you might as well add this to your list. Fast climbers might condense the suffering into a single day. Start below a flake crack at the far left side of the wall. **Pitch 1:** (5.8 A3) Climb the flake and cut right to a bolt. Hard aid past a couple bolts leads to an optional belay. Continue nailing an overhanging dihedral to easy free moves and an anchor. **Pitch 2:** (5.6 A2) Traverse right on mixed free and aid to a hanging belay at the lip of a huge roof. **Pitch 3:** (5.8 A3) Free moves lead to awkward nailing up the Seagull Flake. A dirty water groove ends at an anchor above the roof. **Pitch 4:** (5.6 A3+) Hard nailing and hooking past quarter-inch bolts give way to more junky rock ending at a sloping ledge.

Pitch 5: (5.8 A2) Easy free moves lead past a couple bolts to a scary traverse to a low-angle crack. Finish with mixed aid and free on bad rock in an awkward flare.

37. Sad But True (5.10d) * Mixed to 2.5 inches. The final route along the left base of Picnic Lunch Wall receives little attention. Begin with the obvious flake crack at the start of *Journey to Ixtlan* and continue past a few bolts to a crux, sport climbing finish.

38. Ryan's World (5.10d A3) * Aid rack to 3 inches. Above the free pitch lurks an unmistakable, overhanging flake crack. Someday the route might continue to the top of the cliff, with most (maybe all) pitches free. **Pitch 1:** (5.10d A3) Climb *Sad But True* to the first set of anchors, then take out your hammer and beat the hell out of a shallow corner, ending at the base of a foreboding flake. **Pitch 2:** (5.6 A2) Spectacular, awkward aid leads out the massive flake to an easy slab and a belay. **Pitch 3:** (A2) Aid the obvious dihedral to a bolt marking the current highpoint.

39. Voyage of the Cow Dog (5.9) *** Bolts. The voyage up the southeast flank of Picnic Lunch Wall possesses more character than your average 5.9. Hand-drilled on lead, it's a little sporting in places, but the hardest moves are totally safe. You'll love the massive exposure on the solid final pitch—unless you're scared of heights. Approach by hiking to Table Scraps Wall (see below), skirting right along the base to a dark gully splitting the cliff line. **Pitch 1:** (5.9) 9 bolts. Ascend a junky slab on the right side of the gully to a big ledge. **Pitch 2:** (5.2) 4 bolts. Step right to simple climbing and clip a few easily missed bolts. Belay at a large shelf. **Pitch 3:** (5.9) 9 bolts. Exposed rock leads to a crux high-step on the last move. Either walk off or rap the route.

SHIPROCK

This landmark tower rises left of Picnic Lunch Wall. Originally named Red Fin, it consists of a dramatically different rock type than the tuff. Shiprock's rhyolite is extremely hard but heavily fractured and sharp-edged. Despite its central location, generations steered clear of this shattered monolith for good reason.

40. East Chimney (5.7 R) Gear to 4 inches. This hideous ordeal starts at the base of the obvious chimney system separating Shiprock from Picnic Lunch Wall. A large gendarme at the notch prevents a finish to the summit. **Pitch 1:** (5.6) Squirm up an ugly chimney to a belay spot. **Pitch 2:** (5.7) Continue through even worse rock to the notch. Descend a crumbling chimney on the backside.

41. West Chimney (5.7 X) Gear to 3 inches. Uncommonly serious for the grade, the only route to the summit was the first recorded rock climb in what is now Smith Rock State Park. To approach, hike scree along the western base of the formation to a shallow chimney. **Pitch 1:** (5.6) Climb a fractured trough to a belay notch. **Pitch 2:** (5.7) Ascend appalling rock on the east side of the arête and follow the path of least resis-

tance, finishing on the west side. From the top an optional fourth-class scramble leads to the lower eastern summit. **Descent:** Rotted slings and cords encircle the western summit. In a form of ritualistic celebration, most successful parties add their own loop. Rappel with double ropes off the south side.

42. Project (5.10?) The south buttress inexplicably attracted the attention of some of Smith's leading climbers in the late 1970s. The retreat from 75 feet off the deck was the only sensible part of the escapade. The rotted back-off sling awaits any fool intent on pushing the route higher.

Shiprock

Picnic Lunch Wall

Table Scraps Wall

39. Voyage of the Cow Dog 5.9
41. West Chimney 5.7 X
42. Project 5.10?

THE WOODEN SHIPS AND THE GULLIES

Sean Olmstead was trying to toprope Aggro Monkey *(5.13b) one day, although back then it didn't have a name since it hadn't been done. I was belaying, and a constant stream of rock shards rained from the sky. Sean asked me to take it tight, and I made the mistake of looking up, filling my eyes with tiny pieces of the route he seemed so intent on climbing. Suddenly, with a whoosh and a crash, a larger chunk of rock exploded into the scree behind me. I was about to tell Sean to quit wasting our time when he looked down with a big grin on his face, saying, "This thing is really gonna be good!"*

After turning the corner below the ominous tower of Shiprock, Smith's most popular cliffs come into view, extending one after another toward Asterisk Pass. The first crags are the Wooden Ships—two massive ribs split by a narrow gully. They might not be the most aesthetically pleasing landmarks in the park, but their true beauty lies in both the quality of the climbing and the magnitude of the numbers. In this context these homely cliffs are radiant jewels, with the highest concentration of extreme routes anywhere at Smith.

Although the Eastern Ship sits to the right, and the Western Ship to the left, these crags are better recognized by three gullies cutting through the cliff line. The heavily developed right side of the Eastern Ship borders the Shipwreck Gully, capped by Table Scraps Wall. Between the two crags looms the renowned Aggro Gully, with its overhanging routes on either side. Bordering the left face of the Western Ship is the Cocaine Gully, best known for its collection of popular vertical faces. The layout of these corridors makes the Wooden Ships a good choice year-round. You can usually find sun in the winter and avoid it during the summer, by merely stepping across to the other side of the gully.

While most routes on Smith tuff required cleaning, the cliffs here—especially in the Aggro Gully—seemed almost hopelessly loose and dirty. On the hardest first ascents, climbers spent hours scouring the rock with a brush, pulling off scores of loose flakes, and reinforcing holds with epoxy. Even with such fanatical cleaning, early ascents rained rock scraps. Yet over time the stone magically improved, eventually becoming as solid as anything else at Smith. These routes opened the eyes of anyone who thought only the best rock could yield good lines. Overnight, the amount of climbable stone seemingly increased ten-fold.

Since the Wooden Ships offered few obvious crack lines and no summit spires, early climbers ignored it. After Dean Fry climbed the grubby main faces of both formations in 1973, everyone looked elsewhere for new routes. The first ascent of *Cocaine Crack* (5.11b) a few years later only confirmed the opinions of those who thought the rock wasn't suitable for climbing. As

5.	Blue Light Special 5.11b	
17.	Tsunami 5.12c	
A.	Lysergic Roof V3	
32.	White Wedding 5.13d	
45.	Kill the Hate 5.13a	
B.	Honeycomb Wall	
51.	Toxic 5.11c	
57.	The Burl Master 5.13c	
C.	Western Ship–River Face	
D.	Pharaoh Boulders	
70.	Vomit Launch 5.11b	
E.	Tuff Nuggets Wall	

late as 1987, not a single sport route existed anywhere on the Wooden Ships. As Smith's more classic lines dwindled, climbers reluctantly took a closer look at these formations. Kent Benesch's *Vomit Launch* (5.11b) on the Cocaine Wall started the sport climbing era

here, and a new route explosion followed.

With a strong anti-gullies attitude among Smith locals, foreign visitors first explored the steepest lines. Eager to add to the wave of new routes at Smith, Michael Keiss and Martin Grullich turned to the Aggro Gully

The Wooden Ships and the Gullies Right Side Overview

A. Shipwreck Wall–River Face
B. Shipwreck Wall–Center Face
C. Shipwreck Wall–Upper Face
D. Aggro Gully–Left Wall
E. Western Ship–River Face

in late 1987. Locals laughed as Keiss and Grullich spent days knocking off loose rock, but in the end they uncovered a couple real gems. Despite their efforts they came away empty-handed, as Keiss narrowly failed on his creation—known later as *White Wedding*. Grullich managed two lackluster lines at the entrance to the gully, but never succeeded on what came to be known as *Aggro Monkey*.

With the word out, 1988 was the year of the gully routes. Over a few months *Power* (5.13b), *Time's Up* (5.13a), *Slit Your Wrists* (5.13b), and *Aggro Monkey* (5.13b) fell in

short order. The best ascent came in early June, as Jean-Baptiste Tribout succeeded on *White Wedding* (5.13d), originally hailed as one the country's first 5.14s. These impressive routes instantly brought the Gullies to the attention of climbers everywhere.

The decade of the 1990s helped realize the full potential of the Wooden Ships, with ascents of *Bad Man* (5.14a), *Repeat Offender* (5.14a), and *Mr. Yuk* (5.14a), though the standards rose the most in relatively recent times. The most difficult ascent was *Shock and Awe* (5.14c), pioneered in 2003 by Scott

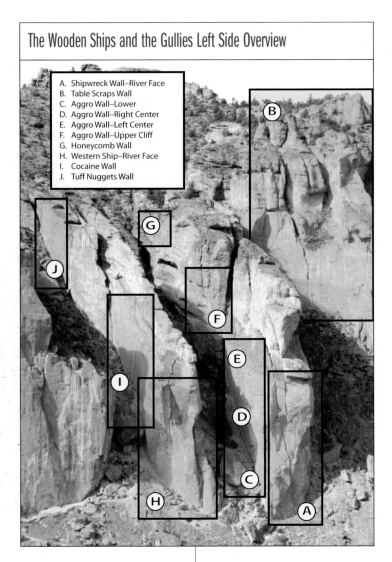

The Wooden Ships and the Gullies Left Side Overview

A. Shipwreck Wall–River Face
B. Table Scraps Wall
C. Aggro Wall–Lower
D. Aggro Wall–Right Center
E. Aggro Wall–Left Center
F. Aggro Wall–Upper Cliff
G. Honeycomb Wall
H. Western Ship–River Face
I. Cocaine Wall
J. Tuff Nuggets Wall

Milton. This link-up of *Repeat Offender* and *Villain* eclipsed *Just Do It* as the hardest route at Smith Rock. In 2007 Ian Caldwell continued the parade of high-level routes with another Aggro Wall link-up called *Shotgun Wedding* (5.14b). But the grandest prize—a link-up of the crux sections of *Repeat Offender, Villain,* and *White Wedding*—still awaits someone with a body of solid muscle. It'll likely hold the coveted title of "Smith's hardest route" for many years into the future.

Finding the crags: From the main parking area, enter the canyon and turn left along the river trail after crossing the bridge spanning the Crooked River. Hike upstream around the base of Shiprock and follow the first staircased path uphill to the base of the crags. **Descent:** Very few routes ascend to the top of these formations. For those that do, hike down the Aggro Gully between the two Wooden Ships.

EASTERN SHIP AREA

The first major crag beyond Shiprock is the Eastern Ship, split by a prominent river-face crack system. On the right rises the Shipwreck Gully, capped by Table Scraps Wall. On the left looms the narrow Aggro Gully, with its ominous overhanging walls.

Shipwreck Wall

This sport cliff includes the entire river face of the Eastern Ship and the left side of the Shipwreck Gully. These routes were rubbish when first climbed, but hundreds of ascents later they're popular for good reason. With midday shade, the uphill routes attract crowds on warm afternoons. The routes start

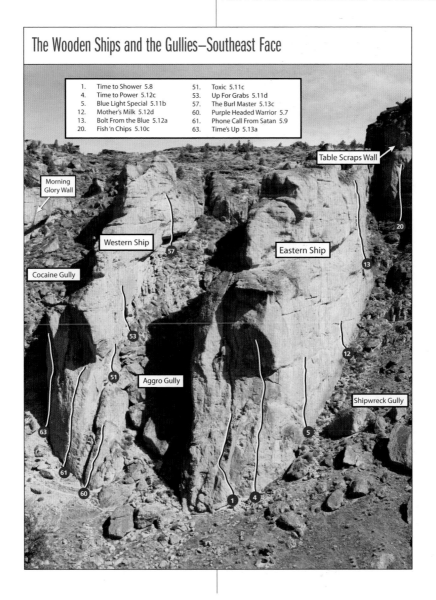

The Wooden Ships and the Gullies—Southeast Face

1.	Time to Shower 5.8	51.	Toxic 5.11c
4.	Time to Power 5.12c	53.	Up For Grabs 5.11d
5.	Blue Light Special 5.11b	57.	The Burl Master 5.13c
12.	Mother's Milk 5.12d	60.	Purple Headed Warrior 5.7
13.	Bolt From the Blue 5.12a	61.	Phone Call From Satan 5.9
20.	Fish 'n Chips 5.10c	63.	Time's Up 5.13a

Table Scraps Wall

Morning Glory Wall

Western Ship

Cocaine Gully

Eastern Ship

Aggro Gully

Shipwreck Gully

Shipwreck Wall—River Face

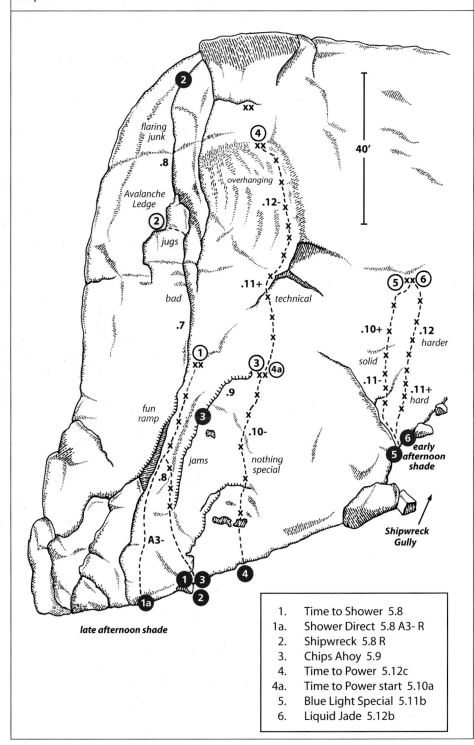

1. Time to Shower 5.8
1a. Shower Direct 5.8 A3- R
2. Shipwreck 5.8 R
3. Chips Ahoy 5.9
4. Time to Power 5.12c
4a. Time to Power start 5.10a
5. Blue Light Special 5.11b
6. Liquid Jade 5.12b

at the base of the river face and continue uphill to the right.

1. Time to Shower (5.8) ★★★ 6 bolts. Although short, this simple route is a lot of fun. Start below a prominent dihedral and gain the pleasant ramp to the left by pulling around a steep section on good holds. A new finish extends the fun a bit farther up the ramp.

1a. Shower Direct (5.8 A3- R) ★ Aid rack to 0.75 inch. The only bolt on this direct variant snapped off long ago. There's no good reason to try it until someone converts it into a moderate sport route.

2. Shipwreck (5.8 R) Mixed to 3.5 inches. This grotesque route follows a traditional line up the only major crack system on the river face. As the namesake of the entire wall, it really doesn't deserve the honor. **Pitch 1:** (5.8) Climb *Time to Shower* and continue in a dirty corridor above the anchor to Avalanche Ledge. **Pitch 2:** (5.8) Grunt up the rotten flaring crack, showering your belayer with rubble. **Pitch 3:** (4th class) Scramble along a ledge above the Aggro Wall to the base of a deep chimney. **Pitch 4:** (4th class) Climb the garbage chute to the top and hike down the Aggro Gully.

3. Chips Ahoy (5.9) ★ Gear to 2.5 inches. A right-arching flake crack splits the base of the river face. A solid starting dihedral gives way to an unnerving, wafer-thin undercling at the top.

4. Time to Power (5.12c) ★★★ 16 bolts. The impressive right side of the river face contains a single sport route capped by an eye-catching overhanging wall. After finessing a technical slab on great rock, the endurance-testing finish powers through good holds. Although first done in two pitches, it's usually climbed in a single push from the ground.

4a. Time to Power start (5.10a) ★ 5 bolts. The lower part of *Time to Power* makes a passable one-pitch route, despite worse-than-average rock.

5. Blue Light Special (5.11b) ★★★★ 6 bolts. If you want to do just one route on the Shipwreck Wall, hike no farther. The only hard move comes at an undercling around a mini-roof at the start. The rest is pure fun on perfect rock.

6. Liquid Jade (5.12b) ★★★ 8 bolts. Excellent rock and a stout crux make this deceptive route worth doing. The moves off the ground are tricky, but almost everyone falls higher, cranking past a small bulge on edges that wear smaller and slicker every year.

7. More Sandy than Kevin (5.11a) ★★★ 6 bolts. This worthwhile climb is a fine example of trash turning into quality with enough traffic. Early ascents suffered through creaky holds and dirty rock. Today the moves are fun and solid.

8. Purple Aces (5.11b) ★★★ 6 bolts. The hardest moves of this enjoyable route pull through some oblong pockets on the left side of the starting bulge. The climbing above eases only slightly, with technical moves on positive edges.

9. Flight of the Patriot Scud Blaster (5.11b) ★★ 4 bolts. Ending shortly after it begins, this diminutive bulge 20 feet off the ground contains a single hard move getting past the second bolt.

10. Marooned (5.11c) ★★ 7 bolts. The perplexing lower half of this innocent-looking route shuts down unsuspecting climbers. The upper portion is much easier but still a little dirty despite countless ascents.

Shipwreck Wall—Center Face

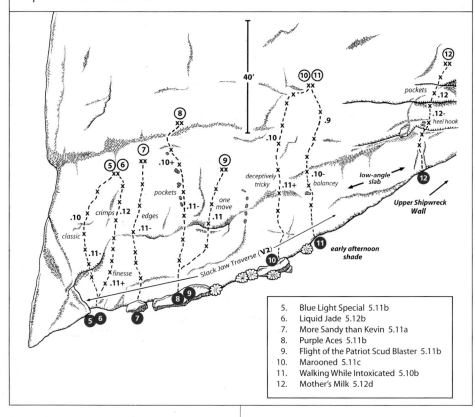

Route list (from topo):

5. Blue Light Special 5.11b
6. Liquid Jade 5.12b
7. More Sandy than Kevin 5.11a
8. Purple Aces 5.11b
9. Flight of the Patriot Scud Blaster 5.11b
10. Marooned 5.11c
11. Walking While Intoxicated 5.10b
12. Mother's Milk 5.12d

11. Walking While Intoxicated (5.10b) ★★★ 6 bolts. One of the easier routes on the Shipwreck Wall features good rock and plenty of bolts. The crux finesses past a steep section low on the route. Start just left of a low-angle, moss-covered slab.

12. Mother's Milk (5.12d) ★★ 6 bolts. A double-tiered overhang marks the left side of a low-level roof extending far uphill. *Mother's Milk* isn't long, but it packs a punch. Above a baffling start the crux clears the final bulge, tugging and throwing between pockets.

13. Bolt From the Blue (5.12a) ★★★ 15 bolts. Marked by a black streak on the upper wall, this long pitch rises far uphill from the lower lines. After a moderate start

the vertical finish blends good rock, big jugs, and a healthy pump. Lower to the ground with a 70-meter rope.

13a. Bolt From the Blue start (5.11a) ★★ 6 bolts. The lower section of *Bolt From the Blue* makes a decent route in its own right. A confusing sequence past a bulge quickly gives way to simple climbing and an anchor.

14. Project (5.11?) This pocketed line right of the finishing headwall of *Bolt From the Blue* should be a little easier than the original route.

15. Project (5.13?) An attractive leaning prow might someday contain the hardest climb on Shipwreck Wall. The crux will be

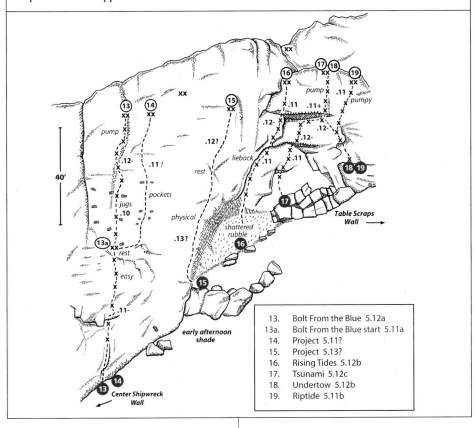

13.	Bolt From the Blue 5.12a
13a.	Bolt From the Blue start 5.11a
14.	Project 5.11?
15.	Project 5.13?
16.	Rising Tides 5.12b
17.	Tsunami 5.12c
18.	Undertow 5.12b
19.	Riptide 5.11b

low on the route with physical side pulls on solid rock.

16. Rising Tides (5.12b) ★★ 8 bolts. There's nothing at Smith like the multi-tiered upper section of the Shipwreck Wall. After a shattered start *Rising Tides* follows a solid leaning flake system leading to a couple small roofs. The pumping lieback at the start does a good job of draining your strength for the crux moves above. Stick-clip the first bolt.

17. Tsunami (5.12c) ★★★ 13 bolts. With its distinctive triple roofs, solid rock, and athletic moves, Tsunami won't disappoint. The hardest section pulls around the middle roof, but anyone lacking fitness will fight

a pump clearing the final roof. Beware of rope drag—using long slings on a few bolts is mandatory.

18. Undertow (5.12b) ★★★ 7 bolts. A slightly less demanding version of *Tsunami* starts off a pile of boulders to the right. Begin with the first three bolts of *Riptide* before veering left past the crux, joining *Tsunami* at the big roof. A final hard move on crimps leads to a jug and a pumping finish.

19. Riptide (5.11b) ★★★ 6 bolts. Sustained moves with an intense crux just below the anchors highlight the petite upper route on the Shipwreck Wall. Begin by scrambling up fractured blocks to a belay bolt.

Table Scraps Wall

Atop the Shipwreck Gully rests this uninspiring cliff. The wall's traditional routes received little attention (for good reason) over the past few decades. Surprisingly, a few recent sport routes, along with the development of the upper Shipwreck Wall, breathed new life into this forgotten crag. **Descent:** Scramble around ledges to the left to an easy downclimb on the backside. Some climbers solo down the chimney immediately left of the wall (4th class). Otherwise hike down the Aggro Gully, farther left.

20. Fish 'n Chips (5.10c) ★★★ 10 bolts. This bolted flake crack splits the left wall of a massive right-facing dihedral. After some easy junk at the start, the quality improves and the pump escalates the higher you go. A quality sport route on Table Scraps Wall— who would have guessed it?

21. Waste Land (5.8) Gear to 5 inches. Wherever you may climb at Smith, it doesn't get much worse than this. Start below a large open book on the left side of the wall. **Pitch 1:** (5.8) Writhe up a nauseating, rotten off-width to a ledge system. Either escape left to a horrid rappel bolt or . . . **Pitch 2:** (4th class) Scramble right along an exposed ledge and hike into a deep gully. **Pitch 3:** (5.6) Follow an easy chimney to the top of the cliff and scramble off the backside.

22. Slab Happy (5.9) ★★ 7 bolts. The bolted slab right of *Waste Land* makes a decent warm-up for nearby lines. The hardest climbing pulls around a vertical section in the middle of the route.

23. Flab Happy (5.11a) ★★ TR. The right of two slab routes is easily toproped after an ascent of *Slab Happy*.

24. Vanishing Uncertainty (5.9) ★ Mixed to 2.5 inches. The original route on the wall sees very few ascents. Adventure climbers might enjoy it—others won't be amused. Begin far left of the obvious face crack. **Pitch 1:** (5.9) Start up *Slab Happy* and traverse right past a spooky bolt to a short flaring crack. Jam and stem to an anchor on the left. **Pitch 2:** (4th class) Scramble up a deep unexposed gully to the base of the finishing chimney. **Pitch 3:** (5.6) Stem the mediocre slot to the top.

24a. Vanishing Variation 5.9 R ★ Gear to 3 inches. You can add a dash of danger to the squalor of the original route by following this multi-pitch variant. **Pitch 1:** (5.9) Follow a groove with poor protection directly into the flaring crack. **Pitch 2:** (4th class) Traverse right into a massive, sagebrush-choked gully. Hike scree into a deep chimney. **Pitch 3:** (5.6) Stem past a steep section and plunge into a heavily vegetated finishing gulch.

25. The Skipper's Little Buddy (5.10d) ★★★ 8 bolts. This bulging water groove in the center of the wall tests your technical skills. There might be more attractive chunks of stone at Smith, but the deceptively tricky moves and solid rock make it worth doing.

26. Project (5.11?) Time will tell if the homely wall right of *The Skipper's Little Buddy* matches the quality of its neighbor.

27. City Dump (5.7 R) ★ Gear to 2.5 inches. The first pitch of the longest route on the crag contains rock so bad it makes the remaining pitches seem good. Begin behind a flake at the base of a filthy, indistinct left-facing corner. **Pitch 1:** (5.7) Climb the cornflake crack to a belay ledge. **Pitch 2:** (5.7) Clamber up a short flaring crack to a low-angle slab. **Pitch 3:** (5.4) Race the

Table Scraps Wall

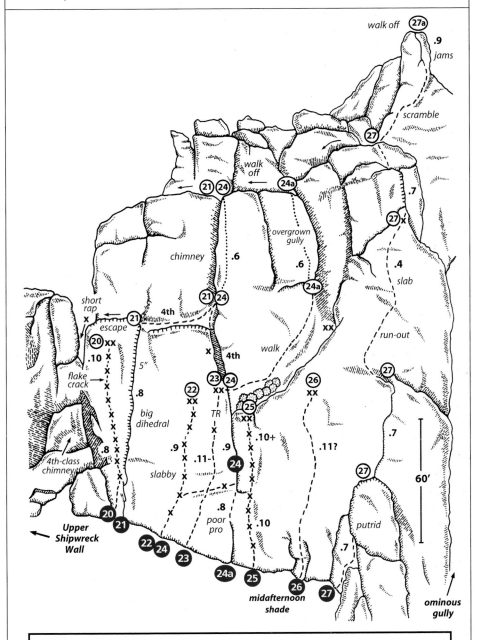

20.	Fish 'n Chips 5.10c	24a.	Vanishing Variation 5.9 R
21.	Waste Land 5.8	25.	The Skipper's Little Buddy 5.10d
22.	Slab Happy 5.9	26.	Project 5.11?
23.	Flab Happy 5.11a TR	27.	City Dump 5.7 R
24.	Vanishing Uncertainty 5.9	27a.	City Dump finish 5.9

unprotected slab to a single-bolt anchor below a right-facing corner. **Pitch 4:** (5.7) Jam to the top.

27a. City Dump finish (5.9) ★ Gear to 2 inches. If you've climbed this far, you might as well add this exposed summit pitch to put an exclamation mark on your effort. From big ledges, scramble up and right to a short, hidden jam crack.

Aggro Gully

The steep-sided, trail-scarred Aggro Gully separates the two Wooden Ships. The gully provides the quickest access to the top of the entire region, including the fastest approaches to Monkey Face and Pleasure Palace. A ramshackle trail leads far uphill to three narrow corridors guarding the top of the gully; take the left one.

The Aggro Wall– Main Cliff

The right wall of the Aggro Gully contains the highest concentration of hard routes at Smith Rock. Some climbers love these overhanging tests of endurance—others hate them. No matter how hard you climb on Smith's vertical faces, you'll get shut down if you don't possess the sheer brawn required here. If you can't climb 5.13, you'll have little reason to visit, other than to sit and watch.

On warm days the best conditions are either before noon or in the evening. Icy winds blow down the gully during the colder months. These same breezes during the warm season make the early morning conditions ideal.

28. Ghost Rider (5.12b) ★ 7 bolts. This ghost town of a route ascends a crumbly prow at the entrance to the gully. If climbed enough, it wouldn't be bad. The awkward crux pulls past a prominent rock jutting out of the upper wall.

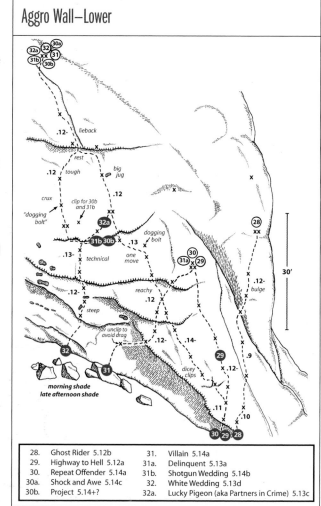

Aggro Wall—Lower

28.	Ghost Rider 5.12b
29.	Highway to Hell 5.12a
30.	Repeat Offender 5.14c
30a.	Shock and Awe 5.14c
30b.	Project 5.14+?

31.	Villain 5.14a
31a.	Delinquent 5.13a
31b.	Shotgun Wedding 5.14b
32.	White Wedding 5.13d
32a.	Lucky Pigeon (aka Partners in Crime) 5.13c

29. Highway to Hell (5.12a) ★★ 6 bolts.
Undercut by a small bulge at the start,
Highway to Hell sees far more traffic than its
neighbor to the right. The hardest section
mixes a hellish clip of the fourth bolt and a
strenuous pull past a bulge.

30. Repeat Offender (5.14a) ★★★ 9 bolts.
This power endurance test ranks among the
hardest routes at Smith. It shares the start
and anchor of *Highway to Hell,* but that's
all the two routes have in common. The
traversing opening sequence is unrelenting,
and the ground is too close for comfort on
the tough clips. The bouldering crux comes
at the fifth bolt, pulling and standing on just
about nothing.

30a. Shock and Awe (5.14c) ★★★ 16 bolts.
One of the country's hardest routes climbs
Repeat Offender before moving left, taking
in the crux and finish of *Villain.* It's pretty
close to linking two 5.14s in a single pitch.
Good luck.

30b. Project (5.14+?) 16 bolts. What this
route lacks in purity of line, it'll more than
make up for in sheer difficulty. There's
nothing original here: Just climb the crux of
Repeat Offender and the crux of *Villain* before
cutting left past a bolt to finish with the
crux of *White Wedding.* It'll easily be Smith's
hardest route when completed.

31. Villain (5.14a) ★★★ 13 bolts. A broken jug
below the crux eliminated a key rest, bumping this route up to the 5.14 level. It received
few attempts and only a single repeat as a
5.13d; perhaps the higher number will attract
more attention. The crux remains the same—
sticking one of Smith's worst holds long
enough to catch a one-finger pocket.

31a. Delinquent (5.13a) ★★ 6 bolts. This
link-up between *Villain* and the finish of
Repeat Offender makes a decent climb in its

own right. By bypassing the hardest climbing on both routes, *Delinquent* provides good
training for the harder lines. If you're short,
you'll have to suffer through a long reach
that taller climbers hardly notice.

31b. Shotgun Wedding (5.14b) ★★★ 15
bolts. The newest link-up on the Aggro
Wall stands near the top of Smith standards.
After cranking the crux of *Villain* (prefer-
ably without the hint of a pump), traverse
straight left past a dedicated bolt and breeze
through the crux and endurance finish of
White Wedding. Reach back to unclip the
first bolt on *Villain,* or face impossible rope
drag higher up.

32. White Wedding (5.13d) ★★★ 11 bolts.
Originally rated 5.14a, this famous route
didn't hold its lofty grade, partly due to a
one-finger pocket that mysteriously appeared
at the crux. Still, the quality only improves
as the once-crumbling rock grows solid.

Ian Yurdin on *White Wedding.* BEN MOON

After a technical crimpy start, you're already starting to tire when you hit the crux in the middle. The pumping sequence above spits off many unfit climbers.

32a. Lucky Pigeon (aka Partners in Crime)

(5.13c) ★★★ 11 bolts. Combining the 5.13 start of *White Wedding* with the best climbing on *Villain* makes one of the better lines of the grade at Smith. This route is especially good for aspiring *White Wedding* climbers; you can dial the start and pumping finish without the midsection crux.

33. Bad Man (5.14a) ★★★★

12 bolts. The best 5.14 on the Aggro Wall rises left of *White Wedding*. Three distinct crux sections on the lower wall provide a classic test of endurance. The final crux, an undercling to a two-finger pocket and a jump for a jug, is one of Smith's most entertaining sequences. Anyone good enough to get this far should have ample staying power for the pumping upper wall.

34. Project (5.14?) 13 bolts. Fully bolted

but not completely cleaned, this steep wall will someday offer yet another way to get pumped silly on the Aggro Wall. It'll likely rate in the middle of the 5.14 grade, and finish via *Mama Docus*.

Aggro Wall–Right Center

wimps* only

.12   reach

crux #3

* unless you're under 5'8"

fitness test

one finger   crux #2

.12   big span

crux #1
.12

.12

.13-

.12+

30'

"basketball"   endurance

.13
long reaches

.12+   side pulls

whew!

technical crux

big jug

.12+

38

sloping ledge

dyno

.11-   reachy

undercling   .13

.14?

37   slab

crimps

.5
low-angle ramp

.13

morning shade

bulge

late afternoon shade

36 35

34 33

33.	Badman 5.14a	36.	Mama Docus 5.13c
34.	Project 5.14?	37.	Crime Wave 5.13c
35.	Aggro Monkey 5.13b	38.	Scene of the Crime 5.13b

35. Aggro Monkey (5.13b) ★★★ 12 bolts.

Disintegrating in the early days but now completely clean, this impressive wall ushered in the Aggro Gully era. Today it's the entrance exam to the higher-level routes. The hardest moves pull around the roof at the start, but you'll probably flame out on the powerful lock-offs higher up.

36. Mama Docus (5.13c) ★★★ 11 bolts. If *Aggro Monkey* doesn't get you worked anymore, cut right after cranking past the starting roof. Sustained side pulls and pockets lead to the crux—moving above a basketball-size knob sticking out from the wall.

37. Crime Wave (5.13c) ★★ 10 bolts. A big number is the best thing the direct start to *Scene of the Crime* has going for it. The reachy crux pulls around the starting roof using a flake that's actually bolted to the wall.

38. Scene of the Crime (5.13b) ★★★ 12 bolts. This stellar route features three crux sections—tweaky pockets at the start, a tendon-straining one-finger pocket in the middle, and a big stretch to a side pull at the top. You can avoid the upper crux by sneaking left, but you'll sleep better knowing you met the challenge head on. Since shorter climbers simply can't span the holds, they can escape left guilt-free.

39. The Quickening (5.12c) ★★★ 10 bolts. A good warm-up for the harder stuff, *The Quickening* sees many ascents. Steep pocket-pulling over the roof leads to a crux on the face above. The jug ladder finish is pure joy—unless you're too pumped to hang on.

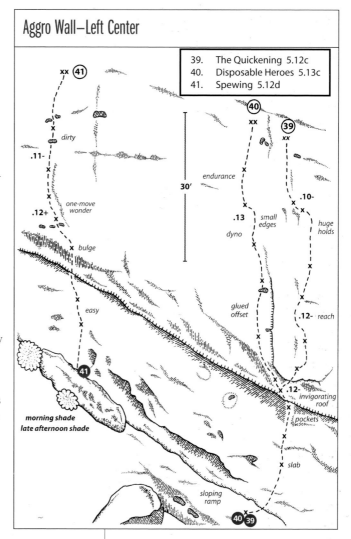

Aggro Wall—Left Center

39.	The Quickening 5.12c
40.	Disposable Heroes 5.13c
41.	Spewing 5.12d

dirty

.11-

one-move wonder

.12+

bulge

easy

endurance

30'

.13   small edges

dyno

glued offset

.10-

huge holds

.12- reach

.12- invigorating roof

pockets

slab

morning shade late afternoon shade

sloping ramp

40 39

40. Disposable Heroes (5.13c) ★★★ 10 bolts. A much harder option shares the same roof start as *The Quickening*, but moves left to an offset. The crux comes in the middle of the route with an intense sequence leading to a pocket. The upper part eases technically, but the rising pump makes it hard to hold on.

41. Spewing (5.12d) ★★ 7 bolts. The farthest uphill route on the main cliff attracts little attention. A single desperate move interrupts a moderate series of good holds.

The Aggro Wall–Upper Cliff

The upper end of the Aggro Wall's main cliff merges into a low-angle corner, leading into a deep chimney. The bulgy section of cliff uphill from this corner features four sport routes and the remnants of the infamous Plastic Area.

The following climbs share the same approach pitch. Hike far up the hillside and step right onto the starting ledge. A short bulge (5.7, 2 bolts) ends at a pleasant ledge below *Caustic* and *Kill the Hate*. To approach *Pouch Whisker* and *Scrotal Avenger*, traverse right from this ledge on good holds past four bolts to an anchor. A foolhardy direct approach climbs into the deep chimney to the right, cutting left without protection to the anchor.

42. Pouch Whisker (5.11b) ★★★ 5 bolts. A sharp edge marks the right boundary of the upper cliff. The solid rock and thoughtful moves will please any Smith arête aficionado. The climb would be far more popular if it didn't involve an approach pitch.

43. Scrotal Avenger (5.12a) ★★★ 10 bolts. A few feet left of the *Pouch Whisker* arête rises another line on naturally solid stone. The hardest section cranks technical edges in the middle of the route.

44. Caustic (5.12b) ★ 9 bolts. Easily missed, an unappealing line right of *Kill the Hate* rarely sports any chalk. Dirty and almost totally ignored, the hardest section pulls over a bulge on blatantly drilled pockets.

45. Kill the Hate (5.13a) ★★★ 10 bolts. Steeper than the average Smith route, this wall of pockets and edges sees many ascents. The moves aren't unreasonably hard, but the pump builds quickly. The strenuous final bulge is the fashionable place to come flying off the rock.

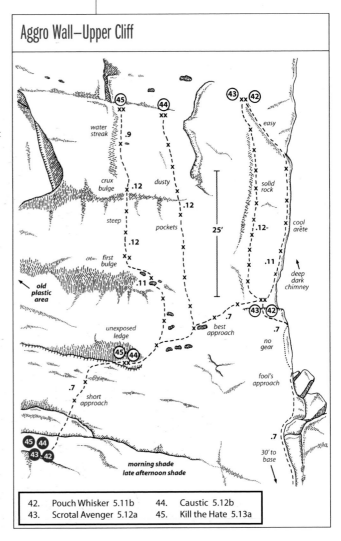

Aggro Wall–Upper Cliff

| 42. | Pouch Whisker 5.11b | 44. | Caustic 5.12b |
| 43. | Scrotal Avenger 5.12a | 45. | Kill the Hate 5.13a |

Plastic Area (1989–1997)

The massive roof at the top of the Aggro Wall was once the scene of Smith's most controversial routes. Demonstrating a world-class lack of judgment, a few leading climbers constructed four routes consisting entirely of bolted-on holds. In retrospect, they jeopardized the future of Smith climbing, set a horrible example for upcoming generations, and wasted time and energy better spent raising the standards of the area. The Plastic Area saw a brief period of popularity in the early 1990s, but once the novelty wore off common sense took over. The holds disappeared in 1997—today no plastic holds adorn any Smith Rock route.

46. Project–Facelift (5.13?) 8 bolts. The easiest of the plastic routes has enough features that it will go free on natural holds. The super-steep, gym-like start leads to a good shake at a big pocket before finishing on a gently overhanging wall on small holds. To reach the base, solo a short fourth-class pitch to a huge ledge.

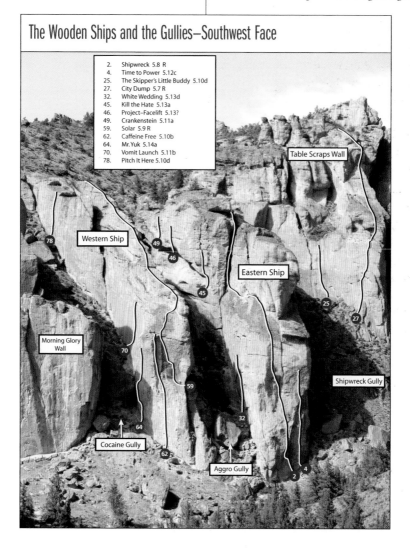

The Wooden Ships and the Gullies–Southwest Face

2.	Shipwreck 5.8 R
4.	Time to Power 5.12c
25.	The Skipper's Little Buddy 5.10d
27.	City Dump 5.7 R
32.	White Wedding 5.13d
45.	Kill the Hate 5.13a
46.	Project–Facelift 5.13?
49.	Crankenstein 5.11a
59.	Solar 5.9 R
62.	Caffeine Free 5.10b
64.	Mr. Yuk 5.14a
70.	Vomit Launch 5.11b
78.	Pitch It Here 5.10d

Table Scraps Wall

Western Ship

Eastern Ship

Morning Glory Wall

Shipwreck Gully

Cocaine Gully

Aggro Gully

Honeycomb Wall

High atop the right side of the Aggro Gully sits this dinky wall. These unique climbs are fun but very short—not many are willing to hike so far for so little. To approach, scramble up the center of three narrow corridors and step right to a sloping ledge.

47. Seasonal Affectiveness Disorder

(5.10b) ★★★ 5 bolts. The energetic right-hand route is the best this wall has to offer. A few technical moves at the start lead to fun jugs around the crux bulge.

48. Skinny Sweaty

Man (5.11a) ★★ 5 bolts. The center route contains a desperate move right off the deck and finishes with a brief flurry of jugs.

49. Crankenstein

(5.11a) ★★ 4 bolts. Strenuous lock-offs on good holds highlight the upper of the three routes on the Honeycomb Wall. The crux cranks past a boulder problem start, though almost everyone ignores the original sequence by using holds to the left. Stick-clip the first bolt.

WESTERN SHIP AREA

Bordered by Cocaine Gully on the left and Aggro Gully to the right, the Western Ship looks like a slender twin of its neighbor to the east. The two gully faces provide totally different climbing experiences.

Aggro Gully–Left Wall

Across the gully from the more famous routes of the Aggro Wall are several lines

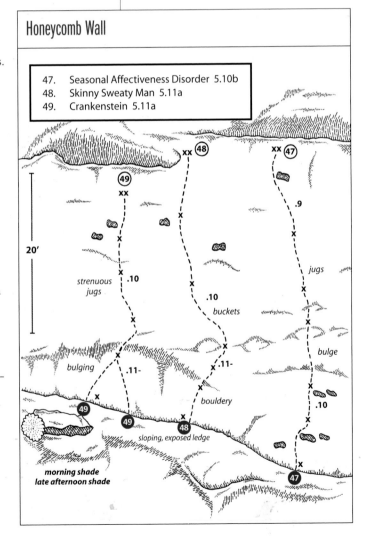

Honeycomb Wall

47. Seasonal Affectiveness Disorder 5.10b
48. Skinny Sweaty Man 5.11a
49. Crankenstein 5.11a

20'

strenuous jugs   .10

.10
buckets

bulging

.11-

.11-

bouldery

sloping, exposed ledge

morning shade
late afternoon shade

.9

jugs

bulge

.10

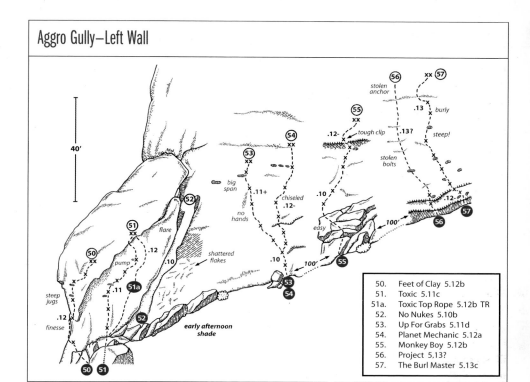

Map labels: stolen anchor; .13 burly; tough clip; .13? steep!; stolen bolts; .12-; big span; .11+; chiseled .12-; .10; no hands; easy; .12-; flare; shattered flakes; pump; .12; .10; .10; 100'; 100'; steep jugs; .11; .12; finesse; early afternoon shade

50.	Feet of Clay 5.12b
51.	Toxic 5.11c
51a.	Toxic Top Rope 5.12b TR
52.	No Nukes 5.10b
53.	Up For Grabs 5.11d
54.	Planet Mechanic 5.12a
55.	Monkey Boy 5.12b
56.	Project 5.13?
57.	The Burl Master 5.13c

described moving uphill, starting from the base of the gully. This side of the Western Ship receives only morning sun, making it a good afternoon destination on a warm day. The first four routes share a common start in a notch right of the midsection of the river face. Approach by entering Aggro Gully on the far right side, before hiking left to a short downclimb leading to a belay slot.

50. Feet of Clay (5.12b) ★★ 5 bolts. This short, intense route ascends the overhanging face around the corner right of *Power*. A delicate crux on the starting arête leads to a physical finish on big holds. Unfortunately, birds find the finishing jugs perfect for nest building.

51. Toxic (5.11c) ★★★★ 6 bolts. The most popular route in the entire Aggro Gully ascends an attractive, overhanging wall directly above the belay slot. The excellent rock and athletic moves captivate everyone. To dyno or not to dyno? That is the question.

51a. Toxic Toprope (5.12b) ★★ TR. A line of holds right of *Toxic* makes a challenging toprope problem. Everyone struggles on an awkward reach-through move at the final bulge; short people just struggle a little more.

52. No Nukes (5.10b) ★ Gear to 2.5 inches. The shattered flakes guarding the entrance to this flaring slot keep all climbers at bay. Still, the dream of the first ascent team holds true—even today there are no nukes anywhere at Smith Rock.

53. Up For Grabs (5.11d) ★★★ 7 bolts. A huge dyno caps this high-quality route, though you can avoid the lunge using holds to the left if you've got a fear of flying. The technical crux comes a few feet lower—finessing a tricky bulge.

54. Planet Mechanic (5.12a) ★★★ 8 bolts. Unfortunate chipped holds keeps this direct line above the start of *Up For Grabs* at a relatively moderate grade. The climbing is good, though we'll never know what might have been.

55. Monkey Boy (5.12b) ★★ 6 bolts. A long roof stretches along the entire upper section of the Aggro Gully's left side. An entertaining line of jugs ascends the left part of this roof. The crux involves a strenuous clip followed by a physical lock-off at the finishing bulge.

56. Project (5.13?) Undercut by a big cave, this partially bolted line immediately left of *The Burl Master* should someday clean into a good route.

57. The Burl Master (5.13c) ★★★ 8 bolts. One of Smith's best endurance tests, this strongly overhanging wall of jugs and edges provides an accurate measure of how burly you really are. The best move throws to a jug in the middle of the route, but the crux comes higher—trying desperately to stick good holds at the final bulge

Western Ship–River Face

The river face of the Western Ship contains many varied routes, ranging from very easy to very hard. Exposed to the elements, the rock is cleaner than the average Wooden Ship wall. Most of the year, sun bakes these lines until late in the day.

58. Power (5.13b) ★★★ 5 bolts. The most impressive feature of the Western Ship's river face is this strongly overhanging wall. The technical crux powers a lock-off to a two-finger pocket, but most climbers plummet from good holds on the dash to the anchor.

The original approach ascended a bolted 5.9 flake beginning above *Purple Headed Warrior*. The best option follows *Phone Call From Satan* to a hanging belay beneath the main wall, though many climbers traverse in from the *Toxic* belay notch.

59. Solar (5.9 R) ★★ Gear to 3 inches. Spectacular yet totally ignored by generations of Smith climbers, *Solar* follows the impressive leaning dihedral high on the river face. Begin in the Aggro Gully at the *Toxic* belay notch. **Pitch 1:** (5.8) A poorly protected hand traverse leads left around the corner to the anchor below *Power*. **Pitch 2:** (5.9) A short pitch moves directly up a broken crack to a cool belay ledge. An easier (5.7) option cuts left to a short left-facing corner. **Pitch 3:** (5.9) Climb the left-leaning dihedral to an anchor. The quickest descent rappels to the ground using double ropes. Early ascents scrambled along the exposed ridge to the top of the formation.

60. Purple Headed Warrior (5.7) ★★★ 5 bolts. A detached slab sits at the right base of the Western Ship's river face. A popular beginner's route ascends simple rock to an anchor.

61. Phone Call From Satan (5.9) ★★★ 9 bolts. The scarred lower slab of the river face offers parallel sport routes. The right route required one of the most extensive cleaning efforts in Smith history. Remarkably, what remains is excellent and extremely popular.

62. Caffeine Free (5.10b) ★★ 8 bolts. The left route on the lower slab isn't as good as *Phone Call From Satan,* but it has a more colorful history. *Caffeine Free* follows an old A4 aid seam called *No Doz*—the first route on the entire Western Ship. Today's free version is far safer, but still a little dirty.

62a. Caffeine Free finish (5.11a) ★ 11 bolts. The exposed, generously bolted upper pitch

Western Ship–River Face

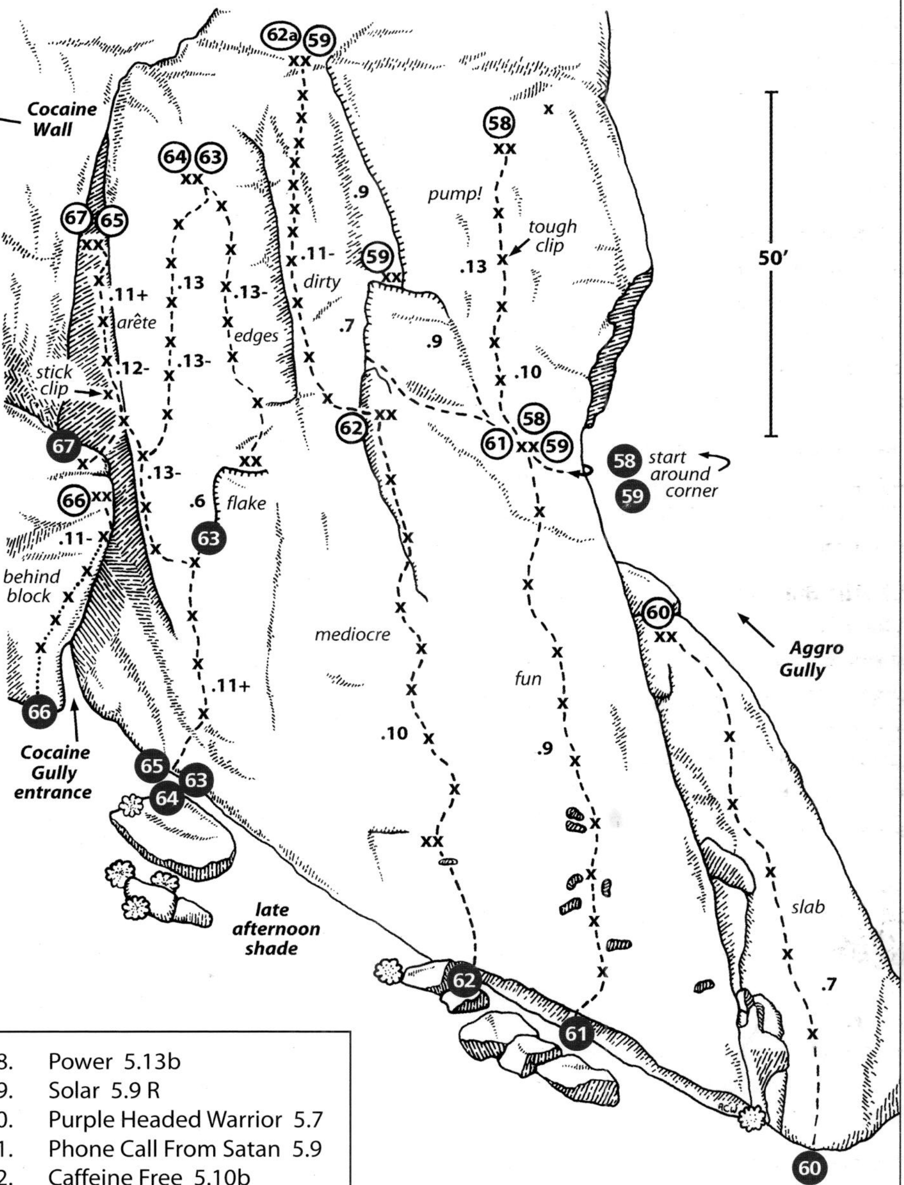

58. Power 5.13b
59. Solar 5.9 R
60. Purple Headed Warrior 5.7
61. Phone Call From Satan 5.9
62. Caffeine Free 5.10b
62a. Caffeine Free finish 5.11a
63. Time's Up 5.13a
64. Mr. Yuck 5.14a
65. Slit Your Wrists 5.13b
66. Skeleton Surfer 5.11b
67. The Blade 5.12a

of *Caffeine Free* sees few ascents. The rock isn't very good, but it'll only get better. The hardest climbing comes in the lower half of the pitch.

63. Time's Up (5.13a) ★★★ 11 bolts. Unlike most other hard lines on the Wooden Ships, this quality route favors technical proficiency over strength. Still, it's plenty pumping as countless airborne climbers discover. The 5.11+ start isn't much fun, but a sit-down rest on a huge flake below the headwall allows a complete recovery.

64. Mr. Yuk (5.14a) ★★★ 13 bolts. The wall left of *Time's Up* shares the same start and anchors, but the similarities end there. The approach climbs the entire crux sequence of *Slit Your Wrists* before stepping right after a rest. A tricky slab leads to a bouldering crux on the main wall, followed by strenuous lock-offs on better holds.

65. Slit Your Wrists (5.13b) ★★★ 12 bolts. The clean overhanging arête left of *Time's Up* succumbs to tenuous slaps with little for the feet. The difficulties ease after the crux, but the final edge of *The Blade* can still foil your redpoint burn.

66. Skeleton Surfer (5.11b) ★★ 5 bolts. Rising from the shadows left of the Cocaine Gully approach chimney is a short overhanging wall. A jungle gym of jugs leads to a crux encounter at the top. Most climbers clip the first bolt and simply hoist themselves to the starting holds. As the ground at the base wears away, the strict bouldering start (5.12) grows more difficult each year.

Cocaine Gully

The gulch between the Western Ship and Morning Glory Wall contains a diverse collection of routes 5.10 and up. A boulder the size of a house blocks the entrance to the gully. The easiest approach scrambles up a simple third-class corridor on the right side. Decades ago, massive blocks plugging this slot fell out during a heavy rainstorm. It's a much easier scramble than before the landslide, but if it happened once, it could happen again. A more stable but seldom-used approach climbs a fourth-class slot on the left side of the house-size boulder.

Cocaine Wall

This classic vertical face on the right side of the Cocaine Gully features many popular routes. Morning shade makes it a good early destination on a hot day.

67. The Blade (5.12a) ★★★ 4 bolts. The far right arête of the Cocaine Wall offers solid rock and bewildering, delicate moves. To approach, step down to a belay bolt from the top of the gigantic boulder and stick-clip the first bolt. A worthwhile alternative begins with *Skeleton Surfer* before stemming over to the arête.

68. Chicken McNuggets (5.10b) ★★★ 9 bolts. Delightful knobs pepper the face right of *Cocaine Crack*. Most of the corrupt nubbins blew off on early ascents, leaving behind a savory route.

69. Cocaine Crack (5.11b) ★★ Mixed to 3 inches. For many years this strenuous crack system was the only route on the wall. Those unfortunate enough to make the epic early ascents inadvertently pulled away all the loose boulders and flakes, leaving a clean but seldom-climbed route. There really aren't any hard moves—the grade comes almost entirely from the pump.

70. Vomit Launch (5.11b) ★★★★ 9 bolts. The best and most popular route on the Cocaine

Cocaine Wall

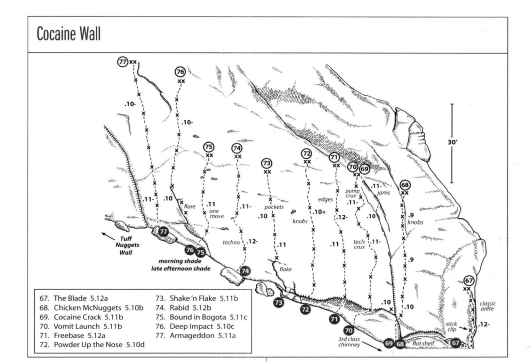

67. The Blade 5.12a
68. Chicken McNuggets 5.10b
69. Cocaine Crack 5.11b
70. Vomit Launch 5.11b
71. Freebase 5.12a
72. Powder Up the Nose 5.10d
73. Shake 'n Flake 5.11b
74. Rabid 5.12b
75. Bound in Bogota 5.11c
76. Deep Impact 5.10c
77. Armageddon 5.11a

Wall is the vertical face immediately left of *Cocaine Crack*. No individual move will throw you much, but the linkage can create a nauseating pump. Fortunately, good holds always appear when you need them most.

71. Freebase (5.12a) ★★★ 7 bolts. A harder version of its neighbor to the right, *Freebase* follows sustained and technical edges. Unlike *Vomit Launch,* good holds don't always appear when you need them most.

72. Powder Up the Nose (5.10d) ★★★ 6 bolts. A narrow swath of knobs follows a water streak in the center of the wall. You'll love the technical climbing if all the nubbins stay put, and hate it if they don't.

73. Shake 'n Flake (5.11b) ★★ 4 bolts. Popular more from its convenient location than the quality of the climbing, this edgy face starts with a loose flake leading to a single hard move.

74. Rabid (5.12b) ★★ 5 bolts. The starting moves on this short wall are a little too crimpy for casual enjoyment. If you can get to the second bolt, the finish seems easy.

75. Bound in Bogotá (5.11c) ★★ 4 bolts. Apart from a tough move above the second bolt, there's little to distinguish this wall of edges and pockets from other routes on the wall.

76. Deep Impact (5.10c) ★★ 8 bolts. A distinctive left-leaning flare splits the base of the left side of the wall. After a strenuous lieback the difficulties ease considerably.

77. Armageddon (5.11a) ★★★ 9 bolts. The leftmost route on the Cocaine Wall originally shared the same start as *Deep Impact.* A new direct start keeps the routes separate. After a boulder problem low, fun climbing on pockets and edges leads to an anchor.

Tuff Nuggets Wall

Far uphill on the right side of the Cocaine Gully are three routes on a mediocre-looking wall. It doesn't come close to matching the quality of the Cocaine Wall, but you might find them worth the slog if you don't have high expectations. Conventional wisdom says they'll get better over time, but after two decades they still aren't very good.

78. Pitch It Here (5.10d) ★ 6 bolts. The longest route on the wall follows a vertical face of pockets and knobs. Start downhill from the other lines with a short offset.

79. Double-Edged Sword (5.10c) ★ 5 bolts. The center of three bolted routes isn't anything special, but indiscriminating climbers might enjoy it. After a crux move on small edges, knobs finish to an anchor.

80. Desmond's Tutu (5.10b) ★ 5 bolts. The upper route on the Tuff Nuggets Wall ascends an ugly face right of a chimney. With poor rock and unnerving knobs, the *Tutu* doesn't have much going for it.

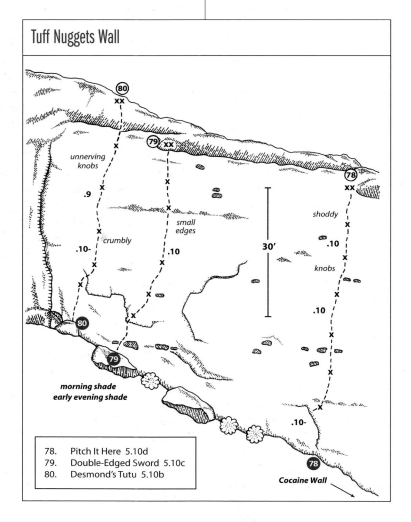

Tuff Nuggets Wall

unnerving knobs

crumbly

small edges

shoddy

knobs

30'

morning shade
early evening shade

78.	Pitch It Here	5.10d
79.	Double-Edged Sword	5.10c
80.	Desmond's Tutu	5.10b

Cocaine Wall

MORNING GLORY WALL AREA

"Spider Dan" Goodwin was one of Smith's most colorful characters. He earned his name after climbing Chicago's Sears Tower in 1981—wearing a Spiderman suit. We all liked Spidey, but he seemed out of place hanging out around the rest of us dirtbags. Meticulously groomed, he wore green contacts that gave his eyes an unnatural sparkle, and he visited a tanning salon throughout the winter. Much to everyone's surprise, Dan pioneered a route between Churning *and* Taco Chips *that was anything but well groomed. No route repelled as much world-class talent, simply because no one could successfully navigate the minefield of exploding edges. Sign of the Times finally met its match after Darius Azin broke off one too many holds trying for a repeat. He simply snapped, yanking all the bolts while cursing the name of Spider Dan.*

The Morning Glory Wall Area appeals to every climber visiting Smith Rock. Whether you enjoy extreme routes, moderate sport climbs, traditional cracks, multi-pitch adventures, or easy toproping, you'll find something to your liking—as long as you don't mind some company. Standing 350 feet tall, the main wall contains some of the most popular and developed sections of stone in the park. The excellent rock, quick approach, and unforgettable routes make Morning Glory Wall one of Smith's most outstanding crags. Since the main cliff gets sun until late in the day, Morning Glory Wall is a wonderful place to climb on clear, cold days—and an oven in the summer. Nonetheless, the routes are popular year-round. If you come seeking solitude, you'll want to avoid the base of the main wall during peak season. But if you're looking to hang out and soak up the local scene, this is the place to be. On hot days smart climbers visit early in the morning or wait patiently for evening shade, while winter visitors bask in the warmth of the sun. Even with below-freezing temperatures, it's short-sleeve weather in the middle of the day as long as the sun shines.

Apart from Morning Glory Wall itself, the area contains several peripheral crags. The rounded boulder of the Peanut sits left of the main wall—it features easy sport routes teeming with climbers. Next in line rises the river face of the Fourth Horseman, with both traditional crack climbs and newer sport routes. Across the river from these crags sits Rope De Dope Rock, a squat blob with throngs of fun sport lines with easy toprope access.

The summit spires of the Four Horsemen attracted the earliest visitors when Jim Ramsey and Bruce Hahn climbed all four pinnacles in 1964. The first ascent of Morning Glory Wall waited until 1967 when Tom and Bob Bauman climbed *Lion's Jaw* (5.8). After aid ascents of the obvious crack systems, Dean Fry and Jeff Thomas ushered out the aid era with a 1973 free ascent of *Zebra* (5.10a). At the time it was the hardest

Morning Glory Wall Area

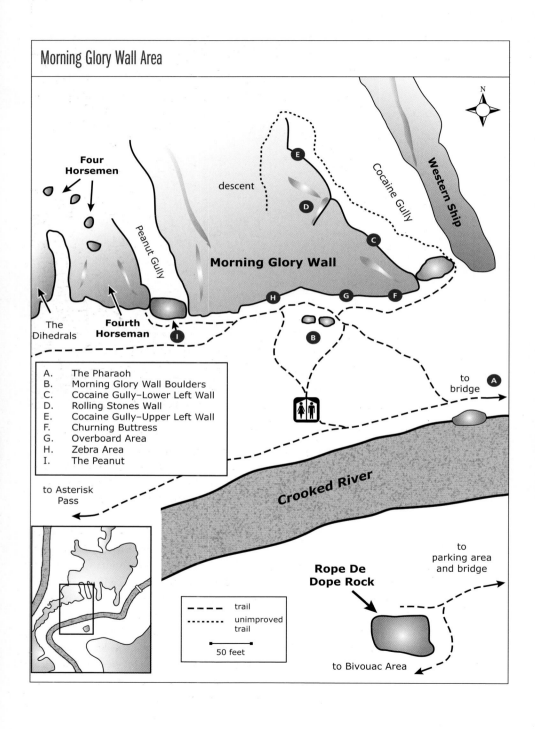

Four Horsemen

descent

Peanut Gully

Cocaine Gully

Western Ship

Morning Glory Wall

E

D

C

H

G

F

B

I

The Dihedrals

Fourth Horseman

A.   The Pharaoh
B.   Morning Glory Wall Boulders
C.   Cocaine Gully–Lower Left Wall
D.   Rolling Stones Wall
E.   Cocaine Gully–Upper Left Wall
F.   Churning Buttress
G.   Overboard Area
H.   Zebra Area
I.   The Peanut

to bridge   A

to Asterisk Pass

Crooked River

to parking area and bridge

Rope De Dope Rock

to Bivouac Area

- - - -   trail

· · · ·   unimproved trail

50 feet

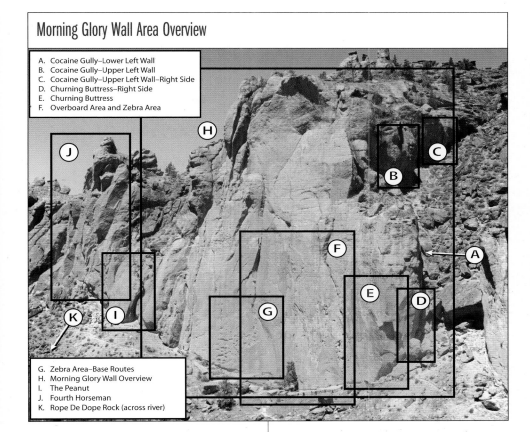

Morning Glory Wall Area Overview

A. Cocaine Gully–Lower Left Wall
B. Cocaine Gully–Upper Left Wall
C. Cocaine Gully–Upper Left Wall–Right Side
D. Churning Buttress–Right Side
E. Churning Buttress
F. Overboard Area and Zebra Area

G. Zebra Area–Base Routes
H. Morning Glory Wall Overview
I. The Peanut
J. Fourth Horseman
K. Rope De Dope Rock (across river)

long free route at Smith. In 1977 Thomas returned, freeing *Lion's Chair* (5.11a). Even today the run-out first pitch earns respect.

During the early boom years of the 1980s, Morning Glory Wall received little notice, as climbers turned their attention to the more natural lines of the Dihedrals and Monkey Face. It wasn't until Jean-Marc Troussier climbed the crumbly *Taco Chips* (5.13a) in 1986 that skeptical locals began giving the cliff a closer look. A short time later, Sean Olmstead and Chris Grover prepared and climbed *Churning in the Wake* (5.13a). The new route race was on—within two years the number of climbs tripled. Several of the best new lines on Morning Glory Wall, including *Oxygen* (5.13b), *Waste*

Case (5.13b), and *Vicious Fish* (5.13c) ranked among Smith's most difficult testpieces. Moderate base routes brought more climbers to the crag, and by the end of the eighties Morning Glory Wall was the place to be seen at Smith Rock.

With most of the best lines climbed, these crags saw little development in the 1990s. The overhanging left wall of the Cocaine Gully was one exception, with Marc Lemenestral's *Runt* (5.13d) being the hardest of several new lines. With a few more moderate base routes on the main wall, and others on the Fourth Horseman, the area seems largely climbed out. Climbers visiting Morning Glory Wall in the future will have to be content following those who arrived first.

Morning Glory Wall

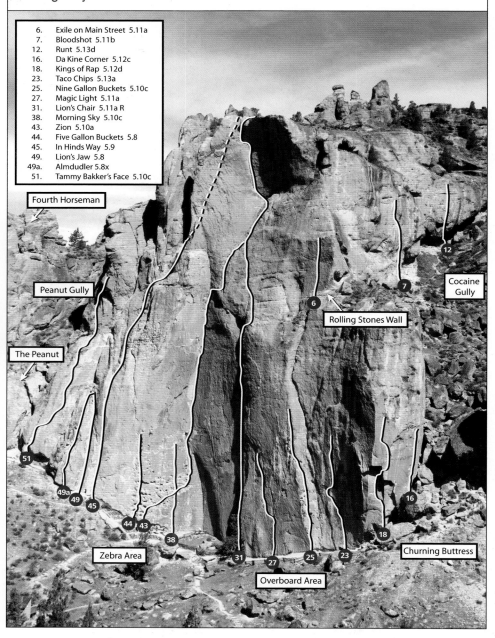

Fourth Horseman

Peanut Gully

The Peanut

Rolling Stones Wall

Cocaine Gully

Zebra Area

Overboard Area

Churning Buttress

MORNING GLORY WALL

After hiking around the bend at Shiprock, Morning Glory Wall dominates the view ahead. Unlike the crumbly looking Wooden Ships with their gully-hidden collection of routes, Morning Glory Wall is beautiful, mostly solid, and instantly appealing.

Finding the crags: Turn left at the bridge and hike downstream around the base of Shiprock. At the end of a boardwalk, just before a restroom the size of a small house, follow wooden stairs uphill to the base of the wall. **Descent:** Few routes ascend to the top of Morning Glory Wall. The best descent walks uphill and enters Cocaine Gully on the right. Walk down a poor trail and plunge through a third-class hole below Cocaine Wall.

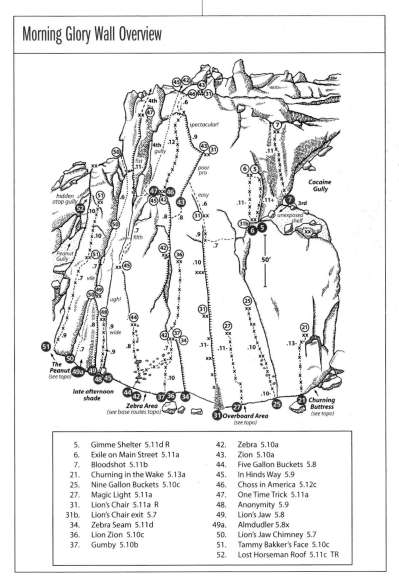

Morning Glory Wall Overview

5.	Gimme Shelter 5.11d R	42.	Zebra 5.10a
6.	Exile on Main Street 5.11a	43.	Zion 5.10a
7.	Bloodshot 5.11b	44.	Five Gallon Buckets 5.8
21.	Churning in the Wake 5.13a	45.	In Hinds Way 5.9
25.	Nine Gallon Buckets 5.10c	46.	Choss in America 5.12c
27.	Magic Light 5.11a	47.	One Time Trick 5.11a
31.	Lion's Chair 5.11a R	48.	Anonymity 5.9
31b.	Lion's Chair exit 5.7	49.	Lion's Jaw 5.8
34.	Zebra Seam 5.11d	49a.	Almdudler 5.8x
36.	Lion Zion 5.10c	50.	Lion's Jaw Chimney 5.7
37.	Gumby 5.10b	51.	Tammy Bakker's Face 5.10c
		52.	Lost Horseman Roof 5.11c TR

Cocaine Gully— Lower Left Wall

The far right side of Morning Glory Wall is also the left wall of the Cocaine Gully. A collection of mediocre routes ascends the short, forgettable section of rock directly across from the Cocaine Wall. Approach through the third-class corridor up the right side of the massive block guarding the base of the gully.

1. Earth 2° (5.10c) ★ 9 bolts. The lowest climb on the left side of the gully follows a line of technical edges crossing over a leaning seam. The rock will inevitably improve after enough ascents, but it'll never be a classic.

2. Baked Mudfest (aka Hobbit's Pockets) (5.10d) ★★ 6 bolts. Deceptively tricky pockets on the starting wall highlight this aptly named route. The finish cuts left around a roof on fun jugs.

3. Hippos on Ice (5.10b) ★ 3 bolts. The original line on this section of cliff won't make much of an impression on anyone. The hardest moves come right at the start.

4. Thieves (5.12a) ★★ 5 bolts. This peculiar route ascends a very short overhanging prow left of a break in the cliff line. After a strenuous traverse on pockets, a boulder crux leads quickly to easy climbing. There's no convenient anchor on top, so most climbers lower from a link on the last bolt.

Rolling Stones Wall

Far off the ground on Morning Glory Wall's main face rises this eye-catching vertical wall. Both routes bake in the sun from early morning until late in the day. Approach via a low-angle gulch splitting the left side of Cocaine Gully.

Cocaine Gully—Lower Left Wall

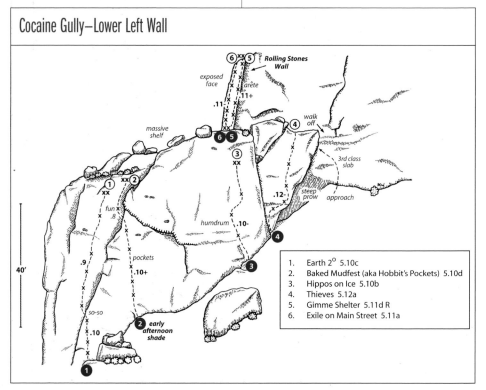

1. Earth 2° 5.10c
2. Baked Mudfest (aka Hobbit's Pockets) 5.10d
3. Hippos on Ice 5.10b
4. Thieves 5.12a
5. Gimme Shelter 5.11d R
6. Exile on Main Street 5.11a

5. Gimme Shelter (5.11d R) ★★ 5 bolts. The right route offers challenging moves slapping up a leaning arête. Blow the dicey second clip, and you'll hit the ground.

6. Exile on Main Street (5.11a) ★★★ 5 bolts. The center of the Rolling Stones Wall features technical crimps on solid stone. The moves are enjoyable, but the brilliant position makes it special.

Cocaine Gully— Upper Left Wall

The upper left side of the Cocaine Gully contains several overhanging routes with the potential for a few more. Visit in the afternoon when the wall sits in the shade.

7. Bloodshot (5.11b) ★★★★ 11 bolts. You wouldn't guess by looking at it, but the first route uphill from a break in the cliff line is a Smith classic. Sustained, appealing moves on solid rock lead to a crux far off the ground.

8. Quest to Fire (5.12a) ★★★ 7 bolts. Ignored for over a decade, this strenuous line became popular when a new bolt eliminated a frightening run-out. The hardest moves come just below the anchor.

9. Crack Babies (5.12b) ★★★ 5 bolts. A few feet left of an ugly overhanging crack rises this steep face/arête. Athletic moves, good rock, and plenty of bolts make it worth doing.

10. Crack Cocaine (5.11d) ★★ 8 bolts. It ain't pretty, but somehow this overhanging crack possesses a perverse charm. With painfully flaring hand jams, *Crack Cocaine* climbs like a bolted trad route. Above the crux, the difficulties and suffering ease greatly.

11. Bongo Fury (5.13a) ★★ 10 bolts. This steeply overhanging wall is Smith's most blatantly chiseled route. The entertaining start pulls drilled pockets ending with "the Frizmo"—a big throw to a natural jug. The crux always came on the finishing slab, but a broken hold makes it a little harder. A

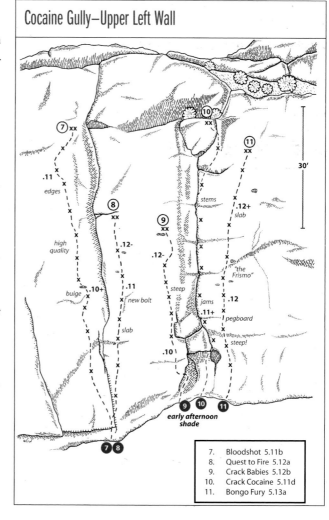

Cocaine Gully–Upper Left Wall

30'

7. Bloodshot 5.11b
8. Quest to Fire 5.12a
9. Crack Babies 5.12b
10. Crack Cocaine 5.11d
11. Bongo Fury 5.13a

worthwhile variant climbs the 5.12c pegboard, lowering off below the slab.

12. Runt (5.13d) ★★★ 9 bolts. A large roof undercuts the bottom of the entire upper section of the wall. Powerful moves clear the roof, followed by a crux of physical lock-offs. A top-notch boulderer will do the route quickly, though the average 5.13 climber will struggle mightily.

13. Project–Bend Over And Receive (5.14?) With drilled pockets and six plastic holds, this former 5.13b free route marked an ethical low point in the history of Smith free climbing. Fortunately, the holds disappeared years ago. With cleaning, a plastic-free variant a few feet left might go completely free at a very high level.

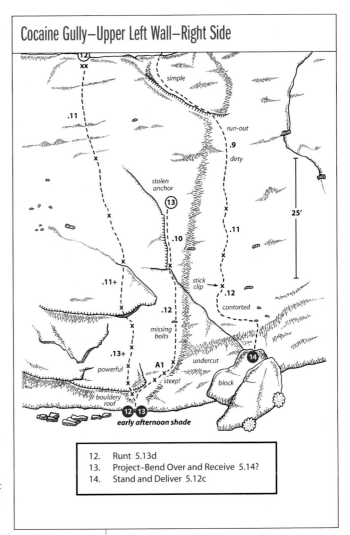

Cocaine Gully–Upper Left Wall–Right Side

12.	Runt 5.13d
13.	Project–Bend Over and Receive 5.14?
14.	Stand and Deliver 5.12c

14. Stand and Deliver (5.12c) ★ 3 bolts. The last route on the left side of Cocaine Gully starts off a pile of boulders a few feet uphill from the preceding lines. After stick-clipping the first bolt, launch into the short crux at the lip of the roof. Footwork is optional.

Churning Buttress

This celebrated buttress at the right base of Morning Glory Wall contains a remarkable concentration of extreme routes. Expect excellent rock, beautiful lines, midday sun, and crowds during peak season.

15. Oxygen (5.13b) ★★★ 5 bolts. At the far right base of the buttress sits a large boulder leaning against the main cliff. *Oxygen* follows a faint seam on the undercut wall right of this block. After traversing in from the boulder, finesse a complex series of pockets, edges, and side pulls.

15a. Jam Master Jay (5.13d) ★★ 7 bolts. This brutal direct start bumps the grade a couple notches higher. A pint-size boulder

problem featuring a
heel hook on a tiny
knob clears the start-
ing bulge, followed
immediately by the
crux of *Oxygen*.

16. Da Kine Corner

(5.12c) **** 4 bolts.
Entertaining side pulls
and pockets on per-
fect rock highlight
this romp up the right
edge of the Churning
Buttress. A mandatory
stick-clip of the first
bolt keeps you off the
starting boulder.

17. White Heat (5.13c)

*** 5 bolts. This offset
seam left of *Da Kine
Corner* features great
rock and a unique crux
move. After the bet-
ter half of a miserable
pocket broke shortly
after the first ascent,
two decades passed
without a repeat.
Recently, in a remark-
able demonstration of
the restorative pow-
ers of nature, the hold

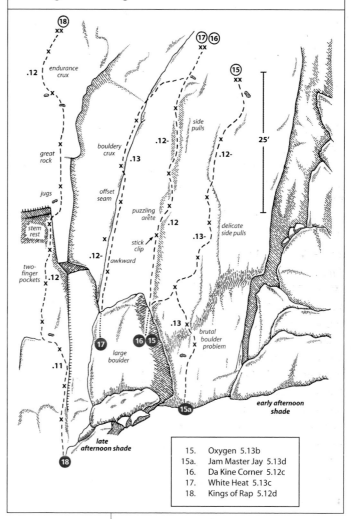

Churning Buttress–Right Side

15.	Oxygen 5.13b
15a.	Jam Master Jay 5.13d
16.	Da Kine Corner 5.12c
17.	White Heat 5.13c
18.	Kings of Rap 5.12d

mysteriously reappeared. You'll still need
to crank for all you're worth on the dinky,
one-finger pocket.

18. Kings of Rap (5.12d) **** 11 bolts.

The best route of the grade at Smith follows a pocketed wall on flawless stone. The
hardest moves crank through two-finger
pockets low on the route, though many
climbers fly off, pumped silly, just below
the anchors. Using long slings on the bolts

below the roof reduces rope drag on the
upper wall.

19. Waste Case (5.13b) **** 10 bolts.

Solid rock, varied moves, and a beautiful
finishing arête highlight this testpiece. *Waste
Case* shares climbing with *Kings of Rap* and
Vicious Fish, with a crux linkage pulling
around a roof. If you're wasted, the highly
technical final moves make a fine place to
let go.

Churning Buttress

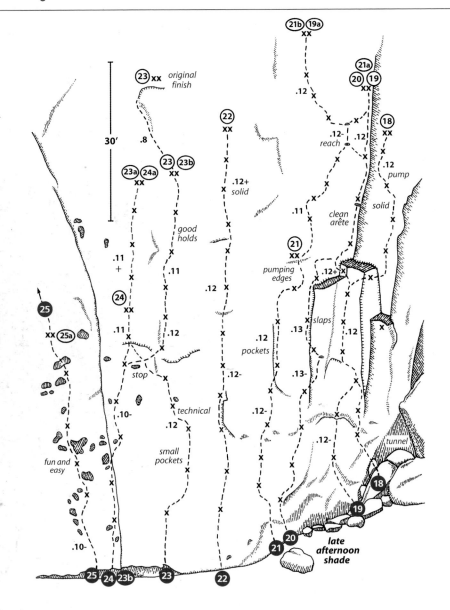

18.	Kings of Rap 5.12d	22.	Sign of the Times 5.13b
19.	Waste Case 5.13b	23.	Taco Chips 5.13a
19a.	Mr. Tapeworm 5.13c	23a.	Nacho Cheese 5.12d
20.	Vicious Fish 5.13c	23b.	Doritos 5.12c
21.	Churning in the Wake 5.13a	24.	Cool Ranch Flavor 5.11b
21a.	Churning Sky 5.13a	24a.	Cool Ranch Flavor finish 5.12a
21b.	Churning in the Ozone 5.13b	25.	Nine Gallon Buckets 5.10c
		25a.	Nine Gallon Buckets start 5.10a

19a. Mr. Tapeworm (5.13c) ★★★ 14 bolts. The grade bumps a notch higher with the pumping *Churning in the Ozone* finish. Step left from the arête after clipping the final bolt on *Waste Case*. Lower with a 70-meter cord.

20. Vicious Fish (5.13c) ★★★★ 10 bolts. This demanding line showcases extreme Smith climbing at its best—the intricate face/arête moves ensure that the brute force approach will end in failure. The hardest climbing comes in the first half of the route, though the artsy final edge often thwarts redpoint burns.

21. Churning in the Wake (5.13a) ★★★★ 7 bolts. By far Smith's most popular 5.13, this gently overhanging wall sees almost nonstop traffic during peak season. The popularity comes from the convenient location, the excellent rock, and the nature of the climbing. With no single move especially hard, *Churning* makes a perfect choice for the 5.12 climber breaking into the higher grades. The pump builds in a memorable sequence of pockets, side pulls, and edges, peaking on the final moves to the anchor.

21a. Churning Sky (5.13a) ★★★★ 13 bolts. An excellent though rarely climbed finish cuts across the upper headwall to the *Vicious Fish* arête. A good rest makes the *Sky* only slightly harder than the original route.

21b. Churning in the Ozone (5.13b) ★★★ 15 bolts. This extended finish avoids the *Vicious Fish* arête, adding a pumping 5.12 section onto *Churning Sky*. Despite

the excellent climbing, the *Ozone* sees few ascents. Use a 70-meter rope to lower off.

22. Sign of the Times (5.13b) ★★★ 11 bolts. Much maligned and eventually chopped after only two ascents, this homely wall never deserved such bad treatment. Fortunately, a rebolting and massive cleaning effort two decades after the first ascent uncovered a route worthy of the Churning Buttress. The newer version bears little resemblance to the

Alan Watts on *Vicious Fish*. CATHY BELOEIL

5.12d original route, as the loose flakes—large and small—are no longer there.

23. Taco Chips (5.13a) ★★★ 10 bolts.

Cleaning off the grunge took hundreds of ascents, but today the original route on the wall is perfectly solid, with a technical line of small pockets and edges. Expect two distinct cruxes, split by an excellent shake above the fifth bolt. If not for this rest, the grade would be a solid notch higher.

23a. Nacho Cheese (5.12d) ★★ 10 bolts.

An easier version of *Taco Chips* completely avoids the upper crux by cruising past the anchor of *Cool Ranch Flavor* to the left, before finishing at a higher set of bolts.

23b. Doritos (5.12c) ★★★ 10 bolts. A

more enjoyable mini-version of *Taco Chips* avoids the techno lower crux by starting with the *Cool Ranch Flavor* buckets on the left. Join the regular line at the rest jug below the upper crux.

24. Cool Ranch Flavor (5.11b) ★★ 6 bolts. A

continuation of a junky old route called *Slum Time* is worth doing. Cleaned, retro-bolted jugs lead to a crimpy crux just below the first set of anchors. Some climbers tone down the hardest moves by straying left.

24a. Cool Ranch Flavor finish (5.12a) ★★★

10 bolts. The original version stops prematurely after a couple hard moves above the buckets. A much improved finish continues via the upper wall of *Nacho Cheese*.

Overboard Area

The heavily chalked wall immediately left of the Churning Buttress is called the Overboard Area. Most of these routes are immensely popular, with big holds, solid rock, and lots of bolts. They all feature multiple midpitch anchors; the lower sections see

far more traffic as the rock typically deteriorates above. You'll typically need two ropes to descend from the highest anchors.

25. Nine Gallon Buckets (5.10c) ★★★ 12

bolts. This delightful line makes a great warm-up for the harder lines. The crux finesses side pulls and edges above the first anchor. The first ascentionist was so ashamed of his poorly cleaned creation, he immediately pulled the bolts in an effort to escape criticism. Only after a thorough scrubbing and rebolting more than a decade later did it become instantly popular.

25a. Nine Gallon Buckets start (5.10a) ★★★

4 bolts. For many years *Nine Gallon Buckets* went no higher than the first anchor. With a bouldering crux right off the ground, the short line of buckets seem easy for the grade.

26. Overboard (5.11c) ★★★ 8 bolts. This

wall of jugs was once Smith's most popular 5.11. The popularity waned as snapped holds raised the grade and finesse-level a couple notches. An insecure barn-door lieback at the crux surprises anyone expecting a cruise.

26a. Overboard extension (5.11d) ★★★ 12

bolts. Almost no one continued above the first set of bolts until a new convenience anchor allowed a quick descent with a 70-meter rope. The moves are less technical but more pumping than the start.

26b. Overboard finish (5.11d) ★★ 14

bolts. The original finish adds little to the difficulty and offers nothing but a nerve-wracking assortment of Smith knobs. Rap with two ropes.

27. Magic Light (5.11a) ★★★ 9 bolts. Good

luck getting on this route during peak season. A long line of jugs and side pulls interrupted by a few crimps generates a healthy pump. It makes a good introduction to the

Overboard Area and Zebra Area

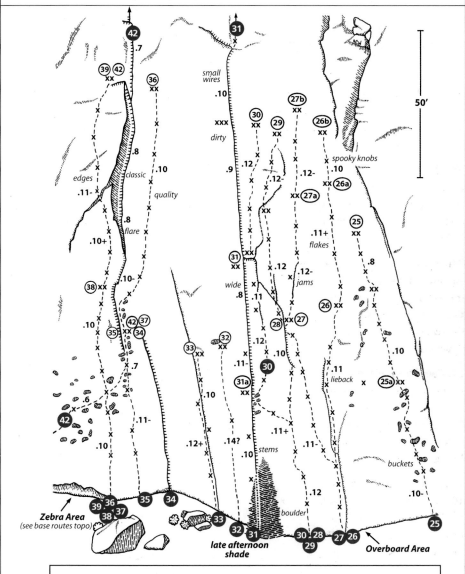

50'

25.	Nine Gallon Buckets 5.10c	31.	Lion's Chair 5.11a R
25a.	Nine Gallon Buckets start 5.10a	31a.	Lion's Chair start 5.10c
26.	Overboard 5.11c	32.	Project 5.14?
26a.	Overboard extension 5.11d	33.	Dandy Line 5.12d
26b.	Overboard finish 5.11d	34.	Zebra Seam 5.11d
27.	Magic Light 5.11a	35.	Zebra Direct 5.11a
27a.	Magic Light extension 5.12a	36.	Lion Zion 5.10c
27b.	Magic Light finish 5.12b	37.	Gumby 5.10b
28.	Energy Crisis 5.12b	38.	Morning Sky 5.10c
29.	Sketch Pad 5.12d	39.	CAT Scan 5.11b
30.	Mane Line 5.13a	42.	Zebra 5.10a

grade since any 5.10 climber can easily do every move.

27a. Magic Light extension (5.12a) ★★★ 14 bolts.
Above the first set of bolts, the jugs end, and strenuous finger jams/edges lead onto the upper wall. With the addition of a new anchor, most climbers avoid the more-difficult original finish by lowering to the ground with a 70-meter rope.

27b. Magic Light finish (5.12b) ★★ 17 bolts.
The entire line sees few ascents. A hard face move just below the top provides a final obstacle. Rap off with double ropes.

28. Energy Crisis (5.12b) ★★★ 7 bolts.
The starting moves are a little too crimpy to make this climb popular. The level eases to 5.11 after the first bolt—this section sees many toprope ascents from the *Magic Light* anchor. After failing repeatedly on the start, the pioneering climber became convinced that the only path to success was through weight loss. After fasting for an entire week, the emaciated German somehow cranked the moves, earning a place in Smith folklore.

29. Sketch Pad (5.12d) ★★★ 15 bolts.
Although rarely climbed, this finish to *Energy Crisis* features a unique crux of side pulls followed by an attractive slab. The same starving climber who pioneered the start couldn't summon the endurance to link the entire route, so he simply lowered the anchors to his high-point and claimed success. Someone eventually replaced his bolts and nabbed the first ascent. Climb in one long pitch from the ground.

30. Mane Line (5.13a) ★★★ 15 bolts.
A long sport route right of *Lion's Chair* offers a little bit of everything, except popularity. Begin with *Energy Crisis* and step left into huge potholes. An intense slab leads into a pumping crack followed by a beautiful 5.12 face on great rock.

31. Lion's Chair (5.11a R) ★★★ Mixed to 3.5 inches.
This unmistakable traditional dihedral was one of Smith's first and most respected 5.11s. The run-out crux above the first anchor still frightens most climbers away. The second and third pitches aren't special, but the entire route provides a fine escape from the circus below. **Pitch 1:** (5.11a) Stem, jam, and lieback the corner 90 feet to a hanging belay. **Pitch 2:** (5.10c) A crumbly dihedral leads to an exit right around the roof and easy face climbing. **Pitch 3:** (5.6) Solo up a low-angle face to a hanging belay beneath the final overhanging crack. **Pitch 4:** (5.9) Savor the breathtaking flake crack to a good ledge and scramble to the top.

31a. Lion's Chair start (5.10c) ★★★ Mixed to 1 inch.
The start of the first pitch is one of the better stemming exercises on Smith tuff, with perfect rock and good protection. Most climbers escape to easy jugs after the crux, avoiding a run-out offset finish.

31b. Lion's Chair exit (5.7) ★ Mixed to 2.5 inches.
If you've had enough, you can bypass the upper two pitches. Clip the first bolt over the second-pitch roof and scamper right to the anchor below Rolling Stones Wall. Hike down Cocaine Gully.

Zebra Area

The section of Morning Glory Wall left of *Lion's Chair* offers a dense concentration of moderate routes. If you're a people-person, you'll love the congested atmosphere at the base of the cliff. The short, one-pitch base routes garner most of the attention, though several of the longer climbs are excellent.

32. Project (5.14?)
All but a couple moves on the face left of *Lion's Chair* go free, but the nature of the beast (a vertical slab without holds) appeals to no one. The crimps

are so thin it's hard taking your weight off the rope.

33. Dandy Line (5.12d) ★★ 5 bolts. A bolted seam splits the smooth wall left of *Lion's Chair*. A brief sequence of liebacks and thin edges deteriorates into much easier junk above. Despite the convenient location, it garners little attention.

34. Zebra Seam (5.11d) ★★★ 8 bolts. This highly technical shallow corner mixes liebacks, jams, and small edges with smears for the feet. It evolved from an A4 nail-up into a dangerous trad route before an anonymous line of retro-bolts eliminated any degree of danger.

35. Zebra Direct (5.11a) ★★★ 4 bolts. Don't take this short face lightly—it's no pushover for the grade. Without good footwork the small crimps and greasy side pulls can be a trying experience.

36. Lion Zion (5.10c) ★★★★ 14 bolts. This brilliant route ascends the blank-looking wall right of the *Zebra* dihedral in a single pitch. Climb *Gumby* and step right past the anchor onto the

bolted face. Sustained climbing on great rock leads to an anchor. Rappel with two ropes.

37. Gumby (5.10b) ★★★ 5 bolts. An easier version of *Zebra Direct* follows the short wall to the left. Much like its neighbor, the technical climbing on small holds surprises those expecting a hike. The original route finished

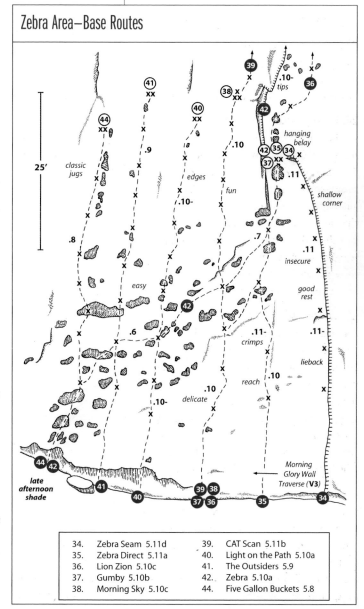

Zebra Area–Base Routes

34.	Zebra Seam 5.11d	39.	CAT Scan 5.11b
35.	Zebra Direct 5.11a	40.	Light on the Path 5.10a
36.	Lion Zion 5.10c	41.	The Outsiders 5.9
37.	Gumby 5.10b	42.	Zebra 5.10a
38.	Morning Sky 5.10c	44.	Five Gallon Buckets 5.8

with easy potholes, though many climbers follow *Morning Sky*.

38. Morning Sky (5.10c) ★★★ 9 bolts. Rather than cutting right into the potholes after the crux on *Gumby,* continue directly up a delightful face on edges and pockets. The higher grade comes more from the pump than any particular move.

39. CAT Scan (5.11b) ★★★ 18 bolts. A one-pitch sport route continues above *Morning Sky,* ending at a good ledge far off the ground. Crumbling holds plagued early ascents, but today it's solid with an airy crux pulling around a small roof. Rappel using two ropes.

40. Light on the Path (5.10a) ★★★ 8 bolts. Nothing better demonstrates the Smith Rock phenomenon of miserable routes being climbed into classics than this extremely popular line. Enough edges pulled off over the years to raise the grade a notch, but the remaining holds aren't going anywhere. With a restored direct start, *Light on the Path* now follows the original line.

41. The Outsiders (5.9) ★★★ 8 bolts. This enjoyable route gives you an opportunity to rub elbows (literally) with climbers on *Light on the Path* and *Five Gallon Buckets.* Solid jugs, knobs, pockets, and edges make it very popular.

42. Zebra (5.10a) ★★★ Mixed to 3 inches. The most obvious line on Morning Glory Wall follows a beautiful right-facing corner. Start with easy potholes or take your pick of *Zebra Seam* (the original aid start), *Zebra Direct,* or *Gumby.* Most climbers avoid the hanging belay by blending a bolted base route and the second pitch into a single lead. **Pitch 1:** (5.7) 5 bolts. Veer right through the huge potholes to a hanging belay. **Pitch 2:** (5.10a) Crux finger jams on perfect rock lead into the awesome corner. Belay at a ledge with two bolts. **Pitch 3:** (5.8) Ascend a flaring crack/corner to a huge ledge (or see *Zion*). **Pitch 4:** (4th class) Step left and hike an ugly gully to the top.

43. Zion (5.10a) ★★★★ Mixed to 3 inches. Almost everyone avoids the final pitch of *Zebra,* wisely opting for this amazing finish. For the grade, nothing compares to the breathtakingly exposed flake crack. Although the entire route is called *Zion* (combining *Zebra* and *Lion's Chair*), many climbers use the misnomer *Zebra Zion.* **Pitches 1 and 2:** (5.10a) Climb the first two pitches of *Zebra.* **Pitch 3:** (5.8) Begin with *Zebra's* third pitch, but step right on airy knobs to a simple unprotected slab ending below an overhanging headwall. **Pitch 4:** (5.9) Spectacular climbing up an overhanging flake crack ends at a ledge a few feet below the top. Finish with an easy scramble.

44. Five Gallon Buckets (5.8) ★★★ 7 bolts. This fun wall of jugs might be Smith's most popular route. Year-round through rain, snow, and triple-digit temperatures, there's almost always someone reaching from bucket to bucket. Although a little too strenuous for most first-timers, it serves as many climbers' introduction to the sport.

45. In Hinds Way (5.9) Gear to 4 inches. Not everything on Morning Glory Wall is a classic. No route demonstrates this better than the repulsive wide crack left of the bolted sport routes. It never gets done, for obvious reasons. **Pitch 1:** (5.9) Grovel up a flaring crack to a bolt belay. **Pitch 2:** (5.7) Easy climbing on rotten rock leads to the large ledge on *Zebra.* Finish with a gully scramble.

The next two routes start far off the ground from the big ledge atop *Zebra*. To approach, climb *Zebra*—or hike to the top via the Cocaine Gully and scramble down the upper chimney.

46. Choss in America (5.12c) ★★★ 13 bolts. The remote location high off the ground is both the charm and curse of this attractive wall. The excellent position, well-protected moves, and solid rock justify the hassle of reaching the base. The pocket-pulling crux comes near the top, just as your forearms start to tire.

47. One Time Trick (5.11a) ★ Gear to 4 inches. Spectacular but forever ignored, this hand/fist crack splits an exposed bulge. Step left from the *Zebra* ledge and jam an overhanging wide crack to a two-bolt belay. Scramble along the ridge to the top.

48. Anonymity (5.9) ★★ 6 bolts. The latest squeeze-job along the base of the Zebra Area follows a shallow arête right of *Lion's Jaw*. It's nothing special, but the line of bolts attracts climbers like bugs to a light.

49. Lion's Jaw (5.8) ★★★ Gear to 2.5 inches. This wonderful right-facing dihedral appeals to traditional climbers for good reason. Fun stems and jams in the solid corner lead to a finishing mini-roof.

49a. Almdudler (5.8 X) ★ Gear to 2 inches. A dangerous variant starts in a mini-flare left of the classic open book. After a crux start on good rock, the quality decreases, and the risk of groundfall increases the higher you go.

50. Lion's Jaw Chimney (5.7) Gear to 4 inches. Around the corner left of *Lion's Jaw* rises one of Smith's most infamous chimneys. The repugnant upper pitches are home to a large percentage of the park's

pigeon population. **Pitch 1:** (5.7) Plunge into the depths of the starting slot and thrash to a ledge. **Pitch 2:** (5.7) Venture into a dark slot and chimney up walls oozing with pigeon poop to a belay slot. **Pitch 3:** (5.6) Writhe up another dismal chimney to the top.

51. Tammy Bakker's Face (5.10c) ★★ Bolts. A buttress sitting on the far left side of Morning Glory Wall features a single route ending just below the top. Early ascents rained a stream of debris, but over the years the crumbling face cleaned nicely. Today it looks far better than the face it was named after. Bring two ropes to descend. **Pitch 1:** (5.9) 7 bolts. Climb a short crack and step right onto a low-angle face with many bolts. **Pitch 2:** (5.10c) 7 bolts. An inside corner leads to a pull over a bulge on creaky holds. A deceptively tricky move ends at an anchor.

52. Lost Horseman Roof (5.11c) ★ TR. A gully plugged by a gigantic boulder called the Peanut marks the left boundary of Morning Glory Wall. High atop the right side of this gully rises an obscure toprope problem weaving through several small roofs.

The Peanut

A 60-foot boulder sits left of Morning Glory Wall. Usually booked solid on any busy weekend, the Peanut offers several enjoyable face routes.

53. Popism (5.11b) ★★ 4 bolts. The rounded right edge of the Peanut provides a brief challenge stretching between pockets. Relocated bolts eliminated any degree of danger—especially with a stick-clip at the start.

The Peanut

55. Peanut Brittle (5.8) ★★★ 6 bolts. Much like its neighbor to the right, the knobby center route became popular only after the addition of several new bolts. Rock that was brittle years ago is solid today.

56. Hop on Pop (5.8) ★★★ 7 bolts. The leftmost route on the Peanut features solid rock and more than enough bolts. Anyone making the second clip will have no trouble with the slabby finish.

The Fourth Horseman

Sitting atop the ridge left of Morning Glory Wall are four squat pillars. Easily the most impressive spire is the Fourth Horseman with its crack-split river face. Recent sport routes and high-quality traditional cracks make it one of the most varied crags in the park. The cracks see far fewer ascents today than they did years ago, but they're worth digging out the gear for. **Descent:** A third-class scramble left leads to a fixed rappel station above *Cinnamon Slab* in the Dihedrals. Two single-rope rappels (or a single rap with a 70-meter rope) end at the base.

51.	Tammy Bakker's Face 5.10c
52.	Lost Horseman Roof 5.11c TR
53.	Popism 5.11b
54.	Pop Goes the Nubbin 5.10a
55.	Peanut Brittle 5.8
56.	Hop on Pop 5.8
57.	Snuffy Smith 5.9

54. Pop Goes the Nubbin (5.10a) ★★★ 7 bolts. The flat face on the Peanut's right side provides a good footwork test. On the first ascent, there were few bolts and plenty of knobs. Today you'll find few knobs and plenty of bolts.

Fourth Horseman

Fourth Horseman

First Horseman

72

52

52.	Lost Horseman Roof 5.11c TR
54.	Pop Goes the Nubbin 5.10a
56.	Hop on Pop 5.8
57.	Snuffy Smith 5.9
59.	No Golf Shoes 5.10c
60.	Friday's Jinx 5.7 R
63.	Calamity Jam 5.10c
64.	The John Galt Line 5.11b
67.	Pack Animal 5.8 R
69.	Headless Horseman 5.10d
72.	Equus 5.11b

Peanut Gully

69

64

63 60

59

57

56   54

67

The Peanut

Fourth Horseman

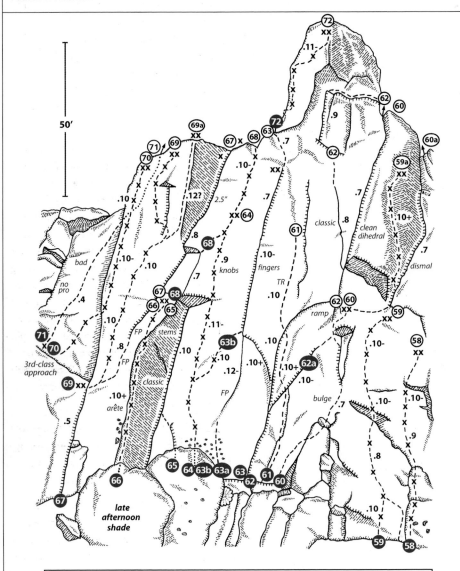

58.	Tuff It Out 5.10a	64.	The John Galt Line 5.11b
59.	No Golf Shoes 5.10c	65.	Pack Animal Direct 5.10b
59a.	No Golf Shoes finish 5.10d	66.	Taiwan On 5.10c
60.	Friday's Jinx 5.7 R	67.	Pack Animal 5.8 R
60a.	Sunday's JInx 5.7	68.	Sundancer 5.10a
61.	Wielded Tuff 5.10c TR	69.	Headless Horseman 5.10d
62.	Crack of Infinity 5.10b	69a.	Project 5.12?
62a.	Infinity Variation 5.10a	70.	Equine-imity 5.10b
63.	Calamity Jam 5.10c	71.	Dead Men Tell No Tales 5.7 X
63a.	Catastrophic Crack 5.12a R	72.	Equus 5.11b
63b.	Sandbag 5.10c R		

57. Snuffy Smith (5.9) ★★ 7 bolts. A few feet left of the Peanut rises a slender column with a distinct upper edge. After some face moves low, avoid the column by climbing a crack to the left. Near the top veer right for a few fun arête moves.

58. Tuff It Out (5.10a) ★★ 7 bolts. The most recent line on the formation starts with big holds, on the right side of a short left-facing corner. Moderate climbing leads to a crux moving through three dinky roofs.

59. No Golf Shoes (5.10c) ★★ 8 bolts. This varied route starts with a crux boulder problem over a bulge and weaves past a roof to another tricky move just below the anchors. The original route (5.10a) bypassed the tough start by traversing in from the right.

59a. No Golf Shoes finish (5.10d) ★★ 14 bolts. You can continue far above the first set of anchors in a single pitch from the ground. The first ascent followed a contrived direct line above the first bolt (5.11a). Everyone else continues up the ramp, stepping onto the face after clipping the second. You can lower to the ground with a 70-meter rope.

60. Friday's Jinx (5.7 R) ★★★ Gear to 2 inches. This unlucky route put several people in the hospital during the 1980s. The accident rate decreased the last couple decades as climbers avoided the *Jinx,* despite its good rock and decent protection. **Pitch 1:** (5.7) Traverse right and pull over a mini-bulge. Climb the corner above and belay at a large block that somehow stays attached to the wall. **Pitch 2:** (5.7) Race up the enjoyable left-facing corner to the top.

60a. Sunday's Jinx (5.7) ★ Gear to 3 inches. If you're foolish, you'll swap the excellent second pitch of *Friday's Jinx* for a forgettable ramp around the column to the right.

61. Wielded Tuff (5.10c) ★★★ TR. Should a new sport route cross the line of an existing trad route? An anonymous bolt chopper voiced his opinion shortly after the first ascent, but you can still toprope *Wielded Tuff* from the anchor on *Calamity Jam*. After a wild sequence up a unique column, cross over *Crack of Infinity* and climb easier rock up the center of the face.

62. Crack of Infinity (5.10b) ★★★ Gear to 3 inches. Each pitch of this enjoyable crack system has a character all its own, with a classic second-pitch flake crack highlighting the adventure. A much easier alternative approaches this crack via *Friday's Jinx* and avoids the final pitch by stepping right. Start below a short dihedral, capped by diverging roof cracks. **Pitch 1:** (5.10b) Jam the overhanging right crack aided by hidden jugs and cut right to the *Friday's Jinx* belay boulder. **Pitch 2:** (5.8) Savor the exposed crack splitting the face and step left to a nut anchor below an overhanging crack. **Pitch 3:** (5.9) Lieback and jam the ominous crack to a ledge and escape right.

62a. Infinity Variation (5.10a) ★★ Gear to 2 inches. An easier and far less intimidating start follows a leaning finger crack to the right of the first-pitch overhang.

63. Calamity Jam (5.10c) ★★★★ Gear to 2 inches. One of Smith's finest cracks splits the center of the wall. Despite the brilliance, the popularity waned after the emergence of sport climbing. Crux underclings and jams in the starting arch lead into a delightful finger crack in a shallow corner. Lower off from a new anchor or continue to the top with the original less-than-classic finish.

63a. Catastrophic Crack (5.12a R) ★★★ Gear to 2 inches. The direct start to *Calamity Jam* strikes fear in the heart of anyone unskilled at placing gear. The dinky wire slots are adequate, but it isn't easy stopping in the middle of a barn-door lieback.

63b. Sandbag (5.10c R) ★★ Mixed to 2 inches. An indistinct right-leaning slash joins *Calamity Jam* past the starting arch. A bolt protects the crux, but nobody enjoys the unnerving traverse to the right.

64. The John Galt Line (5.11b) ★★★ 10 bolts. An enjoyable sport route rises right of a massive open book. A few thin face moves and a strenuous pull over the roof lead to an easier finish on knobs and edges.

65. Pack Animal Direct (5.10b) ★★★★ Gear to 1 inch. For the grade there's no better dihedral on Smith tuff than this attractive line. The easy starting moves protect poorly, but the classic stems and finger jams take good gear. After cutting left at a roof, rappel off or continue via *Pack Animal* or *Sundancer* to the top.

66. Taiwan On (5.10c) ★★★ 6 bolts. Delicate moves on the left edge of the *Pack Animal Direct* dihedral provide a sport climbing alternative. Early ascents faced snapping holds, but the rock has improved greatly in recent years. Climbers sometimes finish to the top in a single lead via *Headless Horseman*.

67. Pack Animal (5.8 R) ★★★ Gear to 2.5 inches. The leftmost of the quality traditional routes on the Fourth Horseman ascends a right-facing corner on the upper half of the cliff. The best approach follows either *Pack Animal Direct* or *Taiwan On*. The easier original start protects with fixed pins placed more than thirty-five years ago. **Pitch 1:** (5.8) Tricky face moves past two dubious pegs lead to a ledge. Clipping the *Headless Horseman* bolts to the left removes the R rating. **Pitch 2:** (5.8) Jam and stem the enjoyable corner to the top.

68. Sundancer (5.10a) ★ Mixed to 1 inch. An alternative to the upper pitch of *Pack Animal* moves right onto a knobby face. The rock deteriorates above a midpitch anchor, spoiling a crux bulge just below the top. Bring a few small nuts for the starting crack or face a long run-out to the first bolt.

69. Headless Horseman (5.10d) ★★★ 9 bolts. The original sport route on the Fourth Horseman ascends the attractive buttress left of *Pack Animal*. Good rock, plentiful bolts, and a blend of face, arête, and stemming moves make it the most popular route to the top of the cliff.

69a. Project (5.12?) A difficult direct finish to *Headless Horseman* will follow a short overhanging arête right of the regular line. The moves go free on toprope.

70. Equine-imity (5.10b) ★★ 9 bolts. A homely sport route rises from the shadows on the far left side of the Fourth Horseman. Despite appearances it's worth doing, with decent rock and an airy position.

71. Dead Men Tell No Tales (5.7 X) Gear to 2.5 inches. This loser follows a dirty, low-angle slab left of the *Headless Horseman* buttress. The crux hand crack at the top protects well, but the 80-foot run-out at the start keeps sane climbers away.

72. Equus (5.11b) ★★ 4 bolts. The river face of the Fourth Horseman's summit block features a single route, high above the ground. Unfortunately, the quality of the climbing doesn't match the exhilarating position, as much of the route trots awkwardly up the left arête.

73. Fourth Horseman (5.7 R) ★ No topo. Gear to 2.5 inches. Anyone interested in standing atop this imposing spire can squirm up a short chimney on the north side.

Rappel down the south face from anchors below the summit.

74. Third Horseman (5.10b R) ★ No topo. Solo. Behind the Fourth Horseman stands a squat tower. The summit comes quickly after soloing a tricky bouldering move on the north side. There's no anchor on top, so don't climb up unless you can climb down.

75. Second Horseman (5.6 R) ★ No topo. Solo. Split by a wide chimney, this unimpressive blob succumbs easily after a moderate scramble. Descend by reversing the route.

76. First Horseman (5.7 R) ★ No topo. Gear to 2 inches. To reach the anchorless summit of the southernmost spire, jam a miniature dihedral leading to a few unprotected face moves.

Riderless Horse (R.I.P.) The first edition of this guide included a route up an "insane spike that looks like it will come tumbling down when the wind blows." During the blustery winter of 1992, that's exactly what happened.

Rope De Dope Rock

Across the river from the Fourth Horseman sits a squarish blob with a prominent crack splitting the river face. The exclusive domain of classes and beginners for many years, today Rope De Dope contains a worthwhile selection of moderate sport routes. Expect mostly solid rock, a quick approach, and a great view of the main climbing area.

A 5.10 boulder problem on the backside provides the quickest route to the top. Fortunately, a permanent aid sling hanging from a bolt bypasses any difficulties. There's an anchor atop almost every route, though some of these aren't easily reached from above. Several bolts on top provide safety while leaning over the edge. Use them.

77. North Slab Crack (5.5 R) ★ Gear to 2.5 inches. Despite unprotected face moves at the start, this flaring crack on the low-angle north side of the block provides an easy path to the top.

78. How Low Can You Go? (5.7) ★★★ 5 bolts. A bolted line in the center of the north slab makes a good beginner's lead. After a tricky start the climbing turns simple, with enough bolts to calm the nerves of any first-timer.

79. Shamu (5.9) ★★★ 6 bolts. The right side of the north slab features another popular route. Deceptively strenuous cranks on good holds give way to a fun, slabby finish.

80. Immortal Beloved (5.9) ★ 5 bolts. The crumbling left arête of Rope De Dope Rock's main face doesn't match the quality of the other lines. After a crux start, easier climbing leads up the right side of the edge.

81. Low Blow (5.10a) ★★ 6 bolts. Right of *Immortal Beloved* rises a mediocre sport route plagued by flaky rock in the middle. The quality improves higher on the wall, with a solid crux just below the top.

82. Float Like A Butterfly (5.10b) ★★★ 5 bolts. Big jugs and side pulls highlight this bulging, solid wall. Muscle through the lower portion and use a little finesse on the crux seam at the top.

83. Sleepy Town (5.10a) ★★★ 5 bolts. A few feet left of *Rope De Dope Crack* sits another enjoyable sport route with plenty of bolts. After an easy slab at the start, fun climbing on big holds ends with face moves cutting left to an anchor.

84. Rope De Dope Crack (5.8) ★★★ Gear to 3 inches. Usually toproped, this unmistakable hand crack jams excellent rock past a strenuous bulge. It protects well for anyone unafraid of the sharp end of the rope.

Rope De Dope Rock

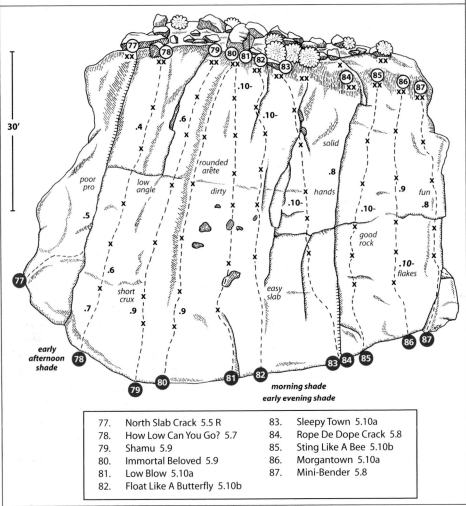

77.	North Slab Crack 5.5 R	83.	Sleepy Town 5.10a
78.	How Low Can You Go? 5.7	84.	Rope De Dope Crack 5.8
79.	Shamu 5.9	85.	Sting Like A Bee 5.10b
80.	Immortal Beloved 5.9	86.	Morgantown 5.10a
81.	Low Blow 5.10a	87.	Mini-Bender 5.8
82.	Float Like A Butterfly 5.10b		

85. Sting Like A Bee (5.10b) ★★★ 5 bolts. This high-quality line ascends the wall immediately right of *Rope De Dope Crack*. Some climbers opt for a harder direct route above the second bolt, though it's more fun skirting left on better holds.

86. Morgantown (5.10a) ★★★ 5 bolts. The rightmost of parallel face routes begins with strenuous side pulls on creaky flakes. The rock turns perfect at a mini-roof in the middle, with a fun finish on good edges.

87. Mini-Bender (5.8) ★★★ 4 bolts. A spirited pull over a crux bulge highlights this pleasant route up the right edge of the block. Great rock, a moderate grade, and quality climbing make it popular.

Hand-drilling bolts was such an unpleasant task I used natural protection whenever I could. But one question haunted me—if I fell, would the miniature wires hold or would the rock rip apart? Heinous Cling (5.12c) gave me the answer. I placed only three bolts on the entire route, relying instead on a hodgepodge of RPs, hexes, and Friends to keep me safe. The first time I linked past the crux, I spent several minutes placing a complex network of wires not far below the top. No single piece inspired much confidence, but I was certain the combination would get the job done. The final moves weren't hard, but I quickly realized that my forearms had nothing left—with a scream I rocketed off into space. Every single RP ripped out of the rock without even slowing me down, and I fell the entire length of the upper pitch until a Friend in a pocket spared my life. When I bolted Darkness at Noon *a few months later, I left the wires behind.*

Serving as center stage to Smith climbing, the Dihedrals offers sublime vertical faces, stunning arêtes, and classic open books. The eye-catching natural lines, solid rock, and wide range of difficulties tantalize both the beginner and world-class climber—and everyone in between. More than any other crag at Smith, the Dihedrals played a key role in the evolution of the sport. It's no exaggeration to say that these routes laid the foundation of sport climbing for the entire country.

Before the development of the Dihedrals, Smith climbers focused on the limited number of cracks and easier faces scattered throughout the park. Once the traditional lines fell, no one saw much future in Dihedrals' free climbing. Without chalk marking the holds, almost everything else looked impossible. Not until 1983 did it finally become clear that the true future of Smith Rock wasn't finishing all the cracks, but tapping the huge volume of untouched faces and arêtes. Rappel inspections began, more from desperation to find something new than a belief that many routes would be possible. Miraculously, usable holds studded every face, and the race was on.

Apart from ascents of the most obvious lines, few climbers visited the Dihedrals in the early days of Smith climbing. Prior to the construction of the bridge in 1975, the remoteness of the area kept most climbers away. The first ascent of the crag occurred in 1963 when George Cummings and John Hall climbed *Rattlesnake Chimney* (5.6). One can only imagine how unpleasant this still-dirty route must have been. The 1972 free ascent of *Moonshine Dihedral* (5.9) by Dean Fry and Jeff Thomas marked the beginning of the free climbing era in the Dihedrals. A year later Fry freed both *Karate Crack* and *Peapod Cave* (both 5.10a). Looking back, the most prophetic routes were the first to venture out of the cracks and onto the steep faces. Dean Fry's unlikely choice of

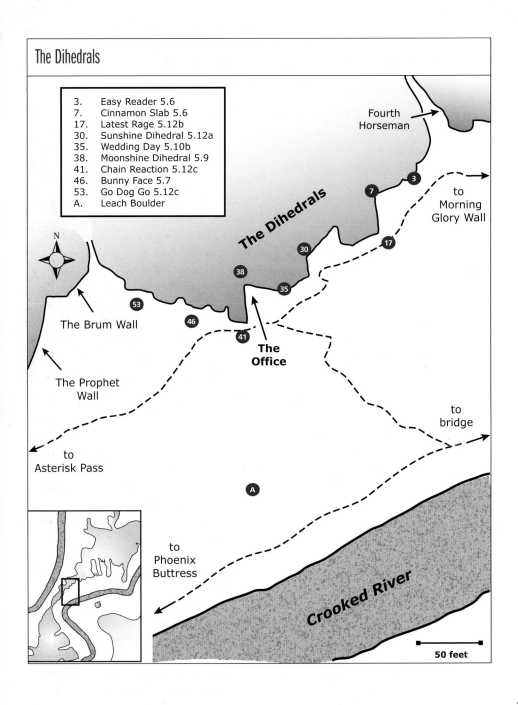

The Dihedrals

3. Easy Reader 5.6
7. Cinnamon Slab 5.6
17. Latest Rage 5.12b
30. Sunshine Dihedral 5.12a
35. Wedding Day 5.10b
38. Moonshine Dihedral 5.9
41. Chain Reaction 5.12c
46. Bunny Face 5.7
53. Go Dog Go 5.12c
A. Leach Boulder

Fourth Horseman

to Morning Glory Wall

The Dihedrals

N

The Brum Wall

The Prophet Wall

The Office

to bridge

to Asterisk Pass

to Phoenix Buttress

Crooked River

50 feet

The Dihedrals Overview

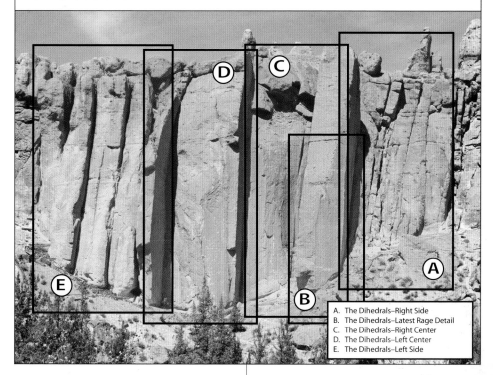

A. The Dihedrals–Right Side
B. The Dihedrals–Latest Rage Detail
C. The Dihedrals–Right Center
D. The Dihedrals–Left Center
E. The Dihedrals–Left Side

Methuselah's Column (5.10a) in 1972 was unlike anything else at Smith—it intentionally avoided easier cracks by searching out a more difficult route to the top. Many years later, ascents of *Karot Tots* (5.11b) and *Sunshine Dihedral* (5.12a) bumped the standards higher. By 1981 the general consensus was that the Dihedrals offered nothing else of interest to free climbers. The cracks all went free and the faces looked unfeasible.

This attitude forever changed in a single month during 1983. *Watts Tots* (5.12b) ushered in the sport climbing era at Smith, and two weeks later *Chain Reaction* (5.12c) also went free. It immediately became apparent that if these lines would go, so would dozens of other face routes around the park. Seemingly overnight Smith Rock went from being climbed out, to holding almost unlimited promise. Within two years the

Dihedrals became the most developed real estate at Smith, with classics such as *Heinous Cling* (5.12c), *Darkness at Noon* (5.13a), *Last Waltz* (5.12c), and *Latest Rage* (5.12b). Many of these original routes avoided the time-consuming placement of hand-drilled bolts by relying heavily on natural gear.

By the time the hoards of visitors first arrived at Smith, most of the classic lines stood ready and waiting. The most obvious new project was the improbable left wall of *Sunshine Dihedral.* The moves went free as early as 1984, but a redpoint ascent seemed years away. Just two years later, French climber Jean-Baptiste Tribout surprised everyone by establishing *To Bolt or Not to Be,* America's first 5.14. This remarkable route matched the highest grade in the world at the time, and validated the controversial tactics of Smith Rock sport climbing.

The Dihedrals cover a surprisingly small section of Smith, stretching only 300 feet from end to end. Yet because of the accordion layout of the cliff, there are more than sixty routes and variations.

Finding the crags: There are two main approaches to the cliff. Either hike along the trail from the base of Morning Glory Wall, or follow a path directly from the river to a flat hangout spot below *Moonshine Dihedral* (known as the Office). For reasons described in How to Use This Book (see Introduction), the routes described below move from right to left, assuming the Morning Glory Wall approach. For anyone using the Office approach, the routes will be in reverse order when walking right. Most climbers adapt, while a very small minority are left completely disoriented.

Descent: Two single-rope rappels from an anchor atop *Cinnamon Slab* reach the ground (or a single rap with a 70-meter rope). Veteran climbers sometimes prefer scrambling down a moderate slab/chimney farther to the right. Anyone unfamiliar with the crag should opt for the rappel.

The slabs on the right side of the Dihedrals are immensely popular with beginners and classes. In peak season, ropes appear early in the morning and stay there all day. On busy weekends instructors should take their groups to other crags.

1. Lichen It (5.8) ★★★ 8 bolts. The often-climbed rightmost route makes a good choice for anyone moving into lead climbing. A tricky move above the first bolt gives way to an enjoyable finish protected by closely spaced bolts.

The Dihedrals–Southeast Face

fixed rap station

1. Lichen It 5.8
5. Night Flight 5.5
7. Cinnamon Slab 5.6
16. Karate Wall 5.12c R
18. Watts Tots 5.12b
28. Powder in the Eyes 5.12c
30. Sunshine Dihedral 5.12a
32. To Bolt or Not to Be 5.14a
35. Wedding Day 5.10b
39. Heinous Cling 5.12c R
41. Chain Reaction 5.12c
50. Helium Woman 5.9

2. Right Slab Crack (5.5) ★★ Gear to 2 inches. A vertical dihedral at the start provides the only challenge on this traditional route. Most climbers forego the lead, toproping after ascents of *Lichen It* or *Easy Reader*. **Pitch 1:** (5.5) Stem and jam the crack to a new anchor. Rappel or . . . **Pitch 2:** (5.2) Continue up easy rock to the top.

3. Easy Reader (5.6) ★★★ 5 bolts. The only tricky part of this popular route is getting off the ground. The remaining slab features solid rock, low-angle climbing, and enough bolts to pacify novices.

4. Left Slab Crack (5.4) ★ Gear to 2.5 inches. This low-angle crack left of *Easy Reader* protects well, but many climbers prefer a toprope after climbing *Night Flight*. The quality doesn't match other nearby lines.

5. Night Flight (5.5) ★★★ 7 bolts. One of Smith's easiest sport routes follows a low-angle seam broken by a ledge system. Anyone searching for a low-key first lead needn't look farther. Expect good rock, plenty of bolts, and consistently simple climbing. Use a 60-meter rope to get down safely.

6. Ginger Snap (5.8) ★★★ 4 bolts. An enjoyable knobby face provides a sport climbing alternative to the first pitch of *Cinnamon Slab*. The hardest moves come at the start of the main wall, leading to a fun finish on great rock. Bring gear if you'd like to protect the scrambling start.

7. Cinnamon Slab (5.6) ★★★ Gear to 3.5 inches. Once the most popular route at Smith, this classic ramp now sees far fewer ascents than the sport climbs to the right. It still makes a great lead for anyone learning the lost art of gear placement. **Pitch 1:** (5.6) Ascend the attractive, easily protected

Cinnamon Slab using jams and face holds, ending at a good belay ledge. **Pitch 2:** (5.5) A tricky move off the ledge leads to an easy finishing dihedral.

7a. Rodney's Chocolate Frosted Love Donut (5.8) ★ 7 bolts. A second-pitch alternative starts with thin moves off the right side of the ledge and follows an easier slab to the top. The rock will improve over time, but the name never will. Some climbers start with *Ginger Snap* in one long pitch from the ground.

7b. Cinnamon Toast (5.7 R) ★ Mixed to 3 inches. This dangerous variation steps left 15 feet up the second pitch of *Cinnamon Slab*. Only two bolts protect the knobby moves, with a crux pulling on loose flakes near the top.

7c. Cry Baby (5.9) ★★★ 6 bolts. A modern alternative follows exposed knobs a few feet left of *Cinnamon Toast*. Much of the face is easy and delightful with a memorable position, though the rock worsens above the last bolt.

8. Karate Crack (5.10a) ★★★ Gear to 3 inches. A classic hand crack splits the vertical face left of *Cinnamon Slab*. The final moves are easy if you're fresh, and desperate if you're pumped. Protect inside the cave, or your partner will freak on the finishing hand traverse.

9. Peapod Cave (5.10a) ★★ Gear to 4 inches. Almost no one ever climbs the chimney above *Karate Crack,* though it isn't that bad; the best climbing exits the slot and scoots right to a belay ledge. Start by stepping left into the chimney partway up *Cinnamon Slab*. A two-pitch version using *Karate Crack* as an approach was originally called *Math Test*.

The Dihedrals—Right Side

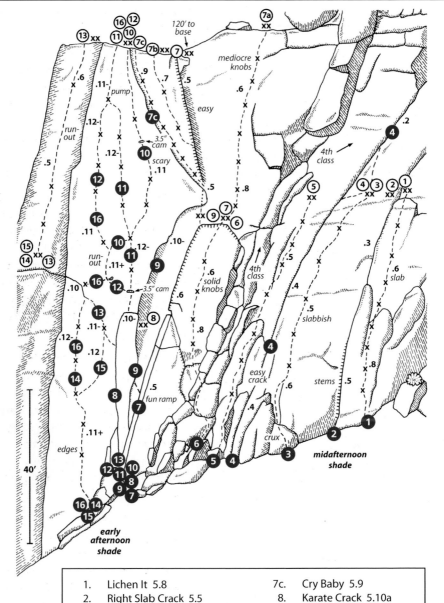

1.	Lichen It 5.8	7c.	Cry Baby 5.9
2.	Right Slab Crack 5.5	8.	Karate Crack 5.10a
3.	Easy Reader 5.6	9.	Peapod Cave 5.10a
4.	Left Slab Crack 5.4	10.	Slow Burn 5.11d R
5.	Night Flight 5.5	11.	Crossfire 5.12b
6.	Ginger Snap 5.8	12.	Power Dive 5.12a R
7.	Cinnamon Slab 5.6	13.	Karot Tots 5.11b
7a.	Rodney's Chocolate Frosted	14.	Firing Line 5.12b
	Love Donut 5.8	15.	Low Profile 5.12c R
7b.	Cinnamon Toast 5.7 R	16.	Karate Wall 5.12c R

The following four routes start with *Karate Crack* and branch off onto the vertical wall. Although first climbed largely with natural gear, most of these lines are fully retro-bolted. An anchor at the top allows easy toproping with double ropes or a single 70-meter cord.

10. Slow Burn (5.11d R) ★★★ Mixed to 4 inches. The original line to the top of the wall sees very few ascents. With the removal of an unfortunate retro-bolt at the lower crux, *Slow Burn* is now unchanged from the days of the first ascent. Bolts on the pumping finish are far apart—don't let go.

11. Crossfire (5.12b) ★★★★ Mixed to 3.5 inches. First climbed with only two bolts and natural gear, the center sport route once boasted a 30-foot run-out. New bolts make it far less serious, but the moves are as brilliant as ever. Bring a 3.5-inch cam for the first big jug above *Karate*. Finish by moving left to the final bolt on *Power Dive*.

12. Power Dive (5.12a R) ★★★★ Mixed to 3.5 inches. The left of three routes above *Karate Crack* will test your endurance, technical skills, and nerve. Apart from the *Karate* approach and single big cam, this wonderful route is now fully bolted. The removal of a retro-bolt restored the demented charms of the lower crux. Anyone carrying a serious pump will likely take a dive from small crimps high on the wall.

13. Karot Tots (5.11b) ★★★★ Mixed to 2.5 inches. The first route venturing onto the blank faces of the Dihedrals, *Karot Tots* (the name rhymes) hinted at the possibilities of the future. It received no attention as an aid climb (called *Euclid's Column*), but became an instant classic after the first free ascent. Great rock and enjoyable moves make it one of Smith's finest 5.11s. **Pitch 1:** (5.11b)

Climb *Karate Crack* and step left below the hand traverse to a bolt. Ascend solid edges to a thin crack and cut around a corner to a belay. **Pitch 2:** (5.6) 3 bolts. Race up easy knobs to the top.

14. Firing Line (5.12b) ★★★ 6 bolts. The attractive line left of *Karate Crack* follows technically demanding edges before cutting left around the corner via the *Karot Tots* crack. The crux at the fourth bolt stretches between crimps with little for the feet. Retro-bolts eliminated the original R rating.

15. Low Profile (5.12c R) ★★★ Mixed to 1.5 inches. A variant to *Firing Line* branches off to the right after the third bolt and climbs without protection on flawless rock to the first bolt on *Karot Tots*. Rarely repeated, it's one of Smith's few serious routes untouched by retro-bolters. Without a skilled belayer, you'll hit the ground on a fall from the last hard move.

16. Karate Wall (5.12c R) ★★★★ 11 bolts. This magnificent route stacks *Power Dive* onto *Firing Line*, connected by a short traverse. Expect nearly perfect rock from bottom to top, with technical moves building into an endurance problem. *Karate Wall* originally had lots of natural protection, few bolts, and even fewer ascents; today it's fully bolted and often climbed.

17. Latest Rage (5.12b) ★★★★ 4 bolts (optional cams to 1.5 inches). One of Smith's finest 5.12s follows the gorgeous edge left of *Karate Wall*. A memorable sequence blends edges, pockets, and slaps up the arête to a crux above the final bolt. The original route included a direct start and finished at the *Karot Tots* belay. Today everyone wisely lowers at the first set of anchors.

17a. Monster Rage (5.12d R) ★★★★ Mixed to 3.5 inches. A new link-up combines *Latest*

Rage with *Karate Wall* in a single pitch to the top. After clipping the fourth bolt on the *Rage* with a long sling, diagonal right and join *Karate Wall* at a big jug. With pumped forearms, all the cruxes seem a little harder.

18. Watts Tots (5.12b)

★★★★ 6 bolts. The beautiful flat face left of *Latest Rage* marked a critical juncture in the evolution of Smith climbing. After decades of mostly traditional cracks, it was the first modern sport route. Today *Watts Tots* remains a test of anyone's technical prowess, with a boulder problem crux above the fifth bolt.

18a. Mega Watts

(5.13b) ★★★ TR. Tightly crammed between *Latest Rage* and *Watts Tots* is a demanding toprope problem. Two distinct cruxes—one low and one high—provide a stiff challenge for the few climbers that try.

19. Fresh Squeezed (5.11a) ★★★ 6 bolts.

The left arête of the *Watts Tots* wall features some of Smith's most squeezed real estate. This aptly named route starts with a direct boulder problem leading to a solid arête. Uncontrived climbing mostly left of the bolt line ends at an anchor.

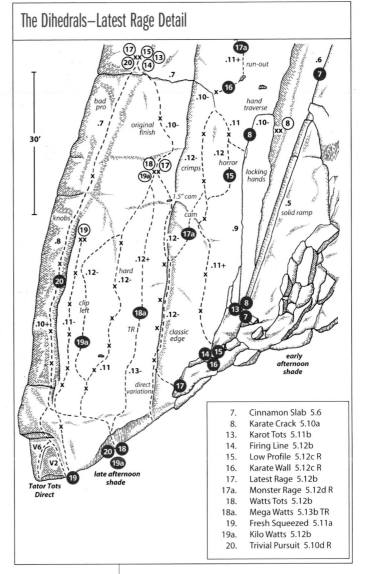

The Dihedrals—Latest Rage Detail

7.	Cinnamon Slab 5.6
8.	Karate Crack 5.10a
13.	Karot Tots 5.11b
14.	Firing Line 5.12b
15.	Low Profile 5.12c R
16.	Karate Wall 5.12c R
17.	Latest Rage 5.12b
17a.	Monster Rage 5.12d R
18.	Watts Tots 5.12b
18a.	Mega Watts 5.13b TR
19.	Fresh Squeezed 5.11a
19a.	Kilo Watts 5.12b
20.	Trivial Pursuit 5.10d R

19a. Kilo Watts (5.12b) ★★★ 6 bolts.

The face left of *Watts Tots* saw a toprope ascent more than two decades ago. You can now lead the original line, clipping the bolts on *Fresh Squeezed* to the left, with a crux veering up and right after the last bolt.

20. Trivial Pursuit (5.10d R) ★ 4 bolts.

Lost amid the better routes, this insignificant arête attracts little attention. A short but strenuous crux on the left side of the edge gives way to long runouts on easy knobs.

21. Tator Tots (5.10a R) ★ Bolts. Long before ascents of the Dihedrals' better known face climbs, *Tator Tots* struck a bold line up an obvious buttress. Bolts safely protect the crux on the left edge of the column, but you'll scrape your face off if you fall on the low-angle knobby finish. **Pitch 1:** (5.10a) 4 bolts. Begin far to the right and foot-shuffle to the main column. Finesse knobs past a bulge and follow spooky nubs to a small belay ledge. **Pitch 2:** (5.6) 3 bolts. An easy bolted slab leads to the top.

22. Latin Lover (5.12a) ★★★ 6 bolts. If you like climbing on tiny edges and pebbles, you'll enjoy this vertical face. If you prefer overhanging jugs, you'll probably hate it. The moves are harder than they once were as some key knobs aren't there anymore.

23. Peepshow (5.12b) ★★ 14 bolts. The continuation of *Latin Lover* climbs the leaning, shadowy wall to anchors just below the top of the crag. Despite solid rock, the position never matches the better Dihedrals'

The Dihedrals—Right Center

20.	Trivial Pursuit 5.10d R	
21.	Tator Tots 5.10a R	
22.	Latin Lover 5.12a	
23.	Peepshow 5.12b	
24.	Upper Ceiling 5.7 R	
24a.	Skag Variation 5.8	
25.	Lester Tots 5.10b R	
26.	Almost Nothing 5.11d R	
27.	Take A Powder 5.12a	
28.	Powder in the Eyes 5.12c	
29.	Little Miss Sunshine 5.14a	
30.	Sunshine Dihedral 5.12a	

routes. The tedious climbing keeps going long after you wish it was over. Bring two ropes to get down.

24. Upper Ceiling (5.7 R) ★ Gear to 3 inches. This unpleasant chimney is a natural chute for the scree slope above the

Dihedrals. Before the arrival of easy bolt routes, it attracted hoards of beginning climbers. Today the native pigeons can once again nest in peace. **Pitch 1:** (5.7) Jam and chimney to a belay anchor. **Pitch 2:** (5.7) Climb to the roof and squeeze through a claustrophobic slot.

24a. Skag Variation (5.8) ★ Gear to 4 inches. A disappointing variant minimizes the amount of time in the line of fire, though it's still not worth doing. **Pitch 1:** (5.8) Jam a fist crack on the right wall of *Upper Ceiling* and traverse along a dirty ramp to the anchor. **Pitch 2:** (5.7) Scramble to the roof and avoid the squeeze chimney by jamming a mediocre crack to the left.

25. Lester Tots (5.10b R) ★ Gear to 1.5 inches. A forgettable, shallow dihedral graces the left wall of the *Upper Ceiling* chimney. The aesthetics aren't stellar— mediocre rock and shaky protection keep all but the foolish away.

26. Almost Nothing (5.11d R) ★★ 5 bolts. Despite no glaring flaws and a convenient location, the flat face left of *Upper Ceiling* receives little attention. The bolts are a little too far apart and the rock too gritty to earn a place on many to-do lists. Nonetheless, the hardest moves are safely protected, and the quality will only improve.

27. Take A Powder (5.12a) ★★★ 8 bolts. As a popular warm-up for the harder routes, this varied climb sees many ascents. A strenuous starting flake gives way to a moderate midsection. The crux comes high on the wall, pulling on tiny edges while standing on nothing substantial.

28. Powder in the Eyes (5.12c) ★★★ 9 bolts. Multiple cruxes on great rock highlight this baffling shallow arête. The insecure pinches aren't great, but they're better than the lousy smears passing for footholds. Start with *Take A Powder,* but step left at the roof.

29. Little Miss Sunshine (5.14a) ★★★ 11 bolts. Smith's most technically demanding route ascends the blank wall right of *Sunshine Dihedral.* It's not nearly as sustained as its more famous neighbor to the left, but a midsection crux devoid of positive holds is far more baffling than anything on *To Bolt.* Originally prepared in 1989, it resisted all attempts until the first free ascent in 2009.

30. Sunshine Dihedral (5.12a) ★★★★ Mixed to 1 inch. Among Smith's finest natural lines, this traditional dihedral was the first 5.12 in the park. Sticky rubber lowered the grade a notch, but a broken flake on the left wall recently restored the original grade. Expect good protection and sustained, thought-provoking climbing. **Pitch 1:** (5.12a) Stem and jam to a hanging belay above all difficulties. Rap with a 70-meter rope or . . . **Pitch 2:** (5.10a) Face climb past a bolt at the roof and follow an easy crack to the top.

31. French Connection (5.13b) ★★★★ Mixed to 1 inch. The original line on the left wall of *Sunshine* ascended the "easy" half of *To Bolt or Not to Be.* The climbing takes in the best of both worlds—a classic traditional dihedral followed by a challenging sport-bolted wall. The hardest moves finesse tricky crimps above the first bolt (the ninth on *To Bolt*), though the real difficulties come from linking the entire upper wall. Lower off with a 70-meter rope.

32. To Bolt or Not to Be (5.14a) ★★★★ 14 bolts. The impossibly blank-looking left wall of *Sunshine* contains one of the world's most historic sport climbs. While other routes slipped a notch, America's first 5.14 still holds its original grade. More than two

The Dihedrals–Left Center

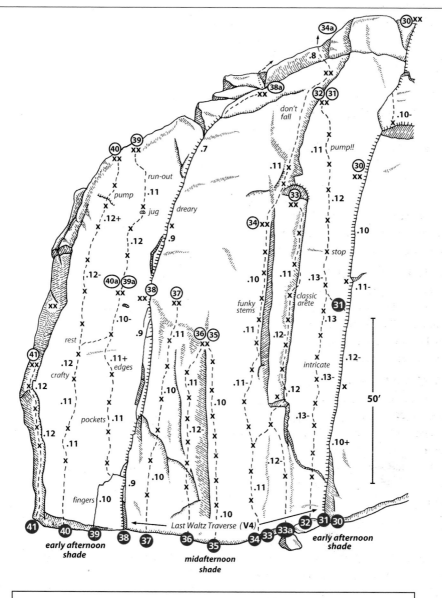

30.	Sunshine Dihedral 5.12a	37.	Middle Aged Vandal 5.11c
31.	French Connection 5.13b	38.	Moonshine Dihedral 5.9
32.	To Bolt or Not to Be 5.14a	38a.	Moonshine Dihedral finish 5.9 R
33.	Last Waltz 5.12c	39.	Heinous Cling 5.12c R
33a.	Last Waltz Direct 5.12c R	39a.	Heinous Cling start 5.12a
34.	Moondance 5.11c	40.	Darkness at Noon 5.13a
34a.	Moondance finish 5.11c R	40a.	Darkness at Noon start 5.12c
35.	Wedding Day 5.10b	41.	Chain Reaction 5.12c
36.	The Flat Earth 5.12a		

Ian Caldwell on *To Bolt or Not to Be.*

decades after the 1986 first ascent, the rare repeats still make news. The climbing is unusual for a hard route—an unrelenting, complex series of crimps, side pulls, and underclings on a wall that doesn't overhang. Success requires excellent technical skills, endurance, and patience—you can fall off almost anywhere. Use a 70-meter rope.

33. Last Waltz (5.12c) ★★★★ 11 bolts. The center of the three classic Dihedrals' arêtes provides the most varied climbing experience. A few crafty edges lead to a tricky sequence skirting the right side of a roof. The best moves weave back and forth on either side of the attractive edge above.

33a. Last Waltz Direct (5.12c R) ★★★ 9 bolts. A high-quality direct start would be the normal approach if it weren't so freakin' scary. Fall near the second bolt and you'll be on the ground. The start itself is only 5.12a—the overall crux comes higher on the original route.

34. Moondance (5.11c) ★★★ 11 bolts. This diverse sport route saw few attempts when five bolts and tiny nuts protected the entire line. Today, with the benefit of a benevolent retro-bolting, it sees many ascents. Don't expect a straightforward line of edges—you'll need to wear your thinking cap on the perplexing dihedral.

34a. Moondance finish (5.11c R) ★ 3 bolts. No one ever climbs the serious summit pitch. Pull over the bolted bulge on suspect rock and run it out to the top.

35. Wedding Day (5.10b) ★★★ 7 bolts. Popular and challenging for the grade, this arête stops many attempts in the first 10 feet. The finishing edges, side pulls, and pinches aren't much easier.

36. The Flat Earth (5.12a) ★ 6 bolts. Just left of the *Wedding Day* arête lurks an uninviting face. The quality of this contrived line doesn't match the typical Dihedrals' sport route. Using the edge within reach to the right knocks a couple letters off the grade.

37. Middle Aged Vandal (5.11c) ★★★ 6 bolts. The wall right of *Moonshine Dihedral* features a fun sport climb. Most of the holds are good, but a bulge above the last bolt weeds out anyone lacking fitness. The bolting of the *Vandal* created a minor controversy when a new ranger threatened a vandalism citation.

38. Moonshine Dihedral (5.9) ★★★★ Gear to 2 inches. The best traditional pitch in the Dihedrals is the lower half of this stunning dihedral. Perfect rock, bombproof protection, and memorable moves make *Moonshine* a winner.

38a. Moonshine Dihedral finish (5.9 R) Gear to 2.5 inches. With bad rock, poor protection, and uninspiring climbing, the

3.	Easy Reader 5.6
17.	Latest Rage 5.12b
21.	Tator Tots 5.10a R
27.	Take a Powder 5.12a
33.	Last Waltz 5.12c
37.	Middle Aged Vandal 5.11c
45.	Bookworm 5.7
46.	Bunny Face 5.7
51.	Captain Xenolith 5.10b
53.	Go Dog Go 5.12c.

upper portion of *Moonshine* is the exact opposite of the start. Climbing to the top in a single pitch makes it easier for your belayer to dodge the inevitable stonefall.

39. Heinous Cling (5.12c R) ★★★★ 9 bolts.

The alluring left wall of *Moonshine Dihedral* features parallel sport routes. The striking right line ascends an assortment of edges and pockets. Originally climbed with three bolts and natural gear, it's now fully bolted. There's a bolt nearby at the crux, but a 5.11 run-out at the top keeps away the timid. A 70-meter rope allows a lower to the ground.

39a. Heinous Cling start (5.12a) ★★★ 5

bolts. One of Smith's most popular (and easiest) 5.12s ascends the lower half of *Heinous Cling*. It makes a good choice for climbers breaking into the higher grades, with sus-tained 5.11 pockets capped by a crux reach between good edges.

40. Darkness at Noon (5.13a) ★★★★ 10 bolts.

A few feet left of *Heinous Cling* soars Smith's first 5.13 face route. Excellent rock, technical moves, and a beautiful line make it a classic of the area. Despite a complete rest after the lower section, most climbers plummet with pumped forearms on the steeper upper wall. Those lacking fitness sometimes drop the grade a notch by cheating over to a good shake on the left arête. Use a 70-meter rope to lower to the ground.

40a. Darkness at Noon start (5.12c) ★★★

5 bolts. The lower part of *Darkness* makes a fine technical exercise in its own right. Expect delicate footwork with an insecure crux above the third bolt.

41. Chain Reaction (5.12c) ★★★★ 4 bolts. This classic knife-edge capped by a roof ranks among the most recognizable sport routes in the world. First climbed in 1983, it marked the beginning of the golden age of Smith sport climbing. A short but packed sequence slaps up the arête, finishing with a crowd-pleasing lunge for a jug over the roof. Believe it or not, *Chain* made the cover of *Newsweek* in 1993.

42. Evil Sister (5.13b) ★★ 4 bolts. A less attractive twin lurks in the shadows left of *Chain Reaction*. The technical crux boulders above the second bolt, but the best sequence dynos past the finishing roof. Completely bypassing a stem to the column on the left bumps the grade up a notch.

43. Rattlesnake Chimney (5.6) ★ Gear to 4 inches. Apart from reliving the first ascent of the Dihedrals, there's no good reason to visit this unpleasant chimney left of *Chain Reaction*. It saw frequent ascents in the pre-sport-route days, but no one bothers anymore. **Pitch 1:** (5.6) Grovel up the dirty chimney to a gravel-covered belay slot. **Pitch 2:** (5.3) Exit the right side of the slot and wander unexposed terrain to the top.

43a. Snakebit (5.7 R) ★ Gear to 4 inches. An upper-pitch variant bypasses the unexposed terrain by climbing an easy leaning dihedral on the right. The crux cranks past a poorly protected bulge on the summit ridge.

44. Ancylostoma (5.9) ★★ 3 bolts. A short line of pockets and knobs leads to the top of a column just left of *Rattlesnake Chimney*. With solid rock and delicate moves, it ends a little too soon. Either lower off or finish via *Bookworm*'s second pitch.

45. Bookworm (5.7) ★★★ Mixed to 3.5 inches. This varied route mixes traditional and sport climbing in a two-pitch line to the top of the cliff. The originally run-out second pitch is now fully bolted, merging with the final pitch of *Bunny Face*. Climbers often forego the first belay and climb in a single pitch. **Pitch 1:** (5.7) After a tricky start, fight up a wide crack to a small ledge. **Pitch 2:** (5.6) 8 bolts. Waltz up wonderful knobs and climb a low-angle slab to the top.

45a. Bookworm Variation (5.7) ★★ Mixed to 3 inches. The original line stepped left about 30 feet up the second pitch, finishing with a solid right-facing corner.

46. Bunny Face (5.7) ★★★ 6 bolts. This delightful, footwork-oriented slab is one of the most popular routes in the park. Expect knobs, pockets, and smears on solid rock, protected by glue-in bolts spaced just far enough apart to make you pay attention. For years a single bolt protected the entire pitch, and loose rock at the top added to the danger. Only after a merciful retro-bolting did the crowds arrive.

46a. Bunny Face finish (5.6) ★★ 4 bolts. The upper pitch of *Bunny Face* receives far less attention, but it's worth doing. From the ledge atop the first pitch, traverse right onto a low-angle bolted slab.

47. Methuselah's Column (5.10a R) ★ 4 bolts. The first bolted route in the Dihedrals ascended a crumbly wall above the *Bunny Face* anchors. Established on lead with quarter-inch bolts in 1973, it remains a serious venture despite modern bolts. After an unnerving start, a much better finish pulls around a solid bulge. Approach via *Bunny Face, Rabbit Stew,* or *Lycopodophyta*.

48. Rabbit Stew (5.7) ★★ Gear to 2 inches. A thin crack borders the left edge of the *Bunny Face* column. The worthwhile jams protect easily, though most climbers prefer the security of a toprope.

The Dihedrals—Left Side

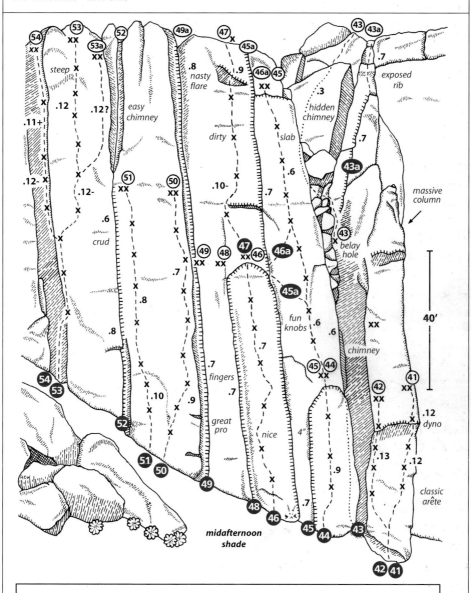

41.	Chain Reaction 5.12c	47.	Methuselah's Column 5.10a R
42.	Evil Sister 5.13b	48.	Rabbit Stew 5.7
43.	Rattlesnake Chimney 5.6	49.	Lycopodophyta 5.7
43a.	Snakebit 5.7 R	49a.	Lycopodophyta finish 5.8
44.	Ancylostoma 5.9	50.	Helium Woman 5.9
45.	Bookworm 5.7	51.	Captain Xenolith 5.10b
45a.	Bookworm Variation 5.7	52.	Deteriorata 5.8
46.	Bunny Face 5.7	53.	Go Dog Go 5.12c
46a.	Bunny Face finish 5.6	53a.	Project 5.12?
		54.	Vision 5.12b

49. Lycopodophyta (5.7) ★★ Gear to 1.5 inches. A full-length crack capped by an overhanging flare splits the cliff left of *Bunny Face*. The first pitch provides a fine introduction to traditional climbing, with good protection and solid rock.

49a. Lycopodophyta finish (5.8) ★ Gear to 3 inches. Unless you're a botanist, avoid the upper-pitch chimney. The odd name comes from a species of moss that once grew high on the route. Avoid a mid-route belay and climb in a single pitch from the ground.

50. Helium Woman (5.9) ★★★ 8 bolts. On the far left side of the Dihedrals looms a mediocre-looking buttress with parallel sport routes. The right line had little going for it in the early days, but now it's solid and well protected with a crux right off the deck.

51. Captain Xenolith (5.10b) ★★ 7 bolts. Much like its neighbor to the right, this knobby face slowly evolved into a worthwhile route as countless ascents scrubbed the junk away. After a few thin moves, the climbing eases quickly above the second bolt.

52. Deteriorata (5.8) ★ Gear to 2.5 inches. Take a hint from the name and avoid this junky dihedral. The moves past the crux roof are worthwhile, but the rock turns to crap near the top.

53. Go Dog Go (5.12c) ★★★ 9 bolts. This cool route combines thin edges and thuggish jugs. The technical crux hits low, but the best moves are on the steep finishing wall. After a memorable throw off a two-finger pocket to a jug, pumping holds lead to an anchor. If you haven't read the book, you're missing out on a real treat.

53a. Project (5.12?) The arête right of the upper part of *Go Dog Go* has seen a toprope reconnaissance from a new anchor right of the original route. It might someday sport a line of bolts.

54. Vision (5.12b) ★★★ 7 bolts. The left arête of the Dihedrals became more popular after a new bolt eliminated an intimidating run-out. With a great position and a fun finish on big jugs, it deserves the increased attention.

Fresh from his repeat of To Bolt or Not to Be, *Scott Franklin arrived in early 1988 intent on freeing the amazing wall left of* Rude Boys. *In the middle of the route was a big flake attached to the wall, with a circus move spanning a 4-foot blank section to a huge jug. To me, this seemed like the saving grace—a heel hook on the jug allowed a good recovery before the hard finish. To Scott, this was a disaster. Nothing but 5.14 would do, so this jug had to go—and the whole flake along with it. I thought he was kidding, but the next day he tried to blow it off with an M-80 that he carried in his pack for just such an occasion. The explosion reverberated through the park, but the flake didn't budge. Since the Terrebonne True Value hardware store was fresh out of dynamite, he had to find another solution. He eventually spent the better part of a day beating it to pieces with a hammer. That's how* Scarface (5.14a) *got its name. Even today you can still see gunpowder marks at the base of the scar.*

Dominating the skyline left of the Dihedrals are the five spires of the Christian Brothers—the Priest, Monk, Friar, Pope, and Abbot. The summits themselves are of little interest to most climbers—the upper reaches of the formation deteriorate into junky rock. But the east wall is a climber's paradise. For top-level athletes, the Prophet Wall offers many hard routes on some of Smith's finest stone. The midsection of the cliff contains attractive cracks for the traditional climber, while the one-pitch sport climbs scattered along the base please just about everyone.

The east side of the Christian Brothers played a major role in the development of Smith climbing. The summits themselves fell to five different parties in 1964—even for the era these ascents weren't major achievements. The first ascent of the east wall came a couple years later when Bob Bauman and Ken Jern pioneered *Gothic Cathedral*. It wasn't until the 1970s that climbers began pushing the level toward the standards of the day at Smith. Tom Rogers's first ascent of *Last Gasp* (5.9) in 1972 and Dean Fry's free ascent of *New Testament* (5.10a) the following year were two of Smith's better ascents of the era. Tim Carpenter's rappel-bolted *Revelations* (5.9) in 1975 wasn't highly respected at the time, but it marked the first hint of rebellion against prevailing ground-up ethics. Two years later Jeff Thomas freed *Shoes of the Fisherman* (5.11b)—the hardest route in the park at the time. His 1978 free ascent of *Wartley's Revenge* (5.11a) further inspired the younger generation and marked the apex of his reign as the most influential Smith climber of the decade.

Thomas's Christian Brothers' routes were quickly eclipsed by far harder lines throughout the park, but the 1984 free ascent of *Double Stain* (5.13a) again brought the crag to the forefront of Smith climbing. While this overhanging wall of pin scars was Smith's first 5.13, the first ascent of *Boy Prophet* (5.12b)

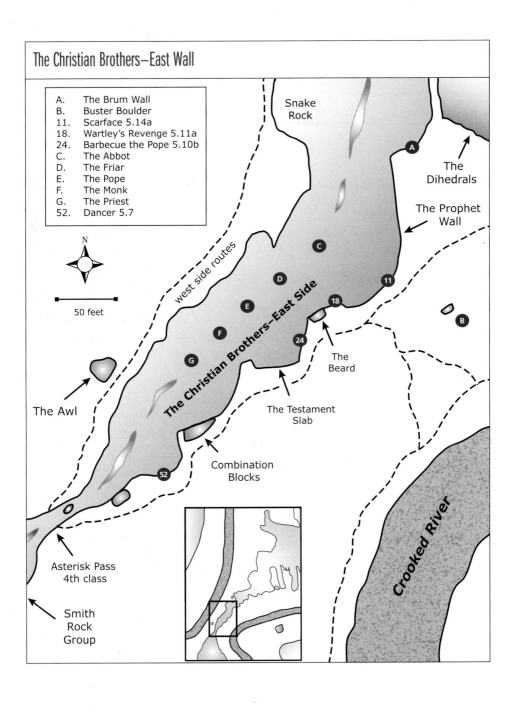

The Christian Brothers—East Wall

A.   The Brum Wall
B.   Buster Boulder
11. Scarface 5.14a
18. Wartley's Revenge 5.11a
24. Barbecue the Pope 5.10b
C.   The Abbot
D.   The Friar
E.   The Pope
F.   The Monk
G.   The Priest
52. Dancer 5.7

N

50 feet

Snake
Rock

west side routes

The Christian Brothers—East Side

The
Dihedrals

The Prophet
Wall

The Beard

The Awl

The Testament
Slab

Combination
Blocks

Asterisk Pass
4th class

Smith
Rock
Group

Crooked River

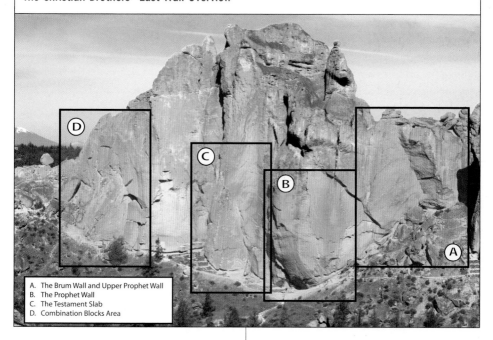

The Christian Brothers—East Wall Overview

A. The Brum Wall and Upper Prophet Wall
B. The Prophet Wall
C. The Testament Slab
D. Combination Blocks Area

a few weeks earlier had a far greater impact on local climbing. Skin-shredding tip cracks with skimpy wires for protection wouldn't bring hoards of climbers to Smith. But the obvious potential of the Prophet Wall would. Routes such as *Dreamin'* (5.12a), *Choke on This* (5.13a), and *Rude Boys* (5.13b) expanded the appeal of the wall, but Scott Franklin's ascent of *Scarface* (5.14a) brought worldwide acclaim. During the past decade climbers realized much of the potential of the Christian Brothers with high-quality new routes—many in the moderate grades. Easily the best effort of the last fifteen years was Scott Milton's ascent of *Chemical Ali* (5.14a) in 2003.

Unlike the nearby Dihedrals, the blank upper walls of the Christian Brothers still hold potential for high-level routes. Since hiking up the backside of the formation isn't an option, climbers looking for new routes usually go elsewhere. This will change in the future. Someday in the twenty-first century, the routes

of the Christian Brothers might again stand atop the climbing world. A fully equipped route left of *Scarface* could conceivably go free somewhere in the 5.15 grade. Eventually it will catch the eye of some mutant teenager.

Early Smith climbers referred to the Christian Brothers, the Awl, Snake Rock, Angel Flight Crags, the Dihedrals, and the Four Horsemen collectively as the Isthmus Group. Here a narrow strip of land only an eighth-mile wide separates the winding Crooked River. As the individual cliffs took on their own identities during the 1970s, the Isthmus Group name faded into history.

The entire east wall of the Christian Brothers catches the first morning sun. The crag goes into the shade by the middle of the day, making it a prime afternoon destination. But the base routes are so popular that many climbers trade the discomfort of climbing in the hot sun for the luxury of shorter waiting times. During winter, with the sun low on the southern horizon, the east wall rarely warms enough for comfortable climbing.

Finding the crags: From the parking lot, enter the canyon and turn left after crossing the bridge. Hike downstream around Shiprock and continue beyond the Dihedrals to a staircased trail leading to the base of the crag. **Descent:** Very few east wall routes top out. Those that do intercept the *Christian Brothers Traverse* (see chapter 7). Continue the traverse moving north, eventually scrambling along an exposed fourth-class ridge to the *Cinnamon Slab* rappel anchor.

THE BRUM WALL

High atop the hillside sits a steep face separating the Dihedrals from the Christian Brothers. The rock quality isn't the best, but the heavily cleaned wall sports the hardest route on the east wall.

1. Deep Splash (5.11d) ★★ 7 bolts. The only "easy" route starts just left of a deep chimney. The hardest moves crank greasy edges above the second bolt, though the pumping finish still burns plenty of energy.

2. La Shootist (5.12d) ★★ 9 bolts. This severely overhanging wall provides a better stamina test than most Smith 5.12s. Begin with a severe boulder problem at the first bolt and climb up and right to a brief shake at jugs on an arête. A physical second crux cuts left to a pumping finish.

3. Chemical Ali (5.14a) ★★★ 10 bolts. The first ascent of this long-standing project moved the Christian Brothers back near the top of Smith's standards. Share the same start as *La Shootist* before veering left on an unrelenting wall packed with desperate moves. After a brutal crux high on the wall, the difficulties ease but the pump only gets worse.

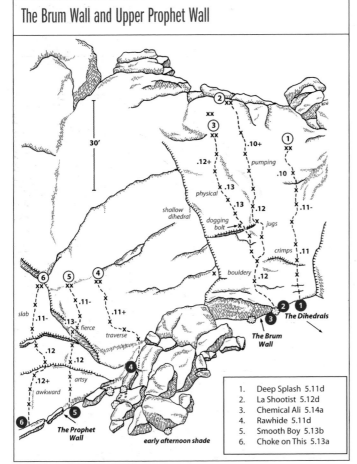

The Brum Wall and Upper Prophet Wall

1. Deep Splash 5.11d
2. La Shootist 5.12d
3. Chemical Ali 5.14a
4. Rawhide 5.11d
5. Smooth Boy 5.13b
6. Choke on This 5.13a

THE PROPHET WALL AREA

A beautiful flat face dominates the northeast side of the Christian Brothers. The Prophet Wall features many difficult routes on perfect rock, starting uphill and continuing down and left along the base of the crag.

4. Rawhide (5.11d) ★★★ 4 bolts. This pumping traverse is fun, with good clings and small edges for the feet. Timid climbers often stick-clip the first bolt.

5. Smooth Boy (5.13b) ★★★ 8 bolts. A prominent diagonal roof slashes along the upper section of the Prophet Wall. The crux of this unique route pulls over the lower right side of the roof using a powerful two-finger pocket. Anticipate nothing straightforward—the moves are insecure and funky from start to finish.

6. Choke on This (5.13a) ★★★ 7 bolts. Another perplexing route starts downhill from *Smooth Boy* and ends at anchors below the diagonal roof. The bizarre crux comes at the start, followed by strenuous underclings; the level eases, but climbers sometimes choke on the finishing slab.

7. Dreamin' (5.12a R) ★★★★ 9 bolts. The starting moves are the hardest on this classic face, but you're dreamin' if you expect a routine finish. Spaced bolts protect the 5.11 slab—long plunges from below the roof are a common occurrence. The roof itself succumbs to a committing blind reach to good

The Christian Brothers–Northeast Face

The Brum Wall

The Testament Slab

The Beard

The Prophet Wall

Buster Boulder

3.	Chemical Ali 5.14a
4.	Rawhide 5.11d
5.	Smooth Boy 5.13b
7.	Dreamin' 5.12a R
9.	Rude Boys 5.13b
11.	Scarface 5.14a
14.	Mystery Aid Seam A5 X
18.	Wartley's Revenge 5.11a
19.	The Right Side of the Beard 5.7
22.	The Clam 5.11d
24.	Barbecue the Pope 5.10b
25.	New Testament 5.10a
26.	Revelations 5.9

holds. Clipping the bolt below the roof with a long sling eliminates oppressive rope drag on the final moves.

8. Boy Prophet (5.12b R) ★★★★ 6 bolts. The original route on the Prophet Wall starts with a devious traverse before launching onto a beautifully solid, run-out face. It makes a good choice for aspiring *Rude Boys* climbers since it shares the same endurance finish. The flawless 5.11 slab both satisfies and terrifies at the same time—bring a 0.75-inch cam or wire if the final piece isn't fixed.

9. Rude Boys (5.13b) ★★★★ 8 bolts. A classic Smith Rock testpiece tacks a direct start onto *Boy Prophet*. The hardest move cranks past the first bolt, but most climbers flame out on a powerful sequence getting to the fourth. The final slab eases considerably, but the building pump makes unfit climbers suffer.

10. Rude Femmes (5.13c) ★★★ 11 bolts. A much more challenging finish to *Rude Boys* steps left after the fourth bolt to a seemingly endless 5.12 slab. Hard enough to keep away the masses, but not hard enough to attract

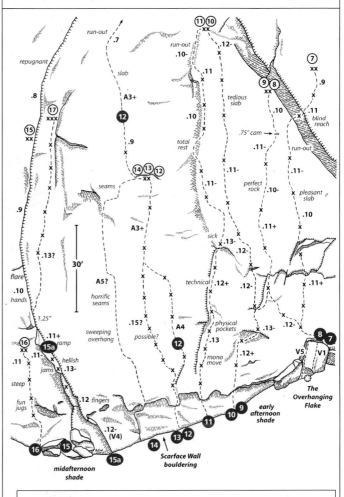

The Prophet Wall

7.	Dreamin' 5.12a R	13.	Project 5.15+?
8.	Boy Prophet 5.12b R	14.	Mystery Aid Seam A5 X
9.	Rude Boys 5.13b	15.	Shoes of the Fisherman 5.11b
10.	Rude Femmes 5.13c	15a.	Project–Toes of the Fisherman 5.13?
11.	Scarface 5.14a	16.	Heresy 5.11c
12.	Air to Spare 5.9 A4 X	17.	Project 5.13?

elite climbers, the entire route sees very few ascents. Guard against impossible rope drag by clipping the third bolt with a long sling. Use a 70-meter rope.

11. Scarface (5.14a) ★★★★ 13 bolts. This sweeping overhang is one of Smith's most impressive lines. The most powerful moves come low, including a crank off a famous one-finger pocket. After a funky midsection the overall crux comes when you're pumped silly, pulling onto the final slab. The finishing slab/arête is relatively easy (5.11a) but nerve-wracking—no one wants to be the first to fall on the dash to the anchors. Lower off with a 70-meter rope.

The eye-catching, rounded overhang left of *Scarface* seems devoid of any climbable features. Two aid routes and a free project are the only lines to date. Beyond the sweeping face are two of the most famous cracks from the early days of Smith free climbing—*Shoes of the Fisherman* and *Wartley's Revenge*.

12. Air to Spare (5.9 A4 X) ★★ Aid rack to 0.75 inch. This fearsome aid line seems out of place surrounded by severe sport climbs. A bolted project largely destroyed this former A5 route, turning a crux knifeblade seam into a bolt ladder. The entire route sees very few (if any) repeats. **Pitch 1:** (A4) Nail incipient seams past hangerless studs, moving left to a reassuring bolt line. **Pitch 2:** (5.9 A3+) Tough aid gives way to progressively easier free climbing. At a dirty ledge, walk left into the Hobbit Hole between the Abbot and Friar.

13. Project (5.15+?) 10 bolts. The fully equipped sport route left of *Scarface* will someday go free, though it'll be far above today's standards. The climber destined to do the first ascent might not be born yet.

14. Mystery Aid Seam (A5 X) ★ Aid rack to 0.25 inch. A mysterious route nails faint seams on the most overhanging section of the wall. Pin scars run almost the entire length of the face, with no bolts or back-off sling in sight. It's either a hoax or the most serious aid route at Smith.

15. Shoes of the Fisherman (5.11b) ★★★
Gear to 3 inches. An ominous crack splits the overhanging wall downhill from *Scarface*. *Shoes* was the hardest route at Smith when first freed in 1977. Awkward and unusually physical for the grade, the crux battles onto a small ledge low on the route; after a good shake, a pumping 1.25-inch crack leads to bomber hand jams in a flaring slot. Rappel with a 70-meter line—don't even think about continuing to the top via a disgusting 5.8 crack. .75 - 3 only (x3?)

15a. Project–Toes of the Fisherman
(5.13?) Mixed to 3 inches. This finger crack/undercling is one of Smith's most peculiar routes. The moves went free long ago, but the contorted climbing discourages redpoint burns. The crux torques a one-finger jam while squeezing the lip of the roof with your thighs. Aspiring climbers should buy a Thigh-Master® immediately.

16. Heresy (5.11c) ★★ 4 bolts. This fun route muscles good holds directly beneath *Shoes of the Fisherman*. Although extremely short it packs a punch with a bouldering crux at the end. You'll need a 12-meter rope to lower down.

17. Project (5.13?) A potential continuation of *Heresy* cuts over *Shoes of the Fisherman*, ascending the overhanging wall to the right.

18. Wartley's Revenge (5.11a) ★★★★ Gear to 2.5 inches. Smith's finest traditional 5.11 follows a striking crack with a prominent diagonal roof flake. After a stemming start, wonderful jams and jugs lead to a strenuous move reaching a ledge. Freed in 1978 it was Smith's most sought after testpiece for many years. #2 at top

18a. Wartley's Revenge finish (5.10a)
★★ Gear to 2.5 inches. The upper pitches receive no attention, but they provide a fine adventure despite a few loose holds. The second pitch involves 5.10a crack/face

The Testament Slab

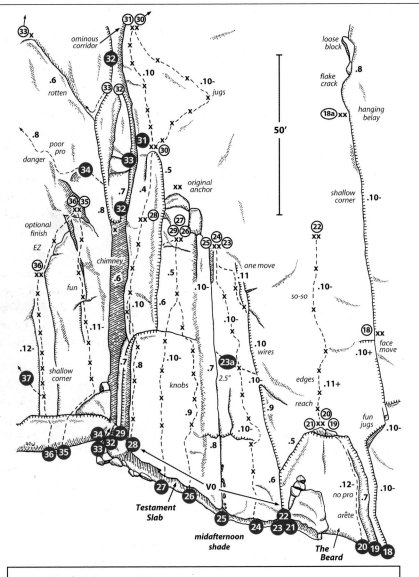

18.	Wartley's Revenge 5.11a	27.	Irreverance 5.10a
18a.	Wartley's Revenge finish 5.10a	28.	Nightingales on Vacation 5.10b
19.	The Right Side of the Beard 5.7	29.	Old Testament 5.7
20.	Risk Shy 5.12a R	30.	Heathen's Highway 5.10a
21.	The Left Side of the Beard 5.6	31.	Via Dolorosa 5.10c
22.	The Clam 5.11d	32.	Gothic Cathedral 5.8 R
23.	Golgotha 5.11b R	33.	Last Gasp 5.9 R
23a.	Temptation 5.10a	34.	Island in the Sky 5.8 X
24.	Barbecue the Pope 5.10b	35.	Blasphemy 5.11a
25.	New Testament 5.10a	36.	Panic Attack 5.12a
26.	Revelations 5.9	37.	Project 5.13?

moves ending at a hanging belay. The 5.8 final pitch jams and liebacks a flake crack, stemming cautiously around a loose block. Cut right to an anchor and scramble into the Hobbit Hole, descending via *Cinnamon Slab*.

The Beard

An unimpressive angular block rests along the base of the wall left of *Wartley's Revenge*. Easy routes ascend cracks up either side to an anchor.

19. The Right Side of the Beard (5.7) ★★ Gear to 2 inches. Deceptively tricky jams highlight this short crack. Beginners frequently arrange a toprope, though it takes excellent protection.

20. Risk Shy (5.12a R) ★★ Solo. The dinky right arête of the Beard offers soloists a few demanding moves. It's a little too long for safe bouldering and too short to bolt.

21. The Left Side of the Beard (5.6) ★★★ Gear to 2.5 inches. A short flurry of hand/ finger jams provide a good introduction to traditional climbing. The hardest moves come right off the ground.

22. The Clam (5.11d) ★★ 6 bolts. The vertical face above the Beard offers a neglected route that keeps getting better and harder as edges snap off. Shorter climbers face a tough stretch reaching the starting holds. The difficulties ease after the first 20 feet, but the crumbly upper wall still requires attention.

THE TESTAMENT SLAB AREA

Just left of the Beard rises an appealing buttress, split by a prominent crack. The wonderful moderate routes attract throngs of climbers on any busy weekend.

23. Golgotha (5.11b R) ★★★ Mixed to 1 inch. A prominent left-leaning seam marks the right border of the Testament Slab. The lower crack protects adequately with nuts, though it makes a poor choice for anyone lacking gear-placement skills. Bolts protect the crux—a bizarre combo of side pulls, crimps, and stems in a mini-corner.

23a. Temptation (5.10a) ★★ Mixed to 1.5 inches. The original route started up *Golgotha* and shuffled left past a bolt, joining *New Testament* below the flare. Without long slings at the start and end of the traverse, rope drag makes it almost impossible to move.

24. Barbecue the Pope (5.10b) ★★★ 7 bolts. This popular slab of edges and knobs humbles many 5.10 climbers. The hardest moves detour around a blank section above the second bolt, though the climbing stays technical to the anchor. Consider stick-clipping the first bolt if the start seems spooky.

25. New Testament (5.10a) ★★★ Gear to 2.5 inches. When first freed in 1973, this attractive hand/finger crack was one of Smith's hardest lines. After a long stretch of pleasantly moderate jams, a deceptively tricky groove near the top routinely spits off anyone celebrating success too soon.

26. Revelations (5.9) ★★★ 6 bolts. This rounded arête was one of Smith's first bolted face climbs. Climbers originally avoided the crumbling edge by staying left, but today it's completely solid. There's a good wire slot on the run-out to the first bolt. Expect a crowd on a busy weekend.

27. Irreverence (5.10a) ★★★ 5 bolts. Delicate knobs and pockets highlight the wall immediately left of *Revelations*. With an ankle-breaking terrace at the base, the first bolt is too far off the deck for anyone questioning their ability.

28. Nightingales on Vacation (5.10b) ★★ 7 bolts. A deceptively tricky crux interrupts easy climbing on this trip up the left arête of the Testament Slab. Despite decent rock, it doesn't match the quality of nearby sport routes.

29. Old Testament (5.7) ★★ Gear to 3 inches. The easiest route on the Testament Slab receives little attention, but it's still worth doing. After crawling right along an awkward ledge, either finish with a pleasant romp up easy knobs or continue in the crack to the anchors atop *Revelations*.

30. Heathen's Highway (5.10a) ★★ Mixed to 3 inches. This multi-pitch adventure ascends to the top of the Friar. The few climbers who try usually lower off after the zigzagging second pitch, though the entire route provides a memorable escape from the bustle below. **Pitch 1:** Climb *Revelations, Irreverence,* or *Nightingales on Vacation* and continue to an anchor at the base of the vertical headwall. **Pitch 2:** (5.10a) 6 bolts. Exciting jugs zig far right and zag back left to a hanging belay. **Pitch 3:** (5.9) Face traverse right to a crack and climb to the gap between the Friar and the Pope. **Pitch 4:** (5.6) Easy climbing on bad rock ends on the summit of the Friar. To descend, rappel north into the Hobbit Hole and make a fourth-class scramble to the *Cinnamon Slab* rappel.

31. Via Dolorosa (5.10c) ★★ 5 bolts. This direct line climbs pockets and edges on the arête left of the second pitch of *Heathen's Highway*. Unfortunately, the rock quality doesn't match the exhilarating position. The most direct approach follows *Nightingales on Vacation* to an anchor below the headwall. With a 70-meter rope you can climb in a single pitch from the ground and lower off.

31a. Project (5.11?) No topo. The steep arête above *Via Dolorosa* will someday feature a spectacular sport route.

A deep chimney marks the left boundary of the Testament Slab. Beyond stretches a blank, undeveloped wall. The following four routes start in the chimney, while two recent sport routes ascend the face just to the left.

32. Gothic Cathedral (5.8 R) Gear to 4 inches. An ominous corridor marked by converging cracks splits the entire east face of the Christian Brothers. Dangerous climbing on poor rock makes it an unusually bad choice for anyone—especially the average 5.8 climber. **Pitch 1:** (5.7) Stem a decent chimney past a roof to an anchor. **Pitch 2:** (5.8) Grovel up the wide right-hand crack to the slot between the Monk and the Friar. Some climbers switch to the left crack near the top. Either see the *Christian Brothers Traverse* (see chapter 7) or rappel with two ropes.

33. Last Gasp (5.9 R) ★ Gear to 6 inches. An impressive see-through-to-the-other-side wide crack/chimney splits the upper face of the Priest. Nicknamed the *Crack of Dawn*, this awe-inspiring pitch has scared away generations of climbers. Modern protection makes it a lot less fearsome, but bad rock awaits anyone who tries it. **Pitch 1:** (5.7) Climb the first pitch of *Gothic Cathedral*. **Pitch 2:** (5.6) Traverse left to a belay below the wide crack. **Pitch 3:** (5.9) Thrash up the *Crack of Dawn* into a spectacular chimney. A rotten exit fol-

The Monk

The Pope

The Friar

The Priest

The Abbot

2.	La Shootist 5.12d
11.	Scarface 5.14a
12.	Air to Spare 5.9 A4 X
15.	Shoes of the Fisherman 5.11b
18.	Wartley's Revenge 5.11a
23.	Golgotha 5.11b R
27.	Irreverance 5.10a
30.	Heathen's Highway 5.10a
32.	Gothic Cathedral 5.8 R
33a.	Safety Valve 5.7 R
40.	Overnight Sensation 5.11a
44.	Double Stain 5.13a
53.	Jeté 5.8
54.	That .10d 5.12a
56.	Kathleen Finds an Edge 5.7

The Brum Wall

The Prophet Wall

Combination Blocks

lowed by a quick face move ends on the summit. Rappel the opposite side with two ropes.

33a. Safety Valve (5.7 R) ★ Gear to 3 inches. If you're trying *Last Gasp* and having second thoughts, *Safety Valve* offers a convenient escape. Rather than committing to the *Crack of Dawn*, continue up a mediocre right-facing corner to the notch between the Priest and Friar.

34. Island in the Sky (5.8 X) ★ Gear to 2.5 inches. If properly cleaned and bolted, this airy traverse would be worth doing. Start up the first pitch of *Gothic Cathedral,* stepping left to a poorly protected traverse on knobs and pockets. Rappel with two ropes.

35. Blasphemy (5.11a) ★★★ 7 bolts. Parallel sport routes ascend the mini-buttress left of

a deep chimney. Expect a struggle if you try to muscle the technical right route. After a fun start on jugs, delicate stems, edges, and side pulls lead over a bulge to an easy finish.

36. Panic Attack (5.12a) ★★★ 9 bolts. A sustained shallow corner sits a few feet left of *Blasphemy*. Complex stems with a bolt every 3 feet end at an anchor. An easy optional finish continues up and right to a higher anchor.

37. Project (5.13?) The impressive wall left of the Testament Slab might someday contain several hard routes. Most of the moves go free on a partially bolted line on the right side of the face, though no one seems interested in completing the long-abandoned project.

COMBINATION BLOCKS AREA

Stacked one atop another on the left side of the Christian Brothers are two massive angular blocks. High-quality routes ascend every side of this unique formation.

38. Private Trust (5.11c R) ★★ 2 bolts. This short route ascends the face a few feet right of Combination Blocks. Stick-clipping the first bolt eliminates any danger at the crux, but the delicate finish isn't much fun.

39. Charlie's Chimney (5.6) ★★★ Gear to 5 inches. The right edge of Combination Blocks forms a distinctive knife-edge flake. A classic lieback at the start leads to a tight squeeze through a narrow slot at the top. Huge cams safely protect the start.

40. Overnight Sensation (5.11a) ★★★ 5 bolts. Great rock and technical moves highlight the main face of Combination Blocks. After a hard move getting to a ledge, the crux finesses greasy slopers on the upper block.

41. Tinker Toy (5.9 X) ★★★ Gear to 3 inches. Two routes climb opposite sides of the striking left edge of Combination Blocks. Only the bold lead the sparsely protected right side, though it makes a fine toprope problem.

42. Double Trouble (5.10b) ★★ 7 bolts. A harder but much safer route ascends the left side of the arête. An intimidating sequence on the upper block liebacks past closely spaced bolts to the top.

43. Bowling Alley (5.5) ★★ Gear to 3.5 inches. The easiest line to the top of Combination Blocks thrashes up a squeeze chimney on the backside of the formation. Climb either crack up the obvious corridor on the left side and fling yourself into the claustrophobic finishing slot.

The following two routes start atop Combination Blocks, tackling the streaked wall above. Approach by climbing any of the routes to the top of the block.

44. Double Stain (5.13a) ★★★ Mixed to 1 inch. Smith's first 5.13 ascends a forgotten pin-scarred crack on an overhanging wall. Despite good rock and a quality position, it receives little attention. Gear placement played a big role in the first ascent, though most modern climbers reduce the difficulty by preplacing every nut. The crux finesses tip scars at the start, leading to a good stop in the middle.

45. Bum Rush the Show (5.13b) ★★ 10 bolts. A more popular sport route climbs the imposing face left of *Double Stain*. Technical moves on small crimps and pockets low on the route lead to better holds on the pumping finish. The huge amounts of epoxy holding everything together give it a gym-like feel.

The fully developed buttress immediately left of Combination Blocks is one of the most popular sections of cliff at Smith. There isn't room for a single new line on the buttress itself, though the wall above holds promise.

46. Toys in the Attic (5.9) ★★ Gear to 4 inches. The wide alley on the left side of Combination Blocks culminates in a massive roof. After jamming the steepening crack, hand traverse down and left to an anchor. Don't forget to protect the traverse for the second; it's scarier to follow than lead.

46a. Child's Play (5.10c) ★★ Gear to 2.5 inches. Hidden from view and rarely climbed, this thin crack branches left midway up *Toys in the Attic*. You won't see the diagonal crack until it's staring you in the face.

47. Hesitation Blues (5.10b) ★★★ Mixed

Combination Blocks Area

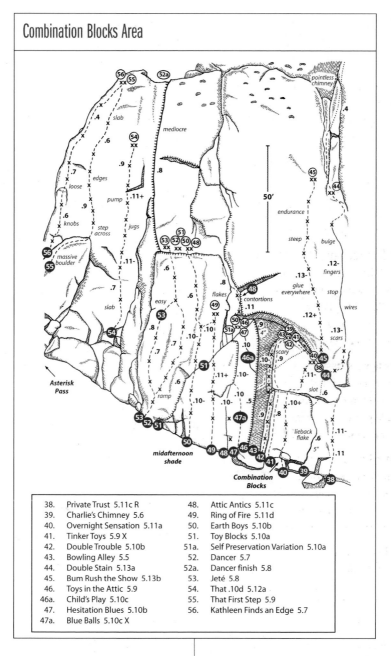

38.	Private Trust 5.11c R	48.	Attic Antics 5.11c
39.	Charlie's Chimney 5.6	49.	Ring of Fire 5.11d
40.	Overnight Sensation 5.11a	50.	Earth Boys 5.10b
41.	Tinker Toys 5.9 X	51.	Toy Blocks 5.10a
42.	Double Trouble 5.10b	51a.	Self Preservation Variation 5.10a
43.	Bowling Alley 5.5	52.	Dancer 5.7
44.	Double Stain 5.13a	52a.	Dancer finish 5.8
45.	Bum Rush the Show 5.13b	53.	Jeté 5.8
46.	Toys in the Attic 5.9	54.	That .10d 5.12a
46a.	Child's Play 5.10c	55.	That First Step 5.9
47.	Hesitation Blues 5.10b	56.	Kathleen Finds an Edge 5.7
47a.	Blue Balls 5.10c X		

to 2 inches. An enjoyable leaning crack ascends the wall left of Combination Blocks. The moves aren't hard, but placing protection expends some energy. The dubious fixed pins are gone, with fresh bolts in their place.

47a. Blue Balls (5.10c X) ★★ Gear to 2 inches. You'll expend no energy placing protection on the direct start since there isn't any. After an unforgiving crux the first placement comes after joining *Hesitation Blues* far off the ground.

48. Attic Antics (5.11c) ★★ Mixed to 2.5 inches. A forgotten finish cranks over the intimidating roof above *Hesitation Blues*. A contorted crux pulling over the lip leads to easier stems and a traverse far left to anchors. Climb in one pitch from the ground.

49. Ring of Fire (5.11d) ★★★ 6 bolts. This popular sport route sees steady traffic on any busy day. Crux crimps with little for the feet stop most attempts. The enjoyable finish cuts across *Toy Blocks* on good holds to a big jug at the anchor.

50. Earth Boys (5.10b) ★★★ 7 bolts. A far less challenging line rises left of *Ring of Fire*. A tricky start gives way to positive holds up the path of least resistance, moving left around the corner after clipping the fifth bolt. Many climbers bypass the exit, veering up and right (5.10c) to the *Ring of Fire* anchor.

51. Toy Blocks (5.10a) ★★ Gear to 2.5 inches. An obvious hand traverse slashes across *Earth Boys* and *Ring of Fire*. The killer blocks disappeared long ago; today the route is relatively safe. The crux comes at the end of the traverse, reaching into locking hand jams with smears for the feet.

51a. Self Preservation Variation (5.10a) ★★★ Gear to 2.5 inches. Instead of pulling into the short hand crack, keep cutting right on good finger jams to the anchors atop *Hesitation Blues*. Good rock and pumping moves go unnoticed as almost no one ever tries it.

52. Dancer (5.7) ★★★ 8 bolts. One of Smith's first rap-bolted routes ascends a wonderful knobby slab. After delicate climbing up the starting ramp, dance up a crux bulge to an easier finish.

52a. Dancer finish (5.8) ★ Gear to 3 inches. An upper pitch sees very few ascents, though it's really not that bad. Climb the left of two uninspiring cracks to the south shoulder of the Priest. Either rappel the route with two ropes or continue via the *Christian Brothers Traverse* (see chapter 7).

53. Jeté (5.8) ★★ 6 bolts. Just a jump left of *Dancer* sits another pleasant knobby face. Once past the difficulties, *Jeté* joins its partner to the right. Confident (and foolish) climbers sometimes stay left on the upper slab, clipping only the final bolt on *Dancer*.

The far left reaches of the Christian Brothers' east side sat ignored until recent development created new interest. Now there are three routes, with potential for at least one more. The easier routes to the left still aren't especially solid. Use care when lowering to avoid raining stones onto climbers at the base of *Dancer*.

54. That .10d (5.12a) ★★★ 8 bolts. With a name guaranteed to confuse generations of climbers, this overhanging wall features great rock and a pumping assortment of cruxes. Begin by scrambling from the left to a belay ledge (bring a 3-inch cam for an optional anchor).

55. That First Step (5.9) ★ 7 bolts. The right of two bolted slabs steps off a big boulder onto a wall of friable edges. You might enjoy yourself if you don't pop off a hold.

56. Kathleen Finds an Edge (5.7) ★ 7 bolts. The south buttress of the Christian Brothers features a lackluster route on substandard rock. Start with good knobs right of an arête and climb past a crumbling ledge to a delicate crux on the slab above. Easy jugs lead far up the buttress to an anchor.

SMITH ROCK GROUP

In 1969 John Haek and I did the first ascent of Snibble Tower's face, spending two nights on the cliff. By today's ultra-gymnastic standards, I suppose this climb is no big deal, but for us at the time it was a great adventure and plenty tough and scary. The first day a 300-pound rock broke loose on the first pitch as I was following, and the only reason I am here to talk about it is because at the last minute, I opted to bring along and wear my motorcycle helmet. The rock glanced off the helmet, knocking me limp and almost unconscious. The second night we were stuck on a ledge only 50 feet or so from the top, and it was so small that only one of us could stoop while the other stood. The icy winds blew up under our jackets, and we were so hypothermic our shiver oscillations were more like spastic fits than shivers. Of course, in true spirit of youth, as soon as we got off the cliff the next morning we thought this was great adventure, even though we could have easily died of hypothermia that night.

Jon Marshall

Especially stunning in the early morning sun, the multicolored cliffs and towering spires of the Smith Rock Group capture the attention of every visitor to the park. Between the east and west sides of the formation, there's more than a mile of cliff line towering as high as 600 feet. Over one hundred routes ranging from 5.1 to 5.13c ascend these crags—sport routes, multi-pitch cracks, adventure routes, good climbs, and bad climbs—you'll find it all here.

You might find it all here, but when it comes to long free routes, the Smith Rock Group literally stands above everything else at Smith. Monkey Face has more classic natural lines, but the longest routes on the Northeast Face of the Smith Rock Group tower more than 200 feet higher. The Monument and Picnic Lunch Wall contend for the title of "Smith's biggest wall," but both monoliths suffer from substandard rock. The Northeast Face isn't flawless, but there are remarkable expanses of bulletproof stone. And nowhere else at Smith does traditional, sport, and big wall climbing blend together so well.

Given the massive amount of rock, the Smith Rock Group is still relatively undeveloped. There are good reasons for this. Grandeur doesn't always translate into high-quality routes—for many years the cliff held more interest for sightseers and bird-watchers than climbers. With only a few exceptions, the early routes on the formation only confirmed suspicions, and climbers looked elsewhere for their adventures. The sheer size of the walls also curtailed activity. These aren't the Dihedrals, where you can hike to the top and rappel to the bottom with a single rope. But hidden among the crumbling walls are large sections of amazing rock. With more development, attitudes are changing about the Smith Rock Group.

The highest spires of the Smith Rock Group surely attracted some of the earliest climbers in the area, though no record exists

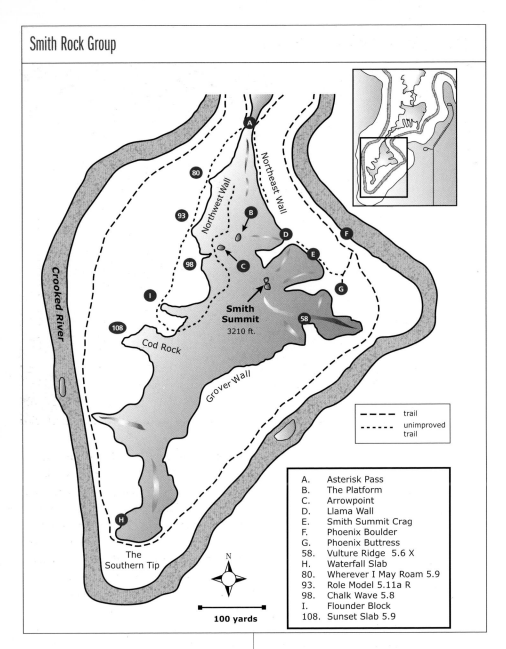

trail
unimproved trail

A.   Asterisk Pass
B.   The Platform
C.   Arrowpoint
D.   Llama Wall
E.   Smith Summit Crag
F.   Phoenix Boulder
G.   Phoenix Buttress
58. Vulture Ridge 5.6 X
H.   Waterfall Slab
80. Wherever I May Roam 5.9
93. Role Model 5.11a R
98. Chalk Wave 5.8
I.   Flounder Block
108. Sunset Slab 5.9

of any ascents prior to 1960. The modern era began in 1968 when Dave Jenson and George Cummings climbed *Sky Ridge* (5.8). Their ascent marked the first time a Smith route saw a top-down preparation, though their original quarter-inch bolts frightened an entire generation. Around the same time the most obvious crack lines on the Northeast Face saw mixed free and aid ascents. The most impressive of these were the multi-pitched adventures of *Snibble Tower* and the bold *Smith Summit–East Wall*. Free climbing standards stayed low—along with several moderate classics like Jeff Thomas's *White Satin* (5.9), the hardest line

Smith Rock Group–Northeast Face Overview

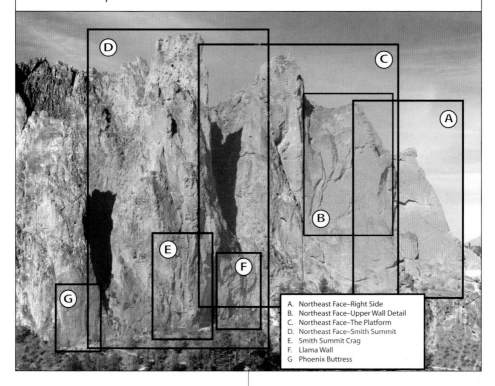

A. Northeast Face–Right Side
B. Northeast Face–Upper Wall Detail
C. Northeast Face–The Platform
D. Northeast Face–Smith Summit
E. Smith Summit Crag
F. Llama Wall
G. Phoenix Buttress

moving into the 1980s was Steve Lyford's 1974 ascent of *Shaft* (5.10b).

This changed quickly over the next several years as climbers pioneered some of the last unclimbed cracks at Smith, including obscure testpieces such as *Tears of Rage* (5.12b) and *Stagefright* (5.12a). These ascents marked the end of an era, just as the new routes in the Dihedrals signaled the beginning of a new one. No longer would gnarled jam cracks be the center of attention. In recent years many single-pitch sport routes on all sides of the formation brought far more climbers to the area. Most of these routes were moderate, with only Brooke Sandahl's *Livin' Large* (5.13a) and Michael Stöger's *100% Beef* (5.13c) cracking the higher grades.

The Smith Rock Group would still be largely unexplored if not for the efforts of Ryan Lawson and Thomas Emde. While everyone else saw nothing but massive work with doubtful returns, Lawson saw opportunity in the virgin walls. After pioneering *Wherever I May Roam* (5.9) on the northwest side, he began exploring the more intimidating northeast wall. The quality of his Smith Summit Crag routes convinced him that the entire cliff held far more potential than anyone else recognized. In 2001 Lawson and Emde climbed a 600-foot route on Smith Summit called *The Struggle Within* (5.11d), but few climbers paid any attention.

The twosome spent days exploring the walls on rappel, searching for lines that linked expanses of brilliant rock while avoiding the inevitable sections of rubble. They employed a style similar to the early years of the Smith sport climbing movement, mixing bolts, traditional gear, and occasional run-outs. Their approach produced results far beyond anyone's expectations. After Emde led routes like *The Good 'Ol Days* (5.11c), *Freedom's Just Another Word For Nothing Left to Lose* (5.12b), and *European Vacation* (5.11a), even the most skeptical Smith locals took notice.

Several routes in the area, especially those near *Sky Ridge,* are sometimes off-limits in the spring and early summer (usually until August 1), as birds of prey nest nearby. The park service posts signs at the parking area, the bridge, and at the base of closed sections of cliff. Regardless of how much you want to climb closed routes, please respect the restrictions—the future of Smith climbing depends upon it.

The east side routes from Asterisk Pass to the Southern Tip are described in order, moving downstream. The only exceptions are the Smith Summit Crag and Llama Wall, which are described moving upstream (the direction of the most common approach). The west-side routes are listed from Asterisk Pass, moving back upstream.

Finding the crags: Approach the Smith Rock Group by turning left at the bridge and walking downstream. Hike uphill to the Christian Brothers for the rightmost Northeast Face routes, and continue over Asterisk Pass for all west-side routes. To approach routes on the center and left portions of the Northeast Face, follow the only graded path branching uphill off the river trail below the Smith Rock Group. This leads directly to the Phoenix Buttress.

ASTERISK PASS

An unmistakable low point on the cliff line separates the Christian Brothers from the Smith Rock Group. This pass provides the easiest access to the west-side routes via an exposed fourth-class scramble down the backside. The descent is simple, but too risky for many beginners and classes. You can always reach any west-side route by hiking the river trail around the Southern Tip.

1. The Asterisk (5.7 R) ★ Solo. No topo. Among Smith's most recognizable features, this bulbous boulder somehow sits atop Asterisk Pass without toppling over. It bears a striking resemblance to Snoopy from the Peanuts comic strip. An exposed move up the back of the head ends on the anchorless summit; the biggest challenge comes from trying to get down.

NORTHEAST FACE

With quality cracks, multi-pitch odysseys, and classic one-pitch sport routes, the ominously beautiful northeast wall is the most outstanding feature of the Smith Rock Group. Since the entire east wall receives first light of day, the best climbing times on warm days are after noon. Most east-side routes make poor choices on winter days—the sun disappears before the rock warms, and icy winds swirl at the base of the wall.

The steep hillside below the Northeast Face is very fragile, and could be destroyed if climbers start cutting up or down the slope. Please approach only by traversing in along the base of the cliff, either from Asterisk Pass (for the first several routes) or from the Phoenix Buttress access trail to the south.

Descent: To hike off routes topping-out, scramble up a third-class gully and continue south around the base of the Platform and Arrowpoint. Eventually a scree chute cuts down the west side to a trail leading back to Asterisk Pass. Don't start down a gully without a clear view of the bottom—several end in steep cliffs. An alternate descent makes three rappels (use a 60-meter rope) down the west side from a fixed station uphill from the top of *Sky Ridge*.

2. Sky Ridge (5.8 R) ★★★ Mixed to 2.5 inches. Two decades before anyone heard of sport climbing, the striking northern arête of the Smith Rock Group saw Smith's first rappel-placed bolts. Despite the great position, it sees relatively few ascents; the bolts are far apart and the moves delicate and frightfully exposed. A rotten start discourages

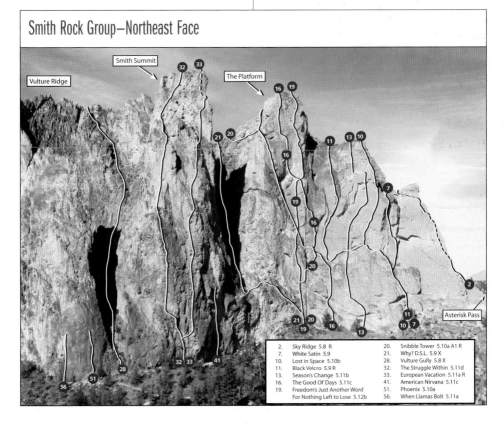

Smith Rock Group—Northeast Face

Vulture Ridge · Smith Summit · The Platform · Asterisk Pass

2.	Sky Ridge 5.8 R	20.	Snibble Tower 5.10a A1 R
7.	White Satin 5.9	21.	Why? D.S.L. 5.9 X
10.	Lost in Space 5.10b	28.	Vulture Gully 5.8 X
11.	Black Velcro 5.9 R	32.	The Struggle Within 5.11d
13.	Season's Change 5.11b	33.	European Vacation 5.11a R
16.	The Good Ol' Days 5.11c	41.	American Nirvana 5.11c
19.	Freedom's Just Another Word	51.	Phoenix 5.10a
	For Nothing Left to Lose 5.12b	56.	When Llamas Bolt 5.11a

Smith Rock Group—Northeast Face—Right Side

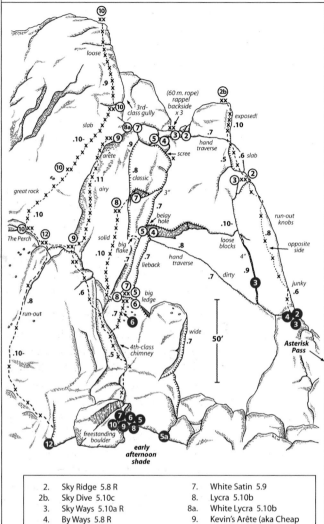

2a. Sky Ridge Variation (5.8 R) ★ Gear to 3 inches. To avoid the best climbing on the first pitch, step right to a junky crack leading directly to a belay higher on the ridge.

2b. Sky Dive (5.10c) ★★★ 6 bolts. The original 1968 finish aided a bolt line on the overhanging summit block. Climb an easy bolted slab above the first-pitch anchor and free a short, knobby bulge with great protection and dizzying exposure.

3. Sky Ways (5.10a R) ★ Gear to 6 inches. An ominous wide crack splits the left wall of *Sky Ridge*. A jumbled section of boulders at a small roof await those foolish enough to try. Finish with either the upper pitch of *Sky Ridge* or *Sky Dive*.

4. By Ways (5.8 R) ★ Gear to 4 inches. An ugly crack slashes across the lower half of *Sky Ridge's* left wall. A mediocre traverse on junky rock ends in a belay hole. Finish with the second pitch of *Sky Chimney*.

5. Sky Chimney (5.7) ★★★ Gear to 3 inches. This attractive crack makes an excellent choice for traditional climbers looking for an easy multi-pitch route. The upper two

2.	Sky Ridge 5.8 R	7.	White Satin 5.9
2b.	Sky Dive 5.10c	8.	Lycra 5.10b
3.	Sky Ways 5.10a R	8a.	White Lycra 5.10b
4.	By Ways 5.8 R	9.	Kevin's Arête (aka Cheap
5.	Sky Chimney 5.7		Polyester) 5.11c
5a.	Sky Chimney Variation 5.7	10.	Lost in Space 5.10b
6.	King Nothing 5.7	12.	Grettir's Saga 5.10a R

some, but the rock improves farther up the edge. Start by scrambling up the ridge on Asterisk Pass to a belay niche. **Pitch 1:** (5.8) Climb entirely on the right wall to a belay on the crest of the ridge. **Pitch 2:** (5.7) Amble up an easy crack on the left to an airy hand traverse below the summit block.

pitches are solid, well protected, and far off the ground. Some climbers avoid the claustrophobic belay hole by combining the second and third pitches into one. Approach by cutting left across the hillside below Asterisk Pass to a distinctive boulder at the base of the wall. **Pitch 1:** (5.5) Bolts protect the entrance into a deep chimney. Scramble up decent rock to a massive ledge. **Pitch 2:** (5.7) Lieback a solid right-facing corner to a roof and disappear into a tight belay hole. **Pitch 3:** (5.7) Fly up the quality dihedral to a scree-covered belay ledge just below the top.

5a. Sky Chimney Variation (5.7) ★ Gear to 6 inches. This variant avoids the starting chimney by climbing a far more disgusting corner to the right.

6. King Nothing (5.7) ★★ 9 bolts. An obscure but worthwhile sport route exits the starting chimney via a solid wall on the right. It's also the highest quality approach to *Sky Chimney*, *White Satin*, or *Lycra*.

7. White Satin (5.9) ★★★ Gear to 3 inches. A brilliant overhanging dihedral highlights the best multi-pitch traditional route in the Smith Rock Group. The first two pitches aren't special, but the final pitch shouldn't be missed. **Pitch 1:** (5.5) Follow the *Sky Chimney* approach chimney or the *King Nothing* sport route. **Pitch 2:** (5.7) Ascend a shallow inside corner and hand traverse around a large flake to a belay slot. **Pitch 3:** (5.9) Glide up an elegant corner on perfect rock to a crux bulge at the top.

8. Lycra (5.10b) ★★★ 10 bolts. The left wall of *White Satin* offers a sport route ending halfway up the face. The entire wall would go free at a much higher grade. **Pitch 1:** (5.7) Approach via *King Nothing*. **Pitch 2:** (5.10b) Good edges on solid rock lead to an anchor. Rappel the route.

8a. White Lycra (5.10b) ★★★★ Mixed to 3 inches. An outstanding alternative steps right from the *Lycra* anchor, finishing with the charming upper pitch of *White Satin*. Climb in one long pitch from the big ledge atop the approach chimney.

9. Kevin's Arête (aka Cheap Polyester) (5.11c) ★★★ Bolts. This attractive line ascends great rock on the arête left of *White Satin*. The approach pitch isn't special, but the long upper pitch is memorable, with airy moves and many bolts. **Pitch 1:** (5.6) 10 bolts. Begin with the *Sky Chimney* approach, but follow the left rib to an anchor atop the highest ledge. **Pitch 2:** (5.11c) 14 bolts. Technical moves lead up the face right of the edge. Near the top veer left, finishing on the arête itself. Lower to the starting anchor and rappel to the ground using double ropes.

10. Lost in Space (5.10b) ★★★ 10 bolts. This recent multi-pitch sport route will see many ascents. The easy approach and the exposed finishing buttress aren't special, but the middle two pitches are great fun on perfect rock. **Pitch 1:** (5.6) 10 bolts. Climb the starting pitch of *Kevin's Arête* and step left along the Perch to an anchor on the right side of a boulder. **Pitch 2:** (5.10c) Bolts. A vertical face above the boulder leads to easier climbing on a slab. Another steep section ends at an anchor. **Pitch 3:** (5.10b) Bolts. A pleasant slab of solid edges leads to the base of a rounded buttress. **Pitch 4:** (5.9) 10 bolts. The finish doesn't match the quality of the rest of the route, but the outstanding position makes up for the less-than-stellar stone.

11. Black Velcro (5.9 R) ★ Mixed to 2.5 inches. A distinctive arching dihedral system offers a rarely climbed line to the top of the cliff. For decades it was the only route in the vicinity, before recent sport climbs opened the wall to the masses. The lower corner

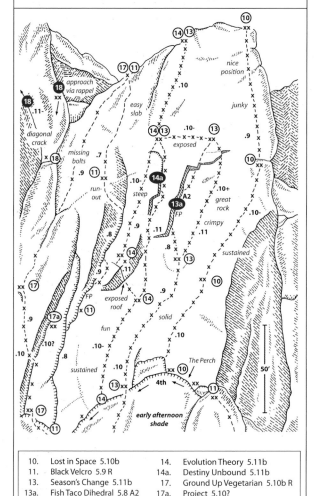

easy slab

nice position

junky

approach via rappel

diagonal crack

missing bolts

run-out

steep

exposed

great rock

crimpy

sustained

exposed roof

solid

fun

sustained

The Perch

50'

4th

early afternoon shade

10.	Lost in Space 5.10b	14.	Evolution Theory 5.11b
11.	Black Velcro 5.9 R	14a.	Destiny Unbound 5.11b
13.	Season's Change 5.11b	17.	Ground Up Vegetarian 5.10b R
13a.	Fish Taco Dihedral 5.8 A2	17a.	Project 5.10?
		18.	Farewell to Smith 5.11a

right past a couple bolts. Step lightly up a moderate corner and escape left on junky rock to old anchor bolts. **Pitch 5:** (5.7) Climb past a single bolt and run it out to the top.

12. Grettir's Saga (5.10a R) ★

Mixed to 2.5 inches. A forgotten route starts 20 feet downhill and left of the detached pillar at the base of *Sky Chimney*. Jam a short left-facing corner and cut left onto an unattractive face. Fighting rope drag, climb crumbly rock past too few bolts to an anchor. Rappel with two ropes.

13. Season's Change (5.11b)

★★★ Bolts. This multi-pitch sport route follows a meandering line up the Northeast Face of the Smith Rock Group. The rock quality runs the gamut from utter crap to absolute brilliance, though it'll only improve as the fine position and ample bolts attract climbers. Begin behind a juniper tree below a crumbling left-arching flake. **Pitch 1:** (5.10a) 7 bolts. The abysmal starting flake has nothing going for it, though the pitches above more than make up for it. A boulder move off the ground gives way to a grim traverse on horrific rock. **Pitch 2:** (5.10b) 12 bolts. Wander up a better quality wall to the Perch—a ledge running across the entire cliff. **Pitch 3:** (5.10c) 10 bolts. Hard moves at the start lead to fun climbing on the clean wall. Belay at a small sickle-shaped ledge. **Pitch 4:** (5.11b) 11 bolts. Classic climbing on perfect rock leads past a distinctive "eye," finishing with

is solid, but a run-out crux pitch makes it a poor choice for developing 5.9 climbers. **Pitch 1:** (5.6) Climb the bolted first-pitch rib of *Kevin's Arête* to an anchor, or follow the original line with a deep chimney a few feet right. **Pitch 2:** (4th class) Walk along the Perch to a short downclimb and belay beneath a right-facing, curving corner. **Pitch 3:** (5.8) Ascend the attractive dihedral to a belay bolt. **Pitch 4:** (5.9) Continue up the dihedral until forced to face climb up and

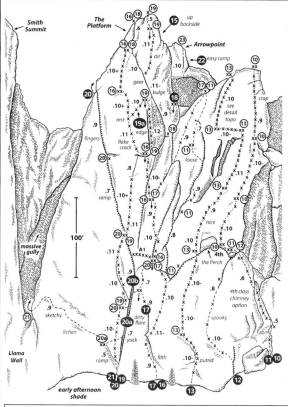

Smith Rock Group–Northeast Face–The Platform

10.	Lost in Space 5.10b	
11.	Black Velcro 5.9 R	
12.	Grettir's Saga 5.10a R	
13.	Season's Change 5.11b	
15.	Southwest Side 5.2	
16.	The Good Ol' Days 5.11c	
17.	Ground Up Vegetarian 5.10b R	
18.	Farewell to Smith 5.11a	
19.	Freedom's Just Another Word For Nothing Left to Lose 5.12b	
19a.	Good 'Ol Variation 5.11b	
20.	Snibble Tower 5.10a A1 R	
20a.	Snibble Tower original start 5.7 R	
20b.	Snibble Free 5.9 R	
21.	Why? D.S.L. 5.9 X	
22.	Northwest Corner 5.2	
23.	Shaft 5.10b	

past a few bolts to easy nailing in a leaning right-facing corner. A couple more bolts up the slab to the right lead to a finishing roof.

14. Evolution Theory (5.11b)

★★★ Mixed to 3 inches (single 5-inch piece optional). A diagonal roof crack highlights this varied line to the top of the Northeast Face. It's largely a sport route, but you'll remember the traditional roof long after the memories of the bolted pitches fade. To approach, either follow *Season's Change,* or walk left along the Perch from atop the opening pitch of *Kevin's Arête.* **Pitch 1:** (5.10a) 9 bolts. Starting on the left side of the Perch, ascend an attractive slab to an anchor below a left-leaning roof crack. **Pitch 2:** (5.11d) Move past a bolt and attack the spectacular crack with a puzzling combination of jams and edges. Ignore a bolt above the lip leftover from the original aid ascent. **Pitch 3:** (5.10a) 8 bolts. Easy slab moves lead to a vertical finish on good rock. **Pitch 4:** (5.10b) 11 bolts. Follow the final pitch of *Season's Change* to the top.

14a. Destiny Unbound (5.11b) ★★★ 12 bolts.

The shallow dihedral directly above the first-pitch anchor on *Evolution Theory* offers a direct, sport-bolted variant to the leaning roof crack. A slabby start leads to crux face climbing past a bulge. Finish with an easier right-facing corner and rejoin the regular route below the final pitch.

a small roof. **Pitch 5:** (5.10a) 4 bolts. Avoid bad rock by making an exposed traverse straight left to an anchor. **Pitch 6:** (5.10b) 11 bolts. Well-protected moves on lackluster rock lead to the top. Hike off the backside.

13a. Fish Taco Dihedral (5.8 A2) ★★ Aid

rack to 2 inches. Until someone frees this fourth-pitch variant, it'll hardly attract a glance despite high-quality stone. From the third-pitch anchor, move up and left

SMITH ROCK GROUP PINNACLES

Capping the northern end of the Smith Rock Group are the Platform, Arrowpoint, and the twin pinnacles of Smith Summit. The northeast face of these spires feature some of the most impressive routes at Smith. From the backside these same spires are little more than insignificant hummocks.

To approach any backside route, hike over Asterisk Pass and walk upstream along a rough trail leading up the hillside between Flounder Block and Cod Rock. At the plateau atop the hill, Smith Summit rises straight ahead with Arrowpoint sitting to the left, hiding the Platform from view.

The Platform

Viewed from the Dihedrals, the Platform towers impressively above the cliff line. An unmistakable diagonal crack slashes across the entire river face. The 550-foot river face features amazing multi-pitch free routes, while the disappointing backside offers a single route.

15. Southwest Side (5.2) ★ No topo. Gear to 2.5 inches. A magnificent view awaits anyone willing to scramble 40 feet up lousy, but mercifully unexposed, rock on the southwest face of the spire. Few climbers brave the backside approach hike—the infrequent ascents usually come after topping-out on nearby routes.

16. The Good Ol' Days (5.11c) ★★★ Mixed to 3 inches. One of Smith's finest multi-pitch sport/adventure routes ascends the impressive east face of the Platform. It's almost entirely bolted, with only a few pieces of gear required. The lower pitches aren't great, but the upper wall is solid and spec-

tacular, with massive exposure. Start right of a pine tree at the base of the wall below an obvious flare. **Pitch 1:** (5.11a) 12 bolts. Boulder to a dirt-covered ledge and follow a simple ramp to a distinctive flare. Step right to crux crimps and follow a pocketed water streak past many bolts. Easy climbing up and left ends at an anchor. **Pitch 2:** (5.10b) Follow a solid right-facing dihedral past three bolts to a crux exit left. Move past several more bolts to an anchor. **Pitch 3:** (5.10a) Start up another right-facing dihedral and cut left to solid moves on an exposed prow. Belay beneath an attractive arête. **Pitch 4:** (5.11c) 9 bolts. Step left to a spectacular flake crack. Pumping moves lead to a much-appreciated no-hands rest. Strenuous liebacks on great rock end at an anchor. **Pitch 5:** (5.10d) 7 bolts. Face climb good rock with major exposure to a belay above all difficulties. **Pitch 6:** (5.6) Junky scrambling ends on the summit. Don't attempt to rappel the route—instead, scramble down the backside.

17. Ground Up Vegetarian (5.10b R) ★ Mixed to 4 inches. In a throwback to the 1970s, this multi-pitch adventure has all the elements of old-time Smith routes—bad rock, poor protection, rope drag, and stomach-churning climbing. Throw in many missing bolts (the first ascent team used removable rebolts), and you've got a climb forever doomed to obscurity. Share the starting moves with *The Good Ol' Days*. **Pitch 1:** (5.9) Unappetizing climbing leads to a ledge below an obvious dirt-choked flare. Ignoring bolts to the right, flail up the flare past a missing bolt and step left to an anchor. Meander past another empty hole to a belay beneath a right-facing corner. **Pitch 2:** (5.10b) The only good climbing follows the second pitch dihedral/exit on *The Good Ol' Days*. **Pitch 3:** (5.9) Climb past a lone bolt to a slabby, pocketed crack leading into a bowl. Exit to the right and climb a long slab past several empty bolt holes to an anchor on a large purple boulder. Hike down the backside.

17a. Project (5.10?)

The right-facing dihedral on the second pitch continues another 20 feet above the left exit. No one knows how the old anchor got there, but this short stint would go free at a reasonable grade.

18. Farewell to Smith

(5.11a) ★★★ Gear to 3.5 inches. This striking diagonal crack cuts across the upper part of the Platform hundreds of feet off the deck. A spectacular pitch on great rock rewards anyone enduring the involved approach. Begin by hiking up the backside and boulder up to an exposed, oddly located anchor. A short rappel leads to the base of the crack.
Pitch 1: (5.11a) Solid jams cruise past a crux bulge on good rock. Bring lots of gear.
Pitch 2: (5.6) The difficulty eases and the rock turns to crap on the mandatory summit pitch. Downclimb the backside.

19. Freedom's Just Another Word For Nothing Left to Lose (5.12b) ★★★★ Mixed to

3 inches. This impressive route ranks among Smith's finest free walls. The position keeps

Tim Garland on *Freedom's Just Another Word For Nothing Left to Lose.*

getting better the higher you go, capped by a pitch so far off the ground it'll send chills down your spine. Although primarily a sport route, traditional climbers will take pleasure in exposed jams high on the wall. Most surprising is the quality of the stone. With the exception of a few small patches, the rock is nearly perfect from bottom to top. Bring a full rack of gear. **Pitch 1:** (5.10a) 6 bolts. Start left of an unmistakable chimney and climb moderate rock to an anchor. **Pitch 2:** (5.11c) 10 bolts. Insecure face moves lead to a clean, leaning dihedral. The hardest climbing comes above the corner on a bulging wall. **Pitch 3:** (5.11b) Hard moves at the start gain a flat face split by a seam. Climb past several bolts to a naturally protected 5.8 crack. Step right to an anchor. **Pitch 4:** (5.12b) 6 bolts. Cautiously balance atop a pillar to clip the first bolt and finesse the right side of a classic Smith arête. Be wary of the sketchy second clip. **Pitch 5:** (5.11c) An unprotected step right leads into *Farewell to Smith.* Jam through the crux and escape right to a line of bolts on the summit headwall. Spectacular climbing on good rock ends at an anchor just below the top. Either make six single-rope rappels to the ground (use a 70-meter rope) or go for the summit. **Pitch 6:** (5.5) Simple junk leads a few feet to the top. Downclimb the easy backside of the formation.

19a. Good 'Ol Variation (5.11b) ★★★★ 8

bolts. An easier alternative bypasses the crux arête pitch. Step left and follow the bolted flake crack of *The Good Ol' Days* until an exposed line of bolts cuts back right to the anchor atop the classic edge. The grade goes down a few notches, but the quality doesn't suffer at all.

20. Snibble Tower (5.10a A1 R) ★★★ Clean

to 3 inches. If right off the ground, the fifth pitch of this adventurous route would be a four-star classic. The approach pitches aren't special, but a new sport start makes the entire route far more attractive. Start below a foreboding chimney system left of a pine tree. **Pitch 1:** (5.10a) 6 bolts. Avoid the obvious chimney by ascending the first pitch of *Freedom's Just Another Word For Nothing Left to Lose.* **Pitch 2:** (5.7) Step right to a crumbling flare and escape right

to an anchor. Follow the run-out path of least resistance to an anchor below a right-facing dihedral. **Pitch 3:** (5.6 A1) A bolt line cuts across the face to the left, rejoining the crack system. **Pitch 4:** (5.7) Climb the solid ramp, stepping around a few bulges to a belay beneath the classic open book. **Pitch 5:** (5.9) Jam and stem incredibly good rock to a ledge. **Pitch 6:** (4th class) Scramble to the summit or traverse down and left to a rubble-filled gully. Walk off to the west.

20a. Snibble Tower original start (5.7 R)

Mixed to 3 inches. The disgusting original start to *Snibble Tower* tarnished the entire route. With the new bolted option, the rotted chimney collects cobwebs. **Pitch 1:** (5.5) An easy lichen-covered ramp diagonals left to an anchor. Belay here, or suffer horrendous rope drag. **Pitch 2:** (5.7) Traverse right and grovel up a run-out flare. Escape right, clipping a new anchor, and wander to a belay ledge.

20b. Snibble Free (5.9 R) Gear to 3 inches.

The entire climb goes free by avoiding the third-pitch bolt line, instead following a direct path up an abysmal corridor. It makes far more sense to forgo the free ascent by following the regular route.

21. Why? D.S.L. (5.9 X) Gear to 3 inches.

An unusually dangerous route climbs the massive gully separating the Platform from Smith Summit. It was free soloed on the only ascent. Dumb? Stupid? Lucky? Or all of the above? **Pitch 1:** (5.9) Follow the original starting ramp of *Snibble Tower* past an anchor to poorly protected garbage. After a crux mantel, downclimb into the heavily vegetated gully. **Pitch 2:** (3rd class) Fight your way through the bushes to the base of a wall. **Pitch 3:** (5.8) Climb through a run-out cliff band. **Pitch 4:** (4th class) Scramble up decomposing trash to the top.

Arrowpoint

From the east this diminutive spire hides anonymously behind the Platform; viewed from the west, Arrowpoint dominates the skyline. Named for a perfect arrowhead found on the first recorded ascent, it features the best rock of any of the summit spires.

22. Northwest Corner (5.2) ★★ Gear to 3 inches. A simple route follows a quaint crack on the northwest side. After enjoying the summit experience, reverse the moves to the base or put your life on the line and rap off two rusted bolts.

23. Shaft (5.10b) ★★ Gear to 1.5 inches. Believe it or not, this secluded thin crack on the north side of Arrowpoint once ranked among Smith's hardest free routes. You'll feel shafted if you endure the hike for this puny route alone, but it makes a worthwhile detour after topping-out on nearby climbs.

24. South Face (5.4 A1) ★ No topo. Aid rack to 1 inch. A left-leaning seam splits the puny but solid south side of Arrowpoint. An old aid route nails a short, free-climbable pitch to the top.

Smith Summit

The highest point of the Smith Rock Group is Smith Summit with its impressive twin spires. The striking east wall stands in sharp contrast to the diminutive backside of the towers. Of all the idiotic Smith-related questions asked by local non-climbers, the most annoying is, "Have you ever climbed Smith Rock?" Only by climbing to the top of Smith Summit can you finally answer, "Yes!"

Backside Routes

Two recent backside routes provide access to both summits. Rock doesn't get much worse

than this, but the position can't be beat, with an amazing view of the main area far below. Save a life and avoid these spires on all but the least crowded days. The sport routes of the Phoenix Buttress are in the line of fire far below.

25. West Tower (5.4 A1) ★ No topo. Clean to 2.5 inches. Aid a short bolt line on terrible rock up the south side of the tower. A simple first free ascent awaits someone with very low standards. Rappel from a two-bolt anchor or see the *East Tower.*

26. East Tower (5.5 R) No topo. 4 bolts. An ascent of the east spire adds an extra dash of adventure (and misery) to its twin to the west. Begin by climbing the *West Tower.* Rappel along a crumbling, frightfully exposed ridge to an anchor at the notch between the pinnacles. Leave the rope fixed for the exit. Climb more appalling rock past several bolts to the top. Descend by rapping to the notch and jumar the fixed line back to the west summit.

East Wall

Towering 600 feet feet above the base, the east wall contends for the title of Smith's biggest wall. Despite recent multi-pitch sport routes, the entire monolith sees very few ascents.

27. Death By Vulture (5.8 X) Gear to 6 inches. The gigantic gulch left of Smith Summit offers a dream-come-true for adventure climbers. Approach by scrambling to the top of the scree-filled gully below an unappetizing chimney. **Pitch 1:** (5.8) Chimney to an off-width bulge and step right to a ledge. **Pitch 2:** (5.8) Step left and follow a chimney/wide crack to an obvious squeeze behind a flake. Continue with scant protection to a ledge. **Pitch 3:** (5.8) Climb a left-facing corner and battle through bushes

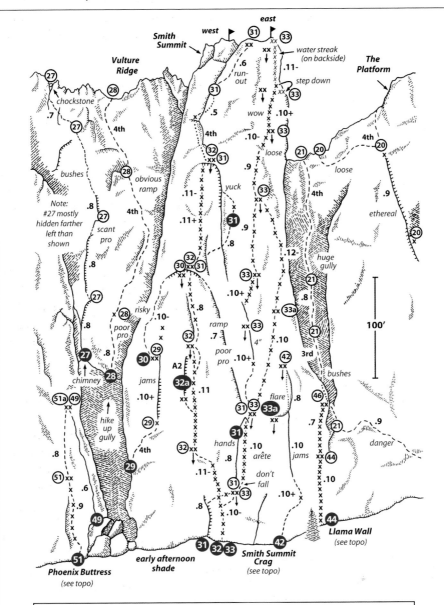

20.	Snibble Tower 5.10a A1 R	33.	European Vacation 5.11a R
21.	Why? D.S.L. 5.9 X	33a.	No Vacation 5.12a
27.	Death By Vulture 5.8 X	42.	The Dobby Brothers 5.10c X
28.	Vulture Gully 5.8 X	44.	Llama Enlightenment 5.10c
29.	Dyer's Eve 5.10d	46.	Seekers of Enlightenment
30.	X-Files 5.10a X		and Choss 5.7
31.	Smith Summit–East Wall 5.8 X	49.	Carabid 5.6 R
32.	The Struggle Within 5.11d	51.	Phoenix 5.10a
32a.	Antisocial Behavior 5.6 A2	51a.	Phoenix finish 5.8 R

and dirty ledges to a belay. **Pitch 4:** (5.7) Move left, passing cracks and steep corners to a ledge. Tunnel under a massive chockstone and scramble off along the top of Vulture Ridge.

28. Vulture Gully (5.8 X) Gear to 4

inches. Another horrendous option to the top of the gully starts downhill right of the opening chimney on *Death By Vulture*. You can climb the steepest rock in many places, including unprotected jugs on the right. Finish with miles of easy, unexposed third- and fourth-class squalor to the top of Vulture Ridge.

29. Dyer's Eve (5.10d) ★★★ Gear to 2 inches.

An unexpectedly high-quality traditional route jams a shallow left-facing corner near the left side of the east wall. With good protection, solid stone, and a crux pulling past a small roof, it deserves more repeats. Approach by hiking into Vulture Gully, traversing right (4th class) to a ledge with a belay bolt.

30. X-Files (5.10a X) Gear to 1.5 inches.

If you're looking for trouble, you'll find more than your share on the long pitch above *Dyer's Eve*. Begin by moving left to a detached slab resting in a dihedral and follow the line of least resistance past a refrigerator-size loose block (you'll need to foot-shuffle along the top of it). Finish with a 50-foot run-out in a groove capped by a rotted boulder problem. Make three rappels to the ground using a 60-meter rope.

31. Smith Summit–East Wall (5.8 X) ★

Mixed to 3 inches. Perhaps the most feared long free route from the early 1970s is this multi-pitch saga up one of Smith's biggest walls. It isn't all bad, but there's enough loose rock and poor protection to scare away almost everyone. Wear a helmet

and carry a rabbit's foot. Start left of the bolted sport routes below a colorful lichen-covered corner. **Descent:** Getting down is an adventure in itself. Make two rappels into the massive amphitheater to the south. Either escape up the gully or scramble down to a short rappel off a single bolt. A safer alternative rappels with two ropes down *The Struggle Within*. **Pitch 1:** (5.8) Climb a shallow corner and traverse across to the base of an imposing hand crack. Bolts now make this pitch perfectly safe. **Pitch 2:** (5.8) Jam the strenuous crack on solid rock to an anchor. The dihedral to the left sports a couple fixed pins and may have seen an aid ascent (A3?) long ago. **Pitch 3:** (5.7) Romp up a dangerous ramp 160 feet and cut left to a ledge. **Pitch 4:** (5.8) Cut right to a filthy crack leading into a rubble-filled corridor. Belay at a huge ledge. **Pitch 5:** (5.5) Scramble up a gully and enter a hidden chimney to the right. Choose a belay spot. **Pitch 6:** (5.6) Run-out rock ends atop the east spire of Smith Summit.

32. The Struggle Within (5.11d) ★★★ Bolts.

One of Smith's most impressive free lines climbs the daunting east face of Smith Summit. With a line of bolts stretching far out of view, it's hardly a traditional route. But the spectacular position, optional summit pitches, and long rappels make it more of an adventure climb than a typical sport route. *The Struggle* features mostly good rock, diverse climbing, idyllic belay ledges, and safe protection. Start below a small, hanging tooth flake. **Descent:** Rappel with two ropes to an anchor atop the third pitch (the ropes are hard to pull). Three more careful rappels with a 60-meter rope lead back to the base. **Pitch 1:** (5.11a) 10 bolts. Simple jams lead to stems followed by a crux stepping left. Avoid the bolted arête by traversing left to a ledge. **Pitch 2:** (5.11c) 11 bolts.

A bolted crack leads to pumping face climbing on fantastic rock. A slightly easier alternative ignores the last bolt, stepping right to 5.8 moves with a 30-foot run-out. **Pitch 3:** (5.8) 4 bolts. Easy climbing on the right side of an arête ends at a big ledge. Optional cams to 2.5 inches protect the opening moves. **Pitch 4:** (5.11d) 10 bolts. The hardest climbing comes far off the ground, clearing a small roof on a vertical face. Belay at another massive ledge. The true adventure climber won't be content to stop here with the summit so close. If you choose to make a dash for the top, follow the final two pitches of *Smith Summit–East Wall* (gear to 3 inches).

32a. Antisocial Behavior (5.6 A2) ★★ Aid rack to 1 inch. An unmistakable left-facing corner sits left of the second pitch of *The Struggle Within*. Begin with the bolted crack and move left to moderate nailing in the remarkably solid dihedral.

33. European Vacation (5.11a R) ★★★★ Mixed to 4 inches. This spectacular adventure continues the tradition of astounding multi-pitch free routes on the Northeast Face of the Smith Rock Group. There's nowhere else at Smith where you can experience the thrill of high-level free climbing so far above the ground. The mandatory seven-rappel descent only adds to the mystique. Use a 70-meter rope, or you'll need to haul a second rope to get down. **Pitch 1:** (5.10a) 4 bolts. Jam past the first four bolts of *The Struggle Within* and step right to belay bolts beneath the second-pitch crack of *Smith Summit–East Wall*. **Pitch 2:** (5.10c) 8 bolts. Risking a nasty fall, make a 5.10 boulder move up and right and join the bolted second-pitch arête of *Eye of the Beholder*. **Pitch 3:** (5.10d) Naturally protected 5.7 climbing leads to a tricky, bolt-protected move. Follow a wid-

ening face crack to a hanging belay. You can combine the third and fourth pitches into a single lead, but you'll need a sizable rack of large gear. **Pitch 4:** (5.10c) Jam the moderate 4-inch crack and veer right to a sport climbing finish past a bulge. Belay at a comfortable ledge. **Pitch 5:** (5.9) 4 bolts. Easy face climbing on imperfect rock leads to another anchor. **Pitch 6:** (5.10a) 5 bolts. A bolted face gives way to an unavoidable dose of bad rock. Fortunately, the finishing knobs are solid and fun. **Pitch 7:** (5.10d) 7 bolts. The highlight of your European vacation ascends great rock high on the finishing tower. At the arete, clip a bolt for your second and step down around the edge to a ledge. Do not attempt to rappel from this anchor! **Pitch 8:** (5.11a) Step right to a bolted water streak and stem dubious rock to a much better finish. The anchor is on the actual summit, far back from the end of the hard climbing. To descend, locate an anchor above the northeast arete (a short fourth-class downclimb). Begin with a rappel to an anchor left of pitch 7 and finish with six more raps directly down the route.

33a. No Vacation (5.12a) ★★★★ Bolts (optional gear to 1 inch). A more difficult option turns *European Vacation* into Smith's longest sport route. Most will argue it's even better than the original line. Despite the sport route billing, you might want to include a small rack for optional pro between bolts. Begin by climbing the first two pitches of the regular route. **Pitch 1:** (5.10b) 6 bolts. Avoid the wide crack by following a bolted slab to the right. **Pitch 2:** (5.12a) 9 bolts. A moderate ramp leads right to a brilliant stretch of climbing on perfect stone, joining *European Vacation* at the end of the fourth pitch. Either rappel off or continue three more pitches to the top.

SMITH SUMMIT CRAG

One of the most unexpected discoveries in Smith history was the wonderful climbing of the Smith Summit Crag. This section of solid stone offers a high concentration of sport routes, including the hardest climbs in the entire Smith Rock Group. Save the hillside by approaching via the Phoenix Buttress and walking right along the base of the cliff. The routes are listed in order moving upstream.

34. The Struggle Within original start

(5.11a) ★★★ 13 bolts. *The Struggle Within* was originally a one-pitch sport route before evolving into a multi-pitch adventure. The entire first pitch is excellent, with a technical stemming section leading to a crux pocket pull. Finish with a delightful arête on solid stone.

35. Harvester of Sorrow (5.11d) ★★★

14 bolts. Split by good rests, this high-quality line features excellent rock and

multiple cruxes. Start with the same bolted crack as *The Struggle Within*, leading to a tough undercling on a right-leaning offset. After a tricky midsection the pumping finish follows a clean arête.

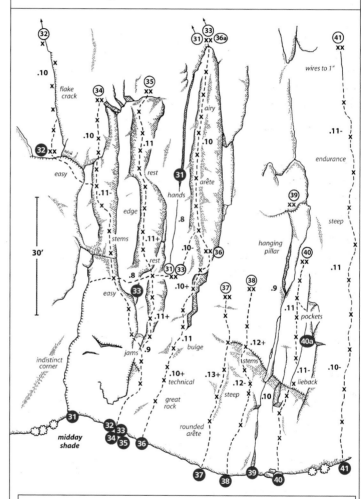

Smith Summit Crag

31.	Smith Summit–East Wall 5.8 X	36a.	Eye of the Beholder finish 5.10c
32.	The Struggle Within 5.11d	37.	100% Beef 5.13c
33.	European Vacation 5.11a R	38.	Livin' Large 5.13a
34.	The Struggle Within original start 5.11a	39.	Condor 5.10c
		40.	Blackened 5.11d
35.	Harvester of Sorrow 5.11d	40a.	Lightly Toasted 5.11b
36.	Eye of the Beholder 5.11c	41.	American Nirvana 5.11c

36. Eye of the Beholder (5.11c) ★★★ 8 bolts. Just right of a bolted flake crack rises another great climb on perfect stone. Intricate moves on positive edges lead past a crux bulge. A still-demanding finish steps right over a small roof to an anchor.

36a. Eye of the Beholder finish (5.10c) ★★ 8 bolts. An impressive arête soars far above the anchors on *Eye of the Beholder.* The exposed position easily compensates for imperfect rock. With more ascents it'll be as good as everything else on the wall. You can climb in a single pitch and lower to the ground with a 70-meter rope.

37. 100% Beef (5.13c) ★★★ 5 bolts. Downhill right of *Eye of the Beholder* are parallel sport routes on perfect rock. The left line powers through intense bouldering moves up an overhanging prow. If you don't live up to the name, you'll get shut down.

38. Livin' Large (5.13a) ★★★ 6 bolts. The right line finesses an awkward move low, before cutting left to insecure stems. The crux pulls over the lip of a petite roof on small edges.

39. Condor (5.10c) ★★ Gear to 3 inches. An intimidating crack splits the right side of the Smith Summit Crag. *Condor* begins with parallel cracks and soars up high-quality rock, ending with jams on the left side of a huge hanging tooth.

40. Blackened (5.11d) ★★★ 9 bolts. The attractive wall right of *Condor* features a fun sport route on solid rock. Lieback a right-leaning crack over a small roof and step left at the fifth bolt to a crux finish on a pocketed wall.

40a. Lightly Toasted (5.11b) ★★ 9 bolts. Nervous climbers often refuse to leave the security of the crack, clipping bolts far to the left on *Blackened* while bypassing the hardest moves. This lowers both the grade and quality.

41. American Nirvana (5.11c) ★★★★ Mixed to 1 inch. Surprisingly, the dark wall right of *Blackened* features one of the better routes of the grade at Smith. Pumping climbing on great rock leads past ten bolts to a single piece of gear in the finishing crack. You can lower to the ground with a 70-meter rope.

42. The Dobby Brothers (5.10c X) ★★ Mixed to 6 inches. Though less stellar than its sport neighbor to the left, this fearsome line is the longest single-pitch route at Smith. Start up *American Nirvana,* but don't clip any bolts (to avoid rope drag). Instead traverse right across an easy slab to a crux protected by a lone bolt. With the hardest moves below, the real difficulties begin as a long flake crack eventually gives way to a run-out death march up a flaring chimney. To descend, rappel with a 70-meter cord to the *American Nirvana* anchor. One more rappel ends on the ground.

LLAMA WALL

Beyond *American Nirvana* the nearly flawless rock of the Smith Summit Crag gives way to the homely Llama Wall. Developed prior to the high-quality lines to the left, these heavily scrubbed routes only confirmed the suspicions of those who turned up their noses at Smith Rock Group sport routes. The cliff rests directly below the massive gully separating the Platform and Smith Summit. Approach via the Phoenix Buttress trail and hike upstream to a scrawny juniper tree.

43. Entering Relativity (5.11a) ★★
14 bolts. With varied climbing and a pumping finish on good rock, this unremarkable route sees many ascents. After a generously bolted pint-sized starting corner, the rock unfortunately deteriorates in the middle. A killer block plaguing early ascents disappeared long ago.

44. Llama Enlightenment (5.10c)
★★ 16 bolts. The best route on the wall follows a homely face, starting behind a skinny tree. Start with crumbling jugs and cut left to a stem rest

under a roof. The crux steps right with good edges on better rock. Most climbers avoid the simple, bolt-sprayed upper slab.

45. When Llamas Need Protection (5.10a)
★ Mixed to 2.5 inches. One of the few distinguishing features of the Llama Wall

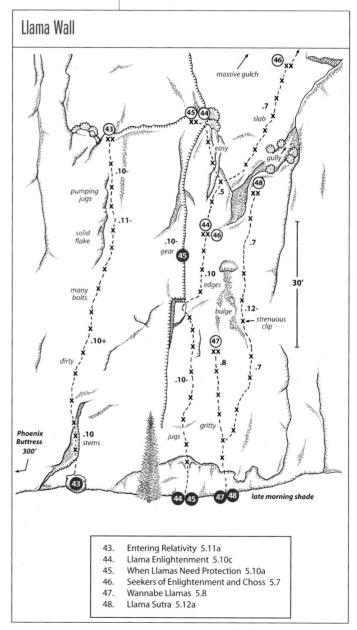

Llama Wall

43.	Entering Relativity 5.11a
44.	Llama Enlightenment 5.10c
45.	When Llamas Need Protection 5.10a
46.	Seekers of Enlightenment and Choss 5.7
47.	Wannabe Llamas 5.8
48.	Llama Sutra 5.12a

a lightning bolt crack split by a small roof. This mini right-facing corner won't appeal to many climbers, despite decent rock and good protection. Start either with *Llama Enlightenment,* or step across from the anchors atop *Wannabe Llamas.*

46. Seekers of Enlightenment and Choss

(5.7) ★★ 8 bolts. An easy sport route cuts right from the upper pitch of *Llama Enlightenment,* following a heavily bolted slab to a higher anchor. It makes a fine beginning lead, but the mandatory 5.10 approach weeds out those who would benefit the most.

47. Wannabe Llamas (5.8) ★★ 5 bolts. The

diminutive original line on the wall features big holds, gritty rock, and bolts every 5 feet. Whether you like it or not, it'll be over in the blink of an eye.

48. Llama Sutra (5.12a) ★★ 10 bolts. The

rightmost route shares the start with *Wannabe Llamas* but veers right to a bulging, black-streaked overhang. After a tough clip a physical crux leads to a simple finish.

PHOENIX BUTTRESS

Sitting at the left base of Vulture Gully is an attractive wall of reddish-purple stone. By far the most popular section of stone in the Smith Rock Group, this buttress features a first-rate collection of moderate routes. The crag goes into the shade by the middle of the day, making it a fine afternoon destination on a hot day.

49. Carabid (5.6 R) ★★ Gear to 2.5 inches.

A pleasant traditional line follows a broken crack system left of the entrance to Vulture Gully. Despite good rock, *Carabid* sees few ascents—it's too run-out for beginners and too easy to attract those climbing nearby sport routes. Two raps end on the ground.

50. Drill 'Em And Fill 'Em (5.10a) ★★ 5

bolts. The rightmost sport route rises above a large detached flake at the base of the wall. Technical moves off the starting flake quickly give way to easier climbing on the slab above.

51. Phoenix (5.10a) ★★★ 5 bolts. The origi-

nal route on the buttress blends great rock and a delightful mix of incut edges, side pulls, and pockets. The grade rose a notch after a large jug pulled off above the fourth bolt, creating a new crux on small holds. An optional cam protects the easy opening sequence.

51a. Phoenix finish (5.8 R) ★ Gear to 2

inches. Early ascents continued up mediocre cracks far above the current anchors to the *Carabid* belay. Deteriorating rock and sparse protection keep everyone away.

52. License to Bolt (5.11c) ★★★ 5 bolts. The

hardest route on Phoenix Buttress follows technical edges and pockets on solid stone. A long reach to a two-finger pocket at the start gives many climbers fits.

53. Fred on Air (5.10d) ★★ 6 bolts. The pocketed face left of *License to Bolt* makes a worthwhile jaunt on good rock. The original line stayed right on the lower part of the wall, but almost everyone climbs bigger holds to the left.

54. Jim Treviso Memorial Route (aka J.T.'s Route) (5.10b) ★★★★ 7 bolts. A wonderful route ascends a shallow arête just right of a low-angle slab. Expect solid rock with positive edges and exhilarating moves. The crux comes at the top, pulling over a bulge on good side pulls.

55. Scary Llamas (aka Hissing Llamas) (5.8) ★★★ 9 bolts. The easiest route on the buttress receives countless ascents. It makes an excellent introduction to the grade with good rock, plenty of bolts, and a single crux move interrupting an otherwise easy slab.

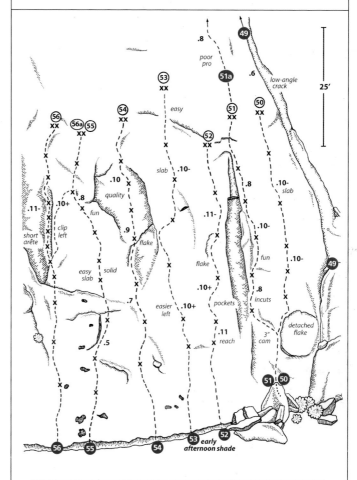

Phoenix Buttress

49.	Carabid 5.6 R		54.	Jim Treviso Memorial Route
50.	Drill 'Em and Fill 'Em 5.10a			(aka J.T.'s Route) 5.10b
51.	Phoenix 5.10a		55.	Scary Llamas (aka Hissing
51a.	Phoenix finish 5.8 R			Llamas) 5.8
52.	License to Bolt 5.11c		56.	When Llamas Bolt 5.11a
53.	Fred on Air 5.10d		56a.	Llamas on the Edge 5.10d

56. When Llamas Bolt (5.11a) ★★ 11 bolts. A short arête sits atop a slab on the left side of Phoenix Buttress. Closely spaced bolts protect an intense sequence on the left side of the edge. Technical moves low give way to strenuous cranks on good holds near the top.

56a. Llamas on the Edge (5.10d) ★★ 10 bolts. A peculiar variant climbs the right side of the arête, clipping the same bolts. The crux finesses a holdless slab, escaping up and right before joining *Scary Llamas*.

Left of Phoenix Buttress rests a huge expanse of rock stretching several hundred yards to the south. Someday climbers will uncover something worth climbing here, but it hasn't happened yet. An attractive face far to the south called the Grover Wall saw limited exploration (but no new routes) in the late 1980s. It drifted into obscurity long ago.

57. Flake Chimney (5.6 R) No topo. Gear to 4 inches. A massive flake leans against the wall 100 feet left of Phoenix Buttress. For reasons unknown, someone once climbed a miserable corridor up the right side of this flake, rappelling from a sling wrapped around the top.

58. Vulture Ridge (5.6 X) ★ No topo. Gear to 3.5 inches. One of Smith's most adventurous routes treads lightly along the crest of the multi-spiked ridge extending east from Smith Summit. It makes a deadly choice for the beginner, with terrible rock and worse protection, though more experienced climbers enjoy the magnificent position. To approach, hike around the corner 0.25 mile beyond the Phoenix Buttress and scramble up the first gully to the right. Veer right to the ridge and weave through spires to the top.

59. Vulture Ridge Spire (5.6) ★★ No topo. Mixed to 3 inches. Only the most demented adventure climbers will make the trek to the top of the largest of the Vulture Ridge pinnacles. Approach via the same disintegrating gully as *Vulture Ridge* and traverse along a third-class ledge to the east notch. Simple, bolt-protected scrambling leads to the summit. Rappel from an anchor just below the top.

SOUTHERN TIP

At the southern end of the Smith Rock Group, the Crooked River turns 180 degrees, heading back along the west side of the formation. The Southern Tip features surprisingly solid stone far from the crowds, with enough worthwhile routes to justify the hike. The Tip receives early shade; after baking in the midday sun, the shade returns to much of the cliff in the late afternoon

60. Sabotage (5.11c) ★★★ 10 bolts. A roof undercuts the right half of the Southern Tip. After stick-clipping the first bolt, a bouldering crux of flaring finger and hand jams at the lip leads to a good shake. The best climbing comes at the top, with pumping edges and liebacks on great rock. Avoiding the permanent pile of cheater stones (starting in the back of the cave) raises the grade a couple notches.

61. Yoderific (5.11d) ★★ 8 bolts. An impressive open book dominates the center of the Southern Tip. The right wall sports an ignored route on mediocre rock. A crux of very thin crimps past the third bolt gives way to more enjoyable face climbing above.

62. Kunza Korner (5.10c) ★★★★ Gear to 2 inches. This brilliant dihedral stands in sharp contrast to the rubble found for hundreds of yards to either side. Perfect rock, intellectual moves, and good protection make *Kunza* (coon-zuh) *Korner* one of the best open books on Smith tuff. The stemming crux comes at a small bulge just below the anchors.

62a. Kunza Korner finish (5.7 A3-) ★ Aid rack to 2 inches. The original aid ascent continued above the anchor, nailing past a roof to a short stint of free climbing ending on the top of the cliff.

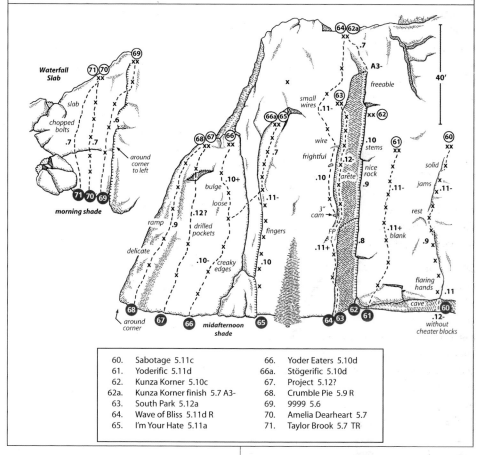

60.	Sabotage 5.11c	66.	Yoder Eaters 5.10d
61.	Yoderific 5.11d	66a.	Stögerific 5.10d
62.	Kunza Korner 5.10c	67.	Project 5.12?
62a.	Kunza Korner finish 5.7 A3-	68.	Crumble Pie 5.9 R
63.	South Park 5.12a	69.	9999 5.6
64.	Wave of Bliss 5.11d R	70.	Amelia Dearheart 5.7
65.	I'm Your Hate 5.11a	71.	Taylor Brook 5.7 TR

63. South Park (5.12a) ★★★ 8 bolts. Two routes sharing the same start ascend either side of the attractive arête left of *Kunza Korner*. *South Park* stays primarily on the right side of the edge, with excellent slaps and edges ending at an anchor below the top of the crag.

64. Wave of Bliss (5.11d R) ★★★ Mixed to 3 inches. The original route on the arête starts with crux moves right of the edge, before finishing on the left side. Despite good rock and engaging moves, a lack of decent protection on 5.10 sections in the middle keeps the faint-hearted away.

65. I'm Your Hate (5.11a) ★★ 11 bolts. A small right-facing corner graces the lower portion of the wall 40 feet left of *Kunza Korner*. Stems and jams in the dihedral lead to a crux exit on face holds. Finish by moving back right to a hidden ledge and follow an easy ramp to an anchor.

66. Yoder Eaters (5.10d) ★ 6 bolts. The disappointing wall left of *I'm Your Hate* offers a few junky lines holding little appeal. The right-hand route edges delicately on creaky holds over a bulge.

66a. Stögerific (5.10d) ★★ 9 bolts. A clever combination starts with *Yoder Eaters* and diagonals right, joining the upper part of *I'm Your Hate*. It's better than the original route, but nothing special.

67. Project (5.12?) Three bolts and several drilled pockets litter the crumbly wall left of *Yoder Eaters*. This aborted project serves as a reminder that some sections of stone at Smith are best left untouched.

68. Crumble Pie (5.9 R) ★ 5 bolts. Around the corner to the left of the preceding lines looms another unremarkable sport route. A delicate slab leads past widely spaced bolts to an anchor.

Waterfall Slab

The west side of the Southern Tip features an insignificant slab named in honor of a seasonal rimrock waterfall fed by irrigation runoff. There isn't much here, but beginning climbers can develop their skills in relative privacy.

69. 9999 (5.6) ★★ 4 bolts. The best line on the slab follows good holds into a simple left-facing dihedral. Cut right near the top to an anchor.

70. Amelia Dearheart (5.7) ★★ 5 bolts. A sport climb up the center of the slab contains a few artsy moves at the start. The difficulties ease quickly on the brief jaunt to the anchors.

71. Taylor Brook (5.7) ★ TR. We all have bad days, but somehow the innocent left-most slab infuriated a climber so much he yanked all the bolts. At the risk of sending yourself into a bolt-chopping rage, you can still toprope the original line.

WEST SIDE ROUTES

The west side of the Smith Rock Group pales in comparison to the massive walls to the east. Nonetheless, both traditional routes and newer sport climbs provide a haven from the madness of the main area. The west side contains three cliffs—the impressive northwest wall, the diminutive Flounder Block, and the square-cut Cod Rock. To approach all west-side routes, scramble over Asterisk Pass and follow a trail upstream along the base of the cliff.

Northwest Wall

The relatively remote northwest wall of the Smith Rock Group contains something for everyone—except the extreme climber. The ancient traditional testpieces, long sport routes, and easy bolted base routes are all worth doing. The entire wall stays in the shade until past noon; even during summer the morning temperatures are pleasant. **Descent:** The old rappel route down *Bits and Pieces* no longer exists. The new rap station is about 30 feet uphill to the south. You'll need a 60-meter line for the three single-rope rappels. Some climbers forego the rappels by hiking up a third-class gully, passing below the western base of the Platform and Arrowpoint. Eventually a scree chute cuts down the west side to a trail heading back to Asterisk Pass.

72. Sky Slab (5.10a) ★ TR. The lower reaches of *Sky Ridge's* west side contains a knobby face sampled only on toprope. To set a rope, follow the first 50 feet of *Sky Ridge* to a double-bolt anchor.

73. Skylight (5.10c) ★★ Gear to 3 inches. Despite a solid and wildly exposed finish, no one appreciates the lackluster starting pitches

A. Northwest Face–Left Side
B. Northwest Face–Center
C. Northwest Face–Right Side
D. Flounder Block and Cod Rock

of this overlooked route. Start at a juniper tree on the far left side of the wall. **Pitch 1:** (5.6) Detour right around a bulge on run-out knobs and scamper to a ledge with a single-bolt anchor. **Pitch 2:** (5.7) Continue up a long crack system before circling right to an anchor atop huge hanging boulders. **Pitch 3:** (5.10c) Move left to locking hand slots in an overhanging corner. The crux exits right on awkward finger jams.

74. Stagefright (5.12a) ★★ Mixed to 1 inch. A remote location high off the ground is both the charm and the curse of this wildly overhanging thin crack. The rock isn't perfect, but the position ranks with the most memorable at Smith, with a bolt-protected lunge to a jug with nothing but air below. Most climbers prefer approaching from above, with a short downclimb of the upper part of *Bits and Pieces*.

75. Serendipity (5.9 X) ★ Mixed to 4 inches. This meandering route seems destined to become the latest chapter in a long list of ignored trad routes in the Smith Rock Group. Begin below a bulge at an insignificant left-leaning seam a few feet right of the start to *Skylight*. **Pitch 1:** (5.9) Crank past a mediocre crux bulge and bypass a roof to the right on good holds. Face climb to a ledge with a single-bolt anchor. **Pitch 2:** (5.6) Continue up an easy lichen-covered slab until a roof forces a long traverse to the right. Set a natural anchor and belay below the wide crack on *Bits and Pieces*. **Pitch 3:** (5.7) Follow the second pitch of *Bits and Pieces* and step left near the top to a run-out slab/arête protected by a lonely bolt.

76. Bits and Pieces (5.7 X) ★ Mixed to 4 inches. The first ascent of the northwest wall followed a distasteful route guaranteed

The Platform

Arrowpoint

Asterisk Pass

2.	Sky Ridge 5.8 R	87.	Taste the Pain 5.10a R
2b.	Sky Dive 5.10c	89.	Fall For Anything 5.10c
73.	Skylight 5.10c	90.	Of Wolf and Man 5.6 R
76.	Bits and Pieces 5.7 X	92.	Thieves Like Us 5.10d
80.	Wherever I May Roam 5.9	93.	Role Model 5.11a R
83.	No Brain, No Pain 5.11a	94.	Cryptesthesia 5.11a
84.	No Pain, No Gain 5.11c	97.	Pocket Pool 5.11b
85.	Why Art Thou? 5.8	98.	Chalk Wave 5.8

to scare the daylights out of any beginning climber. For good reason, the long upper pitch never became popular. **Pitch 1:** (5.5) 9 bolts. Enjoy the sport-bolted start and move right on a bolted ramp to a higher anchor. **Pitch 2:** (5.7) Crux jams in a dirty crack lead into a corridor. You'll have an option of ascending a wide crack or circling around to the left on decent rock with no protection. Finish up a simple groove.

76a. Bits and Pieces start (5.5) ★★★ 5
bolts. The low-angle opening groove makes an excellent lead for beginning climbers. Delightful knobs lead past closely spaced bolts to an anchor at the start of a chimney.

76b. Bits of Feces (5.8) ★★ Gear to 2.5
inches. Since the new rappel route for the entire crag now goes directly down this slab

crack, it's far cleaner today than on early ascents. Still, few climbers bother. Approach by exiting the *Bits and Pieces* chimney to the anchor atop the third pitch of *Wherever I May Roam*.

77. Stained (5.9) ★★★ 7 bolts. A few feet
right of the start to *Bits and Pieces* rises another bolted water streak. The entertaining knobs and edges on great rock are very popular.

77a. Confused and Disfigured (5.10b R) ★★
Mixed to 3 inches. A harder version shares the same start as *Stained* before traversing right to a bolted rib. A cam in a pocket protects the hardest move.

78. Earthtone (5.10a) ★ Mixed to 2 inches.
The face right of the *Bits and Pieces* chimney features a less-than-perfect sport pitch followed by a traditional dihedral. Flaking rock

and poorly placed bolts detract from the experience. **Pitch 1:** (5.9) 7 bolts. Ascend *Stained* and step right to a higher anchor. **Pitch 2:** (5.10a) 12 bolts. The rock slowly improves the higher you meander on this knobby wall. Continue beyond an anchor on *Wherever I May Roam* to bolts below a short dihedral. **Pitch 3:** (5.9) Jam and stem to the top.

79. Adventurous 9904

(5.8) ★★ 7 bolts. If you're looking for a quickie, make a date with *Adventurous 9904*. Don't be discouraged by the homely appearance—the fun knobs and edges are better than they look. Begin below a short left-facing corner splitting a squat pillar at the lowest part of the cliff line.

80. Wherever I May Roam (5.9) ★★★★ Bolts.

Wherever you may roam at Smith, you won't find a better easy long sport route than this five-pitch odyssey. With closely spaced bolts, excellent rock, and a sublime position, you can't go wrong. The popularity and quality grows with each passing year. **Descent:** From the top, rap off the backside to the fixed rap anchor for the

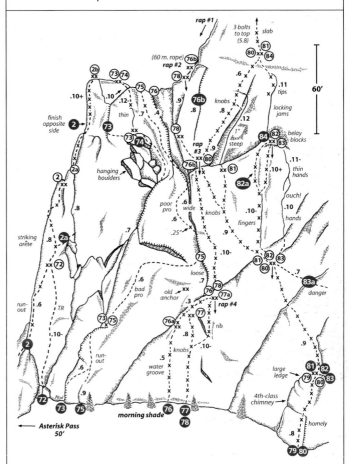

Smith Rock Group—Northwest Face—Left Side

2.	Sky Ridge 5.8 R	77a.	Confused and Disfigured 5.10b R
2a.	Sky Ridge Variation 5.8 R	78.	Earthtone 5.10a
2b.	Sky Dive 5.10c	79.	Adventurous 9904 5.8
72.	Sky Slab 5.10a TR	80.	Wherever I May Roam 5.9
73.	Skylight 5.10c	81.	Tears of Rage 5.12b
74.	Stagefright 5.12a	82.	The Unforgiven 5.10d
75.	Serendipity 5.9 X	82a.	Unforgiven Variation 5.10b
76.	Bits and Pieces 5.7 X	83.	No Brain, No Pain 5.11a
76a.	Bits and Pieces start 5.5	83a.	No Brain original start 5.7 X
76b.	Bits of Feces 5.8	84.	No Pain, No Gain 5.11c
77.	Stained 5.9		

northwest wall. Three more rappels with a 60-meter rope end on the ground. **Pitch 1:** (5.8) 7 bolts. Climb *Adventurous 9904* and step across to a large shelf. **Pitch 2:** (5.9) 9 bolts. Follow a water steak veering left to an anchor. **Pitch 3:** (5.9) 9 bolts. Cut left and follow a long line of bolts on big knobs to an anchor left of an arête. **Pitch 4:** (5.9) 10 bolts. After a tricky start exposed moves lead to an easy finish on a slab. **Pitch 5:** (5.8) 5 bolts. A simple slab ends with a short finishing headwall.

81. Tears of Rage (5.12b) ★★★ Mixed to 2 inches. This overhanging arch high off the ground is one of the hardest non-pin-scarred cracks at Smith. The jams are good, but placing gear burns a lot of energy. For two decades the grotesque approach via *Bits and Pieces* kept everyone away. Perhaps the new direct start will bring greater popularity. Start by scrambling up a fourth-class chimney ending at a large shelf. **Pitch 1:** (5.9) 9 bolts. Follow the second-pitch water streak of *Wherever I May Roam*. **Pitch 2:** (5.9) 8 bolts. Continue with the third pitch, but follow a direct line of bolts to a hanging belay below the arching crack. **Pitch 3:** (5.12b) Pumping 0.75- to 1-inch jams lead to a hard exit left. Easy slab climbing ends at an anchor. **Pitch 4:** (5.8) 5 bolts. The final pitch of *Wherever I May Roam* ends atop the cliff. Rappel or walk right around a fourth-class gendarme and hike down.

82. The Unforgiven (5.10d) ★★★ 8 bolts. With a fun flake crack leading to a high-quality arête, this exposed route deserves more attention. Approach via *Adventurous 9904* or scramble up the chimney behind the pillar. The second pitch of *Wherever I May Roam* ends at an anchor below the crack. Descend via a double-rope rappel.

82a. Unforgiven Variation (5.10b) ★★★ 8 bolts. An easier variant jams and liebacks the bolted crack at the start, finishing with a 5.8 flake crack to the left.

83. No Brain, No Pain (5.11a) ★★ Gear to 3 inches. This skin-shredding hand crack

enjoyed a brief flurry of popularity in the early 1980s before drifting into eternal obscurity. The original start effectively guarded the crack for decades, keeping almost everyone away. The new approach via *Wherever I May Roam* might attract a new generation of trad climbers. The pumping crux hits near the top with a diagonal stretch of thin hand jams. Rappel with two ropes or see *No Pain, No Gain*.

83a. No Brain original start (5.7 X) Gear to 2.5 inches. Hard-core traditional climbers might prefer the dangerous original start. Begin with a short corner on the right side of the *Adventurous 9904* pillar and scramble up an easy corridor to an anchor. Traverse far left without protection on easy, lichen-covered stone to the base of the crack.

84. No Pain, No Gain (5.11c) ★★ Mixed to 2.5 inches. A harder finish rises above the ledge atop *No Brain, No Pain*. Painful, strenuous hand/finger jams on a strongly overhanging wall lead to bolted tip slots at the crux. With new convenient access via *The Unforgiven*, it might receive more than two ascents per decade. Finish to the top with the final pitch of *Wherever I May Roam*.

85. Why Art Thou? (5.8) ★★ 7 bolts. The first bolted line right of the *Adventurous 9904* pillar doesn't look like much, but the bulging start provides some thuggish fun. Finish with a simple slab past an anchor, stepping across a gap to higher bolts.

86. Stand For Something (5.7) ★ 4 bolts. Immediately right of *Why Art Thou?* sits another short line. Positive holds on mediocre rock end quickly at the first anchor.

87. Taste the Pain (5.10a R) ★★ Gear to 3 inches. An impressive overhanging hand crack plugs a corner above the preceding two routes. Avoid bad rock by detouring

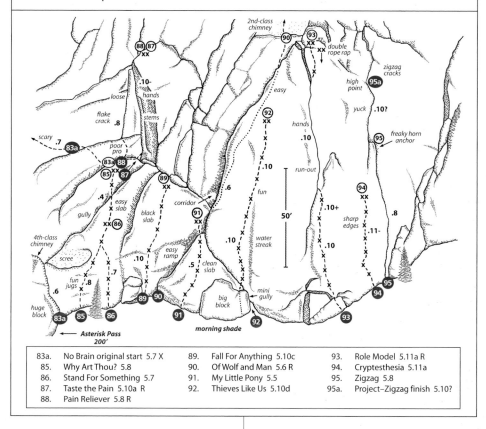

83a.	No Brain original start 5.7 X	89.	Fall For Anything 5.10c
85.	Why Art Thou? 5.8	90.	Of Wolf and Man 5.6 R
86.	Stand For Something 5.7	91.	My Little Pony 5.5
87.	Taste the Pain 5.10a R	92.	Thieves Like Us 5.10d
88.	Pain Reliever 5.8 R		

93.	Role Model 5.11a R
94.	Cryptesthesia 5.11a
95.	Zigzag 5.8
95a.	Project–Zigzag finish 5.10?

left before cutting back right on unprotected lichen to the box corner. Chimney and stem to strenuous hand jams ending at an anchor.

88. Pain Reliever (5.8 R) ★ Gear to 2.5 inches. A less impressive line ascends an unappealing crack left of *Taste the Pain*. Poorly protected holds lead into a leaning crack capped by grisly rock.

89. Fall For Anything (5.10c) ★★ 5 bolts. A few feet left of a right-leaning ramp rises a bolt line with a vertical start. The only hard moves crank past the starting bulge, though the dark finishing slab provides the best climbing.

90. Of Wolf and Man (5.6 R) ★ Gear to 3.5 inches. You'll never have to wait in line for the only route to the top of the northwest wall's right side. Adventure climbers enjoy the alpine setting—everyone else stays away. Start below a right-leaning ramp. **Pitch 1:** (5.6) Climb the ramp past an anchor and jam past a bulge to a decomposed corridor. **Pitch 2:** (2nd class) Walk up the scree slope to the base of a wall. **Pitch 3:** (5.6) Follow the line of least resistance on less-than-perfect rock to the top. Walk off to the south.

91. My Little Pony (5.5) ★★★ 5 bolts. This perfect beginner's route ascends big knobs on a low-angle slab. Even the most timid first-timers find the solid rock and numerous bolts to their liking.

92. Thieves Like Us (5.10d) ★★★ 10 bolts.
The impressive buttress on the right side of the northwest wall features two full-length climbs. The left route starts in a narrow slot behind a boulder. Delightful knobs on the high-quality streak lead to a vertical finish far off the ground.

93. Role Model (5.11a R) ★★★ Mixed to
3.5 inches. Much like routes of yesterday, the most obvious natural line on the buttress combines sporting face climbing and a traditional crack. After starting with bolted edges right of a faint arête, step left around the corner to a run-out ramp. Soar up locking jams in the naturally protected crack and avoid junky rock by exiting right to finishing face holds. Rappel with two ropes.

94. Cryptesthesia (5.11a)
★★ 6 bolts. Beyond *Role Model* the cliff line quickly recedes. A short sport route ascends sharp, technical edges left of a prominent zigzag crack.

95. Zigzag (5.8) ★ Gear to
3.5 inches. An obvious crack system splits the right side of the northwest wall. An ignored route climbs the lackluster crack to a sling wrapped around a horn.

95a. Project–Zigzag finish (5.10?) The zigzagging
finish awaits a first ascent, but loose rock thwarts the few attempts.

A short, streaked wall sits about 150 feet uphill from the lowest part of the buttress, slightly left of the entrance to a big gully. It contains a project and a sport route, with little potential for anything else. Avoid a horrible scree slope by following the trail uphill past the wall and switchback left to the base.

96. Project (5.10?) A moderate project on
the left side of the wall crosses a leaning offset to an anchor. It would be worth doing if someone slammed in a few bolts.

97. Pocket Pool (5.11b) ★★ 5 bolts. The
only completed route on the wall follows pumping pockets on the right side of the

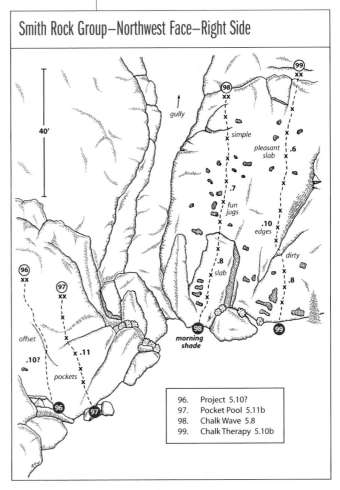

Smith Rock Group–Northwest Face–Right Side

96.	Project 5.10?
97.	Pocket Pool 5.11b
98.	Chalk Wave 5.8
99.	Chalk Therapy 5.10b

face. The crux pulls past a small bulge on positive holds.

A narrow gully splits the right side of the northwest wall. An attractive slab to the right features two worthwhile routes, with obvious potential for more. Avoid tearing up the hillside by hiking uphill on the main trail before backtracking left to the base.

98. Chalk Wave (5.8) ★★★ 9 bolts. A delightful route on good rock graces the left side of the cliff. Begin with a crux sequence up a detached slab and finish with huge jugs.

99. Chalk Therapy (5.10b) ★★ 10 bolts. Right of *Chalk Wave* rises a lower-quality line of jugs. After a junky start the crux finesses technical edges on the left side of a rounded arête. The difficulties ease and the quality improves on the juggy finishing slab.

100. Culls in Space (5.10c) ★★ Gear to 2.5 inches. Just before the northwest wall fades away, a left-leaning crack in a shallow corner comes into view far uphill. A neglected hand traverse powers up this overhanging crack to a rubble-plugged mantel at the top. Walk off to the right.

Flounder Block

About 100 yards beyond the northwest wall, the trail passes below a puny crag broken by an obvious dihedral. There's not enough here to attract many visitors.

101. Flounder Crack (5.6) ★ Gear to 2.5 inches. A few feet left of a sport route sits a dinky crack. Despite some passable finger jams there's no reason to bother, except to set a toprope on the following two routes.

Flounder Block and Cod Rock

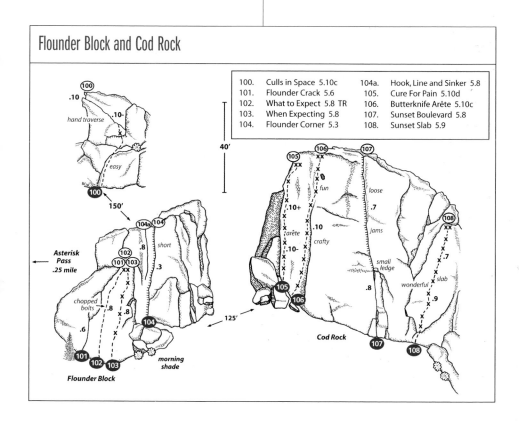

100.	Culls in Space 5.10c	104a.	Hook, Line and Sinker 5.8
101.	Flounder Crack 5.6	105.	Cure For Pain 5.10d
102.	What to Expect 5.8 TR	106.	Butterknife Arête 5.10c
103.	When Expecting 5.8	107.	Sunset Boulevard 5.8
104.	Flounder Corner 5.3	108.	Sunset Slab 5.9

102. What to Expect (5.8) ★ TR. The same day the bolts disappeared on the Southern Tip's *Taylor Brook,* the bolt chopper managed a rare double—the erasing of two harmless sport routes in a single day. Of course, the line still exists and is easily toproped from anchors atop *When Expecting.*

103. When Expecting (5.8) ★★ 4 bolts. A better quality climb to the right somehow escaped the wrath of the bolt chopper. Ascend small holds on good rock past four bolts to an anchor. These two routes are over in the blink of an eye.

104. Flounder Corner (5.3) ★ Gear to 2.5 inches. The original route on the block follows a low-angle dihedral with few redeeming qualities. It's best just to walk on by.

104a. Hook, Line and Sinker (5.8) ★ Gear to 2.5 inches. High on *Flounder Corner* a short crack branches off to the left. Contrived jams mercifully end very quickly.

Cod Rock

After passing beneath Flounder Block, the last developed crag on the west side of the Smith Rock Group comes into view. Three enjoyable sport routes are popular for good reason.

105. Cure For Pain (5.10d) ★★ 7 bolts. The far left arête follows technical edges almost entirely on the right wall. The rock quality isn't the best, though the thoughtful climbing makes up for this shortcoming.

106. Butterknife Arête (5.10c) ★★★ 10 bolts. A better route climbs the edge a few feet right of *Cure For Pain.* Pleasant, artful moves on good rock make it worth doing.

107. Sunset Boulevard (5.8) ★ Gear to 2.5 inches. The first route on the entire west side of the Smith Rock Group followed a homely crack splitting the center of Cod Rock. Second-rate rock keeps all but Smith historians away.

108. Sunset Slab (5.9) ★★★★ 9 bolts. An attractive face on the right side of Cod Rock justifies the hike all by itself. Perfect rock, closely spaced bolts, and charming climbing make this meticulously cleaned slab very popular.

WEST SIDE CRAGS

The sharp arête right of Cling On *captured everyone's imagination in the early 1980s. In the old days we all wore EBs—canvas high-top shoes with hockey puck rubber soles. I pieced together a feasible sequence but couldn't come close to doing the first move, as my feet skated hopelessly on the smooth rock. I came back a few times, but finally crossed it off my list until John Bachar showed up one day with a secret pair of shoes with rubber as sticky as tree sap. I waited months for my first pair of Fires, and quickly headed over Asterisk Pass to give it a try. I could hardly believe it—I did the start first go wearing the magic shoes. It took several more tries, but before long I clipped the anchors and checked* Split Image (5.12d) *off my list.*

Standing in contrast to the amusement park environment of the main area, the West Side Crags offer top-notch climbing without the crowds. Stepping over Asterisk Pass to the west side is like moving back in time. Vegetation still grows at the base of some of the crags, and large expanses of rock remain untouched. The longer approach weeds out convenience-minded climbers. The isolation doesn't appeal to those who feed off the energy of the Smith scene—on the west side there is no scene. During the middle of the week, you might have the whole area to yourself.

The seclusion isn't the only reason why the development lags behind Smith's more popular areas. With a few notable excep-

tions, these crags lack the clean lines found on the east side. Most of the routes involve knobby slabs, vertical faces, or traditional cracks, with few overhanging walls. While recent new routes continually expand the appeal of these crags, the west side simply doesn't have the potential to be the next Dihedrals area—much to the relief of those who enjoy climbing here.

Spread over a half mile of varied terrain, the West Side Crags consist of several independent cliffs. Just over Asterisk Pass rises the leaning spike of the Awl, with the west face of the Christian Brothers towering above. Farther north along the trail sit the high-quality Snake Rock, the Angel Flight Crags, and the first-rate routes of the Spiderman Buttress. After the dominating 350-foot Mesa Verde Wall, the cliff line eventually recedes into the short climbs of the Pleasure Palace. To the north rises the amazing spire of Monkey Face, detailed in the next chapter.

The routes of the West Side Crags appeal primarily to moderate-level climbers. Of the more than one hundred climbs, only six are 5.12 or harder. But don't confuse the lack of difficulty with a lack of quality—many routes are classics or near-classics. Anyone looking for lower-grade climbs will find as many good options here as on the other side. The entire area makes an excellent morning destination on any warm day; most climbs stay in the shade past noon—even on 100-degree days the early temper-

West Side Crags

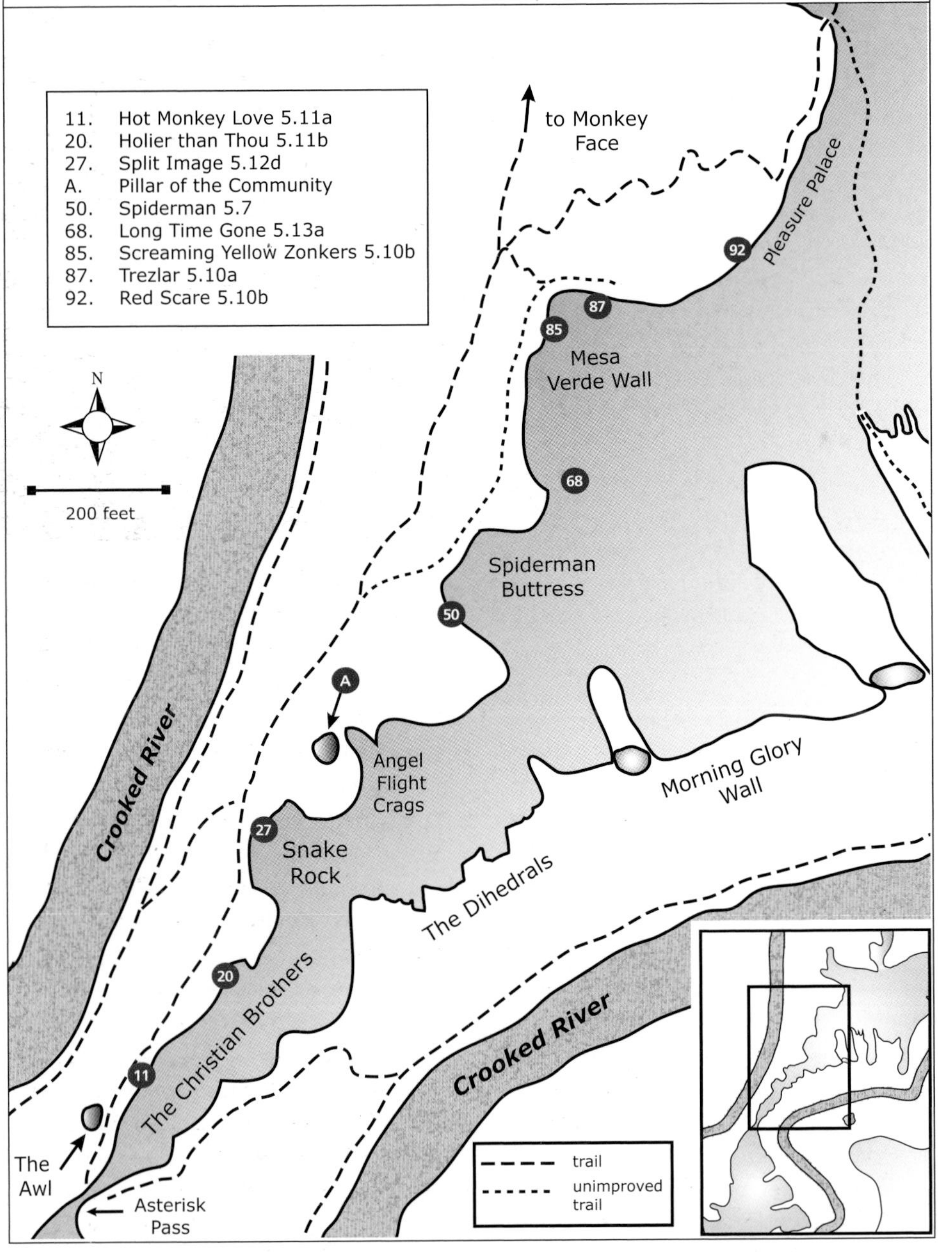

11.	Hot Monkey Love 5.11a
20.	Holier than Thou 5.11b
27.	Split Image 5.12d
A.	Pillar of the Community
50.	Spiderman 5.7
68.	Long Time Gone 5.13a
85.	Screaming Yellow Zonkers 5.10b
87.	Trezlar 5.10a
92.	Red Scare 5.10b

to Monkey Face

Pleasure Palace

92

Mesa Verde Wall

87

85

N

200 feet

68

Spiderman Buttress

50

Crooked River

A

Angel Flight Crags

Morning Glory Wall

27

Snake Rock

The Dihedrals

20

The Christian Brothers

Crooked River

11

The Awl

Asterisk Pass

– – –	trail
··········	unimproved trail

West Side Crags–South Overview

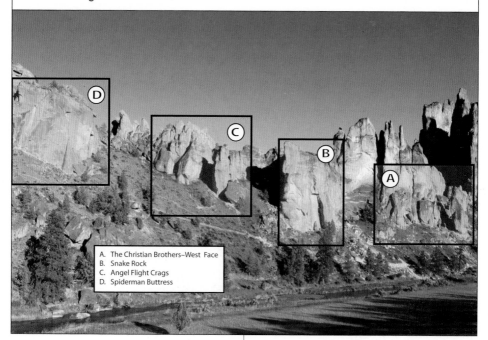

A. The Christian Brothers–West Face
B. Snake Rock
C. Angel Flight Crags
D. Spiderman Buttress

atures are tolerable. By the same token, the prevailing west winds that provide relief in the summer virtually shut the crags down in midwinter.

The isolation of the west side brings greater risk, especially for beginning climbers. Twisted ankles or broken legs are swiftly dealt with in the main area—here they can turn into full-day rescues. For no good reason a disproportionate number of the fatalities at Smith involved west-side accidents. Most of these routes are as safe as any others in the park, but beginning climbers might prefer learning in less remote locations.

The first exploration of the West Side Crags came in 1961 when Jim and Jerry Ramsey climbed the Awl. In a remarkable effort a few months later, Jim returned and freed the starting dihedral (5.10c). Originally graded 5.9, Ramsey's ascent was the best of the decade at Smith. After Kim Schmitz's repeat ascent in 1964, no one exceeded this

standard anywhere on Smith tuff until 1975. By comparison, the first ascents of the five summits of the Christian Brothers in 1964 seemed like child's play. A generation later the standard finally increased with Mike Smelsar's ascent of *Explosive Energy Child* (5.10d) in 1977.

Free ascents of *Minas Morgul* and *Tarantula* (both 5.11d) raised the standard a full number grade in 1981. Three years later the standards shot up another number grade with an ascent of *Split Image* (5.12d). For a few months this gorgeous arête was Smith's hardest route. Over the next several years, climbers explored the vast amounts of untouched rock, and the number of routes doubled with dozens of sport routes in the 5.10 and 5.11 range. But as the standards continued to shoot through the roof elsewhere at Smith, another decade passed until *Long Time Gone* (5.13a) became the first and only 5.13 in the area. During the next

A. Spiderman Buttress and Mesa Verde Wall
B. Mesa Verde Wall–Center Base Routes
C. Mesa Verde Wall–Left Side
D. Pleasure Palace

decade the level will inevitably increase as climbers turn to some of Smith's cleanest sections of untapped stone.

Finding the crags: The only practical approach to most of the West Side Crags is via Asterisk Pass. Since the exposed fourth-class downclimb can freak out anyone with a fear of heights, the west side makes a poor choice for classes or beginners. A much longer alternative hikes all the way around the Southern Tip to an uphill trail joining the cliff line near Snake Rock.

THE AWL

Just beyond Asterisk Pass rises a leaning 60-foot spire with an obvious short dihedral on the south side. This historic pinnacle sees surprisingly few ascents—despite obvious potential, there's only one free route to the top. **Descent:** a free rappel off the overhanging uphill face.

1. Inside Corner (5.10c) ★★★ Mixed to 0.75 inch. Humbling generations of climbers, this puny 20-foot dihedral was the hardest free route on Smith tuff for fifteen years. Clip a bolt off the starting ledge and jam, stem, lieback, and claw your way to a good ledge. Easy moves on a slab lead to the captivating summit.

1.	Inside Corner 5.10c	13.	Modern Zombie 5.10d
7.	Lunatic to Love 5.10a	14.	Midriff Bulge 5.10a
8.	Christian Brothers Traverse 5.10d (or 5.7 A1) R	17.	Benedictine Punk 5.7
10.	Roots of Madness 5.11a R	18.	Bare Midriff 5.10a R
11.	Hot Monkey Love 5.11a	20.	Holier than Thou 5.11b
12.	Fallen Angel 5.10c R	21.	Monk Chimney 5.7 R

2. Project (5.14?) No topo. The pocketed southeast prow of the Awl isn't fully prepared, but there might be enough holds for a free ascent. It awaits some teenage kid with inhuman finger strength.

3. Merkin's Jerkin (A2) ★ No topo. Aid rack to 0.5 inch. An aid seam followed by quarter-inch studs ascends right of the overhanging prow. No one gives it a second glance.

4. Project (5.12?) No topo. An abandoned project on the overhanging uphill face of The Awl hasn't captured anyone's attention. The upper portion looks good, but the flawed start will require aggressive cleaning.

THE CHRISTIAN BROTHERS— WEST FACE

The west face of the Christian Brothers stands in contrast to the more popular east side. The jumbled, lichen-covered rock lacks the obvious clean lines found elsewhere on the formation, though several sport routes are top-notch. With most climbs ascending huge blocks leaning against the base of the cliff, the promising upper wall remains undeveloped. **Descent:** The few routes to the top of the west wall intercept the *Christian*

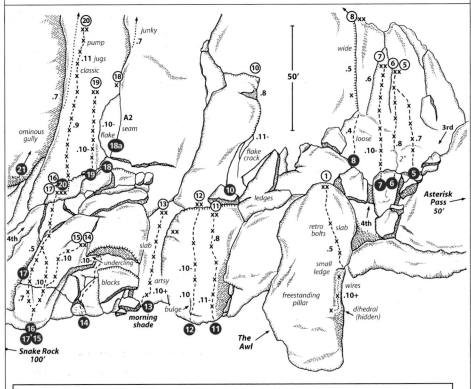

1.	Inside Corner 5.10c	11.	Hot Monkey Love 5.11a	17.	Benedictine Punk 5.7
5.	Little Indian Princess 5.7	12.	Fallen Angel 5.10c R	18.	Bare Midriff 5.10a R
6.	Am I Evil? 5.8	13.	Modern Zombie 5.10d	18a.	Bare Variation 5.5 A2
7.	Lunatic to Love 5.10a	14.	Midriff Bulge 5.10a	19.	Get on the Ball 5.10b
8.	Christian Brothers Traverse	15.	Manic Nirvana 5.10c	20.	Holier than Thou 5.11b
	5.10d (or 5.7 A1) R	16.	Innocent Victim 5.10b	21.	Monk Chimney 5.7 R
10.	Roots of Madness 5.11a R				

Brothers Traverse. You can rap the west side with two ropes, or continue along the traverse, eventually rappelling from an anchor on the north side of Snake Rock.

The far right side of the cliff offers three short sport routes and the starting point for a multi-pitch adventure. The best approach scrambles north along the crest of Asterisk Pass through a notch to a short third-class downclimb.

5. Little Indian Princess (5.7) ★★ 5 bolts. This diminutive sport climb begins with amusing knobs. Finish by veering left to an anchor atop a flake crack.

6. Am I Evil? (5.8) ★★ Mixed to 1.5 inches. The center route starts with a crux lieback followed by an easy slab. A bolted flake crack ends at an anchor. A cam protects the opening moves.

7. Lunatic to Love (5.10a) ★★★ 8 bolts. The left sport route is the best of the bunch. A tricky start on a vertical wall gives way to fun knob-hopping on excellent rock.

8. Christian Brothers Traverse (5.10d [or 5.7 A1] R) ★ Mixed to 3 inches. Anyone bored with the usual routine of crowded sport routes might enjoy traversing the summits of the Christian Brothers—the Priest, Monk, Pope, Friar, and Abbot. Bad rock and sketchy protection make it far too serious for the beginner—retreat isn't as simple as lowering to the ground. Still, the fine position and beautiful scenery make the traverse worth doing once in every adventure climber's lifetime. Avoid the traverse on any busy day—the rubble you knock off might kill someone hundreds of feet below. Start left of the cluster of sport routes near Asterisk Pass, below an obvious crack system. **Pitch 1:** (5.5) Easy climbing on crumbling rock leads to diverging cracks. Ascend huge knobs next to the wide crack on the left or grovel up a flake crack (5.6) on the right. Belay at bolts on the Priest's south buttress. A sport option begins with *Kathleen Finds an Edge* (see chapter 5). **Pitch 2:** (5.4) Romp up fun potholes and leap across a frightening gap to a low-angle slab. Climb big holds to a belay on the crest of the ridge. **Pitch 3:** (5.7) Gain the highest point of the ridge, either directly or by a miserable crack to the left. A bolt-protected face move ends on the summit of the Priest. Rappel north into a notch. **Pitch 4:** (5.6) A scary traverse right leads to a squeeze chimney between the Monk's twin summits. Writhe up the slot to the top and rappel into another low notch to the north. It's possible to bypass the Monk by continuing the starting traverse to the Monk/Pope notch. **Pitch 5:** (5.4) Climb an unprotected chimney and a crumbling slab to the top of the Pope. Rappel into a slot at the base of the Friar. The original route bypassed the Pope with a face traverse to the left. **Pitch 6:** (5.6) Stroll up rotten rock past comical bolts to the top of the Friar. Rappel

north into the Hobbit Hole—an unexposed amphitheater between the Friar and Abbot. A third-class traverse leads along the east side of the Abbot to the base of the northeast face. **Pitch 7:** (5.10d) The miniature summit of the Abbot sees very few ascents. The summit bulb seems frightfully perched atop a slender column. It might stay put for thousands of years or it may fall over tomorrow. If you'd like to speed up the process, climb past a bolted crux bulge to a lichen-plastered slab. Simple junk leads to a 5.7 boulder move to the summit. Adventure climbers lacking 5.10 skills can easily reduce the grade to 5.7 A1 with aid slings.

8a. The Abbot–Pot Belly (5.6 A1) No topo. Bolts (missing). The original route to the top defied common sense by bolting the line of greatest resistance over a big bulge on the east side. Most of the bolts disappeared long ago.

9. Christian Brothers Reverse (5.10d [or 5.7 A1] X) ★ No topo. Mixed to 1 inch. The north-to-south traverse of the Christian Brothers appeals to fewer climbers than the original route, since most of the summits succumb to mindless bolt ladders. The position is just as memorable as the normal line, and demented adventure climbers will find the repugnant rock even more to their liking. Approach from atop the Dihedrals via a fourth-class traverse along an exposed ridge. **Pitch 1:** (5.10d) Free or aid (5.7 A1) to the summit of the Abbot. A short rappel from the top down the northeast side leads to an anchor on the right side of a ledge. A second rap ends at an anchor at the notch between the Abbot and the Friar. **Pitch 2:** (5.0) A simple, lichen-covered traverse leads far left past a single bolt to a belay bolt in a shallow cave. **Pitch 3:** (5.3 A1) Clip a mixture of original and new bolts over a bulge to the summit of the Friar. Belay at the lower summit ridge anchor and rappel diagonally to the Friar/Pope notch. **Pitch 4:** (5.7) A brief stint of squalor leads to a bolt and a fun ridge ending atop the Pope. Don't fall—the hardest climbing comes before the first clip. Rappel to the notch between the Pope and the Monk. **Pitch 5:** (5.4 A1) Chimney to the start of a bolt ladder. Clip good bolts and bad bolts up a disintegrating streak to the double summits of the Monk. Rappel to the Monk/Priest notch, finishing with a scary traverse past a massive loose flake. **Pitch 6:** (A1) Aid an uneventful bolt ladder to the summit of the Priest. Two rappels with double ropes down the west face of the Priest lead to the ground.

9a. The Friar–Northeast Arête (5.6 X) No topo. Gear to 2 inches. A free alternative to the summit of the Friar ascends directly up the exposed northeast ridge. After climbing to the notch between the two formations, solo to the top. Falling is not an option.

9b. The Birthday Start (5.7) ★ Gear to 4 inches. An alternate start to the *Christian Brothers Reverse* ascends a short, unappealing groove between the Abbot and the Friar. Approach from the top of the Dihedrals and skirt around the western base of the Abbot.

THE CHRISTIAN BROTHERS—WEST FACE BASE ROUTES

The following routes ascend directly above the trail skirting the western base of the Christian Brothers. The sport routes are all worth doing—the few traditional climbs aren't.

10. Roots of Madness (5.11a R) ★ Gear to 2.5 inches. A distinctive right-arching crack system rises from a stack of blocks above the Awl. Expect difficult protection, friable flakes, and a bad anchor.

11. Hot Monkey Love (5.11a) ★★★ 6 bolts. Just beyond the Awl sits the appealing Fallen Angel Block. The solid right arête begins with a bouldering sequence and finishes with delightful knobs.

12. Fallen Angel (5.10c R) ★★ 3 bolts. A sparsely bolted route ascends the center of the block. Getting to the first bolt isn't easy, with a crux cranking on good knobs over the obvious bulge. A poorly located second bolt forces a tricky move before making the clip.

13. Modern Zombie (5.10d) ★★★ 6 bolts. Tucked left of the Fallen Angel Block is a narrow low-angle face with a well-scrubbed swath of knobs up the center. The crux traverse at the start finesses underclings, edges, and small knobs; the finishing nubbins are fun and much easier.

14. Midriff Bulge (5.10a) ★★ Gear to 1.5 inches. The only decent traditional route on the west side of the Christian Brothers climbs over an unmistakable roof. A short but intense undercling leads to an awkward crux skirting the lip. Lower from an anchor to the left or continue up junk to a large ledge.

15. Manic Nirvana (5.10c) ★★ 6 bolts. A kooky route traverses above the lip left of the *Midriff Bulge* roof. The lower knobs are enjoyable, but the contrived crux defies logic. The much easier line of least resistance traverses just a few feet higher.

16. Innocent Victim (5.10b) ★★ 9 bolts. A more sensible line starts with *Manic Nirvana* before veering up and left to a simple finish on good knobs. The small nubbins are unnerving, though the bad ones likely snapped off years ago.

17. Benedictine Punk (5.7) ★★★ 10 bolts. This excellent slab makes a fine choice for any beginner. Start with a short crack and race up solid knobs on a carefully scrubbed face to an anchor.

The following four routes start from the left end of a ledge system running across the midsection of the wall. Approach by scrambling in from the left (3rd class), or climb *Midriff Bulge, Innocent Victim,* or *Benedictine Punk.*

18. Bare Midriff (5.10a R) ★ Gear to 3 inches. Above *Midriff Bulge,* a frightfully thin flake leads into a gully ending in the notch between the Monk and the Priest. On granite the flake would be classic, but at Smith it's freaky. From the finishing notch either

see the *Christian Brothers Traverse* or rappel the route with two ropes.

18a. Bare Variation (5.5 A2) ★ Aid rack to 1 inch. The original route nailed a seam to the right of the flake before joining the gully on the regular line. It would obviously go free at a reasonable grade, though better routes are everywhere.

19. Get on the Ball (5.10b) ★★★ 7 bolts. A shallow arête rises a few feet left of the *Bare Midriff* flake crack. A tricky opening sequence on good rock leads to an easier knobby finish.

20. Holier than Thou (5.11b) ★★★★ 12 bolts. This brilliant route climbs the center of an attractive face. It looks blank from the ground, but jugs appear on the upper wall just when they're needed most. Perfect rock, great moves, and a memorable position make it one of Smith's finest 5.11s.

21. Monk Chimney (5.7 R) Gear to 4 inches. An ugly corridor splits the entire northwest face of the Christian Brothers. An abysmal route follows double cracks on terrible rock to the notch between the Monk and the Pope. Descend with a double-rope rappel or continue along the *Christian Brothers Traverse.*

SNAKE ROCK

Beyond the Christian Brothers stands a large buttress split by an obvious crack system. The cliff's name comes from a small snake-head boulder guarding the base of the wall. Varied sport routes on solid rock make it a popular stop. **Descent:** Few routes go to the top of Snake Rock. For those that do, rappel from an anchor atop the north end of the cliff.

22. The Snake (5.9) ★★ Gear to 5 inches. The original route on Snake Rock follows the prominent crack splitting the south side of the buttress. Unfortunately, a grubby finish detracts from an otherwise decent climb. Bring big cams or face a long run-out on the first pitch. **Pitch 1:** (5.7) An easy crack leads to a strenuous lieback ending at an anchor. **Pitch 2:** (5.9) Stem the short crux and slither up a flaring chimney to the top.

22a. Venom (5.10b) ★ Gear to 5 inches. Closely spaced parallel cracks rise a few feet right of the regular line. Painful thin hand jams deteriorate into a mediocre flare above.

23. Don't Tread on Me

(5.8) ★★ 8 bolts. A low-angle slab/arête rises a few feet left of *The Snake*. The imperfect rock will only improve after an inevitable onslaught from climbers lured by the plentiful bolts and low grade.

23a. Don't Tread on Me finish (5.10b) ★ 2 bolts. A direct finish continues up a short, technical wall to a higher anchor. The only thing wrong with this crimpy variant is a total lack of fun moves.

24. Reptile (5.8) ★★ Gear to 2.5 inches. A shallow dihedral splits the wall around the corner from *Don't Tread on Me*. The pleasant moves protect easily, though most climbers opt for a toprope.

Snake Rock

22.	The Snake 5.9	27.	Split Image 5.12d
22a.	Venom 5.10b	28.	Made in the Shade 5.12c
23.	Don't Tread on Me 5.8	29.	Cling On 5.9
23a.	Don't Tread on Me finish 5.10b	30.	A Desperate Man 5.9
24.	Reptile 5.8	31.	Hemp Liberation 5.10d
25.	Iquanas on Elm Street 5.10c	32.	Lords of Karma 5.12c
26.	The Golden Road 5.11b	33.	Strung Out 5.9
		34.	Struck Out 5.6 X

Snake Rock and Angel Flight Crags

Angel Flight Crags

The Abbot

Follies of Youth Block

Angel Flight Buttress

Pillar of the Community

Snake Rock

8.	Christian Brothers Traverse	33.	Strung Out 5.9
	5.10d (or 5.7 A1) R	34.	Struck Out 5.6 X
9b.	The Birthday Start 5.7	35.	La Nina 5.10b
25.	Iquanas on Elm Street 5.10c	37.	Project 5.13?
27.	Split Image 5.12d	38.	Heaven Can Wait 5.7 R
29.	Cling On 5.9	39.	Angel Flight Buttress 5.8 R
31.	Hemp Liberation 5.10d	43.	Youthful Indiscretion
32.	Lords of Karma 5.12c		(aka Wisdom of Age) 5.9

25. Iquanas on Elm Street (5.10c) ★★★ 6 bolts. Crammed tightly left of *Reptile* is the best moderate route on the crag. Fun moves on side pulls and good edges lead to a delicate crux above the fourth bolt.

26. The Golden Road (5.11b) ★★ 3 bolts. Originally rated 5.10d, this attractive golden face grew harder as almost every hold snapped off. Today the remaining edges are solid, though the delicate footwork and crimps at the crux hold little appeal for many climbers. A stick-clip makes the start a lot safer.

27. Split Image (5.12d) ★★★★ 5 bolts. There are longer and steeper arêtes at Smith, but this showpiece of the West Side Crags ranks with the very best. After a baffling technical crux at the first bolt, easier moves on flawless rock lead to an intricate finishing sequence. For a few months during 1984 it was the

hardest route in the park. The first ascent climbed almost entirely on the right side of the arête; repeat ascents discovered an easier line on the left wall. Expect a tricky second clip unless you follow the original line.

28. Made in the Shade (5.12c) ★★★ 4 bolts. The wall left of *Split Image* would be an excellent 5.11 if not for a tip-splitting boulder problem. After a micro-crimp crux below the first bolt, the moves are fun and much more enjoyable.

29. Cling On (5.9) ★★ Gear to 4 inches. An impressive dihedral capped by a huge roof dominates the center of Snake Rock. The great rock and varied climbing curiously attract very little attention. The short first pitch makes a fine traditional lead in its own right. **Pitch 1:** (5.8) Race up a high-quality flake crack to a ledge. **Pitch 2:** (5.9) Either jam or lieback the overhanging crack and traverse right to the anchor atop *Don't Tread on Me*. Rappel or continue to the top via the upper pitch of *The Snake*.

30. A Desperate Man (5.9) ★★ Gear to 1 inch. A large boulder leans against the clean left wall of the *Cling On* dihedral. A few feet left of this block rises a modest flake crack. A brief flurry of jams on good rock end at anchors not far off the ground.

31. Hemp Liberation (5.10d) ★★★ 5 bolts. Shortly before the cliff line recedes, a final line of bolts stretches toward the sky. *Hemp Liberation* pulls around the right side of a small roof, ending at a midpitch anchor. Although intimidating, good holds appear in all the right places.

32. Lords of Karma (5.12c) ★★★ 13 bolts. A much harder continuation to *Hemp Liberation* attacks the sweeping wall above the anchor. Despite decent rock, lots of bolts, and intense climbing, it sees few attempts. To climb in one long pitch, use a long sling on the bolt under the lower roof and unclip the first bolt past the lip.

33. Strung Out (5.9) ★ Gear to 5 inches. Walking uphill around the bulging north face of Snake Rock, the rock quickly deteriorates. The only route of any consequence ascends an ominous flare. This full-body workout starts with hand jams in a wildly overhanging bombay chimney and ends after a short off-width, with nothing but suffering in between.

34. Struck Out (5.6 X) Gear to 2.5 inches. Uphill from *Strung Out* rises a low-angle flaring crack with a face climbing start to the left. Expect thick lichen, junky rock, and poor protection—three strikes and you're out.

ANGEL FLIGHT CRAGS

North of Snake Rock, the unbroken cliff line gives way to smaller gully-split crags. Pillar of the Community dominates, while the Angel Flight Buttress and Follies of Youth Block sit to the left. Lichen grows heavy, but several routes are marginally worth doing.

Pillar of the Community

Easily the most impressive of the Angel Flight Crags is this large chunk of rock with a gently overhanging river face. Despite some untapped potential, there's almost no reason to visit.

35. La Nina (5.10b) ★ 6 bolts. A really junky route ascends the southeast arête of the pillar. Wait a few years and *La Nina* might improve—for now it's one of Smith's least pleasant sport climbing experiences.

36. Up the Backside (5.3 R) ★ Gear to 2.5 inches. The only route to the summit starts with simple jugs on the uphill side of the formation, leading to an old bolt on top. Reverse the route or rappel from an anchor a few feet upstream.

37. Project (5.13?) 7 bolts. The appealing arête on the downhill side of the block sports a fully prepared project. A severe bouldering sequence at the start provides the biggest obstacle. It might be a free route by the time you visit.

Angel Flight Buttress

A prominent low-angle buttress extends down the hillside across the gully from Pillar of the Community. The small collection of routes receive very few ascents. **Descent:**

Angel Flight Crags

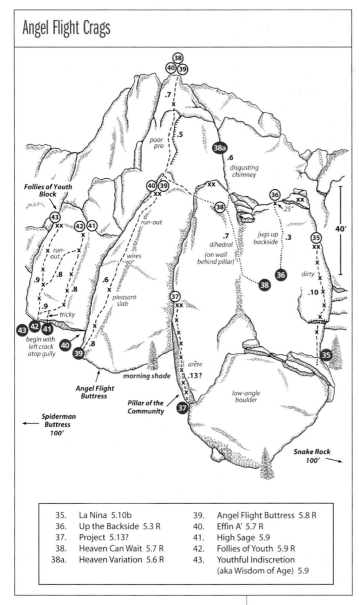

35.	La Nina 5.10b	39.	Angel Flight Buttress 5.8 R
36.	Up the Backside 5.3 R	40.	Effin A' 5.7 R
37.	Project 5.13?	41.	High Sage 5.9
38.	Heaven Can Wait 5.7 R	42.	Follies of Youth 5.9 R
38a.	Heaven Variation 5.6 R	43.	Youthful Indiscretion (aka Wisdom of Age) 5.9

Walk downstream into a gully right of Spiderman Buttress. Scramble down a short fourth-class section.

38. Heaven Can Wait (5.7 R) ★ Mixed to 1.5 inches. Hidden from view until you're standing at the base, this uninspiring route starts behind Pillar of the Community. It's not worth walking uphill for. **Pitch 1:** (5.7) Traverse left along a ledge and jam a low-angle inside corner. **Pitch 2:** (5.7) Merge with *Angel Flight Buttress* to the left and finish with a bolt-protected boulder move.

38a. Heaven Variation (5.6 R) Gear to 3 inches. A grotesque alternative avoids the upper pitch of *Angel Flight Buttress* with a disintegrating chimney rising above the first belay.

39. Angel Flight Buttress (5.8 R) ★★ Mixed to 1 inch. An enjoyable route ascends the downhill face of the buttress. If better protected, this lichen-covered slab might become popular; currently few climbers try. Start uphill and left of the lowest point on the buttress. **Pitch 1:** (5.8) After a tricky start easier knobs lead past a couple bolts to a simple crack. Continue up the slab to a bolt belay. **Pitch 2:** (5.7) A crumbly face move past a single bolt ends on top.

40. Effin A' (5.7 R) ★ Mixed to 3.5 inches. Double cracks separate Angel Flight Buttress from Follies of Youth Block to the left. An obscure trad route starts with the left crack and jams to a slabby traverse to the right

crack. After a bulge, hand traverse right to the anchor atop the first pitch of *Angel Flight Buttress*. Follow the original route to the top.

Follies of Youth Block

The squarish chunk of rock at the left side of Angel Flight Crags offers two worthwhile sport routes, along with the remnants of the original line.

41. High Sage (5.9) ★★ 4 bolts. The rounded right edge of the block offers fun climbing, though it lacks a good start. An undercut boulder problem is too hard for 5.9 climbers, while the only moderate option traverses in from the left. Long ago, a hard direct sequence began after balancing atop sagebrush. With the sagebrush flattened, the holds are now out of reach.

42. Follies of Youth (5.9 R) ★★ 3 bolts. You can still climb the original route, though better-protected lines on either side make much better choices. Start by climbing to the second bolt on *Youthful Indiscretion* and cut up and right across the face without protection to the last bolt on *High Sage*.

43. Youthful Indiscretion (aka Wisdom of Age) (5.9) ★★★ 4 bolts. The best climb on the block shares the same start as the other two routes but follows a direct line to the left. Expect excellent rock and enjoyable moves with a few stretches between good holds.

SPIDERMAN BUTTRESS

After skirting the base of Snake Rock, the trail diagonals uphill past the Angel Flight Crags to the impressive Spiderman Buttress. This popular crag features good rock, morning shade, and many high-caliber moderate routes. **Descent:** Most routes end on top of the crag. Descend by dropping into a gully on the right to a short fourth-class downclimb.

44. Common Household Fly (5.5) ★ Gear to 3 inches. At the far right side of the buttress are parallel low-angle cracks barely deserving a glance. The right line succumbs to a short stint of jams.

A triangular roof rises above a large square block pasted against the right base of the buttress. After a short starting pitch (5.5) up a clean chimney, the following two routes undercling around opposite sides of this roof.

45. Arachnid Boogie (5.9) ★ Gear to 3 inches. Cutting right around the big roof provides a few entertaining moments, but the finish deteriorates into a losing battle against bad rock and rope drag.

46. Tarantula (5.11d) ★★ Mixed to 2.5 inches. This intimidating pitch once ranked among the hardest climbs in the park. Today it collects cobwebs. Despite good rock and an exhilarating lieback above the roof, the contorted crux at the lip stays in your mind long after the good memories fade.

47. Imaginary Spider (5.4 A3+ R) ★ Aid rack to 1 inch. An obscure aid seam ending at a single bolt splits the start of the blank wall left of *Tarantula*. The entire wall will inevitably go free someday, perhaps using this line as a start.

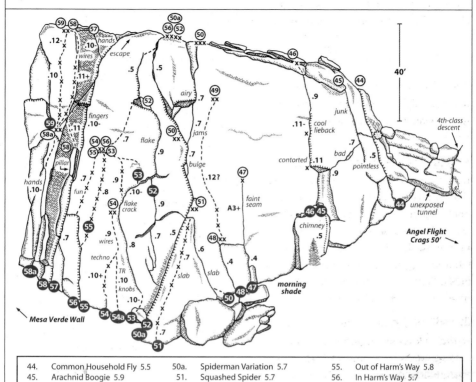

44.	Common Household Fly 5.5	50a.	Spiderman Variation 5.7	55.	Out of Harm's Way 5.8
45.	Arachnid Boogie 5.9	51.	Squashed Spider 5.7	56.	In Harm's Way 5.7
46.	Tarantula 5.11d	52.	Widow Maker 5.9 R	57.	Little Feat 5.10b R
47.	Imaginary Spider 5.4 A3+ R	53.	'Best Left to Obscurity 5.10a R	58.	Cornerstone 5.11d
48.	First Ascent Crack 5.4	54.	Explosive Energy Child 5.10d R	58a.	Cornerstone Variation 5.10a
49.	Project 5.12?	54a.	More or Lester 5.10c TR	59.	Death Takes a Holiday 5.12a
50.	Spiderman 5.7				

48. First Ascent Crack (5.4) ★★ Gear to 2.5 inches. This very short route scrambles 25 feet up a low-angle crack to an anchor. It makes a good introduction to traditional climbing, with easy protection and simple moves. The harder knobs to the left provide a fun toprope exercise (5.7).

49. Project (5.12?) An aborted free project follows a seam above *First Ascent Crack* past two bolts before hitting a dead end. The intended line would follow face holds uncomfortably close to *Spiderman* to an anchor below the top.

50. Spiderman (5.7) ★★★★ Gear to 3 inches. An unmistakable low-angle buttress leans against the lowest part of the cliff. One of Smith's best traditional routes jams the right side of the buttress and the clean crack above in two fun-filled pitches. Great rock, a fine position, and exhilarating moves make it the best climb on the crag. **Pitch 1:** (5.7) Cruise a fun crack and pull past an intimidating bulge to belay bolts on a slab. **Pitch 2:** (5.7) Jam an exposed crack to a memorable lieback around the right side of a roof. Simple scrambling on imperfect rock ends on top.

Spiderman Buttress and Mesa Verde Wall—Southwest Face

Pleasure Palace

95

68

69

66

84

Mesa Verde Wall

71

79   76

58   56

52

51   Spiderman Buttress

50

46

46.	Tarantula 5.11d	68.	Long Time Gone 5.13a
50.	Spiderman 5.7	69.	Palo Verde 5.6 A2+
51.	Squashed Spider 5.7	71.	Cows in Agony 5.11a
52.	Widow Maker 5.9 R	76.	Desolation Row 5.11a
56.	In Harm's Way 5.7	79.	Tale of Two Shities 5.10a
58.	Cornerstone 5.11d	84.	Moons of Pluto 5.10d
66.	Western Chimney 5.5 R	95.	Bop 'Till You Drop 5.11a

50a. Spiderman Variation (5.7) ★★★ Gear to 3 inches. A less exciting version of *Spiderman* offers unnerved climbers an easy escape from the second-pitch roof. The position of the upper section doesn't match the original line, but it still warrants attention. **Pitch 1:** (5.7) Climb the solid dihedral on the left side of the low-angle buttress, joining the regular route below the crux bulge. **Pitch 2:** (5.5) Ascend the ramp around a corner to the left and frolic up a mediocre crack system to the top.

51. Squashed Spider (5.7) ★★★ 7 bolts. Starting from the lowest part of the buttress, this fun sport route ascends solid knobs on an attractive low-angle face. Originally led with no bolts, it became popular only after a compassionate retro-bolting.

52. Widow Maker (5.9 R) ★★★ Gear to 2 inches. This strenuous flake crack leads past

two small roofs on the vertical wall left of *Spiderman*. The sustained climbing protects reasonably well, if you have the endurance to stop in the middle of the pumping moves. **Pitch 1:** (5.9) Begin with the left-hand start to *Spiderman* and step over to the crack. Committing liebacks and jams end at a small ledge. **Pitch 2:** (5.5) Waltz up easy cracks to the top.

53. Best Left to Obscurity (5.10a R) ★ Gear to 1.5 inches. The worst route on the buttress features a dangerous encounter with teetering blocks. Start with a hard move above a small block and climb a right-arching crack. Pull lightly on loose boulders and traverse left to an anchor, fighting rope drag the whole way

54. Explosive Energy Child (5.10d R) ★★★ Mixed to 1 inch. When first climbed in

Spiderman Buttress and Mesa Verde Wall—Northwest Face

Pleasure Palace

Mesa Verde Wall

Spiderman Buttress

50a.	Spiderman Variation 5.7	69.	Palo Verde 5.6 A2+
55.	Out of Harms Way 5.8	73.	Juniper Face 5.12b
57.	Little Feat 5.10b	82.	Minas Morgul 5.11d
61.	Dr. Doom 5.9	85.	Screaming Yellow Zonkers 5.10b
65.	Captain Fingers 5.10a	87.	Trezlar 5.10a

1977, this short wall of miniature nubbins was Smith's hardest face route. Bolts protect the delicate edging at the crux, but expect a run-out on the much easier seam above. Avoid the hanging belay in the middle by linking both pitches together—or simply ignore the upper pitch. **Pitch 1:** (5.10d) Tiptoe up micro knobs to a leaning seam and a hanging belay. **Pitch 2:** (5.9) Follow a flake crack and exit left past two bolts. Traverse far left to an anchor.

54a. More or Lester (5.10c) ★★ TR. A worthwhile toprope problem follows knobs right of the regular line, joining the start of the leaning seam.

55. Out of Harm's Way (5.8) ★★★ Mixed to 1.5 inches. One of the best pitches on the crag follows a delightful knobby face left of *Explosive Energy Child*. Although largely a sport route, the shallow right-facing dihedral at the start requires gear.

56. In Harm's Way (5.7) ★★★ Mixed to 2 inches. Long ago, the first pitch of *In Harm's Way* was the only bolted free route on the entire west side. You'll enjoy the huge knobs on the lower slab, but the lackluster upper pitch has few redeeming qualities. Start in the same right-facing corner as *Out of Harm's Way*. **Pitch 1:** (5.7) Jam the miniature dihedral to a large ledge and wander past classic knobs to an anchor. Rappel if you're smart or . . . **Pitch 2:** (5.7) Move right and make one awkward move to junky cracks.

57. Little Feat (5.10b R) ★★ Gear to 2.5 inches. An obvious right-facing corner dominates the left side of Spiderman Buttress. This varied route weathers a little rotten rock at the start before launching into crux

Spiderman Buttress and Mesa Verde Wall

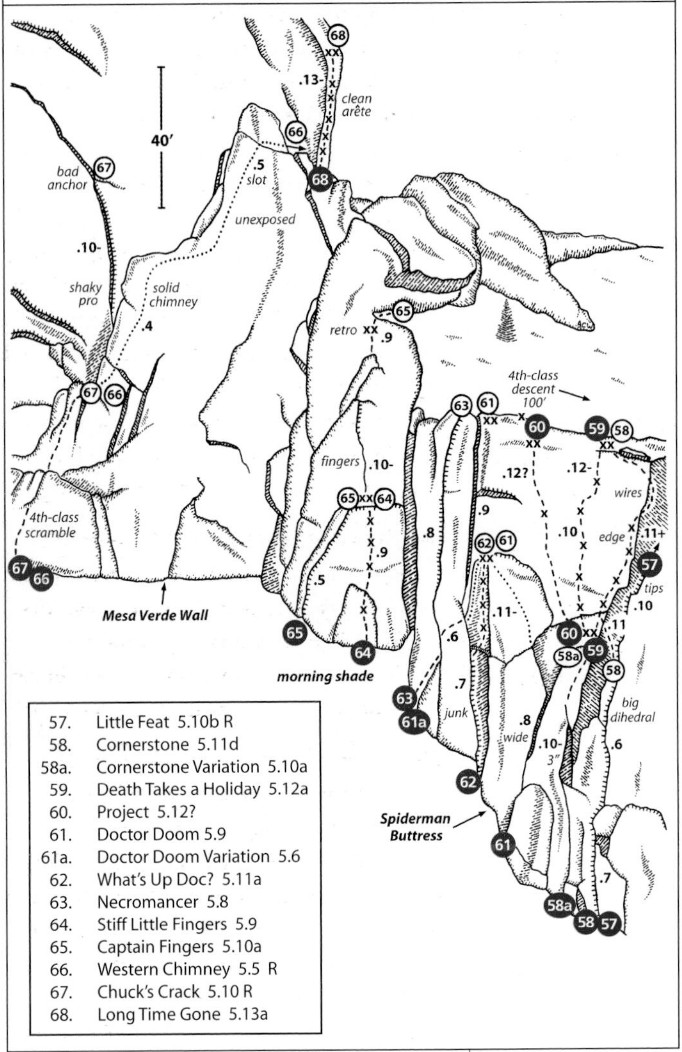

(topo diagram labels:)

68 XX
.13-
clean arête
66
.5 slot
68
bad anchor
67
40'
unexposed
.10-
shaky pro
solid chimney
.4
67 66
4th-class scramble
67 66
Mesa Verde Wall
retro XX
.9
65
4th-class descent 100'
fingers .10-
63 61 60 59 58
XX XX
.12?
.12-
wires
65 XX 64
.9
.8
.9
62 61
.10-
edge .11+
57
tips
.10
.5
60 XX .11
58a 59
65
.6
58
64
.11-
morning shade
63
61a
junk
.7
.8 .10-
wide 3"
big dihedral
.6
62
Spiderman Buttress
61
58a
.7
58 57

57.	Little Feat 5.10b R
58.	Cornerstone 5.11d
58a.	Cornerstone Variation 5.10a
59.	Death Takes a Holiday 5.12a
60.	Project 5.12?
61.	Doctor Doom 5.9
61a.	Doctor Doom Variation 5.6
62.	What's Up Doc? 5.11a
63.	Necromancer 5.8
64.	Stiff Little Fingers 5.9
65.	Captain Fingers 5.10a
66.	Western Chimney 5.5 R
67.	Chuck's Crack 5.10 R
68.	Long Time Gone 5.13a

sport climbers. **Pitch 1:** (5.7) Climb the *Little Feat* dihedral to a belay atop a pedestal. **Pitch 2:** (5.11d) Make a few hard moves (5.11c) protected by wires to a large ledge. Fully rested, finesse past four bolts on the crux arête to a naturally protected finish.

58a. Cornerstone Variation (5.10a) ★★ Gear to 3 inches. The original line bypassed the hard moves off the pedestal by climbing a sweeping hand crack to the left.

59. Death Takes a Holiday (5.12a) ★★★ 5 bolts. The wall left of *Cornerstone* contains the hardest route on the buttress. Reasonable moves on a gently overhanging face culminate in a strenuous crux just below the top. The inaccessible location keeps most climbers away, though the exposure only adds to the charm. Approach from above with a short rappel.

60. Project (5.12?) There's room left of *Death Takes a Holiday* for a couple more quality routes. A few bolts remain from an early reconnaissance.

61. Doctor Doom (5.9) ★★★ Gear to 6 inches. An unmistakable wide crack splits

finger jams on great rock. Finish with a short overhanging hand crack on the left, or weasel off to the right.

58. Cornerstone (5.11d) ★★ Mixed to 1.5 inches. A forgotten route follows the arête left of *Little Feat*. The upper pitch contains two distinct crux sections separated by a ledge. The entire line protects well, though the small nuts might spook today's gym-bred the far left side of the Spiderman Buttress. Modern gear safely protects the ominous upper pitch, but the moves are as awkward as ever. Start on the right side of a large pillar. **Pitch 1:** (5.8) Climb a short fist crack leading into a chimney. Belay atop a massive flat-topped block. **Pitch 2:** (5.9) Step left and thrash to the top on high-quality rock.

61a. Doctor Doom Variation (5.6) Gear to 3 inches. An alternate start scrambles up easy trash on the left side of the starting pillar. You can climb *Dr. Doom* in a single pitch using this variant.

62. What's Up Doc? (5.11a) ★★ Mixed to 3.5 inches. A sharp arête sits below the wide crack of *Dr. Doom*. It would be popular if fully bolted, but a miserable approach up a dirty trad crack guards the base.

63. Necromancer (5.8) ★★ Gear to 3 inches. With a solid finishing dihedral, the far left corner on the Spiderman Buttress might raise your spirits, despite an opening sequence plowing through garbage.

MESA VERDE WALL

The majestic Mesa Verde Wall dominates the skyline left of Spiderman Buttress. With pleasant modern and traditional lines, this monolith makes a good choice on a summer morning—many routes stay shaded well past noon. **Descent:** From the top of the cliff, hike downhill to the right and scramble down a fourth-class gully right of Spiderman Buttress. Traditional routes on the northwest side end below the summit at a massive ledge system stretching across the face. To descend from these routes, scramble left around a corner to an exposed slab (4th class) ending at a single bolt. Rappel or downclimb the chimney below and hike down easy ledges.

64. Stiff Little Fingers (5.9) ★★ 4 bolts. A lackluster wall rises above the high point of the hillside between Spiderman Buttress and Mesa Verde Wall. A second-rate sport route leads to a ledge below an obvious thin crack. Either lower off or continue via the following route.

65. Captain Fingers (5.10a) ★★ Mixed to 2 inches. A painful thin crack splits the wall above *Stiff Little Fingers*. The original start scrambled up a rotten left-facing corner (5.5), though most climbers opt for the direct start. A new anchor atop a pedestal just below the top completely changed the character of the route. Today most climbers lower off before what was once an unnerving boulder-problem finish.

66. Western Chimney (5.5 R) ★★★ Gear to 3 inches. A gigantic flake system leans against the right side of Mesa Verde Wall, creating a hidden chimney. Good rock and enjoyable climbing make it unlike the typical Smith rubble chimney. Approach via a simple fourth-class scramble.

67. Chuck's Crack (5.10b R) ★ Gear to 1.5 inches. Immediately left of *Western Chimney* with little for the feet. A physical final clip adds to the difficulty. Approach via Cocaine Gully or scramble up the hillside above Spiderman Buttress.

69. Palo Verde (5.6 A2+) ★★ Aid rack to 1.5 inches. The only route on the imposing main face of Mesa Verde Wall follows an obvious crack system up the center of the cliff. Except for some junk at the top, it features better-than-average rock for a Smith aid route. It will soon go free, with a brilliant 5.12 pitch capped by a 5.11 finish. **Pitch 1:** (4th class) Scramble to a large ledge system stretching across the base of the wall. **Pitch 2:** (5.6 A2+) Nail a shallow dihedral past a small roof to a hanging belay. **Pitch 3:** (A2+) A long pitch of moderate pin-pounding gives way to a stint of bad rock just below the top.

69.	Palo Verde 5.6 A2+	75.	Project 5.11+ ?
70.	Petroglyph Crack 5.7	76.	Desolation Row 5.11a
71.	Cows in Agony 5.11a	77.	Shadow of Doubt 5.12a
72.	Cliff Dwelling Crack 5.8	78.	Reason to Be 5.11a
73.	Juniper Face 5.12b	79.	Tale of Two Shities 5.10a
74.	Chimney De Chelly 5.10a R		

rises a shallow left-facing corner. After a tricky start with freaky protection, jam to a questionable anchor.

68. Long Time Gone (5.13a) ★★★ 5 bolts. An attractive arête sits high atop the right flanks of Mesa Verde Wall. The crux comes near the top, with intense pinches and side pulls

70. Petroglyph Crack (5.7) ★ Gear to 3 inches. Below the main face of Mesa Verde Wall are two flake cracks ending at a long ledge. The uninspiring right-hand route climbs short triple cracks past eerie blocks.

71. Cows in Agony (5.11a) ★★★ 6 bolts. Right of an obvious flake crack rises an enjoyable sport route on solid rock. You'll raise the grade a notch if you stay right at the lower crux, though almost everyone uses better holds to the left. After a fun midsection, finish with a tough move above the last bolt.

72. Cliff Dwelling Crack (5.8) ★★ Gear to 5 inches. This obvious flake crack sees few ascents despite good rock and a cool lieback crux. Big cams safely protect the wide section at the top.

73. Juniper Face (5.12b) ★★★ 7 bolts. A demanding sport route ascends the right wall of a massive dihedral. If it weren't hidden from view by a juniper tree, this hyper-technical wall might receive more attention. Many 5.12 climbers walk away bewildered and defeated.

74. Chimney De Chelly (5.10a R) ★★ Mixed to 2.5 inches. A multi-pitch route follows the unmistakable dihedral system bordering the left side of the main face. A loose second pitch unfortunately detracts from an otherwise quality climb. **Pitch 1:** (5.10a) Technical finger jams at the start give way to easy potholes. A new bolt on *Juniper Face* protects a tricky face move cutting right to an anchor. **Pitch 2:** (5.9) Balance atop a loose pillar and boulder past a bolt to easy climbing on trashy rock. Belay at an anchor below a large dihedral. **Pitch 3:** (5.8) Stem a fun corner leading into a pleasant finishing chimney. Descend the north-side ledges.

75. Project (5.11+?) An intriguing thin crack slashes across the wall above the first-pitch anchor of *Chimney De Chelly*. Three bolts protect the hardest section, but without a better approach it will never get done. The best option would clean and retro-bolt the second pitch of *Chimney De Chelly* leading into the high-quality leaning crack.

76. Desolation Row (5.11a) ★★★ Mixed to 2.5 inches. A thrilling lieback around a triangular roof highlights this two-pitch jaunt on great rock. Unfortunately, the awkwardly flaring section below the roof isn't much fun. **Pitch 1:** (5.11a) Tricky moves at the start lead to unpleasant finger jams in the back of a deep flare. Clip a bolt at the roof and race to a belay ledge. **Pitch 2:** (5.8) Follow the excellent third-pitch corner of *Chimney De Chelly* to the top.

77. Shadow of Doubt (5.12a) ★★★ 5 bolts. The attractive wall left of *Chimney De Chelly* offers a challenging sport route. Relentless, delicate moves end prematurely with a traverse left to an anchor. A higher anchor awaits someone with technical skill and a power drill.

78. Reason to Be (5.11a) ★★★ 4 bolts. With perfect rock and thoughtful moves, this sharp arête is one of the better sport routes on Mesa Verde Wall. Either start directly up the edge or traverse in from the right.

79. Tale of Two Shities (5.10a) ★★★ Mixed to 2.5 inches. The best multi-pitch route on the main wall offers varied climbing on solid rock. The excellent second-pitch dihedral contains the most physical moves, though technically challenged climbers might find the upper pitch more demanding. Start uphill from the lowest part of the wall below a miniature left-facing corner. **Pitch 1:** (5.7) Jam discontinuous cracks to a belay spot below the attractive dihedral. **Pitch 2:** (5.10a) Strenuous jams on great rock end at a small ledge. **Pitch 3:** (5.9) 2 bolts. An exposed, delicate ramp leads past two bolts to a run-out finish on easier knobs. Descend the north-side ledges.

80. Sundown (5.9) ★★★ Gear to 2 inches. A high-quality traditional route ascends locking jams in a shallow dihedral. Start right of a

Mesa Verde Wall—Left Side

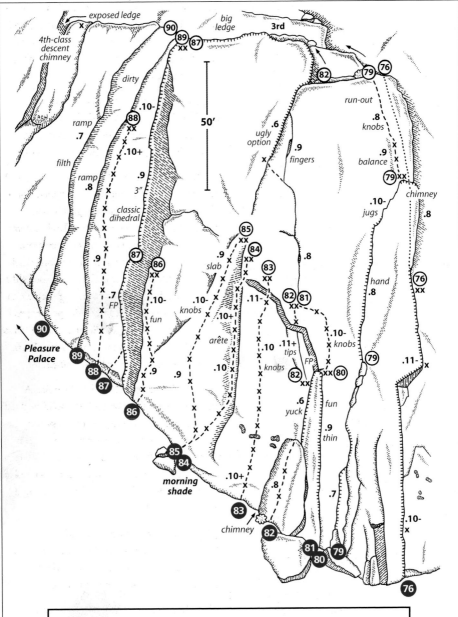

76. Desolation Row 5.11a	85. Screaming Yellow
79. Tale of Two Shities 5.10a	Zonkers 5.10b
80. Sundown 5.9	86. Cosmos 5.10a
81. Down's Syndrome 5.10a R	87. Trezlar 5.10a
82. Minas Morgul 5.11d	88. Planet Luxury 5.10c
83. Bad Moon Rising 5.11a	89. Four Fs 5.8
84. Moons of Pluto 5.10d	90. Lichen Persuasion 5.7

massive block with either a 5.10 direct line or easier face holds to the left. A convenient new anchor eliminates the old hand traverse finish.

81. Down's Syndrome (5.10a R) ★★★ Mixed to 2 inches. Rather than lowering off at the top of the *Sundown* dihedral, attack the face above in one long pitch. Spooky knobs and spaced bolts make it more challenging than most routes of the grade.

82. Minas Morgul (5.11d) ★★★ Mixed to 2.5 inches. In 1981 this overhanging thin crack matched the highest grade in the park. Placing gear burns so much energy that many climbers plummet from good holds pulling around the finishing roof. Start at a large block leaning against the wall. **Pitch 1:** (5.8) Climb knobs to the top of the block and endure junky rock leading to a hanging belay. **Pitch 2:** (5.11d) Jam painful slots on the overhanging wall to another hanging belay over the roof. Lower off or . . . **Pitch 3:** (5.9) Stroll up a low-angle crack on good rock past a small roof and jam a steep finger crack to the top. Fools bypass the final crack by climbing a slovenly corner (5.6) to the left.

83. Bad Moon Rising (5.11a) ★★★ 11 bolts. A few feet left of a huge boulder rises a high-quality flat face capped by a small roof. A perplexing start frustrates anyone who can't reach the holds, but the crux at the roof pleases almost everyone.

84. Moons of Pluto (5.10d) ★★★★ 9 bolts. With great rock, delicate moves, and an exciting position, this classic edge is one of the finest routes on the west side. Anyone lacking in technical skills won't be totally enamored—there aren't many holds at the insecure crux. After cranking around a fun roof at the top, rappel with a 60-meter cord.

85. Screaming Yellow Zonkers (5.10b) ★★★★ 9 bolts. There's no better knobby face at Smith than this colorful wall. The meandering knobs and pockets are tailor-made for climbing, and the many bolts pacify anyone uncomfortable with Smith nubbins. A 60-meter rope barely reaches the starting ledge.

86. Cosmos (5.10a) ★★★ 7 bolts. Another delightful sport route ascends fun knobs a few feet right of an arête. The crux clears a bulge on positive nubbins just below the anchors.

87. Trezlar (5.10a) ★★★★ Gear to 2.5 inches. A beautiful dihedral dominates the shaded north side of Mesa Verde Wall. Originally named *Raindance,* the locking jams and flawless stems protect easily. The grade comes more from the continuity than the difficulty of any single move. Start slightly uphill from the base of the corner. **Pitch 1:** (5.7) Traverse right across the slab to a dirty crack and stem the poorly protected corner to a ledge. **Pitch 2:** (5.10a) Savor the impressive dihedral to a bolt belay. Walk left and descend the north-side ledges.

88. Planet Luxury (5.10c) ★★★ 11 bolts. A charming sport route ascends the solid wall left of *Trezlar.* After starting with an easy slab, the face steepens and the holds dwindle until an arête on the left comes to the rescue. The crux blends delicate pinches and insecure face holds just below the anchor. Lower to the ground with a 70-meter rope.

89. Four Fs (5.8) ★ Gear to 2 inches. Immediately left of *Planet Luxury* are two shallow dihedrals. The lichen-choked right corner succumbs to a single pitch of nastiness.

90. Lichen Persuasion (5.7) ★ Gear to 2 inches. This unappealing line ascends the left of two tight corners next to *Planet Luxury*. The large amounts of lichen will likely persuade you to look elsewhere for your next route.

PLEASURE PALACE

Moving uphill, the north face of Mesa Verde Wall quickly peters out. Beyond lies a broken section of reddish-purple rock with a worthwhile selection of short sport routes. The quickest approach from the parking area hikes up and over Cocaine Gully. If approaching from the West Side Crags, follow the trail toward Monkey Face until a staircase cuts uphill to the right. The following three routes ascend the large purplish wall on the right side of the Pleasure Palace. **Descent:** Most routes end at convenient sport anchors. For those that don't, hike downstream to a second-class break in the cliff line.

91. Watermark (5.9) ★★ 6 bolts. This low-angle wall capped by a couple small roofs

rises above the right base of the crag. Start with fun edges and pull over mini-roofs on huge holds.

92. Red Scare (5.10b) ★★★ 7 bolts. Energetic cranks over bulges near the top highlight this enjoyable line up the center of the face. It's the best route on the right side of the wall.

93. We Be Toys (5.10a) ★★ 5 bolts. The left of three lines ascends a technical seam to an easier low-angle slab. There are more pleasurable routes in the Palace, but it's still worth doing.

The left side of the Pleasure Palace contains several short routes on heavily featured blocks split by shallow corridors.

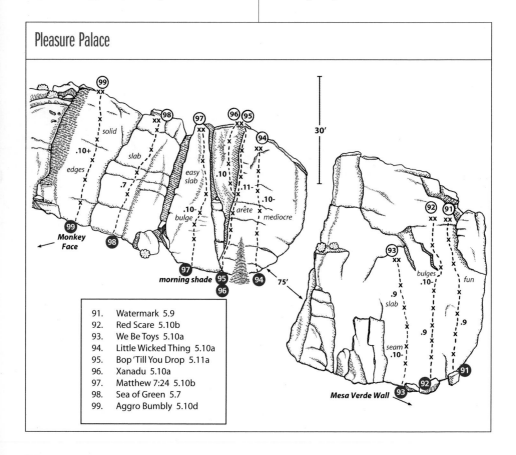

Pleasure Palace

91.	Watermark 5.9
92.	Red Scare 5.10b
93.	We Be Toys 5.10a
94.	Little Wicked Thing 5.10a
95.	Bop 'Till You Drop 5.11a
96.	Xanadu 5.10a
97.	Matthew 7:24 5.10b
98.	Sea of Green 5.7
99.	Aggro Bumbly 5.10d

94. Little Wicked Thing (5.10a) ★★ 4 bolts. Just right of a clean arête rises a short, strenuous route on blocky rock. Expect nothing special.

95. Bop 'Till You Drop (5.11a) ★★★ 5 bolts. The best route on the crag follows an appealing overhanging edge. The solid rock and pumping pockets and pinches justify the long uphill slog.

96. Xanadu (5.10a) ★★★ 6 bolts. If the arête on *Bop 'Till You Drop* proves too intimidating, cut left after the third bolt to solid face holds on the left wall. Fun moves past three more bolts end on top.

97. Matthew 7:24 (5.10b) ★★ 5 bolts. This short, triangular buttress starts with steep cranks on good holds and finishes with a simple arête. With plenty of bolts and a bouldering crux, it's a great place to bag your first 5.10.

98. Sea of Green (5.7) ★★ 4 bolts. The only easy route on the Pleasure Palace climbs the low-angle wall a few feet left of an ugly chimney. The solid rock and plentiful bolts make *Sea of Green* a fine beginner's lead.

99. Aggro Bumbly (5.10d) ★★★ 5 bolts. The leftmost route on the Pleasure Palace climbs the center of the crag's best-looking chunk of rock. Avoid a tempting block right of the crux; the direct line is safer and more enjoyable.

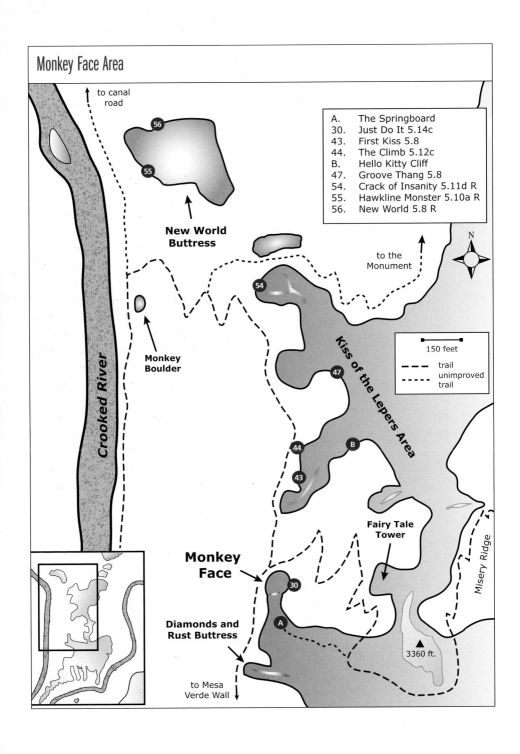

Monkey Face Area

A.	The Springboard
30.	Just Do It 5.14c
43.	First Kiss 5.8
44.	The Climb 5.12c
B.	Hello Kitty Cliff
47.	Groove Thang 5.8
54.	Crack of Insanity 5.11d R
55.	Hawkline Monster 5.10a R
56.	New World 5.8 R

to canal road

New World Buttress

to the Monument

N

Crooked River

Monkey Boulder

Kiss of the Lepers Area

150 feet

— — — trail
· · · · · unimproved trail

Monkey Face

Fairy Tale Tower

Misery Ridge

Diamonds and Rust Buttress

3360 ft.

to Mesa Verde Wall

I always dreamed of putting a route up the underside of the Monkey's chin, but there was something about Close Shave *(5.12d) that unnerved me. With only four bolts, there were places I simply didn't want to fall, never knowing how the rope would fare rubbing against the sharp arête. The crux was safe, but exposed like nothing else at Smith. A bizarre foot hook under the chin allowed me to stick a two-finger pocket with my right hand. I slapped up the arête with my left hand, pumped, and fired as hard as I could—feet off the rock—to a good hold. With so much air below, it was hard finding the motivation to throw hard enough, and I kept coming up short. I finally pacified my fears by using double 11mm ropes, and soon enough* Close Shave *was in the bag.*

The stark beauty of Monkey Face makes it one of the most recognizable landmarks in Oregon. When viewed from the south, this four-sided natural wonder looks remarkably like a grinning monkey—complete with mouth, nose, and eyes. While everyone appreciates the majesty, Monkey Face holds a special place in the hearts of climbers. Amazing knife-edges, clean overhanging faces, beautiful crack systems, and dizzying exposure appeal to the instincts of every climber. Nothing else at Smith compares to the position of these extraordinary lines.

The lower portion of the 350-foot main spire consists of solid, light-colored stone with sharp-cut edges and few pockets.

Higher up it changes into a heavily featured, reddish-purple rock bulging dramatically on all sides. The combination makes every route to the top highly diverse, as clean cracks and small-edged vertical faces give way to overhanging thuggery on big holds. For traditional climbers the attractive multi-pitch cracks make Monkey Face the best destination at Smith, with routes ranging from 5.7 to 5.13d. Sport climbers find some of the hardest and most impressive routes anywhere. With these impressive credentials, Monkey Face should be teeming with activity, but the long walk provides an effective barrier against overcrowding.

The dramatic setting makes Monkey Face the place of choice for screwballs seeking an adrenaline rush. A solo ascent of the *Pioneer Route* from the ground in nine minutes, weddings on the summit, fornicating in the caves, nude ascents, BASE jumps, 50-meter roped free-falls out of the West Face Cave, and massive swings off the Springboard from ropes strung above the east face are some of the many stunts. The best non-climbing effort came when Adam Grosowsky strung a tight wire between the Springboard and the Monkey's mouth. After several rehearsals he walked across the span without a safety line. Witnesses reported that the solo walk was shaky and agonizing to watch, as his usual impeccable form disintegrated into a panicky fit of wobbles.

Monkey Face Area Overview

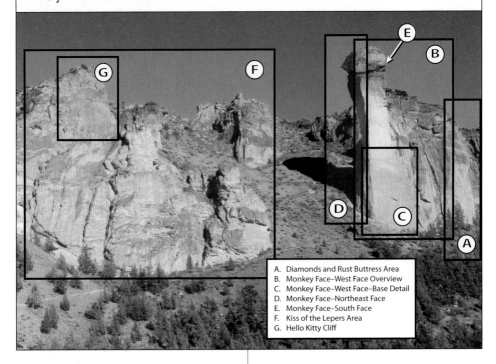

A. Diamonds and Rust Buttress Area
B. Monkey Face–West Face Overview
C. Monkey Face–West Face–Base Detail
D. Monkey Face–Northeast Face
E. Monkey Face–South Face
F. Kiss of the Lepers Area
G. Hello Kitty Cliff

The easiest route to the summit follows the legendary *Pioneer Route*. It looks terrifying, but bolt ladders and great belay ledges remove any degree of difficulty—the only challenge is from exposure unlike any other beginning route at Smith. Smart climbers practice basic aid climbing techniques, free rappels, and multi-pitch routes in more friendly surroundings before giving Monkey Face a whirl. Backing off halfway up the *Pioneer Route* isn't easy.

For four decades Monkey Face played a leading role in Smith climbing; no other crag matched the steady stream of influential, standard-setting routes. It all began in late 1959 when Dave Bohn, Jim Fraser, and Vivian Staender began a lengthy assault on the summit. After seven days of work, they succeeded on the *Pioneer Route* on January 1, 1960. Even for the times, their effort wasn't

any breakthrough in standards, as they drilled and aided bolt ladders the entire way, but the team deserves credit for their ingenuity and perseverance.

During the 1960s the main faces succumbed to hammer-swinging, Yosemite-inspired hardmen. Soon every face featured at least one aid route to the summit, including the West Face, East Face, North Face, and Northwest Passage. Free climbing began in the mid-60s with ascents of the obvious moderate crack lines on the west side. It wasn't until Jeff Thomas's impressive free ascent of the third-pitch dihedral of the *Southwest Corner* (5.11a) in 1977 that the new generation began taking the first steps toward freeing the most impressive aid lines. The most obvious prize was a free ascent of Monkey Face itself, by whatever route held the most promise. In 1979 Chris Jones teamed with

Bill Ramsey, succeeding on *Monkey Space* (5.11b), Smith's first multi-pitch 5.11. A few months after this breakthrough ascent, Jones freed a thin crack on the east side of the spire. His ascent of *Rising Expectations* (5.11d) raised Smith standards by two.

At the same time as sport climbing was evolving in the Dihedrals, the aid lines began falling to free climbers, one pitch at a time. After free ascents of *Astro Monkey* (aka *Southwest Corner*) (5.12a), *Northwest Corner* (5.12a), and *Northwest Passage* (5.12c), the best ascents of the era took place in the mid-1980s. In August 1984 Alan Watts redpointed the wildly overhanging upper pitch of the *East Face* (5.13c) with no preplaced gear. With pumping moves and physically difficult gear placements, this pin-scarred crack was arguably the hardest route in the United States. One year later he returned, freeing the entire route in one push (5.13d). He also added other lines, including *Young Pioneer* and *Close Shave* (both 5.12d).

In 1989 Mike Hoover filmed a segment at Smith Rock for NBC's *Sportsworld*. The storyline involved a free ascent of an extreme route by Wolfgang Gullich, Ron Kauk, and Alan Watts. In charge of picking the line, Watts carefully prepared a beautiful wall left of the *East Face*. With the arrival of the team, the first day's effort involved lots of hanging and little climbing—it quickly became clear that the overhanging wall was far harder than anticipated. Fearing a TV ratings disaster, the team turned to *The Backbone* (5.13a), with Kauk coming away with the first free ascent.

Shortly after the film crew left, the east-side project attracted attention. After failed efforts by several top climbers, Jean-Baptiste Tribout began a massive series of attempts, finally succeeding on *Just Do It* (5.14c) in April 1992. Once again Monkey Face contained the hardest route

in the country. Despite stacks of attempts, Tribout's route saw only two repeats until 1997, when Chris Sharma climbed the route with minimal effort. Fast teenage ascents by other rising stars proved that *Just Do It* was no longer the hardest—but it remains one of the most influential routes in the history of American free climbing. And there's no reason to believe that *Just Do It* will be the hardest route on Monkey Face forever—the potential exists for several lines in the 5.14 to 5.15 range. Tommy Caldwell's ascent of the entire arête of *Spank the Monkey* (5.13d) in 2004 points to a good future for Monkey Face climbing. If the spire weren't so far from the parking lot, all four faces would feature standard-setting routes; these lines remain as prizes for a future generation.

Finding the crags: There are three approach options for Monkey Face—each involving a lot of hiking. Anyone averse to hiking uphill will prefer scrambling over Asterisk Pass (4th class) and following a trail along the base of the West Side Crags. This approach makes the most sense for any of the base routes on the west wall. The usual approach used by sightseers and most climbers is the switchbacked path over Misery Ridge. This option features the only graded trail, but it maximizes the amount of uphill walking. Some climbers prefer hiking up a decrepit trail in Aggro Gully. At the top of the gully, keep hiking uphill until the unmistakable spire comes into view.

In contrast to the splendors of Monkey Face, this chapter also includes several nearby crags with less attractive qualities. Diamonds and Rust Buttress, Fairy Tale Tower, and the New World Buttress are some of Smith's least popular destinations for good reason. However, recent activity in the mostly abysmal Kiss of the Lepers Area uncovered some surprisingly good multi-pitch sport routes.

DIAMONDS AND RUST BUTTRESS

Separated from Monkey Face by a dark gulch, this prominent multi-spiked rib marks the southern boundary of the Monkey Face complex. Despite sections of good rock, the buttress never captured the attention of area locals. Adventure climbers might enjoy the multi-pitch grungefests to the top of the cliff.

Descent: Walk off to the right along the base of Pleasure Palace to a carefully constructed trail leading back to the base.

1. Slow Train (5.7 R) ★★ 7 bolts. The surprisingly solid wall at the base of the buttress contains a forgotten sport route. After a tricky start fun climbing leads far up the face to a big ledge. Although reasonably safe, the bolts are a little too far apart for casual enjoyment.

2. Diamonds and Rust (5.8 X) ★ Gear to 2.5 inches. Apart from quality climbing on the starting pitch, this escapade to the top of the buttress has little to offer. Poor rock and long run-outs are par for the course. Begin below an obvious roof at the base of the but-

tress. **Pitch 1:** (5.8) Undercling the crux roof and wander up a solid face with very little protection to a massive shelf. **Pitch 2:** (5.7) Good holds lead directly over a bulge to a higher shelf. Continue up simple junk to a belay spot. **Pitch 3:** (5.5) A low-angle slab leads to the top of a pillar. Step across to the other side and wander up poorly protected rubbish to the top.

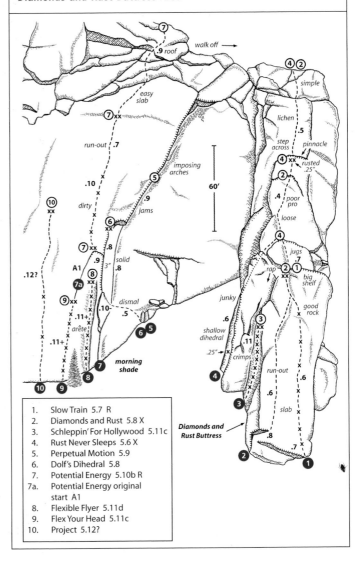

Diamonds and Rust Buttress Area

1.	Slow Train 5.7 R
2.	Diamonds and Rust 5.8 X
3.	Schleppin' For Hollywood 5.11c
4.	Rust Never Sleeps 5.6 X
5.	Perpetual Motion 5.9
6.	Dolf's Dihedral 5.8
7.	Potential Energy 5.10b R
7a.	Potential Energy original start A1
8.	Flexible Flyer 5.11d
9.	Flex Your Head 5.11c
10.	Project 5.12?

3. Schleppin' For Hollywood (5.11c) ★ 7 bolts. The shaded left side of the Diamonds and Rust Buttress features a decent sport route on a flat face. Highly technical edges lead to an anchor in the middle of hard climbing. Big holds a few feet higher would make a more logical stopping point.

4. Rust Never Sleeps (5.6 X) Mixed to 2.5 inches. The first ascent of the buttress followed a horrid route starting a few feet uphill from *Schleppin' For Hollywood*. You'll be scraping the bottom of the barrel if you find yourself racking up for this loser. **Pitch 1:** (5.6) Follow a wretched inside corner past a primordial bolt to an unexposed ledge on the ridge. **Pitch 2:** (5.4) Join the second pitch of *Diamonds and Rust* but climb higher to a fearsome two-bolt anchor just below a pinnacle. **Pitch 3:** (5.5) Step across a gap and climb the final pitch of *Diamonds and Rust* to the top.

MONKEY FACE

Beyond the Diamonds and Rust Buttress rises Monkey Face, the most celebrated chunk of stone at Smith. During the warmer months, there's no better place to climb—cooling breezes make afternoon temperatures bearable (and sometimes chilly) on all but the hottest days. But the exposed position and bitter winds shut Monkey Face down during the winter.

The spire itself sits atop the north side of the expansive west wall. The lower cliff contains several sport climbs and the starting points for some of Smith's best longer lines. The first several routes start about 150 feet right of the main spire below an unmistakable arching crack system. **Descent:** Every route to the summit shares the same descent. Two ropes are mandatory (even a 70-meter rope won't get the job done). From the top, make a short rappel south, stepping awkwardly over the lip of a cave and past the massive nose boulder to an anchor. Next comes the 140-foot free rappel that many *Pioneer Route* climbers consider the highlight of the entire climb. The free rappel ends at another anchor on a good ledge. Either rappel another 45 feet to the ground or scramble down an exposed fourth-class ramp to easy ledges.

5. Perpetual Motion (5.9) ★ Gear to 2.5 inches. The only route on the white-streaked arch jams solid rock to an anchor far below the top. Unfortunately, a dreadful starting traverse from the right sours the experience.

6. Dolf's Dihedral (5.8) ★★ Gear to 2.5 inches. This brilliant crack sits in a corner a few feet left of *Perpetual Motion*. Rock doesn't get any better than this, but a lousy traverse guards the base, and the locking jams end shortly after they begin.

Monkey Face–West Face

5.	Perpetual Motion 5.9	16.	West Face Variation 5.8
7.	Potential Energy 5.10b R	16b.	West Face Variation Direct 5.8
9.	Flex Your Head 5.11c	18.	Moving in Stereo 5.11d
11.	King Kong 5.9	19.	Astro Monkey (aka SW Corner) 5.12a
12.	Godzilla 5.9	22.	West Face 5.12a A1
14.	Blow Cocoa 5.11d	33.	Pioneer Route 5.7 A1

7. Potential Energy (5.10b R) ★★ Mixed to 3.5 inches. A respectable second pitch highlights the only route to the top of the west wall's southern flank. Bolts safely protect the hardest moves, though the scantily protected slab above requires attention. Fortunately, the rock is solid when it matters most. **Pitch 1:** (5.10a) A strenuous left-leaning flake leads to a short stint of perfect jams in *Dolf's Dihedral*. Mantle onto a ledge to the left and belay at two bolts. **Pitch 2:** (5.10b) Dirty rock at the start leads to a hard move on solid stone.

A long run-out up an easy slab ends at an anchor. **Pitch 3:** (5.9) Ramble up and right on low-angle ramps and pull over a couple small finishing roofs.

7a. Potential Energy original start (A1) ★ Clean to 1 inch. The original start aided a direct line up a seam. Today most of this pitch goes free via *Flex Your Head*. The remaining aid would easily go, but the razor-edged jams wouldn't be fun.

8. Flexible Flyer (5.11d) ★★★ 6 bolts. A bolted arête rises behind a juniper tree. With great rock, plentiful bolts, and engaging climbing, it's one of the better Monkey Face base routes.

9. Flex Your Head (5.11c) ★★ 6 bolts. A series of delicate, technical edges lead up a seam starting behind a juniper tree. The crux comes in the middle of the route, finessing past a new bolt.

10. Project (5.12?) Several bolts pepper the blank wall left of *Flex Your Head*. Although long forgotten, it'll someday offer a hard pitch of tiny edges.

Several of the multi-pitch routes on the west wall end at a low notch separating the main spire from the parent cliff. From the notch there are two options: Either continue to the summit via a south face route, or escape off the backside. Descent: Rappel or downclimb (5.5) to a slanting ramp running along the entire east wall. Scramble down fourth-class ledges or rappel from anchor bolts.

11. King Kong (5.9) ★★

Mixed to 8 inches. This multi-pitch adventure contains a little of everything—cracks, knobs, chimneys, and off-widths. The rock and protection are good, with a crux traversing miniature nubbins. The memorable third pitch protects with huge cams, though the off-width thrashes anyone unskilled at the technique. Start below overgrown double cracks. **Pitch 1:** (5.8) Scamper up cracks past a bulge to belay bolts. **Pitch 2:** (5.9) 3 bolts. Sidestep right and move down to an anchor. **Pitch 3:** (5.8) A solid chimney squeezes into a sinister wide crack. At the top, cut far left to a good ledge. **Pitch 4:** (5.8) Finish to the notch via an exposed traverse. Continue to the summit or descend the east side.

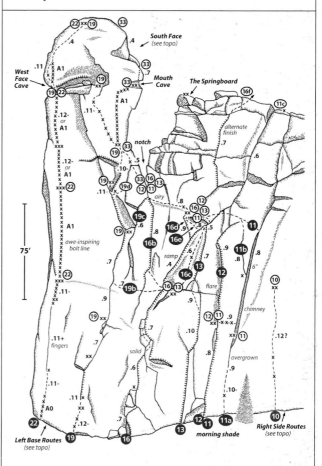

Monkey Face—West Face Overview

10.	Project 5.12?		16d.	Roof Variation 5.9
11.	King Kong 5.9		16e.	Manslaughter 5.8 X
11a.	King Kong Direct 5.10a R		16f.	Finish Variation 5.7
11b.	King Kong Escape 5.8		19.	Astro Monkey (aka Southwest
11c.	King Kong original finish 5.6			Corner) 5.12a
12.	Godzilla 5.9		19b.	Second Pitch Connection 5.7
13.	Smaug 5.10b R		19c.	Escape Variation 5.6
16.	West Face Variation 5.8		19d.	Southwest Corner Traverse 5.11b
16b.	West Face Variation Direct 5.8		22.	West Face 5.12a A1
16c.	Slab Variation 5.6 X		33.	Pioneer Route 5.7 A1

beneath the foliage is a three-star series of face and crack moves.

11a. King Kong Direct (5.10a R) ★ Mixed

to 2.5 inches. Don't even consider trying this variant without first pulling all the weeds and bushes plugging the upper crack. Hidden

11b. King Kong Escape (5.8) ★★ Gear to 3.5

inches. Anyone suffering from offwidthaphobia should bypass the third-pitch wide crack with this flake crack to the left.

11c. King Kong original finish (5.6) ★

Gear to 2.5 inches. The first ascent team skipped the fourth-pitch traverse, following an ordinary crack system to the top of the parent cliff.

12. Godzilla (5.9) ★ Gear to 3 inches. A

monstrous second-pitch chimney detracts from this otherwise decent route. It's still worth doing if you're not allergic to pigeon crap. **Pitch 1:** (5.8) Ascend the first pitch of *King Kong*. **Pitch 2:** (5.9) Flail up the disgusting chimney until an invigorating undercling cuts around a small block. Scramble to a belay platform. **Pitch 3:** (5.8) An exposed traverse left ends at the notch.

13. Smaug (5.10b R) ★ Gear to 1.5 inches.

If someone pried the loose blocks off the crux pitch, this shallow inside corner would be worth doing. The hardest moves are solid, with technical stems followed by runout jugs. **Pitch 1:** (5.10b) Climb the right-facing corner, moving cautiously around shaky flakes, and muscle committing jugs to a belay. **Pitch 2:** (5.6) Step right into a poorly protected corner and skirt the right side of a roof to a belay ledge. **Pitch 3:** (5.8) Traverse left to the notch.

14. Blow Cocoa (5.11d) ★★ 6 bolts. A bolted

wall of micro-edges rises left of the starting corner of *Smaug*. Most of the friable crimps snapped off years ago; today the climb is technical and solid, but still not much fun.

15. Monkey Farce (5.10b R) ★★ Mixed to

1.5 inches. This unlikely route cuts across the lower reaches of Monkey Face to a small ledge below the *West Face* bolt line. The most popular version ignores this serious traverse by finishing with the *West Face Variation*. Start below a diagonal thin crack left of the *Blow Cocoa* bolt line. **Pitch 1:** (5.10b) A hard face move past a new bolt

leads to an excellent finger crack. Finish by traversing left on an unnerving ramp plastered with lichen. **Pitch 2:** (5.9) Face traverse left on low-angle knobs past an anchor to dangerous moves ending at a small ledge. Rappel with two ropes.

16. West Face Variation (5.8) ★★★★ Mixed

to 2.5 inches. The best and most popular of the easy free routes on Monkey Face makes a fine choice for traditional climbers. Despite an unavoidable encounter with rope drag on the second pitch, the climbing is charming and the rock nearly perfect. Finishing to the summit via the *Pioneer Route* is one of Smith's most memorable experiences for any developing climber. With a slew of potential variations, there are virtually unlimited combinations. Start on the left side of neatly stacked blocks. **Pitch 1:** (5.7) Swing right around a blind corner to easy cracks and a ledge. Jam a clean dihedral and weave past a couple bulges to a belay anchor. **Pitch 2:** (5.5) Step left and hike an easy slab until forced to circle right around a roof to a ledge. **Pitch 3:** (5.8) A deceptively tricky move leads past a bolt to an airy traverse ending at the notch. If you're heading for the summit, don't belay at the notch but continue to Bohn Street.

16a. Start Variation (5.8) ★★ Gear to 2

inches. A more difficult and less pleasant variant ascends a diagonal crack on the right side of the starting block.

16b. West Face Variation Direct (5.8) ★★★★

Gear to 2 inches. The quickest route to the notch bypasses the upper pitches with a direct line to the left. Expect perfect rock, excellent protection, and crux finger jams in the back of a flare. If continuing to the summit, ignore the notch belay and continue directly to Bohn Street.

Monkey Face–West Face–Left Base Routes

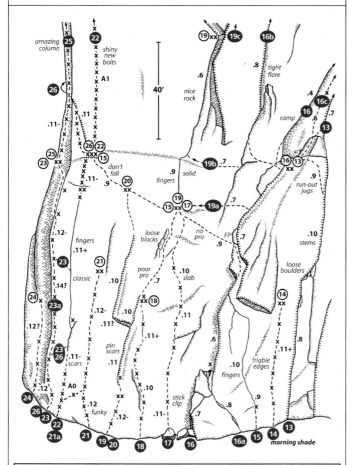

amazing column
shiny new bolts
40'
nice rock
A1
tight flare
ramp
.11
.11-
.11
don't fall
fingers
.11-
.9
.9 solid
fingers
run-out jugs
.12-
fingers
.11+
loose blocks
no pro
.9
FP
.7
.10 stems
classic
.14?
poor pro
.7
.10 slab
loose boulders
.12-
.10
.11?
.11
.10
fingers
.11+
pin scars
.11
.6
friable edges
.11-
scars
.11
.10
.12
A0
.10
stick clip
.9
.12
funky
.12-
.11-
.7
.8
morning shade

13.	Smaug 5.10b R	19b.	Second Pitch Connection 5.7
14.	Blow Cocoa 5.11d	19c.	Escape Variation 5.6
15.	Monkey Farce 5.10b R	20.	Project 5.12- ?
16.	West Face Variation 5.8	21.	Pose Down 5.12c
16a.	Start Variation 5.8	21a.	Pose Down Variation 5.12a A0
16b.	West Face Variation Direct 5.8	22.	West Face 5.12a A1
16c.	Slab Variation 5.6 X	23.	Sheer Trickery 5.12c
17.	Drug Nasty (aka Dean's Dream) 5.11c	23a.	Project 5.14?
18.	Moving in Stereo 5.11d	24.	Project 5.12?
19.	Astro Monkey (aka SW Corner) 5.12a	25.	The Backbone 5.13a
19a.	First Pitch Bypass 5.7 R	26.	Northwest Passage 5.12c

16d. Roof Variation (5.9) ★★ Gear to 1 inch. Instead of bypassing the second-pitch roof, an intimidating direct option jams a thin crack in a corner and mantels onto the belay ledge.

16e. Manslaughter (5.8 X) Gear to 3 inches. This suicidal variant pulls the second-pitch roof by crawling right to left along a detached flake the size of a Coke® machine.

16f. Finish Variation (5.7) ★★ Gear to 2 inches. An alternate finish forgoes the third-pitch traverse by climbing a right-facing corner to the top of the cliff.

17. Drug Nasty (aka Dean's Dream) (5.11c) ★ 7 bolts. The wall left of *West Face Variation* features a below-average sport route. Unnerving nubbins and tedious moves keep most climbers away. Consider yourself lucky if you don't pop a single hold. Stick-clip the first bolt or risk a broken ankle on the starting block.

18. Moving in Stereo (5.11d) ★★★ 7 bolts. Far better than its neighbor to the right,

16c. Slab Variation (5.6 X) ★★ Mixed to 2 inches. A second-pitch variation climbs good rock on a low-angle slab to the right. You'll avoid the rope drag, but the only bolt sticks halfway out the hole.

this left-leaning offset comes highly recommended. Fun moves on good rock lead to a perplexing crux reaching right to a crack. A new bolt eliminates the original run-out to the anchor.

19. Astro Monkey (aka Southwest Corner) (5.12a) ★★★★

Mixed to 2 inches. One of Smith's finest long free routes combines the *Southwest Corner* with *Monkey Space* in six unforgettable pitches to the top of the spire. As tiny knobs snap over the years, the technical first pitch slowly grows harder—some climbers prefer starting with *Moving in Stereo*. The remaining pitches are varied and spectacular on nearly perfect rock. **Pitch 1:** (5.12a) Deceptively tricky face moves give way to pin scars in a shallow corner. After skirting around a roof, a run-out slab leads past loose boulders to an anchor. **Pitch 2:** (5.9) Jam a brilliant finger crack and scamper up easy rock to a belay beneath an overhanging dihedral. **Pitch 3:** (5.11a) Locking finger jams in the corner lead to breathtaking jugs moving left around an exposed roof. **Pitch 4:** (5.10a) Stem a short dihedral and swing right around a roof, mindful of a rope-eating slot. Belay on Bohn Street. **Pitch 5:** (5.11a) 6 bolts. Follow *Monkey*

Monkey Face–Northwest Face

2.	Diamonds and Rust 5.8 X
3.	Schelppin' For Hollywood 5.11c
4.	Rust Never Sleeps 5.6 X
9.	Flex Your Head 5.11c
11.	King Kong 5.9
12.	Godzilla 5.9
16.	West Face Variation 5.8
19.	Astro Monkey (aka SW Corner) 5.12a
21.	Pose Down 5.12c
22.	West Face 5.12a A1
27.	Northwest Corner 5.12a

Diamonds and Rust Buttress

Space into the West Face Cave. **Pitch 6:** (5.11b) 3 bolts. Continue up *Monkey Space* to the top.

19a. First Pitch Bypass (5.7 R) ★★ Gear to

2 inches. You can reduce the grade to 5.11b by joining *Astro Monkey* at the first belay. Climb the first pitch of *West Face Variation* past the final bulge and traverse 30 feet left on solid rock.

19b. Second Pitch Connection (5.7) ★★

Gear to 2 inches. A higher traverse from the top of *West Face Variation*'s first pitch joins *Astro Monkey* above the second-pitch finger crack. Climbers sometimes combine this connection with the *Escape Variation,* creating an easy option to the notch.

19c. Escape Variation (5.6) ★★ Gear to 2.5 inches. If the third pitch proves too intimidating, escape right up a short box corner. Follow a low-angle ramp to the notch and descend the backside.

19d. Southwest Corner Traverse (5.11b) ★★★ Mixed to 2 inches. The original aid route cut right, not left, at the third-pitch roof. This short traverse on pin scars is harder, though not as exhilarating as the regular line. Set an anchor with nuts after the traverse or face intolerable rope drag on the easy scramble to Bohn Street.

20. Project (5.12-?) A new line cuts around the left side of the first-pitch roof on *Astro Monkey.* The roof itself will be easier than the approach.

21. Pose Down (5.12c) ★★★ 9 bolts. Most climbers don't make it past the second bolt on this high-quality route. After a confusing crux of underclings and side pulls, continue with an enjoyable box corner on good rock.

21a. Pose Down Variation (5.12a A0) ★★ 9 bolts. Bypassing the crux by aiding bolts to the left drops the grade a couple notches, while preserving the quality upper section.

22. West Face (5.12a A1) ★★★★ Clean to 2 inches. Nothing at Smith compares to the only route up the blank west side of the main spire. A testament to the power of the drill, the wall features perfect rock, an incredible position, and one of the longest unbroken bolt ladders you'll see anywhere. The original line of the second pitch will never go free, but the other three pitches feature brilliant free climbing (or simple aid). With fully replaced bolts, it's one of the safest aid routes in the world. The first ascent

followed the *South Exit* out of the West Face Cave. Now everyone uses the direct line out the north side. **Pitch 1:** (5.12a A0) Aid a short bolt line and free the classic finger crack to a face climbing finish. A totally free variant (5.12c) boulders left of the original start, via *Sheer Trickery.* **Pitch 2:** (A1 23) Bolts. Clip handsome new bolts on a featureless wall to a ledge. **Pitch 3:** (5.12a) 19 bolts. Wildly exposed free moves on great rock lead past a ledge to an energetic finish into the West Face Cave. **Pitch 4:** (5.11b) 3 bolts. Power out the cave on overhanging pockets or aid the original bolt ladder a few feet right. Easy scrambling ends at bolts just below the summit.

23. Sheer Trickery (5.12c) ★★★ Mixed to 1.5 inches. A prominent arête rises left of the *West Face's* first pitch. A comical line frees a bouldery start and jams 30 feet of the *West Face* crack before cutting back left to the arête. Descend with a double-rope rappel.

23a. Project (5.14?) 12 bolts. The entire edge of *Sheer Trickery* remains undone. The moves still don't go free on a bleak section between the sixth and eighth bolts, nor will they anytime soon.

24. Project (5.12?) A few bolts litter the face around the corner left of the *Sheer Trickery* arête. A decent route awaits anyone willing to scrub lichen from the finishing dihedral.

25. The Backbone (5.13a) ★★★★ Bolts. Perhaps the most impressive natural line at Smith is this gorgeous arête separating the west and north faces. With unforgettable moves and dizzying exposure, the second-pitch backbone is unlike anything you've ever seen. Several ledges on the left side of the arête provide complete rests—otherwise the grade would be a couple notches higher. The hardest climbing slaps desperately up the

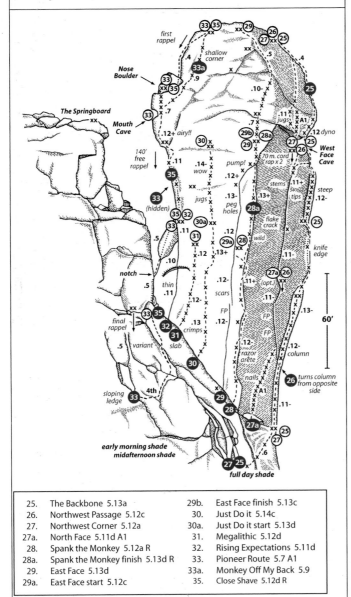

first rappel

shallow corner

Nose Boulder

33a

33

35

The Springboard

33

Mouth Cave

.12+ airy!!

140' free rappel

.11

.14– wow

.12+

.7

.9

.10–

.11 jugs

.7

A1

12 dyno

25

26

27

West Face Cave

70 m. cord rap x 2

pump!

stems

.11+

steep

.12–

35

33 (hidden)

35 32

33

30a

jugs

.13–

peg holes

.13+

tips

.12

wild

.11–

flake crack

25

knife edge

.11

.12

.13+

.12–

scars

.11+ (opt.)

.11–

25

notch

.5

thin .11

.12–

FP

.13–

60'

final rappel

33 35

32

31

30

.13 crimps

.12–

.12–

FP

FP

.12– column

.5 variant

slab

.12– razor arête

nails

A1

turns column from opposite side

sloping ledge

33

4th

29

28

27a

.11–

25

27

.6

early morning shade
midafternoon shade

full day shade

25.	The Backbone 5.13a	29b.	East Face finish 5.13c
26.	Northwest Passage 5.12c	30.	Just Do it 5.14c
27.	Northwest Corner 5.12a	30a.	Just Do it start 5.13d
27a.	North Face 5.11d A1	31.	Megalithic 5.12d
28.	Spank the Monkey 5.12a R	32.	Rising Expectations 5.11d
28a.	Spank the Monkey finish 5.13d R	33.	Pioneer Route 5.7 A1
29.	East Face 5.13d	33a.	Monkey Off My Back 5.9
29a.	East Face start 5.12c	35.	Close Shave 5.12d R

(5.12a) 10 bolts. Step right to the *West Face* bolt line and crank good holds on steep purple rock into the cave. **Pitch 4:** (5.12b) 3 bolts. Start right of the usual exit with an unexposed dyno and monkey up the overhanging wall to the top.

26. Northwest Passage (5.12c) ★★★★

Mixed to 2.5 inches. Smith's finest long traditional route combines the best climbing on the *West Face* and *Northwest Corner* in four distinctive pitches. With a classic finger crack, a razor-edged arête, a pumping flake crack, and a bouldery finish, it appeals to every high-level trad climber. The exposed position makes for chilly climbing on a cool day, so leave this well-shaded route for warmer times. Even in midsummer it remains cool and breezy, as long as you do the first pitch early. **Pitch 1:** (5.12c) Climb the first pitch of the *West Face* starting with the *Sheer Trickery* variant. **Pitch 2:** (5.11c) A nerve-wracking lieback up an exposed edge leads around the corner to the *Northwest Corner* flake crack. You can continue to the West Face Cave in a single

right edge on the widest part of the column. **Pitch 1:** (5.12c) Either climb *Sheer Trickery* or hike in (2 bolts) from the northeast corner of the spire (5.6). **Pitch 2:** (5.13a) 13 bolts. Soar up the breathtaking arête past many bolts to an anchor at a small ledge. **Pitch 3:**

pitch (5.12a), though most pumped climbers gladly stop at a hanging belay. Use a 60-meter rope. **Pitch 3:** (5.11d) Directly above the hanging belay, jam the intense flake crack, stepping right to the West Face Cave. **Pitch 4:** (5.11b) 3 bolts. A brief stint of pure thuggery ends on the summit.

27. Northwest Corner (5.12a) ★★★★ Mixed to 2.5 inches. An unmistakable flake crack splits Monkey Face's north wall. Originally freed in two pitches to the cave, the best version eliminates the hanging belay using a 60-meter rope. The first 20 feet above the midpitch anchor protects stubbornly, but the upper part eats small wires. **Pitch 1:** (5.6) 2 bolts. Start below the northeast corner of the spire and traverse right on bad rock to an anchor. **Pitch 2:** (5.12a) Step right and climb the arête past a few bolts into the flake crack. Never-ending jams and liebacks lead to a crux move just before escaping right into the West Face Cave. An optional (5.10a) direct finish pulls over a frightful bulge protected by a cam. **Pitch 3:** (5.11b) 3 bolts. Muscle up a short overhang and scramble to the top.

27a. North Face (5.11d A1) ★★★ Clean to 1 inch. For reasons unknown, the first ascent team avoided the natural line with a row of prehistoric bolts arching in from the left. With the all-free *Northwest Corner* so close, few climbers follow the original line. **Pitch 1:** (5.11a A1) Aid dreadful nails (you really can't call them bolts) leading to a classic flake crack. Charming jams and liebacks end at a hanging belay. **Pitch 2:** (5.11d) Follow the third-pitch flake crack of the *Northwest Passage* into the West Face Cave. **Pitch 3:** (5.11b) 3 bolts. Crank the usual cave exit.

28. Spank the Monkey (5.12a R) ★★★★ 6 bolts. A classic arête separates the overhanging east wall from the north face. Bolts safely

Renan Ozturk on *Northwest Corner*.

protect the hardest moves, but the mental factor makes it one of Smith's most demanding lower-end 5.12s. Expect long run-outs, a razor-sharp edge, and lots of air.

28a. Spank the Monkey finish (5.13d R) ★★★★ 13 bolts. The overhanging continuation of *Spank the Monkey* is a product of a new generation of climbers unafraid of cranking intense moves with chilling run-outs. If you don't possess these same qualities, you'll want to stay away. Climb in one long pitch from the ground, weaving back and forth on either side of the arête, tugging on pinches and pockets while fighting a massive pump. Using double ropes reduces the danger from the alarmingly sharp edge.

29. East Face (5.13d) ★★★★ Mixed to 2 inches. When first freed in 1985, this former nail-up was the hardest climb in the United

Monkey Face–Southeast Face

Nose Boulder

The Springboard

Bohn Street

33a

29

37

35

28a

New World Buttress

33

30

29

28

28.	Spank the Monkey 5.12a R
28a.	Spank the Monkey finish 5.13d R
29.	East Face 5.13d
30.	Just Do It 5.14c
33.	Pioneer Route 5.7 A1
33a.	Monkey Off My Back 5.9
35.	Close Shave 5.12d R
37.	Monkey Space 5.11b

lead to a small ledge. Free a short bolt ladder on good holds and hike a lichen-covered slab to the top.

29a. East Face start

(5.12c) ★★★ Gear to 2 inches. The gently overhanging thin crack ending at the first set of anchors makes an excellent traditional lead with bombproof protection. Many climbers settle for a toprope after an ascent of *Spank the Monkey*. After starting with good locks and big edges, strenuous tip jams lead to a juggy finish.

29b. East Face finish

(5.13c) ★★★ Mixed to 0.5 inch. The original second pitch of the *East Face* was once the hardest redpoint in America. Climbed in a single push with all gear placed on lead, it was a landmark ascent in Smith history. Approach by climbing the *East Face* start, and arrange a hanging belay.

30. Just Do It (5.14c) ★★★★ 17 bolts. The east wall of Monkey Face features one of the most renowned free climbs on Earth. For many years *Just Do It* was the undisputed hardest route in the country. It probably isn't even Smith's hardest anymore, but nothing matches the sheer magnetism of this sweeping overhang. Climbers sometimes make the hike just to gaze at the line of quickdraws hanging in space. The lower wall contains

States. Despite the fame, it sees few ascents; traditional gear and technical finger jams keep most sport climbers away. Physical nut placements are as much a part of the route as the moves themselves—preplacing gear drops the grade a full letter. The lower crack provides a pleasant warm-up for the real business—powerful jams capped by a pumping traverse on the overhanging purplish wall. **Pitch 1:** (5.13d) Jam the beautiful thin crack past anchors and veer right to the finishing arête. Rappel with two ropes or . . . **Pitch 2:** (5.10b) 5 bolts. Simple face moves the hardest technical moves, but the intimidating finishing bulge requires rare levels of fitness. Convenience-minded climbers use an 85-meter rope.

30a. Just Do It start (5.13d)
★★★ 9 bolts. Even without the finish, the lower wall of *Just Do It* challenges most elite climbers. There are two distinct crux sections—horrible crimps at the start and an extremely difficult span of a blank section (the thimble move) above the eighth bolt. Lower off from an anchor below the color change.

31. Megalithic (5.12d) ★★ 7
bolts. An attractive sport route starts in a small offset left of *Just Do It*. Sharp holds and an odd finish detract from an otherwise worthwhile route on great rock. The hardest move comes right at the anchor.

32. Rising Expectations (5.11d)
★★★★ Gear to 2 inches. At the end of the 1970s, this classic finger crack was the hardest route at Smith. The varied moves on solid stone are enjoyable from start to finish. After demanding tip slots at the start, the sinker jams and big holds disappear at the final bulge when they're needed most.

33. Pioneer Route (5.7 A1) ★★★★ Clean to
2 inches. The original route to the summit offers beginning climbers a chance to get scared out of their wits with minimal risks. It's like a roller-coaster ride—thrilling, safe, and open to anyone with the courage to climb aboard. Every section has its charms— reaching the notch and instantly feeling the

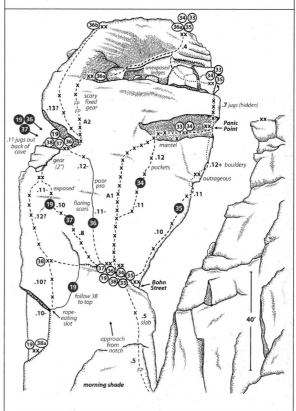

Monkey Face—South Face

19.	Astro Monkey (aka Southwest Corner) 5.12a	36a.	South Exit 5.4 A2
33.	Pioneer Route 5.7 A1	36b.	Project 5.13?
34.	Young Pioneers 5.12d	37.	Monkey Space 5.11b
35.	Close Shave 5.12d R	38.	Project 5.12?
36.	Bohn Street West Face Cave 5.12a R	38a.	Project 5.10?

exposure; clipping up the bolt line with aiders swinging in the breeze; stepping out over the void on Panic Point; and spinning in the air on the free rappel. Approach by hiking up scree on the backside of the spire to a large ledge. **Pitch 1:** (4th class) Step across a gap to easy scrambling up a slanting ramp. **Pitch 2:** (5.5) Stem to the notch and face climb to a ledge called Bohn Street. **Pitch 3:** (A1) 20 bolts. Clip the Chrome-Moly bolt line to an awkward entrance into the mouth. The moves went free eons ago, but the pitch still hasn't seen a recorded redpoint ascent

(5.13+?). **Pitch 4:** (5.7) 4 bolts. Step out of the east side of the mouth and tremble past several bolts to a ledge at the monkey's nose. **Pitch 5:** (5.4) Step right or climb directly over a huge boulder to an unexposed ledge. Easy, unprotected moves end on top. Two ropes are mandatory on the descent.

33a. Monkey Off My Back (5.9) ★★ 7 bolts.
If you can't get enough of the Panic Point exposure, step right and follow jugs to a crux move in a shallow dihedral. The rock isn't perfect, but the dramatic setting makes it worth a go.

34. Young Pioneers (5.12d) ★★★ 11 bolts.
This pumping alternative free climbs into the Mouth Cave a few feet right of the Chrome-Moly bolt line. The crux launches from small pockets for the lip of the cave, followed by a strenuous mantel. You'll find better rock elsewhere on Monkey Face, but you can't deny the spectacular position.

35. Close Shave (5.12d R) ★★★★ 8 bolts.
This amazing line ascends the underside of the Monkey's neck and chin. Although seriously run-out in places, the hardest moves protect safely. The crux finesses unique pockets, pinches, and toe hooks capped by an all-out lunge—with nothing but air below. At the mouth, race through the Panic Point jugs to the anchor at the nose boulder.

36. Bohn Street West Face Cave (5.12a R)
★★ Mixed to 1 inch. When first climbed in 1963, this seam leading from Bohn Street into the West Face Cave was Smith's hardest aid route. Two decades of repeat ascents left grotesque piton scars for today's free climbers to wrestle with. Unfortunately, the many small wires refuse to set properly in the flaring holes, adding an unwelcome element of peril. **Pitch 1:** (5.5) Ascend to Bohn Street. **Pitch 2:** (5.12a) Step left and jam the spine-tingling seam past a bulge. Clip a bolt and fight left into the West Face Cave. **Pitch 3:** (5.11b) 3 bolts. Walk to the backside of the cave and crank a short wall of steep pockets.

36a. South Exit (5.4 A2) ★ Aid rack to
0.75 inch. The original exit from the West Face Cave followed a line of shaky pins and antique bolts out the south side of the cave. It would go free at a high level—just don't expect the existing gear to stop a fall.

36b. Project (5.13?) A potential free line left
of the original finish offers a dramatic exit from the cave. Three bolts tempt anyone unafraid of the nauseating exposure.

37. Monkey Space (5.11b) ★★★★ Mixed
to 2 inches. Almost every free ascent of Monkey Face follows this impressive line left of the *Pioneer Route*. There are better 5.11s at Smith, but none come close to matching the position of this classic. The memorable second pitch traverses over nothingness from Bohn Street into the West Face Cave. The hardest moves exit the north side of the cave with intimidating exposure. **Pitch 1:** (5.5) Climb to Bohn Street. **Pitch 2:** (5.11a) 6 bolts. Move left past several bolts to a strenuous pull over a small bulge. An easy flake crack (with optional gear) ends in the cave. **Pitch 3:** (5.11b) 3 bolts. Gorilla up a short wall past two bolts to the top.

38. Project (5.12?) 6 bolts. A direct line left
of *Monkey Space* will be even more dramatic than the regular route. Approach with a traverse directly left from Bohn Street to a hanging belay.

38a. Project (5.10?) An alternate approach
will connect *Astro Monkey* with the project above. Face climb directly above the fourth-pitch roof past a couple bolts to an exposed hanging belay.

Fairy Tale Tower

Hello Kitty Cliff

39.	Chicken Little 5.6	44.	The Climb 5.12c
40.	Mr. Toad's Wild Ride 5.9 R	45.	Dreams That I Carry 5.10a
41.	Funguy Roof 5.10c X	47.	Groove Thang 5.8
43.	First Kiss 5.8	54.	Crack of Insanity 5.11d R

FAIRY TALE TOWER

Near the top of the scree slope uphill from Monkey Face rests a large hunk of stone, reeking of rotten rock. No one ever does the following two routes.

39. Chicken Little (5.6) ★ Gear to 2 inches. It's not the sky that's falling . . . only stones from above. Start below a prominent dihedral on the left side of the buttress and climb two lackluster pitches to the top.

40. Mr. Toad's Wild Ride (5.9 R) ★ Mixed to 2.5 inches. This humdrum route starts on face holds right of the *Chicken Little* dihedral. Scamper right past too few bolts and scramble to the top.

KISS OF THE LEPERS AREA

To the north of Monkey Face lies a huge amount of mostly unexplored stone. Named for head-shaped "kissing" spires, much of the rock mass is completely unsuitable for climbing. Although scorned by generations of climbers, several new lines are nothing less than brilliant. The main wall towers over 400 feet above the scree, offering several long sport climbs. **Descent:** From the top of the formation, you'll have the option of walking off the backside (exposed fourth class) or rappelling. Rappel with two ropes (or a 70-meter line) from a fixed anchor, veering right to a widening ledge below Hello Kitty Cliff. Scramble off unexposed rock to the right. Some climbers prefer rappelling the entire wall via *The Climb* (two ropes mandatory).

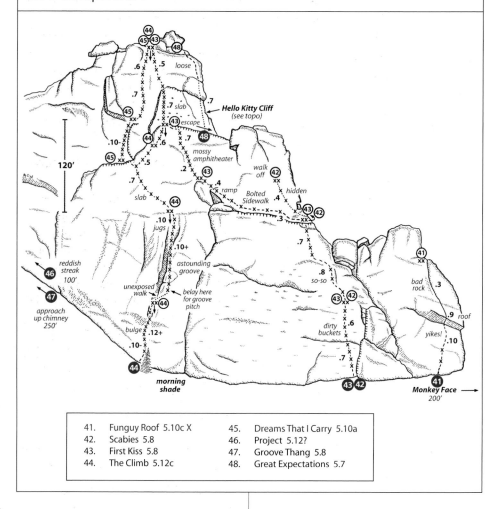

41.	Funguy Roof 5.10c X	45.	Dreams That I Carry 5.10a
42.	Scabies 5.8	46.	Project 5.12?
43.	First Kiss 5.8	47.	Groove Thang 5.8
44.	The Climb 5.12c	48.	Great Expectations 5.7

41. Funguy Roof (5.10c X) ★ Mixed to 2.5 inches. A prominent crack-split roof sits at the right base of the Kiss of the Lepers Area. The roof hardly presents an obstacle, but you'll want to be in peak form for the dangerously run-out wall below. If you pop off just below the roof, you'll be pulling scree out of your ass. Descend with a two-rope rappel or an easy scramble off the backside.

42. Scabies (5.8) ★★ Bolts. The original route on the main wall of the Kiss of the Lepers Area wandered up potholes about 100 feet left of the *Funguy Roof*. *Scabies* suffered from the usual assortment of maladies for a bad route—awful rock, poor protection, and thick lichen. Twenty-five years later a careful scrubbing, retro-bolting, and new finish provided a cure. **Pitch 1:** (5.7) 8 bolts. Start below a left-facing corner and climb mediocre buckets to an anchor. **Pitch 2:** (5.8) 7 bolts. Veer left to a short prow ending at a ledge. Continue higher on better rock to a spacious ledge. The original route bypassed this pitch by traversing right into a gully. **Pitch 3:** (5.4) 3 bolts. Move right and scramble up simple rock to a short finishing slab.

43. First Kiss (5.8) ★★★ Bolts. The longest route on the formation meanders more than 500 feet to the top. With decent rock and more bolts than you can count, it's the perfect sport/adventure route for entry-level climbers. Despite a long approach hike, *First Kiss* attracts more climbers each year as the stone steadily improves and the lichen disappears. **Pitch 1:** (5.7) 8 bolts. Climb the first pitch of *Scabies*. **Pitch 2:** (5.8) 7 bolts. Follow *Scabies* to the second-pitch anchor. **Pitch 3:** (5.4) 9 bolts. Take a stroll left along the infamous Bolted Sidewalk to easy climbing on a ramp. **Pitch 4:** (5.7) 10 bolts. Climb into an amphitheater and exit via a solid rib of rock on the left. A short, vertical section ends at a long ledge. **Pitch 5:** (5.7) 11 bolts. A brilliant finishing pitch follows fun jugs on the left side of a slab. Finish by veering up and left past easier ledges.

44. The Climb (5.12c) ★★★ Bolts. The best route in the Kiss of the Lepers Area follows a remarkable chimney system cut deep into the lower part of the cliff. There's nothing at Smith that compares to this solid groove. The remaining route isn't exceptional, but an endless line of bolts compensates for imperfect rock. Most climbers aid the crumbling starting pitch. Begin behind a tree blocking the opening moves. **Pitch 1:** (5.12c) 9 bolts. Power past an unfortunately dirty bulge, entering a chimney.

Belay here and then walk deep into the groove to another anchor. **Pitch 2:** (5.10d) 10 bolts. Stem the one-of-a-kind slot past a crux bulge and continue with a fun exit on good holds. **Pitch 3:** (5.7) 9 bolts. Follow a mediocre slab up and left to a bulge and climb back right to an anchor. Belaying here reduces rope drag. **Pitch 4:** (5.7) 14 bolts. A short wall leads past an anchor to the outstanding final pitch of *First Kiss*.

45. Dreams That I Carry (5.10a) ★★ Bolts. An alternate ending to *The Climb* won't see many ascents. The crux slab/corner still needs cleaning, and the fun upper pitch isn't as good as the original finish. Approach by stepping left to anchors after the third-pitch bulge on *The Climb*. A faster option rappels diagonally from an anchor on the left side of Hello Kitty Cliff. **Pitch 1:** (5.10a) 7 bolts. Smears on a low-angle, gritty slab lead into a left-facing corner. Step right to an anchor. **Pitch 2:** (5.7) 10 bolts. Move right to an easy wall with steep sections interrupted by ledges.

46. Project (5.12?) The massive wall left of *The Climb* offers little of interest. An abandoned reddish streak rising above the ground might see an ascent in the distant future.

47. Groove Thang (5.8) ★★★ 8 bolts. Smith's most secretive route ascends a surprising one-pitch groove starting far up a chimney atop the gully left of *The Climb*. You'll think you're the victim of a cruel hoax until you spot the hidden line of bolts. Save the hillside—approach and descend along the base of the cliff.

HELLO KITTY CLIFF

There are three crags rising like a gigantic staircase atop the ridge north of Monkey Face. The highest crag is Hello Kitty Cliff, with its pocketed river face towering high above the main wall of the Kiss of the Lepers Area. With an unmatched view of Monkey Face and the Oregon Cascades, the Hello Kitty Cliff will inevitably attract attention. Two of the better lines still need bolts, and harder possibilities to the right await first ascents.

To approach, ascend the trail on the uphill side of Monkey Face and cut north to a third-class scramble. A quicker alternative hikes over Misery Ridge. Until the construction of a suitable trail, use good judgment and avoid cutting directly down the hillside.

48. Great Expectations
(5.7) ★★ Gear to 2.5 inches. The first route ever climbed in the Kiss of the Lepers Area followed a clean right-facing corner at the right side of the cliff. After gliding up the pleasant corner, the rock unfortunately goes bad on the easier finish.

49. Guinness (5.7) ★★★
5 bolts. A left-leaning crack slashes across the river face of Hello Kitty Cliff. Easy, bolted climbing on solid stone leads to a simple finish on a prow.

50. Redundant (5.7) ★★★ TR.
A fun line of pockets pepper the wall immediately left of *Guinness*. Originally led on rebolts, the quality of the climbing easily justifies permanent bolts.

51. Lucky Girl (5.7) ★★★ TR.
Another winning line of jugs joins *No Expectations* just below the top of the slab. You'll need to settle for a toprope ascent until someone fires in a few bolts.

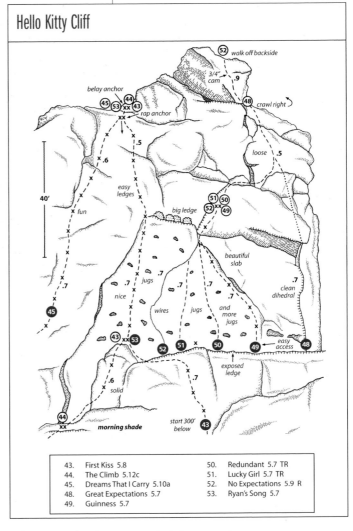

Hello Kitty Cliff

43.	First Kiss 5.8	50.	Redundant 5.7 TR
44.	The Climb 5.12c	51.	Lucky Girl 5.7 TR
45.	Dreams That I Carry 5.10a	52.	No Expectations 5.9 R
48.	Great Expectations 5.7	53.	Ryan's Song 5.7
49.	Guinness 5.7		

52. No Expectations (5.9 R) ★★ Gear to 2.5 inches. A naturally protected thin crack meanders through the pockets to the same anchor as the preceding three routes. You'll have good memories if you stop here. A perilous summit pitch awaits anyone unafraid of bad rock and sparse protection. **Pitch 1:** (5.7) Climb the high-quality thin crack on the pocketed slab to an anchor. Lower off or . . . **Pitch 2:** (5.9) Veer right on mediocre rock, ending at a ledge below the summit block. A dangerous boulder move protected by a cam ends on top. Descend by scrambling down the backside.

53. Ryan's Song (5.7) ★★★ 11 bolts. When climbed as a one-pitch sport route, the excellent upper pitch of *First Kiss* and *The Climb* is called *Ryan's Song*. To approach, traverse along an exposed ledge to an anchor. A wonderful stint of jugs leads up the slab past ledges to an anchor on top. You can lower off (barely) with a single 70-meter rope.

Apart from the main wall, the remaining rock in the Kiss of the Lepers Area is utterly dismal. The only climb in this long stretch of scum ascends one of Smith's most wretched-looking lines.

54. Crack of Insanity (5.11d R) Gear to 4 inches. This grotesque roof crack looks like it came from the bowels of hell. Keeping walking along the base of the Kiss of the Lepers Area looking for your worst nightmare—you'll know it when you see it. **Pitch 1:** (5.9) Climb a high-risk, blocky corner to a belay bolt on a ledge. **Pitch 2:** (5.11d) Step right to a flare dripping with bird shit and gain courage for the 20-foot roof crack. Jams, underclings, full body stems, and other contortions lead to the lip, with an awkward fist crack finish as your reward. Rappel with two 60-meter ropes from ring anchors.

NEW WORLD BUTTRESS

Far north of everything else rises a massive chunk of rock split by several cracks. Two routes of mixed quality provide little reason to visit. Descending via the backside only adds to the adventure.

55. Hawkline Monster (5.10a R) ★★ No topo. Gear to 2.5 inches. The best line on the New World Buttress follows the right of two massive corners on the river face. Despite sections of amazing rock, there's enough garbage to keep almost everyone away. **Pitch 1:** (5.9) Follow the left-facing dihedral past a ledge to a bolt belay. **Pitch 2:** (5.10a) Jam a crux finger crack to a rotten ramp and move up and left to an anchor. **Pitch 3:** (5.8) Face climb to the top of the buttress.

56. New World (5.8 R) ★ No topo. Gear to 2.5 inches. This five-pitch odyssey mixes solid rock with lots of junk. Start on the north side of the buttress with a short traverse right and climb to the top via an obscure crack system. The enjoyable third pitch splits a clean slab, but it's not enough to rescue *New World* from eternal obscurity.

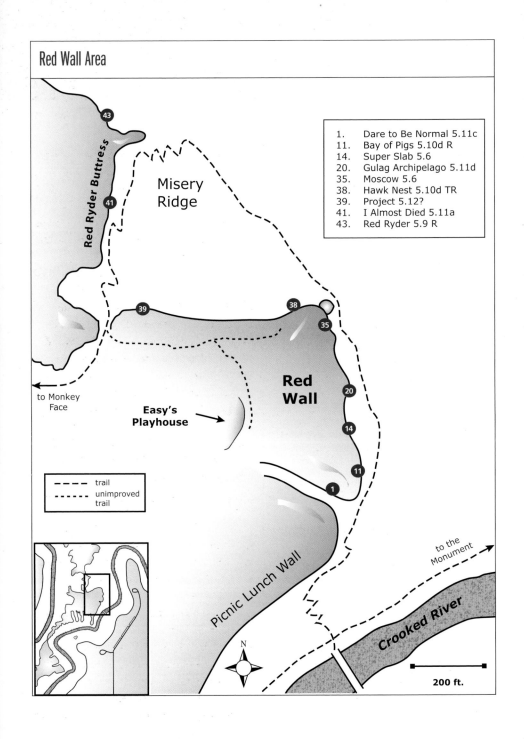

Red Wall Area

1. Dare to Be Normal 5.11c
11. Bay of Pigs 5.10d R
14. Super Slab 5.6
20. Gulag Archipelago 5.11d
35. Moscow 5.6
38. Hawk Nest 5.10d TR
39. Project 5.12?
41. I Almost Died 5.11a
43. Red Ryder 5.9 R

Misery Ridge

Red Ryder Buttress

Red Wall

Easy's Playhouse

to Monkey Face

trail
unimproved trail

Picnic Lunch Wall

to the Monument

Crooked River

N

200 ft.

After washing down some amphetamines with a bottle of red wine, we foolishly hiked up to Red Wall. I was belaying off a small ledge with a lousy anchor as Danny led the final pitch. He hadn't placed any gear, and was shaking and gripped on the final moves far above—one slip from taking us both to the ground.

Steve Strauch after climbing *Amphetamine Grip* in 1970

With hues of red and purple in the morning sun, the beautiful 350-foot Red Wall dominates the western skyline from the turnaround parking area. The high-quality routes and short approach make it a prime destination for moderate-level climbers. With nothing harder than 5.11, most routes follow heavily featured slabs or clean cracks. The lack of hard lines doesn't discourage those who list Red Wall among their favorite destinations. With the higher-level Smith crags packed with difficult sport routes and teeming with climbers, Red Wall is relatively undeveloped and usually free of crowds.

The iron-rich rock offers a different climbing experience than typical tuff. The lower reaches of the cliff are more Smith-like, with light-colored stone peppered with sharp, friable edges. The uniquely colorful upper portion sets Red Wall apart from other crags—only the small Phoenix Buttress comes close to duplicating the unusually solid stone. For traditional climbers Red Wall contains some of the best easy multi-pitch routes at Smith. *Super Slab* and *Moscow,* for instance, are justifiably popular with lower-level climbers—both are safe, solid, and immensely fun. The many one-pitch sport lines receive more ascents each year, as do the newer multi-pitch sport routes to the top of the cliff.

Unlike Smith's more famous crags, Red Wall contains few historically significant routes. Since the crag doesn't culminate in a summit spire, early climbers ignored the obvious crack lines until Pat Callis and Mickey Schurr ascended *Moscow* (5.6) in 1965. The best ascent of the decade came four years later when Tom Bauman led *Peking* (5.9). During the next several years the remaining cracks saw ascents, but it wasn't until the late 1970s that Red Wall had its brief claim to fame. In 1978 Jeff Thomas freed a short dihedral on Red Ryder Buttress called *I Almost Died* (5.11a), and the next year he added the smooth-sided *Chairman Mao's Little Red Book* (5.11a) on the main cliff. These short routes ranked near the top of Smith standards at the time. Despite these promising beginnings, development fizzled in the next two decades—apart from a spattering of simple base routes, the main wall saw little activity. Only recently did climbers take a closer look at the large amounts of untouched stone. Jeff Frizzell and Jim Ablao's 2003 ascent of the multi-pitch *Gulag Archipelago* (5.11d) makes the short list of Smith's best long sport routes

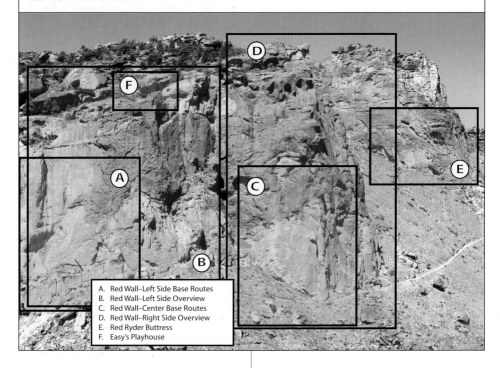

Red Wall Area Overview

A. Red Wall–Left Side Base Routes
B. Red Wall–Left Side Overview
C. Red Wall–Center Base Routes
D. Red Wall–Right Side Overview
E. Red Ryder Buttress
F. Easy's Playhouse

and points to greater possibilities. In coming years the sections of untouched stone will inevitably produce higher-level climbs. An overhanging face in the center of the cliff holds the greatest promise; a fully prepared sport route will someday introduce Red Wall to the 5.13 grade.

Oregon State Parks protects active nesting areas by sometimes closing portions of Red Wall from March through July. The closed sections vary from year-to-year—a decade or more may pass without any closure. Signs at the parking area and the bridge detail the restricted sections of cliff, and the ranger can provide additional information on what routes are off-limits. Please use restraint during these months and go elsewhere—the future of Smith climbing depends on it.

This chapter also includes two lesser nearby crags. The large Red Ryder Buttress contains a small group of mostly traditional routes, while Easy's Playhouse features the only high-level sport routes in the vicinity. The entire region gets early morning sun, with much of the cliff baking until midafternoon. The wall makes a good afternoon choice during the warmer months and a poor option during winter. Except for the far left side of the cliff, the winter sun disappears long before the rock warms enough for comfortable climbing.

Finding the crags: Enter the canyon and cross the bridge below Picnic Lunch Wall. Follow the switchbacked Misery Ridge Trail uphill to the base of the Red Wall.

RED WALL

Stretching over a quarter mile from end-to-end, Red Wall is one of Smith's largest unbroken chunks of stone. The best sections are remarkably solid with terrific beginning cracks and moderate bolted faces. **Descent:** Many of the more popular routes top out. Fixed anchors atop *Amphetamine Grip* allow a quick descent with two double-rope rappels for any route on the left side of the crag. The common descent for any climb topping-out on the right side of the cliff follows the Misery Ridge Trail. From the top of the cliff, weave uphill through junipers, sagebrush, and a small rock band looking to the right for the unmistakable switchbacked path heading back to the base.

1. Dare to Be Normal

(5.11c) ★★ Mixed to 2.5 inches. A deep gully separates Red Wall from Picnic Lunch Wall to the left. High on the right side of the gully sits a short sport route on good rock. Despite a memorable position far off the ground, very few climbers dare. Start from the left side of the long ledge below Bill's Flake. **Pitch 1:** (5.5) Step left around the corner into a low-angle, flaring chimney. Stem and scramble far up the gully, exiting right

to a large ledge. Find a belay bolt hidden to the right. **Pitch 2:** (5.11c) 4 bolts. After an unnerving first clip, follow a technical seam finishing with a small crux bulge. Descend with two rappels down the main face.

2. Titanium Jag (5.10b R) ★★★ Mixed to 2 inches.
An impressive arching dihedral dominates the upper part of Red Wall's far

Red Wall—Left Side Base Routes

1.	Dare to Be Normal 5.11c	7.	Orgasmagoria 5.10c
2.	Titanium Jag 5.10b R	8.	Pop Art 5.10b
3.	Project 5.11+ ?	9.	Dances With Clams 5.10a
4.	Bill's Flake 5.10a	10.	Paper Tiger 5.10a
5.	Finger Puppet 5.10a	10a.	Karl Marx Variation 5.10a R
6.	Phantasmagoria 5.10c	11.	Bay of Pigs 5.10d R
6a.	Jag Connection 5.10c		

left side. A worthwhile route ascends this corner in three varied pitches to the top of the cliff. The most memorable sequence pulls around an exposed roof at the top of the arch. Despite reasonable protection, a second-pitch fall caused a tragic fatality in 1998. Start by scrambling to a ledge left of Bill's Flake. **Pitch 1:** (5.8) Climb an indistinct seam past a fixed pin to the crest of the ridge. Simple moves lead left around the corner to easy scrambling and a belay bolt. **Pitch 2:** (5.9) Scamper up an attractive ramp past a bolt to a small ledge in a left-facing corner. **Pitch 3:** (5.10b) Edge up the face past three bolts to a crux move around the roof. Easy climbing ends at an anchor just below the top.

3. Project (5.11+?) 12 bolts. When completed, the friable edges left of Bill's Flake will test both your technical skills and patience. The crux cranks past a small roof at the start, but the climbing stays difficult from bottom to top.

4. Bill's Flake (5.10a) ★★ Gear to 2.5 inches. This obvious circular flake rests on a ledge system at the base of Red Wall's left side. A short but intense route underclings and jams great rock on the left side.

5. Finger Puppet (5.10a) ★★★ 3 bolts. A short line of edges leads up the face of Bill's Flake. The hardest move balances past the starting arête, but the fun starts higher on the delightful finishing holds.

6. Phantasmagoria (5.10c) ★★★ 9 bolts. An excellent sport route follows the vertical face above Bill's Flake. Start with *Finger Puppet* and step right past the second bolt to a wall packed with delicate, unrelenting moves. Crumbling holds plaguing early ascents are now perfectly solid, though they're not as sharp-edged as they once were.

6a. Jag Connection (5.10c) ★★★ Mixed to 2 inches. An excellent combination connects *Phantasmagoria* with the upper part of *Titanium Jag*. The only independent climbing on the connection follows a short face (5.7) above the *Phantasmagoria* anchor. **Pitch 1:** (5.10c) Climb *Phantasmagoria* and continue above the anchor into the left-facing corner on *Titanium Jag*. **Pitch 2:** (5.10b) Ascend the quality upper pitch of the *Jag* to the top.

7. Orgasmagoria (5.10c) ★★★ Bolts. Another winning combination adds a new sport pitch right of the *Titanium Jag* dihedral. With a satisfying position and great rock, the long finishing pitch shouldn't be missed. **Pitch 1:** (5.10c) 9 bolts. Climb *Phantasmagoria* to the hanging belay. **Pitch 2:** (5.10c) 14 bolts. Veer right on an attractive wall and climb moderate rock on big holds to a hard move at the "blonde bulge" near the top.

8. Pop Art (5.10b) ★★ 3 bolts. Just off the trail below Bill's Flake are parallel bolt lines on an undersize pillar. The short left route follows fun knobs past a crux bulge to an anchor.

9. Dances With Clams (5.10a) ★★ 4 bolts. The right of two bolt lines ascends simple edges to an exciting finish on jugs. Despite a few good moments, it ends shortly after the fun begins.

10. Paper Tiger (5.10a) ★★ Mixed to 2.5 inches. The original route to the top of Red Wall's southern flank followed an obvious traditional crack. The first ascent bypassed the crux pitch by scrambling left from *Super Slab* along a large ledge system. A direct option (originally called *Paper Lion*) provides a more logical start, though the impressive upper wall still highlights the outing. Start at a short right-facing corner next to a bolted pillar. **Pitch 1:** (5.10a) Scurry up the corner to a slot and jam a solid crack to an alcove.

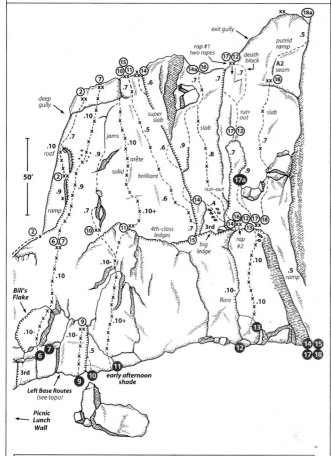

2.	Titanium Jag 5.10b R
6.	Phantasmagoria 5.10c
7.	Orgasmagoria 5.10c
9.	Dances With Clams 5.10a
10.	Paper Tiger 5.10a
11.	Bay of Pigs 5.10d R
12.	'Till the Cows Come Home 5.10a R
13.	Animal Farm 5.10c
14.	Super Slab 5.6
14a.	Panama Express 5.9 R
15.	A Stroke of Brilliance 5.7
16.	Panama Red 5.8 R
17.	Amphetamine Grip 5.7 R
17a.	Gripped 5.9
18.	Red Rover 5.7 R
18a.	Red Rover finish 5.5 A2

avoids the simple corner at the start with run-out edges to the right. After clipping the first bolt on *Bay of Pigs,* quickly cut up and left to the security of the regular route.

11. Bay of Pigs (5.10d R) ★★★★ Bolts. An excellent sport route ascends the attractive left portion of Red Wall. The shining new bolts and solid rock should attract many climbers. The opening pitch isn't exceptional, but the finishing wall dazzles everyone. Unfortunately, the start of the final pitch adds a needless degree of risk. **Pitch 1:** (5.10c) 12 bolts. Follow edges and pockets up a technical wall capped by a bulge. Veer right to an anchor. **Pitch 2:** (5.10d) 13 bolts. Climb great rock to a shallow arête capped by an exposed prow. Expect many tricky moves split by good shakes. Don't fall getting to the second bolt.

Bolts protect an intimidating crux bulge leading up and left to an anchor. **Pitch 2:** (5.9) Cut left on unprotected buckets and move right past sagebrush to a small roof. Step around the roof to the left and climb the enjoyable crack to the top.

10a. Karl Marx Variation (5.10a R) ★ Mixed to 2.5 inches. A moronic variant

12. 'Till the Cows Come Home (5.10a R) ★ Gear to 3 inches. Much like any Smith crag, Red Wall contains good routes and bad routes. This is one of the bad ones. The only good climbing shares the second pitch of *Amphetamine Grip.* Begin behind a boulder below a homely right-facing corner. **Pitch 1:** (5.10a) Awkward stems lead past a bulge on junky rock. Continue to a huge

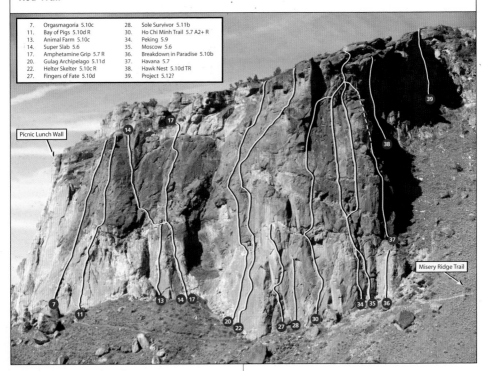

Red Wall

7.	Orgasmagoria 5.10c	28.	Sole Survivor 5.11b
11.	Bay of Pigs 5.10d R	30.	Ho Chi Minh Trail 5.7 A2+ R
13.	Animal Farm 5.10c	34.	Peking 5.9
14.	Super Slab 5.6	35.	Moscow 5.6
17.	Amphetamine Grip 5.7 R	36.	Breakdown in Paradise 5.10b
20.	Gulag Archipelago 5.11d	37.	Havana 5.7
22.	Helter Skelter 5.10c R	38.	Hawk Nest 5.10d TR
27.	Fingers of Fate 5.10d	39.	Project 5.12?

Picnic Lunch Wall

Misery Ridge Trail

ledge. **Pitch 2:** (5.7) Climb the second-pitch flake crack of *Amphetamine Grip*. **Pitch 3:** (5.7) Scamper directly up a run-out slab and climb cautiously past a dangerously hollow flake. Hand traverse straight left to the top.

13. Animal Farm (5.10c) ★★ 9 bolts. A decent sport route ascends the wall right of the first pitch of *'Till the Cows Come Home*. A tricky start gives way to an easier midsection, followed by a second crux reaching between positive edges.

14. Super Slab (5.6) ★★★★ Gear to 2.5 inches. Far and away the best traditional pitch of the grade at Smith is the finishing slab of this popular route. The lower pitches aren't special, but the elegant finish features wonderful rock, aesthetic moves, and a fine sense of exposure. Most climbers rappel off

using two ropes. The original exit dropped into a gully on the backside, scrambled up a deceptively difficult (5.7) unexposed slab, and hiked down Misery Ridge. **Pitch 1:** (5.5) Start left of a shattered amphitheater and ascend a ramp past a mini-bulge to a ledge. **Pitch 2:** (5.4) Step left to a big ledge and climb run-out potholes to a belay slot behind a block. **Pitch 3:** (5.6) Delightful climbing up the super slab ends on top.

14a. Panama Express (5.9 R) ★★ Mixed to 2.5 inches. If *Super Slab* seems too easy for your tastes, you can step right low on the third pitch. Scamper up a shallow corner to a ramp ending at a massive block. Detour right and face climb to the top.

15. A Stroke of Brilliance (5.7) ★★★★ 8 bolts. An enjoyable sport route follows the low-angle face left of *Super Slab*'s final pitch.

The hardest climbing comes right off the starting ledge with a short, bolted crack. After veering left onto the face, a delightful slab leads to another crux just below the top. Approach via the first pitch of *Super Slab* and walk left along an unexposed ledge.

16. Panama Red (5.8 R) ★★★ Mixed to 2.5 inches. The slab right of *Super Slab*'s third pitch features a high-quality though seldom-climbed route. A perilous run-out getting to the first of five bolts discourages many climbers.

17. Amphetamine Grip (5.7 R) ★★★ Gear to 2 inches. Highly varied and challenging for the grade, the *Grip* follows a meandering crack above the first belay on *Super Slab*. A fall on the upper pitch wouldn't be pretty, though anyone solid at the grade will enjoy the pleasant climbing. **Pitch 1:** (5.5) Romp up the first pitch of *Super Slab*. **Pitch 2:** (5.7) An easy scramble gives way to a left-leaning flake crack. Fun jamming and liebacking around a bulge ends at a small belay ledge. **Pitch 3:** (5.7) Simple moves lead to a traverse left and a delicate finish up a corner of light rock.

17a. Gripped (5.9) ★★ Gear to 2 inches. A less enjoyable second-pitch alternative pulls around an awkwardly flaring slot to the right.

18. Red Rover (5.7 R) ★★ Mixed to 2.5 inches. The ignored rightmost slab would receive more attention if not for long run-outs past two newly replaced bolts. Approach with the first pitch of *Super Slab* and scramble up huge blocks to the base of a faint prow.

18a. Red Rover finish (5.5 A2) ★ Aid rack to 2 inches. Twenty-five years after the first ascent, historians discovered that *Red Rover* actually finished to the top. Another twenty-five years might pass before anyone bothers repeating it. Aid a short seam above the second-pitch anchor and shuffle right

along a disintegrating ramp to a simple finish in a groove.

19. Papillion (5.8) ★★ 10 bolts. An easy new sport line starts with buckets downhill to the right of *Super Slab*'s start. A shallow dihedral in the middle of the pitch gives way to a finesse finish.

20. Gulag Archipelago (5.11d) ★★★★ Bolts. The most impressive line on Red Wall attacks the ominous wall above a massive amphitheater. With three pitches of 5.11, it's easily the hardest route on the cliff. Solid rock, a great position, appealing cruxes, and plenty of bolts make *Gulag* one of Smith's finest long sport routes. Most climbers descend via the Misery Ridge Trail, though you can rappel the route with a 60-meter rope. First, scramble down the gully to the anchor atop the third pitch and rappel to an anchor in the middle of nowhere. A second rappel ends atop the first pitch, and one more puts you back on the ground. **Pitch 1:** (5.11b) 12 bolts. Follow technical face holds right of the bucket start to *Papillion* and veer right to an anchor. You can belay at higher bolts, but it puts you at risk of getting smacked by a falling leader. **Pitch 2:** (5.11d) 14 bolts. Intimidating climbing leads past a crux bulge and traverses left over nothingness to a small belay hole. **Pitch 3:** (5.11a) 10 bolts. Follow a water streak past a small roof to an anchor at the base of a gully. **Pitch 4:** (5.9) 4 bolts. Step right and savor the exposed headwall on big edges.

21. Iron Curtain (5.9 R) ★★ Gear to 1.5 inches. A shallow left-facing corner rises in the midst of bolted sport routes. After finessing crux stems and finger jams, finish on creaky flakes to a large ledge. Lower off with a 60-meter line.

22. Helter Skelter (5.10c R) ★★ Mixed to 2.5 inches. The original route to the top of Red Wall's imposing midsection ascends four

Red Wall–Center Base Routes

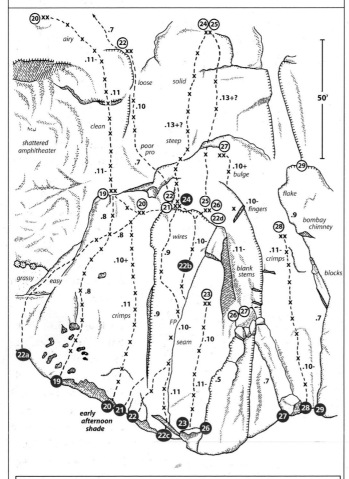

19.	Papillion 5.8	23.	Ride the Lightning 5.11b
20.	Gulag Archipelago 5.11d	24.	Project 5.13+?
21.	Iron Curtain 5.9 R	25.	Project 5.13+?
22.	Helter Skelter 5.10c R	26.	Chairman Mao's Little
22a.	Helter Start Variation 5.8		Red Book 5.11a
22b.	Helter Direct Finish 5.10b	27.	Fingers of Fate 5.10d
22c.	Helter Direct Start 5.11b	28.	Sole Survivor 5.11b
22d.	If Six Were Nine 5.10b	29.	Gone With the Flake 5.9 R

flake. **Pitch 1:** (5.10a) Cut right to a small ledge and face climb a bolted seam. Leave the security of the bolt line by moving left to run-out edges up discontinuous cracks. **Pitch 2:** (5.10c) Move up and left with poor protection to three welcome bolts. Run-out junk ends at a pleasant ledge. **Pitch 3:** (5.7) A terminal run-out diagonals far left to a bolt inches right of the third pitch of *Gulag*. Cut back right (finding a bolt if you're lucky) to a belay spot on the upper slab. **Pitch 4:** (5.8) Scramble up the simple slab and jam a short left-facing corner to the top.

22a. Helter Start Variation (5.8) ★ 4 bolts. The first ascent of the upper pitches bypassed the first pitch with a traverse from the left. Begin by scrambling into a large amphitheater and cut across *Papillion* and *Gulag Archipelago* to the belay ledge.

adventure-filled, rarely climbed pitches. It offers a taste of Smith climbing 1970s-style—despite protection at the crux, other sections are painfully run-out. Retro-bolts removed much of the sting from the first pitch. Start right of *Iron Curtain* below a short curving

22b. Helter Direct Finish (5.10b) ★★★ 6 bolts. A sport climbing variant bypasses the run-out first-pitch finish with a direct line of edges to the right. Continue to the top or lower off with a 60-meter rope.

Red Wall—Right Side Overview

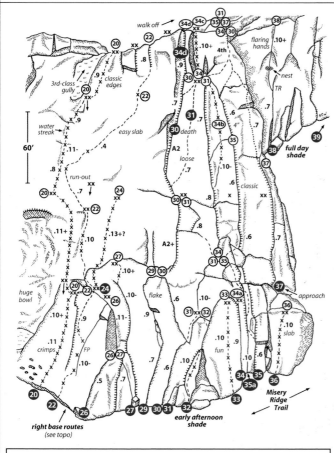

20.	Gulag Archipelago 5.11d	34a.	Chouinard's Crack 5.9
22.	Helter Skelter 5.10c R	34b.	Burma Buttress 5.10a
24.	Project 5.13+ ?	34c.	Straight Outta Peking 5.10d
26.	Chairman Mao's Little Red Book 5.11a	34d.	Beijing Finish 5.9
27.	Fingers of Fate 5.10d	35.	Moscow 5.6
29.	Gone With the Flake 5.9 R	35a.	Mongolians 5.10b R
30.	Ho Chi Minh Trail 5.7 A2+ R	36.	Breakdown in Paradise 5.10b
31.	Shanghai 5.10a X	37.	Havana 5.7
32.	Cartoon Deficiency 5.10c R	38.	Hawk Nest 5.10d TR
33.	Let's Face It 5.10b	39.	Project 5.12?
34.	Peking 5.9		

22c. Helter Skelter Direct Start (5.11b) ★★
7 bolts. A direct start to the first pitch crimps up an obvious seam. Despite solid rock, the sharp edges aren't a lot of fun.

22d. If Six Were Nine (5.10b) ★★ Mixed to 1 inch. A traditional ending to the first pitch

ignores the bolted line by continuing up the right-leaning seam. The deceptively tricky crux pulls over a small roof just below the belay ledge. Lower to the ground with a 60-meter rope.

23. Ride the Lightning (5.11b) ★★★
5 bolts. The original sport route on Red Wall follows a short line of sharp edges left of a small inside corner. The crimping crux comes in the first 15 feet.

24. Project (5.13+?) 9 bolts. The fully prepared face directly above *Helter Skelter's* first pitch will someday bring Red Wall into the modern era. With excellent rock and continuously difficult climbing, it'll easily be the hardest route on the cliff.

25. Project (5.13+?)
The high-quality project to the right won't get done anytime soon. Begin from the right of two anchors atop the starting pitch of *Helter Skelter.*

26. Chairman Mao's Little Red Book (5.11a) ★★★ Gear to 1 inch. The hardest traditional route on Red Wall follows a short, polished dihedral guaranteed to bewilder most sport climbers. Expect top-notch rock, decent protection, and no holds. **Pitch 1:** (5.6) Stroll up a left-facing corner right of *Ride the Lightning* to the base of the *Little Red Book.* **Pitch 2:** (5.11a) Jam and stem the smooth-sided dihedral and step left to an anchor. Rappel with a 60-meter rope.

27. Fingers of Fate (5.10d) ★★★ Mixed to 2 inches.
You wouldn't guess it from below, but this forgotten route contains one of the better finger cracks on Red Wall. Although a traditional lead, the hardest climbing powers through a bolt-protected boulder problem just below the anchors. Rappel with two ropes or a single 70-meter line. **Pitch 1:** (5.7) Start on the right side of a small buttress and climb a short leaning crack to a ledge below the *Little Red Book.* **Pitch 2:** (5.10d) Step right and jam a left-arching crack on great rock. Mantel to a jug, clip a bolt, and crank on creaky edges to an anchor.

28. Sole Survivor (5.11b) ★★★ 8 bolts.
This wall of knobs and crimps starts slightly right of the lowest part of Red Wall. A run-out above the first bolt deters some climbers, though the rest of the route is safe and enjoyable. The hardest and least pleasant moves come at the very top.

29. Gone With the Flake (5.9 R) ★ Gear to 4 inches.
An unmistakable block-plugged flake crack rises right of *Sole Survivor.* After tugging warily on loose blocks, strenuous moves enter a memorable bombay chimney. Rappel with two ropes (or a 70-meter line) from a huge horn wrapped with slings.

30. Ho Chi Minh Trail (5.7 A2+ R) ★ Aid rack to 2.5 inches.
One of Red Wall's few aid routes wouldn't stay that way for long if a good free climber went to work. The hardest section follows a left-facing corner above *Gone with the Flake.* Start below a short right-leaning crack. **Pitch 1:** (5.6) Scramble up the easy crack and climb a wide groove on the right side of a huge flake to an anchor. **Pitch 2:** (A2+) Move right and nail an inside corner to a belay beneath the final slab. **Pitch 3:** (5.7 A2) Low-angle aid and free moves ascend the prominent right-facing dihedral. Cut right to an anchor. **Pitch 4:** (4th class) Step right and weave through boulders to the top.

31. Shanghai (5.10a X) ★ Gear to 3 inches.
Without rival, this multi-pitch adventure is the worst line to the top of Red Wall. Apart from an excellent 15-foot hand crack on the second pitch, there's nothing but loose rock and long run-outs. This might change with a careful scrubbing and retro-bolting—the fourth-pitch slab could be classic. **Pitch 1:** (5.6) Start up the same crack as *Ho Chi Minh Trail,* but avoid the big flake by stepping right to an anchor on a slab. **Pitch 2:** (5.10a) Jam the brilliant crack and grovel into an awkward slot. Easy scrambling up a rotten corridor ends at a ledge. **Pitch 3:** (5.8) Ramble left to an undercling around an obvious roof and continue to a belay ledge. **Pitch 4:** (5.7) Follow the *Ho Chi Minh Trail* dihedral for a few feet and traverse right onto the unprotected slab-of-death. Belay at a new anchor below a bolted arête. **Pitch 5:** (4th class) Traverse right and scramble to the top.

32. Cartoon Deficiency (5.10c R) ★★ Mixed to 1.5 inches.
An insignificant right-leaning corner rises above broken boulders. It's the hardest free route at Smith protected by quarter-inch bolts; expect them to barely slow you down if you fall. After finishing the corner with finger jams, easy rock leads to a traverse left to an anchor.

33. Let's Face It (5.10b) ★★★ 6 bolts.
This pleasant route ascends the attractive wall left

of *Chouinard's Crack*. Enjoyable knobs and edges on great rock make it one of Red Wall's better sport climbs.

34. Peking (5.9) ★★★ Gear to 2.5 inches. Parallel crack systems running from bottom to top split the right side of Red Wall. The less popular left crack doesn't match the quality of its neighbor, though it's still worth doing. You can bypass the challenging opening pitch by starting with *Moscow* to the right. **Pitch 1:** (5.9) Hand traverse left to an elegant crack and jam perfect stone past an anchor to a higher ledge. **Pitch 2:** (5.8) Begin the prominent left-facing corner with a crux bulge and follow a long moderate pitch to a two-bolt anchor. **Pitch 3:** (4th class) Traverse right to easy scrambling to the top.

34a. Chouinard's Crack (5.9) ★★★★ Gear to 2 inches. The lower half of *Peking*'s starting pitch is called *Chouinard's Crack*. The flawless stint of jams routinely shuts down anyone lacking crack experience. The Yosemite legend nailed 15 feet up this unclimbed crack in a 1969 aid demonstration for a group of college students. A few days later, local Tom Bauman did the first ascent, using no aid at all.

34b. Burma Buttress (5.10a) ★★ Mixed to 4 inches. A second-pitch alternative to *Peking* steps right to a short lieback flake. Above the crack, wander past six bolts on a low-angle slab and either cut left to the anchor on *Straight Outta Peking* or exit right with fourth-class scrambling. With enough ascents the lichen-plastered slab could transform into a classic.

34c. Straight Outta Peking (5.10d) ★★★ 5 bolts. Far off the ground an attractive arête rises above the *Peking* dihedral. Approach via *Peking* or *Burma Buttress* and belay at bolts

Wayne Arrington on *Chouinard's Crack*.

below the edge. A short but demanding sequence on solid stone makes this a must-do summit pitch.

34d. Beijing Finish (5.9) ★★ Gear to 2.5 inches. A traditional finish avoids the fourth-class scramble on *Peking* by climbing a short corner to the top of Red Wall. Step left from the anchor below *Straight Outta Peking* and follow the obvious dihedral.

35. Moscow (5.6) ★★★★ Gear to 3.5 inches. The original route to the top of the cliff follows the right side of parallel crack systems. With great rock and enjoyable climbing, it's one of the finest easy traditional routes at Smith. The high-quality second pitch highlights the outing, though every section has its charms. Start below an obvious blocky dihedral. **Pitch 1:** (5.6) Crank fun jugs up the steep starting corner and either jam the excellent dihedral (5.7) or bypass it to the left. Avoid bad rock by stepping left and scramble to a ledge. **Pitch 2:** (5.6) Cut right and jam the attractive left-facing dihedral to a belay ledge. **Pitch 3:** (5.6) Finish the corner with a low-angle wide crack. **Pitch 4:** (4th class) Scramble to the top on easy rock.

35a. Mongolians (5.10b R) ★★ Gear to 1 inch. A comical variant begins left of the starting inside corner. *Moscow* climbers find the poorly protected seam far too difficult, while higher-level climbers have little interest in the remaining route.

36. Breakdown in Paradise (5.10b) ★★★ 6 bolts. At the right edge of the main wall sits an unimpressive, heavily featured block. A simple-looking sport line routinely spits off climbers expecting a cruise.

37. Havana (5.7) ★★ Gear to 4 inches. A completely ignored route wanders up an obscure crack system on the north face of Red Wall. Start uphill right of *Breakdown in Paradise* below an ugly trough. **Pitch 1:** (5.7) Follow a flaring crack to a ledge. **Pitch 2:** (5.7) Jam and lieback to an unexposed shelf. **Pitch 3:** (4th class) Scramble to the top.

38. Hawk Nest (5.10d) ★ TR. An obscure toprope problem starts farther uphill on the shattered north side of Red Wall. Begin with mediocre leaning cracks and climb past an abandoned nest to an overhanging flaring hand crack.

39. Project (5.12?) 10 bolts. Far up Misery Ridge, just before the cliff fades away, a spectacular prow with a shining line of bolts captures your attention. The overhanging, physical climbing bears little resemblance to other routes on the crag. Unfortunately, the rock doesn't match the typical Red Wall quality.

RED RYDER BUTTRESS

Near the top of the hill right of Red Wall rests a massive, dismal buttress. No route ascends the main face—except for some quality stone along the base, the rock stinks. The long approach up Misery Ridge discourages most climbers. The first two routes rise above the trail moving left along the base of the buttress.

40. Metamorphic Maneuvers (5.9 R) ★ Gear to 2 inches. Somehow this insignificant left-facing corner caught someone's attention long ago. A poorly protected crux off the ground leads to 8 quality feet in a leaning dihedral. After a blocky exit easier moves past a peg end at an anchor.

41. I Almost Died (5.11a) ★★★ Gear to 2.5 inches. The only eye-catching feature along the left base of the buttress is a short, roof-capped corner. Locking jams on perfect rock followed by classic hand slots over the roof make it worth the hike for any traditional climber. Descend by walking left.

The next five routes ascend a flat slab on the right side of Red Ryder Buttress. Approach via the Misery Ridge Trail and step right at the switchbacks before the trail cuts left. Scramble up scree to a narrow ledge skirting the base of the slab.

42. Flex (5.9) ★★★ Gear to 0.75 inch. An enjoyable low-angle seam with decent protection splits the left side of the slab. Deceptively tricky jams end far too soon at the first set of bolts.

43. Red Ryder (5.9 R) ★★ Mixed to 1.5 inches. Despite good rock and crafty moves, many climbers find this short face a little too sporting. You can easily combine both

Red Ryder Buttress

40.	Metamorphic Maneuvers 5.9 R
41.	I Almost Died 5.11a
42.	Flex 5.9
43.	Red Ryder 5.9 R
44.	Desperately Seeking Shade 5.8
45.	The Young and the Restless 5.9 R
45a.	Pink Squirrel 5.7 R

Red Ryder Buttress

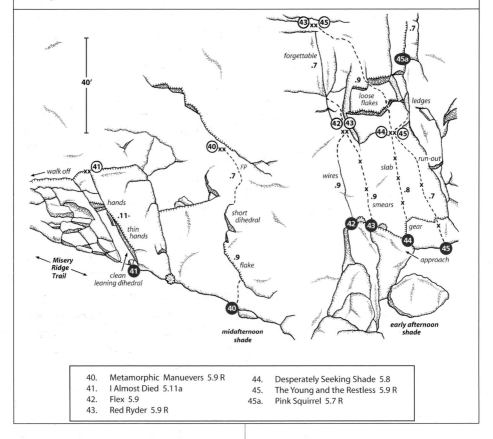

40.	Metamorphic Manuevers 5.9 R	44.	Desperately Seeking Shade 5.8
41.	I Almost Died 5.11a	45.	The Young and the Restless 5.9 R
42.	Flex 5.9	45a.	Pink Squirrel 5.7 R
43.	Red Ryder 5.9 R		

pitches into one, though a smarter option avoids the trashy finish by lowering from the first set of anchors. **Pitch 1:** (5.8) 2 bolts. Smear past widely spaced bolts on the left side of the wall to an anchor. **Pitch 2:** (5.7) Step left and scramble up a lousy crack to a rappel anchor.

44. Desperately Seeking Shade (5.8) ★★★
Mixed to 1.5 inches. The center of the slab offers a quality route devoid of positive edges. After starting with a leaning crack, friction past three bolts on great rock to an easy finishing finger crack.

45. The Young and the Restless (5.9 R) ★
Mixed to 2.5 inches. The most common ver-

sion of this unusual route lowers off after the sparsely bolted first pitch. Loose flakes and poor protection spoil the traversing finish. **Pitch 1:** (5.7) 2 bolts. Start on the right side of the slab and climb lichen-covered knobs to a ledge. Rappel or . . . **Pitch 2:** (5.9) Cut left on dangerous flakes and pull around two intimidating roofs. Continue traversing left to the anchor atop *Red Ryder*'s upper pitch.

45a. Pink Squirrel (5.7 R) ★
Gear to 3 inches. A grotesque alternative to the upper pitch grovels directly up a dismal crack system to the top of the cliff. Scramble far left from the summit to the Misery Ridge descent trail.

EASY'S PLAYHOUSE

A small overhanging cliff packed with powerful sport routes sits atop the gully separating Red Wall from Picnic Lunch Wall. The athletic moves and closely spaced bolts make it a popular destination—despite the monster approach. The easiest option hikes to the top of Misery Ridge, dropping left on a faint trail at the end of the uphill slog. Walk downhill along a slab to the base of the undercut wall.

46. Bee's Nest (5.12a) ★★ 3 bolts. The rightmost line doesn't match the quality of everything else, but it's still worth doing. The holds don't always follow the line of bolts. The grade and contrivance level goes up a couple notches if you strictly follow the bolt line.

47. Bugging Out (5.12d) ★★★ 5 bolts. The hardest line on Easy's Playhouse follows a jungle gym of good holds right of an obvious dihedral. The awkward crux enters and exits a sloping scoop.

48. Boys in the Hood (5.11d) ★★★★ 4 bolts. The best route on the crag rises immediately left of a steep inside corner. The relentless moves on perfect rock provide a rare Smith experience—big holds on a super-steep wall. Unfortunately, it ends after just 40 pumping feet.

48a. Adam Splitter (5.12c) ★★★ TR. A much harder toprope variant powers through overhanging pockets a few feet left of *Boys in the Hood*. Although not nearly as good as the regular line, it would be popular if bolted.

49. Big Boss Man (5.12c) ★★★ 5 bolts. The most physical route on the wall begins deep in the cave with a crux bouldering start. Traverse left on jugs to a line of bolts and finish to the top on easier but radically steep incuts.

50. Straight Outta Madras (5.12c) ★★★ 4 bolts. The left route cranks through underclings and athletic jugs on a wall so steep it feels like a roof. Begin with a leap off the ground using a pocket.

Easy's Playhouse

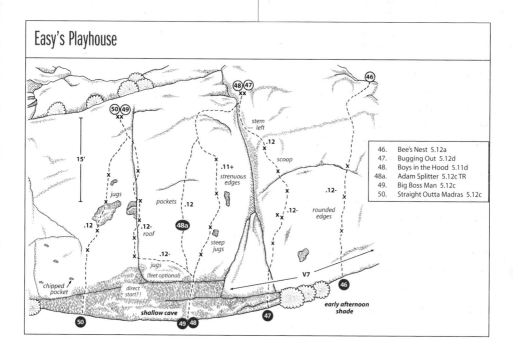

46.	Bee's Nest 5.12a
47.	Bugging Out 5.12d
48.	Boys in the Hood 5.11d
48a.	Adam Splitter 5.12c TR
49.	Big Boss Man 5.12c
50.	Straight Outta Madras 5.12c

The Monument Area and Staender Ridge

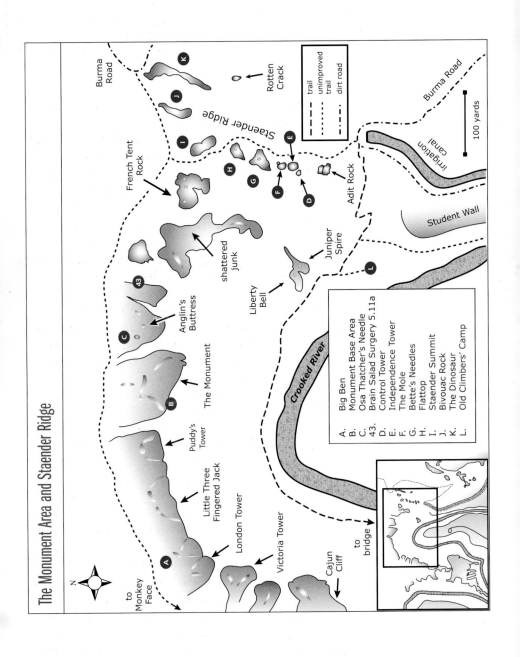

Burma Road

Staender Ridge

Rotten Crack

trail
unimproved trail
dirt road

Burma Road

irrigation canal

100 yards

French Tent Rock

Adit Rock

Student Wall

shattered junk

Anglin's Buttress

The Monument

Juniper Spire

Liberty Bell

Puddy's Tower

Little Three Fingered Jack

London Tower

Victoria Tower

Cajun Cliff

to Monkey Face

Crooked River

to bridge

A. Big Ben
B. Monument Base Area
C. Osa Thatcher's Needle
43. Brain Salad Surgery 5.11a
D. Control Tower
E. Independence Tower
F. The Mole
G. Bette's Needles
H. Flattop
I. Staender Summit
J. Bivouac Rock
K. The Dinosaur
L. Old Climbers' Camp

N

THE MONUMENT AREA AND STAENDER RIDGE

It was the closest I ever came to getting killed climbing. The main feature on the wall was a long crack leading into a flaring chimney. The chimney was easy, but getting to the crack was the crux of the whole route, with a pendulum in from the right. I swung across, hammering a pin into the crumbling stone, but it didn't hold my weight. I tried again, stacking pins this time, until I finally got them to stick. I was standing in my aid slings, when to my horror I realized that my rope had somehow unclipped from my harness! I was hanging off of the worst pins imaginable, unroped, 300 feet off the ground. I lunged at the rope before it swung away and clipped it back into my harness. Before I could even breathe a sigh of relief, the pins pulled out, and I swung across the face.

Ted Davis after the 1966 first ascent of the *Southeast Face* of the Monument

Upstream right of Red Wall lies a picturesque array of imposing faces and spires, curving around a sharp bend in the Crooked River. Despite their rugged beauty, rotten bands of rock split the highest walls, making them unusually dangerous ventures. Fortunately, hidden amid the rubbish are several gems that somehow escaped the dole of bad rock. Even the best of these lines attract little attention—on many days you won't see another soul. With a history dating to the 1940s, these cliffs offer a glimpse back to the earliest days of Smith climbing. You'll marvel over sightings of rusting "bolts" with homemade hangers—and fret if you have to use them.

Walking right from the bridge, the rock beyond Red Wall degenerates into crumbly gullies and unappetizing faces. The small Cajun Cliff is the only worthwhile section of rock in this large expanse. Shortly before the bend in the river, the faces grow more impressive with the striking wall of Little Three Fingered Jack and the 600-foot south face of the Monument. Farther right the rock again worsens as the imposing faces give way to ugly gullies and shattered rhyolite plugs. Just after the river finishes its 180-degree turn, the pinnacles of Staender Ridge rise in a tidy row left of the switch-backed Burma Road.

In the decades prior to the construction of the hiking bridge across the Crooked River, these crags were the most popular climbing destination at Smith. While picnickers and sightseers visited today's main parking area, climbers drove along Burma Road—parking either at the base or top of Staender Ridge. A pleasant setting amid the pines at the northern bend of the Crooked River became the camping area of choice. From this undeveloped campground, the pioneers set off on expeditions to first reach the summits and later pioneer the massive cliffs. This idyllic age ended with the closing of the Burma Road and the park's ban on camping in the canyon. Today there's little evidence of the Old Climbers' Camp apart from a few blackened fire pits beneath scattered boulders.

The easiest spires surely saw exploration from early adventurers prior to World War II. The first recorded ascents in the 1940s were nothing more than simple scrambles to the most prominent summits. In the mid-1950s Vivian and Gil Staender climbed several spires on the ridge that today bears their name. By the sixties, with most of the summits already climbed, a new generation turned their attention to the unclimbed faces. Bruce Hahn and Jim Ramsey climbed *Bruce's Traverse* (5.8) in 1963, and three years later Ted Davis and Willy Zeigler climbed a perilous route up the southeast side of the Monument. The most impressive effort came in 1970 when Steve Strauch and Danny Gates pioneered *Abraxas,* likely Smith's biggest wall climb.

As free climbing grew more popular in the early seventies, these crags saw some of the best ascents of the era. Del Young's free ascent of *Sunjammer* (5.10b) in 1972 ranked near the top of Smith standards. In 1976 Jeff Thomas bumped the level higher when he polished off *Brain Salad Surgery* (5.11a). This overhanging wide crack was the first 5.11 anywhere on Smith tuff. In the early 1980s a new generation of boulderers became intrigued with a short aid roof on the west side of Staender Summit. *Smut* (5.12d) stopped many attempts until Alan Watts succeeded in early 1981. Although more of a boulder problem than a real route, *Smut* pushed Smith standards higher by nearly a full number grade. While the rest of Smith boomed during the 1980s, almost no one visited these crags, and new route activity abruptly ceased. During the following decade several sport routes finally broadened the appeal. Easily the finest of these was Tom Egan's ascent of *The Product* (5.13a) in 1990. Thomas Emde's and Michael Stöger's recent development of a sport climbing zone on Big Ben should finally lure more climbers to the area.

With plenty of south-facing cliffs and shady backsides, this area offers year-round climbing. The exposed pinnacles of Staender Ridge are intolerably cold on a windy day in winter, but they provide a respite from the heat during the warmer season. The approach hike varies from twenty minutes for the Cajun Cliff to forty-five minutes to the top of Staender Ridge. A quicker alternative during low-river conditions fords the river below the Northern Point. To use this approach, park at the turnaround and hike north toward the Monument, dropping down to the left along an obvious trail. Walk upstream about 100 yards to a suitable crossing spot. If the river crossing looks questionable from the rim, don't even try. The deceptively swift water and polished boulders make a dangerous combination.

The Little Three Fingered Jack area, the Monument, and Osa Thatcher's Needle area are typically closed from February 1 to August 1 every year to protect active nesting sites. Expect these closures to continue, so climb elsewhere during these months.

Finding the crags: Descend into the canyon from the parking lot and turn right after crossing the bridge. As you follow the trail upstream, you'll see Little Three Fingered Jack and the Monument directly ahead. Continue farther upstream around the northern bend of the Crooked River for the Staender Ridge routes.

LITTLE THREE FINGERED JACK AREA

North of Red Wall rests a huge volume of gully-split walls. There's not much eye-catching in a quarter-mile expanse of crumbling stone, but eventually the spires distinguish themselves with clean river faces and some of the largest virgin walls at Smith. Moving downstream, Cajun Cliff, Victoria Tower, London Tower, Big Ben, Little Three Fingered Jack, and Puddy's Tower offer a combination of base routes and full-length adventure climbs.

Cajun Cliff

In the midst of a wide section of nondescript squalor lies a short patch of surprisingly clean rock called the Cajun Cliff. The following two routes receive minimal attention, but they make a fine change of pace from the hubbub. To approach, turn right at the bridge and walk along the river one-third mile to a massive pine tree. A quick scramble up scree ends at the base of the streaked crag.

1. Definitely Cajun (5.12a) ★★★ 5 bolts. The most appealing line on the wall follows a water streak up a shallow arête. The crux finesses side pulls past the second bolt, though climbers often fail on the pumping edges above.

2. Pleasure Principle (5.10d) ★★ 7 bolts. The bolted face on the right side of the cliff doesn't match the quality of its neighbor, although the rock improves with each ascent. The delicate moves on small edges appeal to technical specialists.

Little Three Fingered Jack Area—Left Side

2. Pleasure Principle 5.10d
3. Oh Oh Climax 5.9
5. The Safe Zone 5.10a
6. Catherine's Ridge 5.6 R
8. London Tower 5.10a R
11. Chocolate and Cheese 5.9 R
13. Alpen Symphony 5.12a

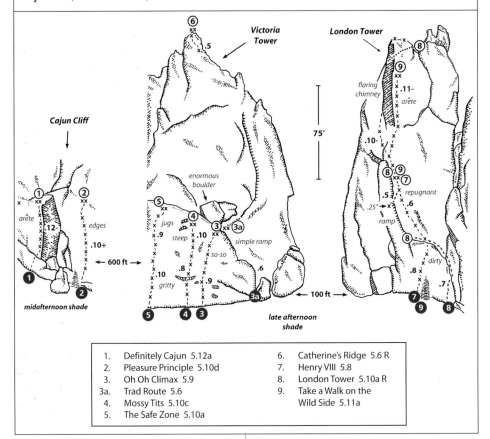

1. Definitely Cajun 5.12a
2. Pleasure Principle 5.10d
3. Oh Oh Climax 5.9
3a. Trad Route 5.6
4. Mossy Tits 5.10c
5. The Safe Zone 5.10a
6. Catherine's Ridge 5.6 R
7. Henry VIII 5.8
8. London Tower 5.10a R
9. Take a Walk on the Wild Side 5.11a

Victoria Tower

A massive chunk of jumbled stone with a broad base and slender summit rises across the gully left of London Tower. The following four base lines will eventually earn an extra star once the rock improves.

3. Oh Oh Climax (5.9) ★ 7 bolts. Massive potholes guard the lower section of Victoria Tower. A less-than-stellar sport route stretches between big jugs and grit-covered slopers. It will only get better as time passes.

3a. Trad Route (5.6) ★ Gear to 2.5 inches. A simple route ending at the anchor above

Oh Oh Climax follows a short right-facing corner leading to a low-angle ramp.

4. Mossy Tits (5.10c) ★★ 8 bolts. Just left of *Oh Oh Climax* rises another potholed route. Mediocre starting moves lead to a fun, physical finish cranking through incuts on an overhanging wall.

5. The Safe Zone (5.10a) ★★ 10 bolts. This generously bolted route (you can almost clip the first bolt standing on the ground) should eventually become popular. The quality improves the higher you go, with a delightful finish on solid jugs.

6. Catherine's Ridge (5.6 R) ★ Mixed to 4

inches. Adventure climbers might enjoy a complicated alpine scramble ending atop the summit spire. Approach up the gully right of the formation and cut left to a belay bolt on a chossy ledge. **Pitch 1:** (5.5) Stem a solid 30-foot dihedral, ending at an anchor atop the lower of two summits. Rap into the notch between the pinnacles and traverse rotted ledges to another anchor. **Pitch 2:** (5.6) Climb past a bolt to a ledge and clip a second bolt before traversing left to a detached block. Easy scrambling ends at a belay bolt on the junky summit. Rappel with double ropes from a two-bolt anchor down the south side of the tower.

London Tower

An obvious crack system splits the river face of the attractive spire across the gully right of Victoria Tower. A single full-length route and two newer sport lines see limited traffic. To reach the summit, hike up the gully to the left and scramble to the summit ridge.

7. Henry VIII (5.8) 9 bolts. Few sport routes at Smith match the nastiness of this grit-covered face. Start behind a juniper tree and stagger past many bolts on rock that starts bad and only gets worse. Rappel with two ropes.

8. London Tower (5.10a R) ★ Mixed to 4 inches. The only route to the top of the cliff receives, at best, one ascent every decade. If you'd like to get in on the action, start below a trough right of *Henry VIII*. **Pitch 1:** (5.7) Enter the trough by bouldering on the left and hike to a big ledge leading left across the face. **Pitch 2:** (5.5) Climb a simple ramp to a quarter-inch bolt atop a pillar. Step right on horrid rock, joining *Henry VIII* just before the anchor. **Pitch 3:** (5.10a) Follow a newly bolted dihedral and cut left to crux face moves protected by modern bolts. Step

back right and stem a corner leading into a flaring chimney.

9. Take a Walk on the Wild Side (5.11a) ★★★ Bolts. An awe-inspiring arête soars far off the ground on the upper reaches of London Tower. A spectacular sport climb on great rock graces this edge. A much more difficult continuation to the top awaits a first ascent. **Pitch 1:** (5.8) 9 bolts. Suffer through *Henry VIII* and belay at two bolts in a trough. **Pitch 2:** (5.11a) 9 bolts. Step right and follow the edge. The position and climbing gets better the higher you go. Rap with two ropes.

Big Ben

This massive crag split by ominous cracks towers right of London Tower. With two full-length routes and a growing collection of bolted lines at the base, it's becoming an increasingly popular destination. The south-facing cliff makes a good choice on the cold, clear days common during a Smith winter, as the cliff warms to short-sleeve temperatures.

10. Dead Baby Bubbas (5.10a) ★★ Gear to 2 inches. At the base of Big Ben sits a short, south-facing finger crack with locking jams on surprisingly solid rock. Rappel from two bolts, or continue via *Chocolate and Cheese*.

10a. Project (5.12?) The polished wall right of *Dead Baby Bubbas* might someday contain a challenging route; currently it sports a single reconnaissance bolt.

11. Chocolate and Cheese (5.9 R) ★★ Mixed to 1 inch. The attractive slab above *Dead Baby Bubbas* features some of the best rock in the entire Little Three Fingered Jack Area. Unfortunately, the run-outs will traumatize budding 5.9 climbers. **Pitch 1:** (4th class) Hike up dirty buckets to an anchor. **Pitch 2:** (5.9) Edge past four bolts and a

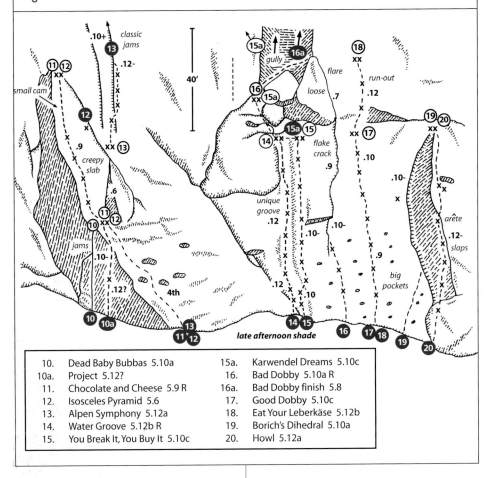

10.	Dead Baby Bubbas 5.10a	15a.	Karwendel Dreams 5.10c
10a.	Project 5.12?	16.	Bad Dobby 5.10a R
11.	Chocolate and Cheese 5.9 R	16a.	Bad Dobby finish 5.8
12.	Isosceles Pyramid 5.6	17.	Good Dobby 5.10c
13.	Alpen Symphony 5.12a	18.	Eat Your Leberkäse 5.12b
14.	Water Groove 5.12b R	19.	Borich's Dihedral 5.10a
15.	You Break It, You Buy It 5.10c	20.	Howl 5.12a

crucial small cam placement to an anchor. Rappel with two ropes.

12. Isosceles Pyramid (5.6) ★ Mixed to 2.5 inches. A ramp right of *Chocolate and Cheese* won't appeal to many climbers. Start with an easy fourth-class scramble to an anchor. Solid jams give way to a low-angle groove with a bolt in the middle.

13. Alpen Symphony (5.12a) ★★★ Mixed to 2.5 inches. One of Smith's best multi-pitch routes ascends an unmistakable dihedral system up the awe-inspiring main face of Big Ben. Consistently overhanging, naturally

solid rock blends sport climbing cruxes with perfect jam cracks. To descend, traverse 20 feet along the summit ridge to an anchor and make two single-rope rappels into the big gully between Big Ben and Little Three Fingered Jack. Hike downhill and rappel from anchors at the bottom of the gully. **Pitch 1:** (5.6) Scramble up the slab to a bolt and continue up *Isosceles Pyramid* to an anchor. **Pitch 2:** (5.12a) Easy, naturally protected moves lead to four bolts in a right-facing corner. Decipher a short, perplexing crux and finish up a beautiful 5.10d crack on perfect stone. Belay at two bolts on a good ledge. **Pitch 3:** (5.10d) Wildly exposed climbing past a few bolts leads to a traverse left to a complete rest. Jam an easier overhanging crack to a belay anchor on a slab. **Pitch 4:** (5.10a) Easy face climbing and stems up a corner lead to a short stretch of loose rock just below the summit.

14. Water Groove (5.12b R) ★★★ 8 bolts.

An unmistakable water-worn groove features a highly technical sport route. A bizarre combination of contortions, stems, and crimpy edges climbs more like Upper Gorge basalt than typical Smith tuff. There are two distinct cruxes, with 5.11 stems in the middle, followed by a sporting finish.

15. You Break It, You Buy It (5.10c) ★★

8 bolts. The rounded arête right of *Water Groove* doesn't match the quality of the streak, but it'll improve quickly with more ascents. The moves are fun and sustained from bottom to top, with a technical crux getting past the second bolt.

15a. Karwendel Dreams (5.10c) ★★★ Mixed

to 2.5 inches. This multi-pitch finish to the top of Big Ben shouldn't be missed. The fully bolted final pitch features good rock with an amazing position, far off the ground. Begin from a hanging belay atop *You Break It, You Buy It*. **Pitch 1:** (5.7) Traverse directly left 10 feet without protection to an anchor and scramble to higher bolts at the base of a massive gully. By starting with *Water Groove* you can completely avoid this traverse. **Pitch 2:** (5.10c) Walk up scree 50 feet and climb a short right-facing corner to

Little Three Fingered Jack Area

7. Henry VIII 5.8	16a. Bad Dobby finish 5.8
9. Take a Walk on the Wild Side 5.11a	21. Victory of the Proletarian
11. Chocolate and Cheese 5.9 R	People's Ambition Arete 5.7 X
13. Alpen Symphony 5.12a	21a. The Quickie 5.6
15. You Break It, You Buy It 5.10c	21b. Adams/Emde Variation 5.8 X
15a. Karwendel Dreams 5.10c	22. Bruce's Traverse 5.8 R
16. Bad Dobby 5.10a R	22a. Bruce's Variation 5.8 R

a bolted crux over a small roof. Step left to a ledge and continue past several more bolts to an anchor. **Pitch 3:** (5.10b) 8 bolts. After a hard move at the start, the climbing eases and the exposure increases on the long dash to the summit. Don't attempt to rappel the route. Instead, scramble 15 feet along the summit ridge to an anchor and make two single-rope rappels into the gully between Big Ben and Little Three Fingered Jack. Walk down the scree and make one more rappel to the ground.

16. Bad Dobby (5.10a R) ★ Mixed to 4 inches. Despite some entertaining moments, *Bad Dobby* won't attract many repeats. A bolted wall of pockets leads to a traditional flake crack with a thin hand crux. The crack widens and the rock deteriorates into a grotesque finishing slot.

16a. Bad Dobby finish (5.8) ★ Gear to 3 inches. You can turn *Bad Dobby* into even more of an adventure by adding a traditional pitch deep in the back of the gully. Follow a right-facing corner to an anchor on a flat ledge. Either rappel or continue to the top via the finishing pitches of *Victory of the Proletarian People's Ambition Arête*.

17. Good Dobby (5.10c) ★★ 7 bolts. The better of neighboring *Dobby* routes ascends a heavily pocketed wall on decent rock. The big jugs at the start grow scarce the higher you go, until they disappear completely at an edgy crux just below the anchor.

18. Eat Your Leberkäse (5.12b) ★★★ 10 bolts. An intimidating bulge sporting two bolts rises above the *Good Dobby* anchors. It's short, but it'll kick your ass unless you've got enough brawn to crank the strenuous slopers. Climb in a single pitch from the ground.

19. Borich's Dihedral (5.10a) ★ Mixed to 2.5 inches. This prominent left-facing corner

attracts little attention. Start with easy run-out jugs leading past a bolt to a thin crack/stemming crux just below the anchor.

20. Howl (5.12a) ★★★ 6 bolts. For nearly two decades, this ignored line was the only sport route on the crag. Today it finally has some company. The unnerving, technically oriented slaps up the left side of the edge should please any arête aficionado.

Little Three Fingered Jack

The highest and most massive of the unclimbed faces is Little Three Fingered Jack. There are two main summits—an attractive spire to the left and the actual summit to the right. Both offer simple backside scrambles to the top. Two lines ascend the impressive river face, though the most obvious weakness—a gigantic leaning dihedral—remains unclimbed. **Descent:** Either walk left to an easily hiked gully downstream from London Tower or hike right to the gully left of the Monument.

21. Victory of the Proletarian People's Ambition Arête (5.7 X) Mixed to 3 inches. Originally billed as a "route for the common man" this multi-pitch venture is anything but that. The dismal rock, poor protection, and unaesthetic climbing can turn a pleasant day into an ordeal for any novice. Start below a ramp on the left side of Little Three Fingered Jack's main face. **Pitch 1:** (5.6) Climb a rotted trough to an anchor directly below a right-leaning dihedral plugged with a massive eagle's nest. **Pitch 2:** (5.7) Move up and left past widely spaced bolts, until it's possible to step left to a two-bolt belay. **Pitch 3:** (5.4) Wander far left through massive potholes on good rock past a few bolts to an anchor on the wall's left arête. **Pitch 4:** (5.6) Either ascend an easy chimney and traverse far left on a ledge, or turn a bulge on the right, clipping a lone bolt before following a gully. **Pitch 5:** (5.7) The best pitch on the route follows the path of least resistance to the top.

21a. The Quickie (5.6) Gear to 3 inches ★ The crumbling first-pitch corridor was done about a decade before the rest of the route. It's nothing special, but far less dangerous than the full version.

21b. Adams/Emde Variation (5.8 X) Mixed to 3 inches. You can make an already bad route much worse by following this dangerous variation. From the anchor atop *The Quickie*, step left and climb past two bolts before stepping back right to a flake system. Climb a freaky, hollow-sounding flake the size of a Boeing 737's wing and traverse left across a crumbling slab, arranging a sketchy belay anchor. Traverse far left on easy rock (5.4) before joining the third pitch of the regular route.

22. Bruce's Traverse (5.8 R) ★ Gear to 2.5 inches. A prominent left-leaning slash cuts across the upper wall of Little Three Fingered Jack. When first climbed in 1963, this forgotten route was Smith's hardest long free climb. Approach by scrambling into a gully right of the main face. **Pitch 1:** (5.7) Climb a long slab on the left; despite some big run-outs, the hardest moves protect well. **Pitch 2:** (5.8) Follow the ramp diagonally across the face past some spooky loose features to a cool belay alcove. **Pitch 3:** (5.6) Fun face climbing on a solid slab leads to an exposed hand traverse on a loose flake. Scramble into the finishing gully.

22a. Bruce's Variation (5.8 R) ★★ Gear to 2.5 inches. A better exit steps right after the solid slab on the third pitch to a belay ledge below an attractive dihedral. Easily protected

climbing in the solid corner leads to an exposed traverse left to an exciting but rotten finish.

23. Northwest Ridge (3rd class) ★ No topo. Solo. The highest finger involves nothing trickier than a lot of uphill walking. Approach this blob by scrambling up the gully left of the Monument and skirt west behind the cliff line. Simple hiking along the backside ridge ends on top.

24. Chockstone Chimney (5.0) ★ No topo. Gear to 2.5 inches. A longer option starts 40 feet below the left side of the backside ridge. Follow a simple left-leaning flake and finish with a chockstone-plugged chimney.

Puddy's Tower

The first tower left of the Monument, named in memory of Mike Puddy, features three one-pitch base routes. Despite obvious potential, the menacing river face still hasn't seen an ascent. Adventure climbers should relish the challenge. The summit consists of two pinnacles, one tucked behind the other. The highest is an unimpressive blob, reached via a third-class backside scramble. A more dramatic spire atop the river face might be unclimbed.

25. Miller Pillar (5.7 R) ★ Gear to 2 inches. A scrawny spire with a webbing-wrapped summit rises across the gully upstream from Little Three Fingered Jack. Either follow a loose direct line on the river face or scramble up the gully to the backside of the pinnacle. A bouldering move ends on top.

26. A Little Dementia (5.9 A3+ R) ★ Aid rack to 2 inches. An attempt on the river face of Puddy's Tower ended after one pitch. The wall above looks horrifying, but the start could become a decent free route

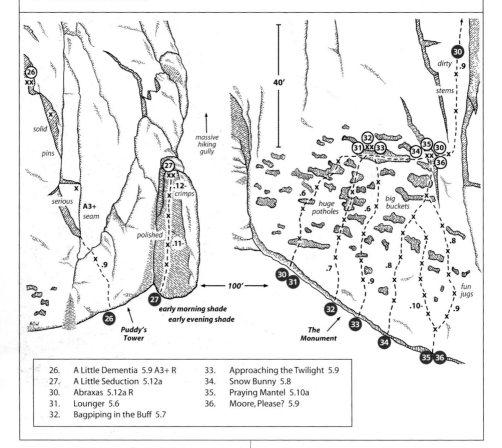

26.	A Little Dementia 5.9 A3+ R	33.	Approaching the Twilight 5.9
27.	A Little Seduction 5.12a	34.	Snow Bunny 5.8
30.	Abraxas 5.12a R	35.	Praying Mantel 5.10a
31.	Lounger 5.6	36.	Moore, Please? 5.9
32.	Bagpiping in the Buff 5.7		

with a little preparation. Start left of a huge detached boulder at the base of the cliff.

27. A Little Seduction (5.12a) ★★★ 4 bolts. An oversize detached flake with an overhanging downhill face sits at the base of Monument Gully. An enjoyable route cranks good edges to a crimping crux just below the anchor. The unusually polished stone makes it unlike anything else at Smith.

THE MONUMENT

This beautiful Smith Rock landmark towers over 600 feet above the northern bend of the Crooked River. The three full-length routes up the main wall see very few ascents—despite sections of good rock, rotten bands turn most routes into epics. Recent sport climbs at the base of the wall attract far more attention than the other routes combined. **Descent:** Reverse the *North Ridge* by scrambling down an unexposed chimney.

28. North Ridge (5.1) ★★ No topo. Gear to 3 inches. The easiest route to the top of the

The Monument Area

The Monument

Anglin's Buttress

Osa Thatcher's Needle

Puddy's Tower

25.	Miller Pillar 5.7 R	37.	Sands of Time 5.7 A4 X
26.	A Little Dementia 5.9 A3+ R	38.	Project 5.12?
27.	A Little Seduction 5.12a	39.	Southeast Face 5.7 A3 X
30.	Abraxas 5.12a R	41.	Bird Dung Chimney 5.4 X
30a.	Tombstone Wall 5.10d	42.	Deception Crack 5.10a R

Monument Base Area

Monument scrambles up the simple backside. Walk up the third-class gully to the left of the tower and follow the north ridge before moving right to a finishing chimney. The climbing isn't special, but the summit makes a fine rest day destination.

29. North Ridge Direct (5.5 R) ★★★ No topo. Solo. The best easy option to the summit stays on the crest of the north ridge. The only difficulties crank past unprotected pockets on a short wall of solid stone.

30. Abraxas (5.12a R) ★★★ Mixed to 3.5 inches. By far the best multi-pitch route on the Monument tackles the impressive southwest face. The entire line goes free, though clean aid ascents are far more common. The highlight of the adventure comes high off

the ground, jamming the beautiful *Tombstone Wall*. A recent cleaning, new anchors, and many replaced bolts make the entire route worth doing, despite some imperfect stone and dubious original bolts. **Pitch 1:** (5.6) 5 bolts. Start on the left side of huge potholes and climb past several bolts, traversing right to an anchor. **Pitch 2:** (5.9) Step right to a shallow chimney and climb dreadful rock past quarter-inch bolts to a hand traverse left to a new anchor. You can combine the first two pitches into one by starting with your choice of sport routes directly up the huge potholes. **Pitch 3:** (5.11a) Climb straight up from the belay to a hard move past a new bolt. Follow the original line of bolts to another new anchor. **Pitch 4:** (5.12a) Climb a 5.10 face protected by old bolts to

Adam Knoff on *Tombstone Wall*.

two fixed pins. Pull over the overhanging crack/bulge to an anchor below the headwall. **Pitch 5:** (5.10d) Step right and jam the spectacular *Tombstone Wall* in one long pitch to an anchor. **Pitch 6:** (5.5) An easy ramp ends on top. Either hike down the backside or rappel the entire route with two ropes (you'll find the first anchor down and about 20 feet upriver from where you top out).

30a. Tombstone Wall (5.10d) ★★★★ Gear to 3 inches. This gently overhanging hand crack on perfect rock rivals the most spectacular pitches on Monkey Face. Climbers occasionally hike to the summit and rappel (two double-rope raps) just to take a crack at this single-pitch gem.

31. Lounger (5.6) ★★ 4 bolts. The originally run-out first pitch of *Abraxas* now features retro-bolts and a new name. Beginners will appreciate the giant holds and safe protection. Rather than traversing far to the right, lower off from a convenient new anchor.

32. Bagpiping in the Buff (5.7) ★★ 4 bolts. The buckets to the right of *Lounger* are so big you can crawl inside of them. The hardest moves are at the start before the bathtubs begin.

33. Approaching the Twilight (5.9) ★★ 5 bolts. The third bolt line from the left starts with a crux face move at the first bolt. The climbing eases considerably wandering the jugs to the anchor.

34. Snow Bunny (5.8) ★★ 6 bolts. Another line of jugs meanders up and right to a different anchor than the preceding three routes. Like everything else on the face, the hard moves come before the big jugs begin.

35. Praying Mantel (5.10a) ★★ 8 bolts. The hardest of the base routes begins with crux stretches between positive edges. Beyond all difficulties, join the *Snow Bunny* bolt line on the left. Despite the name, there aren't any mantels.

36. Moore, Please? (5.9) ★★ 7 bolts. The farthest right of the sport routes shares the same first bolt as *Praying Mantel* but veers up and right on fun jugs. The dubious rock should improve with more ascents.

37. Sands of Time (5.7 A4 X) Aid rack to 3 inches. The most difficult aid line on the Monument likely still awaits a repeat. Soloed in a single push with two bivouacs, it ascends a prominent crack system right of *Abraxas*. Literally tons of rock rained down on the epic ascent—climbing solo was risky, but it eliminated the threat of a partner getting killed by rockfall. Expanded nailing on a delicately perched block the size of an

SUV nearly brought the effort to a catastrophic end.

38. Project (5.12?) A project to the left of the *Southeast Face*'s starting chimney saw toprope attempts in the late 1980s. Long abandoned, this smooth slab could someday feature a worthwhile sport route.

39. Southeast Face (5.7 A3 X) Aid rack to 3.5 inches. Any list of Smith's worst routes would be incomplete without this appalling climb. The adventure begins in a deep chimney on the right side of the wall and wanders up several dangerous pitches to the top. The cadaverous rock, grisly protection, and inadequate anchors are the stuff of nightmares. After unfounded rumors spread of an attempting climber dying in the early 1970s, the *Southeast Face* earned such a strong reputation that generations steered clear.

ANGLIN'S BUTTRESS

Right of the Monument rests a massive, undeveloped formation. It was named in honor of Smith pioneer Jim Anglin, who wouldn't have shied away from the crumbling stone. A slender spike clings precariously to the left side of the buttress, while several gullies split the rubble to the right. The two highest summits of this monolith look impressive from the river, but they are nothing more than third-class backside scrambles.

40. Osa Thatcher's Needle (5.7 X) No topo. Gear to 1 inch. This detached spire juts out from the left side of Anglin's Buttress. The unimposing backside offers a simple route to the top. Hike up the second-class gully next to the Monument and make a complex fourth-class scramble to a notch. Clip an ancient peg and boulder to the summit.

41. Bird Dung Chimney (5.4 X) Gear to 4 inches. One look should change your mind if you've somehow developed an interest in doing this piece of crap. Midway up the gully right of the Monument, climb the obvious chimney joining the backside route below the notch.

42. Deception Crack (5.10a R) ★ Gear to 3 inches. This prominent crack separates Osa Thatcher's Needle from Anglin's Buttress. Sandwiched between a junky approach and a garbage finish is a single pitch of high-quality climbing. Approach by hiking up the gully east of the Monument. **Pitch 1:** (4th class) Wade through bad rock to the base of a clean crack. **Pitch 2:** (5.10a) Solid jams lead to an anchor in a chimney. **Pitch 3:** (5.7) Climb a glum corridor, raining scraps of rock onto your helpless belayer. **Pitch 4:** (5.7) From the summit notch, boulder to the top of Osa Thatcher's Needle. Rap the backside and scramble off.

43. Brain Salad Surgery (5.11a) ★★★ No topo. Gear to 6 inches. On the right side of Anglin's Buttress are several gully-split rubble cliffs. Remarkably, amid some of the worst rock on Earth rises a rare jewel. Don't let the wide crack scare you away—the entire route goes without a single off-width move. Instead, a bizarre sequence of liebacks, underclings, and edges enter a moderate finishing flare. Hike up the third gully right of the Monument and look left for the unmistakable crack.

44. Street Walker (5.6) ★ No topo. Gear to 3 inches. Downhill from *Brain Salad Surgery* sits a sordid left-leaning crack. After a quick encounter in the corner, get off by scrambling up an easy ridge.

LIBERTY BELL AND JUNIPER SPIRE COMPLEX

Beyond the Monument the trail curves around the bend in the Crooked River, passing across a scree slope. Nestled in the pines and junipers to the right is the Old Climbers' Camp. The pinnacles of Liberty Bell and Juniper Spire tower above the trail.

Liberty Bell

This dark, double-peaked lump sits west of the slender spike of Juniper Spire. The upper portion of Liberty Bell is extremely solid, but bad rock guards the lower reaches. **Descent:** There's no rappel anchor on the actual summit, so downclimb west to a sling-wrapped horn.

45. Juniper Gully (5.6 A1 R) ★ Clean to 2.5 inches. Start on the downhill side of the formation left of an impressive bolted arête. Enter the gully between Liberty Bell and Juniper Spire and climb so-so rock past an anchor to a notch below the summit. A single aid bolt leads to an unprotected arête ending on the lower summit. It would easily go free—just don't fall on the ancient bolt.

46. Liberty Bell Chimney (5.5 R) ★ No topo. Gear to 2.5 inches. The original route to the top stemmed a wide chimney on the uphill side of the crag. After pulling over a chockstone, squeeze through a hole and scramble to the shattered summit.

Liberty Bell, Juniper Spire, Adit Rock

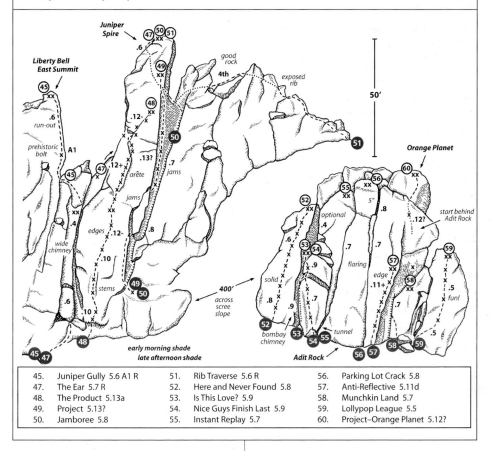

45.	Juniper Gully 5.6 A1 R	51.	Rib Traverse 5.6 R
47.	The Ear 5.7 R	52.	Here and Never Found 5.8
48.	The Product 5.13a	53.	Is This Love? 5.9
49.	Project 5.13?	54.	Nice Guys Finish Last 5.9
50.	Jamboree 5.8	55.	Instant Replay 5.7

56.	Parking Lot Crack 5.8
57.	Anti-Reflective 5.11d
58.	Munchkin Land 5.7
59.	Lollypop League 5.5
60.	Project–Orange Planet 5.12?

Juniper Spire

Immediately right of Liberty Bell rises a distinctive, willowy tower with a gorgeous south face. Unusually solid rock makes most routes worth doing. **Descent:** From the summit, rappel with double ropes down the overhanging south wall.

47. The Ear (5.7 R) ★★ Gear to 2.5 inches. Start on the downhill side and climb the trough between Liberty Bell and Juniper Spire to a single bolt at the notch. The unnerving crux pitch climbs a delicate arête up the right side of the notch, passing behind a small "ear"

to a finishing crack. Simple scrambling along the backside summit ridge leads to the top.

47a. Ear Variation (5.4) ★ No topo. Gear to 3 inches. If the ear pitch seems too creepy, you can escape right with an easy finish up a shattered chimney.

48. The Product (5.13a) ★★★★ 20 bolts. One of Smith's finest pitches follows an exquisite arête on Juniper Spire's south face. There are three distinct sections split by good rests—varied climbing leading to the edge, a wonderful arête, and a powerful finish up a diagonal crack. Despite perfect rock, cerebral moves, and closely spaced bolts, it sees few attempts. A 70-meter rope allows a simple descent.

49. Project (5.13?) The right edge of Juniper Spire's south face will someday produce another extraordinary route. It's one of Smith's finest unclimbed arêtes.

50. Jamboree (5.8) ★★ Gear to 2 inches. A crack in a shallow corner separates the southeast side of Juniper Spire from the connecting rib uphill to the right. A flurry of jams and stems on decent rock end on the backside ridge.

51. Rib Traverse (5.6 R) ★★★ Gear to 2.5 inches. The easiest route to the summit scrambles along a rib on the uphill side of tower. After weaving past several gendarmes on great rock, fun face moves end on the appealing summit.

Tom Egan on the first ascent of *The Product* (5.13a), 1990. TOM EGAN COLLECTION

STAENDER RIDGE

Rising above the irrigation tunnel left of the Burma Road are a row of pinnacles known as Staender Ridge. From bottom to top, Adit Rock, Control Tower, Independence Tower, the Mole, Bette's Needles, Flattop, and Staender Summit sit neatly along the crest of the ridge. Nearby are French Tent Rock, Rotten Crack, the Dinosaur, and Bivouac Rock. Long ago, Smith climbing focused on these remote spires when the Burma Road provided simple access to both the lower and upper portions of the ridge. After the earliest pioneers reached the summits, climbers turned their attention to every conceivable crack—many so short they barely qualify as legitimate routes. Today these traditional lines are well suited for beginning climbers who prefer alpine surroundings to the mob scene common at Smith's most popular areas.

With the Burma Road closed, the long uphill slog ensures that overcrowding will never be a problem. The hike varies from thirty to forty-five minutes depending on how far you venture up the ridge. To approach, follow the trail right from the bridge on a mile-long jaunt around the northern bend of the river. Beyond Juniper Spire the path veers uphill and switchbacks to the first of the pinnacles. At the end of the day, please refrain from careening down the massive scree scar below Staender Summit; instead follow the indistinct trail along the east side of the ridge.

A word of warning for dog owners: At the base of Staender Ridge, the irrigation canal flows into a claustrophobic concrete tunnel more than two-thirds of a mile long. Thirsty dogs sometimes jump into the canal to cool off, only to get sucked into the shaft. The author's dog, Buster, survived a trip through the blackness of the tunnel, arriving on the other side exhausted but alive. If your dog takes the plunge, race 2 miles up and over the Burma Road. With luck you'll greet your no-longer-thirsty hound at the tunnel exit in Sherwood Canyon.

Adit Rock

Sitting at the base of the ridge, Adit Rock offers outstanding rock and a small selection of pleasant routes. It's far and away the most popular destination on Staender Ridge. A chimney splits the crag into two portions—a downhill chunk containing most of the routes and a rounded uphill boulder with limited potential. **Descent:** Most routes have sport anchors. The backside offers a simple descent via a short chimney or easy slab.

52. Here and Never Found (5.8) ★★★ 9 bolts. The left side of Adit Rock features an outstanding sport route on a perfect slab. After a physical crux at the start, savor easy climbing past many bolts to an anchor.

53. Is This Love? (5.9) ★★ Mixed to 3.5 inches. A bombay chimney on the left side of Adit Rock enjoyed a brief stint of popularity. Unfortunately, Smith's resident route-chopper took offense, removing the bolts. No one ever climbs it anymore, despite decent natural protection.

54. Nice Guys Finish Last (5.9) ★★★ 4 bolts. A fun route follows a pillar leaning against the main wall. Easy climbing on great rock leads to a deceptively hard move pulling past an undercut. Either lower from anchors or

Staender Ridge—West Side

Flattop
Bette's Needles
The Mole
Independence Tower
Control Tower
Adit Rock
89
78
79
75
67
66
61
52
Liberty Bell
Juniper Spire
46
48

46. Liberty Bell Chimney 5.5 R
48. The Product 5.13a
52. Here and Never Found 5.8
61. Out of Control 5.10c
66. D.A.R. Crack 5.10a
67. Sunjammer 5.10b
75. Easy Street 5.7 R
78. Limestone Chimney 5.3
79. Juniper Snag 5.7 R
89. South Buttress 5.3 X

Staender Ridge–South Side

French Tent Rock

Staender Summit

Bivouac Rock

The Dinosaur

99

95

101

Bette's Needles

Flattop

108

106

82

Rotten Crack

76

102

56.	Parking Lot Crack 5.8
76.	Thrasher 5.8 A2
82.	Lost Fox 5.9
95.	Northwest Corner 5.3
99.	Milwaukee's Best 5.7
101.	South Bowl 5.5 X
102.	Rotten Crack 5.8 R
106.	Brown Cow 5.7 R
108.	The Long Walk 5.7

56

Adit Rock

continue up a simple, naturally protected crack to the top.

55. Instant Replay (5.7) ★★★ Gear to 1.5 inches. The left of parallel cracks on the downhill side starts behind a leaning pillar. Solid rock and good protection make it a fine beginner's route.

56. Parking Lot Crack (5.8) ★★ Gear to 5 inches. The right of Adit Rock's parallel cracks was once the closest route to the old parking area. You can bypass the finishing off-width with good face holds on the right.

57. Anti-Reflective (5.11d) ★★★ 5 bolts. The hardest sport route on Staender Ridge climbs the attractive edge on the right side of Adit Rock. The rock is nearly perfect on the arête itself, though crumbling edges lure pumped climbers left.

58. Munchkin Land (5.7) ★★ Gear to 2 inches. A miniature leaning corner cuts across the right side of Adit Rock. On the positive side it features great rock, fun liebacks, and sinker protection. There's only one negative—the fun ends just 20 feet after it begins.

59. Lollypop League (5.5) ★★★★ 4 bolts. A detached pillar with a single sport route balances right of Adit Rock. Enchanting pockets and edges on brilliant rock make it the perfect first lead.

60. Project–Orange Planet (5.12?) The only prospect on the bulbous uphill block of Adit Rock follows a rounded arête right of a chimney. A short, bouldery sequence on great rock awaits a power drill–toting climber.

Uphill from Adit Rock are two unnamed, 15-foot pillars with simple third-class boulder problems to the top. Next in line are two larger pinnacles—Control Tower on the left and Independence Tower on the right.

Control Tower

A prominent wavy crack splits the south side of this small pinnacle. The backside offers a simple third-class scramble, while the longer west face contains the following route.

61. Out of Control (5.10c) ★★ Mixed to 2.5 inches. This strenuous crack cuts across the bulging west side of the formation. A bolt protects a boulder problem crux at the start, though many climbers lose control in a pumping flurry of jams above. Lower off from a new anchor.

Independence Tower

A few feet uphill from Control Tower lurks a large chunk of rock capped by a slender pillar. There's nothing eye-catching on the east side, though a huge dihedral dominates the west face. **Descent:** Make a short rappel off the uphill side.

62. Free Spirit (5.8) ★★ Gear to 2 inches. A pleasant finger crack on good rock splits the southwest corner of the spire. Reach the base by scrambling down a crumbling

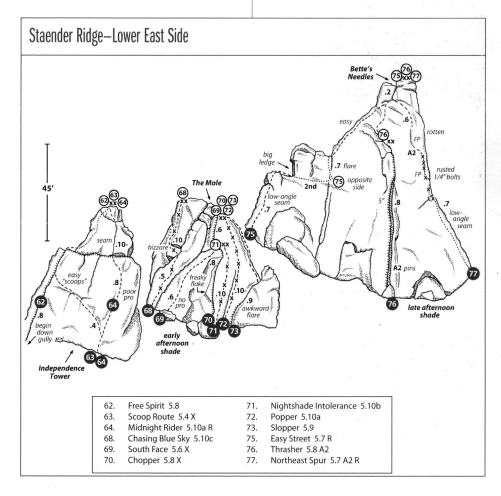

Staender Ridge–Lower East Side

62.	Free Spirit 5.8	71.	Nightshade Intolerance 5.10b
63.	Scoop Route 5.4 X	72.	Popper 5.10a
64.	Midnight Rider 5.10a R	73.	Slopper 5.9
68.	Chasing Blue Sky 5.10c	75.	Easy Street 5.7 R
69.	South Face 5.6 X	76.	Thrasher 5.8 A2
70.	Chopper 5.8 X	77.	Northeast Spur 5.7 A2 R

gully between Independence Tower and Control Tower.

63. Scoop Route (5.4 X) ★★ Gear to 2 inches. A simple route follows the path of least resistance up ledges on the south side. You'll encounter good rock as you essentially solo to the top.

64. Midnight Rider (5.10a R) ★ Gear to 1 inch. Apart from solid, unprotected face moves at the start, this direct line on the south face of the tower has nothing going for it. The crux boulders a miserable seam above a large ledge just below the summit.

65. North Side (5.5) ★★ Gear to 2 inches. The original route to the top of the spire provides the best option for beginners. The hardest moves are right off the ground on the diminutive uphill side of the pinnacle.

66. D.A.R. Crack (5.10a) ★★ Gear to 4

inches. Easily the most impressive line on Independence Tower is a large right-facing dihedral on the west face. Unfortunately, the rock quality doesn't match the appearance. Begin with face holds leading to jams and stems, finishing with a lieback up a short off-width.

The Mole

Next in line above Independence Tower sits the rounded Mole. Despite its humble stature, this block contains a first-rate selection of fun routes. **Descent:** From routes ending on the summit, descend by rappelling from an anchor on the east side, or downclimb the *North Ramp*.

67. Sunjammer (5.10b) ★★★ Gear to 1 inch. One of Staender Ridge's better traditional routes jams great rock in an overhanging dihedral on the southwest side of the Mole.

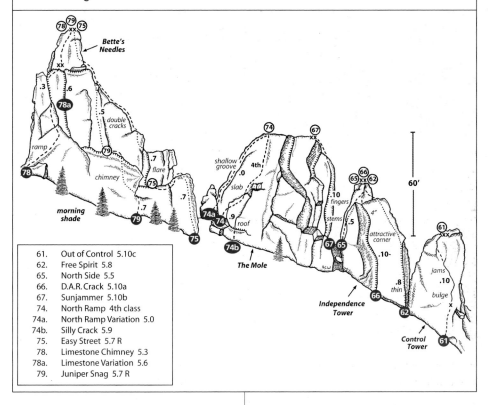

61.	Out of Control 5.10c
62.	Free Spirit 5.8
65.	North Side 5.5
66.	D.A.R. Crack 5.10a
67.	Sunjammer 5.10b
74.	North Ramp 4th class
74a.	North Ramp Variation 5.0
74b.	Silly Crack 5.9
75.	Easy Street 5.7 R
78.	Limestone Chimney 5.3
78a.	Limestone Variation 5.6
79.	Juniper Snag 5.7 R

Start at the notch between Independence Tower and the Mole, and step across to the base of the corner.

68. Chasing Blue Sky (5.10c) ★★★ 5 bolts. The southern edge of the Mole features a surprisingly good sport route. After an easy start a baffling crux clears a roof on the left before finishing on entertaining jugs.

69. South Face (5.6 X) ★★ Gear to 2.5 inches. Begin off a boulder and face climb with minimal protection up the southeast side of the block. Finish with a short hand crack above *Chopper*.

70. Chopper (5.8 X) ★★★ Gear to 2.5 inches. An attractive corner plugged with a detached pillar dominates the east side of the Mole. The well-protected jams and stems are

charming as long as the pillar stays in place. If the pillar comes down, you'll be dead— along with your partner.

71. Nightshade Intolerance (5.10b) ★★ 3 bolts. Despite good rock, the short sport route on the wall right of *Chopper* leaves a lingering feeling of guilt. The best climbing follows a harder direct line near the top, though everyone uses big holds on the right.

72. Popper (5.10a) ★★★ 6 bolts. A miniature right-facing corner right of *Nightshade Intolerance* makes a better choice. After crux jams and liebacks at the start, much easier face moves on good rock end at the summit anchor.

73. Slopper (5.9) ★ Gear to 1 inch. A few feet right of *Popper* sits a short right-leaning arch. Apart from good rock, Slopper offers nothing positive—the moves are awkward and unrewarding.

74. North Ramp (4th class) ★★ Solo. The quickest route to the top follows an effortless ramp on the uphill side of the block.

74a. North Ramp Variation (5.0) ★★ Gear to 3 inches. An easy alternative marches up a short flaring crack a few feet left.

74b. Silly Crack (5.9) ★★ Gear to 2.5 inches. Right of the *North Ramp* sits a miniscule crack splitting a bulge. Tricky thin hand jams at the start quickly give way to easy scrambling.

Bette's Needles

Uphill from the Mole rises the largest and most spectacular of the Staender Ridge spires. The 150-foot south face towers impressively above the trail. The rock quality doesn't match the nearby pinnacles, but the summit experience reigns supreme. **Descent:** Rappel from an anchor on the summit down the northwest side of the tower.

75. Easy Street (5.7 R) ★ Gear to 3 inches. This circuitous route winds along the south arête of the tower. A pleasant slab at the start protects poorly, while the poor upper pitch protects pleasantly. Start left of the ridge below double seams. **Pitch 1:** (5.7) Follow low-angle cracks and traverse a big ledge along the west face to a chimney. **Pitch 2:** (5.7) Double cracks in a short overhanging slot end on the south buttress. Romp up simple rock to the top.

76. Thrasher (5.8 A2) ★ Aid rack to 6 inches. An appropriately named, right-facing corner splits the southeast side of Bette's Needles. Bad rock and a pitiful off-width

discourage all levelheaded climbers. The entire route will go free, but it'll always be a thrash session. **Pitch 1:** (5.8 A2) A short section of nailing leads into a grotesque wide crack. Brawl to a good belay ledge. **Pitch 2:** (5.2) Scramble up easy rock to the top.

77. Northeast Spur (5.7 A2 R) Aid rack to 1.5 inches. A mystery route from Smith's early days ascends the prominent buttress on the east side of Bette's Needles. Begin uphill on the north side of the rib and free climb a low-angle seam. Many rusted quarter-inch bolts and fixed pins lead through horrific rock to the top.

78. Limestone Chimney (5.3) ★★ Gear to 1.5 inches. The easiest route to the summit follows a simple chimney system on the uphill side of the tower.

78a. Limestone Variation (5.6) ★ Gear to 2 inches. A more challenging variant climbs an inside corner slightly right of the regular line.

79. Juniper Snag (5.7 R) ★★ Gear to 2.5 inches. The best route on the spire ascends inside corners on the west face. Start at a gnarled juniper snag, halfway down the western base of the formation. **Pitch 1:** (5.7) Boulder up a tricky groove to a scree-covered ledge and climb a tight open book to a belay spot. **Pitch 2:** (5.5) Jam double cracks up a flaring chimney and scamper to the top.

Flattop

Next in line above Bette's Needles rests an aptly named, square-cut block. The west-side routes are extremely short, though the east face offers some longer climbs. The bulbous summit sits atop the north side of a flat plateau. Gently overhanging on all sides, this 10-foot pillar offers three options up the northwest, west, and southeast sides (all

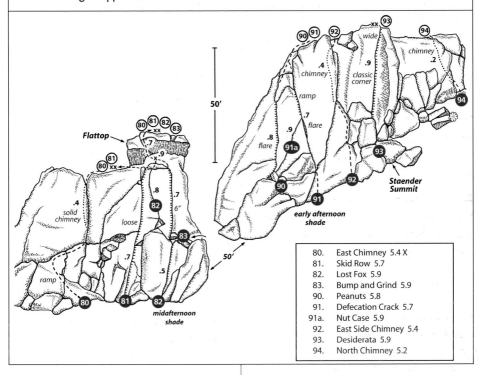

80.	East Chimney 5.4 X
81.	Skid Row 5.7
82.	Lost Fox 5.9
83.	Bump and Grind 5.9
90.	Peanuts 5.8
91.	Defecation Crack 5.7
91a.	Nut Case 5.9
92.	East Side Chimney 5.4
93.	Desiderata 5.9
94.	North Chimney 5.2

5.7). Most climbers crank the boulder problem once, settling for the summit plateau on future ascents. All grades assume a finish on the plateau rather than the actual top—otherwise every low-end route would have the same grade. **Descent:** Either rappel off the west side from the summit or from an anchor on the plateau above *Prune Face*.

80. East Chimney (5.4 X) ★★★ Gear to 1
inch. It looks like any other rubble-chute, but this short chimney is solid and entertaining—just don't expect much protection. Start up a zigzag ramp on the east side and stem huge knobs to the flat bench below the summit block.

81. Skid Row (5.7) ★ Gear to 2 inches.
The obvious left-facing dihedral on the east side of the block doesn't rank with the best Staender Ridge routes. The crux at the start

is solid, but the rock deteriorates in the corner above.

82. Lost Fox (5.9) ★★★ Mixed to 2.5 inches.
An appealing crack splits Flattop's east buttress. After enjoyable 5.8 jams, step left to an awkward crux below the summit block.

83. Bump and Grind (5.9) ★★ Mixed to 6
inches. An off-width in a right-facing corner lurks on the uphill side of the east face. Lieback and stem solid rock on the 5.7 crack before traversing left to the same bouldering crux as *Lost Fox*.

84. Deliverance (5.9) ★ TR. A freestanding slab on the miniature northwest side of Flattop offers an unlikely toprope problem. From the summit anchor, run the rope over the top of the slab and finesse tricky face moves on small edges.

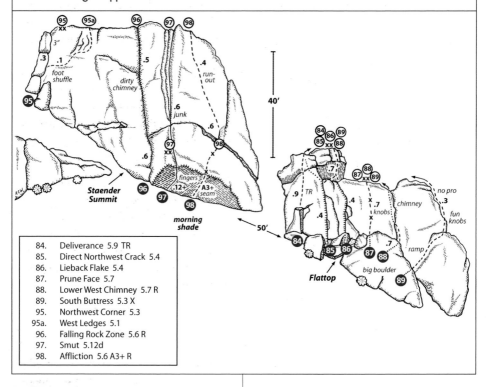

Staender Ridge–Upper West Side

84. Deliverance 5.9 TR
85. Direct Northwest Crack 5.4
86. Lieback Flake 5.4
87. Prune Face 5.7
88. Lower West Chimney 5.7 R
89. South Buttress 5.3 X
95. Northwest Corner 5.3
95a. West Ledges 5.1
96. Falling Rock Zone 5.6 R
97. Smut 5.12d
98. Affliction 5.6 A3+ R

85. Direct Northwest Crack (5.4) ★ Gear to 2 inches. The name sounds impressive, but this dinky route up the left of parallel cracks on the west face is laughably short. Below the summit block, either cut left or right to the top.

86. Lieback Flake (5.4) ★ Gear to 2 inches. Neither a lieback nor a flake, this block-plugged corner splits the center of Flattop's pint-size west face.

87. Prune Face (5.7) ★★ 2 bolts. The only sport route on the formation follows good knobs past two bolts to the summit plateau. If you take your time, it provides about forty-five seconds of pure fun.

88. Lower West Chimney (5.7 R) ★ Gear to 3 inches. The counterpart to the *East Chimney* climbs the opposite side of the same slot. An annoyingly tricky entrance gains the simple unprotected chimney.

89. South Buttress (5.3 X) ★★ Gear to 1 inch. This enjoyable route storms the diminutive south buttress. A quick traverse right along a ledge leads to solid, unprotected knobs ending on the summit shelf.

Staender Summit

A large chunk of stone with a distinctive low-level roof caps Staender Ridge. Traditional routes ascend the many cracks splitting every side of the block. **Descent:** Scramble down the simple *North Chimney* or rappel from new anchor bolts.

90. Peanuts (5.8) ★★ Gear to 2.5 inches. The left of several crack lines on

Staender Summit's east side jams great rock up an opening flare. Finish with a left-facing corner.

91. Defecation Crack (5.7) ★★ Gear to 2.5 inches. Far better than the name implies, this worthwhile line follows a short flare leading to a left-leaning ramp.

91a. Nut Case (5.9) ★★ Gear to 2.5 inches. A pleasant starting alternative to *Defecation Crack* jams good rock up a right-leaning crack to the finishing ramp.

92. East Side Chimney (5.4) ★ Gear to 3 inches. A dismal corridor splits the center of Staender Summit's east wall. There's nothing pleasant about it, but at least the double cracks protect easily.

93. Desiderata (5.9) ★★★ Gear to 4 inches. An attractive dihedral dominates the east side of the crag. Delightful stems and jams on perfect rock unfortunately end with an awkward grovel in a short off-width. The elegance of the corner more than makes up for this brief indignity.

94. North Chimney (5.2) ★★ Gear to 2.5 inches. The original route to the top of Staender Summit followed a short groove on the uphill side of the block.

95. Northwest Corner (5.3) ★★ Gear to 3 inches. A short hand crack on the tiny north face of the formation splits the right side of a pillar.

95a. West Ledges (5.1) ★ Gear to 3 inches. A simple alternative foot-shuffles right to a huge ledge system just below the summit.

96. Falling Rock Zone (5.6 R) Gear to 3 inches. If not for hideous rock, meager protection, distasteful moves, and a claustrophobic setting, this flaring chimney left of *Smut* would be excellent.

97. Smut (5.12d) ★★★ Gear to 2 inches. Whether you call it a 5.12d trad route or a V6 boulder problem, this finger crack roof once stood atop Smith free-climbing standards. The first ascent started off the dirt with a pull-up on horrible jams followed by a dyno into a sharp slot. Cheater stones lower the grade considerably. Originally led with protection, the second ascent free-soloed to the summit. Ignore the junky (5.6) finish by lowering from bolts over the lip.

98. Affliction (5.6 A3+ R) ★ Aid rack to 1 inch. If aid bouldering sounds like fun, consider this faint roof seam right of *Smut*. Nothing will keep you off the deck if (when) a pin pulls. Belay in an alcove over the lip and exit a scoop to an easy, unprotected finishing slab.

French Tent Rock (aka No Name)

This multi-peaked spire sits across the gully left of Staender Summit. The most distinctive feature is a slender pinnacle to the west, though the actual summit sits to the east. To reach the highest spire, either make a quick third-class backside scramble or head up the following sport route:

99. Milwaukee's Best (5.7) ★★ 4 bolts. A fun sport route ascends a short low-angle slab up the northeast side of the formation. The approach hike will weed out all but the most hardy, but the good rock, reassuring bolts, and great vista make it a perfect beginner's lead.

The following two routes ascend the obvious spire jutting out from the west side of French Tent Rock. **Descent:** Cross your fingers and rappel from primeval bolts down the north side of the spire.

100. North Ledge (5.6 R) ★ No topo. Gear to 3 inches. The only sensible route to the top of the spire starts on the backside. After liebacking a short left-facing corner, follow the easy west ridge to the summit.

101. South Bowl (5.5 X) Gear to 2.5 inches. If the sight of this slag heap doesn't scare you away, nothing will. Approach by circling below the *North Ledge* to the south side of the spire. Start with a short scramble and climb an obvious flare on some of Smith's worst rock (that's really saying something) to an unexposed bowl. Finish by cutting left to the summit ridge.

Rotten Crack

Right of Staender Ridge, about midway up the hillside, lurks an isolated pinnacle. The two routes to the summit are awful. **Descent:** Make a short rappel down the west side from bolts placed during the early years of the Eisenhower administration.

102. Rotten Crack (5.8 R) Gear to 1 inch. The original route to the top followed a lousy seam on the west side of the tower. Add to the misery with a direct start up a wide crack, or minimize it by stepping in from the backside to poorly protected finishing moves.

103. Friction Arête (5.4 X) Solo. This unpleasant route climbs boldly up the downhill arête. The unprotected moves are easy, but the crumbling rock makes it a gamble for anyone.

The Dinosaur

This unusual formation sits above Rotten Crack, just left of the crest of the Burma Road. Split into two distinct segments, the upper part is a small pinnacle, while the low-angle slab of the Dinosaur's tail extends far downhill. **Descent:** Scramble down third-class rock on the uphill side.

104. Orange Peel (5.6 X) No topo. 3 bolts. A lousy route follows a low-angle slab on the west side of the Dinosaur's tail. Start uphill from the lowest of several juniper trees and traverse right into a scoop. Friction moves lead past quarter-inch bolts (without hangers) to an easy scramble along the top of the ridge. Ignore the upper pinnacle by hiking down a simple groove.

105. Lemon Peel (5.8 X) ★ No topo. 2 bolts. About 20 feet uphill from *Orange Peel,* behind a second juniper tree, sits this dirty slab. Unpleasant smears lead to a meandering crack ending at the crest of the ridge. Hike down an easy groove.

106. Brown Cow (5.7 R) Gear to 3 inches. A grotesque chimney splits the south side of the Dinosaur's upper pinnacle. A tormenting pitch on bad rock ends on top.

107. Cow Pie (5.6 R) No topo. Gear to 1 inch. The west face of the Dinosaur's upper segment offers a second ugly chimney. Enter the slot with a face move to the left and wallow up a low-angle, sparsely protected groove.

Bivouac Rock

A large blob of undeveloped rock sits between the Dinosaur and Staender Summit. The uphill side is nothing more than a simple scramble, while the upper east side contains a recent sport climb.

108. The Long Walk (5.7) ★★ 4 bolts. You'll be disappointed if you make the uphill trek just for this route, but the uniquely featured wall provides a few moments of fun for anyone in the vicinity. Lower off from a two-bolt anchor atop a boulder.

THE MARSUPIAL CRAGS AND SURROUNDING AREAS

I was at a hanging belay with quarter-inch bolts, with Dean Fry nailing the crux of the whole route, right over my head. He placed a line of RURPs above the anchor, and I started panicking, realizing that if he fell, we'd probably both go to the ground. I was so scared I begged him to place a bolt, and he finally agreed—most likely to ease my nerves, not his.

Jack Barrar after the first ascent
of *C.L. Concerto* in 1972

There's more to Smith Rock climbing than visiting the Dihedrals every weekend. The outlying region contains large expanses of high-quality rock, hindered only by a long approach. By far the best routes are on the Marsupial Crags, a group of spires and walls dominating the hillside east of the park. Every visiting climber gazes at these landmarks, but relatively few visit. The long approach discourages some, while others make the mistake of listening to climbers who dismiss the area without ever giving it a chance.

As late as 1994 there wasn't a whole lot here apart from novelty routes leading to the summits. Today the Marsupials offer one of the better assortments of easy to moderate sport routes at Smith. The hike will forever keep these climbs from attracting the mobs found at the base of Morning Glory Wall, but anyone making the trek won't leave disappointed. Since the Marsupial Crags sit high above the rest of the park, an added bonus is the marvelous view of Smith Rock far below,

with the pastoral high desert and snowcapped Cascades serving as an idyllic backdrop.

Among the most widely held myths of Smith climbing is that the tuff in the Marsupial Crags doesn't match the quality of the main area. There's often some truth behind a myth, and it's easy to see how this falsehood began. Much like the rest of Smith, climbers making bad choices will suffer—the worst Marsupial routes are intensely unpleasant. There's no denying the wretchedness of early routes such as *Catfight Cracks* and the Kangaroo's *North Ledges Traverse*. But the truth is that the stone here compares favorably to anywhere else at Smith.

With the Marsupials attracting more attention every year, reclusive climbers might consider hiking even farther. The pinnacles of Indian and Mendenhall Ridge dominate the skyline far north of the state park. These spires are the most prominent landmarks at Smith, visible on the horizon for 40 miles to the north and south. The rock quality isn't special, but visitors can experience climbing unchanged from the days of the earliest pioneers. Even more secluded is a crag called the Zoo, tucked away in a hidden valley a mile east of the Wombat. Almost completely undeveloped, this cliff holds potential for many unique sport routes.

Early explorers found great appeal in the summit pinnacles of the Marsupials and Indian/Mendenhall Ridge. There's reason to believe that local settlers scrambled to the

The Marsupial Crags

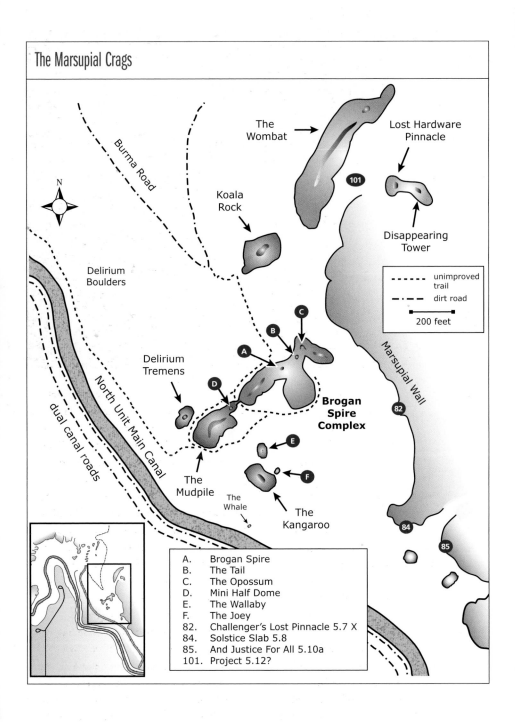

The Wombat

Lost Hardware Pinnacle

Burma Road

Koala Rock

Disappearing Tower

N

Delirium Boulders

101

unimproved trail

dirt road

200 feet

Delirium Tremens

C

B

A

D

Brogan Spire Complex

Marsupial Wall

82

E

The Mudpile

The Whale

F

The Kangaroo

84

85

A.   Brogan Spire
B.   The Tail
C.   The Opossum
D.   Mini Half Dome
E.   The Wallaby
F.   The Joey
82. Challenger's Lost Pinnacle 5.7 X
84. Solstice Slab 5.8
85. And Justice For All 5.10a
101. Project 5.12?

North Unit Main Canal

dual canal roads

The Marsupial Crags Overview

A. Koala Rock–South Face
B. Koala Rock–West Face–Base Detail
C. Koala Rock–West Face Overview
D. Koala Rock–Southeast Face
E. Brogan Spire–North Face
F. Brogan Spire Complex–South Face
G. The Mudpile Area–North Face
H. The Mudpile Area–Base Detail
I. The Wombat–Lower Northwest Face
J. The Wombat–Upper Northwest Face

top of the easiest landmarks early in the century. The first recorded ascent occurred in 1935, when Johnny Bissell reached the top of Squaw Rock. Fourteen years later, Ross Petrie led the nearby Poplar on Mendenhall Ridge. Recorded activity in the Marsupials began much later, with the first ascent of the Opossum in 1960 by Jim and Jerry Ramsey. That same year the Ramsey brothers turned back just short of the summit of Brogan Spire during a violent lightning storm.

With no virgin spires remaining after the 1964 ascent of the Thumb, climbers turned their attention to the walls. In 1967 Jon Marshall led the first ascent of the Wombat's main face via *Green Gully,* while Steve Heim and Jim Neiland nailed the awe-inspiring *Great Roof* on Brogan Spire. The first golden age of Marsupial climbing ended with a flurry of significant ascents in 1972. First, Dean Fry and Jack Barrar succeeded on *C.L. Concerto* (5.9 A4), taking the path of most resistance up the Wombat's blank northwest face. With ascents of Jeff Thomas's *Desert Solitaire* (5.10a), Dean Fry's *Catfight Cracks* (5.10a), and Del Young's *Delirium Tremens* (5.10b), the Marsupials contained some of Smith's hardest free climbs. After these ascents new route activity slowed to a trickle. The closing of the Burma Road access and the opening of the new bridge below Picnic Lunch Wall effectively put Marsupial climbing into a two-decade hibernation.

With the advent of sport climbing, it was only a matter of time before power drill–packing climbers scoured the Marsupial Crags for new lines. To the surprise of many Smith veterans, the rumors of crumbling cliffs proved largely unfounded, and during the 1990s dozens of high-quality lines arose out of nowhere. Bill Soule pioneered several sport routes in the middle of the decade, but only through the tireless labors of Ryan Lawson did the Marsupials become a trendy destination. In a whirlwind effort beginning with *Ryan's Arête* in 1997, Lawson bolted nearly forty routes and spread the word through a new-route update. While Lawson deserves most of the credit for the wave of popularity, the attention of the entire sport climbing world focused on the Marsupials in 2004. After six weeks of effort, Beth Rodden succeeded on a free ascent of the opening pitch of *The Great Roof.* She named her route *The Optimist*—appropriate given that no one else seriously thought the pitch would go free. At 5.14b, it was the hardest free route ever pioneered by a female in the history of climbing. No matter how you sliced it, Marsupial climbing was no longer a joke.

Rodden's ascent alone did little to entice high-level climbers to the Marsupials. Even today there are only four routes graded harder than 5.11. There's no reason why this shouldn't change in the future—

many difficult possibilities should attract future climbers. Already the base of the Mudpile contains a wall of dangling quickdraws that will change the mind of anyone convinced that there's nothing truly steep at Smith. In September 2006 Michael Stöger powered his way up one of these lines, creating *Climb Like A Bomb* (5.13a). The large expanses of untouched stone suggest that the best may be yet to come.

Finding the crags: Approach the Marupial Crags by turning right at the bridge below the main parking area. Walk around the northernmost bend of the Crooked River and hike up the gulch between Staender Ridge and the Student Wall to the irrigation canal. Walk up the Burma Road to the prominent switchback and cut uphill on a poor trail to Koala Rock, the first of the Marsupial Crags. During low-river conditions, a much shorter approach drops into the canyon from the turnaround parking area and hops boulders below the Student Wall. Don't take chances unless the water level is very low—the river runs fast and the boulders are smooth as glass.

THE MARSUPIAL CRAGS

Towering high on the hillside east of the parking lot are the Marsupial Crags. These remote cliffs contain diverse routes amid the best setting in the entire region. A view like this doesn't come without sacrifice—it takes nearly forty minutes to reach the base of Koala Rock. With the addition of so many quality routes, the crags attract far more climbers than ever before, though there will never be an over-crowding problem.

Koala Rock

The 250-foot-high chunk of square-cut stone nearest the Burma Road is the most popular destination in the Marsupial Crags. Packed with easy to midlevel routes, Koala Rock ranks among the finest at Smith with unusually solid and well-featured stone. While almost everything here is worth climbing, the multi-pitch lines are especially memorable. The routes described below begin on the south wall and circle the block moving clockwise. **Descent:** From the summit, either downclimb a short third-class ramp on the backside or

make a quick rappel from an anchor. Return to the base of the formation after scree surfing down the southern base of the block, or follow a long switchback heading to Brogan Spire and back to Koala Rock.

1. Ryan's Arête (5.10c) ★★★ 8 bolts. A large dihedral capped by a roof dominates the south face of Koala Rock. The original route on the right edge avoids major difficulties by traversing high from the starting crack, ignoring the first two bolts on the actual arête. The fun upper part cranks between big

Koala Rock–Southwest Face

1.	Ryan's Arête 5.10c
4.	Cool Air 5.11a
6.	Suck My Kiss 5.10a
7.	Thin Air 5.10b
14.	Round There 5.7
15.	Desert Solitaire 5.10a R
16.	Round River 5.4 R
16a.	Round River Direct 5.8
25.	King of Pain 5.11b

Koala Rock—South Face

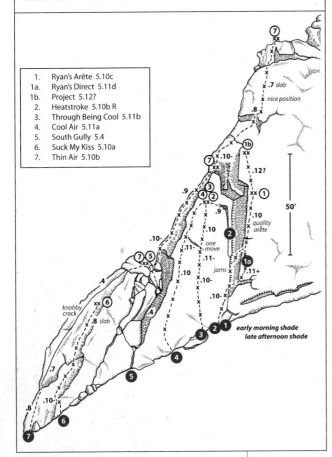

1. Ryan's Arête 5.10c
1a. Ryan's Direct 5.11d
1b. Project 5.12?
2. Heatstroke 5.10b R
3. Through Being Cool 5.11b
4. Cool Air 5.11a
5. South Gully 5.4
6. Suck My Kiss 5.10a
7. Thin Air 5.10b

.7 slab
nice position

50'

.12?

.10 quality arête

one move

jams

knobby crack
.8 slab

early morning shade
late afternoon shade

holds on great rock to an anchor below the final roof.

1a. Ryan's Direct (5.11d) ★★★ 9 bolts. A challenging variant confronts the real difficulties by cranking through side pulls and smears before joining the regular line.

1b. Project (5.12?) 2 bolts. The short blank face above the anchors will offer a challenging, first-rate finish to *Ryan's Arête*.

2. Heatstroke (5.10b R) ★★ Mixed to 1.5 inches. This obvious dihedral follows uniquely polished rock to a freaky face traverse left below a roof. Begin with

the bolted lower crack of *Ryan's Arête*—only the upper part demands gear-placement skills.

3. Through Being Cool (5.11b) ★★★ 9 bolts. The attractive slab left of *Heatstroke* follows unrelenting 5.10 edges, interrupted by a single desperate move on great rock. The less-than-vertical wall isn't pumping, but the crux requires more brainpower than the average route of the grade.

4. Cool Air (5.11a) ★★★ 9 bolts. This clean arête sits left of *Through Being Cool*. Unlike its neighbor, there's no clear crux; instead a complicated series of mostly 5.10 moves weave from side-to-side on edges and pinches.

5. South Gully (5.4) ★ Gear to 3 inches. A traditional line provides quick access to the anchor atop the first pitch of *Thin Air*. Follow jumbled rock up the obvious weakness on the south side of the formation.

6. Suck My Kiss (5.10a) ★★★ 6 bolts. A delightful sport route rises right of the lowest stretch of Koala Rock. After a quick crux stepping left above the first bolt, amazing knobs lead past several bolts to an anchor. Combining this route with the upper two pitches of *Thin Air* makes a four-star sport climb.

7. Thin Air (5.10b) ★★★★ Mixed to 2.5 inches. For the grade, multi-pitch routes at Smith don't get any better than this. Memorable climbing, top-notch rock, great protection, and a magnificent position make *Thin Air* a must-do. The first pitch highlights the adventure, though the exposed upper pitches only add to the charm. Start below a thin crack at the lowest part of Koala Rock. **Pitch 1:** (5.8) Finger jams and incuts on perfect rock lead over a small roof. Simple hand locks and huge knobs end at an anchor on a jumbled ledge. **Pitch 2:** (5.10a) 5 bolts. A tricky start gives way to easier edges on a slab ending at a higher ledge. **Pitch 3:** (5.10b) 8 bolts. Good knobs lead over an intimidating bulge directly above the anchor. The climbing eases and the exposure increases on the fun finishing slab.

Koala Rock—West Face Base Detail

6.	Suck My Kiss 5.10a	10.	Catty Corner 5.8
7.	Thin Air 5.10b	11.	Crazies 5.7
7a.	Changing Lanes 5.8	12.	Round Here 5.6
8.	Here Today, Gone Tomorrow 5.10c TR	13.	Cool Hand Luke 5.5 R
9.	Buffalo Power 5.10c	14.	Round There 5.7
9a.	Chipmunk Power 5.10d TR		

7a. Changing Lanes (5.8) ★★★ Mixed to 2.5 inches. Climb to the first-pitch roof of *Thin Air* and hand jam far to the right. A few face moves merge into the knobby finish of *Suck My Kiss*.

8. Here Today, Gone Tomorrow (5.10c) ★★ TR. The arête left of *Thin Air* once sported a single-pitch sport climb. Offended by shared holds, the Koala Rock route patrol pulled the bolts. It still makes an enjoyable toprope problem, though the lack of a convenient anchor limits the number of ascents.

9. Buffalo Power (5.10c) ★★★ 8 bolts. The left wall of the *Thin Air* buttress contains a justifiably popular face climb. Fun moves on good edges lead to a finish roaming up big knobs.

9a. Chipmunk Power (5.10d) ★★ TR. After lowering off *Buffalo Power,* you might as well toprope a slightly harder variant to the left. Begin with a crack leading to a delicate ramp and finish with a shallow arête leading to knobs.

10. Catty Corner (5.8) ★ Gear to 5 inches. Parallel cracks in a left-facing corner split the lower flanks of Koala Rock. The forgettable right crack jams awkwardly past a few blocks to the anchor atop the first pitch of *Thin Air.* Rappel, downclimb ledges to the left, or continue to the top.

11. Crazies (5.7) ★★ Gear to 3 inches. The left of parallel cracks at the base of the formation tackles a fun flake ending with a low-angle lieback. A killer block once guarded the middle of the route; today its remnants litter the base.

12. Round Here (5.6) ★★ 6 bolts. The low-angle slab at the base of Koala Rock is perfect for beginning climbers. The rightmost line doesn't match the quality of its neighbor, but the rock improves with each ascent.

13. Cool Man Luke (5.5 R) ★★★ Gear to 1 inch. A short seam rises slightly right of the *Round There* bolt line. After a naturally protected start, run it out

on the simple slab to the anchor. Beginners should steer clear, but you can eliminate ground fall risk by clipping bolts to the left.

14. Round There (5.7) ★★★★ 7 bolts. There's no better easy sport climb at Smith than the left of parallel bolt lines at the base of Koala Rock. Expect wonderfully solid, heavily featured rock with a crux move right at the start.

15. Desert Solitaire (5.10a R) ★★ Mixed to 2.5 inches. This intimidating route follows a direct line up the center of Koala Rock. The 1972 first ascent was a bold

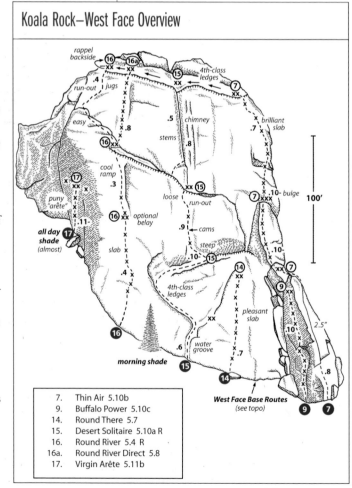

Koala Rock–West Face Overview

7.	Thin Air	5.10b
9.	Buffalo Power	5.10c
14.	Round There	5.7
15.	Desert Solitaire	5.10a R
16.	Round River	5.4 R
16a.	Round River Direct	5.8
17.	Virgin Arête	5.11b

West Face Base Routes
(see topo)

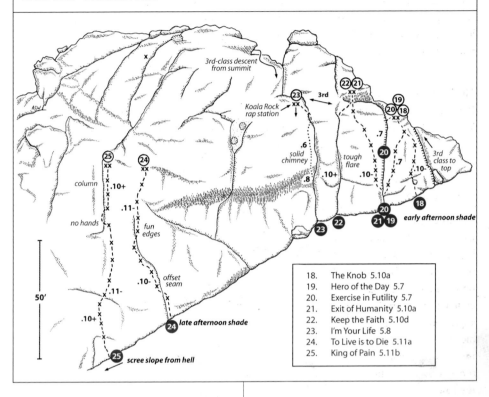

3rd-class descent from summit

Koala Rock rap station

3rd

solid chimney

tough flare

.6

.8

.10+

.10-

.7

.7

.10-

3rd class to top

early afternoon shade

column

.10+

.11-

no hands

fun edges

offset seam

.10-

.11-

.10+

50'

late afternoon shade

scree slope from hell

18.	The Knob 5.10a
19.	Hero of the Day 5.7
20.	Exercise in Futility 5.7
21.	Exit of Humanity 5.10a
22.	Keep the Faith 5.10d
23.	I'm Your Life 5.8
24.	To Live is to Die 5.11a
25.	King of Pain 5.11b

undertaking—imagine starting up the overhanging second pitch with nothing more than a hammer, hooks, pins, and a quarter-inch bolt kit. Replaced bolts reduce the danger, but falls are best avoided. Start below a short, water-stained groove. **Pitch 1:** (5.6) Solo up a deceptively tricky slot and zigzag along unexposed ramps to a ledge beneath an ominous bulge. **Pitch 2:** (5.10a) Incut holds lead past two bolts to the base of an inside corner. Fortunately, you can sink a good cam between the bolts. **Pitch 3:** (5.8) Enter the final crack from the left and romp up a chimney to the top.

16. Round River (5.4 R) ★★★★ Mixed to 1.5 inches. Beginning climbers looking for a safe entrance to the sport should look no farther than the opening pitch of this fine route—

the rock and protection are first-rate. The entire route is Smith's best easy line, though run-out sections on the upper two pitches might frighten novices. Climbers often combine the first two pitches using a 60-meter rope. Start behind a small juniper tree. **Pitch 1:** (5.4) 6 bolts. Ramble up enjoyable, low-angle rock to an anchor. **Pitch 2:** (5.3) Move past a bolt to a fun slab with huge pockets. **Pitch 3:** (5.4) Wander along a simple ramp on the north face and move up and right on run-out jugs to the top.

16a. Round River Direct (5.8) ★★★ 7 bolts. No one ever climbed this dangerous third-pitch variant until a fresh line of bolts removed the X from the rating. Now it only adds to the quality of the original route.

17. Virgin Arête (5.11b) ★★ 3 bolts. The only route on the north face of Koala Rock crimps a diminutive "arête" on great rock. The bouldering crux comes below the first bolt—either use a stick-clip or risk hobbling all the way back to the parking lot.

The short uphill side of Koala Rock contains several worthwhile routes. By far, the best approach follows any of the multi-pitch routes up the main face and rappels or scrambles down the backside. Hiking up the scree slope on the south side of the formation is a miserable experience.

18. The Knob (5.10a) ★★ 4 bolts. This petite route will take about two minutes out of your day. The one-move crux cranks past a slick knob the size of a beach ball.

19. Hero of the Day (5.7) ★★ 4 bolts. Crammed tightly between *The Knob* and *Exercise in Futility,* this stunted route follows fun edges and pockets. It makes a fine first lead for any beginning climber.

20. Exercise in Futility (5.7) ★★ Gear to 3 inches. Fleeting jams and edges polish off the right of three short cracks on the backside of Koala Rock. It provides a good toprope exercise for climbers who left their rack in the car.

21. Exit of Humanity (5.10a) ★★ 6 bolts. The left of three pint-size sport routes pulls through a contrived crux on mediocre rock. The climbing quickly eases, and the rock improves on the dash to the anchor.

22. Keep the Faith (5.10d) ★★ Gear to 2.5 inches. Awkward finger/hand jams lead into a flare up the center of three parallel cracks. Fortunately, good edges on either side reduce the struggle to tolerable levels. Most sport climbers prefer the security of a toprope from the *Exit of Humanity* anchors.

23. I'm Your Life (5.8) ★★ Gear to 3 inches. The left of three backside cracks ain't pretty, but it's the best of the bunch. Easy jams enter a flare followed by fun stems on good rock.

24. To Live is to Die (5.11a) ★★★ 9 bolts. A short scramble down the south-side scree slope leads to an offset seam. Mostly solid rock, great protection, and unique moves make it a worthwhile venture.

25. King of Pain (5.11b) ★★★ 12 bolts. This bulging wall doesn't look great, but appearances can deceive—expect sustained climbing and high-quality stone. After a crux lower section, the crowning moment comes on the clean finishing column.

BROGAN SPIRE AREA

Across the hillside right of Koala Rock sits a large expanse of rock. The main feature is the Brogan Spire Complex, with the triple peaks of the Opossum, the Tail, and Brogan Spire dominating the skyline. Downhill sits Mini Half Dome, the Mudpile, and Delirium Tremens. To approach these routes, hike up the Burma Road to the obvious switchback below Koala Rock and follow an indistinct trail across the hillside ending at the north side of Brogan Spire. Anyone visiting only Delirium Tremens and the Mudpile might prefer hiking along the east side of the canal, cutting uphill below the crags.

Brogan Spire Complex

A slender, flat-topped summit caps the most appealing of the three spires. With an over-hanging north face and a distinctive buttress extending far south from the summit spire, Brogan Spire ranks with Koala Rock as the best of the Marsupial Crags.

Brogan Spire–North Face

26. Knuckle-Draggers Anonymous 5.6 A3+ X
27. Project 5.13?
28. The Optimist 5.14b
28a. The Great Roof 5.6 A2+
29. Project 5.13?
30. Pouches 5.11c
31. Pin Bender 5.8 A2
32. Nice Beak A3+ R
33. Project 5.12?
34. Perry Masonry A4- X

Brogan Spire– North Face

The overhanging north wall offers some of the better rock in the area. Apart from two sport routes, it currently appeals mainly to aid specialists. This should eventually change as some of the enticing lines go free. **Descent:** From the summit, rappel west to the anchor atop the second pitch of *The Great Roof*. A double-rope rappel down the north face ends on the ground.

26. Knuckle-Draggers Anonymous (5.6 A3+ X) ★
Aid rack to 3 inches. Only knuckleheads will consider this dangerous aid line up the purple-streaked wall left of *The Great Roof*. Despite better than usual rock for a Smith nail-up, a frightening encounter with a loose flake takes much of the fun away. **Pitch 1:** (5.6 A3+) Start by nailing a crux seam past two bolts and gingerly free

The Opossum

The Tail

Brogan Spire

Mini Half Dome

The Mudpile

45

48

28

30

35

50

51

55

57

Delirium Tremens

74

28.	The Optimist 5.14b
30.	Pouches 5.11c
35.	West Face 5.5 X
45.	North Face Traverse 5.3 R
48.	Dogfight Crack 5.8 R
50.	Spankies Quest for the Nectar Hole 5.10c
51.	Tuff Shit 5.10b
55.	Kid-Packed Mini-Van from Hell 5.11a
57.	Lusty Lady 5.8
74.	Delirium Tremens 5.10b

a creepy flake. Aid a left-leaning crack and drop down around a hanging tooth before moving up to the summit ridge. **Pitch 2:** (5.4) Simple free climbing ends on top.

27. Project (5.13?) The eye-catching wall left of *The Great Roof* features flawless rock begging for a sport climb. An anchor in the middle of nowhere marks the end of what might someday be a classic high-end route.

28. The Optimist (5.14b) ★★★★ 8 bolts. What was once Smith's last great problem is now one of the hardest crack climbs in the world. The physical blend of tip jams and liebacks demand high levels of technical wizardry and fitness—few 5.14 climbers find much reason for optimism. With almost nothing but smears for the feet, the powerful lock-offs quickly sap your strength. The intricate pin-scarred crux comes in the first 50 feet, but

the pumping liebacks above will severely test your staying power.

28a. The Great Roof (5.6 A2+) ★★★ Clean to 1 inch. The entire route will see far more aid ascents than free ones in the years to come. With many bolts and good nut slots, it easily goes clean on aid. Avoid massive doses of bad karma—leave your hammer and pins at home. The disappointing roof pitch traverses around the huge ceiling instead of attacking it directly. **Pitch 1:** (A2+ or 5.14b) Free climbing (yeah, right) or clean aid ends at a hanging belay. **Pitch 2:** (5.6 A2-) A few aid placements lead to a traverse out the right wall on bolts. Exit around the corner and move right to an anchor. **Pitch 3:** (5.4) Simple scrambling on good stone leads to the top.

29. Project (5.13?) The clean wall right of *The Great Roof* holds promise for an extreme route sometime in the future. The first two bolts are already there, beginning with a short right-leaning flake.

30. Pouches (5.11c) ★★★ 8 bolts. The only "easy" free route on the north wall follows entertaining jugs on an overhanging wall. Snapping holds at the crux wreaked havoc with the grade, but now the stone seems rock solid.

31. Pin Bender (5.8 A2) ★ Aid rack to 1 inch. Fifty feet right of *The Great Roof* lurks an indistinct aid seam lacking in physical charms. The scarcity of pin scars prove that very few climbers bother. Start behind a juniper tree on a pocketed wall. **Pitch 1:** (5.8 A2) Nail a seam and shallow right-facing corner to an anchor. **Pitch 2:** (5.8) Bolt-protected face moves give way to easier climbing.

32. Nice Beak (A3+ R) ★ Aid rack to 1 inch. Downhill right of *Pin Bender* rises a perilous aid line ending at a single-bolt anchor. Clipping the bolts on the free project to the right greatly increases the odds that you'll live to see another day.

33. Project (5.12?) The blank section of cliff downhill from *The Great Roof* might have enough holds to host several extreme free climbs. An abandoned project between two aid seams sports several bolts and an anchor high above.

34. Perry Masonry (A4- X) ★ Aid rack to 1 inch. A faint seam right of *Nice Beak* provides a few moments of terror. Using beaks, masonry nails, and other aid toys, engineer a line to a bolt about 50 feet up and lower off.

Brogan Spire—South Side

The southern side of the Brogan Spire Complex offers climbers a far broader selection than the north face. The nor-mal approach scrambles through a notch between Brogan Spire and Mini Half Dome. **Descent:** From the summit, first rappel east to the notch between Brogan Spire and the Tail. Second, rappel down a low-angle groove to unexposed ledges. Finally, make a short rappel east down the first pitch of *The Cave Route.*

35. West Face (5.5 X) ★★★ Mixed to 3 inches. The downhill ridge of Brogan Spire offers a delightful romp up mostly solid rock. Much of the route protects poorly, though you'll find a bolt on the hardest move. Start at the Mini Half Dome notch. **Pitch 1:** (5.5) Climb a short stretch of poor rock past a replaced bolt and scramble up easy stone to a belay spot with a gear anchor. **Pitch 2:** (5.3) Easy scrambling ends at a huge shelf. Walk uphill 100 feet to an anchor. Some climbers combine the first two pitches with a long rope. **Pitch 3:** (5.4) Stroll directly up the pinnacle on solid, unprotected rock to the summit.

36. Smash the Silence (5.10c) ★★ 13 bolts. A single route ascends the main spire's south wall. Begin atop a small boulder, crank a crux move right off the deck, and climb some of Smith's most massive huecos to the shelf below the summit. The rock would be better if it saw more traffic. Rappel off with two ropes or continue to the top via the *West Face.*

37. West Gully (5.10d) ★★★ Gear to 1 inch. If not for a physical boulder problem out the starting cave, the *West Gully* would be a fine beginner's route. It almost never gets done—beginners can't do the start, and those who can rarely hike to the base. Begin at the highest point of the hillside in a massive amphitheater on the west side of the Brogan Spire Complex. **Pitch 1:** (5.10d) Power up the overhanging cave on positive holds and

The Wombat

Brogan Spire
The Tail
The Opossum

The Kangaroo

The Mudpile

46

The Joey   36

Marsupial Wall

81

39   40

73

71   80

36.	Smash the Silence 5.10c	71.	Edge of the World 5.10b
39.	Barred Reality 5.10a	73.	Loose Hookers 5.7 A2- R
40.	South Buttress 5.5 X	80.	South Face 5.8 X
46.	Living Blindly 5.7	81.	Southwest Side 5.4 R

stroll to a unique hole. Belay here, or continue up a simple (5.4) groove to anchors on the summit ridge. **Pitch 2:** (5.4) Wander up great rock with little protection to the summit.

37a. West Gully Variation (5.7) ★ No topo. Gear to 3 inches. A short crack on the left bypasses the bouldering start. Apart from providing easy access to the finishing groove, it holds little appeal.

38. Death of a Raven (5.8) ★★★ 9 bolts. Just right of the *West Gully* boulder problem rises a gently overhanging sport route. Buckets at the start lead to fun pockets and a steep finish on good holds. Lower off, or take your pick of summit routes.

39. Barred Reality (5.10a) ★★★ Bolts. A long sport route on Brogan Spire's southern buttress features solid rock and tame climbing for the grade. Apart from short bouldering

cruxes, it's a breeze. Start on the lowest flank of rock right of the *West Gully*. **Pitch 1:** (5.10a) 8 bolts. Strenuous moves on the starting wall lead to easy scrambling and an anchor on a large ledge. **Pitch 2:** (5.10a) 2 bolts. Crank past an unexposed bulge and hike to an anchor near a natural tunnel. **Pitch 3:** (5.5) 6 bolts. Step left to a low-angle wall and race past several bolts on big holds to the summit.

40. South Buttress (5.5 X) ★★★★ Mixed to 2 inches. A charming route follows the low-angle southern rib of the Brogan Spire Complex. With excellent rock and pleasant climbing, the only thing missing is decent protection. Still, it makes a great choice for anyone comfortable soloing at the grade. Start at the far south end of the buttress near a burnt-out juniper snag. **Pitch 1:** (5.5) A short crux leads to an easy scramble as far

Brogan Spire Complex—South Face

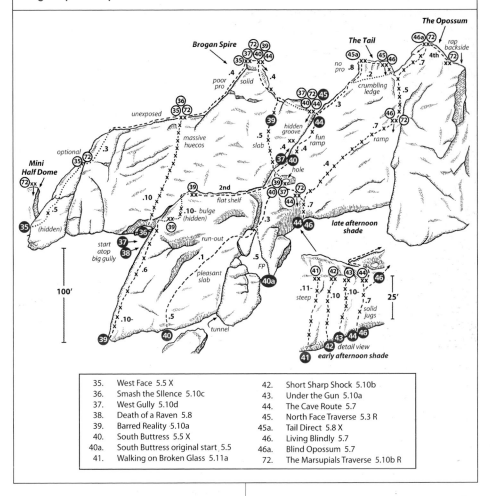

35.	West Face 5.5 X	42.	Short Sharp Shock 5.10b
36.	Smash the Silence 5.10c	43.	Under the Gun 5.10a
37.	West Gully 5.10d	44.	The Cave Route 5.7
38.	Death of a Raven 5.8	45.	North Face Traverse 5.3 R
39.	Barred Reality 5.10a	45a.	Tail Direct 5.8 X
40.	South Buttress 5.5 X	46.	Living Blindly 5.7
40a.	South Buttress original start 5.5	46a.	Blind Opossum 5.7
41.	Walking on Broken Glass 5.11a	72.	The Marsupials Traverse 5.10b R

as a rope will reach. You'll need to rely on your route-finding skills. **Pitch 2:** (5.4) 2 bolts. Pass over the top of a tunnel and climb a classic ramp to an anchor on the summit ridge. **Pitch 3:** (5.4) Stroll up perfect rock to the top.

40a. South Buttress original start (5.5) ★★
Gear to 1.5 inches. A lesser-quality variant starts on the uphill side of a natural tunnel. Follow a left-leaning crack past an old fixed pin to the crest of the buttress and join the regular route.

The uphill face of Brogan Spire's south buttress contains a small selection of steep routes, highlighted by unusual wafer-thin jugs. Approach by skirting the southern flanks of the Brogan Spire Complex, passing through a small tunnel along the way.

41. Walking on Broken Glass (5.11a) ★★
4 bolts. The longest and leftmost of the sport lines powers through an exceptionally featured overhanging wall. Every hold is a jug, but the angle generates a healthy pump, peaking on the final moves.

42. Short Sharp Shock (5.10b) ★★★ 4 bolts. A few feet uphill to the right sits another steep line studded with big holds. Expect good rock and energetic moves.

43. Under the Gun (5.10a) ★★★ 4 bolts. Although shorter than the routes to the left, this steep wall is just as much fun. With big holds, solid rock, and safe protection it makes a good introduction to the 5.10 grade.

44. The Cave Route (5.7) ★★★★ Mixed to 2 inches. The best route to the summit of Brogan Spire follows three memorable pitches starting with a vertical wall of good holds. Despite the quality, the long approach and unprotected crux pitch kept everyone away for decades. Today, with new bolts and the resurgence of Marsupial climbing, it's finally receiving long-overdue attention. **Pitch 1:** (5.7) 2 bolts. Climb a short pitch of perfect rock to an anchor. **Pitch 2:** (5.4) 2 bolts. Scramble over a tunnel and race up a clean slab to an anchor on the summit ridge. **Pitch 3:** (5.4) Enjoy a stretch of good holds ending on top.

The Tail

For good reason, the upper two summits of the Brogan Spire Complex receive far less attention than the namesake. Everyone ignored the Tail until a popular sport route on the south face provided a good reason to visit. Early ascents either traversed across from Brogan Spire or rappelled into a notch from the summit of the Opossum. **Descent:** Rappel from the summit down *Living Blindly* to an anchor atop the second pitch. A second rap with a 60-meter rope barely reaches the ground.

45. North Face Traverse (5.3 R) ★ Gear to 2 inches. The easiest line to the summit scrambles up the ridge from the Brogan

Spire notch, before cutting north along an exposed, rotted ledge. A couple easy moves above the Opossum notch end on top.

45a. Tail Direct (5.8 X) ★★ Gear to 1 inch. A high-risk, higher-quality option follows a direct line from the Brogan Spire notch. You won't want to plummet from the unprotected bouldering finish.

46. Living Blindly (5.7) ★★★ Bolts. This long route to the top of the Tail gained instant popularity due to easy climbing, high-quality rock, and cushy protection. Some climbers prefer splitting the first pitch into two, belaying below the tunnel on *The Cave Route*. **Pitch 1:** (5.7) 11 bolts. Follow the short first pitch of *The Cave Route* and veer right across the face to an anchor on a small ledge. **Pitch 2:** (5.5) 6 bolts. Easy climbing leads to the summit ridge. Step left to an anchor atop the Tail.

The Opossum

Climbers rarely visited the upper spire of the Brogan Spire Complex before *Living Blindly* provided easy access. The 1960 first ascent was the first recorded route anywhere in the Marsupials. **Descent:** Backside routes rap the uphill face from an old anchor on the exposed summit ridge. Most modern climbers rappel from the summit of the Opossum and scramble up to the anchor atop the Tail. Make two rappels down *Living Blindly*.

46a. Blind Opossum (5.7) ★★ 8 bolts. An alternate finish to *Living Blindly* ignores the summit of the Tail, opting instead for the Opossum. Bolts safely protect the originally frightening slab.

47. Diagonal Crack (5.4 R) ★ Gear to 3 inches. The first ascent of the Opossum followed an insignificant, poorly protected slash cutting across the uphill face. Walk, crawl, and hand traverse along the increasingly difficult ramp to the top.

48. Dogfight Crack (5.8 R) Gear to 2.5 inches. An unusually dismal route jams a harrowing crack on the northeast corner of the Opossum. It's worth walking by the base, if only to marvel at the depths that some climbers will sink to.

Mini Half Dome

A rounded block below the lowest point of the Brogan Spire Complex vaguely resembles Yosemite's Half Dome. In an ethical travesty, a sweeping overhang on the north face once sported a line of gaudy artificial holds—fortunately this eyesore disappeared long ago. **Descent:** Make a short rappel down the east side.

49. Mini Half Dome (5.8) ★★ 5 bolts. The original route to the top follows technical holds past newly replaced bolts on the uphill side of the block.

50. Spankies Quest for the Nectar Hole (5.10c) ★ 9 bolts. This peculiar line follows a minefield of petrifying knobs on the north side of Mini Half Dome. Edge cautiously on exploding nubbins around two arêtes and finish with hidden jugs over a small roof.

The Mudpile

The massive chunk of rock below the Brogan Spire Complex offers more variety than most Smith crags. There's not much middle ground with the Mudpile; the rock is either solid or junk; the routes are gentle slabs or vicious overhangs; the grades are pleasantly moderate or radically hard. The

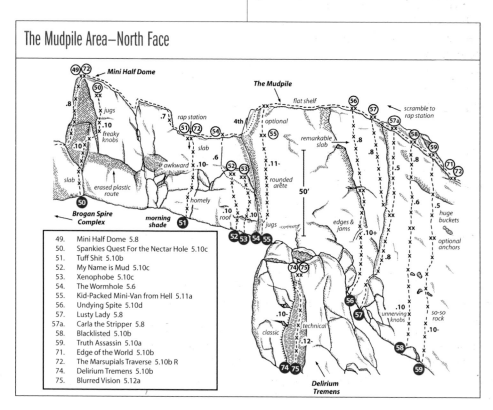

The Mudpile Area–North Face

49.	Mini Half Dome 5.8
50.	Spankies Quest For the Nectar Hole 5.10c
51.	Tuff Shit 5.10b
52.	My Name is Mud 5.10c
53.	Xenophobe 5.10c
54.	The Wormhole 5.6
55.	Kid-Packed Mini-Van from Hell 5.11a
56.	Undying Spite 5.10d
57.	Lusty Lady 5.8
57a.	Carla the Stripper 5.8
58.	Blacklisted 5.10b
59.	Truth Assassin 5.10a
71.	Edge of the World 5.10b
72.	The Marsupials Traverse 5.10b R
74.	Delirium Tremens 5.10b
75.	Blurred Vision 5.12a

north wall features the best rock on the formation, with little opportunity for future development. The steepest part of the undercut river face might someday contain a dense concentration of hard routes, though currently almost nothing goes free.

Many climbs on the north side of the formation have two sets of anchors, but they are best done in a single pitch. The first anchors allow a single-rope descent after the crux sections. The routes start uphill on the north side and descend in order around the base to the south.
Descent: From the top of the cliff, scramble uphill toward Brogan Spire along a fourth-class ridge. Drop down slightly and find rap hangers near the top of *Tuff Shit*. Rappel off the north side with one rope.

51. Tuff Shit (5.10b) ★★ 6 bolts. The farthest uphill route on the north side of the crag

makes a good introduction to the unique world of Mudpile climbing. The lower section ascends rock that somehow sticks together—despite appearances. The crux comes higher with an uncommonly awkward move pulling over a bulge onto the solid finishing slab.

52. My Name is Mud (5.10c) ★★ 5 bolts. Two goofy-looking routes undercut by a roof rise left of a chimney. The left route cranks through crux jugs to a much easier slab finish.

53. Xenophobe (5.10c) ★★ 5 bolts. The right of two identical oddball routes cranks over a physical roof on jugs. The climbing eases considerably on the slab above.

54. The Wormhole (5.6) ★ Gear to 2.5 inches. The first ascent of the Mudpile followed a deep chimney separating the upper

The Mudpile Area—West Face

Mini Half Dome

The Mudpile

The Kangaroo

The Wallaby

Delirium Tremens

51   54

56

78

58

76   59

74   60

67

51.	Tuff Shit 5.10b	60.	Project 5.12?
54.	The Wormhole 5.6	67.	Jacobs-Strain Line 5.12c
56.	Undying Spite 5.10d	74.	Delirium Tremens 5.10b
58.	Blacklisted 5.10b	76.	South Side 5.10d
59.	Truth Assassin 5.9	78.	North Wall 5.10a

part of the wall from the larger lower section. Start with jugs on the right wall and writhe up a slot to a ledge. Cut left past sagebrush and follow a thin crack to a single-bolt anchor on the ridge.

55. Kid-Packed Mini-Van from Hell (5.11a) ★★★ 8 bolts.
The rounded arête right of *The Wormhole* sports one of the better routes on the Mudpile. Sustained, fun moves on decent rock end at an anchor just below the summit ridge.

56. Undying Spite (5.10d) ★★ 14 bolts.
An easy finish on a beautiful slab high off the ground highlights this worthwhile route. The much more difficult lower portion isn't special, with a crux bulge mixing edges and finger jams. The rock runs the gamut from bottom to top, beginning with rubbish and ending with excellence.

57. Lusty Lady (5.8) ★★★★ 14 bolts.
A remarkable finishing slab highlights the best route to the top of the Mudpile. With great rock, plenty of bolts, and a superb setting, *Lusty Lady* is one of the Marsupial's unknown treasures. Her opening sequence isn't the best, but she improves the higher you go. Start on the left side of a large flake leaning against the base of the wall.

57a. Carla the Stripper (5.8) ★★★ 11 bolts.
This lesser variant follows *Lusty Lady* to the midpitch anchors, but continues in an easier direct line to the summit. *Carla* was the original line on the main wall of the Mudpile, though she lost popularity with the emergence of her more attractive neighbor.

58. Blacklisted (5.10b) ★ 14 bolts.
Technical, friable nubbins at the start detract from this otherwise worthwhile route. The best climbing cruises fun jugs above the midpitch anchor, though the start weeds out those who would enjoy it the most.

59. Truth Assassin (5.10a) ★★ 11 bolts.
Just right of *Blacklisted* sits a similar but more enjoyable route. After an unnerving start the climbing improves greatly as the nubbins give way to big jugs.

The following several lines ascend the strongly overhanging base of the Mudpile. These climbs bear absolutely no resemblance to the other routes on the formation. All ethics went down the toilet in the preparation, but there's nothing steeper anywhere at Smith.

60. Project (5.12?)
The most obvious natural weakness on the downhill side of the Mudpile is a shallow dihedral guarded by an overhanging start. For now there's nothing but a bolt about 40 feet up

61. Project (5.13?) 5 bolts.
A bolt line on the left side of the cliff might go free, though it pales in comparison to the impressive routes farther right.

62. Climb Like A Bomb (5.13a) ★★ 8 bolts.
The first of hopefully many 5.13s starts with technical, physical moves leading to a roof with good pockets. The crux comes in the finishing right-facing corner, cranking past a glued-on chunk of rock.

63. Project (5.13?) ★★ 7 bolts.
A harder variant starts a few feet right before joining the right-facing corner above the roof. All the moves go free, and it'll likely be the next completed route on the wall.

64. Project (5.14?) 10 bolts.
A less-than-obvious connection begins with the preceding route before traversing right along the lip of the roof to an extreme finish. It might be the hardest of all the projects at the base of the Mudpile.

65. Project (5.13+?) 10 bolts.
Another option starts atop a big boulder, clearing the

The Mudpile Area—Base Detail

Delerium Tremens

50'

.7 to top

peculiar traverse

funky arête

edges

morning shade
late afternoon shade

morning shade

The Mudpile

shallow cave

big boulder

unique jugs

crumbling buckets

tricky slab

right-leaning crack 150'

midafternoon shade

60.	Project 5.12?	68.	Project 5.13?
61.	Project 5.13?	69.	Rampage 5.11a
62.	Climb Like A Bomb 5.13a	70.	Marsupial Madness 5.11c
63.	Project 5.13?	71.	Edge of the World 5.10b
64.	Project 5.14?	72.	The Marsupials Traverse 5.10b R
65.	Project 5.13+?	73.	Loose Hookers 5.7 A2- R
66.	Project 5.14?	76.	South Side 5.10d
67.	Jacobs-Strain Line 5.12c	77.	Airstream 5.11d

roof directly above and traversing left along the lip to the right-facing corner finish.

66. Project (5.14?) 11 bolts. The purest new line starts inside a shallow cave on a boulder and follows a direct route over the roof to a high set of anchors. Apparently enough holds exist, though the long spans will challenge even the best teenage mutants.

67. Jacobs-Strain Line (5.12c) ★★★ 9 bolts. The original base route clears the big roof following a short offset to a pumping finish that gives even the fittest climbers the

blues. The overhanging wall looks harder than the grade.

68. Project (5.13?) 7 bolts. One final project starts right of the roof from a pile of rocks. Hard bouldering on the lower wall leads left, finishing with the upper part of the *Jacobs-Strain Line.*

69. Rampage (5.11a) ★★ 6 bolts. There's nothing else at Smith quite like the overhanging wall of jugs on the southwest side of the Mudpile. After enduring crumbling rock for much of the route, the pumping crux above the last bolt turns solid. The experience somehow leaves you disgusted and satisfied at the same time.

70. Marsupial Madness (5.11c) ★★ 4 bolts.
The lower south face contains two sport routes on the sort of rock that gave the Mudpile its name. The left route starts with deceptively tricky moves on sharp crimps, finishing with unique jugs. Climbers sometimes enjoy the madness, though few have any interest in returning.

71. Edge of the World (5.10b) ★★ Bolts.
A more enjoyable route starts uphill from *Marsupial Madness*. Be leery of the opening traverse unless both climbers are solid at the grade—following is more challenging than leading. **Pitch 1:** (5.10b) 8 bolts. Traverse far left past an anchor on so-so rock, eventually veering up and right to a higher set of bolts. Belay here or face impossible rope drag. **Pitch 2:** (5.7) 4 bolts. Step left and wander up easy rock to a belay in a groove. Make two single-rope rappels to the ground.

72. The Marsupials Traverse (5.10b R)
★★★ Mixed to 2.5 inches. No route at Smith covers as much real estate as *The Marsupials Traverse*. There's very little original here; except for a pitch to the summit of Mini Half Dome, it combines existing lines. Adventure climbers will enjoy the literal ups and downs of the journey. Starting with *Lusty Lady* drops the grade a couple notches, but increases the quality. **Pitches 1 and 2:** (5.10b) Climb *Edge of the World* to the top of the Mudpile. **Pitch 3:** (4th class) Hike along the top and descend to the anchor above *Tuff Shit*. **Pitch 4:** (5.7) Boulder past a bolt to a flat-topped summit. Downclimb and step across a chasm to an easy slab ending atop Mini Half Dome. Rappel into the notch below Brogan Spire. **Pitches 5, 6, and 7:** (5.5) Follow the *West Face* to the top

of Brogan Spire. You can easily combine the fifth and sixth pitches into one with a long rope. Rappel into the Tail's notch and make a second rappel south down a corridor. Pass through a tunnel to an anchor on the opposite side. **Pitches 8 and 9:** (5.7) Join *Living Blindly* and climb two pitches to the top of the Tail. **Pitch 10:** (5.7) Follow *Blind Opossum* to the summit of the Opossum. Continue past the anchor to a traverse along a knife-edge ridge. Rappel down the backside from old bolts.

73. Loose Hookers (5.7 A2- R) ★ Aid rack to 3 inches. A secluded aid climb follows a peculiar crack slashing across a shallow amphitheater on the southeast side of the Mudpile. Either approach through the notch between Mini Half Dome and Brogan Spire or slog up scree along the south side of the formation. **Pitch 1:** (5.7 A2-) Aid past a small roof to a thinning diagonal crack. A few unnerving hooks mixed with free moves lead to a more conventional finish past a couple mini-roofs. Avoid intense rope drag by setting a belay on a ledge above all difficulties. **Pitch 2:** (5.2) A simple slab with minimal protection ends at an anchor on top. Either rap the opposite side via *Tuff Shit* or rappel the route with two ropes.

Delirium Tremens

A square pillar with an unmistakable north-side dihedral rises nearest the canal, just left of the Mudpile. The routes are short, but the rock ranks with the very best. The puny uphill side succumbs to a quick third-class scramble. **Descent:** All routes lower from anchors below the summit.

74. Delirium Tremens (5.10b) ★★★★ Gear to 2.5 inches. This beautiful bulging dihedral is one of the best traditional pitches at Smith.

Expect flawless rock and unrelenting jams and stems.

75. Blurred Vision (5.12a) ★★ 4 bolts. Despite massive development, the first sport route in the Marsupial Crags is still one of the hardest. The ultra-technical crimps up the wall right of *Delirium Tremens* are solid and well protected, but unfortunately not much fun.

76. South Side (5.10d) ★★ 4 bolts. The backside of Delirium Tremens contains two short sport climbs. The left route weaves along an arête, with a perplexing crux traverse just below the anchor.

77. Airstream (5.11d) ★★★ 7 bolts. The best sport route on the formation follows great rock on the right side of the south face. The deceptive crux cranks sloping edges off the starting ledge, while the easier finish generates a pump for anyone lacking fitness.

The Maruspial Spires

Three pinnacles rise near the canal right of the Mudpile. Farthest north sits the bulbous-topped Wallaby, while the massive Kangaroo towers to the right. The Joey lies hidden from view on the Kangaroo's backside. These spires appeal only to climbers willing to suffer for their summits.

The Wallaby

The only route to the top of this distinctive spire sees very few ascents, and the few potential new lines make the original look like a classic. **Descent:** Rappel the north side.

78. North Wall (5.10a) ★ 8 bolts. With freshly replaced bolts, more climbers should weather the crumbling rock for a chance to stand atop the Wallaby. Start on the north

ridge and cautiously edge up a bolt ladder to a belay below the summit block. Circle to the east side and make a deceptively tricky boulder move to the top.

The Kangaroo

Despite potential, this massive pinnacle offers nothing but trouble. The two routes to the summit are unusually dangerous, with loose rock and dubious protection. **Descent:** Traverse south on the summit ridge. Administer last rites and rappel with double ropes from slings wrapped around a flake.

79. North Ledges Traverse (5.7 R) No topo. Mixed to 3 inches. Don't let the grade fool you—this intimidating route makes a very poor choice for any beginner, despite freshly replaced bolts. Start with pockets on the backside leading into an amphitheater and scramble to the notch between the Kangaroo and the Joey. Crawl and hand traverse along a dirty right-leaning ramp to the top.

80. South Face (5.8 X) Mixed to 2 inches. The only other option to the summit of the Kangaroo follows a line just as miserable as the preceding route. Start below the south side and traverse left past a bolt on repugnant rock onto the low-angle south face. Fighting rope drag, follow the line of least resistance to the top in two pitches.

The Joey

From most vantage points, this insignificant gendarme on the east side of the Kangaroo goes unnoticed. The following route might make you wish you hadn't noticed it either. **Descent:** Rappel from suspicious bolts.

81. Southwest Side (5.4 R) 1 bolt. Boulder into a gully and scramble up junky flakes to a notch between the two pillars. Easy moves on putrid rock lead past a lone bolt to the top.

Marsupial Wall

Above and south of the Brogan Spire Complex stretches a large expanse of bad rock. Despite the huge volume of stone, this cliff offers nothing good except two routes on the far south end of the cliff.

82. Challenger's Lost Pinnacle (5.7 X) ★

Mixed to 2 inches. Across the scree slope east of the Brogan Spire Complex sits a dangerous route ending at an anchor atop a slender pinnacle. With only three bolts and mediocre rock, this line receives no attention whatsoever.

82a. Challenger's Lost Pinnacle finish (5.7 X)

No topo. Gear to 2.5 inches. If you've got a death wish, you can climb the miserably rotten, poorly protected wall rising above the notch separating the spire from the parent cliff.

83. Project (A4?) No

topo. No route ascends the largest part of the Marsupial Wall. The only attempt ended at a bolt 15 feet off the ground. Enough said.

84. Solstice Slab (5.8) ★★ Gear to 2 inches.

An isle of decent rock in a sea of trash lurks a quarter mile south of the Kangaroo. *Solstice Slab* rests at the entrance to the northernmost hiking gully extending through the cliff line. A freaky face move at the start leads to good jams ending at a rappel block.

85. And Justice For All (5.10a) ★★ 5 bolts.

On the left side of a hiking gully at the southern end of the cliff line rests a surprisingly solid, sport-bolted slab. It might be popular if not for the remote location.

The Wombat and Marsupial Wall—South Side

The Wombat

Lost Hardware Pinnacle

Disappearing Tower

The Thumb

102

101

104

The Opossum

86

47

Marsupial Wall

82

85

84

47.	Diagonal Crack 5.4 R		86.	Catfight Cracks 5.10a X
82.	Challenger's Lost Pinnacle 5.7 X		101.	Project 5.12?
84.	Solstice Slab 5.8		102.	Wombat Chimney 5.6 R
85.	And Justice For All 5.10a		104.	Over the Hill 5.7 X

The Wombat

This foreboding monolith dwarfs the other members of the Marsupial Crags. Perched atop the hillside far above the Burma Road, it's one of Smith's most impressive landmarks. The remote location is both the best and worst part of the Wombat experience. The magnificent setting offers a bird's-eye view of the entire Central Oregon region. The never-ending approach weeds out all but the most determined, though anyone enduring the scree slog finds ample rewards. The monolith offers a little of everything—cracks, sport routes, and aid lines on rock varying from terrible to wonderful.

Descent: From the summit, scramble down a short fourth-class ridge on the east side.

86. Catfight Cracks (5.10a X) Gear to 3 inches. The longest route on the Wombat follows an unpleasant crack system on the southwest side of the monolith. The second pitch was one of the most dangerous leads in Smith history when first done in 1973 with almost no protection. Modern gear may (or may not) reduce the seriousness, though the rock is as bad as ever. Start at the lowest part of the Wombat below a disgusting groove. **Pitch 1:** (5.7) Climb a dirty flare to a bolt belay. **Pitch 2:** (5.10a) Step across to the miserable right crack and fight to a belay stance. **Pitch 3:** (5.8) Traverse right onto the south face of the Wombat and climb to the notch behind an obvious detached spire called the Thumb. **Pitch 4:** (5.7) An unexposed boulder move leads into a deep trough. Using a 60-meter rope, follow the path of least resistance to an anchor. **Pitch 5:** (4th class) A never-ending scramble along the summit ridge leads to the top. The

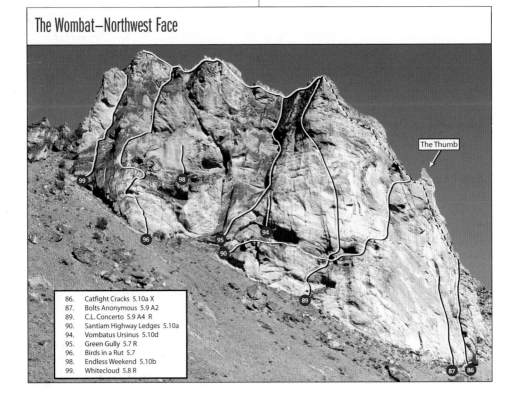

The Wombat–Northwest Face

The Thumb

86.	Catfight Cracks 5.10a X
87.	Bolts Anonymous 5.9 A2
89.	C.L. Concerto 5.9 A4 R
90.	Santiam Highway Ledges 5.10a
94.	Vombatus Ursinus 5.10d
95.	Green Gully 5.7 R
96.	Birds in a Rut 5.7
98.	Endless Weekend 5.10b
99.	Whitecloud 5.8 R

moves are never hard, but climbers often use a rope for the most exposed sections.

87. Bolts Anonymous

(5.9 A2) ★ Aid rack to 1 inch. A pointless row of bolts mars the lower reaches of the Wombat's main wall. Oddly, the party backed off as soon as they reached a natural crack system. **Pitch 1:** (5.9 A2) A bouldering start gives way to a long string of bolts, interupted by a few pin placements. A final free move ends at an anchor. **Pitch 2:** (A1) Continue clipping bolts to a bail-off point.

88. Deffenbaugh Flake

(5.10a) ★★ Gear to 4 inches. A few feet left of *Bolts Anonymous* rises an unmistakable flake crack in a left-facing corner. A fleeting flurry of jams and liebacks ends at a single bolt on a small ledge.

89. C.L. Concerto (5.9 A4 R) ★ Aid rack

to 4 inches. An impressive aid climb follows a direct line up the largest face on the monolith. Nothing comes easy—the lengthy approach, rotten rock, and unnerving nailing consume a long, trying day. Ascents are as rare as a crowded day on the Wombat. Start below a homely flaring crack left of a dark, sagebrush-covered ledge. **Pitch 1:** (5.9) Thrash up a short crack and scramble

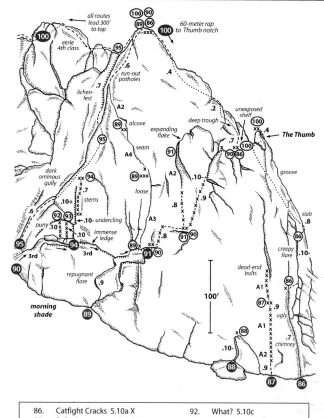

The Wombat—Lower Northwest Face

86.	Catfight Cracks 5.10a X	92.	What? 5.10c
87.	Bolts Anonymous 5.9 A2	93.	Where? 5.10b
88.	Deffenbaugh Flake 5.10a	94.	Vombatus Ursinus 5.10d
89.	C.L. Concerto 5.9 A4 R	95.	Green Gully 5.7 R
90.	Santiam Highway Ledges 5.10a	100.	The Thumb 5.7 R
91.	The Scab 5.8 A2		

to a bolt on a big ledge below the main wall. **Pitch 2:** (A3) Nail repugnant seams to bolts and a hanging belay. **Pitch 3:** (A4) Difficult aid leads up and left to an anchor in an alcove. **Pitch 4:** (5.6 A2) Continue aiding left and move around a corner to run-out potholes. **Pitch 5:** (4th class) Scramble up the exposed ridge to the summit.

90. Santiam Highway Ledges (5.10a) ★★

Mixed to 3 inches. This adventurous route sees few ascents, despite reasonable rock and an exposed position. A line of horrifying protection "nails" kept almost everyone away for decades, but modern bolts now make it much safer. Start at a huge ledge system running across the lower reaches of the main wall. **Pitch 1:** (3rd class) Walk along the massive ledge to an anchor at the far right end. **Pitch 2:** (5.8) 3 bolts. Creaky edges lead past a couple bolts to a higher ledge. Traverse right to the base of a bolt line. **Pitch 3:** (5.10a) Face climb past replaced bolts to a crux move reaching an unmistakable crack. Traverse right to a notch behind the Thumb. A short stint to the top of this spire (5.4) makes a fine detour. **Pitch 4:** (5.7) An unexposed boulder problem leads into a deep gully. Easy run-out scrambling ends at an anchor. **Pitch 5:** (4th class) Eerie fourth-class climbing leads hundreds of feet along the summit ridge to the top.

91. The Scab (5.8 A2 to highpoint) Aid rack to 4 inches. An unmistakable sickle-shaped flake hangs from the upper wall of the Wombat's main face. After a free climbing start, aid the crack to a back-off sling. The terrifying, expanding finish awaits someone unafraid of the great beyond.

The following three routes start from the left side of a massive ledge stretching across the lower flanks of the Wombat.

92. What? (5.10c) ★★ 3 bolts. The better of two midget-size routes follows technical edges past bolts to a single-bolt anchor. The final moves are trickier than they look, as good holds give way to blank stone.

93. Where? (5.10b) ★ 3 bolts. The right of two bolted sport routes disappoints anyone expecting more than 18 feet of climbing. A better name for this microscopic route would be "Why?"

94. Vombatus Ursinus (5.10d) ★★ Mixed to 2.5 inches. Right of two miniscule sport

routes looms a unique line combining trad and sport climbing. The start makes a fine traditional pitch (5.10a) with an undercling cutting around a big roof. The bolted moves above the anchor blend stemming, thin jams, and face climbing. Use long slings under the roof or face crippling rope drag at the crux.

95. Green Gully (5.7 R) ★ Gear to 3 inches. A menacing gully overgrown with fluorescent green lichen splits the entire northwest face of the Wombat. The short stretch of good rock on the second pitch isn't worth the ordeal getting there. **Pitch 1:** (5.6) Scramble up a dirty corridor and thrash through a groove to a belay below diverging cracks. **Pitch 2:** (5.7) Step left and jam a lichen-covered corner to the summit ridge. **Pitch 3:** (4th class) Scramble several hundred feet along the exposed ridge to the top.

96. Birds in a Rut (5.7) ★★★ Mixed to 3 inches. The most enjoyable route on the Wombat climbs six fun pitches to the summit. Excellent protection, solid rock, and spacious ledges make it a safe and enjoyable experience for lower-level climbers. Apart from the approach, the only negative is the prodigious amount of lichen growing everywhere. Start left of a small juniper tree below a bolted slab. **Pitch 1:** (5.7) 6 bolts. Wander up a low-angle slab, veering left to an anchor in a shallow hole. **Pitch 2:** (5.6) 4 bolts. Step left and face climb up and right to a huge ledge. **Pitch 3:** (2nd class) Walk right and switchback left along unexposed ledges to an anchor. **Pitch 4:** (5.7) Cut left and jam a short fist crack. Finish with low-angle lichen-smearing past several bolts to another huge ledge. **Pitch 5:** (5.7) Jam and stem the obvious inside corner to an anchor. Some climbers descend from here by making three single-rope rappels to the ground. First, rappel the dihedral to a big ledge. Second, rap-

The Wombat–Upper Northwest Face

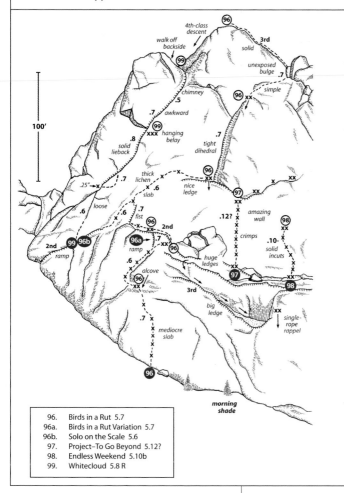

96.	Birds in a Rut 5.7
96a.	Birds in a Rut Variation 5.7
96b.	Solo on the Scale 5.6
97.	Project–To Go Beyond 5.12?
98.	Endless Weekend 5.10b
99.	Whitecloud 5.8 R

96b. Solo on the Scale

(5.6) ★ 5 bolts. A quick variant avoids the first three pitches by traversing in farther up the hill. Start by walking right along a ledge to an exposed face move protected by a bolt. Veer right and join the fourth pitch of *Birds in a Rut* above the fist crack.

The following two routes ascend a beautiful streaked wall rising above a large ledge system on the Wombat's northwest face. This smooth face is one of the finest at Smith, with a gently overhanging expanse of flawless rock. The two routes barely scratch the surface of the potential here. The best approach follows the first two pitches of *Birds in a Rut*. To descend from the base of the wall, walk down to an anchor on the right side of the lowest ledge and rappel with a single rope to the ground.

97. Project–To Go Beyond

(5.12?) 7 bolts. The left side of the wall offers a fully prepared sport route. Technical moves on good rock lead to a crux just below the anchor.

98. Endless Weekend

(5.10b) ★★★ 5 bolts. The right side of the wall contains a short line of gently overhanging jugs. The brilliant stone and pumping moves make it one of the Marsupials' finest routes.

pel down an attractive wall to a bigger ledge. Finally, weave down ledges to a final anchor and rappel to the ground. **Pitch 6:** (5.7) Unexposed hiking leads to a short bouldering sequence past a bulge. Easy scrambling ends on the summit.

96a. Birds in a Rut Variation

(5.7) ★ Gear to 2 inches. Instead of belaying at the second anchor, continue via a short dihedral to the anchor atop the third pitch. This short-lived variant completely eliminates the second-class pitch.

99. Whitecloud (5.8 R) ★★ Mixed to 3 inches. This remote route makes a good choice for climbers wanting to get away from it all. The run-out start isn't special, but a spectacular dihedral comes to the rescue. Start from a good ledge sprouting a small tree. **Pitch 1:** (5.8) Climb a grungy crack to a quarter-inch bolt and smear right to the start of the fun. High-quality jams lead to an inconvenient hanging belay. **Pitch 2:** (5.7) An awkward flare immediately above the anchor leads to an easier finishing chimney. Walk off the backside.

100. The Thumb (5.7 R) ★★ Gear to 2 inches. Only the most adventurous climbers will consider spending a day exploring this small spire jutting out from the southwest side of the Wombat. The Thumb itself entails just 20 feet of exposed climbing, while the approach and retreat set new standards of complexity. After hiking to the top of the Wombat, scramble hundreds of feet (4th class) down the exposed, unforgiving summit ridge to an anchor. A 60-meter rappel ends at an unexposed notch. The classic summit is just a short stroll away (5.4). The pocketed crux comes on the retreat with a bouldering move right off the ledge. Easy climbing with poor protection reverses the rappel and retreats along the endless summit ridge.

101. Project (5.12?) A horrific-looking inside corner splits the entire southeast face of the Wombat. Just to the right soars a shallow arete on uniquely featured stone. Given the remote location, decades might pass before anyone finishes this impressive line.

102. Wombat Chimney (5.6 R) Gear to 4 inches. Higher up the Wombat Gully, behind a lone juniper tree, rises an obscure chimney that no one will care to repeat. After a single pitch of squalor, walk left along a ledge to the summit ridge and finish to the top.

Lost Hardware Pinnacle and Disappearing Tower

Hidden behind the Wombat atop the ridge to the south are two puny spires joined by a connecting rib. Lost Hardware Pinnacle is the highest peak, while Disappearing Tower sits down the ridge. From the west these pinnacles are impressive, but the backside view will make you wonder why you bothered hiking here. The quickest approach scrambles up the third-class gully right of the Wombat—allow an hour and fifteen minutes from the parking lot. **Descent:** Make short rappels down the backside from anchors atop each summit.

103. Lost Hardware Route (5.7 R) ★ No topo. Gear to 1.5 inches. Begin on the short uphill side of the spire and foot-shuffle right along a ledge to the southwest corner. An exposed face move leads to an easy final slab. The curious name came from a rack of vintage gear discovered on the first free ascent.

104. Over the Hill (5.7 X) ★★ Mixed to 2 inches. This frightening route climbs the obvious arête on the downhill side of Lost Hardware Pinnacle. The crux near the top protects with a hidden bolt around the corner to the right.

105. The Far Side (5.10a R) ★★ No topo. 3 bolts. Immediately right of *Over the Hill* lurks a spooky face protected by widely spaced bolts. Move left near the top, avoiding the final arête.

106. Disappearing Tower (5.8 X) ★ No topo. Gear to 3 inches. The only route to the top of this pillar starts at the notch between the two spires. After a dangerous move into a miniature corner, a short crack leads to the teetering summit.

The Tasmanian Devil and the Zoo

Two of Smith's most remote crags, the Tasmanian Devil and the Zoo, sit hidden from view more than a mile east of the Wombat. The remote location guarantees that only climbers with a thirst for adventure (and a good set of legs) will ever visit. The most common approach hikes for more than an hour from the main parking area. Begin by hiking to the top of the Burma Road and follow an excellent trail across the northern hillside until the Tasmanian Devil comes into view. The Zoo lies hidden down a draw to the south. An alternate approach from the Skull Hollow Campground isn't any faster.

Tasmanian Devil

A pillar of decent rock sits along the crest of the ridge far from the center of the Smith Rock universe. The lack of routes will only disappoint anyone making the trek. **Descent:** Reverse the *Pocket Hold Route.*

107. Pocket Hold Route (5.4 R) ★★ No topo. Gear to 3 inches. The only route to the top follows good holds on the east side to a finishing slot. Rappel from a new anchor.

108. Devil in Disguise (5.11c R) ★ No topo. Gear to 1 inch. A short crack splits the lower portion of the Tasmanian Devil's north face. Tip jams with mar-

ginal protection lead to an anchor below a dangerous flake guarding the summit.

The Zoo

Completely hidden from view in a tranquil gully, this secluded crag surprises even the most seasoned Smith veterans. Overhanging and covered with huge jugs, the Zoo holds potential for dozens of routes. The rock isn't perfect, but a little cleaning would uncover some real gems. To approach the Zoo, hike to the Tasmanian Devil and follow a rough road leading downhill to the south. It seems like a wild goose chase until a large cliff appears on the left side of the

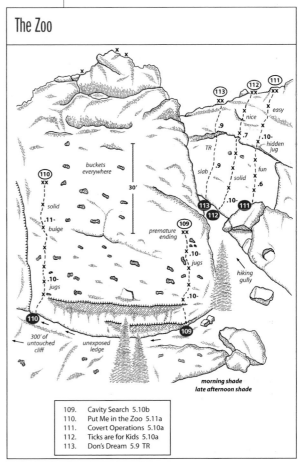

The Zoo

buckets everywhere

30'

solid

.11- bulge

premature ending

.10- jugs

.10- jugs

.10-

.9

.7

.10-

TR

slab .9

solid

fun

.6

.10-

nice

easy

.10- hidden jug

hiking gully

300' of untouched cliff

unexposed ledge

morning shade
late afternoon shade

109.	Cavity Search 5.10b
110.	Put Me in the Zoo 5.11a
111.	Covert Operations 5.10a
112.	Ticks are for Kids 5.10a
113.	Don's Dream 5.9 TR

draw. The following two routes rise above a large ledge on the southernmost part of the crag. **Descent:** All the routes have sport anchors.

109. Cavity Search (5.10b) ★★ 4 bolts. The right route isn't special, but the quality quickly improves after some junk down low. The crux cranks over a bulge on big holds. The wall above the anchor deteriorates, but heavy cleaning might uncover a worthwhile finish.

110. Put Me in the Zoo (5.11a) ★★★ 6 bolts. The left route rewards anyone making the long trek. Search for a line of bolts starting slightly right of an inside corner. The dirty jugs at the start give way to solid rock above, with a strenuous crux bulge above the fifth bolt.

The three remaining routes ascend a wonderful slab on the cliff behind *Cavity Search*. Approach by scrambling up a gully, looking right for two sport routes on pocketed rock. Easily arranged topropes make it a good practice area, though too advanced for most neophytes.

111. Covert Operations (5.10a) ★★★ 6 bolts. The right route starts with fun holds leading to a crux reach to a hidden jug. Above the roof, easier climbing ends at an anchor.

112. Ticks are for Kids (5.10a) ★★★ 5 bolts. The best route on the slab starts with a crux boulder problem right off the ground. Entertaining pockets and jugs on great rock lead to the top.

113. Don's Dream (5.9) ★★ TR. The leftmost route deserves bolts as much as the others, though you can easily set a toprope from an anchor atop the left side of the cliff. Expect a clean slab leading to a crux move at the obvious roof.

INDIAN AND MENDENHALL RIDGE

Smith's earliest climbs took place on the isolated pinnacles of Indian and Mendenhall Ridge, far north of today's state park. The rock on these weathered spires doesn't compare with Smith's main area, but the alpine position is unmatched.

Indian Ridge

From Smith's main parking lot, the politically incorrect Indian Ridge dominates the distant northern horizon. Everyone notices these spires, but almost no one visits. From bottom to top, Gunsight Rock, Squaw Rock, Leaning Brave, Little Big Horn, and the Papoose rise above a variety of lesser, unnamed blobs. Approach from the park by scrambling up the gully left of the Monument, and trek down across Sherwood Canyon to the north. Allow one and a half hours each way.

Gunsight Rock

The first pillar of any consequence on the lower reaches of Indian Ridge is this aptly named tower. There are better nearby spires, but you might as well scramble to the top as you hike up the ridge toward Squaw Rock. **Descent:** There's no anchor on top—reverse the route.

114. North Side (5.3 R) ★ No topo. Solo. Zigzag up easy ledges on the north side to the notch between the two peaks and climb big holds on good rock to the summit.

Squaw Rock

Smith's most visible spire overlooks the entire Central Oregon area. If you like alpine settings, you'll enjoy spending a day

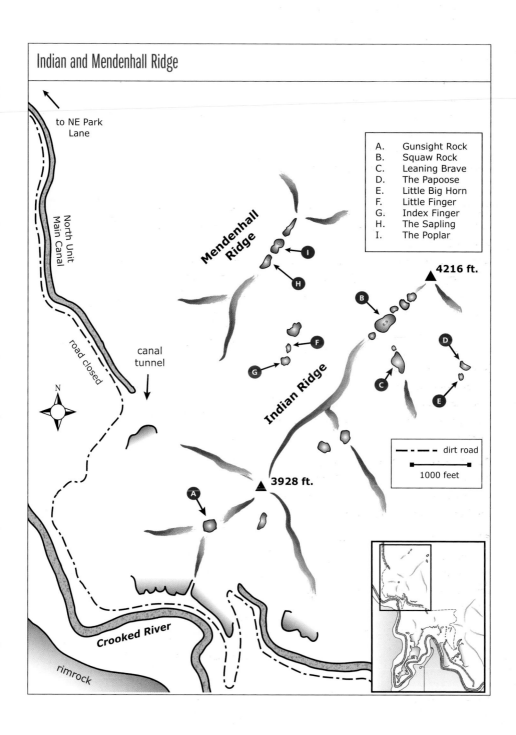

Indian and Mendenhall Ridge

to NE Park Lane

North Unit Main Canal

road closed

canal tunnel

N

Mendenhall Ridge

Indian Ridge

4216 ft.

3928 ft.

A.   Gunsight Rock
B.   Squaw Rock
C.   Leaning Brave
D.   The Papoose
E.   Little Big Horn
F.   Little Finger
G.   Index Finger
H.   The Sapling
I.   The Poplar

I

H

F

G

B

D

C

E

A

- · -   dirt road

1000 feet

Crooked River

rimrock

Squaw Rock

Leaning Brave

115. Spiral 5.2 R
116. South Spiral 5.3 R
117. South Face 5.3 X
118. North Face 5.8 X
119. Pale Face 5.10a
120. South Buttress 5.8 TR

climbing this landmark. Besides, you can't call yourself a true Smith Rock veteran until you stand atop the proud summit. Anyone offended by the insensitive name might choose to boycott the summit. **Descent:** As with many alpine climbs, there aren't any rappel anchors. Fools rappel from slings draped around loose boulders, but smart climbers reverse *Spiral*.

115. Spiral (5.2 R) ★★★ Gear to 2 inches. This best route on the monolith ascends good rock along a spiraling ledge. There's almost no protection, so climbers often third class to the summit. The moves are easy and rarely exposed, but it's steep enough to warrant belays for novices. Start left of a juniper tree, near the east corner of the pillar. The hardest climbing comes right off the ground, moving left and back right to a large ledge. Hike right along a ramp to

the west face and race up solid face holds to the top.

115a. Direct Variation (5.5 R) ★ Gear to 3 inches. A more difficult variant follows a direct line up the east face. Begin below an ugly groove a few feet right of the regular start. **Pitch 1:** (5.5) Climb the awkward crack to a large ledge at the Squaw's lap. **Pitch 2:** (5.5) Follow a mediocre crack splitting the east face directly to the summit.

116. South Spiral (5.3 R) ★ Gear to 2.5 inches. Similar to the original route, this series of ledges winds the opposite direction to the summit. Use the same start but cut left to a crumbly right-facing corner. Circle across the south side to the west face and scramble to the top.

117. South Face (5.3 X) ★★ Gear to 2.5 inches. This intimidating route-finding

Squaw Rock–East Face

115a
116
115
115a

115.	Spiral 5.2 R
115a.	Direct Variation 5.5 R
116.	South Spiral 5.3 R

exercise follows easy ledges directly up the southwest face. Surprisingly solid rock and enjoyable moves make it worth doing, despite poor protection. Start at the crest of the ridge below the lowest point of the spire.

Near Squaw Rock are three spires sitting south of Indian Ridge. Downhill rests the Leaning Brave, while the twin spires of the Papoose and Little Big Horn sit farther away to the southeast.

Leaning Brave

If this tower sat atop Indian Ridge, it would dominate the skyline just as much as Squaw Rock; instead it rises anonymously to the south. The 1963 first ascent was one of the better free climbs of the era. **Descent:** Make two single-rope rappels on the north side.

118. North Face (5.8 X) ★ Gear to 1.5 inches. The dangerous original route begins by traversing from the uphill ridge to a notch below the north side. The crux skirts right to a large ledge cutting across the face. Easy scrambling past a primordial bolt finishes to the top.

119. Pale Face (5.10a) ★★ Mixed to 2 inches. A better alternative follows a mostly bolted face starting below and right of the original route. Anyone willing to hike this far will enjoy the two pitches to the top. **Pitch 1:** (5.8) Face climb past three bolts to easy scrambling ending at an anchor. **Pitch 2:** (5.10a) Tricky, bolt-protected face moves lead up a mini-ramp to the summit.

120. South Buttress (5.8) TR. If you enjoy bad rock, you'll love the 175-foot south side of Leaning Brave. A toprope route wanders up hopeless stone to the summit.

The Papoose and Little Big Horn

Twin spires stand about a quarter mile southeast of Squaw Rock. The highest tower is the Papoose, with the smaller Little Big Horn rising slightly downhill. If you only have time to climb one of the spires, you'll face a tough choice—both are utterly dreadful. **Descent:**

You won't find any anchors on the summits. The crux of both routes comes on the downclimb.

121. Papoose, Southeast Ridge (5.2 X)
Gear to 2 inches. A terrible route follows junky rock on the southeast edge to the shattered summit.

122. Little Big Horn
(5.3 X) Gear to 2 inches. Lunkheads sometimes climb suicidal flakes on the east side to the summit. Everyone else stays away.

Indian Ridge/ Mendenhall Ridge Gully

The Papoose and Little Big Horn—Southwest Face

The Papoose

Little Big Horn

121

122

121. Papoose, Southeast Ridge 5.2 X
122. Little Big Horn 5.3 X

Smith's most obscure spires rise anonymously on the right side of the draw between Indian Ridge and Mendenhall Ridge. They aren't worth a special trip by any stretch of the imagination, but they make a fun detour. There are several blobs here—mostly second and third class—and the following slender spires. **Descent:** Neither pinnacle has a rappel anchor on top—instead, reverse the moves.

123. Little Finger (5.7 R) ★★★
No topo. Solo. Hidden from view downhill from a large rock mass balances this delightful needle. A great route on the south arête follows 25 feet of solid rock to the top.

124. Index Finger (5.4 R) ★
No topo. Solo. This slender spire capped by a small boulder

sits near the bottom of the cluster. Simple but unprotected moves scramble 30 feet up the east side to the top.

Mendenhall Ridge

Mendenhall Ridge rises across the draw to the north of Indian Ridge. Two spires dominate the skyline—the spike-topped Sapling and the classic Poplar. A few other rock masses (3rd class) make simple scrambles if you'd like to tick the entire ridge. Some climbers make a two-hour hike north from the Smith parking area. A much shorter option approaches from the north. Turn east off U.S. Highway 97 onto Park Lane just north of the Crooked River Gorge. Drive 2 miles east and park at a gate beyond the canal road. A one-hour cross-country hike leads up the north side of Mendenhall Ridge. Do not approach along the canal road itself—this is private property!

The Sapling

A distinctive summit horn caps the lower of two neighboring spires atop Mendenhall Ridge. The two short routes to the top are far below par. **Descent:** There's no anchor on the actual summit. Reverse the final moves of *Tilted Slab* to an anchor.

125. Tilted Slab (5.3 R) Solo. Start on the uphill side of the pinnacle and face climb unprotected junk 25 feet to the tilted slab. Circle around and scale the precarious spike from the south.

126. Tilted Mud (5.7) 2 bolts. A new route rises where you'd least expect it. Start right of *Tilted Slab* and climb loose holds past two bolts before joining the original line.

The Poplar

One of Smith's most slender spires balances atop Mendenhall Ridge uphill from the Sapling. When driving along US 97 south of the Crooked River Gorge, this bulbous pinnacle stands out on the horizon. **Descent:** Rappel down the uphill side with a single rope.

127. South Chimney (5.7 R) ★ Gear to 3 inches. An obvious slot splitting the south face of the tower provides an easy route to the summit. The crux stems past the starting bulge on bad rock before plunging into the finishing chimney.

128. North Chimney (5.10a) ★ Mixed to 5 inches. Smith routes don't get any more isolated than this. A steep wall guards the northern entrance into the chimney splitting the Poplar. Follow the right crack past an overhang and move to the left crack past a second bulge. Clip a bolt at the final bulge and finish with a simple chimney.

Mendenhall Ridge–South Side

The Poplar

The Sapling

125.	Tilted Slab 5.3 R
126.	Titled Mud 5.7
127.	South Chimney 5.7 R
128.	North Chimney 5.10a

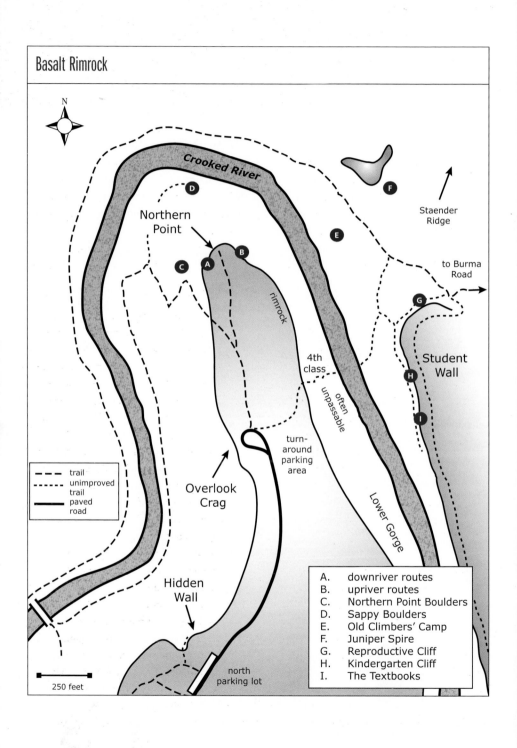

Basalt Rimrock

Crooked River

N

Northern Point

Staender Ridge

to Burma Road

D

B

A

C

E

F

G

Student Wall

rimrock

4th class

often unpassable

H

I

turn-around parking area

Overlook Crag

Lower Gorge

Hidden Wall

north parking lot

- - - trail
- - - unimproved trail
— paved road

250 feet

A. downriver routes
B. upriver routes
C. Northern Point Boulders
D. Sappy Boulders
E. Old Climbers' Camp
F. Juniper Spire
G. Reproductive Cliff
H. Kindergarten Cliff
I. The Textbooks

BASALT RIMROCK

*I was hiking along the base of the Northern
Point on a 100 degree afternoon, checking out
possible lines. Without thinking I started up
a puny route right of the approach chimney
(Jersey Shore, 5.7). I didn't have my chalk
bag and was wearing Air Jordans instead of rock
shoes, but it was just an easy scramble—until I
reached a short box corner at the top. My shoes
weren't smearing worth a damn—they might
have worked wonders for Michael on the hard-
wood, but they weren't getting the job done on
the basalt. I tried to retreat, but I was greasing
out of the finger jams so badly I realized that
the safest option was to go for the top. By now I
was dripping sweat all over the rock and getting
that "I wish I wasn't here right now" feeling. I
knew my best chance was to ditch my Nikes, so
I reached down one hand at a time to untie my
double-knotted shoes. After a few tense, contorted
minutes, I kicked my clunky shoes into the boulder field below. With nothing but socks on my
feet, I stemmed and manteled to the top, embar-
rassed, but glad to be alive.*

Barely noticed against the backdrop of
towering walls, the basalt rimrock lining
the Crooked River gets little respect. Most
climbers don't even give these puny cliffs a
second glance, though they provide a pleasant alternative to Smith's more crowded
areas. While there isn't much to capture the
attention of the elite climber—only a couple
lines extend into the 5.13 grade—everyone
else can find something of interest. For

beginners and classes, the basalt provides a
perfect skill-building opportunity, with good
rock and easily arranged topropes. And no
one complains about the shortest approaches
at Smith Rock.

Of the miles of rimrock along the
Crooked River, only two sections, on opposite sides of the river, contain a significant
collection of routes. The first grouping of
broken rimrock, known collectively as the
Practice Area, stretches from north of the
campground to beyond the turnaround parking area. By far the best section of rim here
is the Northern Point. A flat two-minute
approach makes this Smith's most accessible
crag. The second rimrock cliff, the Student
Wall, sits across the river slightly upstream
from the Northern Point. This collection of
attractive cracks on weathered basalt features
the highest quality rimrock at Smith.

The first recorded exploration of the
Student Wall occurred in 1957, as a rock
climbing practice outing curiously appeared
on the Mazama schedule. No one knows
what they climbed, but these were likely
the first routes at Smith not ending on a
summit. Throughout the 1960s the convenient location below the canal access road
attracted anonymous climbers, though first
ascent information went entirely unrecorded.
Perhaps climbers of the day felt that these
short routes didn't deserve the formality of
a name. This changed in 1971 when Del
Young freed two difficult cracks. His ascent

of *Theseus* (5.10c) matched the highest level at Smith Rock, while *Minotaur* (5.11a), a Yosemite-style tips crack, was Smith's first 5.11. These routes deserved testpiece status, but the prevailing attitude of the day— "basalt routes don't really count"—denied Young his rightful place in Smith history for decades. The Northern Point received even less attention; after Wayne Arrington pioneered most of the traditional cracks in the mid-1970s, few climbers visited.

In the early 1990s two events finally brought greater attention to Smith rimrock. First, Jeff Frizzell and Chip Brejc bolted several high-quality sport routes on the Northern Point and Student Wall. Second, the first edition of this book came out—for the first time names and grades appeared in a guide. Within a few years the popularity of the rimrock increased dramatically. The best ascents came in 1993 when Mark Huth freed *Havana Smack* and *The Heathen* (both 5.13a) on the Northern Point.

Although most lines are easily led, many climbers prefer a toprope. Anchors along the top of the rim provide simple access to the most popular routes, including every sport climb. Less popular routes aren't as easily equipped with a toprope, though juniper trees provide solid anchors. Always bring an extra junk rope, as the trees sit far back from the rim.

PRACTICE AREA

The basalt rimrock of the Practice Area stretches for nearly a mile, starting north of the campground and ending far upstream at the start of the columnar basalt of the Lower Gorge. The rock doesn't match the quality of the Student Wall, let alone the Gorge, but it's more solid than much of the tuff. The first three cliffs—Lost Crag, Hidden Wall, and Overlook Crag—offer few options, but good routes pack the Northern Point.

Lost Crag

The first cliff of any consequence sits atop the hillside upstream from Rope De Dope Rock. Approach via the gravel-covered sightseers' path heading west from the southern end of the first parking lot. After strolling 150 yards, veer right off the trail to a lower shelf and skirt along the base of the cliff.

A unique chasm behind the rim provides several beginning toprope problems. The best section lies 50 feet west of the bolted routes. The aesthetics aren't pleasant, but anyone willing to climb in a graffiti-littered pit will find several short cracks ranging from 5.6 to 5.9. The easiest approach hikes along the top to the end of the rift and tunnels through a pile of blocks.

1. Lost in Montana (5.9) ★★ No topo. 6 bolts. The left of two routes starts next to a jumbled crack and veers right on incut edges to an easier jamming finish. Expect good rock, fun moves, and plenty of bolts.

2. Laid-Back Screaming (5.11a) ★ No topo. 5 bolts. A bolted off-width rises above a pile of sand around the corner right of *Lost in Montana*. Fear not—a strenuous liebacking crux completely avoids the indignity of flailing up the 6-inch crack. Easier jugs and hand jams lead to the anchor chains.

Hidden Wall

This puny crag sports a single route reached after Smith's shortest approach. There are other untouched lines here, though they aren't especially eye-catching. Approach via a paved path from the final day-use parking area before the turnaround. After walking 100 feet, cut downhill along a fence to the base of the wall; allow sixty to ninety seconds each way, depending on weather conditions and fitness.

3. Soft Asylum (5.12b) ★★ No topo. 5 bolts. A forgotten but worthwhile route powers up an overhanging arête rising above a massive boulder. Start with insecure stems and crank through a crux blending small pockets, crimps, and slaps.

Overlook Crag

With Red Wall dominating the view to the west and the Monument towering to the north, the turnaround parking area makes a popular scenic stop for anyone visiting Smith Rock. The insignificant cliff immediately below the viewpoint is the Overlook Crag. Apart from a challenging toprope problem, there's no reason to visit. Approach by hiking down the south side and boulder hopping upstream through a scattering of tourist-tossed litter to the following routes.

4. Flicker Flash (5.10a) ★ No topo. Gear to 3 inches. The disappointing first line on the broken rimrock jams a right-leaning hand crack rising above a pile of boulders. It's short, loose, and unaesthetic, but you might impress sightseers when you pull over the top.

5. Flash in the Pan (5.11b) ★ No topo. TR. Immediately left of *Flicker Flash* are parallel right-leaning seams. The tricky right crack succumbs to short-lived liebacks, stems, and edges.

6. Lightning (5.11a) ★ No topo. TR. Strenuous liebacks, finger jams, and high steps polish off the left of parallel mini-seams. Finish with a fight through sagebrush guarding the top.

7. Rambo Roof (5.12b) ★★★ No topo. TR. The best section of the Overlook Crag is about 100 feet upstream from the preceding routes. The *Rambo Roof* rises above a large pyramid block. The wimp-proof crux comes right at the start, dead-hanging a distinctive detached stone and a flaring jam with feet bicycling in the air. With no convenient anchor on top, few climbers go through the hassle of setting a toprope.

8. Project (5.12?) No topo. Left of *Rambo Roof* rises a promising-looking arête sporting a few bolt holes. Surprisingly, it still awaits a first ascent.

The Northern Point

Smith's most accessible climbing area overlooks the Monument and the northern bend of the Crooked River. Here the scattered sections of jumbled rimrock finally consolidate into a cliff offering dozens of short sport and traditional routes. Numerous anchors atop the cliff make toproping easy for anyone unsure of their basalt climbing skills. Since almost every route faces north, the Point makes a fine afternoon destination on a hot day.

To approach the crag from the turnaround parking area, hike north toward the Monument along a well-worn path.

Continue to the northern rim and peer over the edge, looking upstream for a large, weathered snag leaning against the wall. Slightly downstream from this snag is a break in the rimrock; an easy third-class scramble down a jumbled chimney leads to the base of the crag. The chimney isn't difficult, but beginners and classes sometimes prefer eliminating any degree of risk by veering left into the canyon on the approach hike. At the first switchback, hike uphill past a few boulders to the base of the downriver routes. If using this approach, the downriver routes will be in reverse order.

Downriver Routes

Moving downstream from the approach chimney are the least impressive lines on the Northern Point. Most of these routes are safely led, though climbers usually arrange a toprope.

9. Greenhouse (5.8 X) ★ Gear to 2 inches. Much better toproped than led, this pint-size route starts above blocks right of the approach chimney. Pull past an energetic bulge on moss-covered ledges and master a crux face move at the top.

10. Jersey Shore (5.7) ★★ Gear to 2.5 inches. The first crack right of the approach chimney cuts around the left side of a small fin. After an entertaining lieback clears a bulge, thin jams end at a crux mantel.

10a. Rossi's Variation (5.8 R) ★ Gear to 2.5 inches. An awkward, poorly protected variant climbs around the right side of the fin.

11. Lean Cuisine (5.6) ★★ Gear to 3 inches. Next in line beyond *Jersey Shore* are under-

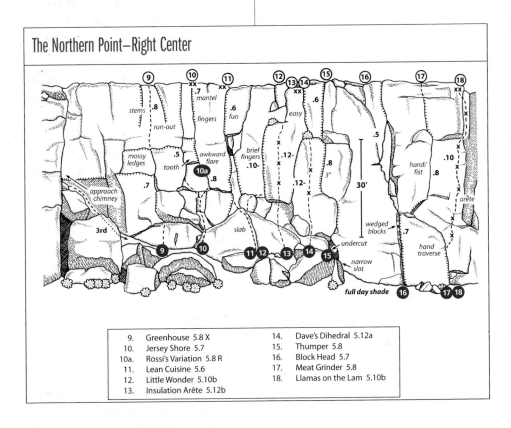

The Northern Point—Right Center

9.	Greenhouse 5.8 X
10.	Jersey Shore 5.7
10a.	Rossi's Variation 5.8 R
11.	Lean Cuisine 5.6
12.	Little Wonder 5.10b
13.	Insulation Arête 5.12b
14.	Dave's Dihedral 5.12a
15.	Thumper 5.8
16.	Block Head 5.7
17.	Meat Grinder 5.8
18.	Llamas on the Lam 5.10b

size, left-leaning double cracks. Despite appearances, expect charming stems and jams on good rock.

12. Little Wonder (5.10b) ★★ Gear to 0.75 inch. Although laughably short, this thin crack in a shallow open book is no pushover. Start atop a block right of a broken left-leaning crack and jam 15 desperate feet to easy climbing.

13. Insulation Arête (5.12b) ★★ Mixed to 2 inches. Short parallel sport lines ascend arêtes on either side of an inside corner. Begin with a crux bouldering sequence past three bolts and finish with easy trad climbing.

14. Dave's Dihedral (5.12a) ★★ Mixed to 2 inches. The right of parallel sport routes ascends past two bolts to a simple traditional ending. Lower from chains below the top of the cliff.

15. Thumper (5.8) ★★ Gear to 3 inches. Exciting liebacks mixed with hand jams tame this appealing line. Begin by stepping off a boulder across a void to a small corner and hand traverse left to the base of a vertical crack.

16. Block Head (5.7) ★ Gear to 3 inches. Downhill a few feet beyond *Thumper* lurks a fractured corner. After cranking on wedged blocks at the start, lieback around an easier bulge to the top.

17. Meat Grinder (5.8) ★★ Gear to 3.5 inches. An arching hand traverse at the start distinguishes this energetic route. Make an awkward exit move, then jam, stem, and lieback the finishing fist crack.

18. Llamas on the Lam (5.10b) ★★ 6 bolts. This short sport route ascends the prominent arête left of a break in the cliff line. Delicate moves on great rock give way to stems just below the top.

19. Double Time (5.7) ★ Gear to 2.5 inches. An obvious weakness splits the rimrock beyond a sharp arête. After starting with a clean jam crack, scramble into the slot. *Double Time* avoids the simple chimney by cutting right and stemming to a crux mantel.

20. Devil's Delight (5.9 R) ★ Gear to 4 inches. This overhanging, block-filled wide crack rises around the corner right of a break in the rimrock. Scramble to a ledge and tempt fate by cranking on rattling blocks wedged in the crack.

21. Swan Song (5.10b) ★★ Gear to 2 inches. Flanked by wide cracks, *Swan Song* jams a strenuous crack splitting a short wall. Unfortunately, a detached block at the crux takes some of the fun away.

22. Big Bad Wolf (5.10d) ★ Gear to 3 inches. A killer block plugging this leaning crack disappeared long ago. Today the moves entering the awkward flare are safe, but harder.

23. Microcosm (5.11b) ★★ 4 bolts. A technical sport route sits a few feet right of *Big Bad Wolf*. After an insecure side-pulling crux, the climbing eases until a tough stemming finish.

24. Jiminy Cricket (5.9) ★★ Gear to 2 inches. This highly varied crack rises left of a large boulder, about 15 feet right of *Microcosm*. Somehow, in the course of 30 feet, it includes finger/hand jams, face moves, stems, and liebacks.

25. Phantom (5.10a) ★ Gear to 4 inches. Beyond huge blocks obstructing the path, a short wide crack near the top of the cliff comes into view. Begin with an easy flare before launching into an intimidating off-width. If spooked, step left to an easy escape.

26. A Little Twisted (5.11a) ★★ 5 bolts. An entertaining sport route follows bolts left

The Northern Point–Right Side

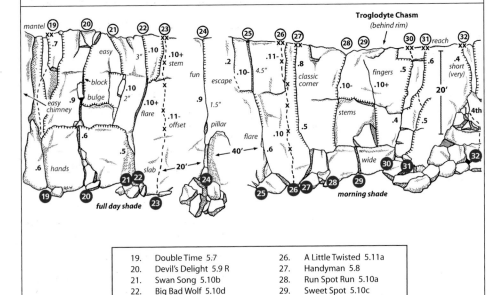

19.	Double Time 5.7	26.	A Little Twisted 5.11a
20.	Devil's Delight 5.9 R	27.	Handyman 5.8
21.	Swan Song 5.10b	28.	Run Spot Run 5.10a
22.	Big Bad Wolf 5.10d	29.	Sweet Spot 5.10c
23.	Microcosm 5.11b	30.	Pumpkin Patch 5.5
24.	Jiminy Cricket 5.9	31.	Jurassic Park 5.6
25.	Phantom 5.10a	32.	Winnie the Pooh 5.4

of an obvious inside corner. A tough bouldering start leads to crux stems just below the anchor.

27. Handyman (5.8) ★★★ Gear to 2.5 inches. The best easy lead on the Northern Point follows an attractive crack set in a shallow dihedral. Big face holds slash the difficulty as delightful stems and jams give way to a crux finish. An anchor at the top allows easy toproping.

28. Run Spot Run (5.10a) ★ Gear to 2.5 inches. A short right-facing corner cuts over a mini-roof right of *Handyman*. After an easy stemming start, the only hard moves jam past the roof.

29. Sweet Spot (5.10c) ★★ Gear to 1.5 inches. This tricky problem jams a short diagonal crack above a small roof. Reach the starting slots by balancing atop an obvious

triangular block. The pull around the roof comes easily, but the crux hits hard on the final moves.

30. Pumpkin Patch (5.5) ★ Gear to 3.5 inches. Nearing the end of the rimrock, a low-angle crack system splits a patch of orange rock right of *Sweet Spot*. An easy scramble leads to a single muscle move cutting left at the top.

31. Jurassic Park (5.6) ★ Gear to 3.5 inches. A section of jumbled rock a few feet right of *Pumpkin Patch* was a dubious sport route until the bolts mysteriously disappeared. Today it's a trad route, with the only tricky move coming at a vertical section near the top.

32. Winnie the Pooh (5.4) ★ Gear to 3 inches. The last route before the rimrock disappears follows a very short corner plugged by a block. The anchor on top makes it a fine toprope exercise for beginners and kids.

Troglodyte Chasm

A narrow, 20-foot-deep crevice behind the preceding routes provides fun for classes, kids, and first-timers. Unlike a similar formation behind the Lost Crag, the walls here are free of graffiti. Climbers seeking anonymity can totally disappear from view in the chasm while practicing cracks and chimneys. The four sets of anchors recently disappeared, so bring a few nuts along.

Upriver Routes

The upriver routes are longer and steeper, with the best collection of sport climbs on Smith rimrock. After scrambling down the third-class approach chimney, walk toward the massive snag leaning against the rimrock.

33. Who Pudding (5.8 R) ★ Gear to 2.5 inches. Near the upstream exit of the approach chimney are two puny lines not worth bothering with. The first route starts below a small inside corner plugged by a miniature spike. A few jams mixed with good jugs tame the right-leaning crack.

33a. Who Hash (5.8 R) ★ Gear to 2.5 inches. The second of two insignificant routes follows the line of least resistance left of *Who Pudding*. After an awkward crux cranks past a seemingly detached block, cut right and finish on easier rock.

34. Moni's Line (5.7) ★★ Gear to 2.5 inches. Directly under the tip of a massive leaning snag is Smith's only route with a memorial plaque. Traverse in from the right and hand

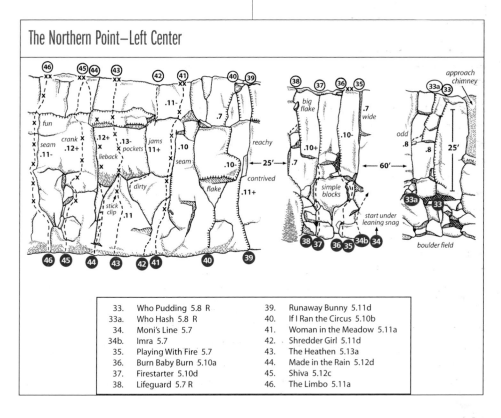

The Northern Point—Left Center

33.	Who Pudding 5.8 R	39.	Runaway Bunny 5.11d
33a.	Who Hash 5.8 R	40.	If I Ran the Circus 5.10b
34.	Moni's Line 5.7	41.	Woman in the Meadow 5.11a
34b.	Imra 5.7	42.	Shredder Girl 5.11d
35.	Playing With Fire 5.7	43.	The Heathen 5.13a
36.	Burn Baby Burn 5.10a	44.	Made in the Rain 5.12d
37.	Firestarter 5.10d	45.	Shiva 5.12c
38.	Lifeguard 5.7 R	46.	The Limbo 5.11a

jam over a bulge. Step past the marble slab and continue to an anchor.

34a. It's All About Me (5.10a) ★★ No topo. Gear to 2.5 inches. Instead of traversing left at the start of *Moni's Line*, follow deceptively tricky side pulls and stems directly above. Almost everyone opts for a toprope from bolts on the rim.

34b. Imra (5.7) ★★ Gear to 3 inches. Start downhill and left of *Moni's Line* and crank through a small flake roof at the start. Easy scrambling leads to a thin hand crux at the top.

35. Playing With Fire (5.7) ★★ Gear to 4 inches. Just past the leaning snag are several worthwhile cracks. The first line stems and liebacks a surprisingly easy off-width.

36. Burn Baby Burn (5.10a) ★★★ Gear to 2.5 inches. Around the corner left of the obvious wide crack rises a shallow dihedral. Start with a simple scramble to a hole, then lieback and jam the high-quality crux to the top.

37. Firestarter (5.10d) ★★ Gear to 2 inches. The left of three parallel cracks is by far the most challenging. If you miss the critical face holds past the undercling at the crux, you'll probably plummet.

38. Lifeguard (5.7 R) ★ Gear to 2.5 inches. This moderate climb follows an easy line left of three attractive cracks. Start behind a juniper tree and scramble to a deceptive crux that catches unwary climbers off guard. Say a prayer and pull softly around a massive block at the top.

39. Runaway Bunny (5.11d) ★★ Gear to 2 inches. Slightly right of a roof sits a contrived route in a shallow corner. After desperate moves on polished rock, finish with long stretches between positive holds. Purists

totally ignore the hand crack only inches to the left.

40. If I Ran the Circus (5.10b) ★★★ Gear to 3 inches. Among the best and most obvious lines on the Northern Point is this undercling around a roof. Start with a few jams up an inverted triangular block and launch into energetic moves past the roof to a liebacking crux.

41. Woman in the Meadow (5.11a) ★★★ 5 bolts. Far better than it looks, this enjoyable line follows a gray seam splitting the face. It makes a good warm-up for the harder climbs, as big holds at the start gradually shrink to a crux move just below the anchor.

42. Shredder Girl (5.11d) ★★ Gear to 2.5 inches. A meandering trad route follows the path of least resistance left of *Woman in the Meadow*. The sandy rock isn't perfect at the start, but the moves are strenuous and enjoyable. Dinky wires protect the crux at the start—the level eases and the gear improves on the dash to the rim.

43. The Heathen (5.13a) ★★★ 5 bolts. The hardest route on Smith rimrock attacks the attractive wall rising above a sweeping triangle. Stick-clip the first bolt and crank through powerful moves to a low-percentage dynamic near the top. Finish with a sketchy mantel.

44. Made in the Rain (5.12d) ★★ 3 bolts (optional gear to 1 inch). An unusually physical route follows the overhanging dihedral left of *The Heathen*. Powerful liebacks and jams lead to face holds pulling around a roof. If you fall clipping the last bolt, you might hit the deck.

45. Shiva (5.12c) ★★★ 4 bolts (optional gear to 1 inch). To the left of *Made in the Rain* rises a bolted line on a rounded bulge. It

Ed Friesen on *The Heathen.* BEN MOON

resisted several attempts until an anonymous person improved a critical pocket. Awkward moves low give way to a potent crux reach near the top. Some climbers prefer placing a piece of gear on the final moves to the top.

46. The Limbo (5.11a) ★★★ 6 bolts. Beyond the steepest section of rimrock, the cliff returns to a more tolerable angle. A high-quality sport route follows a leaning seam, blending edges, side pulls, and jams.

47. Dat Be Up Da Butt, Bob (5.11c) ★★ 5 bolts. Just right of an unmistakable roof crack sits a line of cold shuts. The crux cranks through crimps cutting right around a corner before giving way to a much easier finish. Rumor has it the name comes from a contestant's answer to a question once asked on the *Newlywed Game,* "What's the strangest place you've had sex with your husband?"

48. Hang it Loose (5.10b) ★★ Gear to 3 inches. This flaring roof crack was one of the earliest routes on the Northern Point. After romping up a slab-plugged corner, crank the memorable roof on great holds. The deceptive crux comes with a tricky high-step safely protected by a new bolt.

49. Lamoidian Power Dance (5.11b) ★★ 6 bolts. Left of *Hang it Loose* rises a one-move-wonder of a sport route. The reach-dependent crux underclings past a roof—it might seem easier or harder depending on your wingspan.

50. Morning Dew (5.9) ★★ Gear to 2 inches. A left-leaning crack follows an awkward corner to a face-climbing finish. Bolts protected early ascents, but they disappeared long ago. Most climbers prefer toproping instead of fiddling with tiny wires at the crux.

51. Metamorphic Dawning (5.10c) ★★ 7 bolts. This enjoyable sport route begins left of the bolt line with a bouldering crux and ends with crimpy edges on the bulge near the top. The first ascent stayed left at the start, while most climbers finessed easier moves to the right. A broken flake now forces everyone to tackle the original start.

51a. Ledges (5.10c) ★★ TR. A fun toprope problem starts with *Metamorphic Dawning* and wanders up edges and ledges to the right. Use the easily accessible anchors atop *Morning Dew.*

52. Sidewinder (5.11a) ★★ Gear to 2.5 inches. Traditional climbers might enjoy this strenuous crack. Expect good rock with locking jams over a bulge leading to crux face moves protected by wires.

53. Jungle Fever (5.11b) ★★ 5 bolts. This bolted seam starts up a pillar and follows pumping liebacks and edges to a crux

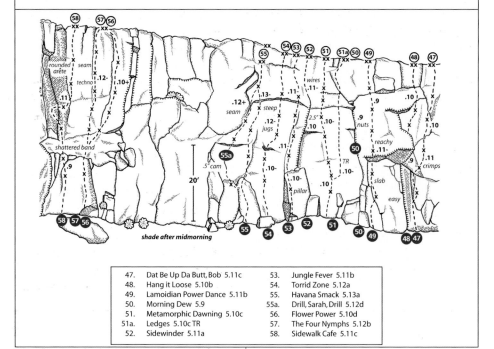

47.	Dat Be Up Da Butt, Bob 5.11c	53.	Jungle Fever 5.11b
48.	Hang it Loose 5.10b	54.	Torrid Zone 5.12a
49.	Lamoidian Power Dance 5.11b	55.	Havana Smack 5.13a
50.	Morning Dew 5.9	55a.	Drill, Sarah, Drill 5.12d
51.	Metamorphic Dawning 5.10c	56.	Flower Power 5.10d
51a.	Ledges 5.10c TR	57.	The Four Nymphs 5.12b
52.	Sidewinder 5.11a	58.	Sidewalk Cafe 5.11c

reach past the final bulge. The original line cranked directly, but most climbers cut left at the top.

54. Torrid Zone (5.12a) ★★★ 5 bolts. Gym-rats love this steep wall of jugs. Unlike the usual basalt finesse routes, technique is optional on the *Torrid Zone*—strength is not.

55. Havana Smack (5.13a) ★★★ 4 bolts. This high-quality route attacks the eye-catching overhang left of *Torrid Zone*. Sustained, sequential moves lead to an off-balance deadpoint crux just below the last bolt.

55a. Drill, Sarah, Drill (5.12d) ★★★ 4 bolts (optional gear to 2 inches). After an easy start, crank powerful moves up a steep right-leaning seam. Veer right, clip the final bolt on *Havana Smack,* and muscle to the anchor.

56. Flower Power (5.10d) ★★ 5 bolts. About 50 feet beyond *Havana Smack* are a few large, flat-topped boulders at the base of the rim-rock. Above are the final three climbs on the Northern Point. The right route starts with an arête and cuts right through fractured rock to crux stems and edges in a shallow corner.

57. The Four Nymphs (5.12b) ★★ 6 bolts. The center route starts with the same arête as *Flower Power* but attacks the seam directly above. Sustained, insecure moves on sloping holds and smears appeal only to technical wizards.

58. Sidewalk Café (5.11c) ★★ 6 bolts. A short fingertip traverse to a rounded arête highlights the last route on the Northern Point. Start with easy shattered jugs leading into a corner and commit right to the crux moves.

STUDENT WALL

Across the river upstream from the Northern Point stretches the high-quality, weathered basalt of the Student Wall. A popular destination with classes for the past fifty years, this crag contains Smith's finest rimrock climbing. Since the entire crag faces west, it makes a good morning choice in the summer and an afternoon destination on a sunny winter day. The shortest approach cuts across the river upstream from the Northern Point and hikes uphill to the base. During high-river conditions this crossing becomes extremely dangerous. Instead, hike around the bend upstream from the bridge below Picnic Lunch Wall. Anyone visiting with a class of students should always use the longer approach.

Reproductive Wall

The left side of the crag contains the longest routes on the Student Wall. It doesn't receive nearly as much attention as the Textbooks to the right, despite some fine crack lines. The few bolted routes are the best on the entire Student Wall. The following climbs start on the upper left side and continue in order moving right along the base.

59. Spring Break (5.5) ★ Gear to 3 inches. The easiest route on the wall follows a short left-facing corner on the far left side. Begin by scrambling up simple boulders and finish with fun jams and stems.

60. Flunked Out (5.6) ★★ Gear to 3 inches. This simple climb wanders up the easiest path above a band of reddish dirt at the base

Reproductive Wall–Left Side

59.	Spring Break 5.5	63.	Frat Jerks 5.8
60.	Flunked Out 5.6	64.	Bonfire 5.8
61.	Cram Session 5.8	65.	Passing Grade 5.9
61a.	Cram Variant 5.10c	66.	Puppet Master 5.11a TR
62.	Fist Fight 5.8	67.	Pop Quiz 5.11c

of the cliff. After a crux traverse moving right from the starting corner, simple rock leads to the top.

61. Cram Session (5.8) ★ Gear to 2.5 inches. Several parallel jam cracks split the left portion of Reproductive Wall. The left crack begins with a water-worn groove and jams around the left side of a hanging column to jugs.

61a. Cram Variant (5.10c) ★★ Gear to 2.5 inches. A harder option steps right, jamming directly over a small roof formed by a hanging column.

62. Fist Fight (5.8) ★★ Gear to 2.5 inches. The neighbor to *Cram Session* shares the same start but jams and liebacks a higher-quality hand crack to the right.

63. Frat Jerks (5.8) ★★ Gear to 4 inches. A wide crack set in a right-facing corner looks intimidating, but stems and liebacks avoid any unpleasantness. Begin with a simple trough directly below the chockstone-plugged crack.

64. Bonfire (5.8) ★★ Gear to 3.5 inches. Tucked in a left-facing corner right of *Frat Jerks* is an appealing line. After a simple scramble, fun jams lead to a short wide section.

65. Passing Grade (5.9) ★★★ Mixed to 3 inches. One of the better routes on the crag starts at yellow splotches of lichen and jams a short, attractive crack. Edges lead past two bolts to an enjoyable flurry of jams up a left-facing dihedral.

66. Puppet Master (5.11a) ★★★ TR. If bolted, this meandering seam would be one of the best sport routes on Smith rimrock. As a toprope problem it sees very few attempts. After crux liebacks and awkward edges at the start, the difficulties ease and the fun begins on the delightful finish. Start

downhill and around the corner right of several parallel cracks.

67. Pop Quiz (5.11c) ★★ Gear to 3 inches. The most imposing crack on the Reproductive Wall is this unmistakable arch. Unprepared climbers flunk out on the contorted thin hand jams at the start.

68. Fight Song (5.10a) ★★★ Gear to 2 inches. Left of a gray bolted wall rises this exceptional flake crack. An awkward start up a short right-leaning corner gives way to exciting jams and liebacks at the crux.

68a. Sorority Girl (5.12b) ★★★ Gear to 2 inches. After cruising through the crux jams of *Fight Song,* step right to a diagonal seam protected by small wires. Technical moves protected by physical wire placements make it the most difficult line on the Student Wall.

69. Embryonic (5.11d) ★★★ 9 bolts. The center of the Reproductive Wall offers two high-quality sport climbs. The left route starts with a bolted crack and attacks a pocketed wall before pulling over a sequential bulge near the top.

70. Drilling Zona (5.11c) ★★★★ 9 bolts. The best face route on Smith rimrock attacks the striking buttress in the center of the wall. Start up the same crack as *Embryonic* but veer right on fun pockets until a crux move gains the arête. Exciting moves on big holds lead to a second crux just below the anchors.

70a. Project (5.13?) A direct start to *Drilling Zona* could someday be the hardest line on the Student Wall. Start with jumbled rock to a roof and levitate 20 feet up a featureless dihedral before joining the regular line.

71. Class Dismissed (5.12a) ★★ Mixed to 1 inch. For twenty-seven years this attractive tips crack was the hardest route on

Reproductive Wall–Right Side

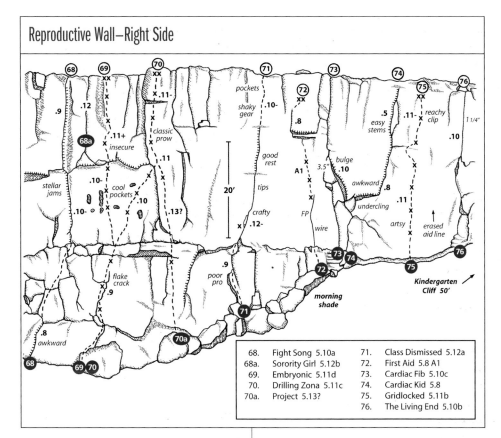

68.	Fight Song 5.10a	71.	Class Dismissed 5.12a
68a.	Sorority Girl 5.12b	72.	First Aid 5.8 A1
69.	Embryonic 5.11d	73.	Cardiac Fib 5.10c
70.	Drilling Zona 5.11c	74.	Cardiac Kid 5.8
70a.	Project 5.13?	75.	Gridlocked 5.11b
		76.	The Living End 5.10b

the Student Wall. Today it has to settle for second place. Begin with heavily featured, poorly protected rimrock leading to a crux lieback past a bolt. Most sport climbers will flail on the technical jams above.

72. First Aid (5.8 A1) ★★ Clean to 2.5 inches. A line of bolts and fixed pins garnish the wall right of *Class Dismissed*. It makes a good place to sample aid climbing, but expect strenuous free moves pulling around the finishing roof. Lower off from bolts below the rim.

73. Cardiac Fib (5.10c) ★★ Gear to 3.5 inches. An overhanging crack splits the inside corner right of the *First Aid* bolt line. After jamming around a heart-stopping bulge, cruise easier rock to the top.

74. Cardiac Kid (5.8) ★★ Gear to 3 inches. This peculiar line starts below *Cardiac Fib* and underclings right to an annoyingly awkward crux exiting a small roof. Finish with simple stemming in a corner.

75. Gridlocked (5.11b) ★★★ 6 bolts. The flat face on the right side of Reproductive Wall once sported a grid pattern of dozens of quarter-inch studs. Today the offensive bolts are gone, replaced by a single sport route. The highly technical sequence isn't strenuous in the slightest degree, but the moves are delicate and insecure from bottom to top.

76. The Living End (5.10b) ★★ Gear to 2 inches. The last climb of any consequence on Reproductive Wall follows humbling inch-and-a-quarter jams rising above a boulder-plugged slot.

Kindergarten Cliff

The 200-foot midsection of the Student Wall contains dozens of options, from simple scrambles to tough boulder problems. Ranging from 15 to 25 feet high, this puny cliff is too short for legitimate routes and too high for safe bouldering. You'll find traverse potential, high-ball boulder problems, and the following route on the right side of the wall.

77. Kindergarten Crack (5.5) ★★ Gear to 2 inches. With unprotectable seams splitting most of the miniature corners of the Kindergarten Cliff, a fun jam crack provides the only beginner-level route on the wall. You can arrange a toprope from a cluster of three bolts on the rim.

The Textbooks

The right side of the Student Wall contains the finest selection of moderate cracks on Smith rimrock. Perfect basalt, varied

climbing, and convenient anchors make it a wonderful place to develop crack climbing skills; most routes protect easily, though almost everyone takes out a toprope. The Textbooks start right of a fourth-class descent chimney, just as the trail along the base drops downhill.

78. Cheat Sheet (5.11b) ★★ Gear to 2.5 inches. Ten feet right of a break in the rimrock sits this short thin crack beginning with a mini right-facing corner. Expect potent liebacks and edges along with long reaches between flaring jams.

79. The Fire Within (5.11b) ★★ Gear to 2.5 inches. Left of an obvious inside corner sits a serious-looking route. Fortunately, the moves getting to the only bolt aren't difficult and the finishing crack protects easily.

80. School's Out (5.7) ★★ Gear to 3 inches. Double cracks split the first inside corner on the left side of the Textbooks. Most climb-

Student Wall–The Textbooks–Left Side

77. Kindergarten Crack 5.5	84. Rage 5.7
78. Cheat Sheet 5.11b	85. Dunce Cap 5.8 R
79. The Fire Within 5.11b	86. Boys Visit Charm School 5.10b
80. School's Out 5.7	87. Bad Manners 5.7
81. Chalkboard 5.10c	88. Panic Seizure 5.11b
82. Prom Night 5.7	89. Little Black Sambo 5.9 X
83. Doorknob People 5.7	90. Global Motion 5.10b
83a. Slam Dance 5.8	91. Homecoming Queen 5.7

ers stem across to the off-width on the right, though jamming either crack separately provides more of a challenge (5.10a left, 5.8 right).

81. Chalkboard (5.10c) ★★ 3 bolts. The Textbooks' only pure sport route follows good holds on the right wall of the *School's Out* dihedral. Good rock, fun moves, and reassuring bolts provide a fine diversion from the line of jam cracks.

82. Prom Night (5.7) ★★ Gear to 1.5 inches. This agreeable route follows locking finger jams up a shallow corner, aided by huge face holds. Begin with a boulder move onto a large square ledge.

83. Doorknob People (5.7) ★★ Gear to 3 inches. An ominous-looking chimney in a deep-set corner gets little attention, though the moves aren't bad. Stems and jams exit a flaring crux slot just below the top.

83a. Slam Dance (5.8) ★ Gear to 3 inches. Don't be lured by a hand traverse midway up *Doorknob People*. The cleaner rock doesn't make up for the annoying struggle entering the finishing groove.

84. Rage (5.7) ★★ Gear to 1.5 inches. A few feet right of the *Doorknob People* chimney are two routes sharing the same start in a very short arch. The easier left crack follows face holds and jams in a shallow right-facing corner.

85. Dunce Cap (5.8 R) ★★ Gear to 1 inch. After starting up *Rage,* continue up a seam to scary face moves at the finish. It makes a fun toprope problem but a dangerous lead for any 5.8 climber.

86. Boys Visit Charm School (5.10b) ★★ Mixed to 1.5 inches. This short, bolted wall begins with a tricky move off a boulder. After pulling onto a big ledge, finish with much easier thin hand jams in a small corner.

87. Bad Manners (5.7) ★★ Gear to 3.5 inches. An obvious chimney slices through the rimrock immediately left of a gray wall. Despite its slovenly appearance, the stems and knobs in the flaring slot aren't bad.

88. Panic Seizure (5.11b) ★ Gear to 3.5 inches. The Textbooks are exceptionally solid except for this dirty section of gray rock. An unappetizing route plows around a bulging sand dune on hand jams to a solid finish. The confusing crux comes near the top, with desperate edges and side pulls above a crucial one-finger pocket.

89. Little Black Sambo (5.9 X) ★★ Gear to 1 inch. Distinguished by a big oblong hole 10 feet off the ground, this sparsely protected route follows a leaning crack above a bouldering start.

90. Global Motion (5.10b) ★★★ Gear to 3 inches. Shortly before a large boulder blocks the path, a right-leaning crack splits the rimrock. The high-quality crux reaches between good slots in the starting corner.

91. Homecoming Queen (5.7) ★★ Gear to 2 inches. Beyond a massive block at the base of the cliff lurks a crack plugged by an angular block. After a short lieback enters a slot, step past the loose flake to a crux finish up either of two cracks.

92. Silly Boy (5.10c) ★★★ Gear to 2.5 inches. Left of an unmistakable inside corner rises an attractive crack. A challenging undercling at the start leads to solid jams and liebacks. Above a ledge, choose between an easy finish to the left or a tougher direct line.

93. Heart Throb (5.7) ★★★ Gear to 3 inches. The most conspicuous route on the Textbooks is this short dihedral capped by a roof. A pleasant crack ends far too quickly at an anchor 30 feet off the

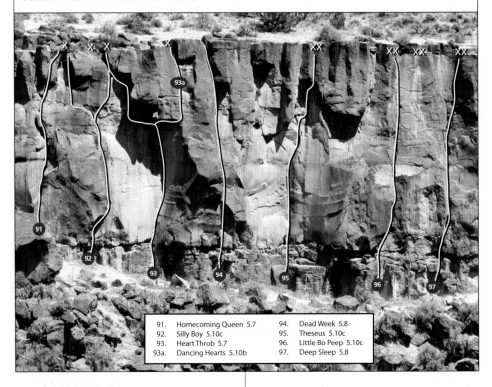

91.	Homecoming Queen 5.7	94.	Dead Week 5.8
92.	Silly Boy 5.10c	95.	Theseus 5.10c
93.	Heart Throb 5.7	96.	Little Bo Peep 5.10c
93a.	Dancing Hearts 5.10b	97.	Deep Sleep 5.8

ground. Many climbers lower off here, but the finish cuts left on jugs around an intimidating roof.

93a. Dancing Hearts (5.10b) ★★ Gear to 2 inches. An alternate finish underclings around the strenuous right side of the roof.

94. Dead Week (5.8) ★★ Gear to 3 inches. Ten feet right of *Heart Throb* sits a run-of-the-mill right-facing corner. Begin atop a small block and lieback to easier climbing.

95. Theseus (5.10c) ★★★ Gear to 2 inches. This demanding line helped boost standards in the early 1970s. Along with nearby *Minotaur,* it stood near the top level of Smith free climbing for several years. After storming the attractive crux finger crack, finish by cutting right past a fixed pin.

96. Little Bo Peep (5.10c) ★★★ Gear to 2.5 inches. Tough moves up a prominent right-leaning corner highlight this enjoyable crack. Cut right near the top when the holds disappear.

97. Deep Sleep (5.8) ★★★ Gear to 3 inches. A fun route jams a locking hand crack in a shallow corner right of *Little Bo Peep*. Finish by finessing solid face moves.

98. The Virgin Slayer (5.9) ★★★ Gear to 3.5 inches. The most impressive feature on the right side of the Textbooks is an imposing triangular roof capping a short right-facing corner. The easiest route weasels awkwardly left around the roof and jams an exquisite hand/finger crack.

99. Labyrinth (5.10b) ★★★ Gear to 3 inches. A burly undercling cuts right around an

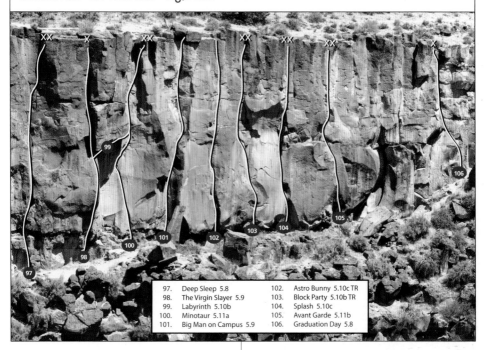

97.	Deep Sleep 5.8	102.	Astro Bunny 5.10c TR
98.	The Virgin Slayer 5.9	103.	Block Party 5.10b TR
99.	Labyrinth 5.10b	104.	Splash 5.10c
100.	Minotaur 5.11a	105.	Avant Garde 5.11b
101.	Big Man on Campus 5.9	106.	Graduation Day 5.8

intimidating roof to a strenuous exit. Finish with easier double cracks in a corner.

100. Minotaur (5.11a) ★★ Gear to 2 inches. A low-angle, leaning tips crack splits the smooth face right of *Labyrinth*. In 1971 this innocent-looking route became Smith's first 5.11. Sticky rubber helps with the insecure toe jams, but it still sees few clean leads.

101. Big Man on Campus (5.9) ★★★ Gear to 1 inch. Behind a tilted freestanding pillar sits this high-quality line. Start by squirming up a unique slot and execute tricky face moves to the top.

102. Astro Bunny (5.10c) ★★ TR. Right of a detached pillar rises a right-arching inside corner. After a crux of side pulls, thin jams, and stems, perplexing face moves finish to the rim.

103. Block Party (5.10b) ★★ TR. If someone pried off a killer block in the middle, this route would make a fine toprope problem. Start with a shallow groove and detour left around the flake, finishing with wonderful jugs.

104. Splash (5.10c) ★★ Gear to 2 inches. Tough thin hand jams in an offset corner highlight this attractive route. Move cautiously past loose blocks after the crux and follow moderate edges to the top.

105. Avant Garde (5.11b) ★★ Gear to 2 inches. The last route of any consequence on the right side of the Textbooks jams a parallel-sided finger crack right off the deck. Thin-crack masters hike the crux, but everyone else struggles.

106. Graduation Day (5.8) ★ Gear to 3 inches. Uphill around the corner 30 feet right of *Avant Garde* sits an inconsequential dihedral. Easy scrambling leads to stems just below the top.

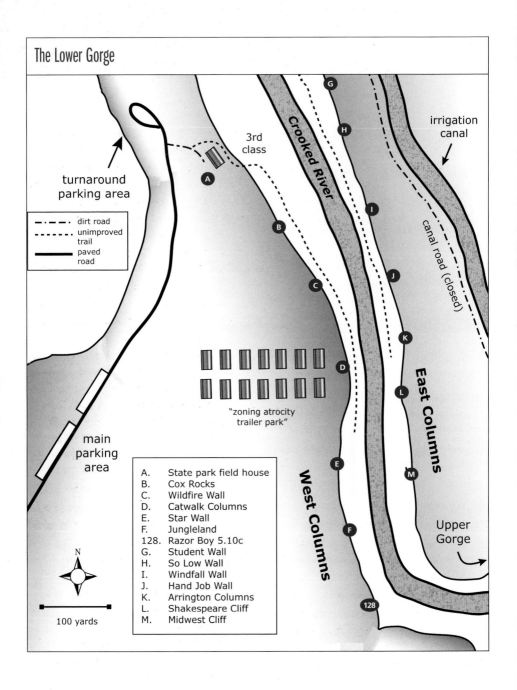

The Lower Gorge

turnaround
parking area

3rd
class

- - · - · dirt road
· · · · · · · · unimproved
         trail
─────── paved
         road

main
parking
area

N

100 yards

Crooked River

irrigation
canal

canal road (closed)

East Columns

West Columns

Upper
Gorge

"zoning atrocity
trailer park"

A.   State park field house
B.   Cox Rocks
C.   Wildfire Wall
D.   Catwalk Columns
E.   Star Wall
F.   Jungleland
128. Razor Boy 5.10c
G.   Student Wall
H.   So Low Wall
I.   Windfall Wall
J.   Hand Job Wall
K.   Arrington Columns
L.   Shakespeare Cliff
M.   Midwest Cliff

THE LOWER GORGE

Wayne Arrington thrived on climbing. He once told me that climbing was "an activity that has come to be a central pursuit in my life, one that has given me more satisfaction than any other activity I have encountered." Wayne made decisions in the moment. He wasn't easily excitable or given to emotions, and he exuded a quiet intensity. I remember him commenting on doing forty first ascents in the Lower Gorge, many of them solo. Many of these routes were subsequently done and claimed as first ascents by other climbers. In later years he told me that one of the reasons he never wrote anything down was to give other climbers the feeling of doing a first ascent.

Tom Rogers

Hidden in the canyon upstream from Smith's more famous climbs are the remarkable basalt columns of the Gorge. With over 300 routes ranging from 5.7 to 5.13c, the entire Gorge would be a respected climbing area in its own right. Combined with the cliffs of welded tuff, the columnar basalt brings Smith unmatched diversity. Although both rock types are volcanic in origin, they couldn't be more different. You won't find any nubbins or overhanging pocketed lines—instead the Gorge features traditional cracks, calf-burning stemming corners, delicate faces, and outrageous arêtes, with routes every 6 feet or so for hundreds of yards. The square-cut edges and wavy, textured ripples make even the blankest faces possible.

There are two sections of columnar basalt, separated by a 90-degree bend in the Crooked River—the mostly traditional Lower Gorge and the sport climber's paradise of the Upper Gorge (see chapter 14). As the rest of Smith becomes more of a sport crag each year, the Lower Gorge remains the domain of traditional climbers. Sport climbs account for less than 10 percent of the 220 routes and variants. These bolted lines add to the appeal of the area, but the elegant jam cracks set the Lower Gorge apart from everything else. Without rival they are the finest at Smith Rock.

Despite the quality, Gorge climbing isn't for everyone. The steepness and isolation of the routes, coupled with the boulder-hopping approach, make a very bad choice for beginners or classes. The better climbs start at 5.10, and many of the easier lines protect poorly. The rimrock of the Northern Point and the Student Wall (see chapter 12) provide a safer introduction to basalt for the novice. For experienced climbers the vertical routes require little in the way of physical prowess. Flexibility, creativity, footwork, and patience come into play more than strength—anyone relying on brute force will leave the Gorge frustrated and bewildered. While some feel that the basalt gets repetitive after awhile—since one column resembles another—others get so addicted to the intellectual moves they rarely venture elsewhere. For everyone the Gorge provides a fine departure from tendon-tweaking pockets.

Lower Gorge climbing requires more than mere technical mastery. Since most routes protect naturally, gear-placement skills are an essential key to success. The majority of these lines protect easily, though several of the more difficult routes are both technically demanding and tricky to protect. It's not easy stopping in the middle of a finesse move, feet smearing on nothing, while fiddling with a small wire—but it's just part of the game. A complete range of cams and wires suffice for most routes. Don't even consider venturing onto the harder traditional routes without the latest in high-tech gear. The newest ultra-small cams can sometimes turn the most serious old lines into routine leads.

Traditional and sport climbs coexist better in the Lower Gorge than anywhere else at Smith. While most bold lines on tuff long ago fell victim to retro-bolters, the routes in the Gorge are mostly unchanged from the days of the first ascents. Despite the temptations of the power drill, the overwhelming majority of Gorge climbers prefer leaving the older routes as they are. The only exception is the replacement of fixed pins. Rusted pegs placed twenty-five years ago still protect the cruxes of many of the older testpieces. Others fell out long ago. The freezing and thawing of the columnar joints inevitably loosens any fixed pin, making these routes potentially dangerous. Rather than replacing the old pins with new ones, it makes more sense to drill a bolt. Still, once climbers replace the suspect pins, the traditional lines—no matter how run-out—should be left as they are.

The earliest basalt climbers visited the Student Wall in the late 1950s, but it wasn't until the early seventies that climbers ventured into the Gorge. Wayne Arrington was the first of many climbers to become obsessed with Smith basalt, pioneering forty routes in the Lower Gorge alone. Trained as a helicopter pilot in Vietnam, and on the basalt cracks of Eugene's Skinners Butte Columns, he was perfectly suited to the early days of Gorge climbing. In a harrowing tour of duty where he was shot down six times, he learned to control his fears and emotions in the face of grave danger. The unprotected climbs in the Gorge required the same discipline, except now there wasn't anyone trying to shoot him out of the sky. In this environment Arrington thrived when most climbers withered. His most audacious route, *Titus* (5.10b), was typical of the climbs that built his reputation as Oregon's boldest climber. Before wide crack protection, the last placement was less than halfway up this 70-foot crack. Facing an unprotectable off-width, with the certainty of grounding out onto a razor-topped flake, retreat was the only sensible option. Arrington never hesitated and calmly ran it out to the top.

Although Arrington led the way, other climbers also explored the Gorge. Tom Rogers's *As You Like It* (5.10b), Mike Seeley's *Cruel Sister* (5.10b), and Jeff Thomas's *Blood Clot* (5.10b) were the best early ascents. The biggest breakthrough came in March of 1975, when Paul Landrum and Ken Currens settled for a week at Smith after getting washed out in Yosemite. Under rainy skies they boosted the standards of Gorge climbing with several first ascents, including *Wildfire* (5.10b), *Prometheus* (5.10b), and *Morning Star* (5.10c). After Jeff Thomas pioneered a 1.25-inch crack called *Original Sin* (5.10c), the Gorge contained more 5.10 routes than the rest of Smith combined.

Along with everything else at Smith, Gorge climbing really took off during the 1980s. Chris Grover's ascent of *On the Road* (5.11a) in 1980 marked the beginning

Chuck Buzzard, 1981.

arrival of R.P.s from Australia, the Gorge was the primary testing ground for three-cam-units and Sliders (the precursor of today's Ball Nuts), developed by a fledging local garage shop called Metolius.

Finally, a Redmond-based climber named Chuck Buzzard devoted himself to the basalt columns like no one before, pioneering more than sixty routes in three years. His climbs weren't the hardest of the time, but he was the first to realize the true potential of the Gorge. Rarely venturing elsewhere Buzzard painstakingly cleaned overgrown walls, hacked trails through the brush, and self-published "Basalt and Boulders," his cryptic guide to Central Oregon basalt. With his religion-based route names and lack of interest in Smith tuff, Buzzard never gained the full acceptance of many climbers of the era. But in retrospect he made a greater impact on Lower Gorge climbing than anyone else.

By the end of 1984, the traditional era of Gorge climbing came to a close. After the well-protected cracks fell, climbers turned to thinner seams protected by miniature wires. Watts's ascents of *Jonny and the Melonheads* and *Masquerade* (both 5.12b) marked the end of this high-risk evolution. With sport climbing gaining momentum on the tuff, the best climbers turned away from the increasingly serious ventures on basalt. Again, Gorge development might have floundered if not for the arrival of John Rich and his power drill.

Rich first made his mark with *Cry of the Gerbil* (5.12b) in 1986, but his biggest influence was bringing modern sport climbing to the Gorge. The shift to bolt-protected routes came without any controversy—the handful of critics no longer visited Smith, and everyone else welcomed the drill with open arms—especially those who had tried hand-drilling

of a four-year flurry of new routes. The most significant ascents of the early eighties occurred on the Star Wall, when Alan Watts freed both *Dark Star* (5.11d) and *Neutron Star* (5.12a). He also toproped an unheralded column left of *Cruel Sister* called *Child Abuse* (5.12b). These routes put the Gorge back at the top of Smith climbing.

Despite the promise of these early routes, Gorge climbing might have stagnated if not for three key factors. First, the introduction of Boreal Fires, the original sticky-rubber shoes that made a noticeable difference on the tuff, dramatically changed the nature of Gorge climbing. Virtually every route in the Gorge dropped a full letter grade overnight. Second, technological advances in gear opened up dozens of previously unprotectable routes. Along with the basalt. Rich pioneered *Resuscitation* (5.12c) and *The Caning* (5.12b), along with many easier lines. Others followed his lead, and soon the new sport routes became as popular as the clean cracks. Today, with most classic lines already climbed, the days of explosive growth are over, but the coming years will surely see more activity as the magnetism of the basalt attracts a new generation of climbers.

Despite the undeniable charm, several annoyances plague Gorge climbing. The most troublesome issue involves land ownership. Most of the west side of the Lower Gorge is privately owned. Climbing got off to a rocky start in the 1970s, when a landowner fired warning shots at early pioneer Steve Strauch. Fortunately, for the last three decades there haven't been any problems. The state park owns the only access to the Lower Gorge, including a recently acquired section of land extending beyond Cox Rocks. The acquisition of the entire East Columns by Oregon State Parks further reduced the chances of a confrontation. If climbers respect the rights of landowners by entering the Gorge only from the designated areas and never topping-out on any west-side routes, there shouldn't be any problems. If you're ever confronted by a landowner, please be polite and respect their wishes—

future access may depend on your behavior.

A more repugnant annoyance also afflicts the Lower Gorge. Over the past several decades, environmental Neanderthals living above the west rim sometimes used the Gorge as a garbage dump. Rather than taking an old tire or washing machine to the landfill, they'd push them off the top of the cliff. Instead of observing more traditional rituals, they'd opt for the fling-the-dead-cat-into-the-canyon method of burial. This is far less of a problem than it once was, as the worst offenders either moved away, died off, or changed their disposal methods. Still, an overgrown collection of junk—especially below the Catwalk Columns—spoils the otherwise pristine surroundings.

A final aggravation is the amount of vegetation along the base of the cliff. This isn't a problem in much of the Lower Gorge, but lush overgrowth along the base of Jungleland and upstream from the Midwest Cliff makes hiking a challenge for all but the most hardened jungle travelers. Choked with stinging nettles and other foliage, the overgrowth usually returns every season—despite the efforts of machete-wielding climbers.

Finding the crags: See descriptions for individual areas.

WEST COLUMNS

Rising above the western bank of the Crooked River is a quarter-mile stretch of some of the best columnar basalt in the country. The perfect rock, attractive cracks, featured faces, and solid arêtes appeal to both traditional and sport climbers. The afternoon shade and frequent breezes make it an excellent destination on a warm day—and an icebox in the winter.

To approach all West Column routes, drive past the main parking area to the turn-around parking lot. Few climbers use the original approach chimney, which sports three rebar rungs and a homemade wooden ladder. The modern approach follows a driveway east toward a house owned by Oregon State Parks. Continue to the rim and hike upstream until a third-class stack of columns leads into the canyon. Although simple, there's enough exposure to warrant attention on the descent. Hop boulders upstream to the first wall.

Cox Rocks (aka Parched Cat Cliff)

Jutting out from the hillside at the end of the boulder field are Cox Rocks. The small collection of mediocre routes doesn't come close to matching the quality farther upstream. Despite solid rock, the cracks are a little too painful for fun climbing.

1. The Lonesome Crowded West (5.9) ★★★ Gear to 1 inch. A pleasing trad route ascends a slender north-facing wall, slightly left of a chimney. Avoid the columnar basalt by scrambling uphill to a belay bolt and follow discontinuous cracks past a crux bulge to an anchor just below the top.

2. Edgewise (5.10d) ★★★ 6 bolts. The best route on Cox Rocks follows a bolted arête

on the upper reaches of the crag. Hike uphill to a belay bolt beneath a chimney and step left to fun edges and pinches. Rappel from an anchor on top with a 70-meter rope.

3. Little Orphan Jammies (5.10d) ★ Gear to 2.5 inches. This forgettable line features a short blend of stems and painful slots. Jam a starting thin crack to a ledge and move right to a crack-split dihedral. Finish with a traverse left to an anchor.

4. Squeal and Peel (5.11c) ★★ Gear to 2 inches. A brief crux of delicate stems highlights this ignored route. After jamming dirty converging cracks, cut right to a ledge and storm the blank corner above.

5. Cretin's Retreat (5.10c) ★★ Gear to 2.5 inches. The most prominent dihedral on the cliff looks appealing, but the razor-sharp jams can shred your fingers. The first ascent team retreated at a bolt below the current anchors, naming the route after their aborted effort.

6. Oriface (5.10b) ★★★ Mixed to 2.5 inches. Best done in a single pitch from the ground, the vertical wall above *Cretin's Retreat* combines good edges, solid rock, and a rare dose of Gorge exposure. There are only two bolts—bring nuts for supplemental protection.

7. The Ferret's Dead (5.9) ★★ Gear to 2.5 inches. An appealing crack splits the upper slab left of *Cretin's Retreat,* providing a painless alternate approach to *Oriface.* Begin with a brief struggle in an awkward crack.

8. Cox Rocks (5.8) ★ Gear to 4 inches. The original route on the cliff never received much attention. After the same ungainly start as *The Ferret's Dead,* thrash up an off-width in a right-facing corner.

9. Three Fingered Hack (5.10c) ★★ Gear to 3 inches. A pleasant finger crack splits the column face left of the *Cox Rocks*

Cox Rocks (aka Parched Cat Cliff)

1. The Lonesome Crowded West 5.9
2. Edgewise 5.10d
3. Little Orphan Jammies 5.10d
4. Squeal and Peel 5.11c
5. Cretin's Retreat 5.10c
6. Oriface 5.10b
7. The Ferret's Dead 5.9
8. Cox Rocks 5.8
9. Three Fingered Hack 5.10c
10. Hack Attack 5.12a TR
11. Vulture Crest 5.9
12. Terrorbonne 5.10a R
13. Physical Abuse 5.10a

bordering razor-edged flakes. Above a pedestal, finish with simple jams to an anchor.

12. Terrorbonne

(5.10a R) ★ Gear to 3 inches. Immediately left of *Vulture Crest* are sharp flakes splitting a flat face. After shaking through the crux, climb an easy crack to a rappel anchor.

13. Physical Abuse

(5.10a) ★★ Gear to 2.5 inches. The last route on Cox Rocks follows a very short crack splitting two detached columns. The moves are as good as any Gorge classic, but there just aren't enough of them.

Wildfire Wall

The real climbing in the Gorge starts beyond Cox Rocks. The Wildfire Wall contains an uninterrupted stretch of full-length parallel cracks. The right section features great crack climbs, while the midportion offers difficult stemming corners and bolted sport routes. Far to the left the wall fizzles out at a narrow passage called the Catwalk.

off-width. Jam a starting hand crack, moving left under a block, and savor the shallow crux corner above.

10. Hack Attack (5.12a) ★★ TR. The direct start to *Three Fingered Hack* follows a dirty seam in a blank corner. Without bolts and a complete scrubbing, it'll be nothing more than an overlooked toprope problem.

11. Vulture Crest (5.9) ★ Gear to 3.5 inches. On the left side of Cox Rocks are two unappealing flake cracks starting off a 15-foot column. A useless route starts up the right side of this column and jams a crack

14. Byrne's Revenge (5.11b R) ★★

Mixed to 1 inch. At the right side of the Wildfire Wall are several curved corners split by seams. *Byrne's Revenge* starts left of a detached pillar and finesses past a bolt-protected crux. The difficulty eases, but the risk increases on the sparsely protected finishing corner.

15. Mad Man (5.8 R) ★★
Gear to 8 inches. This unmistakable wide crack/squeeze chimney was the first recorded route in the Gorge. The infrequent early ascents were almost completely unprotected. Modern technology solved this problem, though the moves are as uncomfortable as ever.

16. Wildfire (5.10b) ★★★★
Gear to 2.5 inches. With flawless rock and sinker protection, the first of the classic Gorge routes shouldn't be missed. The hardest climbing stems and jams a tight flare at the start, leading to an appealing finger crack. Finish by cutting right around a blind corner to an anchor.

17. La Vie Dansante (5.11d R) ★★ Gear to 2 inches. The poorly protected, chalk-free seam left of *Wildfire* attracts little attention. The few attempts usually rely on a toprope. To finish, either cut right or move left to a higher anchor.

18. Crime Wave (5.11b) ★★★ Gear to 1.5 inches. This enjoyable route begins below a missing chunk of column. Jam around a starting roof to a charming crux mixing tip slots and edges. The first ascent bypassed the final corner by traversing left to *Gruff;* a higher anchor allows a direct finish.

19. Gruff (5.10a) ★★★ Gear to 3 inches. The most locking jams you'll ever experi-

Wildfire Wall–Right Side

14.	Byrne's Revenge 5.11b R	19.	Gruff 5.10a
15.	Mad Man 5.8 R	20.	Rim Job 5.10b
16.	Wildfire 5.10b	21.	Iron Cross 5.11b
17.	La Vie Dansante 5.11d R	22.	Neutral Zone 5.11a
18.	Crime Wave 5.11b		

ence highlight this well-protected route. No move is hard, but the entire sequence builds a pump. Begin directly with harder finger slots, or hand traverse in from the left.

20. Rim Job (5.10b) ★★★ Gear to 3 inches. An appealing corner with a technical crux at the start rises left of *Gruff*. The upper section looks tough from below, but hidden ledges slash the grade.

21. Iron Cross (5.11b) ★★ Gear to 3 inches. Until someone replaces a missing fixed pin with a bolt, this unusual route will see only

Wildfire Wall–Right Center

22.	Neutral Zone 5.11a	28.	Titus 5.10b R
23.	Organ Grinder 5.10a	29.	Split Decision 5.12a
24.	Badfinger 5.10b	30.	Pure Palm 5.11a
25.	Soft Touch 5.10d	31.	Cornercopia 5.10b
26.	On the Road 5.11a	32.	The Caning 5.12b
27.	Edge of the Road 5.12c TR	33.	Teachers in Space 5.11d R

management somehow misses the best parts of three separate routes. Start with the converging cracks of *Neutral Zone* and cut left past *Badfinger,* finishing with *Soft Touch*'s upper corner.

24. Badfinger (5.10b)

★★★★ Gear to 2.5 inches. A longtime Gorge classic, this attractive face crack features excellent rock, bomber protection, and three intriguing bulges. Start left of an obvious wide slot.

25. Soft Touch (5.10d)

★★ Gear to 3 inches. The right-facing dihedral left of *Badfinger* doesn't match the quality of nearby routes, though it's far safer today than on early ascents. A massive guillotine flake once guarded the hardest moves.

26. On the Road (5.11a)

★★★ Gear to 2.5 inches. The Gorge's first 5.11 follows a varied crack splitting an attractive buttress. The technical crux exits a flare on painful tip jams low on the route. Above, the pumping crack slowly widens from finger jams to hand slots.

toprope ascents. The one-move palming crux at midheight requires more agility than the typical 5.11.

22. Neutral Zone (5.11a) ★ Gear to 3 inches.

Left of *Iron Cross* are converging cracks forming a wide slot between two columns. After stemming the simple chimney, painful finger jams in a shallow dihedral lead to an easy traverse left to an anchor.

23. Organ Grinder (5.10a) ★ Gear to 3

inches. This meandering lesson in rope drag

27. Edge of the Road (5.12c) ★★★ TR.

First done more than twenty-five years ago, this rarely tried toprope problem still matches the hardest grade in the Lower Gorge. Start atop a precariously balanced pillar left of *On the Road* and crank through a tough crimping move on the razor-edged arête. The difficulties ease only slightly through the midsection before the holds disappear just below the top.

28. Titus (5.10b R) ★★ Gear to 8 inches. This obvious wide crack was one of the most respected and dangerous testpieces from the early days of the Gorge. The crack widens from fist jams at the start to a squeeze chimney finish, with nothing but agony in between.

29. Split Decision (5.12a) ★★★ Gear to 1 inch. Challenging for the grade, this shallow dihedral left of *Titus* sees few ascents. Start atop a detached pillar and step across to a thin crack. The difficulties slowly mount, capped by a 20-foot sequence of delicate stemming. Unfortunately, someone stole four critical fixed pins—use a toprope until they're replaced with bolts.

30. Pure Palm (5.11a) ★★★ 8 bolts. There's nothing quite like this perfect box corner. Finesse climbers love the unrelenting sequence of stems and palms. The average gym climber won't find much to like—there isn't a cling hold on the entire route.

31. Cornercopia (5.10b) ★★★ Mixed to 1.5 inches. Left of *Pure Palm* rises a similar but much easier stemming box. A bolt-protected bouldering crux at the start leads to easier jams and stems.

32. The Caning (5.12b) ★★★ 9 bolts. One of the harder sport routes in the Lower Gorge ascends great rock to a midpitch crux. The moves favor those with a good reach— shorter climbers might find the route a notch harder. In the more-than-you-wanted-to-know department, caning is the technique of striking someone with a cane (most commonly on the buttocks) for erotic pleasure. Coincidentally, this challenging route whacks most climbers in the ass.

Marie Andree Cloutier on *Pure Palm*. BEN MOON

33. Teachers in Space (5.11d R) ★ Gear to 1 inch. Underneath a coating of bat crap lies a formerly worthwhile route. Painfully wide stems at the start give way to a crux on positive edges. For reasons unknown this shallow dihedral is a favorite place for the furry creatures to relieve themselves—just look at the ground below the corner. With *The Caning* so close, *Teachers in Space* hardly exists anymore.

34. Bold Line (5.10d) ★★ Gear to 2.5 inches. Left of *Teachers in Space* are three hanging columns. An intimidating but surprisingly moderate route jams a face crack and cuts right under these columns. Pull over a small roof and stem to an anchor.

34a. Passover (5.10d) ★★ Gear to 2.5 inches. An alternate finish cuts left around the roof to a couple bolts. The original line stopped here, but a new ending pulls around a second roof to a higher anchor.

Wildfire Wall—Left Center

34.	Bold Line 5.10d	37a.	White Trash finish 5.10d
34a.	Passover 5.10d	38.	Lion of Judah 5.11d
35.	Resuscitation 5.12c	38a.	Judah Direct 5.12b
36.	Project 5.12?	39.	Cry of the Poor 5.11a
37.	White Trash 5.12a		

ing column the size of a couple Coke® machines might fall out someday.

37. White Trash

(5.12a) ★★★★ 7 bolts. Technical and highly varied, this classic line is one of the finest in the Gorge. A new bolt graces the formerly pin-protected crux. Start atop a small block leaning against the wall.

37a. White Trash finish (5.10d) ★★★ 5 bolts.

A fun finish through the rimrock adds to the variety of the original line. Power through overhangs on good holds and lower to the ground with a 60-meter rope.

38. Lion of Judah

(5.11d) ★★★ 8 bolts. This open book rises above an obvious roof at the base of the cliff. Stick-clip the bolt at the lip and bypass the roof with crux face holds to the left. After a good rest, unrelenting stemming in a tight corner leads to the anchor.

35. Resuscitation (5.12c) ★★★ 7 bolts. The hardest route in the Lower Gorge ascends an attractive rippling wall. Start atop a pile of rubble and finesse unrelenting edges and side pulls to a crux move getting past the fourth bolt. There's little chance to catch your breath on the sustained dash to the anchors.

36. Project (5.12?) Left of *Resuscitation* sits an anchor atop an abandoned corner. The shallow dihedral would obviously go free, but there's reason to believe that a hang-

38a. Judah Direct (5.12b) ★★ 8 bolts. A much harder variation pulls directly over the starting roof. Begin in a short inside corner, exiting left using a critical undercling/side pull with nothing for the feet. To lead this roof, stick-clip the first two bolts.

39. Cry of the Poor

(5.11a) ★★★★ Gear to 2 inches. Arguably the best traditional 5.11 in the Gorge follows a delightful seam left of *Lion of Judah*. The rock and protection are nearly perfect, with a thin-edged crux in the middle of the route.

40. Just Say Yes

(5.12a) ★★★ 9 bolts. The flat face left of the *Lion of Judah* roof features an engaging sport route. Start with a dihedral on the left, clipping a bolt before veering right past another bolt to good edges. After a moderate midsection, master a delicate crux just below the top. The original toprope line (5.12b) included a desperate direct start—leading this variant requires a second bolt stick-clip.

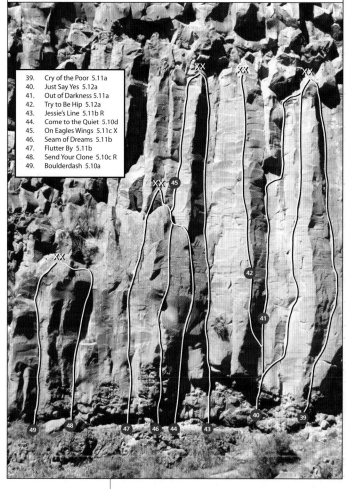

Wildfire Wall—Left Side

39.	Cry of the Poor 5.11a
40.	Just Say Yes 5.12a
41.	Out of Darkness 5.11a
42.	Try to Be Hip 5.12a
43.	Jessie's Line 5.11b R
44.	Come to the Quiet 5.10d
45.	On Eagles Wings 5.11c X
46.	Seam of Dreams 5.11b
47.	Flutter By 5.11b
48.	Send Your Clone 5.10c R
49.	Boulderdash 5.10a

41. Out of Darkness

(5.11a) ★★★ Mixed to 2 inches. A quality stemming corner rises between two bolt lines. After a fun dihedral the first crux comes before a traverse under a roof protected by a peculiar retro-bolt drilled in the bottom of a hanging column. Finish with an insecure palming move in the corner to the right.

42. Try to Be Hip

(5.12a) ★★★★ 8 bolts. Another winning sport route starts with the first 20 feet of *Out of Darkness* before stepping left onto an attractive column. Split by good rests, the enchanting series of intellectual cruxes never let up until you clip the anchors.

43. Jessie's Line

(5.11b R) ★★ Gear to 4 inches. The last unbroken dihedral on the Wildfire Wall might receive more attention if not for a scary start protected by a dubious cam in a bombay slot. Most climbers skirt right around a thin section at the crux; others prefer a direct line (5.11c) on sharp tip jams.

44. Come to the Quiet

(5.10d) ★★ Gear to 1.5 inches. Beyond *Jessie's Line* the full-length corners give way to a row of shorter columns. The first of these condensed routes jams a thin crack to an awkward, committing crux pulling around a bulge.

45. On Eagles Wings (5.11c X) ★ Gear to
1 inch. Above the *Come to the Quiet* anchor lurks a short, nightmarish dihedral. There isn't a single decent nut placement on the route, and a sharp-edged, ankle-shattering pillar awaits anyone popping off the insecure stems. Modern gear might completely eliminate any degree of danger, though the safest option avoids it altogether.

46. Seam of Dreams (5.11b) ★★ Gear to 1
inch. An obscure, chalk-free seam splits the face left of *Come to the Quiet*. After starting up jumbled jugs, technical moves lead up a low-angle, wire-eating crack.

47. Flutter By (5.11b) ★★ Mixed to 1 inch.
If not for a bolt 20 feet off the deck, no one would ever give this puny face a second glance. The moves past the bolt aren't hard, but the crux comes a little higher above a critical small wire slot.

48. Send Your Clone (5.10c R) ★ Gear to
1.5 inches. An overgrown relic from the past, this dirty right-leaning thin crack isn't worth lacing your shoes for. A rusted fixed pin protects the crux sequence. Appearances can deceive, but in this case they don't.

49. Boulderdash (5.10a) ★ Gear to 1.5
inches. This stunted line ascends the last crack before the Catwalk. The brief flurry of jams won't leave much of an impression on you.

Catwalk Columns

Beyond the Wildfire Wall the trail narrows to a small ledge skirting precariously above the water. Known as the Catwalk, this passage leads to the outstanding routes of the Catwalk Columns. The unbroken stretch of basalt offers several new sport routes, along with the finest cracks in the entire Gorge. The best routes are on the right and center portions of the wall. To the left the cliff deteriorates into shorter cracks often sprouting vegetation.

50. Project (5.11?) Above the Catwalk the
beautiful columns of the Wildfire Wall give way to a small patch of jumbled rock. A toprope problem follows a shallow corner just left of the fractured stone.

51. Crossroads (5.11b) ★★★ Mixed to 2.5
inches. The first sport route on the Catwalk Columns follows an attractive line immediately beyond the Catwalk. It's entirely bolted except for a single piece of gear.

52. Prometheus (5.10c) ★★★ Gear to 2.5
inches. The first traditional route beyond the Catwalk follows an obvious crack leading to a stemming box. Moderate jams at the start give way to a delicate crux high on the route.

53. Northern Lights (5.11d) ★★★ 7 bolts.
This enjoyable sport route ascends an attractive seam splitting the prominent column left of *Prometheus*. Entertaining crack and face moves lead to an unusual crux stretching past a blank bulge at the fifth bolt.

54. Last Chance (5.10c) ★★★★ Gear to 2
inches. Traditional climbers shouldn't miss this sustained open book. Perfect rock, bomber protection, and locking fingers jams make it a Gorge classic. You won't find any hard moves, but climbers with pumped forearms sometimes fail near the top.

55. Strike Force (5.12a R) ★★ Gear to 1.5
inches. Left of *Last Chance* rises another dihedral guarded by a roof at the base. The short-lived crux cranks through a flaring

50.	Project 5.11?	55.	Strike Force 5.12a R
51.	Crossroads 5.11b	56.	Silent Holocaust 5.11c
52.	Prometheus 5.10c	57.	Mid-Life Celebration 5.11c
53.	Northern Lights 5.11d	58.	Diminishing Returns 5.10c
54.	Last Chance 5.10c	59.	Spiritual Warfare 5.11a

tected by two pathetic knifeblades, today bolts safely protect the once-frightening start. Moderate climbing above the roof leads right to *Strike Force.*

57. Mid-Life Celebration (5.11c)

★★★ 8 bolts. This eye-catching, roof-capped column features a quality sport route. Start with the same crux as *Silent Holocaust* before stepping left to fun moves on great rock.

58. Diminishing Returns (5.10c) ★★

Gear to 4 inches. A meandering route takes in part of *Silent Holocaust* and finishes with *Strike Force,* after traversing right from double wide cracks.

59. Spiritual Warfare

(5.11a) ★★ Gear to 3 inches. Deceptively tricky jams over a daunting bulge highlight this unremarkable route. Start up the same easy wide crack as *Diminishing Returns,* but instead of stepping right, battle directly to an anchor.

60. The Pearl (5.11b) ★★★★ Gear to 2.5

inches. This high-quality seam left of converging wide cracks ranks with the best traditional 5.11s in the Gorge. The three crux sections protect well, with a stopper move just below the roofs.

lieback to an inelegant face move on a blank wall. The upper corner eases quickly, ending with a traverse up and right to an anchor. The dubious pin at the crux wasn't that good when it was first placed twenty-five years ago.

56. Silent Holocaust (5.11c) ★★ Mixed to 1.5

inches. Much like its neighbor to the right, the crux of *Silent Holocaust* cranks around an awkward roof near the ground. Long pro-

Catwalk Columns–Right Center

59.	Spiritual Warfare 5.11a	65.	Bat Flake 5.10a
60.	The Pearl 5.11b	66.	Satan's Awaiting 5.11b
61.	Nuclear 5.11d	67.	Rising Star 5.10b
62.	Full Court Press 5.12a	68.	White Dwarf 5.11b R
63.	Baby Fit 5.11c	69.	Night Shift 5.11b
64.	Pet Semetery 5.11b		

the continuously difficult moves. Stick-clip the first bolt.

63. Baby Fit (5.11c)
★★ Mixed to 1 inch. An odd route starts with a shallow corner skirting imperfect rock. The unusual crux jogs left to a fixed pin and cuts back right on thin edges. Clip the pin with a very long sling, or face maddening rope drag on the finish.

64. Pet Semetery
(5.11b) ★★ 8 bolts. It might not be the most attractive route in the Gorge, but this newer line is worth doing. Sandy rock at the start detracts from the appeal, but the crux finish will restore your faith in the quality of Smith basalt.

65. Bat Flake (5.10a) ★
Gear to 2.5 inches. The worst route on the right side of the Catwalk Columns skirts a filthy crack on the right side of a two-tiered roof before finishing on a solid right-leaning flake.

66. Satan's Awaiting (5.11b) ★★ Gear to
1.5 inches. This rarely climbed crack splits the center of double-tiered roofs. The roofs aren't hard, but expect hellish finger jams in the final corner.

67. Rising Star (5.10b) ★★ Gear to 2.5
inches. A unremarkable route pulls around the left side of the obvious gray roofs. After

61. Nuclear (5.11d) ★★★ Mixed to 2
inches. The blank corners left of *The Pearl* feature several mostly fixed routes. The right line starts with a mini box corner protected by a bolt and finesses past pegs and nuts to a crux move at a patch of rough rock. Finish by cutting left around a distinctive triple roof.

62. Full Court Press (5.12a) ★★★ 8 bolts.
The hardest section of this quality sport route edges past the third bolt, but the bigger challenge comes from linking together

clearing the second roof, jam a pleasant crack to the anchors.

68. White Dwarf

(5.11b R) ★★ Gear to 2 inches. Left of *Rising Star* looms a dangerous open book starting on pocketed rock. The delicate stems in the lower corner protect with spooky wires. Purists raise the grade a notch by ignoring the final section of *Rising Star;* everyone else grabs everything within reach.

69. Night Shift (5.11b)

★★★ Gear to 2 inches. An intricate seam splits the shallow corner left of *White Dwarf.* A crux lieback protects well if you can hang out long enough to place the tiny wires. Tall climbers won't even notice the second crux—a long stretch between good holds.

70. Ground Zero (5.11a) ★★★ Gear to 1.5

inches. Improved small-wire technology long ago eliminated any degree of seriousness from this technical corner. The crux masters a ticklish blend of edges and stems.

71. Quasar (5.10a) ★★★ Gear to 2.5 inches.

A short crack rises above a blocky start on sharp rock. After soloing easy jugs, jam charming hand/finger slots past the original anchor to higher bolts atop the column.

Catwalk Columns—Left Center

70.	Ground Zero 5.11a		77.	Child Abuse 5.12b
71.	Quasar 5.10a		78.	Taxtor 5.9 R
72.	Erogenous Zone 5.10c		79.	Southern Cross 5.11a
73.	Battle of the Bulge 5.10a		80.	Harvest 5.11b
74.	Blood Clot 5.10b		81.	Grim Tales 5.11a
75.	Crack-a-no-go 5.11b		82.	Patent Leather Pump 5.9
76.	Cruel Sister 5.10b			

72. Erogenous Zone (5.10c) ★★ Gear to 2

inches. Immediately left of *Quasar* lurks a shallow inside corner above a square ledge. The hardest moves stretch between good jams right off the deck.

73. Battle of the Bulge (5.10a) ★ Gear to

4 inches. Beyond *Erogenous Zone* are a few overgrown cracks capped by small roofs. A rarely climbed off-width splits the left side of this mediocrity—the only highlight pulls around a measly roof.

74. Blood Clot (5.10b) ★★★★ Gear to 3 inches. Locking finger jams and sinker hand slots on terrific rock make this one of the Gorge's finest cracks. After a complete rest in the middle, a much easier crack finishes to a ledge.

75. Crack-a-no-go (5.11b) ★★★ Gear to 3.5 inches. Sandwiched between two classic lines, this tips crack protects well, though most climbers settle for a toprope. The lower section packs a punch with edges, side pulls, and thin jams. The wide crack above presents few obstacles.

76. Cruel Sister (5.10b) ★★★★ Gear to 3.5 inches. There's no better hand crack at Smith than this attractive line. Set in a shallow corner, the elegant crack widens gradually from thin hand jams, through a locking section, to a few fist jams on the final bulge. Unlike *Blood Clot* to the right, no rests interrupt the escalating pump.

77. Child Abuse (5.12b) ★★★★ 7 bolts. For several years the brilliant sport route on the column left of *Cruel Sister* was the hardest technical exercise on Smith basalt. Long a testpiece on toprope, sticky rubber slashed the grade, and bolts turned it into a challenging lead. Good shakes on square-cut edges break an onslaught of unique moves. The crux comes right at the top with an extended reach to a side pull with nothing for the feet.

78. Taxtor (5.9 R) ★★ Gear to 6 inches. The taxing wide crack on the left side of the *Child Abuse* column sees very few ascents. Only off-width aficionados will appreciate the awkward climbing.

Beyond *Taxtor* the attractive cracks of the Catwalk Columns deteriorate into dirty, overgrown corners. Despite appearances several of these lines are worth climbing, and they offer the West Column's easiest routes. In a gar-dening effort of legendary proportions in the early 1980s, Chuck Buzzard transformed this vertical jungle into a legitimate crag. Since almost no one climbs here, some of the vegetation has returned in recent years.

79. Southern Cross (5.11a) ★★ Gear to 2 inches. The best route on the left side of the Catwalk Columns follows a dihedral left of *Taxtor*. If not for a few stubborn plants, it would surely attract more attention. A tricky start past a missing fixed pin gives way to pleasant moves in a well-protected corner. A fun toprope problem (5.11d) starts atop a short flat-topped column to the left, before moving right to a shallow arête.

80. Harvest (5.11b) ★★ Gear to 2.5 inches. An obscure seam splits the column left of the *Southern Cross* dihedral. Start with the right of two cracks above a flat-faced pillar. Improbable moves lead to a delicate crux just below the top. Cut right to the *Cruel Sister* anchor.

81. Grim Tales (5.11a) ★ Gear to 2.5 inches. This uninviting route crammed tightly in a small corner left of *Harvest* wasn't especially good when clean. Today the assortment of foliage plugging the crack appeals only to florists.

82. Patent Leather Pump (5.9) ★★ Gear to 3 inches. Diverging cracks mark this popular warm-up in an inside corner. Hanging vines made it a grotesque struggle on early ascents, but a prodigious gardening effort uncovered a decent route. Lower off from bolts at the top.

83. Old and In the Way (5.10c) ★★ Gear to 2 inches. Left of a vegetated double-crack corner rises a worthwhile thin crack. A pumping start leads to a technical crux on rough rock at midheight.

Catwalk Columns—Left Side

82.	Patent Leather Pump 5.9	88.	Brain Death 5.11b	94.	Greasy Spoon 5.10a
83.	Old and In the Way 5.10c	89.	On the Spot 5.9	95.	Dire Wolf 5.8
84.	Father Mercy 5.11b	90.	Wasted Words 5.10a	96.	Delicatessen 5.8
85.	Conversion Excursion 5.10a	91.	Lost Souls 5.9	97.	Fast Food Junky 5.8
86.	Bean Time 5.10d	92.	Religious Fervor 5.10a	98.	Phallic Symbol 5.7
87.	Lava Tube 5.7 X	93.	Sitting Duck 5.9	99.	Chimney of Ghouls 5.7 R

84. Father Mercy (5.11b) ★★ Gear to 1.5 inches. An obscure seam splits a flat, dark wall right of a dihedral. Mercifully, the crux at the start protects easily with small wires and the upper part isn't especially difficult.

85. Conversion Excursion (5.10a) ★★ Gear to 3.5 inches. A gloomy open book plugged with two closely spaced cracks rises above jumbled columns. Lackluster jams in the corner end with a traverse left to an anchor.

86. Bean Time (5.10d) ★ Gear to 1.5 inches. Right of a menacing chimney sits a contrived corner. Ignoring the column to the left, jam and stem sustained moves past a bush to an anchor.

87. Lava Tube (5.7 X) ★ Gear to 2 inches. Despite the grade, this obvious slot makes a poor choice for beginners. An overgrown entrance, awkward squirming, and bad protection provide a negative learning environment.

88. Brain Death (5.11b) ★★ Gear to 4 inches. A prominent detached column split by a crack juts out from the left side of the Catwalk Columns. Begin atop a massive block and boulder past an awkward crux to an easy wide crack.

89. On the Spot (5.9) ★ Gear to 3 inches. The left side of the *Brain Death* column offers an unremarkable jamming exercise. Most climbers bypass a block-plugged wide crack at the start by stepping in from the pillar to the right.

90. Wasted Words (5.10a) ★ Gear to 4 inches. The right of two closely spaced cracks veers past blocks to a short, sickle-shaped fist crack. Above a ledge simple jams end at an anchor.

91. Lost Souls (5.9) ★★ Gear to 3 inches. The left of parallel cracks jams awkwardly past the same loose blocks as *Wasted Words,* but finishes with an enjoyable face crack in a shallow corner. Move up and left to an anchor.

92. Religious Fervor (5.10a) ★★ Gear to 4 inches. This obvious wide crack splits a left-facing corner. After a committing lieback at the start, moderate finger/hand jams finish.

93. Sitting Duck (5.9) ★ Gear to 3 inches. Just left of *Religious Fervor* rises a hand crack. Awkward, dirty jams at the start give way to a finish on textured rock. Avoiding the crack to the right near the top bumps the grade up a notch.

94. Greasy Spoon (5.10a) ★★ Gear to 4 inches. A small white-capped pillar rests in a corner below three cracks. The right line starts with a crux finger crack and ends with an easy wide crack.

95. Dire Wolf (5.8) ★ Gear to 1.5 inches. An unremarkable thin crack sits in a shallow inside corner directly above a small pillar. Finger jam to a dicey encounter with a guillotine flake and cut left to bolts.

96. Delicatessen (5.8) ★★ Gear to 4 inches. A low-angle hand/fist crack branches left from the start of *Dire Wolf.* A massive bush once blocked the start, forcing the first ascent party to foot-shuffle in from the left.

97. Fast Food Junky (5.8) ★ Gear to 4 inches. A bland route follows double wide cracks in a block-capped slot. Jam the left crack to easy stemming below the roof. Cut left if you've had your fill, or pull around to the right if you crave more.

98. Phallic Symbol (5.7) ★ Gear to 2.5 inches. A 15-foot column sits below short, unappealing double cracks. Climb either side of the starting pillar and jam past a slender namesake block to an anchor.

99. Chimney of Ghouls (5.7 R) ★ Gear to 4 inches. Around the corner left of *Phallic Symbol* lurks an ominous wide crack marking the end of the Catwalk Columns. Difficult protection takes some of the fun away from pleasant stems and liebacks.

Star Wall

After the disappointing left side of the Catwalk Columns, the quality returns with the exceptional routes of Star Wall. The shorter climbs to the right aren't special, but the full-length lines beyond are some of the finest in the Gorge. In the early 1980s, this wall contained Smith's hardest routes.

100. Old Trouble's Number Seven (5.10b) ★★ Gear to 2.5 inches. Star Wall begins with an ugly section of dark rock overgrown with shrubbery. About 20 feet left of *Chimney of Ghouls* rises a respectable hand crack leading to a foliage-covered ledge.

101. Pink Roadgrader (5.10d) ★ Gear to 1.5 inches. This lush route begins left of *Old Trouble's Number Seven.* After pulling around a blank crux, bulldoze through weeds to the top.

102. Kneegobee (5.8) ★★ Gear to 4 inches. Right of a block-plugged wide crack sits a left-facing corner. The moves look desperate, but stems to the left slash the difficulty.

Star Wall–Right Side

100.	Old Trouble's Number Seven 5.10b	106.	Levitate 5.11d
101.	Pink Roadgrader 5.10d	107.	Turning Point 5.10a
102.	Kneegobee 5.8	108.	St. Paddee's Day 5.10a
103.	Jenga 5.9	109.	Lethal Dose 5.11a R
104.	Left Wing 5.10c	110.	Mantra 5.10a
105.	Last Days 5.10a	111.	Tantra 5.12a TR

103. Jenga (5.9) ★ Gear to 6 inches. This distinctive, flake-plugged wide crack won't receive many ascents. Take a hint from the name—the stack of blocks in the middle of the route are precariously perched.

104. Left Wing (5.10c) ★★★ Mixed to 1 inch. The best warm-up for the more difficult routes on Star Wall mixes a traditional start with a sport-bolted finish. Begin with a clean finger crack and step right onto a column. Quality climbing leads over a crux bulge to an anchor.

105. Last Days (5.10a) ★★★ Gear to 2.5 inches. Beyond a couple easy unclimbed(?) cracks is a left-facing corner that receives little attention, despite fun climbing. A flurry of entertaining finger/hand jams on good rock ends at an anchor.

106. Levitate (5.11d) ★★ Mixed to 1 inch. An attractive starting arête highlights this varied line. The sport climbing crux leads to a good ledge and an easier finish of stems and finger slots.

107. Turning Point (5.10a) ★★ Gear to 4 inches. Double wide cracks lurk in a dark, ugly corner. After an awkward start the turning point comes with excellent finger jams above.

108. St. Paddee's Day (5.10a) ★★ Gear to 4 inches. Long guarded by a massive sticker bush at the start, this wide crack once again is open for traffic after a prodigious gardening effort. You'll want to tick this one off your list quickly, before the foliage returns.

109. Lethal Dose (5.11a R) ★★ Gear to 2 inches. Filthy rock and creepy wires keep almost everyone away from this serious route. Above the crux start, the rock and protection improve greatly on the 5.10 finish.

110. Mantra (5.10a) ★★★ Gear to 3 inches. Don't let the sandy start scare you away

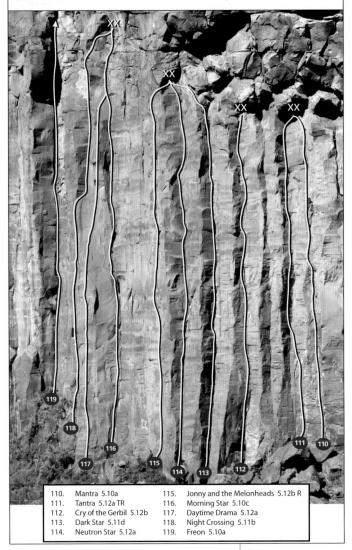

Star Wall—Left Side

110.	Mantra 5.10a	115.	Jonny and the Melonheads 5.12b R
111.	Tantra 5.12a TR	116.	Morning Star 5.10c
112.	Cry of the Gerbil 5.12b	117.	Daytime Drama 5.12a
113.	Dark Star 5.11d	118.	Night Crossing 5.11b
114.	Neutron Star 5.12a	119.	Freon 5.10a

112. Cry of the Gerbil

(5.12b) ★★★ 8 bolts. The hardest sport route on Star Wall follows a shallow, highly technical dihedral. After a gritty start delicate stems give way to a baffling crux above the sixth bolt. There are better sport routes in the Lower Gorge, but almost nothing matches the sustained difficulties of this intense wall.

113. Dark Star (5.11d)

★★★ Gear to 0.75 inch. When pioneered in July 1981, this attractive corner was the first 5.12 on Smith basalt. Within a few years the arrival of sticky rubber stripped the insecure smears of their original grade. You'll need gear for the low-end 5.11 stems and jams at the start, but four fixed pins protect the hardest moves near the top.

114. Neutron Star

(5.12a) ★★★★ Mixed to 0.75 inch. From the same era as *Dark Star* comes this wonderful face climb. After a couple nuts at the start, a line of fixed gear protects the sustained climbing. The hardest sequence cranks positive edges past a bolt, followed by an awkward entrance into a flaring slot.

from this delightful route. The charm of the finger/hand jams more than make up for the imperfect beginning.

111. Tantra (5.12a) ★★ TR. The inside corner immediately left of *Mantra* provides some toproping fun. It's a little close to *Mantra,* but someone will inevitably spray it with a line of sport bolts.

115. Jonny and the Melonheads (5.12b R) ★★★ Gear to 1 inch. The most challenging lead on Star Wall combines desperate stems/edges with physically difficult gear placements. The crux pulls around a strenuous bulge low on the route, though the pin-protected finish in a shallow dihedral spits off anyone lacking stemming skills.

116. Morning Star (5.10c) ★★★★ Gear to 2.5 inches. During the late 1970s, this popular crack was the hardest in the Gorge. Along with almost every other Gorge route, the grade fell a notch with new shoe technology. After a 1-inch crack at the start, the climbing eases slightly but the pump builds on the unrelenting jams above. An anonymous sculptor left his mark on the base of the cliff by carving a likeness of a climber into the stone.

117. Daytime Drama (5.12a) ★★★ 9 bolts. Left of *Morning Star* rises a delightful sport route. A finesse crux low gives way to pure fun on the finishing column. As with every Gorge classic, you'll find flawless stone and creative moves.

118. Night Crossing (5.11b) ★★ Gear to 2.5 inches. A face seam leading into a deep dihedral lurks left of *Daytime Drama*. After an annoyingly hard blind-reach off an undercling, easy stems above a big ledge lead to the anchor.

119. Freon (5.10a) ★ Gear to 4 inches. A conspicuous wide crack marks the end of Star Wall. Unfortunately, grit clinging to the rock turns any ascent into a trying ordeal.

Jungleland

For about 200 feet beyond Star Wall, the columns are short and broken—stacked one atop another. A prominent chimney marks the beginning of Jungleland, the final cliff on the West Columns. To date, a lack of clean lines and a horrific bushwhack along the base keep all but the most persistent climbers away. Good luck finding the following lines—the undergrowth makes it nearly impossible to see exactly what you're starting up.

120. Whispers (5.10a) ★★ Gear to 3.5 inches. Fifteen feet right of Jungleland's first chimney rises a hand crack. After scrambling up broken columns, jam to a finish around a blocky section. To descend, traverse far left to the anchors atop *Masquerade*.

121. Tree Route (5.9) ★ Gear to 3.5 inches. Around the corner downhill from the beginning chimney of Jungleland are triple cracks, starting off a short stack of columns. A sickly tree grows to the left. After climbing the cracks, cut left to fun hand/fist jams.

122. Hand Jive (5.9) ★ Gear to 3.5 inches. Forty feet left of the *Tree Route,* beyond closely spaced parallel cracks, rises this forgotten line. Solid jams lead past some blocks into a flare. After finishing up a slot, walk left to an anchor.

123. Herky Jerky (5.9) ★ Gear to 4 inches. A distinctive zigzagging wide crack splits a dark face right of a massive column. Start to the right and move left past some trees to the crux jams.

124. Judas (5.10a) ★ Gear to 3 inches. Another loser starts 15 feet right of an unmistakable chimney and jams double cracks on ominous, dark rock to a better finish. Expect nothing good, and you won't feel betrayed.

125. Big Chimney (5.7 X) ★★★ Gear to 2 inches. A pillar split by an alluring thin crack stands apart from the main cliff. Despite sparse

Jungleland

120.	Whispers 5.10a	125.	Big Chimney 5.7 X
121.	Tree Route 5.9	126.	Masquerade 5.12b R
122.	Hand Jive 5.9	127.	Bush Doctor 5.10a
123.	Herky Jerky 5.9	128.	Razor Boy 5.10c
124.	Judas 5.10a		

protection, chimney enthusiasts love slithering up the narrow corridor behind this column.

126. Masquerade (5.12b R) ★★★★ Gear to 1 inch. A remarkable seam splits the main face of the *Big Chimney* column. It's worth hacking through the jungle, if only to gaze at the most attractive line in the Lower Gorge. Unrelenting, technical moves and challenging natural protection make it the most respected traditional lead in the Gorge. The crux comes near the start, fiddling with miniature wires and pulling on make-believe holds.

127. Bush Doctor (5.10a) ★★★ Gear to 3 inches. About 30 feet beyond *Masquerade*, around the corner left of an unclimbed off-width, rises a fun hand/finger crack. The thick undergrowth prevents any good views of the route, but after emerging from the foliage the climbing won't disappoint.

128. Razor Boy (5.10c) ★★ Gear to 2.5 inches. The last route on the West Columns requires the maximum amount of jungle travel. *Razor Boy* sits right of a prominent green pillar, but you won't catch a glimpse until you're standing beneath it. A few razor jams at the start lead to a crux skirting a small diagonal roof.

EAST COLUMNS

The east side of the Lower Gorge offers more than eighty under-appreciated routes, on rock every bit as solid as the more popular columnar basalt across the river. Despite the quality, the basalt doesn't match the variety found on the west side; with only four sport routes, it appeals mostly to traditional climbers. The best lines are long and diverse, with smooth-sided jam cracks giving way to edges and pockets on the finishing rimrock. Since the entire East Columns are part of Smith Rock State Park, there aren't any awkward ownership issues; climbing to the top of the rim isn't a problem. The standards don't match the west side, but 5.9 to 5.11 climbers will find plenty to hold their interest.

With a sometimes problematic approach, the East Columns sees far fewer visitors than the west side. During low-water conditions the routes are just a boulder-hop away (the best crossing is below the Shakespeare Cliff). More often than not this won't be possible, as the river runs perilously fast. The only dependable option hikes thirty minutes upstream from the bridge below Picnic Lunch Wall, passing under the Student Wall. Beyond the puny So Low Wall, a narrow path hacked through a jungle of stinging nettles leads to the better climbs. The route descriptions assume this approach—they're listed moving upstream, beginning with the far left side of the columns.

So Low Wall

A pint-size cluster of columns sits near the river, upstream from the Student Wall. These cracks are so short they barely qualify as routes, but many of them make excellent miniatures of the longer Gorge classics. For climbers unsure of their abilities, they provide low-stress training for the real thing.

129. Little Weenie (5.7) ★ Gear to 3 inches. A laughably short crack rises right of a small pillar. Fifteen feet of hand jams prove that in rock climbing, size really does matter.

130. Runt's Grunt (5.7) ★ Gear to 4 inches. A short wide crack splits the leftmost inside corner. After an awkward entrance move, simple liebacks and stems end quickly at an anchor.

131. Sawed Off Runt (5.8) ★★ Gear to 3 inches. Parallel hand cracks ascend opposite sides of a hanging column. The enjoyable left crack concludes after a fleeting series of locking jams.

132. Pipsqueak (5.8) ★★★ Gear to 3 inches. Although length-challenged, this sublime crack is the best route on the wall. It hardly justifies a visit by itself, but anyone passing by won't leave disappointed. Bomber hand jams breeze the right side of a hanging column to anchor bolts.

133. Little Squirt (5.9) ★★ Gear to 2.5 inches. Sinker finger jams highlight this face crack left of an off-width. Unfortunately, the route ends abruptly after only a quick spurt of pleasure.

134. Dwarf's Delight (5.8) ★★ Gear to 4 inches. Tucked in a 4-foot-wide slot are an off-width and a thin crack. At first glance the *Dwarf* looks anything but delightful, though the stems between both walls are a lot of fun.

135. Short Man's Complex (5.9) ★ Gear to 3.5 inches. Around a sharp corner right from *Dwarf's Delight* are diverging cracks. The left line jams awkwardly up a right-facing dihedral and muscles past a bulge to an anchor.

129.	Little Weenie 5.7		135.	Short Man's Complex 5.9
130.	Runt's Grunt 5.7		136.	Stunted Growth 5.8 R
131.	Sawed Off Runt 5.8		137.	Napoleon Complex 5.10d
132.	Pipsqueak 5.8		138.	Short Stuff 5.10b
133.	Little Squirt 5.9		139.	Punk Kid 5.11c TR
134.	Dwarf's Delight 5.8			

136. Stunted Growth (5.8 R) ★★ Gear to 3 inches. Enjoyable hand jams up a heavily textured face highlight the right of two diverging cracks. The fun ends cutting left on face holds around an intimidating bulge.

137. Napoleon Complex (5.10d) ★★ Gear to 3 inches. Desperate stems and tip jams right off the deck highlight this tight dihedral. Above the crux, veer left to an anchor.

138. Short Stuff (5.10b) ★ Gear to 2 inches. On the right side of the So Low Wall are parallel cracks rising above blocks scattered at the base. The locking finger jams up the left crack might be worth doing if they weren't choked with dirt.

139. Punk Kid (5.11c) ★ TR. The last route on the So Low Wall follows an innocent-looking crack. If scrubbed the grade would drop; for now the filthy flares are a real struggle.

Windfall Wall

Beyond So Low Wall a path hacked through sticker bushes leads to the Windfall Wall. The full-length columns at the left end of the crag are the best on the east side of the river, offering a variety found nowhere else in the Lower Gorge. Unlike the usual route ending atop the columnar basalt, these climbs continue through the rimrock to the top of the cliff. A fixed anchor on the rim allows a two-rope rappel back to the base. Anchors atop the columnar basalt allow an easy retreat, though the

Windfall Wall–Left Side

140.	Emmaus 5.10a	145.	Fool's Pleasure 5.10a
141.	Zealot 5.12a	146.	Llama Momma 5.10b
142.	Midnight Creeper 5.8	147.	Baby Walks 5.10a R
142a.	Jeepers Creepers 5.8 X	148.	Windfall 5.11b
143.	Across the Water 5.9	149.	Hard Attack 5.11a
144.	Margo's Madness 5.10b		

follows a short seam tucked in a shallow corner right of *Emmaus*. Only climbers adept at placing small wires off flaring jams and nebulous stems should consider this testpiece. Above the corner, step right to the *Midnight Creeper* anchor.

142. Midnight Creeper (5.8) ★★ Gear to 3 inches. Far better than it looks, this block-plugged wide crack starts above a staircase of columns. You won't face a single off-width move thanks to a finger crack inches to the left. Almost everyone lowers from an anchor atop a pillar, but you can finish to the top by veering left to the finish of *Emmaus*.

142a. Jeepers Creepers (5.8 X) ★★★ Gear to 3 inches. A terrifying ending diagonals above the *Midnight Creeper* anchor across a quality face to an easy corner. A bone-breaking fall awaits anyone unfortunate enough to pop off the good holds.

143. Across the Water (5.9) ★★ Gear to 4 inches. The right side of the *Midnight Creeper* pillar offers a stemming problem between two wide cracks. Good stems eliminate the need to plunge into the depths of the off-width. Lower off, or see *Jeepers Creepers*.

rimrock finishes are best done in a single rope length from the ground.

140. Emmaus (5.10a) ★★ Gear to 2.5 inches. The far left route walks up a staircase of broken pillars before cruising sharp finger/hand jams in a left-facing corner. Crank past a fun bulge and hand-shuffle right. Continue up junky blocks (5.7) to the top of the cliff.

141. Zealot (5.12a) ★★★ Gear to 1 inch. The hardest traditional route on the East Columns

144. Margo's Madness (5.10b) ★★★ Gear to 3 inches. This gorgeous face crack splits the center of the column right of *Across the Water*. After an awkward entrance from either side, memorable finger stacks and thin hand jams quickly give way to a moderate flare. Step left to anchor chains.

145. Fool's Pleasure (5.10a) ★★★ Gear to 4 inches. Widening slowly from finger slots at the start to fist jams near the top, this attractive crack plugs a right-facing corner right of *Margo's Madness*. Lower off from the column-top anchor.

146. Llama Momma (5.10b) ★★★ Gear to 4 inches. A high-quality left-facing dihedral highlights this varied route. Start from the left with a scramble up broken columns, or take a poorly protected direct line. Hand/fist jams lead to a finger crack crux. Either lower off from anchor bolts or finish with a solid inside corner.

147. Baby Walks (5.10a R) ★★★ Gear to 3.5 inches. Another winning route follows an attractive crack right of an off-width. Begin with a wandering traverse from the left and race up strenuous jams to an anchor. Either rappel off or attack a dangerously run-out direct line on solid face holds (5.9).

148. Windfall (5.11b) ★★★ Gear to 1 inch. This appealing seam rises from the lowest part of the cliff right of several shorter cracks. After finessing a crux flare at the start, you'll have trouble catching your wind on the unremitting finish. Almost everyone raps off from anchor bolts, but a fun finish veers right on good holds to a pocketed, crack-split wall.

149. Hard Attack (5.11a) ★★★ Gear to 2.5 inches. Another high-quality route begins with closely spaced cracks in an inside corner, before cutting left around a tricky roof

to fun stems. You can weasel left to the *Windfall* anchor, but the actual route attacks a breathtaking crack on the rimrock.

150. The Sheepgate (5.11c) ★★★★ Mixed to 2.5 inches. Varied moves on perfect rock make this appealing route the best on the wall. Share the same start as *Hard Attack* but step right around a roof to strenuous tip jams. The hardest climbing comes higher, moving past a pair of roofs protected by three bolts. A convenient anchor above all difficulties allows a quick exit, avoiding a simple finishing scramble. Use a 60-meter rope.

151. Wave of Mutilation (5.12a) ★★★ 5 bolts. The only bolted column on the Windfall Wall makes a fun diversion from the cracks and stemming corners. The hardest moves come right off the deck with a vigorous sequence of side pulls.

152. Mister Reach (5.11b) ★★★ 7 bolts. Butt-ripping stems between widely spaced seams highlight this flexibility test. Swivel-hipped climbers will enjoy the insecure moves; everyone else will suffer. Originally protected by fixed pins and nuts, a line of new bolts takes some of the sting away. A new bolt left of the anchor might allow a connection with the upper part of *The Sheepgate*.

153. Bridge of Sighs (5.10d) ★★ Gear to 2.5 inches. Right of *Mister Reach* are matching seams in a shallow corner. After jamming the cracks, exit right past a blank crux on hidden holds. There's no anchor atop the columns, so veer up and right over intimidating bulges to easy climbing.

154. Genocide (5.10b) ★★ Gear to 3 inches. Left of a dark face lurks a mediocre right-facing dihedral capped by a small roof. Begin with painful hand jams in the corner and move left, joining *Bridge of Sighs* below the finishing bulges.

149.	Hard Attack 5.11a
150.	The Sheepgate 5.11c
151.	Wave of Mutilation 5.12a
152.	Mister Reach 5.11b
153.	Bridge of Sighs 5.10d
154.	Genocide 5.10b
155.	Left Gnarly Crack 5.11a TR
156.	Right Gnarly Crack 5.11a TR
157.	Swallowed 5.9
158.	Dink 5.8

157. Swallowed (5.9) ★ Gear to 3 inches. A miniscule left-arching crack rises above a short stack of columns right of the *Gnarly Cracks*. No one would ever bother if not for a convenient anchor at the top.

158. Dink (5.8) ★ Gear to 3 inches. The far right side of the Windfall Wall consists of nothing but short, insignificant seams devoid of any eye-catching lines. The only route sits at the end of these columns, left of an inside corner plugged with a guillotine flake. The 25 feet of hand jams are fun, but they hardly justify the annoyance of the long third-class scramble to the rim.

155. Left Gnarly Crack (5.11a) ★ TR. The right side of the main cliff features an unusual wall of heavily textured, dark basalt. The left of three cracks starts by scrambling up a column to the left. Reach right and follow skin-shredding jams to an anchor. The crack should protect adequately, though no one has gone for the lead.

156. Right Gnarly Crack (5.11a) ★ TR. Much like its neighbor to the left, the center of three cracks goes free on toprope but hasn't been led. Expect to lose some flesh on the cheese-grater rock.

Hand Job Wall

Beyond the Windfall Wall the full-length columns return with the Hand Job Wall. The best routes are on the higher right side of the cliff, though the shorter lines downstream are worth doing. A short chimney behind the top of the cliff provides an unexposed, third-class downclimb for any routes topping-out nearby.

159. Quickie (5.10b) ★★ Mixed to 2 inches. A single bolt protects the crux of the first route on the wall. A directional bolt down

159. Quickie 5.10b
160. My Friend of Misery 5.10d
161. Independence Day 5.10a
162. Lost and Found 5.8
163. Huckleberry Hound 5.7
164. Gagged and Bound 5.7
165. Lube Me Up, Scotty 5.10b
166. Into White 5.9
167. Strawberry Blonde 5.11c
168. Demander Cody 5.9

and right from the anchor allows a toprope of the shallow arête below.

160. My Friend of Misery (5.10d) ★★ 4 bolts. The only fully bolted sport route on the Hand Job Wall stems a flaring box corner to an anchor below the roof. A higher anchor awaits, but the short rimrock finish needs a protection bolt.

161. Independence Day (5.10a) ★★ Mixed to 2 inches. This varied route starts right of a massive pillar leaning against the wall. After stemming a box corner past a bolt, jam around the right side of a hanging column and face climb past two more bolts to an anchor. A partially bolted second pitch will someday lead over a rimrock roof to the top.

162. Lost and Found (5.8) ★★ Gear to 3 inches. A clean left-facing corner rises 15

feet right of *Independence Day*. Sinker finger jams span between wide sections before cutting right to an anchor.

163. Huckleberry Hound (5.7) ★★ Gear to 3 inches. A shallow corner rises above an unusual cave. A fleeting series of enjoyable stems and hand jams lead to anchor bolts.

164. Gagged and Bound (5.7) ★ Gear to 3.5 inches. Left of a short, bolted arête sits an obvious slot plugged by broken columns. After a simple chimney, either risk getting stuck squeezing through a tight hole or hand traverse left to anchors.

165. Lube Me Up, Scotty (5.10b) ★★ Mixed to 2.5 inches. This tempting arête might be short, but it's worth doing. A bolt-protected crux leads to fun spans between horizontal cracks splitting the column.

166. Into White (5.9)
★★ Gear to 1.5 inches.
Just right of an arête
sits a pleasant inside
corner. The jam crack
at the start gradually
peters out to crux face
holds near the top.

167. Strawberry Blonde
(5.11c) ★★ Mixed to
1 inch. A single bolt
protects the crux of this
shallow dihedral rising
above a leaning block.
At the top of the cor-
ner, either cut left to an
anchor or continue up
and right to the bolts
atop *Demander Cody*.

168. Demander Cody
(5.9) ★★ Gear to 2
inches. Perhaps the
most distinctive feature
on the Hand Job Wall
is a missing chunk of
column, leaving a roof-
capped chimney in its
place. An intimidat-
ing undercling escapes
around the left side of
the roof, leading to an easier finish in a shallow, lichen-covered corner.

169. Mines of Moria (5.8 R) ★★ Gear to
2.5 inches. Nothing at Smith compares to
this claustrophobic chimney. Jam and stem
to a roof and say goodbye to daylight as you
enter an eerie chimney behind a missing
section of column. Squirm toward the light
high above and follow another hidden chimney to the top of the cliff.

170. Cody's Corner (5.8) ★★ Gear to 2.5

Hand Job Wall–Right Side

168.	Demander Cody 5.9	173.	Ugly as Sin 5.11a
169.	Mines of Moria 5.8 R	174.	Hand Job 5.10b
170.	Cody's Corner 5.8	175.	Original Sin 5.10c
171.	McKenzie's Way 5.11b	176.	Blitzkrieg 5.9
172.	Killer Jism 5.11b	177.	Blitzen 5.10c

inches. The right exit around a hanging column reaches blindly to good jams. After clearing the roof, cut right to the finishing corner.

171. McKenzie's Way (5.11b) ★★ Gear to
2 inches. A short crux followed by simple
climbing makes this short-lived route a
natural for anyone looking for a cheap 5.11.
Begin with the starting crack of *Cody's
Corner* and shuffle right to thin jams.

172. Killer Jism (5.11b) ★★ Gear to 1 inch.
This nasty route follows a blackened seam
rising above a small, slanting block. The

insecure stems on flaking rock leave much to be desired.

173. Ugly as Sin (5.11a) ★ Gear to 2.5 inches. An 8-foot flat-topped pillar sits at the base of an ugly inside corner. If thoroughly scrubbed a decent route might emerge; for now expect unforgiving jams and stems on dirt-covered walls.

174. Hand Job (5.10b) ★★★ Gear to 2.5 inches. The best route on the wall jams and stems between double cracks right of a 6-foot chunk of basalt. After a tricky bouldering start, the feel-good finish jams perfect rock with sinker protection.

175. Original Sin (5.10c) ★★★ Gear to 2.5 inches. One of the few 1.25- to 1.5-inch cracks in the Gorge provides training for climbers with Yosemite aspirations. It starts with locking hand jams in a shallow dihedral and slowly narrows to a pumping crux near the top.

176. Blitzkrieg (5.9) ★★ Gear to 4.5 inches. After a quick glance most climbers pass on this zigzagging off-width. If you're looking for a tussle, stem double cracks low and storm awkward moves past a few loose blocks. Escape left, or continue right to anchors.

177. Blitzen (5.10c) ★★ Gear to 3.5 inches. The last route on the wall follows a short right-leaning crack. After scrambling atop a pillar, annoying hand/fist jams give way to crux finger slots near the top.

Arrington Columns

A third-class chimney marks the right boundary of the Hand Job Wall. Beyond are many short, jumbled columns ending at a ledge running along the midsection of the cliff. With only a couple exceptions, these routes don't come close to matching the quality found elsewhere in the Gorge. Most climbers forego the simple rimrock finishes by rappelling from anchor bolts atop the columnar joints.

178. Crunch Time (5.8) ★ Gear to 3 inches. The first route on Arrington Columns jams an undistinguished crack above the highest point on the hillside. A killer block guarding the final moves awaits some unlucky climber. Either rappel from bolts or follow a crack (5.5) to the top.

179. Exiled Man (5.8) ★ Gear to 3 inches. Crammed right of *Crunch Time* is a crack capped by a hanging flake. Fun hand jams lead to a risky encounter at the top.

180. Brother's Child (5.10c) ★★★ Gear to 2.5 inches. Unlike most routes in the Gorge, this line offers two enjoyable pitches. Some climbers rappel after the starting corner, but the best part attacks the overhanging rimrock. Start right of an 8-foot pillar. **Pitch 1:** (5.10b) Contend with flaky rock at the start and you'll be rewarded with fun jams ending at an anchor. **Pitch 2:** (5.10c) Muscle an intimidating crack past a bulge to a finish on big face holds. Descend 100 feet downstream via the Hand Job Wall chimney.

181. Chimney Sweep (5.7 R) ★ Gear to 4 inches. Easy but poorly protected stems between wide cracks lead to a ledge. Either rappel or follow a simple (5.5) second pitch to the left.

182. Master Loony (5.11a) ★★★★ Mixed to 2.5 inches. Unlike anything else in the Lower Gorge, this exceptional route shouldn't be missed. Anyone bored with straight-in cracks and stemming corners will thrill over the exciting jugs at the crux, muscling around a bolted roof. The starting crack (5.10b) makes a fine affair in its own right, but the real fun begins above.

Arrington Columns—Left Side

178.	Crunch Time 5.8		183.	Looney Tunes 5.11b R
179.	Exiled Man 5.8		184.	Tuned Out 5.9 R
180.	Brother's Child 5.10c		185.	Stuffed Turkey 5.8
181.	Chimney Sweep 5.7 R		186.	Off Tempo 5.10a
182.	Master Looney 5.11a		187.	Banana Split 5.8

185. Stuffed Turkey

(5.8) ★ Gear to 5 inches. Poor protection and dirty rock detract from this turkey of a route. Begin by stemming between wide cracks leading into an ending chimney.

The next several routes follow short cracks to a long ledge below the rimrock. Bolts allow a quick descent, but three options await anyone going for the top. A chimney on the left and a ramp to the right are easy, pointless scrambles. The only decent finish stems an inside corner (5.7) between the other exits.

186. Off Tempo

(5.10a) ★★ Gear to 5 inches. An attractive wide crack splits a flat face of great rock between two columns. Despite the quality, few climbers brave the depths of the off-width.

187. Banana Split (5.8) ★ Gear to 4 inches.

Looming above a small, lichen-covered block are clean double cracks. Tolerable stems and liebacks end at an anchor.

188. Chimney Fire (5.7 R) ★ Gear to 4

inches. Another mediocre stemming problem looms between two columns rising above a massive chunk of basalt. Begin with a scramble up the right side of the starting block.

183. Loony Tunes (5.11b R) ★★ Gear to 1.5

inches. Left of a dismal wide crack looms a blank, sparsely protected corner. Sensible climbers stem off a block to the right at the crux, but the first ascent foolishly ignored it completely (5.11c). Atop the crack, either finish to the rim via *Master Loony* or cut left to rappel anchors.

184. Tuned Out (5.9 R) ★ Gear to 6

inches. This awkward, uninspiring slot squeezes past a detached block to a few fist jams. Swing right and finish with a simple chimney.

187.	Banana Split 5.8	191.	Banned For Life 5.10b
188.	Chimney Fire 5.7 R	192.	Shackles and Chains 5.8
189.	Lucky Guy 5.10c	193.	Sleeping Dog 5.7
190.	Common Criminal 5.8	194.	Slasher 5.10a

189. Lucky Guy (5.10c) ★★ Gear to 2.5 inches. A few feet right of a rectangular 10-foot block sits a shallow, lichen-covered corner. Deceptively tricky jams end below an optional rimrock dihedral.

190. Common Criminal (5.8) ★★ Gear to 3.5 inches. A distinctive wedged pillar blocks the upper section of a deep-set corner. After climbing into a slot, locking hand jams escape around the left side of the obstacle.

191. Banned For Life (5.10b) ★ Gear to 2.5 inches. Rising from the left side of a sagebrush-covered ledge is a disappointing thin crack. Begin by finessing past a loose block on finger jams and avoid a blank finish by veering left.

192. Shackles and Chains (5.8) ★★ Gear to 3 inches. A quick hand crack splits the short corner above a sagebrush-capped ledge. Hexes work better than cams in the angular slots.

193. Sleeping Dog (5.7) ★★ Gear to 4 inches. The last of several identical chimneys between widely spaced columns rises above a flat plate of basalt. The moves aren't special, but the right crack eats nuts and the low grade appeals to entry-level Gorge climbers. The easy finish on the rimrock adds to the adventure.

194. Slasher (5.10a) ★★ Gear to 3 inches. The vegetated cracks along the right end of the Arrington Columns offer few options. The only eye-catching line finger jams to

rotted slings and attacks a bulging crack splitting the rimrock. The best climbing comes
on the strenuous finish, though the start
alone makes a good jaunt (5.9).

Shakespeare Cliff

The final full-size East Columns crag contains several excellent cracks. Since the
columns aren't especially steep, you'll find
the best easy routes in the entire Gorge.
The first lines start uphill on the left side
of the wall.

**195. Love Struck
Romeo** (5.8) ★★ Gear
to 3 inches. A hand
crack bordered by an
off-width rises behind
a freestanding pillar at
the start of the cliff.
Locking jams mixed
with optional stems to
the right lead to a fin-
ishing chimney.

196. Big Woody (5.9)
★★ Gear to 3 inches.
Right of a distinctive
balanced column are
double cracks converg-
ing into an inverted
spike. Skirt around the
left side of this tooth and
jam a stiff hand crack to
easy scrambling.

197. Little Stiffy
(5.10b) ★ Gear to 3
inches. The disap-
pointing crack right
of *Big Woody* doesn't
match the quality of
other routes on the
Shakespeare Cliff.

198. As You Like It (5.10b) ★★★ Gear to 2.5
inches. One of the best cracks on the wall
starts off the right side of a small, flat block.
Fly up thin hand slots in a left-facing corner
to a finger jam crux and finish with a crank
around a rimrock bulge.

198a. Yost in Space (5.11a) ★★★ TR. The
enjoyable column a few feet to the right
makes a fun toprope jaunt after an ascent of
As You Like It.

199. Sauron (5.9) ★★ Gear to 4 inches.
Closely spaced cracks split the left side of a

Shakespeare Cliff

195.	Love Struck Romeo 5.8	202.	Puck 5.10a
196.	Big Woody 5.9	203.	Othello 5.9
197.	Little Stiffy 5.10b	204.	Azog 5.9
198.	As You Like It 5.10b	204a.	Midsummer Night's Scream 5.9
198a.	Yost in Space 5.11a TR	205.	Ophelia 5.8
199.	Sauron 5.9	206.	Two Gentlemen's Pneumonia 5.7
200.	Measure for Madness 5.11d	207.	Lust Labours Cost 5.10b
201.	Much Ado About Nothing 5.10d	208.	King Smear 5.11a

massive, flat column. After boorish moves in the starting flare, jam and stem to a final pull over a steep bulge.

200. Measure for Madness (5.11d) ★★★ 8
bolts. Shakespeare Cliff's token sport route ascends a prominent, flat column face. After a low-angle start the column steepens and the difficulties mount with a stylish crux at two-thirds height.

201. Much Ado About Nothing (5.10d) ★★★
Gear to 3 inches. The most varied route on the wall starts from the lowest point of the cliff line, bordering the right edge of *Measure for Madness*. The original route jammed to a premature ending at an anchor (5.9), but the highlight blasts through an intimidating finger crack roof on the finishing rimrock.

202. Puck (5.10a) ★★★ Gear to 2.5 inches.
A varied traditional route ascends the clean crack right of *Much Ado About Nothing*. Atop the crack, muscle through the rimrock crux, clearing a small roof on big holds.

203. Othello (5.9) ★★★ Gear to 2.5 inches.
A shallow right-facing corner offers a pleasant pitch of finger jams and stems. The first ascent climbed through the rimrock to the top. Most climbers prefer joining *Midsummer Night's Scream* to the left.

204. Azog (5.9) ★★ Gear to 3 inches. The first
crack right of *Othello* succumbs to moderate jams. Atop a shallow dihedral, avoid the rimrock by sidestepping right to an anchor.

204a. Midsummer Night's Scream (5.9)
★★★ Gear to 3 inches. The best finish to *Azog* cuts left through the rimrock and mantels to an anchor. Big holds slash the grade but not the thrill of pulling around the exposed bulge (5.7).

205. Ophelia (5.8) ★★★ Gear to 3 inches.
Another desirable, easy option jams closely

spaced double cracks ending at a small bulge. Early ascents continued directly to the top of the cliff, though it's more convenient to cut right to an anchor.

206. Two Gentlemen's Pneumonia (5.7) ★★
Gear to 4 inches. A massive angular block plugs a wide crack on the left side of a pillar. Easy moves lead past this chunk to a short off-width ending at an anchor.

207. Lusts Labours Cost (5.10b) ★★★ Gear
to 3 inches. Parallel cracks split the wall above short, broken columns. Scramble up easy fractured rock to a large ledge and savor enjoyable jams, stepping left to an anchor.

208. King Smear (5.11a) ★ Gear to 3
inches. The smooth-sided corner on the right succumbs to skin-shredding tip jams and blank stems. Save your cuticles and look elsewhere.

Midwest Cliff

Upstream from Shakespeare Cliff the unbroken cliff band finally fades away. Generations surprisingly didn't even notice, but a final crag sits far upstream, just before the bend in the Crooked River. It ain't pretty, but the jumbled cliff contains several recent routes. With anchors atop the rim, all of these routes are easily toproped.

209. Ole' Kentucky (5.8) ★ Gear to 3 inches.
This homely route starts with a short box corner leading to a corridor ending at a small roof. Jam a crack on the right and jog back left to a finishing crack system.

210. Pond Hockey (5.10b) ★ Mixed to 6
inches. The most appealing line on the wall follows a sport-bolted line in the middle of the crag. After a promising start you'll face a finishing wide crack.

Midwest Cliff

209.	Ole' Kentucky 5.8
210.	Pond Hockey 5.10b
211.	Chicago Love Affair 5.10b
212.	Detroit Rock City 5.9
212a.	Twelve Hours to Muncie 5.9

211. Chicago Love Affair (5.10b) ★ Gear to 6 inches. Next up in a row of second-rate routes begins with a short corner just left of a wide crack, leading to a brief hand traverse left of an obvious crack system. Again your reward at the top is a dingy off-width.

212. Detroit Rock City (5.9) ★ Gear to 6 inches. The most obvious line on the wall starts with a crescent-shaped wide crack. The finish, of course, is another off-width.

212a. Twelve Hours to Muncie (5.9) ★ Gear to 6 inches. The last route in the Lower Gorge follows fun jams right of the crescent-shaped crack. Continue to the top of the cliff via the *Detroit Rock City* off-width.

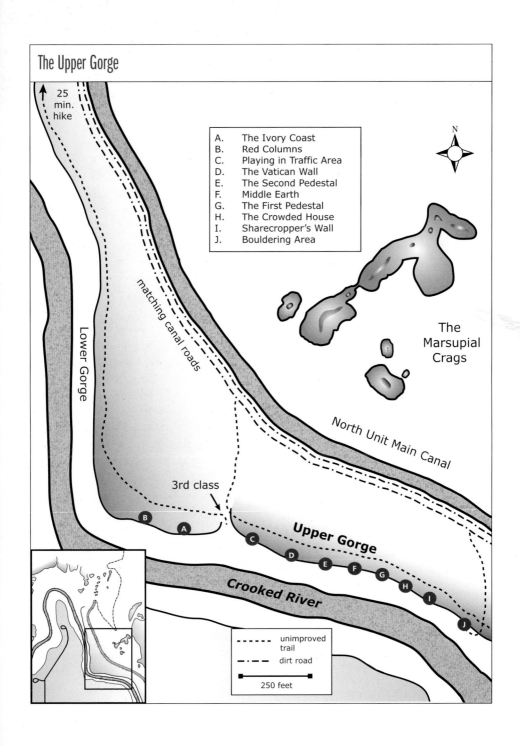

The Upper Gorge

25 min. hike

A. The Ivory Coast
B. Red Columns
C. Playing in Traffic Area
D. The Vatican Wall
E. The Second Pedestal
F. Middle Earth
G. The First Pedestal
H. The Crowded House
I. Sharecropper's Wall
J. Bouldering Area

N

matching canal roads

Lower Gorge

The Marsupial Crags

North Unit Main Canal

3rd class

B

A

C

Upper Gorge

D

E

F

G

H

I

J

Crooked River

- - - - unimproved trail
- · - · dirt road

250 feet

THE UPPER GORGE

Jeff Frizzell was as uniquely suited to the Upper Gorge as I imagine any climber ever has been to any crag. Copious levels of power were often inadequate to ensure success on his testpieces. Warming up on the hangboard one day, I stumbled onto Jeff's strength secret—he didn't have any! "Here's a simple routine that starts out with ten chins," I said. "That may be a problem," came the reply, "I can't do ten chins." I've often replayed that exchange—sitting under one of his projects and wishing for just a little more fitness. Goodness knows what unholy level of kinesthetic talent he must have possessed in order to succeed on some of those routes. Jeff was all about adding up to more than the sum of his parts and beating the odds. Some people climbed a little harder than he did, but I don't think I ever saw anyone climb better.

Paul Marshall

The columns of the Upper Gorge contain one of the most remarkable collections of basalt sport routes in the country. Tucked away in the remote upper reaches of the Crooked River canyon, the quarter mile of flawless columnar basalt is a paradise for technically oriented sport climbers. There's no crag at Smith matching the intense concentration of difficult lines. The elegant arêtes, delicate faces, and precarious stemming problems offer almost unlimited challenges for high-end climbers.

Located upstream and around the bend from the traditional columns, the Upper Gorge is a world all its own. While climbers swarm over Smith's more famous crags, these secluded routes attract surprisingly little attention. Nowhere else on Smith basalt is the sport climbing ethic so fully embraced—except for a handful of easier lines, you won't need the typical Gorge rack of cams and wires. To some climbers the Upper Gorge seems overdeveloped, as a bewildering array of bolts cover the best sections of cliff. But the lines are typically well defined, and the density results more from the nature of the columnar basalt than an overzealous compression of routes. It'll dishearten a staunch traditionalist, but most sport climbers feel like a kid in a candy store, deciding which treat to sample next.

The Upper Gorge caters only to experienced climbers. For many years the sheer difficulty of the climbing limited the number of visitors, but today there's plenty of reason to visit—even if you can't climb 5.12. With over forty-five sport routes under 5.12 (including fifteen 5.10s), it's a great destination for the midlevel climber. Novices, however, should take heed—the Upper Gorge makes an exceptionally poor choice for the beginner. Apart from the lack of low-end routes, it's one of Smith's most isolated crags—if you get hurt, you'll wait hours for a rescue.

Despite the quality and range of difficulties, the Upper Gorge has never gained the acceptance of many elite Smith climbers. Ultimately, the biggest reason for the bias was simple—those accustomed to Smith tuff often found it tough-going on the basalt. The cerebral sequences usually aren't obvious, and the edgy footwork required on the tuff doesn't easily translate to the smears of the basalt. Furthermore, many routes are unusually hard on-sights for the grade—unlocking the solution to the cruxes requires creativity and patience. Some belittle Gorge climbing for the repetition of one blank corner after another. Veteran Upper Gorge climbers know this isn't a fair argument—especially in the higher grades. Each high-level route has a character all its own, every bit as recognizable as the tuff classics.

From the earliest days of Gorge climbing, explorers turned the bend, gazing upon a seemingly endless series of blank corners. Basalt pioneer Wayne Arrington climbed the most obvious cracks in the mid-1970s, including *Land of the Lost* (5.10a) and *Gondor* (5.10b). For the climbers of the era, these jam cracks were the only possible lines, as everything else required bolts. During the boom years of the eighties, Lower Gorge climbers explored upstream, but no one relished the idea of agonizing hand drilling. Still, the legend quickly spread that the "5.12 Wall" held the future of Gorge climbing.

For fifteen years after the earliest ascents, absolutely nothing happened here. This changed with remarkable swiftness in 1989 as motivated climbers arrived equipped with the key to opening the door to the Upper Gorge—the power drill. Over six obsessive months, Jeff Frizzell and Tom Egan established two dozen difficult sport routes, highlighted by Frizzell's *Hot Lava* (5.13b) and Egan's *Controlled Hysteria* (5.13a). Egan eventually moved to the tuff, but Frizzell dedicated himself to realizing the ultimate potential of the crag.

Unusually well suited for the unique world of Gorge climbing, Frizzell possessed all the necessary talents to succeed—technical excellence, flexibility, creativity, and a monomaniacal focus. His final tally was over sixty new routes, including six 5.13s, capped by *Big Tuna* (5.13c), the hardest route anywhere on Smith basalt. Other Frizzell routes such as *Peruvian Skies* (5.13a), *Feminazis* (5.13a), and *Cuban Slide* (5.13b) will both tantalize and torment generations of future basalt climbers. Had Frizzell compiled such an impressive list of first ascents on Smith tuff, he'd be recognized as a pioneer of the sport climbing movement. Instead, he's likely the most underappreciated climber in Smith history.

Jeff Frizzell, 2002. BRENT MCGREGOR PHOTO

Much like its counterpart downstream, the Upper Gorge faces a few vexing problems. Although property boundaries aren't perfectly clear, many downstream routes (including the entire Red Columns) are privately owned. Fortunately, all upriver routes are on Bureau of Land Management (BLM) land. After nearly two decades of trouble-free use, this is less of a problem than originally feared. However, ownership sometimes changes hands—if you're ever confronted, please be respectful and leave. The future of climbing in the entire Gorge might depend on your behavior. Hopefully in the future, climbers, landowners, and Oregon State Parks will arrive at a solution to ensure that this unique recreational resource will forever remain open to the public.

Two additional problems might plague future Gorge climbers. The earliest pioneers faced formidable amounts of undergrowth along the base of the columns, including poison oak and sumac. For more than a decade, their path hacked through the jungle provided pain-free access along the base. Unfortunately, by the summer of 2008, the hike through the Gorge had returned to the pre-climbing days, with head-high stinging nettles and thick overgrowth almost the entire length of the canyon. Hopefully a real trail will someday be blasted through the bushes—until this happens the Upper Gorge's popularity will be limited. A lesser problem is the Crooked River itself. During extremely wet years, the water rises so high you'll need a boat to visit. Fortunately, this happens only once every twenty years or so. When the river floods, walking upstream from the base of the approach gully is impossible.

Sun bathes the Upper Gorge almost all day, making it a fine destination in the winter. You can climb on the coldest days, no matter what the temperature, as long as the sun shines. Like the rest of Smith, the prime seasons for the Upper Gorge are spring and fall; during the summer the sweltering canyon bakes until late afternoon. The harder routes are more condition-dependent than comparable routes on the tuff—the grades increase noticeably on the warmest days. Still, you can hang out comfortably once the sun dips below the rim, as a cooling breeze often blows downstream.

Despite the length, the leisurely forty-minute approach from the parking area is hardly unpleasant, with minimal uphill walking. Turn right at the bridge below Picnic Lunch Wall and hike a mile around the northern bend of the Crooked River. Hike up the draw between Staender Ridge and the Student Wall and cut right on a good trail below the irrigation tunnel. Follow this flat trail along the eastern rim of the Gorge, beyond the bend in the river, to the top of the Upper Gorge entrance gully. Zigzag down third-class ledges to the base of the crag. During the early 1990s everyone approached from the south along the canal road. Locked gates now block access to the bridge spanning the canyon. Please do not use this approach—it might save a few minutes of hiking, but it places future climbing in serious jeopardy.

Finding the crags: The route descriptions assume the most common approach—the entrance gully between the Ivory Coast and the Playing in Traffic Area. If using an alternate approach (entering from either end of the Upper Gorge), either the upstream or downstream routes will be in reverse order.

DOWNSTREAM ROUTES

From the base of the approach gully, the columns extend both upstream and downstream. The downstream columns contain the remarkable routes of the Ivory Coast and Red Columns. Dubbed the 5.12 Wall on a reconnaissance visit in the mid-1980s, these cliffs more than lived up to their original billing. Today they contain one of the most concentrated selections of high-level routes at Smith. Unlike the rest of the Upper Gorge, which rests on BLM land, the downstream routes are privately owned. There are anchors along the rim above every route on these crags, but you'll keep a lower profile if you avoid these. You can always stick-clip your way up any route if you aren't feeling up to an on-sight attempt.

The Ivory Coast

The Ivory Coast stretches from the right side of the cliff to a bolted column route called *The Urge*. Why it arbitrarily ends here is a mystery, but the Red Columns continue to the end of the cliff line. These impressive routes display Upper Gorge climbing at its very best.

1. Shrimpton's Shrine (5.12a) ★ TR. Easy to pass by, this obscure toprope problem isn't worth the hassle of rigging a toprope. Before the better lines start, look for an indistinct right-facing corner distinguished by elongated pockets. Someone will eventually bolt the *Shrine,* but it'll never be a classic.

2. Shame (5.11d) ★★ 8 bolts. The first sport route on the Ivory Coast follows a seam set in a shallow left-leaning corner. Delicate stemming at the start gives way to fun climbing on the arête to the right.

The Ivory Coast–Right Side

1.	Shrimpton's Shrine 5.12a TR	6.	Black Nails 5.10c
2.	Shame 5.11d	7.	The Fugitive 5.11d
3.	Orphan's Cruel 5.12b	8.	Wardance 5.12a
4.	Chillin' in the Penzo 5.12c	9.	Big Tuna 5.13c
5.	Punk Primitive 5.11b	10.	Steaming Café Flirts 5.12c

3. Orphan's Cruel (5.12b) ★★★ 7 bolts. Despite dirty-looking rock at the start, this faint corner is stimulating, sustained, and never dull. It'll improve quickly as more ascents brush clean the sandy stone.

4. Chillin' in the Penzo (5.12c) ★★★★ 11 bolts. The first of many Upper Gorge classics follows the second corner left of *Orphan's Cruel*. The rock at the start might not match the usual Upper Gorge quality, but the moves are diverse and high caliber. Begin with pockets on the left and cut right to buckets leading to a stemming crux at two-thirds height.

5. Punk Primitive (5.11b) ★★★★ 9 bolts. An excellent warm-up tackles the left side of a prominent edge. You'll take in a little of everything, from face moves and stems to finger jams. Finish with an enjoyable romp up the arête to the right.

6. Black Nails (5.10c) ★★ 10 bolts. Compared to everything else on the Ivory Coast, this squeezed route is a walk in the park. It provides a good introduction to Gorge stemming, with a fun finish clearing a couple small roofs.

7. The Fugitive (5.11d) ★★ 10 bolts. Slightly right of the *Wardance* box corner rests a shallow inside corner splitting a patch of filthy gray rock. A lackluster crux on creaky holds leads to a much better finish with stems and edges leading over a dinky roof.

8. Wardance (5.12a) ★★★ 10 bolts. This leg-cramping stem-a-thon will thrill any box corner fanatic. If you're not a member of this club, you'll want to make a different choice. The repetitive nature of the climbing can wear your patience, or whet your appetite, depending on your tastes.

9. Big Tuna (5.13c) ★★★★ 11 bolts. Deserving of far more attention, this amazing column ranks among the finest sport routes at Smith. Brilliant, audacious, and pumping, *Big Tuna* won't disappoint. A bewildering array of bouldery moves keep coming the whole way, but technical prowess alone won't suffice—you'll be hard pressed to hang on as your forearms scream for relief. The start takes a direct line, with an optional first bolt stick-clip.

10. Steaming Café Flirts (5.12c) ★★★ 7 bolts. Immediately left of the *Big Tuna* column sits a vicious stemming problem in a tight inside corner. A bizarre series of technical moves will exhaust your body and fry your brain (and vice versa).

11. Controlled Hysteria (5.13a) ★★★★ 10 bolts. As the most popular 5.13 in the Gorge, this demanding seam is the entrance exam to the harder routes. The hysterical start battles a blend of stems and edges, but you'll fly off higher up if you don't maintain control on the still-tricky finish.

12. Slack Mackerel (5.12b) ★★★ 7 bolts. Tucked right of a sharp arête is a right-facing dihedral. The demanding liebacks and stems are worth doing, but you'll feel squeezed near the top with *Controlled Hysteria* just inches to the right.

13. Project–Savage Truth (5.13?) This sharp arête is arguably the most attractive line in the entire Upper Gorge. Unfortunately, the column isn't wide enough to make it an independent line. As a slightly contrived toprope problem, it remains one of the Gorge's last great problems.

14. New Breed Leader (5.12b) ★★★ 9 bolts. Left of *Savage Truth* looms a striking inside corner marked by an odd slot at the first bolt. The creative stemming at the start provides a good introduction to the mechanics of Gorge climbing. Above the top-notch

The Ivory Coast–Left Side

9.	Big Tuna 5.13c	16.	Cuban Slide 5.13b
10.	Steaming Café Flirts 5.12c	17.	The Urge 5.12d
11.	Controlled Hysteria 5.13a	18.	Colorsplash 5.10b
12.	Slack Mackerel 5.12b	19.	Special Effects 5.11d
13.	Project–Savage Truth 5.13?	20.	Project 5.12+?
14.	New Breed Leader 5.12b	21.	Yellow Fin 5.12b
15.	Peach Nails 5.12c	22.	Bangstick 5.11b

esoteric climbing requires more brainpower than firepower. Stacked with hard moves, you could (and will) fall off almost anywhere.

17. The Urge (5.12d) ★★★★ 7 bolts. This elegant column provides a fine change of pace from the conventional Gorge stemming corner. Good shakes interrupt an enchanting series of baffling boulder problems. Expect a sporting mantel onto a ledge past the fourth bolt.

Red Columns

The Urge marks the left boundary of the Ivory Coast. There's no break in the cliff line, but the attractive downstream routes now comprise the Red Columns. The standards don't match the Ivory Coast, but the quality is every bit as high. Apart from a couple unclimbed corners, this section of cliff is completely climbed out.

crux, the climbing eases greatly with a finish on pumping face holds.

15. Peach Nails (5.12c) ★★★ 10 bolts. This challenging shallow corner keeps dishing it out from bottom to top. The hardest moves aren't far off the ground, but you'll be fighting the entire way to the anchor.

16. Cuban Slide (5.13b) ★★★ 10 bolts. Just right of an obvious flat-faced column rises Smith's hardest stemming problem. The

18. Colorsplash (5.10b) ★★★ Gear to 3 inches. An appealing finger/hand crack splits the yellow face left of *The Urge*. It might be popular if it was in the Lower Gorge, but fate placed it in the middle of a sport crag. Sport climbers never carry a rack, and die-hard traditionalists can't bear looking at the densely bolted cliff.

19. Special Effects (5.11d) ★★★ 8 bolts. The line of bolts left of *Colorsplash* might be easier than most sport routes on the crag, but it'll humble anyone expecting a stroll. The difficulties begin at the fourth bolt and continue unabated to the anchor.

20. Project (5.12+?) 10 bolts. A fully prepared project stems to a hanging column, steps right to a shallow corner, and continues through an intense rimrock bulge to an anchor. It'll be a free climb in the not-too-distant future.

21. Yellow Fin (5.12b) ★★★ 10 bolts. The first edition of this quality route began to the right before cutting left around a hanging column roof. The improved modern version starts with an attractive face to the left joining the original line just past the roof. Enjoyable arête moves lead to a finishing mantel on the rimrock.

22. Bangstick (5.11b) ★★ 9 bolts. This stemming problem sits immediately right of a bolted column. The vigorous stems and palms will please box corner devotees and annoy anyone less enamored with the technique.

23. Shark Infested Waters (5.12b) ★★★ 9 bolts. This alluring, low-tech column should please anyone unfamiliar with the finer nuances of Upper Gorge climbing. The clips require some creativity, but it's all part of the fun. The sharp-toothed crux comes at the top, yanking past a physical bulge.

24. The Big Kill (5.12a) ★★ 8 bolts. Just left of a rare unclimbed dihedral rises this typical Upper Gorge stemming corner. The moves are crafty but not unlike other nearby lines.

25. Screams and Whispers (5.12b) ★★★ 10 bolts. The first corner left of *The Big Kill*

Red Columns

22.	Bangstick 5.11b	28.	Persuasion 5.12a
23.	Shark Infested Waters 5.12b	29.	Atlas Shrugged 5.12c
24.	The Big Kill 5.12a	30.	Slay the Dragon 5.12c
25.	Screams and Whispers 5.12b	31.	Rainbow's End 5.11c
26.	Brazilian Skies 5.12b	32.	Almost Something 5.10c
27.	Red Lilly Q 5.12c		

blends contorted stems with a face climbing finish. The moves are high quality, though you might struggle if you can't twist yourself into a pretzel.

26. Brazilian Skies (5.12b) ★★★ 7 bolts. This worthwhile route blends box corner stemming and technical face climbing. It might be relatively straightforward if it was one or the other, but the transitions provide a constant challenge.

27. Red Lily Q (5.12c) ★★★ 7 bolts. The first corner left of *Brazilian Skies* features a tuff-like one-finger pocket pulling past a tweaky bulge. The artsy climbing above will remind you that you're still in the Gorge.

28. Persuasion (5.12a) ★★★ 7 bolts. Bordered by unclimbed dihedrals to either side, this worthwhile inside corner starts above a small, white-capped slab. If you stick a throw to a sloper you'll be through the crux, but the thought-provoking moves never really let up. Expect a tough clip low on the route.

29. Atlas Shrugged (5.12c) ★★★★ 9 bolts. Arguably the finest Red Column route ascends an alluring corner, left of the last unclimbed dihedral on the cliff. Sustained, precise, and eccentric, *Atlas Shrugged* has a nature all its own. The business comes in the lower half of the route, but it'll stay with you to the very end.

30. Slay the Dragon (5.12c) ★★★ 6 bolts. At the left end of the Red Columns, the beautiful full-length corners give way to less appealing seams. The last attractive corner begins with a crux stem past a flare. The climbing eases briefly, but many gallant efforts end near the top with a blind face move.

31. Rainbow's End (5.11c) ★★ 5 bolts. Around the corner left of *Slay the Dragon* rises a final unbroken corner that doesn't match the quality of its neighbor. The contrived climbing forces you to decide between tricky moves to the right and easier off-route holds to the left.

32. Almost Something (5.10c) ★ 6 bolts. The final route on the Red Columns doesn't match the quality of everything else on the crag. Intended as a warm-up for nearby routes, *Almost Something* is nothing much at all.

UPSTREAM ROUTES

Upstream from the base of the approach gully, an unbroken wall of columnar basalt stretches nearly 200 yards. Unlike the consistently difficult downstream lines, these routes hold wider appeal with many moderate sport routes. Crack climbers might enjoy the small assortment of naturally protected lines, but the sheer number of glittering bolts will offend hardcore traditionalists. You can reach the anchors atop most of these routes from many bolts along the rim.

Playing in Traffic Area

The first section of upstream columns rises above a row of juniper trees and snags. The rock quality doesn't match the usual Upper Gorge crag, but the wide range of difficulties will inevitably attract many climbers. A distinctive jumbled band splits the entire left side of the cliff, breaking the continuity of the first dozen routes. During exceptionally high-water years, the base of the first several routes is submerged.

33. Empty-Headed Hound (5.10b) ★★ 9 bolts. This rambling but worthwhile warm-up bears little resemblance to the average Upper Gorge route. Begin with a short crack and veer left past a mini-roof on good holds. The solid upper slab continues far above to a second crux high on the wall.

34. Dig Dig (5.11d) ★ 6 bolts. Another atypical Gorge route shares the start with the *Hound*. After a contrived crux past the fourth bolt, steep climbing on big holds cuts right past a pumping bulge to anchors. You can toprope the upper section from the anchor atop *Empty-Headed Hound*.

35. The Seep (5.10b) ★★ 5 bolts. This atypical jug-haul hides

Playing in Traffic Area—Left Side

33.	Empty-Headed Hound 5.10b	39.	Talladega 5.11c
34.	Dig Dig 5.11d	40.	Black Orpheus 5.12c
35.	The Seep 5.10b	41.	Calliope 5.10c
36.	Formula One 5.11c	42.	Drepane 5.10d
37.	Racer X 5.11b	43.	Six Hits of Sunshine 5.11c
38.	Sprint Car 5.10b		

ehind a snag. Depending on the season you might be standing in a marsh at the start, but the rock stays dry—it makes a worthwhile warm-up for the harder lines.

36. Formula One (5.11c) ★★★ 9 bolts. You wouldn't guess by looking, but this varied route shouldn't be missed. Insecure moves off the deck lead to fun pockets and a pit stop at a big hueco. Step right to crux edges and weave through a fun overhang to an anchor.

37. Racer X (5.11b) ★★ 6 bolts. A devious move leads into a short but deceptively pumpy box corner. After a rest the crux strikes just below the anchor.

38. Sprint Car (5.10b) ★★ 8 bolts. Delightful pockets on the starting arête highlight this simple sport route. Above, step left to a short box corner and finish high on the solid rimrock.

39. Talladega (5.11c) ★★★ 9 bolts. A more difficult version of *Sprint Car* races up the same shallow arête and steps right to a technical seam in a shallow corner. Above all difficulties, move back left on the rimrock, rejoining *Sprint Car* just before the checkered flag.

40. Black Orpheus (5.12c) ★★★ 11 bolts. There's nothing repetitive about this challenging route. The

character changes from artsy edges at the start to physical cranks on the overhanging rimrock at the top. The easier midsection shares the same shallow seam as *Talladega*.

41. Calliope (5.10c) ★★ 6 bolts. Developing Gorge climbers will enjoy this pint-size version of the more difficult columns. Start behind a cluster of triple snags and climb moderate rock capped by a long reach to a sloper.

42. Drepane (5.10d) ★★ 10 bolts. To keep the grade at a moderate level, *Drepane* intentionally avoids a more direct path. Sustained

Playing in Traffic Area—Right Side

44.	Milky Way 5.11c	47.	Playing in Traffic 5.12b
44a.	Milky Way start 5.10b	48.	Octane 96 5.12b
45.	Virtual Beach 5.11a	49.	Starkist 5.11a
46.	Spellbound 5.11c	50.	Just Do It 5.10a

climbing on the left leads to a crux move just below a jumbled band. Step right and stem a 5.10 box corner to a rimrock finish. Despite the less-than-classic line, the climbing is excellent.

43. Six Hits of Sunshine (5.11c) ★★★ 10 bolts. A more difficult, high-quality counterpart follows a line as whacky as its partner to the left. The lower and upper halves are both 5.11, split by a good rest. Begin with a pocketed left-leaning corner and huck to a midpitch ledge, crossing left over *Drepane.* After a delicate corner, finish with pumping moves on the rimrock.

44. Milky Way (5.11c) ★★ 10 bolts. This bolted column capped by a committing dyno provides many good moments. A no-hands ledge in the middle allows a complete recovery, though the moderate start shouldn't tire you much.

44a. Milky Way start (5.10b) ★★ 5 bolts. One of the easier sport routes in the Upper Gorge ascends the lower half of *Milky Way,* stepping left at the midpitch ledge to an anchor.

45. Virtual Beach (5.11a) ★★ 10 bolts. The first unbroken corner in the Playing in Traffic Area isn't one of the finest, but it's still worth climbing. Grit-covered stems at the start slowly give way to cleaner rock, finishing with a bulge-pull on the rimrock.

46. Spellbound (5.11c) ★★ Mixed to 3.5 inches. An inside corner borders the left side of the *Playing in Traffic* column. Three bolts protect the hardest climbing at the start, but bring gear for the finger/hand crack finish.

47. Playing in Traffic (5.12b) ★★★★ 8 bolts. For many years this wonderful arête was the only sport route on this section of columns. Today it has plenty of company. Begin on

polished rock and frolic through a pumping assortment of fun moves. A complex crux near the top will run you over if you're not on top of your game.

48. Octane 96 (5.12b) ★★★ 8 bolts. Beyond a few virgin corners are parallel sport routes a few feet apart, starting behind a couple small boulders. Expect diverse, attention-grabbing moves climbing more like a face route than a stemming corner.

49. Starkist (5.11a) ★★★ 9 bolts. The inside corner immediately right of *Octane 96* succumbs to enjoyable stems on great rock. For reasons not clearly understood, *Starkist* was first led in the nude, the climber wearing nothing but a harness, chalk bag, and shoes.

50. Just Do It (5.10a) ★★★ Gear to 3 inches. Hidden behind two juniper trees, in the midst of blank corners, is an enjoyable crack. Done in 1989 this was Smith's original *Just Do It,* though the Monkey Face version grabbed all the headlines (it is, after all, 18 grades harder). Start up the right side of a short pillar and step left to fun jams in a shallow corner.

The Vatican Wall

Just Do It marks the end of the Playing in Traffic Area. Beyond is the almost entirely undeveloped basalt of the Vatican Wall. These columns aren't as attractive as others in the area, but they will inevitably see development in the future.

51. Mother Superior (5.11d) ★★ 8 bolts. The right side of the Vatican Wall contains three distinctive stair-stepped columns forming a ledge in the middle of the wall. Immediately right of these stunted columns rises a bolted corner with a face climbing start. Unfortunately, a sit-down rest atop a

The Vatican Wall

50.	Just Do It 5.10a	53.	Hail Mary 5.11d
51.	Mother Superior 5.11d	54.	Land of the Lost 5.10a
52.	The Sign of the Priest 5.10b	55.	Voodoo Child 5.12a

column to the left breaks the continuity of an otherwise decent route.

52. The Sign of the Priest (5.10b) ★★ 7 bolts. Among the easiest sport climbs in the Gorge, this unremarkable route makes a good warm-up. Start with jumbled face climbing immediately right of *Mother Superior* and step across to a finishing dihedral.

53. Hail Mary (5.11d) ★★★ Gear to 1 inch. A quality, high-level traditional route in the Upper Gorge? It's as rare as a game-winning Hail Mary pass. This attractive corner delivers in the clutch, with well-protected climbing similar to many Upper Gorge sport routes.

54. Land of the Lost (5.10a) ★★ Gear to 3 inches. A route from the earliest days of Gorge climbing, this clean hand crack splits a flat face. Look for a distinguishing oval hole on the right wall, just above a broad starting shelf.

55. Voodoo Child (5.12a) ★★ 8 bolts. Rising above a flat-topped column right of *Land of the Lost,* this inside corner capped by a rimrock bulge is worth doing. Begin with exfoliated huecos and master crux stems ending at a rest below a roof. The physical finish will feel easy if you're a powerhouse—and hard if you're not.

The Second Pedestal

The small Second Pedestal contains nothing but two ignored trad routes. If the order seems reversed (given that the Second Pedestal comes before the first), bear in mind that early climbers approached from the opposite direction.

56. Second Pedestal Crack (5.10a) ★★
Gear to 4 inches. Undercut by a roof, this attractive crack splits the face of the Second Pedestal. After a sandy start you'll enjoy the finishing hand/fist crack. There's an anchor along the column tops to the right.

57. Pedal to the Metal (5.11b) ★ Gear to 3 inches. An unfortunate start detracts from this appealing-looking hand crack. The painful tip jams on dirty rock simply aren't any fun. Lower from an anchor, or continue through the rim via *E-Type Shag*.

Middle Earth

A wonderful collection of high-level testpieces extends for about 150 feet upstream beyond the Second Pedestal. These highly developed, full-length columns feature some of the finest and most difficult climbs in the Gorge. Many of the better routes take advantage of the overhanging rimrock capping the columnar basalt; the character instantly changes from technical precision to spectacular thuggery. Middle Earth is the most pleasant place to hang out in the Upper Gorge, as there's minimal undergrowth along the base.

58. E-Type Jag (5.11a) ★★★★ 10 bolts. Unlike anything else at Smith, this bucket arête enjoys a cult following—the spectacular finishing roof attracts more than its fair

The Second Pedestal Area

54.	Land of the Lost	5.10a
55.	Voodoo Child	5.12a
56.	Second Pedestal Crack	5.10a
57.	Pedal to the Metal	5.11b
58.	E-Type Jag	5.11a
58a.	E-Type in Drag	5.10d
58b.	E-Type Shag	5.10a
59.	The Fifth Dimension	5.11d TR
60.	Conflicted Goddess	5.12d

Jeff Frizzell on *E-Type Jag*. BRENT MCGREGOR PHOTO

share of climbers. The slightly contrived original recipe avoided a no-hands rest below the roof and stayed to the right side of the finishing edge. The first bolt protects a mantel onto a pedestal; unclipping it eliminates any rope drag.

58a. E-Type in Drag (5.10d) ★★★ 10 bolts. The most common version of this popular route follows an uncontrived line, benefiting from a stem left to a column top after the hueco arête and a detour left above the roof.

58b. E-Type Shag (5.10a) ★★★ 10 bolts. A much easier version of *E-Type* avoids all the hard moves of the original line. After hiking up the huecos, step left to a no-hands rest on the column top and crank past a roof leading into an inside corner.

59. The Fifth Dimension (5.11d) ★★★ TR. A new anchor to the right provides access to a fun toprope problem after any ascent of *E-Type*. Atop the starting pedestal of *E-Type Jag,* follow a pocketed column leading right to a stemming corner capped by a unique crux arch on the rimrock.

60. Conflicted Goddess (5.12d) ★★★★ 8 bolts. Closely spaced corners ending at an anchor below the rimrock challenge even the finest Gorge climbers. An unremitting blend of stems and edges highlights the remarkable left corner. After weathering a bundle of baffling moves, you'll need to stick a final deadpoint.

61. The Seventh Deadly Sin (5.13a) ★★★ 7 bolts. With the Gorge packed with eccentric moves, nothing scores higher on the techno-scale than this unique testpiece. The start and finish are difficult, but they pale in comparison to the twisted crux. Creativity is a prerequisite.

62. Peruvian Skies (5.13a) ★★★★ 9 bolts. The most varied 5.13 in the Gorge somehow combines easy huecos, artistic stems, bulging rimrock, and a sobering pump into a single pitch. It'll seem like a cakewalk at the start, but the upper half packs a punch. The crux seduces a shallow dihedral, but everyone fails with cramped forearms weaving through the final overhang. Beware of a loose block below the roof.

63. Blame It On Rio (5.12b) ★★★ 8 bolts (optional 3-inch cam). Another route offering a day-and-night mixture of insecure stems and pure thuggery ascends the second corner right of *Peruvian Skies*. The lower wall contains the hardest moves, but the most memorable moment comes pulling around a big roof—with feet swinging in space. A pocketed second pitch (5.10b) finishes past five bolts to the top of the rimrock.

Middle Earth–Left Side

60.	Conflicted Goddess 5.12d
61.	The Seventh Deadly Sin 5.13a
62.	Peruvian Skies 5.13a
63.	Blame It On Rio 5.12b
64.	Bushwhacker 5.11d
65.	Feminazis 5.13a

66.	Tears For Tonya (aka Shut Up and Skate) 5.11d
67.	Tomb of Love 5.11d
68.	Hot Lava 5.13b
69.	Gapers on a Tangent 5.12a
70.	Naxis 5.10b

of beauty. The complex, pumping climbing appeals to a broader audience than the nearby stemming nightmares. The difficulties mount until a reachy crux hits at three-quarters height. Fighting a pump, slap past rounded holds to the top.

66. Tears For Tonya (aka Shut Up and Skate) (5.11d) ★★★ 9

bolts. Another high-quality option follows a varied line right of *Feminazis*. Begin with stems to the right and step left to a fun arête. Veer back to a shallow corner and finish with double roofs on the rimrock.

67. Tomb of Love

(5.11d) ★★★ 10 bolts. This enchanting route ascends a seam around the corner left of *Hot Lava*. A mixture of stems and edges leads to a flaring crux capped by a vigorous pull over a bulge.

64. Bushwhacker (5.11d) ★★ 7 bolts.

Immediately left of a steep arête rises a stemming problem between double seams. Much like Lower Gorge routes from the early 1980s, the first ascent protected entirely with natural gear; today it's fully bolted.

65. Feminazis (5.13a) ★★★★ 10 bolts. With

many routes in the Upper Gorge looking more or less the same, this charismatic arête is a thing

68. Hot Lava (5.13b) ★★★ 7 bolts.

Sophisticated and imaginative, this orange-streaked wall was the Gorge's first 5.13. The moderate start provides a warm-up for the real business. Take a deep breath, detour left to the infamous F.T.D. move, and cut back right to intense deadpoints in a seam. Expect a tricky clip of the sixth bolt.

69. Gapers on a Tangent (5.12a) ★★★ 9 bolts. Capped by a triangular roof, the next in a long string of excellent corners ascends a mystifying blend of stems and edges. Shake out below a roof and storm a strenuous crack on finger stacks.

70. Naxis (5.10b) ★★★ 7 bolts. As if drawn by some magnetic force, this charming route attracts more climbers than anything else in the Upper Gorge. You might as well give in and join the herd. Sustained stems, jams, and edges follow closely spaced cracks through a finishing slot. The original line stepped left to the anchors atop *Gapers on a Tangent*, but the best finish moves right to the *Unique Monique* anchor.

71. Unique Monique (5.12a) ★★★ 9 bolts. This comely dihedral graces the left side of the *Up Country* arête. You'll need to unlock the mysteries of two seductive cruxes in the inside corner. Finish with physical moves on the overhanging upper face.

72. Up Country (5.12a) ★★★ 10 bolts. Despite a dirty-looking start, this appealing arête is a lot of fun. Entertaining jugs give way to increasingly crafty moves broken by good shakes.

73. Groove Cat (5.12c) ★★★ 8 bolts. An attractive flaring seam splits the wall right of *Up Country*. Complicated moves in a pumpy corner lead to a rest. The groovy finish cuts left through the tricky rimrock to the *Up Country* anchors.

74. Natural Art (5.11c) ★★★ 8 bolts. This shallow box corner makes a good introduction to the Middle Earth's harder routes. Artsy stems between widely spaced seams will loosen your muscles and prepare your mind for the nuances of Gorge climbing.

75. Get That Feeling (5.11d) ★★★ 5 bolts. This short pitch of insecure stems will keep you absorbed from the moment you clip the

Middle Earth–Right Side

69.	Gapers on a Tangent	5.12a
70.	Naxis	5.10b
71.	Unique Monique	5.12a
72.	Up Country	5.12a
73.	Groove Cat	5.12c
74.	Natural Art	5.11c
75.	Get That Feeling	5.11d
76.	Isengard	5.10a

first bolt. Begin with easy jams leading into the double-seamed corner.

76. Isengard (5.10a) ★★ Gear to 3 inches. Just left of the detached First Pedestal, tucked in a corner of gray rock, is a right-leaning hand crack. History buffs might enjoy repeating one of the first routes in the Upper Gorge.

The First Pedestal

A prominent freestanding column marks the boundary between Middle Earth and the First Pedestal. Here you'll find a few uninspiring cracks and the bolted columns of the Three Stooges.

77. First Pedestal Crack (5.10a) ★ Gear to 3.5 inches. An obvious crack splits the face of the First Pedestal. The rock improves greatly after a dirty start, but few climbers bother. An awesome display of greenery usually guards the base.

78. Mordor (5.9) ★★ Gear to 3 inches. On the left side of the First Pedestal are three short cracks rising above short double columns. The left of the three cracks succumbs to enjoyable hand slots. Begin with crux jams in a vegetation-choked crack.

79. P.W. (5.9) ★ Gear to 2.5 inches. The center crack looming above a short stack of columns follows locking jams, with optional stems to an off-width. Begin with the same vegetated moves as *Mordor*.

80. Larry (5.12a) ★★ 9 bolts. The first stooge starts with a knuckleheaded crack ending atop a short column. Step right and ascend an attractive buttress on pleasant stone.

81. Moe (5.11d) ★★ 7 bolts. Stooge number two begins on the right side of a short column and veers left to a bolted arête. After

The First Pedestal

76.	Isengard 5.10a	81.	Moe 5.11d
77.	First Pedestal Crack 5.10a	82.	Squeeze Play 5.10c
78.	Mordor 5.9	83.	Curly 5.11b
79.	P.W. 5.9	84.	Gondor 5.10b
80.	Larry 5.12a	85.	Predator 5.12d TR

moderate climbing, throw a "moe" at the top.

82. Squeeze Play (5.10c) ★★ Gear to 2.5 inches. A diminutive dihedral rises above a stunted column. Begin by jamming the right side of the pillar and finish with a mix of stems and finger slots.

83. Curly (5.11b) ★★ 7 bolts. The last of the Three Stooges stumbles up a column right of a hand crack. Crux side pulls give way to a pumpy finish.

84. Gondor (5.10b) ★ Gear to 4 inches. A disappointing crack splits the column left of a deep chimney. Quality jams are unfortunately sandwiched between a grimy start and an awkward finish.

85. Predator (5.12d) ★★ TR. A flat buttress rises between a menacing chimney and a fist crack. You can't fault the quality of the climbing, but the moves are too contrived to merit a sport bolting.

86. Shelob's Lair (5.9 X) ★ Gear to 8 inches. This ominous, cobweb-filled squeeze chimney was the first route ever climbed in the Upper Gorge, and the last route anyone would want to repeat.

The Crowded House

Beyond the First Pedestal is the birthplace of Upper Gorge sport climbing—the Crowded House. The level of difficulty doesn't match the downstream columns, but the quality is just as high. With the original southern entrance rarely used anymore, these routes see less traffic than they once did. Apart from one unfinished project, there's nothing new left to do.

87. Easy For Some (5.11b) ★★ 6 bolts. Tucked in a corner right of *Shelob's Lair* is an easy sport route interrupted by a one-move

crux. You'll cruise if you can make the reach to a hidden hold, and struggle if you can't.

88. Huck Fin (5.11d) ★★★ 6 bolts. The fun ends too quickly on this appealing, flat-faced column. Compelling climbing leads to a cool midpitch huck to a flat edge, followed by an easier finish.

89. Chienne No More (5.12a) ★★ 7 bolts. This prominent right-facing corner features crux stems past a cantankerous bulge. There's nothing wrong with the sustained climbing, but there's little to distinguish it from other Gorge corners. Either lower off or continue through the rimrock via *Always a Bitch*.

89a. Always a Bitch (5.12a) ★★ 2 bolts. An optional finish powers through edges on the wildly overhanging rimrock to a higher anchor. The physical cranks provide a welcome release after the artsy palms of *Chienne No More*.

90. Integrated Imaging (5.12a) ★★★ 8 bolts. There are more attractive lines in the Upper Gorge, but this deceptive face offers high-quality climbing. Start behind a massive sagebrush and finesse artsy moves on awkwardly angled edges.

91. Project (5.12+?) The only unclimbed line on the Crowded House weaves up a pair of shallow inside corners left of the *Mojomatic* arête. After battling up the left corner, take a breather and step across and finesse the corner to the right. All moves go free on toprope.

92. Mojomatic (5.12b) ★★★★ 8 bolts. This captivating arête is the highlight of the Crowded House. A winning series of pinches, slaps, and edges on superior rock lead to an insecure crux near the top. If you want more of a challenge, try a contrived variant using only the arête (5.12c).

The Crowded House

85.	Predator 5.12d TR	91.	Project 5.12+?
86.	Shelob's Lair 5.9 X	92.	Mojomatic 5.12b
87.	Easy For Some 5.11b	93.	Animation 5.11c
88.	Huck Fin 5.11d	94.	Celibate Wives 5.12a
89.	Chienne No More 5.12a	95.	Hieroglyphics 5.11d
89a.	Always a Bitch 5.12a	96.	Blind Dogs Need Bones, Too 5.10d
90.	Integrated Imaging 5.12a	97.	Dances with Dogs 5.11c

bolt, but the bigger challenge comes from staying on the rock the rest of the way.

95. Hieroglyphics

(5.11d) ★★★★ 8 bolts. This classic line follows a seam splitting a flat buttress. Expect a tough-to-decipher crux just below a rest, though the difficulty comes mainly from the continuous nature of the climbing.

96. Blind Dogs Need Bones, Too (5.10d)

★★ 8 bolts. The best warm-up in the Crowded House was once the most popular route in the Upper Gorge. Today other routes receive far more attention. Scramble up stunted columns and follow low-tech stems, jams, and edges to an anchor.

93. Animation (5.11c) ★★ 7 bolts. This typical box corner marked the beginning of the sport climbing frenzy in the Upper Gorge. Within a few months, harder (and better) routes were everywhere. Begin below a curving ramp and make repetitive moves from stem to stern.

94. Celibate Wives (5.12a) ★★★ 7 bolts.

The original Upper Gorge 5.12 follows a shallow dihedral left of staircased columns. The technical crux edges past the fourth

97. Dances with Dogs

(5.11c) ★★ 6 bolts. Atop a staircase of short columns rises an innocent-looking seam. The deceptively tricky crux blends side pulls and smears in a very shallow left-facing corner.

98. This Dog Won't Hunt (5.10c) ★ 5

bolts. This flawed boxed corner borders a wide crack to the right. A single hard move leads into a short finishing groove. Lower from the same anchor as *Dances with Dogs*.

Sharecropper's Wall

The final stretch of columnar basalt in the Upper Gorge features a few short climbs that are little more than afterthoughts.

99. Sink the Sub (5.10a) ★ Gear to 3 inches. Immediately left of a bolted column sits a forgettable hand crack. Traverse in from the left and jam flaking rock, continuing through the rimrock to the top of the cliff.

100. Pruning the Family Tree (5.11c) ★★ 6 bolts. A run-of-the-mill sport route tackles a column right of *Sink the Sub*. After wading through a mediocre crux at the start, the fun begins after stepping right to an attractive finishing buttress.

101. L.K. and Ruby May (5.11c) ★★ 5 bolts. A diminutive route with a face climbing crux follows the third seam right of *Pruning the Family Tree*. Begin to the left and veer

Sharecropper's Wall

97.	Dances with Dogs 5.11c
98.	This Dog Won't Hunt 5.10c
99.	Sink the Sub 5.10a
100.	Pruning the Family Tree 5.11c
101.	L.K. and Ruby May 5.11c
102.	Forty Acres and a Mule 5.10b
103.	Kid'n Play 5.8
104.	Cranking with Kari 5.10c

across to the right side of the corner, finishing with a pull over a small bulge.

102. Forty Acres and a Mule (5.10b) ★★ 5 bolts. The final column in the Upper Gorge makes a fun warm-up with reaches between good holds. Lower from the anchor atop *L.K. and Ruby May.*

Bouldering Area

Beyond the Sharecropper's Wall the columns disappear. High above on the rimrock is the Upper Gorge bouldering area. The best approach is from above, not below. Walk upstream along the rim a couple hundred yards beyond the normal approach gully, patiently waiting for a break in the rimrock. A very short second-class scramble leads to the base. At the downstream side of this heavily featured crag are the following two climbs.

103. Kid'n Play (5.8) ★★ 5 bolts. This simple route is kid's play compared to everything else in the Upper Gorge. Start with a simple crack and move right onto a lighthearted, pocketed buttress.

104. Cranking with Kari (5.10c) ★★ 4 bolts. The left of parallel sport routes on the rimrock ascends a short, flat-faced buttress. The pocketed climbing might be popular if the crag wasn't so isolated.

Smith Bouldering

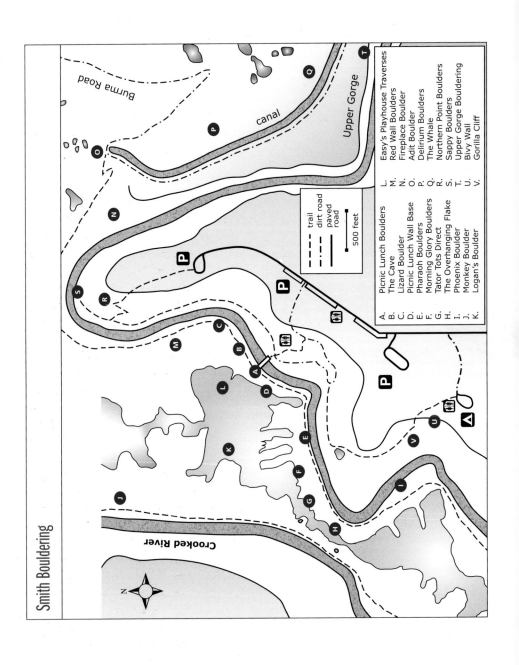

Burma Road

canal

Upper Gorge

Crooked River

N

trail
dirt road
paved
road

500 feet

A. Picnic Lunch Boulders
B. The Cave
C. Lizard Boulder
D. Picnic Lunch Wall Base
E. Morning Glory Boulders
F. Pharaoh Boulders
G. Tator Tots Direct
H. The Overhanging Flake
I. Phoenix Boulder
J. Monkey Boulder
K. Logan's Boulder

L. Easy's Playhouse Traverses
M. Red Wall Boulders
N. Fireplace Boulder
O. Adit Boulder
P. Delirium Boulders
Q. The Whale
R. Northern Point Boulders
S. Sappy Boulders
T. Upper Gorge Bouldering
U. Bivy Wall
V. Gorilla Cliff

BOULDERING

It was midsummer 1979, and Chris Jones and I were working on a direct start to Tator Tots (V6). We had entirely different sequences—I crimped small edges while he spanned harder moves between pinches. For the first time I felt I had a real chance to beat Chris to the punch. I worked a summer job, and as soon as five o'clock arrived I drove out to Smith and ran down the trail. I laced my shoes, chalked up, and stepped to the base. There, to my horror, arranged neatly in the dirt at my feet were small rocks carefully spelling a message meant only for me— "sorry Al." I instantly knew that Chris had already visited Smith earlier in the day and came away with the first ascent. After a few tries I managed the second and rearranged the stones to create my own not-so-polite response in the dirt— "up yours Jones"—a reflection of my frustration trying to compete with someone in an entirely different league.

Smith Rock and world-class bouldering aren't often mentioned in the same sentence. Climbers travel from around the world to test themselves on the famous sport routes, but no one visits for the bouldering. At Smith there are no famous problems—there's no *Midnight Lightning,* no *Thimble,* no *Ripper Traverse.* Even the best local problems normally go unnoticed as climbers marvel at the expanses of golden tuff towering high above.

The time has come to welcome the new era of Smith Rock bouldering. With the attention of so many top climbers

focused on sport routes over the past two decades, new generations have found quiet pleasure in exploring Smith's untapped bouldering potential. It was a slow transformation, but the old stereotype of Smith as a bouldering backwater no longer fits. The first edition of this guide included 100 problems, mainly at the base of today's sport crags. Now there are 322 lines, with most of the growth coming in never-before-included areas such as the Bivy Boulders, Delirium Boulders, and the Northern Point. The best of these modern problems are solid, steep, and difficult.

Bouldering holds a special place in the history of Smith Rock. Long before the power drill, Smith climbers had few options apart from traditional cracks and easy knobby faces. With few chances to develop higher-level skills, they turned to the boulders, soon gaining the strength and confidence needed for the sport routes of the future. Although the earliest Smith climbers practiced the art of bouldering in the Old Climbers' Camp, the first recorded lines arose in 1979 when Mike Adams pioneered at least two dozen problems, including *The Nose* (V2) and the *Adams' Problem* (V4). That same year Chris Jones spent the summer at Smith, instantly vaulting bouldering into modern times. Gifted with astonishing power, he could crank multiple one-arm pull-ups on small edges with lazy ease. With power to spare, the rest of Jones's body seemingly disengaged

Chris Jones on *Tator Tots Direct*. CHRIS JONES COLLECTION

from the process—his legs swung limply as he slowly powered through problems without any visible effort. The not-so-steep bouldering of Smith rarely allowed him to take full advantage of his freakish talents.

Jones's best efforts only hinted at his potential—routes like the *Jones Problem* (V8) and the *Jones Route* variant to *Tator Tots Direct* (V8) required minimal effort. His one-handed ascent of the *Jug Route* (V10) on Red Clot Rock was a more typical Jones problem—easy for him and impossible for everyone else. The fact that he nearly succeeded on a no-feet, one-handed version of this problem gives a better indication of his unique talents. Before moving to Colorado in 1980, he wrote a fourteen-page unpublished guide to Smith bouldering, detailing over one hundred problems.

Mentored by Jones, Alan Watts bouldered more than anyone else at Smith in the first half of the 1980s, developing the strength needed for his future sport climbs. Endurance problems such as the *Combination Blocks Round Trip* (V6) and *Around the Block* (V7) became daily warm-ups. His best ascent came in 1985, when he linked *Under Fire* (V10), a power-endurance problem in the Cave that still sees few repeats.

After these promising beginnings, Smith bouldering stagnated for many years. Ironically, development slowed, at least in part, because the tactics used to develop sport climbing weren't applied to the boulders. Cleaning loose rock on rappel opened the door to high-level Smith climbing, while the lack of cleaning limited the number of new boulder problems. Many of the existing lines were so crimpy they didn't appeal to the new generation of power-oriented climbers. With so many high-level sport routes throughout the park, the boulders sat forgotten.

The unlikely origin of Smith's bouldering renaissance was basalt-specialist Jeff Frizzell. Since the opening of the Smith Rock Bivouac Area in the mid-1980s, climbers had noticed short walls of tuff below the campground, but the rock was far from perfect. For the first time in the history of Smith bouldering, Frizzell approached from above, cleaning off loose rock and scrubbing away lichen from the Bivy Wall and Gorilla Cliff. Soon a group of locals, including Jim Belzer, Larry Brumwell, and Paul Marshall, along with an international contingent of Bivy Area residents, went to work developing the crags. In more recent years, with the growth of Bend-based bouldering, a talented crop of youngsters revisited Smith's potential, led by Will Nazarian, Rio Rose, and Logan Carr, along with veterans

Brooke Sandahl and Michael Stöger. They discovered new pockets of bouldering at Smith, but each kept such a low profile it took years for the word to get out.

The 1992 edition of this book came out before the art of grading boulder problems had fully evolved. Rather than using the familiar B-scale (B1, B2) or the budding V-scale, the original guide used a Smith-specific S-grade system (from S0 to S5). But even as the book went to press, the V-system was emerging as the accepted grading scale throughout the country. Saddled by the arcane S-system, Smith bouldering went unnoticed.

Fortunately the S-grade system is toast, replaced by the now familiar V-grades (with thanks to John Sherman). As much as any single factor, Sherman's V-grading scale led to the immense growth of bouldering in this country. Trying to rate an entire pitch is difficult enough, but accurately rating one or two moves is nearly impossible. Body size alone can make a huge difference— one person's V9 is another person's V6 (and vice versa). John Gill's intentionally vague B-system recognized the inherent absurdity of grading boulder problems. The V-system flies in the face of reality, placing a precise grade on each boulder problem. But Sherman wisely recognized that a climber's need to quantify his/her efforts far outweighed the practical limitations. With a comparable grading scale throughout the country, bouldering flourished.

In all seriousness, the bouldering grades in this book are completely screwed up— they're only rough estimates for an average-size climber and shouldn't be taken too seriously. Your assessment of the level might differ by several V-grades. In part this chaos resulted from the inherent vagaries of any bouldering grading scale, but a greater factor was the challenge of converting the grades of ancient, barely remembered problems into a scale the author had little experience with. With enough feedback, the accuracy of the grades in future editions will only improve.

The V-system doesn't work well with low-end boulder problems. I've used a V0 designation to rate the easier problems, splitting the grade into three levels: V0+, V0, and V0-. Anything rated V0- receives a decimal grade as well (ranging from 5.0 to 5.8). Part of the satisfaction of bouldering is discovering your own solution to a difficult problem. The descriptions help define the problems, but hopefully they won't take the fun away from working out your own sequence. Occasionally sequences are described in greater detail only when it would be impossible to describe the problem otherwise.

This chapter was never intended to present a comprehensive record of Smith bouldering. There are scores of easy lines on the hundreds of boulders at Smith, and several high-end problems at the outer fringes of the Smith Rock region. Also, dozens of contrived variations (often ranking among the hardest at Smith) weren't included, to avoid the challenge of explaining what is and isn't a legal hold. More often than not, the name, grade, and first ascent information of a new sport route is common knowledge among Smith regulars. Bouldering is different. Apart from some of the earliest and most difficult problems, it's rarely clear who did each line first—several recent "new problems" were actually climbed decades ago. To complicate matters further, almost no one gives their problems formal names or grades. Rather than listing a couple hundred problems as unnamed and ungraded, every line in this chapter now has a distinctive name, along with a shot-in-the-dark V-grade.

PICNIC LUNCH BOULDERS

Several dozen boulders of various shapes and sizes rest on the hillside near the bridge. Most of them are crumbling and undeveloped, but there are several worthwhile exceptions. These were some of the first boulder problems at Smith, as the short approach lured bouldering pioneers.

River Boulder

The large boulder nearest the bridge contains several highball lines. Bad rock was part of the challenge in the early days, but today the stone is mostly solid.

1. The Nose (V2 R) ★★★ Ascend the rounded arête on the right. The first and best route on the boulder—just don't fall on the last moves.

1a. Nosed Out (V3) ★★★ Do the start without the right side pull.

1b. By a Nose (V3) ★★ After matching on the starting hold, reach left for a pocket.

1c. Hard Nosed (V4) ★★ Start 8 feet left and traverse right along a seam.

2. Loose Lucy (V2 R) ★ Dangerous and still a little loose, with a committing crux moving right at the top.

3. Black Dike (V2 R) ★★ This 1-foot-wide black streak is unnerving and delicate, with a final crux move.

4. Kent's Big Day (V1) ★★ Ascend side pulls and jugs on much-improved stone.

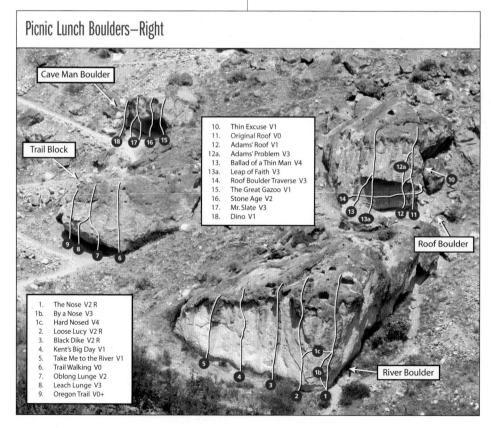

Picnic Lunch Boulders—Right

Cave Man Boulder

Trail Block

10.	Thin Excuse V1
11.	Original Roof V0
12.	Adams' Roof V1
12a.	Adams' Problem V3
13.	Ballad of a Thin Man V4
13a.	Leap of Faith V3
14.	Roof Boulder Traverse V3
15.	The Great Gazoo V1
16.	Stone Age V2
17.	Mr. Slate V3
18.	Dino V1

Roof Boulder

River Boulder

1.	The Nose V2 R
1b.	By a Nose V3
1c.	Hard Nosed V4
2.	Loose Lucy V2 R
3.	Black Dike V2 R
4.	Kent's Big Day V1
5.	Take Me to the River V1
6.	Trail Walking V0
7.	Oblong Lunge V2
8.	Leach Lunge V3
9.	Oregon Trail V0+

5. Take Me to the River (V1) ★★ Edges lead to liebacks up a right-leaning seam.

Trail Block

The first boulder uphill from the bridge is an unimpressive slab with many short, contrived options. The undercut left side offers a few brief problems, though everything else is simple.

6. Trail Walking (V0) ★★ Uncontrived face on the right, with a crux move right off the deck.

7. Oblong Lunge (V2) ★ Dyno from an oblong pocket up and left to a jug.

8. Leach Lunge (V3) ★ A one-move throw to a jug from a left-hand crimp and a right-hand pinch.

9. Oregon Trail (V0+) ★★★ Uncontrived edges on the left.

Roof Boulder

A clean block with a distinctive roof sits directly above the River Boulder. These were some of the earliest recorded problems at Smith.

10. Thin Excuse (V1) ★ Dismal thin crack on the right wall with a bad landing.

11. Original Roof (V0) ★★★ Fun jugs on the arête.

12. Adams' Roof (V1) ★★★ Uncontrived over the roof.

12a. Adams' Problem (V3) ★★ Pull over the roof, reaching to a left-hand sloper and an incut right-hand side pull. Ignore better holds to the right.

13. Ballad of a Thin Man (V4) ★★★ From the wall under the left side of the roof,

stretch to a rounded sloper at the lip and fire for a higher pocket.

13a. Leap of Faith (V3) ★★ An easier but more committing option jumps from a boulder to the same lip holds as *Ballad of a Thin Man*.

14. Roof Boulder Traverse (V3) ★★ This pumping round-trip around a corner makes a good workout.

Cave Man Boulder

Undercut by a cave, this smallish boulder sits at the second switchback above the bridge. There are several possible variants and the following uncontrived lines:

15. The Great Gazoo (V1) ★ One move on the right side.

16. Stone Age (V2) ★★ From a good jug, climb straight up.

17. Mr. Slate (V3) ★★ Start either to the right or left, bouldering past a sloper to the top.

18. Dino (V1) ★★ Climb past a pocket on the left edge.

Circus Boulder

Above the Cave are two massive chunks of stone. Just left of the upper boulder is a remote block with a steep downhill face. No topos.

19. Circus Lunge (V1) ★★★ On the left side, dyno from jugs to a big knob. This was Smith's first named boulder problem.

20. Three Rings (V2) ★★ Start 5 feet right of *Circus Lunge*.

21. Big Top (V2) ★★ Ascend thin flakes on the right.

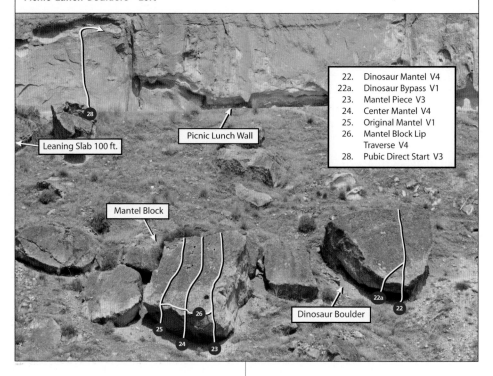

22. Dinosaur Mantel V4
22a. Dinosaur Bypass V1
23. Mantel Piece V3
24. Center Mantel V4
25. Original Mantel V1
26. Mantel Block Lip Traverse V4
28. Pubic Direct Start V3

Leaning Slab 100 ft.

Picnic Lunch Wall

Mantel Block

Dinosaur Boulder

Dinosaur Boulder

At the first switchback past the Cave Man Boulder sits a pointed slab with deceptively tricky mantels at the base.

22. Dinosaur Mantel (V4) ★★ Reach awkwardly for a knob and hump your way over the lip. If you thrive on mantels, you might want to consider a pure press without using the knob.

22a. Dinosaur Bypass (V1) ★ The level drops dramatically when starting a few feet to the left.

Mantel Block

Off the trail to the left, just beyond Dinosaur Boulder, rests this unimpressive blob that delights the rare breed of mantel-loving climbers. You can crank over the lip just about anywhere, but the most distinctive problems are as follows:

23. Mantel Piece (V3) ★★ Jump from the ground and mantel the rounded prow on the right.

24. Center Mantel (V4) ★★ Start with a good right hold 5 feet left of *Mantel Piece*.

25. Original Mantel (V1) ★★★ Pull past circular jugs on the left.

26. Mantel Block Lip Traverse (V4) ★★ Move left to right, with the *Mantel Piece* finish.

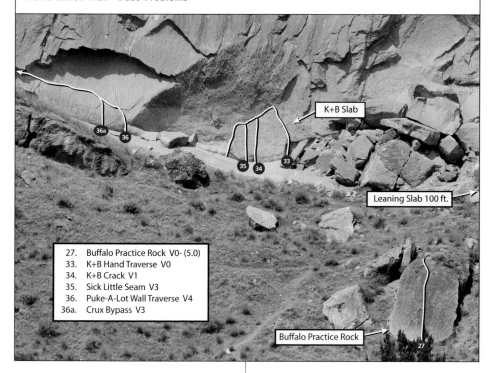

K+B Slab

Leaning Slab 100 ft.

27.	Buffalo Practice Rock V0- (5.0)
33.	K+B Hand Traverse V0
34.	K+B Crack V1
35.	Sick Little Seam V3
36.	Puke-A-Lot Wall Traverse V4
36a.	Crux Bypass V3

Buffalo Practice Rock

Buffalo Practice Rock

27. Buffalo Practice Rock (V0- 5.0) ★
Roughly 150 feet left of Mantel Block are
two square-cut slabs, separated by a narrow
corridor. Only slightly steeper than the surrounding hillside, the left slab is Smith's easiest toprope introduction for young kids and
timid novices. Look for a two-bolt anchor
on top.

PICNIC LUNCH WALL BASE

There are a few problems scattered along the
base of Picnic Lunch Wall. They don't compare with Smith's better lines, but they stay
dry in a heavy rain despite the fact that none
of them are steeper than 90 degrees.

28. Pubic Direct Start (V3) ★★★ The best
base problem on Picnic Lunch Wall is
the opening moves of *Pubic Luau Direct*.
Technical crimps lead to a ledge—either
jump off or hand traverse right to a brief
downclimb.

Leaning Slab

Perched below Snack Crack is an unmistakable slab leaning away from the base of the

wall. The low-angle backside contains simple friction problems, more akin to the Glacier Point Apron than the tuff of Smith Rock. No topos.

29. River Face Crack (V0- 5.8 X) ★★ The unmistakable crack on the downhill face of the Leaning Slab is easy, intimidating, and unforgiving.

30. Right Slab (V0- 5.8 R) ★★★ Backside smears right of the crack—a little spooky at the top.

31. Left Slab (V0- 5.7) ★★★ Edges left of the crack.

32. Leaning Edge (V0- 5.6) ★★★ Fun climbing on the left edge of the backside slab.

K+B Slab

Marked by a faded K+B scraped into the rock, this pointed, crack-split flake balances against the base of Picnic Lunch Wall.

33. K+B Hand Traverse (V0) ★★ Traverse either direction.

34. K+B Crack (V1) ★★★ Jam the crack and reach left to a finishing side pull.

34a. (V3) ★★ Climb the crack strictly without reaching left (statically V4).

34b. (V4) ★ Fingers and feet in crack.

35. Sick Little Seam (V3) ★ Just to the left of *K+B Crack* is a faint seam. Keeping fingers strictly in the seam, you'll need to wedge a single digit into a horrid avulsion slot.

36. Puke-A-Lot Wall Traverse (V4) ★★ If it's raining hard and you want to do some bouldering, you'll inevitably settle for the long traverse along the base of Picnic Lunch Wall. Expect an awkward crux off a small boulder at the far right end. You'll get through this section quickly if traversing right to left—otherwise it's the final move. Whether linking the traverse for the first time or the fiftieth, you'll probably wish you were climbing something else.

36a. Crux Bypass (V3) ★★ Start (or finish) without the crux sequence at the right side of the traverse.

THE CAVE

An unusual cave formed by a deeply under-cut boulder contains some of the hardest problems at Smith. There are several variants at the lip of the roof and a crimpy traverse starting deep in the cave. The holds have changed often over the years—some are better, others worse. To approach, turn right at the bridge and hike 100 feet along the trail.

37. Right Exit (V3) ★ Long ago an anonymous climber aided out the right side of the Cave using two bolts. You can free the bolt ladder by starting off a purple boulder and groveling over the lip.

38. Original Exit (V2) ★★★ From a right-hand edge, spring from the ground and palm the lip with your left hand. Reach over the lip to a jug and pull onto the slab.

38a. (V3) ★★ Leave the ground statically, doing a pull-up off two obvious edges, and huck for the lip.

39. Jones Problem (V8) ★★★ This left-to-right exit was one of the better problems from the late 1970s. Begin from jugs on the left wall and set up on a big undercling. Reach backward with your right hand to a cling, hook a toe, and stretch for a left edge (the same starting holds as the *Original Exit*). Cut loose your feet and crank over the lip. The so-called "no feet" variant avoids any foot hooks after cutting loose your feet, though it adds little to the level.

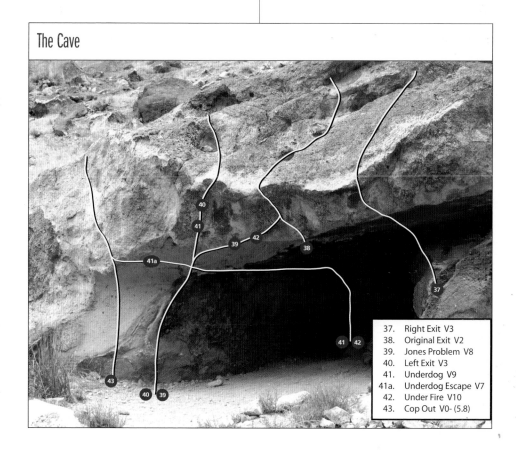

The Cave

37.	Right Exit V3
38.	Original Exit V2
39.	Jones Problem V8
40.	Left Exit V3
41.	Underdog V9
41a.	Underdog Escape V7
42.	Under Fire V10
43.	Cop Out V0- (5.8)

39a. Keeping Up With the Joneses (V8) ★★★ From the undercling at the start, avoid the right cling completely, reaching directly with your right hand to the left of two starting holds on the *Original Exit.* Hook a toe and reach the lip with your left hand.

40. Left Exit (V3) ★★ Jump from the ground, a la the *Original Exit.*

40a. (V7) ★★ Leave the ground statically, reaching from a deteriorated left-hand edge to the lip. You'll need to use a painful knee bar to have any chance.

40b. (V8) ★★ From the big undercling, reach directly to the lip with your right hand.

41. Underdog (V9) ★★★ Start in the back of the Cave and traverse the crimpy inner wall right to left, finishing with your choice of the *Left Exit* options.

41a. Underdog Escape (V7) ★★★ A much less demanding finish continues past the *Left Exit,* finishing instead with *Cop Out.*

42. Under Fire (V10) ★★★★ Traverse the inner wall and crank over the roof via the *Jones Problem.* The same line, finishing with *Keeping Up With the Joneses,* hasn't been done, though the grade would be similar.

43. Cop Out (V0- 5.8) ★ The easiest option completely avoids the Cave itself, using edges to the left.

LIZARD BOULDER (AKA PRACTICE BOULDER)

This massive boulder rests along the trail upstream from the Cave. With two anchors on top, the 25-foot river face is far more popular with classes than boulderers. The lines are easy, but you wouldn't want to pop off near the top. The shorter backside contains several harder problems on great rock.

44. Drill Team (V0 R) ★★★ Gently overhanging wall of incuts on the left.

45. First Timer (V0 R) ★★ Awkward jugs in the center.

46. Practice Slab (V0- 5.8 R) ★★ Wander up the slab, keeping left the higher you go. Don't fall.

46a. Slab Escape (V0- 5.7 R) ★★ When you start getting nervous on the original line, cut right to safety.

47. Lizard Problem (V3) ★★ Start on positive edges at the right base of the boulder and traverse right on slopers, finishing with *Faking It.*

48. Faking It (V1) ★ By sitting down you can almost turn the line of sinker pockets on the right edge of the boulder into a legitimate problem.

49. Making It (V1) ★ A few feet right of *Faking It* is a similar option, done with a sitdown start.

50. Pocket Crack (V0) ★★ Fun moves up a leaning, pocketed crack on the left part of the backside wall.

51. Practice Makes Perfect (V2) ★★ Pull down on edges on the left side of a dark, flat face on the backside.

Lizard Boulder (aka Practice Boulder)

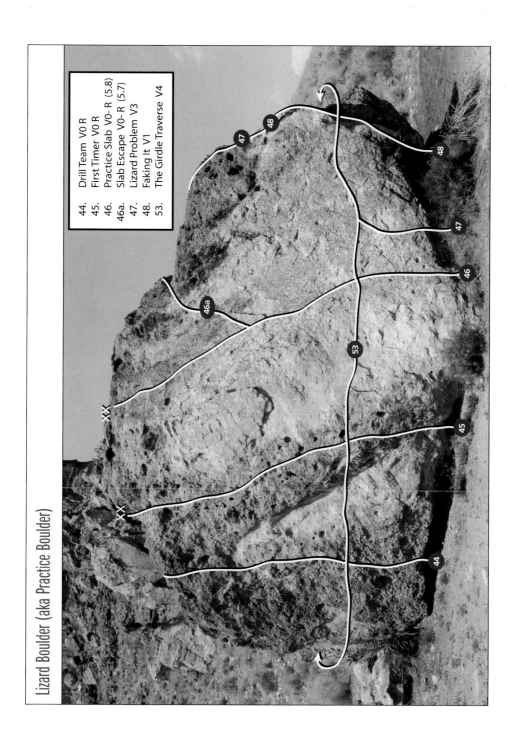

44. Drill Team V0 R
45. First Timer V0 R
46. Practice Slab V0- R (5.8)
46a. Slab Escape V0- R (5.7)
47. Lizard Problem V3
48. Faking It V1
53. The Girdle Traverse V4

Lizard (aka Practice) Boulder–North Side

48.	Faking It	V1
49.	Making It	V1
50.	Pocket Crack	V0
51.	Practice Makes Perfect	V2
52.	Perfect Stranger	V2
53.	The Girdle Traverse	V4

52. Perfect Stranger (V2) ★★ Five feet right is another decent problem, starting with a chalked side pull.

53. The Girdle Traverse (V4) ★★ The circumnavigation of the Lizard Boulder begins wherever you choose and traverses in either direction endlessly. The grade goes way down if you traverse around the right corner on big holds above the *Lizard Problem*.

PHARAOH BOULDERS

After walking around the base of Shiprock, you'll arrive at a small cluster of boulders rising above a boardwalk. There's not enough here to get many climbers to stop on their way to Morning Glory Wall.

The Pharaoh

The most appealing boulder is a pharaoh-head block with a distinctive river-face pocket.

54. King Tut (V2) ★★ Ascend the right arête. It's harder now that someone tore off a big jug.

55. Pocket Hold Route (V2) ★★★★ A Smith Rock classic with small knobs.

55a. (V4) ★★★ Don't use the obvious pocket.

56. Cursed (V5) ★★★ Climb the left arête, avoiding the big pocket.

56a. (V3) ★★ Uncontrived up the left edge.

Carter's Block

Beyond the Pharaoh is a low-angle, 35-foot slab rising directly above the boardwalk. There are two bolts on top for anyone preferring a toprope.

57. Kid's in Action (V0- 5.1 X) ★★ This slab makes a good toprope option for beginners.

58. I Want My Mummy (V1) ★ At the left side of the *Kid's in Action* slab is a mediocre problem pulling over a bulge.

58a. Mummy Variant (V2) ★ It's a little harder starting left with a traverse along big knobs before cranking the crux bulge.

Bonehead Block

An intimidating boulder rests atop the mini-gully left of Carter's Block. You don't want to fall off near the top on either of the following two problems.

59. Where Boneheads Dare (V2 R) ★★ Begin with a tricky move on the uphill part of the face and finish with highball jugs.

60. Where Boneheads Slam (V2 R) ★ Jam the unpleasant, freaky crack at base of block.

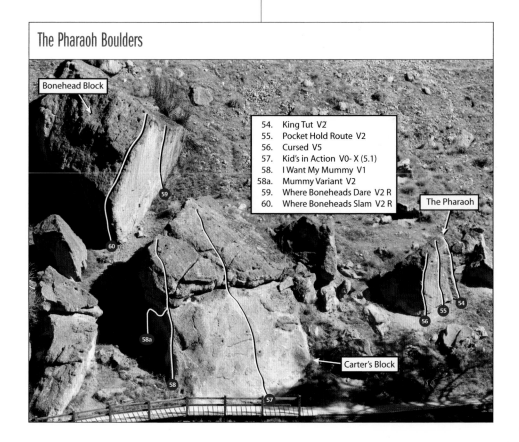

The Pharaoh Boulders

Bonehead Block

54.	King Tut V2
55.	Pocket Hold Route V2
56.	Cursed V5
57.	Kid's in Action V0- X (5.1)
58.	I Want My Mummy V1
58a.	Mummy Variant V2
59.	Where Boneheads Dare V2 R
60.	Where Boneheads Slam V2 R

The Pharaoh

Carter's Block

MORNING GLORY WALL AREA

For good reason, climbers don't often visit Morning Glory Wall for the bouldering alone. The small collection of forgettable traverses and problems gets overshadowed by the magnitude of the longer routes. No topos.

61. Slack Jaw Traverse (V2) ** This long traverse moves uphill along the base of the Shipwreck Wall, starting below *Blue Light Special*. The crux comes quickly, with a tough move skirting a rounded bulge.

62. Lysergic Roof (V3) * Low in the Aggro Gully lurks a shallow cave split by a roof crack. A poor man's *Separate Reality* hand jams to a crux pull around the lip. Expect a gruesome skin-shredding struggle.

MORNING GLORY BOULDERS

Two closely spaced boulders sit at the base of Smith's most heavily traveled real estate. There are two main problems and many possible variants. No topos.

63. Just Say No (V2) * Traverse the undercut river face of the right boulder and finish to the top.

64. Heavenly Blue (V1) * Make a long reach from a sloping platform on the left boulder.

65. Morning Glory Wall Traverse (V3) *** A popular warm-up traverse cuts along the base of the Zebra Area. The traverse typically begins at the *Zebra Seam* and continues across the wall, ending after a tough sequence just left of *Lion's Jaw*. You can continue much farther, ending well past the Peanut.

DIHEDRALS AND CHRISTIAN BROTHERS

You'll find excellent bouldering amid the most heavily developed sport crags in the park. These problems are popular since they make good warm-ups for the bolted routes.

Tator Tots Direct

66. Roof Bypass (V0) ★ No topo. You can completely bypass the roof with edges to the right. This ancient problem is now the start to *Fresh Squeezed*.

67. Tator Tots Direct (V6) ★★★★ No topo. This uncontrived, overhanging line was Smith's quintessential problem in the early days. The hardest moves come below the roof, but the classic jug-hauling finish makes

it special. There are several harder eliminate variants (V7 to V9).

67a. Jones Route (V8) ★★★★ No topo. The first ascent of *Tator Tots Direct* avoided all crimpy holds. From a left-hand side pull, dyno with your right to a pinch and hop your right hand higher to a good hold below the roof. Release your left and reach all the way to the big jug at the lip, using no intermediate holds.

67b. Original Line (V2) ★★★ No topo. The first problem to crank over the actual roof started 5 feet right, before reaching left.

68. Total Eclipse (V5) ★★★★ This long traverse cuts across the heart of the Dihedrals. Start below *Take A Powder* or *Rattlesnake Chimney* and move in either direction. The entire traverse offers a great work-out, but

Moonshine Face

68.	Total Eclipse V5
68b.	Last Waltz Traverse V4
68c.	Moonshine Traverse V4
69.	Right Pockets V4
70.	Center Pockets V3
70a.	Center Right V4
71.	Original Pockets V3
72.	Hand Traverse V0+
72a.	Traverse Variant V0
73.	Nasty Seam V4

two no-hands rests make it little harder than its individual sections. Most climbers don't go for the entire traverse, settling instead for the sections listed below.

68a. Sunshine Traverse (V4) ★★★ No topo. The wall right of *Sunshine Dihedral*.

68b. Last Waltz Traverse (V4) ★★★ The long section between *Moonshine* and *Sunshine*.

68c. Moonshine Traverse (V4) ★★★ Start below *Rattlesnake Chimney* and traverse around the corner to *Moonshine Dihedral* (or vice versa).

Moonshine Face

The pocketed face on the wall left of *Moonshine Dihedral* contains several classic problems and countless contrived variations. A flat landing allows you to throw yourself at these lines with wild abandon.

69. Right Pockets (V4) ★★★ Although difficult on early ascents (V6), the dinky one-finger cranks a few feet left of *Moonshine* somehow grew into two-finger slots.

70. Center Pockets (V3) ★★ Start with pocket pulls and finish by reaching left to the *Hand Traverse*.

70a. Center Right (V4) ★★ It's a little harder veering right at the top.

71. Original Pockets (V3) ★★★ Start just right of the finger crack and crank pockets to a hard last move.

72. Hand Traverse (V0+) ★★★★ Classic finger crack finishing with a downclimb to the right.

72a. Traverse Variant (V0) ★★★ Avoid the crux start by climbing jugs to the left.

72b. (V4) ★ Climb the start one-handed, ending at the traversing crack.

73. Nasty Seam (V4) ★ Keep your fingers in the crimpy seam left of the finger crack.

Leach Boulder

Halfway down the hillside below *Chain Reaction* is a large blob of rock split by a narrow gully. Overhanging problems ascend either side of this gulch.

74. Smokin' (V0+) ★ Muscle through edges on the far left side of the block.

75. Molten Fingers (V3) ★★ Starting from an undercling, reach to a sloping ledge and make a long crank to jugs at the top.

76. Big Al's Arête (V4) ★★ Climb the rounded arête immediately right of the gully.

77. Leach Reach (V2) ★★ On the right side of the boulder, begin with an undercling and make a fingery move to a jug.

77a. Leach Variant (V0) ★ You can start slightly right, avoiding the undercling crux.

Buster Boulder

About 100 feet left of the Leach Boulder sits a peculiar boulder resembling the crest of a wave. Two physical, oddball problems exit the undercut roof. No topos.

78. Go Fetch (V1) ★ Bypass the wave to the left and mantel onto a ledge just over the lip.

79. Phi Slamma Grandma (V2) ★ Start inside the cave and exit the center of the wave, feet flailing in the air.

The Overhanging Flake

The steep flake below the Prophet Wall contains one of Smith's earliest and most climbed boulder problems. No topos.

74.	Smokin' V0+	77.	Leach Reach V2
75.	Molten Fingers V3	77a.	Leach Variant V0
76.	Big Al's Arête V4		

80. The Overhanging Flake (V2) ★★★★
Classic pocket pulling. An optional sit-down start on sharp pockets adds to the length but doesn't bump the difficulty much.

80a. (V4) ★★ No-foot variant, at least until you grab the top of the flake.

81. Penny Pincher (V5) ★★ Ascend the left arête, finishing with a barn-door move to a jug. Rough landing.

Scarface Wall

Downhill left of *Scarface* are heavily chalked edges on a very steep wall. Physical and sharp, these aren't Smith's finest problems, but they provide a good test of your physical prowess. All of these lines were done in the early days of Smith bouldering, but so many edges have broken that today's versions bear little resemblance to the problems of old. No topos.

82. Scar Tissue (V5) ★★ Starting from edges on the right, power directly to a big jug. Once a Smith classic, the fun decreased (and the level increased) as holds snapped away.

82a. Nameless Variant (V3) ★ From the starting edges, traverse left to the final move of *Scarred for Life*.

83. Scarred for Life (V4) ★★ Starting from a side pull flake, spring to a good edge and reach to a good jug on the left.

83a. (V6) ★ Shuffle right along painful edges to the crux move on *Scar Tissue*.

84. Little Friend (V5) ★★ Crank through side pulls just left of *Scarred for Life,* ending at a jug.

85. Toes of the Fisherman start (V4) ★

The roof crack/flaring slot at the base of the wall provides a few moments of awkwardness. Jump off after dangling with both hands from an unmistakable tooth.

Testament Slab Traverse

86. (V0+) ★★★ No topo. An easy warm-up traverse cuts either direction between the *Beard* and *Old Testament*. The terraced shelves below the uphill part create a hazardous landing, so don't fall off.

Combination Blocks Traverse

The best traverse at Smith is this often tried endurance problem; it was one of the better by-products of the early 1980s bouldering frenzy. Several "direct" problems join the traverse along the way.

87. Combination Blocks Traverse (V5)
★★★★ Slightly harder left to right. Finish by reaching the ground without jumping off.

87a. Round Trip (V6) ★★★★ Move left to right, touching a foot to the dirt, then reverse.

87b. Extension (V2) ★ You can make the traverse a little longer by starting on the *Charlie's Chimney* flake to the left and finessing around a corner to a no-hands rest.

88. Butt-Scraping Traverse (V6) ★★ Move
left to right, barely off the deck, finishing at good holds at the right end of *Combination Blocks Traverse*.

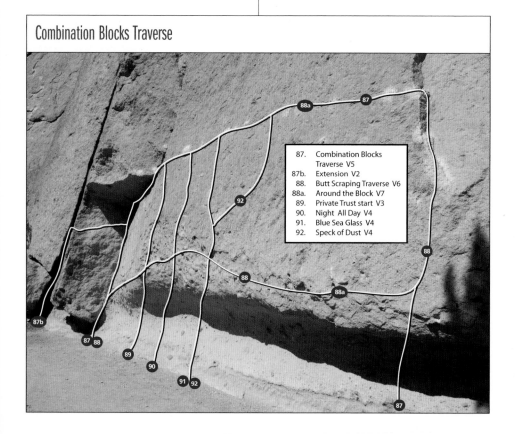

Combination Blocks Traverse

87.	Combination Blocks Traverse V5	
87b.	Extension V2	
88.	Butt Scraping Traverse V6	
88a.	Around the Block V7	
89.	Private Trust start V3	
90.	Night All Day V4	
91.	Blue Sea Glass V4	
92.	Speck of Dust V4	

88a. Around the Block (V7) ★★★ Do the *Butt-Scraping Traverse* and complete the loop by moving left via *Combination Blocks Traverse*.

89. Private Trust start (V3) ★★ Start below the right lip of the roof.

90. Night All Day (V4) ★★ Reach between a pocket and edge.

91. Blue Sea Glass (V4) ★★ Awkward seam.

92. Speck of Dust (V4) ★★ Reach right to a small crimp followed by a high step.

Phoenix Boulder

As you walk downstream heading toward the Phoenix Buttress, you'll spot a solid chunk of rock on your left at the only uphill part of the trail. Just beyond this boulder a path branches off to the left, heading to the river. You'll stumble upon the block to your right. Eons ago this boulder plummeted from the massive wall above—it's composed of the same iron-hard tuff found on the Smith Summit Crags. No topos.

93. Phoenix Problem (V2) ★★★ Follow uncontrived pockets up a shallow dihedral in the center of the block.

94. The Undercling (V3) ★★ Climb the left side, reaching to edges above a unique undercling.

THE SOUTHERN TIP BOULDERS

At the southernmost bend of the Crooked River are several small boulders. You'll find several easy options on these unimpressive blobs, mostly in the V0 to V1 range, though none of them are named.

WEST SIDE PROBLEMS

Scattered on the hillside on the west side of Smith Rock are dozens of boulders, extending from Cod Rock to the south to beyond Monkey Face to the north. Despite the volume of rock, there are very few problems here—most of the boulders have bad landings, are too high, too rotten, or all of the above. Two notable exceptions are the Monkey Boulder and Logan's Boulder.

Monkey Boulder

Along the river trail north of Monkey Face sits one of Smith's finest boulders, with a distinctive 15-foot roof barely off the ground. Remarkably, there are incuts everywhere, and the quality of the stone is way above average.

You'll have the option of soloing to the top after every problem, but everyone jumps off after getting established over the lip. Along with the problems listed below, there are untold eliminator options.

The 2-mile approach all the way around the Southern Tip via the river trail takes forty minutes, but it's flat the whole way. Approaching over Asterisk Pass knocks fifteen minutes off the time. Follow the well-maintained trail along the base of the West Side Crags, past Monkey Face to switchbacks leading back down to the river. Follow the trail upstream 200 feet to the boulder.

95. Ape Shit (V1) ★★ Start just left of a tree on the right side of the boulder and muscle through big holds.

96. Me and My Monkey (V4) ★★ Begin bunched up, clutching holds barely off the

Monkey Boulder

95.	Ape Shit V1	
96.	Me and My Monkey V4	
96a.	My Monkey and I V3	
96b.	My Monkey and Me V2	
97.	Spider Monkey V1	
97a.	Spider Variant V2	
98.	Monkey in the Middle V5	
99.	Monkey See, Monkey Do V3	
101.	Monkey Lip Traverse V7	

deck, and veer right through small pockets.

96a. My Monkey and I (V3) ★★★ Share the same start, but finish slightly left of the pocketed face.

96b. My Monkey and Me (V2) ★★ Same sitting start, but exit to the left.

97. Spider Monkey (V1) ★★★ Start inside the right part of the cave and hand traverse to the lip, moving right on big incuts. This was the original problem from the late 1970s.

97a. Spider Variant (V2) ★★ Traverse the same starting holds, but exit left at the lip.

98. Monkey in the Middle (V5) ★★★ The center roof exit starts deep inside the cave on chalked jugs. Half the problem is keeping your feet off the ground as you reach from incut to incut.

99. Monkey See, Monkey Do (V3) ★★★ Muscle through the first chalked jugs left of *Monkey in the Middle*.

100. Barrel of Monkeys (V3) ★★★ No topo. Begin at a big jug in the left side of the cave and power over the lip on incuts.

101. Monkey Lip Traverse (V7) ★★★ Start in the cave as far to the left as possible and head right, traversing the entire lip of the cave and finishing with *Ape Shit*.

102. Jungle Gym (V0) ★★★ No topo. The vertical north side of the boulder features many sporting options, all on incuts. Pick a line and go.

103. Red Boulder (V2) ★★ No topo. A prominent reddish block hides behind the Monkey Boulder. Follow a vertical line of edges up the center of the face.

Logan Carr on *Logan's Boulder*. BEN MOON PHOTO

Logan's Boulder

Atop the ridge south of Monkey Face, just above *Pleasure Palace,* sits a reddish boulder with a jungle gym of jugs on the southeast side. The unimproved trail up Aggro Gully leads directly to the boulder. Otherwise you'll spot the boulder on your left as you near Monkey Face after hiking up Misery Ridge. No topo.

104. Logan's Problem (V3) ★★★ Start under a small roof and power left through entertaining incuts.

Easy's Playhouse

Above Red Wall rests this small, steep cliff studded with sport routes. Along with the bouldering starts to each route, there are two physical traverses. No topos.

105. Easy's Left Traverse (V6) ★★ The pocketed yellow wall left of Easy's Playhouse features a physical traverse, done from left to right. You'll have the option of finishing to the top of the rock band at the end.

106. Easy's Right Traverse (V7) ★★ A flaring crack with a triangular block at the base splits the middle of Easy's Playhouse. A challenging traverse start at this crack and muscles far right on positive holds.

RED WALL BOULDERS

Many boulders are strewn across the hillside below Red Wall. Most of these are undeveloped, but a collection of boulders near the river are studded with fun problems. The pleasant approach turns right at the bridge, following the trail 200 yards beyond the Lizard Boulder.

Red Clot Rock

Nearest the trail sits this attractive boulder with several problems on perfect rock. The overhanging river face makes it the best of the Red Wall boulders. Before the Smith Rock fire, large pine trees provided shade and a tranquil setting. Today it's more like a war zone littered with charred, uprooted snags.

107. The Jug Route (V1) ★★★ This classic problem cranks between two obvious jugs. You'll get to choose from a static version, jumping off the ground, and many other creative variants, along with the following options:

107a. The Begin Down Under Problem (V3) ★★★ Start sitting down—harder if done statically.

107b. (V3) ★★ Double-handed lunge from the first jug to the second.

107c. (V10) ★ One handed. You can take just enough weight off using your feet to make this possible, but you still need to be freakishly strong.

107d. (V14?) One handed (no feet). This undone problem is the perfect test of raw

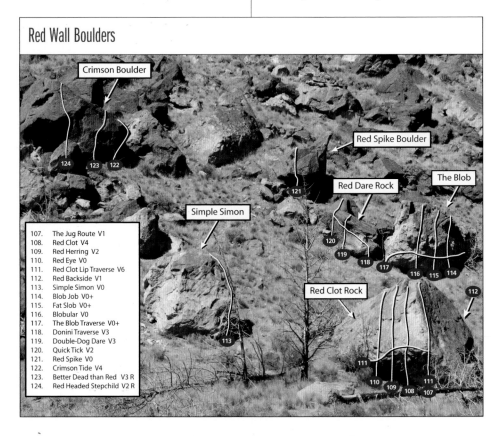

Red Wall Boulders

Crimson Boulder

Red Spike Boulder

The Blob

Red Dare Rock

Simple Simon

Red Clot Rock

107.	The Jug Route	V1
108.	Red Clot	V4
109.	Red Herring	V2
110.	Red Eye	V0
111.	Red Clot Lip Traverse	V6
112.	Red Backside	V1
113.	Simple Simon	V0
114.	Blob Job	V0+
115.	Fat Slob	V0+
116.	Blobular	V0
117.	The Blob Traverse	V0+
118.	Donini Traverse	V3
119.	Double-Dog Dare	V3
120.	Quick Tick	V2
121.	Red Spike	V0
122.	Crimson Tide	V4
123.	Better Dead than Red	V3 R
124.	Red Headed Stepchild	V2 R

power. You'll need to jump to a jug and do a one-arm pull-up with enough momentum to fly for a jug 18 inches above. In the early 1980s Chris Jones missed by less than an inch. Succeed and you are the burliest climber on earth.

108. Red Clot (V4) ★★★ One of Smith's first difficult boulder problems. Start 4 feet left of *The Jug Route* with a miserable cling for your left hand and a pinch for your right.

108a. (V6) ★★ The level increases a couple notches with a sitting start.

108b. (V4) ★★ Jump off the ground, latching a slanting side pull with your left hand and a sloper with your right.

108c. (V5) ★★ Power to the finishing jug with no feet. It's okay using your feet on the upper slab—otherwise you'll be slithering on your belly like a snake.

108d. (V4) ★★★ From the first of two buckets on *The Jug Route,* power left and finish with *Red Clot.*

109. Red Herring (V2) ★ Stretch off the ground for a line of crimpers 4 feet left of *Red Clot.*

110. Red Eye (V0) ★ Crammed near a small snag left of *Red Herring* is an easier line of edges.

111. Red Clot Lip Traverse (V6) ★★ This problem traverses from right to left with hands just over the lip. Begin from the first jug on *The Jug Route* and end at *Red Eye*'s dead snag.

112. Red Backside (V1) ★ There's not much on the short backside apart from a one-move problem off a slimy crimper.

112a. (V0) ★ An easier option pulls through better holds a few feet left.

113. Simple Simon (V0) ★★ Start sitting down left of a hole at the base of the boulder left of Red Clot Rock and muscle through big holds.

The Blob

Behind Red Clot Rock are two closely spaced boulders. The solid right block contains a few fun problems that really aren't much of a problem at all.

114. Blob Job (V0+) ★ Start with a flat cling hold on the right side of the face and race through big holds.

115. Fat Slob (V0+) ★ Solid edges up the center of the wall.

116. Blobular (V0) ★ An easy "groove" to the left with big holds.

117. The Blob Traverse (V0+) ★ Traverse the entire width of the face.

Red Dare Rock

The left of two closely spaced boulders is the appealing Red Dare Rock.

118. Donini Traverse (V3) ★★★ Start right of *Double-Dog Dare* and move uphill on pockets, finishing with *Quick Tick.*

119. Double-Dog Dare (V3) ★★★ Solid edges lead to a finishing mantel on the center of the block.

120. Quick Tick (V2) ★★ Press a fun mantel on the left side of the block without using a small boulder at the start.

Red Spike Boulder

121. Red Spike (V0) ★★ Lieback a short flake on the pointed-topped boulder above Red Dare Block.

Crimson Boulder

This impressive, reddish boulder sits left of the Red Spike Boulder. The lines are more serious than other nearby problems.

122. Crimson Tide (V4) ★★ Follow the short right arête.

123. Better Dead than Red (V3 R) ★★★ Sporting near the top, but it's the best problem on the block.

124. Red Headed Stepchild (V2 R) ★★ Ascend white-capped incuts on the left, hoping that nothing snaps. There was an ankle-wrecking sagebrush at the base, but the 1996 Smith fire conveniently eliminated this hazard.

OLD CLIMBERS' CAMP BOULDERS

Upstream from the Monument, at the northernmost bend of the Crooked River, sits the Old Climbers' Camp. Apart from a blackened fire pit on the north side of the Fireplace Boulder, there's little evidence that for more than a decade it was the camping spot for almost all Smith pioneers. Smith's first boulderers explored the limited options, though no one remembers who did what. Chris Jones made these boulders his personal playground in 1979, climbing every obvious line along with other obscure variants. Approach by following a path veering right just after the river trail crosses a scree slope below Juniper Spire.

Fireplace Boulder

The centerpiece of the Old Climbers' Camp is a blackened boulder with an undercut face. Smith tuff doesn't get better than this.

Fireplace Boulder

125.	Money to Burn V0	129.	Jones Traverse V4
126.	Fireplace Problem V3	130.	Jones Mantel V2
126a.	Fire and Rain V1	131.	The Leg Swing Traverse V3
127.	Light My Fire V0	132.	The Begin Down Under Prow V4
128.	Hot Spot V0	134.	Pioneer Traverse V0+

125. Money to Burn (V0) ★ The leftmost problem on the main face of the Fireplace Boulder begins with a left-hand pinch.

126. Fireplace Problem (V3) ★★★ The blackened fire pit route starts sitting down and ends with a tough move past a mini-undercling.

126a. Fire and Rain (V1) ★★★ Share the same start, but finish with holds a few feet right.

127. Light My Fire (V0) ★★★ Crank distinctive slanting holds to a finishing jug on solid stone.

127a. (V2) ★★ The grade goes up but the fun goes down with a sitting start.

127b. (V3) ★★ From the slanting holds, make a two-handed lunge all the way to the finishing jug. You can drop the grade (and increase the enjoyment) a notch by lunging to a slanting ledge to the right.

128. Hot Spot (V0) ★★ A fun problem shuffles up the right corner of the main face.

129. Jones Traverse (V4) ★★★ Step off a small boulder on the right and traverse the face low on a series of slanting holds, finishing to the left with *Money to Burn*.

130. Jones Mantel (V2) ★ Around the corner right of the attractive main face is a sloping shelf. You can fashion a pure mantel just about anywhere.

131. The Leg Swing Traverse (V3) ★★ Traverse along the lip right of the *Jones Mantel* and pull past the overhang on big holds, dodging an inconvenient tree branch.

132. The Begin Down Under Prow (V4) ★★ Ascend a steep, juggy arête on the back of the boulder with a sit-down start.

133. Fire Nation (V0) ★ No topo. Uncontrived climbing on the right side of the slabby backside of the boulder.

Pioneer Boulder

Immediately left of the Fireplace Boulder is a rounded blob of solid rock with simple scrambles everywhere. You'll find some fun one-handed and even no-handed problems, along with the following three lines.

134. Pioneer Traverse (V0+) ★★ Start close to the Fireplace Boulder and traverse clockwise just a few feet off the deck.

135. Native Son (V0) ★★ No topo. On the undercut main face, start sitting down with both hands on a rail and make one physical reach to good knobs.

136. Old Timer (V0+) ★ No topo. Ascend mediocre rock left of a big tree on the backside of the boulder.

River Rock

Hidden in the trees about 100 feet downstream from the Fireplace Boulder is a small block of yellow tuff. There isn't much here apart from a few historical relics. No topos.

137. Thomas No Hands (V0+) ★ The rightmost backside slab features a novel no-hands problem.

138. River Rock Slab (V0) ★★ This appealing low-angle face on the backside provides a pleasant technical exercise.

138a. (V1) ★ Using one hand provides a stiffer technical challenge.

139. Lucky Charms (V2) ★ The gently overhanging upriver side of the block contains two short problems. The right route begins with positive edges and boulders up the center of the face.

140. Magically Delicious (V2) ★ Just left of *Lucky Charms* is a very short prow.

DELIRIUM BOULDERS

Scattered below the Marsupial Crags are more than a hundred boulders. With the canal access road so close, early Smith pioneers scrambled up the easier lines, but it wasn't until the spring of 1979 that Mike Adams ushered in the modern bouldering era. A few months later Chris Jones spent fifteen days bouldering here, doing dozens of moderate problems and a few difficult lines, including the *Whale's Head* (V8). He named the entire boulder field after a nearby crag and made a detailed map of his problems. With his chalk soon washed away, boulderers from each subsequent generation explored the area, repeating the exact same problems, each thinking they were doing first ascents.

Despite the volume of rock, this isn't a bouldering nirvana—like everywhere else at Smith, most of the boulders leave much to be desired. But the finest chunks of stone are excellent, with the landings usually flat and sandy. The tuff here is different than anything else at Smith—solid and heavily featured with sharp edges everywhere. The nineteen boulders described below range from top-notch to mediocre, but they provide a good sampling of what's here. Attempting to chronicle every problem ever climbed would require a chapter all by itself. Almost all of these unrecorded lines are at the lower end of the V-scale.

To approach, turn right at the bridge and hike upstream around the northern bend of the Crooked River. Hike up the draw between the Student Wall and Staender Ridge to the Burma Road and follow a trail skirting the uphill bank of the canal. Because of the sheer volume, these are some of the harder problems to locate at Smith. Fortunately, there are several distinguishing boulders just above the canal trail that can be used as a reference point. Using the photos you'll have no problem locating each of these boulders (in order of approach): Adams Pillar, Jones Boulder, Gem Boulder, and Delirium Block. Locate these boulders, and you'll find everything else nearby.

Adit Boulder

As you approach the Burma Road, you'll notice several boulders at the base of Staender Ridge. About 100 feet above the trail is the appealing-looking Adit Boulder. There are two chunks of rock— the main boulder and a small slab to the right. No topos.

141. Adit Slab (V0- 5.7) ★★★ Ascend perfect rock on the dinky slab.

142. Subtract It (V0 R) ★★ Start atop boulders on the left side and pull past a small horizontal roof leading to an easy finish.

143. Drift Mine (V0+ R) ★★ The longest problem on the block ascends good holds onto a shelf. Finish with simple pockets high off the ground.

144. Adit Up (V4) ★★★ A fun problem begins sitting down on the uphill side with both hands on a rail, and eases after latching a classic knob. The grade goes down a couple notches if you stem off a boulder to the left.

Ocean Boulder

After leaving the Burma Road the trail heads south, skirting the hillside above the canal. As soon as you turn the corner, moving away from the canal, you'll see the Ocean Boulder directly ahead. Two juniper trees grow uncomfortably close to the base of the

Delirium Boulders

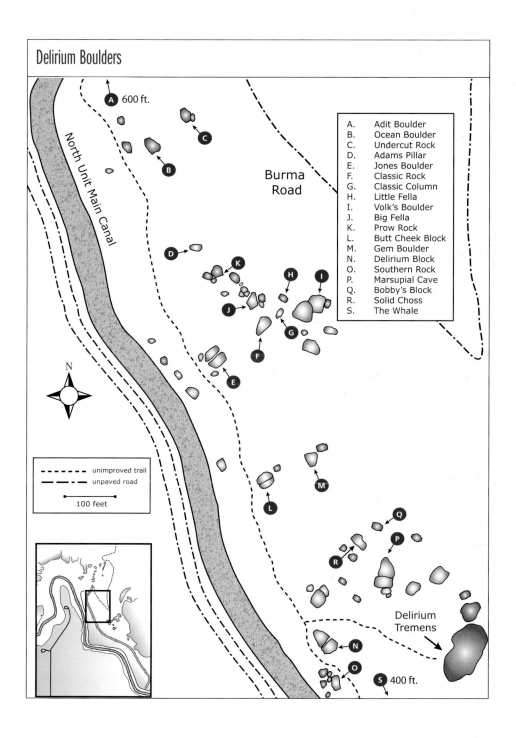

A.   Adit Boulder
B.   Ocean Boulder
C.   Undercut Rock
D.   Adams Pillar
E.   Jones Boulder
F.   Classic Rock
G.   Classic Column
H.   Little Fella
I.   Volk's Boulder
J.   Big Fella
K.   Prow Rock
L.   Butt Cheek Block
M.   Gem Boulder
N.   Delirium Block
O.   Southern Rock
P.   Marsupial Cave
Q.   Bobby's Block
R.   Solid Choss
S.   The Whale

600 ft.

North Unit Main Canal

Burma Road

N

unimproved trail
unpaved road

100 feet

Delirium Tremens

400 ft.

left side of the rounded blob. Most climbers walk by with hardly a glance. No topos.

145. Barnacle Bill (V5) ★★★ The best problem on the boulder slaps up the solid left arête.

146. Pacific Ocean Wall (A1) ★ Smith's version of this El Cap classic clips three quarter-inch bolts up a breathtaking expanse of tuff guarded by a tree. If you can stick a painfully sharp jam, you might be able to free the entire 12-foot wall.

147. Boogie Board (V0+) ★ Ten feet right of the *P.O. Wall,* start with an offset and finish with sharp edges.

148. Seaside Ocean (V0) ★ Ascend the line of good holds up the center of the face, just left of the line of least resistance.

149. Ebby's (V1) ★ Climb edges above an undercut base, just left of the right corner.

150. Salt Water Taffy (V3) ★ Start with a left-hand side pull and crank over a bulge on the right prow.

Undercut Rock

Uphill 150 feet and left of the Ocean Boulder is a blob of rock with an undercut downhill side. There's a single problem that barely justifies walking up the hill. No topo.

151. Underhanded (V2) ★ Begin sitting down with a big undercling at the right corner and reach to a good edge.

Adams Pillar

Walk 100 yards along the trail beyond the Ocean Boulder and look uphill for a pleasant boulder with an obvious prow on the downhill face.

152. Mike's Arête (V2) ★★ Boulder up the left edge.

153. Wild Man (V1) ★★ Climb the right side of the same prow.

Adams Pillar

152. Mike's Arête V2
153. Wild Man V1
154. Addams Family V0
155. Adams Apple V0

154. Addams Family (V0) ★ Begin with a rounded orange knob on the face to the right.

155. Adams Apple (V0) ★★ From an incut rail around the corner to the right, lock off and reach the top.

Jones Boulder

Continuing on the trail past Adams Pillar, you'll soon arrive at the unmistakable Jones Boulder at the base of the most visited section of real estate in the Delirium Boulders. Strewn on the hillside above are many chunks of stone, both large and small. The Jones Boulder offers something for everyone, with problems ranging from easy to hard on decent rock.

156. Alley Traverse (V0) ★ A corridor as wide as a sidewalk divides the Jones Boulder. A low horizontal seam splits the alley of the larger half of the block. The low traverse starts to the right and moves left, hand traversing the low seam.

156a. Alley Cat Traverse (V2) ★ A much harder variant moves left to right along the seam, finishing with *Alley Cat*.

157. Alley Cat (V4) ★★★ The steep downhill side of the Jones Boulder features three higher-level problems. The most attractive line follows the rounded left arête.

158. Indiana Jones (V4) ★★ Ascend the face immediately right of *Alley Cat*.

159. Jonestown (V7 R) ★★★ One of the better problems on the Delirium Boulders powers between good holds up the center of

Jones Boulder

the overhanging downhill face. Reaching two pockets at midheight is the biggest challenge, but the highball finish will test your nerves.

160. Maple Slam (V2) ★★ The vertical south face offers several decent lines. The left route starts just right of the overhanging downhill face.

161. Red Licorice (V1) ★★ The center of three south-side routes follows good edges.

162. Jonesing (V0+) ★★★ One of the earliest problems on the Delirium Boulders climbed a solid rib/seam on the right side of the south face.

163. Too Much Trouble (V0) ★★ A simple seam on the uphill side of the boulder really isn't much trouble at all.

Classic Rock

Directly above the Jones Boulder rests a squarish chunk of rock with an attractive south face. The right side contains several moderate, high-quality lines, while the undercut left side features the best high-end route in the area.

164. Pet Sounds (V2 R) ★★ Ascend the highball left arête of the main face.

165. The Wall (V8) ★★★ The most perplexing Marsupial problem begins with knobs in the center of the wall and makes a long reach to small edges.

166. Sticky Fingers (V3) ★★ Start just left of the rounded right edge and reach left to a side pull.

Classic Rock

Classic Column

Little Fella

164. Pet Sounds V2 R
165. The Wall V8
166. Sticky Fingers V3
167. Abbey Road V2
168. Back in Black V0
169. Classic Column V1
170. Little Fella V0+

167. Abbey Road (V2) ★★ Slap up great rock on the right arête, very close to *Sticky Fingers*.

168. Back in Black (V0) ★★ Good holds on the solid uphill side of the block.

Classic Column

169. Classic Column (V1) ★★★★ One of Smith's most distinctive problems rises above the Classic Rock. The perfectly cleaved column is perfectly suited for climbing, with memorable slaps up both razor-sharp edges.

Little Fella

170. Little Fella (V0+) ★★ Directly above and left of Classic Column is a small boulder composed of solid tuff with an appealing problem up the center.

Volk's Boulder

The massive chunk of rock rising above Classic Column is Volk's Boulder. Despite gorgeous rock on the lower half, it's too high for bouldering—apart from a backside line, there's nothing here. No topo.

171. Volk's Slab (V0- 5.4) ★★ In the early 1980s Mike Volk, founder of Timberline Mountain Guides, took his beginning classes to this small uphill slab. It was an ideal setting to teach first-timers the basics. With the anchor no longer in place, today it's nothing more than a footnote in Smith history.

Big Fella

The boulder immediately left of Classic Column offers three closely spaced problems on the heavily featured north side. No topos.

172. Black Dog (V1) ★★ Climb the right edge.

173. Sneeze Machine (V3) ★★★ Crank pockets in the center of a flat face just left of *Black Dog*.

174. Fella, Not a Wella (V1) ★★ Follow an obvious leaning seam slightly left of the other lines.

Prow Rock

From Big Fella, walk north 50 feet through a gap between two boulders. Directly ahead you'll see a quality problem. No topo.

175. South Corner Overhang (V3) ★★★ Start sitting down below a classic namesake prow on the uphill side of the boulder.

Butt Cheek Block

Continuing 100 yards along the trail south of the Jones Boulder, you'll next pass below a large chunk of stone split by a flaring, block-plugged crack. It doesn't compare favorably with the better nearby boulders. No topos.

176. Preparation H (V1) ★ Muscle through edges to the left of the butt crack.

177. Right Butt Cheek (V0+) ★ Climb the wall right of the flaring crack.

Gem Boulder

Above Butt Cheek Block is a pocketed, triangular boulder composed of reddish stone. There's nothing quite like it among the Delirium Boulders.

178. Emerald Face (V3) ★★★ Begin sitting down below the big pockets on the left side of the boulder, and finish up and right on the main face. Beginning from the jugs drops the grade to V1.

178a. Emerald Edge (V3) ★★★ Share the same sit-down start, but finish up the left

Gem Boulder

178.	Emerald Face V3
178a.	Emerald Edge V3
179.	Sapphire Wall V1
179a.	Sapphire Escape V1
180.	Diamond Face V0+
181.	Jones' Jump V0
182.	Gem Traverse V3

edge. Eliminating the sit-down start drops the grade to V2.

179. Sapphire Wall (V1) ★★ Follow a direct line up the center of the block, topping out at the summit.

179a. Sapphire Escape (V1) ★★ Veer left on good holds, eliminating the highball finish.

180. Diamond Face (V0+) ★★ Ascend the right side of the attractive wall.

181. Jones' Jump (V0) ★ A peculiar line on the low-angle right slab begins with a running jump and finishes up a ramp using no hands.

182. Gem Traverse (V3) ★★★ Start on the right side of the block and traverse left barely off the ground, ending with your choice of *Emerald* finishes.

Delirium Block

183.	Yellow Brick Road V0- (5.7 R)	188.	J-Bru V0
184.	Delirium Traverse V1	189.	Delirium Jam V0- (5.7)
185.	Burning Eyes Red V1	190.	One Piece Truck V0- (5.8)
186.	Sun Cottage V0	191.	Backside Slab V0+
187.	Bury the Egg V0+	192.	Chimney Arête V0

Delirium Block

Continuing along the trail beyond Butt Cheek Block, you'll next pass a massive bulb lacking in decent bouldering lines. Ahead is the Delirium Block, cut in two by a chimney. Each side offers something different—an uphill slab, fun problems on the vertical south side, and freaky solos on the river face.

183. Yellow Brick Road (V0- 5.7 R) ★★★
The low-angle slab on the downhill side of the boulder is a delight, as long as you don't fall off.

184. Delirium Traverse (V1) ★★ You can
traverse the entire south face, starting from jugs near the right corner and ending at the ramp on *One Piece Truck*.

185. Burning Eyes Red (V1) ★★ Ascend
good holds rising above the middle of the steepest part of the *Delirium Traverse* and finish right.

186. Sun Cottage (V0) ★ Scramble up big
holds rising above a left-leaning ramp.

187. Bury the Egg (V0+) ★ Begin with
rounded knobs in the center of the southern face.

188. J-Bru (V0) ★★ Solid rock starting with
a jug just left of a hand crack.

189. Delirium Jam (V0- 5.7) ★★ Jam
and hand traverse the obvious leaning hand crack.

190. One Piece Truck (V0- 5.8) ★★
Follow the ramp/finger crack just right of *Delirium Jam*.

191. Backside Slab (V0+) ★ Balance up knobs on the less-than-vertical wall left of the backside chimney.

192. Chimney Arête (V0) ★ Ascend the left edge of the uphill chimney.

Southern Rock

Just south of the Delirium Block is a cluster of angular boulders. The southeast boulder is the best of the bunch, with several fun problems.

193. Sweet Home Alabama (V0+) ★★ Start with slanting wafer jugs on the uphill face and crank past a bulge.

194. Black Betty (V0) ★★ Five feet left of *Sweet Home Alabama*, ascend a vertical wall starting with a jug.

195. Whipping Post (V2) ★★ The short southern prow features a fun problem.

196. Free Bird (V1) ★ Climb a left-leaning seam on the south side with a sit-down start.

Southern Rock

193.	Sweet Home Alabama	V0+
194.	Black Betty	V0
195.	Whipping Post	V2
196.	Free Bird	V1
197.	Ramblin Man	V2
198.	Dixie Chicken	V0

197. Ramblin Man (V2) ★ Boulder up the short, steep wall just left of *Free Bird*.

198. Dixie Chicken (V0) ★ Begin sitting down with an offset to the left.

Marsupial Cave

About a dozen massive boulders litter the hillside uphill from the Delirium Block. They look impressive, but they remain untouched—the best-looking lines are free solos, not boulder problems, and the lesser boulders lack compelling lines. About 200 feet uphill from the Delirium Block sits the Marsupial Cave, split by a chimney into a lower and upper half. With an anchor on top and a bad landing, the following two routes are usually toproped. No topos.

199. Right Jugs (V2 R) ★ Start deep in the backside cave on jugs coated with crap and power through buckets skirting the right side of the roof.

200. Left Jugs (V3 R) ★ Start in the cave and exit left.

Bobby's Block

Slightly uphill 50 feet north of the Marsupial Cave is a rounded, south-facing boulder composed of solid stone. No topos.

201. The Apple Farm (V0) ★ Begin just left of a creaky flake on the right side of the slab.

202. One Humid Day (V1) ★ Start sitting down in the center of the slab at a light-colored patch of rock.

Southern Delirium Boulders

Marsupial Cave

Solid Choss

Bobby's Block

Delirium Block

Southern Rock

203. Bobby Eat Peaches (V0+) ★★ Start from an incut just off the ground on the left side and crank through big side pulls.

Solid Choss

Forty feet downhill from Bobby's Block sits a heavily featured, west-facing wall. At first glance the rock looks like crap, but it's surprisingly solid. No topos.

204. My Gravy's No Good (V2) ★★ The best option powers up the short right prow, finishing with a mantel.

205. Choss Time (V0) ★ You'll have your choice of many potential lines on the main face. The original problem followed jugs up the center.

The Whale

About 200 yards south of the Delirium Block sits a rounded boulder just above the canal. There's not much here apart from a difficult Jones problem from 1979. No topos.

206. The Whale's Head (V8) ★★ On the north side of the boulder is an overhanging prow capped by a line of incuts. Using a sit-down start, grab horrible holds and fire for a good pocket.

206a. (V3) ★★ The grade goes way down if you ignore the sit-down start, but the finishing jugs are still the best part of the problem.

NORTHERN POINT BOULDERING

The basalt of the Northern Point contains many underappreciated boulder problems. Basalt offers a very different bouldering experience than Smith tuff, with square-cut edges, insecure slopers, and perfect stone. There are three pockets of problems—a long traverse along the base of the cliff, boulders below the downriver routes, and others along the river.

207. The Heathen Traverse (V8) ★★★ No topo. A physical traverse starts off a small ledge below *The Heathen* and ends below *Hang It Loose,* far to the left. Follow the same approach through the rimrock used for all Northern Point routes and hike upstream to the first bolted lines.

Northern Point Boulders

Several boulders rest high on the hillside, just below the downriver routes on the Northern Point. Approach by walking north from the turnaround parking lot, entering the canyon via a trail on your left. At the first switchback, step off the trail and boulder hop upstream 30 feet to the boulder field. No topos.

208. Northstar (V5) ★★★ This impressive problem ascends the overhanging north side of the boulder nearest the switchback.

209. Point Blank (V5) ★★★ The block left of *Northstar* features an appealing problem beginning with a sit-down, left-to-right traverse and finishing with a rounded arête.

210. Point Pleasant (V3) ★★ The second boulder left of *Point Blank* contains a single problem beginning with a stretch to sloping holds at the lip of a mini-roof.

The Sappy Boulders

Three basalt boulders sit among the pines at the base of the hillside at the northern bend of the Crooked River. Approach either by walking upstream from the bridge along the east side of the river or descending the switch-backed path west of the Northern Point.

Sappy Boulder

The uniquely shaped namesake boulder hides behind a massive, sap-dripping pine tree. A burly collection of high-end problems ascend every side of this angular block.

211. The Sappy Traverse (V5) ★ No topo. The unimpressive downriver side of the block features an uphill traverse along the lip of a low-level roof.

212. The Coffin Problem (V5) ★★★ An impressive problem ascends the downhill rib of the Sappy Boulder, with a coffin-shaped boulder at the base. A committing sequence leads over a prominent tooth to a sketchy finish.

212a. Coffin Bypass (V0+) ★★ Avoid the intimidating tooth by climbing sloping ledges to the left.

213. Rose Wall (V3) ★★★ The upstream face of the boulder blends edges and slopers with an insecure crux at the top.

213a. Rose Traverse (V3) ★★ You can start uphill, traversing down and right before joining the regular line. It barely impacts the grade.

214. Feeling Sappy (V5) ★★★ An appealing overhanging prow on the uphill side cranks

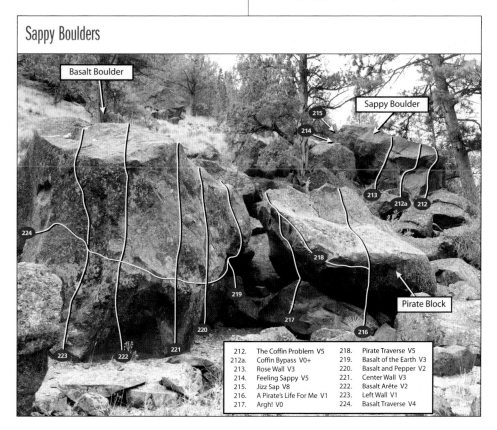

Sappy Boulders

212.	The Coffin Problem V5	218.	Pirate Traverse V5
212a.	Coffin Bypass V0+	219.	Basalt of the Earth V3
213.	Rose Wall V3	220.	Basalt and Pepper V2
214.	Feeling Sappy V5	221.	Center Wall V3
215.	Jizz Sap V8	222.	Basalt Arête V2
216.	A Pirate's Life For Me V1	223.	Left Wall V1
217.	Argh! V0	224.	Basalt Traverse V4

from a jug to a good hold at the lip. You can double the length approaching via the *Rose Traverse*.

215. Jizz Sap (V8) ★★★ The most challenging problem on Smith basalt starts left of *Feeling Sappy* and cranks through horrid pinches and slopers.

Pirate Block

Below and slightly upstream from the Sappy Boulder are two closely spaced blocks with sandy landings. The unimpressive Pirate Block sits to the right.

216. A Pirate's Life For Me (V1) ★ Start to the right and pull over the lip to an awkward finishing mantel.

217. Argh! (V0) ★ Start from a big jug on the left and crank over a mini-bulge.

218. Pirate Traverse (V5) ★ You can contrive a hard problem by starting at an obvious pocket on *A Pirate's Life For Me* and traversing the lip without using the block at the base.

Basalt Boulder

Just left of Pirate Block sits a squarish boulder. The problems are worth doing, with reaches between square-cut edges.

219. Basalt of the Earth (V3) ★★ The right line cranks over a small roof on positive crimps.

220. Basalt and Pepper (V2) ★ Finesse side pulls in the center of the block, making a big stretch to a good hold on top.

221. Center Wall (V3) ★★ Crimp up the vertical face 6 feet right of an arête.

222. Basalt Arête (V2) ★★ Ascend the shallow left arête using edges on either side.

223. Left Wall (V1) ★★ Start from a pocket left of the edge and finish with a mantel.

224. Basalt Traverse (V4) ★★ Start on the far left side of the boulder and traverse right, finishing with *Basalt of the Earth*.

UPPER GORGE BOULDERING AREA

Just below the upstream entrance to the Upper Gorge stretches a unique section of rimrock. Ranging from 15 to 30 feet high and graced with a sandy landing, this heavily pocketed wall contains Smith's most enjoyable basalt bouldering. Most climbers prefer staying close to the ground with a traverse on wonderful pockets.

THE BIVY BOULDERING AREA

The most accessible and popular bouldering in the park is the Bivy Bouldering Area, located near the Smith Rock Bivouac Area. Two overhanging cliff bands and a small group of boulders offer high-level lines, good rock, and an effortless approach. While most Smith bouldering was a product of the pre–sport climbing days, these crags weren't developed until the 1990s. There are several more boulders than described below, mostly downstream, with limited potential.

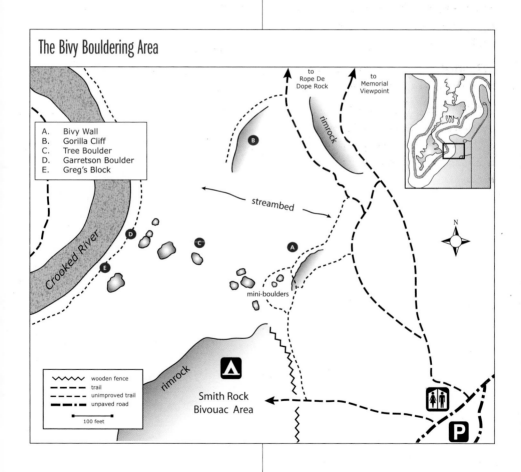

The Bivy Bouldering Area

A. Bivy Wall
B. Gorilla Cliff
C. Tree Boulder
D. Garretson Boulder
E. Greg's Block

to Rope De Dope Rock

to Memorial Viewpoint

rimrock

streambed

Crooked River

mini-boulders

N

wooden fence
trail
unimproved trail
unpaved road
100 feet

rimrock

Smith Rock Bivouac Area

Bivy Wall

A hybrid bouldering/sport crag rests atop the Bivy Bouldering Area. With problems ranging from 15 to 25 feet, it's a little too short for sport routes and too high for casual bouldering enjoyment. A two-minute approach and toproping chains make it popular whether opting for a rope or a bouldering pad. To approach, follow the gravel path from the Bivy Area showers and take the left fork. Either skirt along the top of the crag to your left or descend a couple switchbacks before crossing a piddling stream on fallen timbers.

225. Jughead (V2 R) ★ Race up gnarled jugs and freaky, wafer-thin underclings to a crux side pull at the top.

226. Black Sheep (V4 R) ★★ Ascend highball side pulls just right of a black streak.

Even with a stack of pads, you won't want to fall off at the top.

227. Frizzell's Line (V0+ R) ★★★ An obvious seam with buckets on either side splits the highest part of the wall. Two leads bolts appeared long after the first ascent, along with anchor chains. The "R" grade disappears if you go for the lead.

228. Buckets of Rain (V0 R) ★★★ Just right of *Frizzell's Line* rises a fun line of jugs.

229. Moonbeams (V2 R) ★★ Climb the black streak centered between two lines of buckets. The holds near the top are huge but a little hollow sounding.

230. To Be or Not to Bolt (V3 R) ★★★ The right side of the wall features a sport-bolted line with crux edges leading to buckets. Clipping the bolts removes the "R" grade.

Bivy Wall–Left Side

225.	Jughead V2 R
226.	Black Sheep V4 R
227.	Frizzell's Line V0+ R
228.	Buckets of Rain V0 R
229.	Moonbeams V2 R
230.	To Be or Not to Bolt V3 R
238.	Bivy Wall Traverse V3 R

Bivy Wall–Right Side

230.	To Be or Not to Bolt V3 R
231.	Off the Hook V5 R
232.	The Offset V2 R
233.	Ovaltine V1
233a.	Oval Direct V3
234.	Left Scoop V1
235.	Center Scoop V0
236.	Bivy Seam V0
237.	Right Scoop V1
238.	Bivy Wall Traverse V3

231. Off the Hook (V5 R) ★★ Start left of a leaning offset with a long crank off a side pull and finish right on jugs.

232. The Offset (V2 R) ★★★★ Follow the high-quality offset above a beaten-down tree that probably wishes it had grown somewhere else.

233. Ovaltine (V1) ★★★ Start left and follow the path of least resistance on good edges and pockets, veering right to an oval-shaped jug just below the top.

233a. Oval Direct (V3) ★★ Start right and climb directly on crimps to the oval jug, avoiding bigger holds to the left.

234. Left Scoop (V1) ★ There are three massive scoops on the right side of the cliff. Exit the left scoop and follow an offset to a mossy finish.

235. Center Scoop (V0) ★★ The best scoop problem pulls over a bulge on positive edges to a mossy finish.

236. Bivy Seam (V0) ★ Follow a short seam between the center and right scoops.

237. Right Scoop (V1) ★ Exit the right scoop, pulling over the top on mounds of moss.

238. Bivy Wall Traverse (V3) ★★ Begin at either end and traverse the entire cliff. The more you avoid the low-angle slab running along the base, the higher the grade.

The Gorilla Cliff

About 200 feet below and upstream from the Bivy Wall is a renowned rock band called the Gorilla Cliff. For good reason, this is the most popular bouldering destination at Smith—nowhere else is there such an unbroken stretch of overhanging, high-quality problems. The flat landing, three-minute downhill approach, and big numbers only add to the appeal. The most easily defined problems, all with sitting starts, are listed below, but the potential link-ups and eliminates are nearly infinite.

To approach, follow the trail from the Bivy Area showers and immediately take the left fork leading into the canyon. After descending switchbacked wooden steps, the trail levels out, and you'll soon spot the cliff to your left. The wall itself is over 150 feet long, gradually increasing in height the whole way.

239. One Hit Wonder (V3) ★ No topo. A low-level roof cuts along the left side of the crag. You can mantel over anywhere, but

the first real problem exits the left of two large, circular scoops.

240. Two to Tango (V2) ★ No topo. Ascend the slightly easier right scoop.

241. Three-peat (V0) ★ No topo. To the right of the scoops, climb an inconsequential seam capped by good edges.

242. Final Four (V2) ★★ Start behind a tree with both hands on a rail and crank past the bulge.

243. Five and Dime (V7) ★★★ This small offset doesn't look like much at first glance, but starting in the back of the "mini-cave" makes it surprisingly physical. After latching the holds at the lip, it's hard staying off the ground when cutting loose your feet.

Gorilla Cliff–Left Side

242.	Final Four V2
243.	Five and Dime V7
243a.	Alternate Ending V8
244.	Six Feet Under V10
245.	Seven Dwarfs V7
246.	Eight Mile V7
247.	Revolution 9 V5
247a.	Nine Millimeter V6
248.	Ten Second Rule V2
251.	Friday the 13th V10
256.	The Stöger Traverse V9
256a.	Cliff Notes V8

3 feet

243a. Alternate Ending (V8) ★★ A harder option exits right on sloping edges once you're established on the offset. The lower the exit, the harder the problem.

244. Six Feet Under (V10) ★★ From a good undercling slightly right of *Five and Dime,* reach to small crimps and pull over the lip. It's one of Smith's hardest problems.

245. Seven Dwarfs (V7) ★★ Start off a sinker pocket 3 feet left of a big knob and move past an undercling, reaching to slopers.

246. Eight Mile (V7) ★★ Begin with a huge knob and crank through crimpy edges before veering left to the same slopers as *Seven Dwarfs.*

247. Revolution 9 (V5) ★★★ The short left side of the cliff merges with the higher right part in the middle of the wall. One of the original problems on the crag starts with a mini right-facing corner barely off the ground, eventually escaping left to avoid a lichen-plastered direct finish.

247a. Nine Millimeter (V6) ★★★ A harder start begins a few feet right, reaching to small pockets.

248. Ten Second Rule (V2) ★★ Start on the left side of a big hueco and crank to good pockets below the lichen-covered final bulge. Until someone scrubs the finish, the problem ends here.

249. Eleventh Hour (V2) ★★ Two abbreviated problems start at the base of the undercut, ending at sloping holds 10 feet

Gorilla Cliff–Right Side

248.	Ten Second Rule V2
249.	Eleventh Hour V2
250.	Twelve Angy Men V2
251.	Friday the 13th V10
252.	Fearless Fourteen V6 R
252a.	Fearless Variation V7
253.	Fifteen Minutes of Fame V3
254.	Sweet Sixteen V2
255.	She Was Just Seventeen V5
256.	The Stöger Traverse V9
257.	Waterfall Traverse V5

30 feet

up. The left line begins on the right side of an oversize hueco and veers right.

250. Twelve Angry Men (V2) ★★ The right of two short problems begins sitting down from pockets before cranking up a big rail. Jump off after matching on the same finishing holds as *Eleventh Hour*.

251. Friday the 13th (V10) ★★★ One of Smith's hardest problems climbs *Twelve Angry Men* and then traverses left, keeping your hands above the big huecos—eventually finishing with *Seven Dwarfs*.

252. Fearless Fourteen (V6 R) ★★★★ This dramatic problem finishes to the top of the crag, capped by a big lunge to a jug. Begin with large holds on the right side of a hueco.

252a. Fearless Variation (V7) ★★★ Begin to the right with pockets leading to an undercling, before joining the regular line before the big dyno.

253. Fifteen Minutes of Fame (V3) ★★ Crank through pockets and power through the left side of a hanging tooth. Jump off below the finishing bulge.

254. Sweet Sixteen (V2) ★★ Begin behind a tree and jump off after latching a left-hand cling and right-hand pinch.

255. She Was Just Seventeen (V5) ★★ This full-length problem begins right of a tree and pulls over the lip after a crux dyno.

256. The Stöger Traverse (V9) ★★★★ This amazing 50-meter problem starts at the far right side and traverses uncontrived along the entire length of the Gorilla Cliff.

256a. Cliff Notes (V8) ★★★ This abbreviated version avoids the long crimpy finish, ending instead with *Five and Dime*.

257. Waterfall Traverse (V5) ★ A stream fed by irrigation runoff marks the end of the Gorilla Cliff. A short traverse begins at the farthest right cling hold just before the deluge and moves left until a tree gets in the way.

Tree Boulder

A mediocre boulder with two trees growing uncomfortably close sits 200 feet south, across the hillside from the Gorilla Cliff. You can approach by crossing the overgrown stream beyond the right end of the Gorilla Cliff, or follow an unimproved trail downhill from the right end of the Bivy Wall. Everything begins with a sitting start. No topos.

258. Clear Cut (V2) ★ Starting uphill, traverse right and pull over a bulge on slopers.

259. Tree Hugger (V2) ★ Traverse right along a leaning slash and finish back left on *Clear Cut*.

260. Skewer Problem (V5) ★ Crammed behind a skinny tree is a short crimpfest. Beware of a tree branch spike at the base.

261. Treebeard (V4) ★★ A deceptively difficult problem at the base of the boulder fights awkwardly over a bulge. Scramble to the top through massive mounds of pine needles.

Garretson Boulder

At the bottom of the hill, about 50 feet above the river, the Garretson Boulder offers one high-level problem, with little potential for anything else. Approach from above by bombing down the hillside below the Tree Boulder. No topo.

262. WTF? (V8) ★★ Ascend the overhanging river face, with the hardest moves right off the deck.

Greg's Block

Downstream 200 feet beyond the Garretson Boulder towers a massive boulder with a large flake at the base. The pocketed main face would obviously go, but it would be the freakiest problem at Smith. No topo.

263. Sage Walk (V1) ★ Ascend a prow on the left side of the flake at the base of the wall—you'll have to fight through some vegetation to get to the start.

APPENDIX

FIRST ASCENT INFORMATION

This appendix features a detailed list of all known first ascent information. Smith climbing, as we know it today, reflects the collective efforts of hundreds of people spread over seventy-five years. For some, Smith Rock played a central role in their lives, while for others it was just a place to enjoy a day of climbing. But for almost everyone, Smith Rock made a lasting impression. The evolution of climbing is a cumulative process. The efforts of the earliest pioneers influence future generations, who, in turn, influence the next generation. First ascent information also passes from generation to generation, and I'm indebted to those who came before me—especially anyone who authored a previous guidebook.

Keeping track of who-did-what-when is a never-ending challenge. Decades might pass before definitive information about some unknown route finally comes to light. Others will forever be a mystery. I've done my best, but this section is more prone to error than any other part of the book. If you have information about any first ascent listed as "unknown," please send an email to me at awatts@bendcable .com. I'd also appreciate hearing about any errors (names, spelling, dates, etc.), no matter how small.

I've used a variety of designations, some familiar and some not, to describe the first ascent history of Smith Rock routes. The following definitions will help you decipher my codes:

Prep (Preparation): The person who prepared a route but didn't actually climb it. Given the nature of the rock at Smith, this sometimes involves more effort than the ensuing ascent. The climber may have worked out some parts of the route free, but didn't meet the first ascent criteria.

F.A. (First Ascent): The first to climb a route, whether aid or free. To qualify as a first ascent of a sport route, the climber must climb (not just jumar) the entire line (although not necessarily freeing all moves).

F.F.A. (First Free Ascent): The first to complete a no-falls ascent of a route previously climbed on aid or with hangs.

F.R.A. (First Recorded Ascent): The first person to ascend a route that likely had already received an earlier unrecorded ascent.

F.R.F.A. (First Recorded Free Ascent): The first recorded no-falls ascent of a route that likely had already gone free.

T.R. (Toprope): First ascent done on toprope.

R.B. (Retro-Bolt): The person who added bolts to a route previously climbed with fewer bolts.

B.R. (Bolts Removed): The removal of bolts used on the first ascent.

Lead: The first lead of a route previously done only on toprope.

Solo: The first ascent was done without a partner, using a rope and protection devices.

Free solo: Either the first ascent or the first free ascent was done without the use of a rope or any protection.

CHAPTER 1: PICNIC LUNCH WALL AREA

1. Pisces (F.A. Thomas Emde, Ryan Lawson, Martina Otte, spring 2007)
2. I Lost My Lunch (F.A. Mark Cartier, Jim Anglin, October 19, 1980)

3. Scorpio (F.A. Curt Haire, Ray Stewart, April 1977)

4. Fool's Overture (F.A. Mike Smelsar, Dana Horton, fall 1977)

5. Highway 97 (F.A. Brooke Sandahl, winter 1989)

5a. Highway 97 finish (F.A. Brooke Sandahl, winter 1989)

6. Driveway Gravel (F.A. T.R. Brooke Sandahl, 1990; F.A. lead, Scott Franklin, 1996)

7. La Siesta (F.A. Brents Hawks, winter 1989)

8. Spartacus (F.A. Ed Barry, Tom Herbert, Mark Chapman, fall 1987)

9. Appian Way (F.A. Ed Barry, Tom Herbert, Mark Chapman, fall 1987)

10. No Picnic (F.A. Jim Anglin, Mike Hartley, July 3, 1981)

10a. Bob's World (F.A. Bob McGown, mid-1980s)

10b. Farmer's Variation (F.A. Craig Benesch, Doug Kozlik, fall 1981)

11. Honey Pot (F.A. Ian and Darryn Caldwell, April 25, 2001)

12. Teddy Bear's Picnic (F.A. Mark Whalan, June 1990)

13. Free Lunch (F.A. upper three pitches (via *Unfinished Symphony*), Jeff Thomas, Steve Moore, April 1972; F.F.A. last two pitches (via *Unfinished Symphony*) Dean Fry, Larry Kemp, May 6, 1972; F.A. first two pitches, Dan Foote, Mike Smelsar, Brian Holcomb, fall 1976; F.F.A. entire route, Jeff Thomas, Willis Krause, February 12, 1977)

14. Five Easy Pieces (F.A. Adam Grosowsky, 1992; F.F.A. unknown, late 1990s)

14a. Five Easy Pieces start (F.A. Adam Grosowsky, 1992)

15. Unfinished Symphony (F.A. Kim Schmitz, Dean Caldwell, summer 1965; F.F.A. Alan Watts, May 14, 1982)

15a. Unfinished Symphony finish (F.A. second pitch, Kim Schmitz, Dean Caldwell, summer 1965; F.A. entire route, Jeff Thomas, Steve Moore, April 1972; F.F.A. final two pitches, Dean Fry, Larry Kemp, May 6, 1972)

16. High Noon (F.A. Michael Stöger, October 2008)

17. Project–Rainy Day Diversion (Prep. Ryan Lawson, February 1999)

18. Project (Prep. Ryan Lawson, March 1999)

19. Coleslaw and Chemicals (F.A. Tedd Thompson, fall 1988; F.F.A. Darius Azin, fall 1988)

19a. Project (Prep. Michael Stöger, spring 2009)

20. Pubic Luau (F.A. Brooke Sandahl, spring 1986)

20a. Pubic Luau Direct (F.A. Brooke Sandahl, T.R. spring 1986)

21. Starvation Fruit (F.A. Joe Brooks, October 1997)

22. The Big R (F.A. Darius Azin, fall 1988; F.F.A. Marc Lemenestral, 1995)

23. Zortex Thrux (F.A. to highpoint, Scott Davis et. al., early 1980s)

24. Midnight Snack (F.A. Alan Watts, May 26, 1982)

25. Project (Prep. Ryan Lawson, March 1999)

26. Snack Crack (F.A. Alan Watts, April 1988)

27. Soft Shoe Ballet (F.A. first two pitches, Bill Antel, Bob McGown, Jeff Alzner, Bruce Birchell, November 1978; F.A. entire route, Bill Antel, Bob McGown, spring 1979)

27a. Jim Anglin Memorial Route (F.A. first pitch, Tyler Adams, solo, January 2009; F.A second pitch, Jake Hector, Tyler Adams, February 2009)

28. Project (Prep. Scott Franklin, 1989)

29. Ancient Bolt Line (F.A. unknown, early 1970s; F.R.A. Vince Gonor, 1999)

30. Bubbas in Bondage (F.A. pitch, Alan Lester, Chuck Wheeler, winter 1982; F.F.A. T.R. Ryan Lawson, March 1999; F.F.A. Chris Van Leuren, April 1999)

30a. Masochistic Tendencies (F.A. T.R. Ryan Lawson, March 1999; F.A. lead, Michael Orr, March 1999)

30b. Bubbas in Bondage finish (F.A. Jim Anglin, solo, spring 1983)

31. Out to Lunch (F.A. Sean Moore, winter 2000; F.F.A. Michael Stöger, 2005)

32. Picnic Lunch Wall (F.A. Tom Bauman, Kim Schmitz, October 21-22, 1969; F.F.A. first pitch, Bob McGown, mid-1980s)

33. Wayne's World (F.A. Wayne Wallace, solo, late 1990s)

34. Suicidal Tendencies (F.A. Kurt Smith, spring 1988)

35. Touch (F.A. Kurt Smith, spring 1988)

36. Journey to Ixtlan (F.A. first two pitches, Bob McGown, Jeff Alzner, March 1979; F.A. upper pitches, Bob McGown, Mark Simpson, summer 1981)

37. Sad But True (F.A. Ryan Lawson, December 1998, F.F.A. Chris Van Leuren April 1999)

38. Ryan's World (F.A. to highpoint, Ryan Lawson, 2005)

39. Voyage of the Cow Dog (F.A. Jon Bates, solo, August 2008)

40. East Chimney (F.A. Jim Ramsey, Jerry Ramsey, 1959)

41. West Chimney (F.A. Ross Petrie, Dave Pearson, 1946)

42. Project (F.A. to highpoint, solo, Chris Jones, 1979)

CHAPTER 2: THE WOODEN SHIPS AND THE GULLIES

1. Time to Shower (F.A. Dean Fry, Terri Raider, January 3, 1973; R.B. Ryan Lawson, January 1999)

1a. Shower Direct (F.A. unknown, 1970s)

2. Shipwreck (F.A. Dean Fry, Terri Raider, January 3, 1973)

3. Chips Ahoy (F.A. Avary Tichner, 1981)

4. Time to Power (Prep. Eric Johnson, 1990; F.F.A. John Collins, spring 1992)

4a. Time to Power start (F.A. Eric Johnson, 1990)

5. Blue Light Special (F.A. Tom Egan, December 1990)

6. Liquid Jade (F.A. Tom Egan, Tom Heins, December 6, 1990)

7. More Sandy than Kevin (F.A. Tom Heins, December 1, 1990)

8. Purple Aces (F.A. Jeff Frizzell, December 2, 1990)

9. Flight of the Patriot Scud Blaster (F.A. Tom Heins, Tom Egan, February 1991)

10. Marooned (F.A. Stuart Young, 1992)

11. Walking While Intoxicated (F.A. Tom Heins, Tom Egan, December 7, 1990)

12. Mother's Milk (F.A. Jay Greene, Gary Rall, May 21, 1991)

13. Bolt From the Blue (F.A. Brett Hall, 1996)

13a. Bolt From the Blue start (F.A. Brett Hall, 1996)

14. Project (Prep. Jeff Frizzell, 2002)

15. Project (Prep. Jeff Frizzell, 2002)

16. Rising Tides (F.A. Ted Stahl, Jim Ablao, March 9, 2002)

17. Tsunami (F.A. Ben Moon, July 8, 2002)

18. Undertow (F.A. Ben Moon, May 8, 2004)

19. Riptide (F.A. Ben Moon, June 2002)

20. Fish 'n Chips (F.A. Ben Moon, May 1, 2004)

21. Waste Land (F.A. Jeff Thomas, Steve Lyford, Jack Callahan, March 31, 1974)
22. Slab Happy (F.A. Jim Ablao and Ted Stahl, April 4, 2002)
23. Flab Happy (F.A. T.R. Jim Ablao, Ted Stahl, spring 2002)
24. Vanishing Uncertainty (F.A. Andy Embick, Ted Schuck, 1972; F.F.A. Jeff Thomas, Steve Lyford, March 31, 1974)
24a. Vanishing Variation (F.A. first pitch, Ted Stahl, Jim Ablao, spring 2002; F.A. upper pitches, unknown)
25. The Skipper's Little Buddy (F.A. Ted Stahl, Jim Ablao, spring 2002)
26. Project (Prep. Jim Ablao, Ted Stahl, spring 2002)
27. City Dump (F.A. Steve Lyford, Jack Callahan, Jeff Thomas, March 31, 1974)
27a. City Dump finish (F.A. Thomas Emde, Ryan Lawson, January 2002)
28. Ghost Rider (F.A. Martin Grullich, fall 1987)
29. Highway to Hell (F.A. Martin Grullich, fall 1987)
30. Repeat Offender (F.A. Joe Brooks, April 15, 1998)
30a. Shock and Awe (F.F.A. Scott Milton, spring 2003)
30b. Project (F.F.A. incomplete)
31. Villain (F.A. Geoff Weigand, spring 1990)
31a. Delinquent (F.A. Joe Brooks, April 12, 1998)
31b. Shotgun Wedding (F.F.A. Ian Caldwell, October 27, 2007)
32. White Wedding (F.A. Michael Keiss, fall 1987; F.F.A. Jean-Baptiste Tribout, June 1988)
32a. Lucky Pigeon (aka Partners in Crime) (F.A. Joe Brooks, May 2, 1988)
33. Bad Man (F.A. Alan Watts, summer 1990; F.F.A. Jean-Baptiste Tribout, January 1991)

34. Project (F.A. Joe Brooks, May 6, 1988; F.F.A. incomplete)
35. Aggro Monkey (Prep. Martin Grullich, December 1987; F.A. T.R. Sean Olmstead, spring 1988; F.F.A. Martin Atkinson, May 1988)
36. Mama Docus (F.A. Joe Brooks, April 28, 1998)
37. Crime Wave (F.A. Tom Herbert, October 1991)
38. Scene of the Crime (F.A. Sean Olmstead, spring 1990; F.F.A. Jean-Baptiste Tribout, spring 1990)
39. The Quickening (F.A. Kevin Lawlor, October 1990)
40. Disposable Heroes (F.A. Sean Olmstead, spring 1991; F.F.A. Joe Brooks, April 14, 1997)
41. Spewing (F.A. Colin Lantz, February 22, 1991)
42. Pouch Whisker (F.A. Walter Anyan, February 25, 2001)
43. Scrotal Avenger (F.A. Steve Mrazek, February 18, 2001)
44. Caustic (F.A. Jim Hall, spring 1991)
45. Kill the Hate (F.A. Sean Olmstead, May 1992)
46. Project–Facelift (Prep. Ian Caldwell, fall 2008)
47. Seasonal Affectiveness Disorder (F.A. Pete Keane, February 1991)
48. Skinny Sweaty Man (F.A. Pete Keane, Tom Heins, February 1991)
49. Crankenstein (F.A. Tom Heins, Pete Keane, February 1991)
50. Feet of Clay (F.A. Adam Grosowsky, fall 1989)
51. Toxic (F.A. Colin Lantz, Greg Robinson, fall 1987)
51a. Toxic Toprope (F.A. T.R. Darius Azin, spring 1990)
52. No Nukes (F.A. Avary Tichner, 1981)

53. Up For Grabs (F.A. Sean Olmstead, August 1988)
54. Planet Mechanic (F.A. Kevin Gianino, Cory Jones 1996; F.F.A. John Collins 1996)
55. Monkey Boy (F.A. Sean Olmstead, fall 1989)
56. Project (Prep. Ian Caldwell, 1995)
57. The Burl Master (Prep. Kent Benesch, 1989; F.A. Sean Olmstead, 1992; F.F.A. Will Caitlin, 1994)
58. Power (F.A. Brooke Sandahl, spring 1989)
59. Solar (F.A. upper pitch, via Caffeine Free, Dean Fry, Russ Bunker, February 24, 1973; F.F.A. Jeff Thomas, Steve Lyford, March 11, 1977)
60. Purple Headed Warrior (F.A. Matt Canham, Don Gonthier, March 16, 1996)
61. Phone Call From Satan (F.A. Mike Lewis, Wendy Borgerd, September 4, 1999)
62. Caffeine Free (F.A. first pitch, Dean Fry, Russ Bunker, February 24, 1973; F.F.A. Sean Moore, winter 2000)
62a. Caffeine Free finish (F.A. Sean Moore, winter 2000)
63. Time's Up (F.A. Dan Goodwin, fall 1987; F.F.A. Geoff Weigand, spring 1988)
64. Mr. Yuk (Prep. Kent Benesch, spring 1990; F.A. Joe Brooks, spring 1997; F.F.A. Michael Orr, January 2, 1999)
65. Slit Your Wrists (F.A. Geoff Weigand, spring 1988)
66. Skeleton Surfer (F.A. James Fredericks, Ted Otto, summer 1989)
67. The Blade (F.A. Tedd Thompson, Darius Azin, fall 1987)
68. Chicken McNuggets (F.A. Tom Heins, Pete Keane, March 1, 1991)
69. Cocaine Crack (F.A. Bob McGown, Doug Bower, July 1979; F.F.A. Alan Watts, Kent Benesch, November 13, 1981)
70. Vomit Launch (F.A. Kent Benesch, spring 1987)
71. Freebase (F.A. Dan Goodwin, fall 1987)
72. Powder Up the Nose (F.A. Mark Dube, fall 1987)
73. Shake 'n Flake (F.A. Tedd Thompson, fall 1987)
74. Rabid (F.A. Rick Lince, fall 1987)
75. Bound in Bogotá (F.A. Tom Egan, December 1990)
76. Deep Impact (F.A. Ryan Lawson, December 1999; F.A. direct start, Ryan Lawson, 2000)
77. Armageddon (F.A. Ryan Lawson, December 1999)
78. Pitch It Here (F.A. Tom Heins, August 1990)
79. Double-Edged Sword (F.A. Tom Heins, August 1990)
80. Desmond's Tutu (F.A. Tom Heins, November 1990)

CHAPTER 3: MORNING GLORY WALL AREA

1. Earth 2° (F.A. Cory Jones, Kevin Gianino, March 1997)
2. Baked Mudfest (aka Hobbit's Pockets) (Prep. Tim Olson, winter 1990; F.A. Erik Wolfe, spring 1996)
3. Hippos on Ice (F.A. Cecil Colley, Gary Gallagher, Tim Olson, winter 1990)
4. Thieves (F.A. Clark Shelk, summer 1994)
5. Gimme Shelter (F.A. Kent Benesch, 1984)
6. Exile on Main Street (F.A. Kent Benesch, 1984)
7. Bloodshot (F.A. Kevin Gianino, Cory Jones, spring 1997)

8. Quest to Fire (F.A. John Collins, spring 1991)
9. Crack Babies (F.A. Kevin Lawlor, 1992)
10. Crack Cocaine (F.A. Ryan Lawson, December 1999; F.F.A. Michael Richter, December 1999)
11. Bongo Fury (F.A. Jeff Frizzell, June 1991)
12. Runt (F.A. Jason Karn, spring 1991, F.F.A. Marc LeMenestral, spring 1995)
13. Project–Bend Over and Receive (F.A. Adam Grosowsky, spring 1989; F.F.A. with plastic holds, Geoff Weigand, September 1989; F.F.A. natural rock, uncompleted)
14. Stand and Deliver (F.A. Adam Grosowsky, fall 1988)
15. Oxygen (F.A. Darius Azin, October 1987)
15a. Jam Master Jay (Prep. Darius Azin, 1988; F.A. Jerry Moffatt, November 1988)
16. Da Kine Corner (F.A. Brooke Sandahl, spring 1987)
17. White Heat (F.A. Alan Watts, April 1988)
18. Kings of Rap (F.A. Brooke Sandahl, spring 1987)
19. Waste Case (F.A. Alan Watts, April 1988)
19a. Mr. Tapeworm (F.A. Michael Stöger, 1989)
20. Vicious Fish (F.A. Alan Watts, March 1988)
21. Churning in the Wake (F.A. Sean Olmstead, March 1987)
21a. Churning Sky (F.A. Craig Smith, spring 1987)
21b. Churning in the Ozone (F.A. Geoff Weigand, fall 1988)
22. Sign of the Times (F.A. Dan Goodwin, fall 1987, B.R. Darius Azin, 1988; R.B. Ian Caldwell, spring 2008)
23. Taco Chips (F.A. Jean Marc Troussier, November 1986)
23a. Nacho Cheese (F.A. to old anchor, Ian Caldwell, 2002; F.A. to higher anchor, unknown)
23b. Doritos (F.A. Ian Caldwell, November 21, 2001)
24. Cool Ranch Flavor (F.A. Ryan Lawson, October 8, 1999)
24a. Cool Ranch Flavor finish (F.A. Ian Caldwell, January 25, 2007)
25. Nine Gallon Buckets (F.A. Martin Grullich, spring 1987)
25a. Nine Gallon Buckets start (F.A. Martin Grullich, spring 1987)
26. Overboard (F.A. Martin Grullich, spring 1987)
26a. Overboard extension (F.A. Martin Grullich, spring 1987)
26b. Overboard finish (F.A. Martin Grullich, spring 1987)
27. Magic Light (F.A. Martin Grullich, spring 1987)
27a. Magic Light extension (F.A. Martin Grullich, spring 1987)
27b. Magic Light finish (F.A. Martin Grullich, spring 1987)
28. Energy Crisis (F.A. Martin Grullich, spring 1987)
29. Sketch Pad (F.A. Martin Grullich, spring 1987; F.F.A. Geoff Weigand, fall 1988)
30. Mane Line (F.A. Alan Watts, winter 1989)
31. Lion's Chair (F.A. first two pitches, Phil Dean, Steve Heim, 1968; F.A. upper pitches, Phil Dean, George Selfridge, 1968; F.F.A. second and fourth pitches, Bob McGown, Jeff Thomas, April 1977; F.F.A. entire route, Jeff Thomas, Ted Johnson, June 5, 1977)
31a. Lion's Chair start (F.A. Phil Dean, Steve Heim, 1968; F.F.A. unknown, mid-1970s)

31b. Lion's Chair exit (F.A. Phil Dean, Steve Heim, 1968)

32. Project (Prep. Alan Watts, 1988)

33. Dandy Line (F.A. Dan Goodwin, fall 1987; F.F.A. Alan Watts, January 1988)

34. Zebra Seam (F.A. Bob Martin, Ray Snyder, 1970; F.F.A. T.R. Alan Watts, Bill Ramsey, August 29, 1981; F.F.A. lead, Steve Byrne, 1984; R.B. unknown, 1991)

35. Zebra Direct (F.A. Alan Watts, Bill Ramsey, May 26, 1979)

36. Lion Zion (F.A. Erik Wolfe, spring 1996)

37. Gumby (F.A. Alan Watts, Brooke Sandahl, spring 1987)

38. Morning Sky (F.A. David Tvedt, Dee Tvedt, June 1994)

39. CAT Scan (F.A. Chris Snyder, summer 1989)

40. Light on the Path (F.A. Alan Quine, winter 1988)

41. The Outsiders (F.A. Ryan Lawson, Holly Beck, January 2000)

42. Zebra (F.A. via *Zebra Seam,* Bob Martin, Ray Snyder, 1970; F.F.A. via potholes, Dean Fry, Jeff Thomas, January 14, 1973)

43. Zion (F.A. Jeff Thomas, Chris Mannix, April 24, 1977)

44. Five Gallon Buckets (F.A. Tom Heins, Ryan Palfree, December 1991)

45. In Hinds Way (F.A. Chuck Buzzard, Jerry Radant, 1984)

46. Choss in America (F.A. Duane Raleigh, fall 1988)

47. One Time Trick (F.A. Alan Lester, 1982)

48. Anonymity (F.A. Chip Miller, Doug Phillips, spring 2006)

49. Lion's Jaw (F.A. Tom Bauman, Bob Bauman, 1967)

49a. Almdudler (F.A. Thomas Emde, October 2008)

50. Lion's Jaw Chimney (F.A. first pitch, unknown, late 1960s; F.A. upper pitches, Tom Bauman, Bob Bauman, 1967)

51. Tammy Bakker's Face (F.A. Mike Mahoney, 1988)

52. Lost Horseman Roof (F.A. T.R. Chuck Buzzard, December 1984)

53. Popism (F.A. unknown, 1989; F.F.A. Alan Watts, summer 1989)

54. Pop Goes the Nubbin (F.A. Jeff Thomas, Chris Jones, October 22, 1978; R.B. unknown, late-1980s)

55. Peanut Brittle (F.A. Jeff Thomas, Chet Sutterlin, March 18, 1977; R.B. unknown, late-1980s)

56. Hop on Pop (F.A. Alan Watts, JoAnn Miller-Watts, fall 1989)

57. Snuffy Smith (F.A. Erik Wolfe, January 10, 1996)

58. Tuff It Out (F.A. Erik Wolfe, December 14, 2002)

59. No Golf Shoes (F.A. Erik Wolfe, January 10, 1996)

59a. No Golf Shoes finish (F.A. Erik Wolfe, February 1996)

60. Friday's Jinx (F.A. Dean Fry, Paul Fry, March 10, 1973)

60a. Sunday's Jinx (F.A. Pat Carr, 1977)

61. Wielded Tuff (F.A. Erik Wolfe, Carol Simpson, Steve Ohran, November 20, 2002; B.R. unknown, fall 2003)

62. Crack of Infinity (F.A. second pitch, Bob Grundy, April 7, 1974; F.A. third pitch, Bob McGown, Mike Smelsar, 1976; F.F.A. entire route, Jeff Thomas, Chet Sutterlin, March 19, 1977)

62a. Infinity Variation (F.A. Bill McKinney, Avary Tichner, 1978)

63. Calamity Jam (F.A. Jeff Thomas, Mike Smelsar, March 13, 1977)

63a. Catastrophic Crack (F.A. Alan Watts, March 10, 1983)

63b. Sandbag (F.A. Alan Watts, summer 1987)

64. The John Galt Line (F.A. Erik Wolfe, February 1996)

65. Pack Animal Direct (F.A. Tom Rogers, Jeff Elphinston, 1972; F.F.A. Jeff Thomas, Chet Sutterlin, March 18, 1977)

66. Taiwan On (F.A. Erik Wolfe, April 1996)

67. Pack Animal (F.A. via direct start, Tom Rogers, Jeff Elphinston, November 13, 1972; F.F.A. regular route, Jeff Thomas, Jack Callahan, April 7, 1974)

68. Sundancer (F.A. Tim Olson, Tony Bishop, Cecil Colley, January 28, 1989)

69. Headless Horseman (F.A. Doug Phillips, summer 1987; F.F.A. Greg Phillips, summer 1987)

69a. Project (Prep. Erik Wolfe, spring 1996)

70. Equine-imity (F.A. Erik Wolfe, December 14, 2002)

71. Dead Men Tell No Tales (F.A. Alan Watts, free solo, 1984)

72. Equus (F.A. Alan Watts, August 1987)

73. Fourth Horseman (F.R.A. Jim Ramsey, Bruce Hahn, 1964)

74. Third Horseman (F.R.A. Jim Ramsey, Bruce Hahn, 1964, F.R.F.A. Alan Watts, 1980)

75. Second Horseman (F.R.A. Jim Ramsey, Bruce Hahn, 1964)

76. First Horseman (F.R.A. Jim Ramsey, Bruce Hahn, 1964)

77. North Slab Crack (F.A. unknown, 1970s)

78. How Low Can You Go? (F.A. T.R. unknown, 1970s; F.A. lead, Alan Watts, JoAnn Miller-Watts, June 1, 1991)

79. Shamu (F.A. Alan Watts, JoAnn Miller-Watts, June 1, 1991)

80. Immortal Beloved (F.A. Ryan Lawson, Alan Watts, September 4, 1999)

81. Low Blow (F.A. T.R. Alan Watts, June 1, 1991, F.A. lead, Alan Watts, September 4, 1999)

82. Float Like A Butterfly (F.A. T.R. Alan Watts, June 1, 1991, FA lead, Alan Watts, September 4, 1999)

83. Sleepy Town (F.A. Alan Watts, Ben Watts, August 22, 1999)

84. Rope De Dope Crack (F.A. unknown, 1970s)

85. Sting Like A Bee (F.A. T.R. Alan Watts, 1980, F.A. lead, Alan Watts, Ryan Lawson, September 4, 1999)

86. Morgantown (F.A. T.R. Alan Watts, 1980; F.A. lead, Alan Watts, Ryan Lawson, September 4, 1999)

87. Mini-Bender (F.A. Alan Watts, Ben Watts, August 22, 1999)

CHAPTER 4: THE DIHEDRALS

1. Lichen It (F.A. Alan Watts, JoAnn Miller-Watts, October 17, 1989)

2. Right Slab Crack (F.A. unknown, 1960s)

3. Easy Reader (F.A. Alan Watts, JoAnn Miller-Watts, summer 1989)

4. Left Slab Crack (F.A. unknown, 1960s)

5. Night Flight (F.A. Alan Watts, Ben Watts, August 14, 1999)

6. Ginger Snap (F.A. Alan Watts, JoAnn Miller-Watts, summer 1989)

7. Cinnamon Slab (F.A. Bob Bauman, free solo, mid-1960s)

7a. Rodney's Chocolate Frosted Love Donut (F.A. Matt Canham, Don Gonthier, Rodney Spencer, June 28, 1999)

7b. Cinnamon Toast (F.A. Jeff Thomas, Chet Sutterlin, Tim Carpenter, Roseann Lehman, March 19, 1977)

7c. Cry Baby (F.A. Brooke Sandahl, Tiffany Schwarz, 1998)

8. Karate Crack (F.R.A. Dean Caldwell, Byron Babcock, fall 1966; F.F.A. Dean Fry, Steve Lyford, October 7, 1973)

9. Peapod Cave (F.R.A. Dean Caldwell, Byron Babcock, fall 1966; F.F.A. Dean Fry, Steve Lyford, October 7, 1973)

10. Slow Burn (F.A. Alan Watts, April 2, 1983)

11. Crossfire (F.A. Alan Watts, May 1, 1984, R.B. Alan Watts, 1988)

12. Power Dive (F.A. Alan Watts, April 14, 1984; R.B. Erik von Heideken, 1998)

13. Karot Tots (F.A. Dave Jensen, George Cummings, 1970; F.F.A. Alan Watts, Mark Cartier, October 4, 1980)

14. Firing Line (F.A. Alan Watts, March 24, 1984; R.B. Erik von Heideken, 1998)

15. Low Profile (F.A. Alan Watts, April 18, 1984)

16. Karate Wall (F.A. Alan Watts, May 26, 1984; R.B. Erik von Heideken, 1998)

17. Latest Rage (F.A. Alan Watts, February 18, 1984)

17a. Monster Rage (F.A. Michael Stöger, spring 2005)

18. Watts Tots (F.A. Alan Watts, February 11, 1983)

18a. Mega Watts (F.A. T.R. Alan Watts, 1989)

19. Fresh Squeezed (F.A. Brooke Sandahl, winter 2002; F.F.A. Ben Moon, winter 2002)

19a. Kilo Watts (F.A. T.R. Alan Watts, summer 1987; F.A. lead, Masahiro Eito, spring 2002)

20. Trivial Pursuit (F.A. Alan Watts, November 10, 1983)

21. Tator Tots (F.A. Jeff Thomas, Mike Smelsar, February 26, 1977)

22. Latin Lover (F.A. Jean Marc Troussier, October 1986)

23. Peepshow (F.A. Alan Watts, September 1988)

24. Upper Ceiling (F.A. Dean Caldwell, Jim Kindler 1966)

24a. Skag Variation (F.A. Jeff Thomas, Dean Fry, November 4, 1972)

25. Lester Tots (F.A. Alan Watts, Chris Grover, March 3, 1983)

26. Almost Nothing (F.A. Jean Marc Troussier, October 1986)

27. Take A Powder (F.A. Alan Watts, August 1987)

28. Powder in the Eyes (F.A. Jean Marc Troussier, October 1986)

29. Little Miss Sunshine (F.A. Alan Watts, December 1989; F.F.A. Ian Caldwell, April 1, 2009)

30. Sunshine Dihedral (F.A. first pitch, Tom Bauman, late 1960s; F.A. entire route, Tom Rogers, Dan Muir, Jack Barrar, February 13, 1971; F.F.A. T.R. Chris Jones, Alan Watts, July 6, 1979; F.F.A. lead, Alan Watts, Alan Lester, July 18, 1981)

31. French Connection (F.A. Alan Watts, fall 1984; F.F.A. Jean-Baptiste Tribout, October 1986)

32. To Bolt or Not to Be (F.A. T.R. Alan Watts, fall 1984; F.F.A. Jean-Baptiste Tribout, November 7, 1986)

33. Last Waltz (F.A. Alan Watts, October 8, 1983)

33a. Last Waltz Direct (F.A. Alan Watts, February 1985)

34. Moondance (F.A. Alan Watts, Chris Grover, January 28, 1984; R.B. Kent Benesch, late 1980s)

34a. Moondance finish (F.A. Alan Watts, Chris Grover, January 28, 1984)

35. Wedding Day (F.A. Graeme Aimeer, Grant Davidson, 1984)

36. The Flat Earth (F.A. Eric Horst, May 1991)

37. Middle Aged Vandal (F.A. Alan Watts, November 24, 1996)

38. Moonshine Dihedral (F.A. Dave Jensen, Bob Pierce, 1963; F.F.A. Dean Fry, Jeff Thomas, November 4, 1972)

38a. Moonshine Dihedral finish (F.A. unknown, 1960s; F.F.A. Dean Fry, Jeff Thomas, November 4, 1972)

39. Heinous Cling (F.A. upper part, Alan Watts, March 22, 1984; F.A. entire route, Alan Watts, April 29, 1984; R.B. Darius Azin, 1991)

39a. Heinous Cling start (F.A. Alan Watts, April 25, 1983; R.B. Darius Azin, 1991)

40. Darkness at Noon (F.A. upper part, Alan Watts, May 26, 1984; F.A. entire route, Alan Watts, March 9, 1985)

40a. Darkness at Noon start (F.A. Alan Watts, March 17, 1984)

41. Chain Reaction (F.A. Alan Watts, February 26, 1983)

42. Evil Sister (F.A. Alan Watts, December 1990; F.F.A. Scott Franklin, 1996)

43. Rattlesnake Chimney (F.A. George Cummings, John Hall, May 1963)

43a. Snakebit (F.R.A. free solo, Alan Watts, 1980)

44. Ancylostoma (F.A. Brian Baker, 1988)

45. Bookworm (F.R.A. via variation, Dave Jensen, 1970; F.A. entire route Alan Watts, free solo, 1983; R.B. Kent Benesch, late 1980s)

45a. Bookworm Variation (F.R.A. Dave Jensen, 1970)

46. Bunny Face (F.A. Jeff Thomas, Ken Currens, March 26, 1977; R.B. Dan Carlson, late 1980s)

46a. Bunny Face finish (F.A. JoAnn Miller, Alan Watts, August 1987)

47. Methuselah's Column (F.A. Dean Fry, Paul Fry, March 10, 1973)

48. Rabbit Stew (F.R.A. Randy Hagen, Pat Carr, Alan Watts, December 1975)

49. Lycopodophyta (F.A. Dean Fry, Jeff Thomas, December 17, 1972)

49a. Lycopodophyta finish (F.A. Dean Fry, Jeff Thomas, December 17, 1972)

50. Helium Woman (F.A. Kevin Pogue, Jay Goodwin, April 1990)

51. Captain Xenolith (F.A. Kevin Pogue, Jay Goodwin, March 20, 1991)

52. Deteriorata (F.A. Jeff Thomas, Steve Lyford, March 3, 1974)

53. Go Dog Go (F.A. Alan Watts, September 1988)

53a. Project (Prep. Erik Wolfe, 2006)

54. Vision (F.A. Colin Lantz, spring 1988)

CHAPTER 5: THE CHRISTIAN BROTHERS—EAST WALL

1. Deep Splash (F.A. Tom Egan, April 1991)

2. La Shootist (F.A. Larry Brumwell, October 1999)

3. Chemical Ali (F.A. Scott Milton, April 26, 2003)

4. Rawhide (F.A. Brooke Sandahl, winter 1988)

5. Smooth Boy (F.A. Erik Johnson, winter 1990; F.F.A. Jean-Baptiste Tribout, January 1991)

6. Choke on This (F.A. Kent Benesch, January 1988)

7. Dreamin' (F.A. Brooke Sandahl, February 1988)

8. Boy Prophet (F.A. Alan Watts, April 22, 1984)

9. Rude Boys (F.A. Alan Watts, February 1985; F.F.A. Jean-Baptiste Tribout, October 1986)

10. Rude Femmes (F.A. Alan Watts, October 21, 1988)

11. Scarface (F.A. Scott Franklin, April 1988)

12. Air to Spare (F.A. Jim Anglin, Tom Blust, February 28, 1981)

13. Project (Prep. Joe Brooks, spring 1997)

14. Mystery Aid Seam (F.A. unknown, 1990s)

15. Shoes of the Fisherman (F.A. Jeff Thomas, Ralph Moore, March 31, 1975; F.F.A. Jeff Thomas, April 24, 1977)

15a. Project—Toes of the Fisherman (F.A. Alan Watts, March 10, 1984; F.F.A. uncompleted)

16. Heresy (F.A. Ryan Lawson, May 3, 1999)

17. Project (Prep. Ryan Lawson, 1999)

18. Wartley's Revenge (F.A. Tom Rogers, Wayne Haack, Ken Jern, October 21, 1972; F.F.A. Jeff Thomas, Chris Jones, November 4, 1978)

18a. Wartley's Revenge finish (F.A. Tom Rogers, Wayne Haack, Ken Jern, October 21, 1972; F.F.A. Jeff Thomas, Chris Jones, November 4, 1978)

19. The Right Side of the Beard (F.A. Tom Bauman, Jan Newman, October 13, 1968)

20. Risk Shy (F.A. free solo, Alan Watts, November 14, 1984)

21. The Left Side of the Beard (F.A. Tom Bauman, Jan Newman, October 13, 1968)

22. The Clam (F.A. Doug Phillips, spring 1989; F.F.A. Alan Watts, May 1989)

23. Golgotha (F.A. Alan Watts, Mel Johnson, June 20, 1981)

23a. Temptation (F.A. Alan Watts, Wayne Kamara, March 17, 1981)

24. Barbecue the Pope (F.A. Brooke Sandahl, January 1987)

25. New Testament (F.A. unknown, 1960s; F.F.A. Dean Fry, Larry Kemp, February 18, 1973)

26. Revelations (F.A. Tim Carpenter, John Tyreman, 1975)

27. Irreverence (F.A. T.R. Jeff Thomas, 1977; F.A. free solo, Alan Watts, 1984; R.B. Alan Watts, JoAnn Miller-Watts, August 1988)

28. Nightingales on Vacation (F.A. Alan Watts, Amy Bruzzano, JoAnn Miller-Watts, July 6, 1990)

29. Old Testament (F.A. unknown, late 1960s)

30. Heathen's Highway (F.A. Jim Anglin, Mike Hartley, October 28, 1979)

31. Via Dolorosa (F.A. Jim Davis, John McDaniel, Cyndee McDaniel, 1997)

31a. Project (F.A. T.R. John McDaniel, 1997)

32. Gothic Cathedral (F.A. Bob Bauman, Ken Jern, mid-1960s)

33. Last Gasp (F.A. Tom Rogers, Clay Cox, November 19, 1972)

33a. Safety Valve (F.A. unknown, 1970s)

34. Island in the Sky (F.A. Mike Steele, John Steele, 1981)

35. Blasphemy (F.A. Ryan Lawson, December 1998; F.F.A. Tom Egan, Thomas Emde, February 1999)

36. Panic Attack (F.A. Sean Moore, winter 2000)

37. Project (Prep. Kent Benesch, 1989)

38. Private Trust (F.A. Alan Watts, January 27, 1984)

39. Charlie's Chimney (F.A. Dean Caldwell, Val Kiefer, 1967)

40. Overnight Sensation (F.A. Brooke Sandahl, winter 1987)

41. Tinker Toy (F.A. Jeff Thomas, Alan Watts, Bill Ramsey, February 19, 1978)

42. Double Trouble (F.A. Tom Heins, spring 1990)

43. Bowling Alley (F.A. Dean Caldwell, Val Kiefer, 1967)

44. Double Stain (F.A. Dave Jensen, 1969; F.F.A. Alan Watts, May 22, 1984)

45. Bum Rush the Show (F.A. Brooke Sandahl, March 31, 1991)

46. Toys in the Attic (F.A. Bill Ramsey, Chris Jones, July 19, 1979)

46a. Child's Play (F.A. Alan Watts, Bruce Birchell, July 5, 1980)

47. Hesitation Blues (F.A. Alan Watts, Kent Benesch, August 23, 1980)

47a. Blue Balls (F.A. free solo, Alan Watts, summer 1985)

48. Attic Antics (F.A. Alan Watts, June 10, 1982)

49. Ring of Fire (F.A. Brooke Sandahl, June 1988)

50. Earth Boys (F.A. Alan Watts, Amy Bruzzano, May 1996)

51. Toy Blocks (F.A. Jeff Thomas, Shari Kearney, May 28, 1977)

51a. Self Preservation Variation (F.A. Mike Hartley, Jim Anglin, August 25, 1979)

52. Dancer (F.A. Tim Carpenter, John Tyreman, 1976)

52a. Dancer finish (F.A. Jeff Thomas, Ken Stroud, February 14, 1976)

53. Jeté (F.A. Alan Watts, JoAnn Miller-Watts, August 1988)

54. That .10d (F.A. Larry Brumwell, January 2003)

55. That First Step (F.A. Tom Willard, Matt Canham, September 18, 1999)

56. Kathleen Finds an Edge (F.A. free solo, Chuck Buzzard, September 1984; R.B. Matt Canham, Don Gonthier, Rodney Spencer, June 28, 1999)

CHAPTER 6: SMITH ROCK GROUP

1. The Asterisk (F.A. Jim Ramsey, Jerry Ramsey, 1961)

2. Sky Ridge (F.A. via Sky Dive, Dave Jensen, George Cummings, 1968; F.A. second pitch, Steve Lyford, Scott Schmidt, 1973)

2a. Sky Ridge Variation (F.A. Jeff Thomas, Tim Carpenter, Ed Beacham, August 1972)

2b. Sky Dive (F.A. Dave Jensen, George Cummings, 1968; F.F.A. Tom Blust, Spurge Cochran, February 1981)

3. Sky Ways (F.A. Jeff Thomas, Doug Phillips, Scott Hansen, May 11, 1974; F.F.A. Mark Cartier, Jim Anglin, fall 1981)

4. By Ways (F.A. Jean Yves Poublan, Walt Allegar, July 4, 1980)

5. Sky Chimney (F.A. Dave Jensen, George Cummings, fall 1969; F.F.A. Doug Phillips, Jack Callahan, winter 1974)

5a. Sky Chimney Variation (F.A. Alan Lester, 1979)

6. King Nothing (F.A. Kevin Gianino, March 1997)

7. White Satin (F.A. Jeff Thomas, Doug Phillips, March 11, 1974)

8. Lycra (F.A. Kevin Gianino, Steve Jones, March 24, 1997)

8a. White Lycra (F.A. unknown, late 1990s)

9. Kevin's Arête (aka Cheap Polyester) (F.A. Steve Jones, Kevin Gianino, April 10, 1997)

10. Lost in Space (F.A. final pitch, Mark Deffenbaugh, September 2005; F.A. entire route, Mark Deffenbaugh, Jim Ablao, spring 2008)

11. Black Velcro (F.A. lower three pitches, Bob Johnson, Doug Phillips, 1975; F.A. entire route, Jeff Thomas, Mark Cartier, August 19, 1978)

12. Grettir's Saga (F.A. Mike Steele, 1982)

13. Season's Change (F.A. first four pitches, Mark Deffenbaugh, Bryan Smith, September 28, 2005; F.A. final pitch, Jim Ablao, Moira Armen, June 2008; F.A. entire route, Mark Deffenbaugh, Jim Ablao, summer 2008)

13a. Fish Taco Dihedral (F.A. Tyler Adams, Mark Deffenbaugh, March 2008)

14. Evolution Theory (F.A. Mark Deffenbaugh, Tyler Adams, September 2008)

14a. Destiny Unbound (F.A. Mark Deffenbaugh, 2009)

15. Southwest Side (F.R.A. Jim Ramsey, Jack Watts 1960)

16. The Good Ol' Days (F.A. Thomas Emde, June 27, 2004)

17. Ground Up Vegetarian (F.A. Ryan Lawson, Thomas Emde, October 2003)

17a. Project (F.A. unknown, 1970s)

18. Farewell to Smith (F.A. Thomas Emde, Ryan Lawson, September 2003; F.F.A Thomas Emde, Steve Baldwin, May 2004)

19. Freedom's Just Another Word For Nothing Left to Lose (F.A. Thomas Emde, Jim Ablao, August 6, 2004)

19a. Good 'Ol Variation (F.A. Thomas Emde, 2004)

20. Snibble Tower (F.A. Jon Marshall, John Haek, 1969; F.F.A. fifth pitch, Alan Kearney, Shari Kearney, 1976)

20a. Snibble Tower original start (F.A. John Marshall, John Haek, 1969)

20b. Snibble Free (F.A. Alan Kearney, Shari Kearney, 1976)

21. Why? D.S.L. (F.A. free solo, Blake Hankins, late 1990s)

22. Northwest Corner (F.R.A. Jim Ramsey, Jack Watts, 1960)

23. Shaft (F.A. Steve Lyford, 1974)

24. South Face (F.A. Nick Dodge, Jay Barton, 1963)

25. West Tower (F.A. with bow and arrow, Charles Dotter, Tony Bates, Jeff Dotter, Marcia Bilbao, June 1967; F.A. solo, Brad Englund, August 7, 1994)

26. East Tower (F.A. solo, Brad Englund, September 7, 1994)

27. Death By Vulture (F.A. Jim Ablao, Tyler Kamm, August 2008)

28. Vulture Gully (F.R.A. free solo, Alan Watts, spring 1991)

29. Dyer's Eve (F.A. Ryan Lawson, Thomas Emde, spring 2002)

30. X-Files (F.A. Thomas Emde, Ryan Lawson, spring 2002)

31. Smith Summit–East Wall (F.A. Dean Fry, Wayne Arrington, May 27, 1973; F.F.A. Jeff Thomas, Steve Lyford, February 23, 1974)

32. The Struggle Within (F.A. first three pitches, Ryan Lawson, Thomas Emde, April 15, 2001; F.A. fourth pitch, Ryan Lawson, Thomas Emde, June 2, 2001; F.F.A. entire route, Thomas Emde, October, 2004)

32a. Antisocial Behavior (F.A. Ryan Lawson, Thomas Emde, October 2000)

33. European Vacation (F.A Thomas Emde, Ryan Lawson, October 2007)

33a. No Vacation (F.A. Thomas Emde, 2008)

34. The Struggle Within original start (F.A. Ryan Lawson, June 16, 2000)

35. Harvester of Sorrow (F.A. Ryan Lawson, June 3, 2000; F.F.A. Thomas Emde, 2000)

36. Eye of the Beholder (F.A. Ryan Lawson, May 28, 2000)

36a. Eye of the Beholder finish (F.A. Ryan Lawson, May 28, 2000)

37. 100% Beef (F.A. Brooke Sandahl, spring 1991; F.F.A. Michael Stöger, April 2006)

38. Livin' Large (F.A. Brooke Sandahl, October 17, 1992)

39. Condor (F.A. Jim Anglin, John Rich, 1986)

40. Blackened (F.A. Ryan Lawson, June 18, 2000)

40a. Lightly Toasted (F.A. unknown, 2000)

41. American Nirvana (F.A. Thomas Emde, Ryan Lawson, October 2007)

42. The Dobby Brothers (F.A. Thomas Emde, Ryan Lawson, December 2007)

43. Entering Relativity (F.A. David Tvedt, Dee Tvedt, September 26, 1999)

44. Llama Enlightenment (F.A. Dee Tvedt, David Tvedt, October 29, 1999)

45. When Llamas Need Protection (F.A. David Tvedt, October 29, 1999)

46. Seekers of Enlightenment and Choss (David Tvedt, Dee Tvedt, August 3, 2000)

47. Wannabe Llamas (F.A. David Tvedt, Dee Tvedt, Keenan Tvedt, August 30, 1999)

48. Llama Sutra (F.A. David Tvedt, August 1999; F.F.A. Jeremy Hensel, Ben Moon, September 2001)

49. Carabid (F.A. Chet Sutterlin, Bob Bury, 1977)

50. Drill 'Em and Fill 'Em (F.A. Mike Puddy, Alan Watts, summer 1987)

51. Phoenix (F.A. Ken Currens, winter 1976)

51a. Phoenix finish (F.A. Ken Currens, winter 1976)

52. License to Bolt (F.A. Brooke Sandahl, spring 1987)

53. Fred on Air (F.A. T.R. Brooke Sandahl, Alan Watts, 1987; F.A. lead, Rick Lince, 1987)

54. Jim Treviso Memorial Route (aka J.T.'s Route) (F.A. Bill Soule, January 1992)

55. Scary Llamas (aka Hissing Llamas) (F.A. Dee Tvedt, David Tvedt, August 24, 1994)

56. When Llamas Bolt (F.A. David Tvedt, August 15, 1995)

56a. Llamas on the Edge (F.A. T.R. David Tvedt, August 1994, F.A. lead, Alan Watts, 1996)

57. Flake Chimney (F.A. unknown, 1970s)

58. Vulture Ridge (F.R.A. free solo, Alan Watts, spring 1991)

59. Vulture Ridge Spire (F.A. solo, Brad Englund, November 12, 1999)

60. Sabotage (F.A. Ryan Lawson, April 1999; F.F.A. Michael Richter, December 2000)

61. Yoderific (F.A. Jim Yoder, 1988)

62. Kunza Korner (F.A. Ralph Moore, 1976; F.F.A. Alan Watts, Jeanne Kunza, June 9, 1980)

62a. Kunza Korner finish (F.A. Ralph Moore, 1976)

63. South Park (F.A. John Merriam, Mike Lewis, August 3, 1999)

64. Wave of Bliss (F.A. Brooke Sandahl, spring 1984)

65. I'm Your Hate (F.A. Ryan Lawson, Thomas Emde, December 9, 2000)

66. Yoder Eaters (F.A. Jim Yoder, spring 1990)

66a. Stögerific (F.A. Michael Stöger, spring 2005)

67. Project (Prep. unknown, spring 1990)

68. Crumble Pie (F.A. Jim Yoder, spring 1990)

69. 9999 (F.A. Jim Leland, September 9, 1999)

70. Amelia Dearheart (F.A. Jim Leland, September 4, 1999)

71. Taylor Brook (F.A. Bob Pasic, September 4, 1999; B.R. Matt Canham, 2002)

72. Sky Slab (F.A. T.R. Ted Stahl, Jim Ablao, 2002)

73. Skylight (F.A. Jeff Thomas, Chris Jones, July 1979; F.F.A. Jeff Thomas, Bill Ramsey, July 18, 1979)

74. Stagefright (F.A. Alan Watts, Mike Puddy, April 16, 1983)

75. Serendipity (F.A. Ryan Lawson, Thomas Emde, spring 2002)

76. Bits and Pieces (F.A. Brian Holcomb, Dan Foote, Don Johnson, April 1977)

76a. Bits and Pieces start (F.A. Brian Holcomb, Dan Foote, Don Johnson, April 1977; R.B. unknown, 1990s)

76b. Bits of Feces (F.A. Pat Carr, 1982)

77. Stained (F.A. Jim Ablao, Ted Stahl, 2002)

77a. Confused and Disfigured (F.A. T.R. Jeff Frizzell, 2002; F.A. lead, unknown, 2005)

78. Earthtone (F.A. Mark Deffenbaugh, Terry Schild, April 11, 2005)

79. Adventurous 9904 (F.A. Holly Beck, Ryan Lawson, fall 1999)

80. Wherever I May Roam (F.A. Ryan Lawson, Thomas Emde, January 2000)

81. Tears of Rage (F.A. Alan Watts, Mike Puddy, April 16, 1983; R.B. final pitch, Ryan Lawson, fall 1999)

82. The Unforgiven (F.A. Ryan Lawson, Thomas Emde, January 1, 2000)

82a. Unforgiven Variation (F.A. Ryan Lawson, 2000)

83. No Brain, No Pain (F.A. Jeff Thomas, Bill Ramsey, July 19, 1979; F.F.A. Alan Watts, Alan Lester, April 25, 1981)

83a. No Brain original start (F.A. Jeff Thomas, Bill Ramsey, July 19, 1979)

84. No Pain, No Gain (F.A. Alan Watts, Alan Lester, August 17, 1981)

85. Why Art Thou? (F.A. Ryan Lawson, 2002)

86. Stand For Something (F.A. Jim Ablao, Ted Stahl, 2002)

87. Taste the Pain (F.A. Thomas Emde, Ryan Lawson, spring 2002)

88. Pain Reliever (F.A. unknown, 1980s)

89. Fall For Anything (F.A. Jim Ablao, Ted Stahl, 2002)

90. Of Wolf and Man (F.A. free solo, Ryan Lawson, March 2000)

91. My Little Pony (F.A. Ted Stahl, Jim Ablao, 2002)

92. Thieves Like Us (F.A. Jim Ablao, Ted Stahl, 2002)

93. Role Model (F.A. Ryan Lawson, Thomas Emde, May 20, 2001)

94. Cryptesthesia (F.A. Mike Pajunas, Jim Davis, October 22, 1994)

95. Zigzag (F.A. unknown, 1970s)

95a. Project—Zigzag finish (F.A. to high-point, Thomas Emde, Ryan Lawson, 2001)

96. Project (Prep. Jim Davis, 1996)

97. Pocket Pool (F.A. Jim Davis, Mike Pajunas, John Sprecher, August 4, 1996)

98. Chalk Wave (F.A. Don Cossel, Collette Whelan, 2002)

99. Chalk Therapy (F.A. Don Cossel, Phil Wise, Jory Meade, April 20, 2002)

100. Culls in Space (F.A. Jim Anglin, Mike Hartley, 1980)

101. Flounder Crack (F.R.A. Bob Pasic, July 14, 1997)

102. What to Expect (F.A. Bob Pasic, Jim Leyland, July 14, 1997; B.R. Matt Canham, 2002)

103. When Expecting (F.A. Jim Leyland, Bob Pasic, July 14, 1997)

104. Flounder Corner (F.A. unknown, early 1970s)

104a. Hook, Line and Sinker (F.A. Pat Carr, John Fiala, Randy Hagen, Alan Watts, 1977)

105. Cure For Pain (F.A. Mike Pajunas, Jim Davis, John Sprecher, October 23, 1994)

106. Butterknife Arête (F.A. Tom Heins, 1992)

107. Sunset Boulevard (F.A. Bob Marshall, Wayne Haack, 1972)

108. Sunset Slab (F.A. Dan Carlson, Paul Fry, July 1989)

1. Inside Corner (F.A. Jim Ramsey, Jerry Ramsey 1961; F.F.A. Jim Ramsey, Bruce Hahn, August 1961)
2. Project (Prep. Alan Watts, 1990)
3. Merkin's Jerkin (F.A. Alan Campbell, mid-1970s)
4. Project (Prep. Alan Watts, 1990)
5. Little Indian Princess (F.A. Ryan Lawson, Thomas Emde, January 2000)
6. Am I Evil? (F.A. Ryan Lawson, Thomas Emde, January 2000)
7. Lunatic to Love (F.A. Ryan Lawson, Alan Watts, December 2000)
8. Christian Brothers Traverse (F.A. The Priest: Kim Schmitz, Eugene Dod, Alan Amos, April 5, 1964; F.A. The Monk: Bill Cummins, Jon Marshall, Ted Davis, Ken Wallen, 1964; F.A. The Pope: unknown, mid-1960s; F.A. The Friar: Ted Davis, Bill Cummins, Juli Beall, 1965; F.A. The Abbot: Ryan Hokanson, Kirby Spangler, September 9, 1995)
8a. The Abbot–Pot Belly (F.A. Jon Marshall, Gerald Bjorkman, April 5, 1964)
9. Christian Brothers Reverse (F.A. The Abbot, Ryan Hokanson, Kirby Spangler, September 9, 1995; F.A. The Friar, Ted Davis, Jon Marshall, March 1964; F.F.A. T.R. Brad Englund, November 1997; F.A. entire route, Brad Englund, solo, November 8, 1997.
9a. The Friar–Northeast Arête (F.A. Kim Schmitz, 1964)
9b. The Birthday Start (F.A. Tyler Adams, solo, February 20, 2009)
10. Roots of Madness (F.A. Chuck Buzzard, 1986)
11. Hot Monkey Love (F.A. Mike Pajunas, Jon Sprecher, Jim Davis, April 28, 1991)
12. Fallen Angel (F.A. Mike Smelsar, Nancy Baker, October 1978)
13. Modern Zombie (F.A. Mike Pajunas, June 8, 1991)
14. Midriff Bulge (F.A. Jeff Thomas, Mike Smelsar, February 1977)
15. Manic Nirvana (F.A. Mike Pajunas, Jon Sprecher, May 18, 1991)
16. Innocent Victim (F.A. Ryan Lawson, J. T. Seymore, May 6, 1999)
17. Benedictine Punk (F.A. Ryan Lawson, April 1999)
18. Bare Midriff (F.A. Alan Watts, August 1999)
18a. Bare Variation (F.A. unknown, late 1970s)
19. Get on the Ball (F.A. Ryan Lawson, J. T. Seymore, May 6, 1999)
20. Holier than Thou (F.A. Ryan Lawson, April 1999; F.F.A. Chris Van Leuren, Ryan Lawson, April 1999)
21. Monk Chimney (F.A. Kim Schmitz, Eugene Dod, December 1967)
22. The Snake (F.A. Jeff Thomas, Tim Carpenter, May 26, 1974)
22a. Venom (F.A. unknown, 1980s)
23. Don't Tread on Me (F.A. Ryan Lawson, June 1999)
23a. Don't Tread on Me finish (Prep. Ryan Lawson, June 1999; F.A. Thomas Emde, 1999)
24. Reptile (F.A. unknown, 1970s)
25. Iguanas on Elm Street (Mike Pajunas, Jon Sprecher, April 26, 1992)
26. The Golden Road (F.A. Kent Benesch, Tom Blust, August 1981)
27. Split Image (F.A. Alan Watts, March 3, 1984)
28. Made in the Shade (F.A. Jandy Cox, Steve Zeke, spring, 1989; F.F.A. Alan Watts, John Rich, September 30, 1989)
29. Cling On (F.A. Jeff Thomas, Doug Phillips, Greg Phillips, July 7, 1974)
30. A Desperate Man (F.A. Doug Phillips, 1986)

31. Hemp Liberation (F.A. John Collins, summer 1990)

32. Lords of Karma (F.A. John Collins, March 1991)

33. Strung Out (F.A. Jeff Thomas, Doug Phillips, Greg Phillips, July 7, 1974)

34. Struck Out (F.R.A. Alan Watts, free solo, 1984)

35. La Nina (F.A. Ryan Lawson, April 1999)

36. Up the Backside (F.A. unknown, 1960s)

37. Project (Prep. unknown, 1990)

38. Heaven Can Wait (F.A. Kent Benesch, Chris Haunold, August 1979)

38a. Heaven Variation (F.A. Alan Watts, free solo, 1983)

39. Angel Flight Buttress (F.A. Mike Smelsar, Dick Morse, October 1978)

40. Effin A' (F.A. Nick Dolecek, Rob Hernandez, February 2005)

41. High Sage (F.A. unknown, 1992)

42. Follies of Youth (F.A. Mike Smelsar, Mark Cartier, October 1978)

43. Youthful Indiscretion (aka Wisdom of Age) (F.A. unknown, 1992)

44. Common Household Fly (F.A. Chris Gentry, Dave Francisco, February 1982)

45. Arachnid Boogie (F.A. Chris Gentry, Dave Francisco, February 1982)

46. Tarantula (F.A. Alan Watts, July 12, 1981)

47. Imaginary Spider (F.A. Wayne Wallace, Tim Olson, 1995)

48. First Ascent Crack (F.R.A. John Sedelmeyer, John Pinckney, mid-1990s)

49. Project (Prep. Clark Shelk, summer 1994)

50. Spiderman (F.A. Steve Strauch, Danny Gates, 1969)

50a. Spiderman Variation (F.A. unknown, 1970s)

51. Squashed Spider (F.A. Mike Smelsar, 1978, R.B. John Sedelmeyer, summer 1998)

52. Widow Maker (F.A. Dan Foote, Brian Holcomb, fall 1976)

53. Best Left to Obscurity (F.A. Mike Hartley, Jim Anglin, 1981)

54. Explosive Energy Child (F.A. Mike Smelsar, Bob McGown, fall 1976; F.F.A. Mike Smelsar, John Tyreman, spring 1977)

54a. More or Lester (F.A. T.R. Alan Lester, 1981)

55. Out of Harm's Way (F.A. Paul Fry, 1988)

56. In Harm's Way (F.A. Bob Johnson, Doug Phillips, September, 1975)

57. Little Feat (F.A. Mike Hartley, Jim Anglin, June 16, 1980)

58. Cornerstone (F.A. Chuck Buzzard, 1986)

58a. Cornerstone Variation (F.A. Chuck Buzzard, 1986)

59. Death Takes a Holiday (F.A. Tom Blust, 1988)

60. Project (Prep. unknown, 1991)

61. Doctor Doom (F.A. Jeff Thomas, Steve Lyford, Tim Miller, Tom Minderhout, April 20, 1974)

61a. Doctor Doom Variation (F.A. unknown, 1970s)

62. What's Up Doc? (F.A. unknown, 1991)

63. Necromancer (F.A unknown, 1970s)

64. Stiff Little Fingers (F.A. unknown, mid-1990s)

65. Captain Fingers (F.A. Craig Benesch, Kent Benesch, fall 1980)

66. Western Chimney (F.A. George Cummings, Roger Peyton, April 1963)

67. Chuck's Crack (F.A. Chuck Buzzard, 1986)

68. Long Time Gone (F.A. Alan Watts, Mike Puddy, October 23, 1996)

69. Palo Verde (F.A. Jim Anglin, Mike Hartley, January 1, 1981)

70. Petroglyph Crack (F.A. unknown, 1970s)

71. Cows in Agony (F.A. Tom Feldmann, Mike Paulson, spring 1989)
72. Cliff Dwelling Crack (F.A. unknown, 1970s)
73. Juniper Face (F.A. Matt Kerns, Jim Yoder, 1989)
74. Chimney De Chelly (F.A. Jeff Thomas, Ken Currens, March 25, 1977)
75. Project (Prep. unknown, mid-1990s)
76. Desolation Row (F.A. Alan Watts, Pat Carr, June 27, 1981)
77. Shadow of Doubt (F.A. Greg Collum, Matt Kerns, Jim Yoder, 1988)
78. Reason to Be (F.A. Greg Collum, Matt Kerns, 1988)
79. Tale of Two Shities (F.A. first two pitches, Monty Mayko, Bruce Casey, December 4, 1977; F.F.A. entire route, Jeff Thomas, Chris Jones, Mike Hartley, September 30, 1978)
80. Sundown (F.A. Alan Kearney, Shari Kearney, November 1978)
81. Down's Syndrome (F.A. Chuck Buzzard, winter 1980)
82. Minas Morgul (F.A. solo, Wayne Arrington, 1972; F.F.A. Alan Watts, Chris Grover, May 3, 1981)
83. Bad Moon Rising (F.A. Jerry Messinger, June 1989)
84. Moons of Pluto (F.A. Frank Cornelius, 1984)
85. Screaming Yellow Zonkers (F.A. Kent Benesch, Alan Watts, 1982)
86. Cosmos (F.A. Mike Pajunas, Jon Sprecher, Gary Rall, June 9, 1989)
87. Trezlar (F.A. Tom Rogers, Clay Cox, Bob Johnson, November 12, 1972; F.F.A. Jeff Thomas, Jim Davis, April 3, 1976)
88. Planet Luxury (F.A. Mike Pajunas, Jon Sprecher, June 20, 1992)
89. Four Fs (F.A. Mike Barbitta, fall 1985)
90. Lichen Persuasion (F.A Jon Sprecher, Pat Carr, fall 1978)
91. Watermark (F.A. Bob Durand, Katie Meyers, May 19, 1996)
92. Red Scare (F.A. Mike Pajunas, Jon Sprecher, June 1, 1989)
93. We Be Toys (F.A. Mike Pajunas, Jon Sprecher, June 2, 1989)
94. Little Wicked Thing (F.A. Mike Pajunas, Jon Sprecher, June 2, 1989)
95. Bop 'Till You Drop (F.A. Bruce Casey, 1988)
96. Xanadu (F.A. Bob Durand, Diana Dutton, March 18, 1995)
97. Matthew 7:24 (F.A. Tom Heins, 1990)
98. Sea of Green (F.A. Bob Durand, Dennis Alexander, April 24, 1992)
99. Aggro Bumbly (F.A. unknown, 1990)

CHAPTER 8: MONKEY FACE AREA

1. Slow Train (F.A. Tim Carpenter, Judy Carpenter, 1984)
2. Diamonds and Rust (F.A. Mark Cartier, Mike Smelsar, winter 1979)
3. Schleppin' For Hollywood (F.A. Erik Wolfe, summer 1996)
4. Rust Never Sleeps (F.A. unknown, early 1970s)
5. Perpetual Motion (F.A. Mike Hartley, John Rich, 1980)
6. Dolf's Dihedral (F.A. Bill Ramsey, Mary Ellen Dolf, spring 1980)
7. Potential Energy (F.A. second and third pitches, Alan Lester, Chuck Wheeler, fall 1980; F.F.A. entire route, Alan Watts, John Barbella, July 28, 1981)
7a. Potential Energy original start (F.A. Alan Lester, Chuck Wheeler, fall 1980)
8. Flexible Flyer (F.A. Jim Davis, Mike Pajunas, mid-1990s; F.F.A. unknown, late 1990s)

9. Flex Your Head (F.A. Alan Lester, Chuck Wheeler, fall 1980; F.F.A. Jim Davis, 1988)

10. Project (Prep. Jim Davis, 1989)

11. King Kong (F.A. Scott Arighi, Jim Neiland, 1967; F.F.A. Steve Strauch, Danny Gates, 1970)

11a. King Kong Direct (F.A. Alan Watts, Bill Ramsey, July 27, 1978)

11b. King Kong Escape (F.A. unknown, 1970s)

11c. King Kong original finish (F.A. Scott Arighi, Jim Neiland, 1967)

12. Godzilla (F.A. Tom Bauman, November 26, 1966; F.F.A. Steve Strauch, Danny Gates, 1970)

13. Smaug (F.A. second pitch, Tom Rogers, Al Balmforth, 1970; F.A. entire route, Jeff Thomas, Avary Tichner, September 2, 1978)

14. Blow Cocoa (F.A. Kent Benesch, summer 1989)

15. Monkey Farce (F.A. Jeff Thomas, Mike Smelsar, April 2, 1977)

16. West Face Variation (F.A. Tom Bauman, Bob Ashworth, September 11, 1965; F.F.A. Tom Bauman, Bob Ashworth, April 9, 1967)

16a. Start Variation (F.A. unknown, late 1960s)

16b. West Face Variation Direct (F.A. unknown, late 1960s)

16c. Slab Variation (F.A. unknown, early 1970s)

16d. Roof Variation (F.R.A. Bill Ramsey, Alan Watts, summer 1978)

16e. Manslaughter (F.A. Bill Ramsey, Alan Watts, August 26, 1978)

16f. Finish Variation (F.A. unknown, mid-1960s)

17. Drug Nasty (aka Dean's Dream) (F.A. Dean Hart, 1987)

18. Moving in Stereo (F.A. Kent Benesch, 1986)

19. Astro Monkey (aka Southwest Corner) (F.A. entire Southwest Corner, Tom Bauman, 1970; F.A. fifth pitch, Bob McGown, 1978; F.F.A. second pitch, Mike Seeley, 1972; F.F.A. third and fourth pitches, Jeff Thomas, Mike Smelsar, April 3, 1977; F.F.A. upper two pitches, Chris Jones, Bill Ramsey, April 21, 1979; F.F.A. first pitch, Alan Watts, Tom Blust, June 18, 1980; F.F.A. entire route, Alan Watts, Chris Grover, July 21, 1983)

19a. First Pitch Bypass (F.A. unknown, mid-1970s)

19b. Second Pitch Connection (F.A. unknown, mid-1970s)

19c. Escape Variation (F.A. unknown, mid-1970s)

19d. Southwest Corner Traverse (F.A. Tom Bauman, 1970; F.F.A. Alan Watts, John Barbella, July 27, 1981)

20. Project (F.A. T.R. Jim Davis, 1996)

21. Pose Down (F.A. Kent Benesch, summer 1989)

21a. Pose Down Variation (F.A. Kent Benesch, summer 1989)

22. West Face (F.A. Dean Caldwell, Byron Babcock, Bill Lentsch, 1962, finishing via *South Exit;* F.A. final pitch, Dean Caldwell, Jim Kindler, December 1967; F.F.A. final pitch, Chris Jones, Bill Ramsey, April 21, 1979; F.F.A. first pitch with aid start, Alan Watts, July 26, 1981; F.F.A. third pitch, Alan Watts, summer 1985)

23. Sheer Trickery (F.A. Ron Kauk, Wolfgang Gullich, Alan Watts, June 1989)

23a. Project (Prep. Alan Watts, June 1989)

24. Project (Prep. Robert Rogoz, fall 1989)

25. The Backbone (F.A. first pitch, Ron Kauk, Wolfgang Gullich, Alan Watts, June 1989; F.A. second pitch, Alan Watts, 1987; F.F.A. third pitch, Alan Watts, summer 1985; F.F.A. entire route, Ron Kauk, June 1989)

26. Northwest Passage (F.A. second pitch, Tom Bauman, Bob Ashworth, 1968; F.A. entire route, Jeff Thomas, Steve Moore, April 28, 1973; F.F.A. second pitch, Alan Watts, November 3, 1981; F.F.A. third pitch, Alan Lester, 1983; F.F.A. entire route with aid start, Hidetaka Suzuki, 1985)

27. Northwest Corner (F.A. second pitch, Dean Caldwell, Jim Kindler, December 1967; F.A. entire route, Tom Bauman, Bob Ashworth, March 28, 1969; F.F.A. second pitch, Alan Lester, 1983; F.F.A. entire route, Alan Watts, summer 1985)

27a. North Face (F.A. Dean Caldwell, Jim Kindler, December 1967; F.F.A upper part first pitch, Alan Watts, fall 1981; F.F.A. second pitch, Alan Lester, 1983)

28. Spank the Monkey (F.A. Alan Watts, summer 1985)

28a. Spank the Monkey finish (F.A. Will Nazarian, 1996; F.F.A. Tommy Caldwell, October 2004)

29. East Face (F.A. Kim Schmitz, Gerald Bjorkman, summer 1964; F.F.A. final pitch, Alan Watts, 1983; F.F.A. entire first pitch, Alan Watts, August 31, 1985)

29a. East Face start (F.F.A. Alan Watts, September 24, 1983).

29b. East Face finish (F.F.A. Alan Watts, August 25, 1984)

30. Just Do It (F.A. T.R., Alan Watts, June 1989; F.F.A. Jean-Baptiste Tribout, April 6, 1992)

30a. Just Do It start (F.A. T.R., Alan Watts, June 1989; F.F.A. Jean-Baptiste Tribout, 1991)

31. Megalithic (F.A. Brooke Sandahl, fall 1990)

32. Rising Expectations (F.A unknown, 1960s; F.F.A. Chris Jones, Alan Watts, September 13, 1979)

33. Pioneer Route (F.A. Dave Bohn, Jim Fraser, Vivian Staender, January 1, 1960; F.F.A. Panic Point, unknown, 1960s)

33a. Monkey Off My Back (F.A. Ryan Lawson, Thomas Emde, February 10, 2002)

34. Young Pioneers (F.A. Alan Watts, Chris Grover, August 1985)

35. Close Shave (F.A. Alan Watts, Mike Puddy, August 1985)

36. Bohn Street West Face Cave (F.A. second pitch, Bob Martin, Dave Jensen, January 1963; F.F.A. Alan Watts, Chris Grover, July 15, 1983)

36a. South Exit (F.A. Dean Caldwell, Byron Babcock, Bill Lentsch, 1962)

36b. Project (Prep. Kevin Gianino, spring 1997)

37. Monkey Space (F.A. into West Face Cave, Bob McGown, 1978; F.F.A. entire route, Chris Jones, Bill Ramsey, April 21, 1979)

38. Project (Prep. Kevin Gianino, spring 1997)

38a. Project (Prep. Kevin Gianino, spring 1997)

39. Chicken Little (F.A. Mike Smelsar, Tom Easthope, August 1978)

40. Mr. Toad's Wild Ride (F.A. Mike Smelsar, Tom Easthope, August 1978)

41. Funguy Roof (F.A. Mike Barbitta, 1996)

42. Scabies (F.A. original line, Mike Smelsar, John Tyreman, 1978; R.B. first pitch, Don Cossel, April 2002; F.A. entire route, Don Cossel, Troy Longstroth, Collette Whelan, Tony Sleznick, April 5, 2002)

43. First Kiss (F.A. first pitch, Mike Smelsar, John Tyreman, 1978; F.A. second pitch, Don Cossel, Troy Longstrough, Collette Whelan, Tony Sleznick, April 5, 2002; F.A. final pitch, Ryan Lawson, Thomas Emde, March 31, 2002; Prep. third and fourth pitches, Ryan Lawson, fall 2002; F.A. entire route, Thomas Emde, free solo, November 2002)

44. The Climb (F.A. Ryan Lawson, Thomas Emde, March 31, 2002; F.F.A. Michael Stöger, Thomas Emde, September 2005)

45. Dreams That I Carry (F.A. T.R. Ryan Lawson, fall 2002)

46. Project (Prep. Ryan Lawson, spring 2002)

47. Groove Thang (F.A. Ryan Lawson, Thomas Emde, March 31, 2002)

48. Great Expectations (F.A. Paul Fry, Jeff Thomas, March 6, 1977)

49. Guinness (F.A. Ryan Lawson, Ryan Kerner, May 2002)

50. Redundant (F.A. Ryan Lawson, Ryan Kerner, May 2002)

51. Lucky Girl (F.A. Ryan Lawson, Michelle Weinert, April 2002)

52. No Expectations (F.A. Thomas Emde, Ryan Lawson, March 2002)

53. Ryan's Song (F.A. Ryan Lawson, Thomas Emde, March 31, 2002)

54. Crack of Insanity (F.A. Thomas Emde, Ryan Lawson, 2002; F.F.A. Thomas Emde, Steve Baldwin, June 2004)

55. Hawkline Monster (F.A. Chuck Buzzard, solo, 1980)

56. New World (F.A. Mike Smelsar, Nancy Baker, March 1979)

CHAPTER 9:
RED WALL AREA

1. Dare to Be Normal (F.A. unknown, mid-1990s)

2. Titanium Jag (F.A. Tim Olson, Greg Lyon, Cecil Colley, March 25, 1989)

3. Project (Prep. unknown, 1999)

4. Bill's Flake (F.A. Bill Ramsey, Alan Watts, August 17, 1978)

5. Finger Puppet (F.A. Jim Boucher, May 1988)

6. Phantasmagoria (Tim Olson, Cecil Colley, November 13, 1989)

6a. Jag Connection (F.A. unknown, 1990s)

7. Orgasmagoria (F.A. Ted Stahl, Jeff Frizzell, Brett Yost, February 2003)

8. Pop Art (F.A. Eric Horst, May 1991)

9. Dances With Clams (F.A. Tom Heins, Pete Keane, April 1991)

10. Paper Tiger (F.A. upper pitch via Super Slab, Jeff Thomas, Mark Cartier, August 27, 1978; F.A. entire route, Mike Hartley, Jim Anglin, December 15, 1979)

10a. Karl Marx Variation (F.A. Mike Barbitta, 1988)

11. Bay of Pigs (F.A. first pitch, Ted Stahl, Jeff Frizzell, Jim Ablao, March 2003; F.A. entire route, Jeff Frizzell, Ted Stahl, March 2003)

12. 'Till the Cows Come Home (F.A. second pitch, Danny Gates, Steve Strauch, 1970; F.A. entire route, David Knoll, John Simonson, fall 1997)

13. Animal Farm (F.A. Ted Stahl, Jeff Frizzell, February 2003)

14. Super Slab (F.A. Danny Gates, 1969; F.F.A. Danny Gates, Neal Olsen, 1970)

14a. Panama Express (F.A. Jim Anglin, Mike Hartley, January 2, 1980)

15. A Stroke of Brilliance (F.A. Brooke Sandahl, Doug Phillips, 1995)

16. Panama Red (F.A. Mike Smelsar, Mark Cartier, 1979)
17. Amphetamine Grip (F.A. Danny Gates, Steve Strauch, 1970)
17a. Gripped (F.A. unknown, late 1970s)
18. Red Rover (F.A. Dana Horton, 1980)
18a. Red Rover finish (F.A. Dana Horton, 1980)
19. Papillion (F.A. Jeff Frizzell, Jim Ablao, February 2003)
20. Gulag Archipelago (F.A. Jeff Frizzell, Jim Ablao, February 2003)
21. Iron Curtain (F.A. Jeff Thomas, Chris Mannix, April 24, 1977)
22. Helter Skelter (F.A. first pitch, Jeff Thomas, John Rakovsky, May 8, 1977; F.A. entire route via start variation, Mike Smelsar, Ed Newville, spring 1978)
22a. Helter Start Variation (F.A. Mike Smelsar, Mark Cartier, spring 1978)
22b. Helter Direct Finish (F.A. Will Nazarian, 1998)
22c. Helter Skelter Direct Start (F.A. Will Nazarian, 1998)
22d. If Six Were Nine (F.A. Bruce Birchell, June 1979)
23. Ride the Lightning (F.A. Kent Benesch, Tom Blust, Doug Phillips, 1987)
24. Project (F.A. Will Nazarian, 1998, F.F.A. uncompleted)
25. Project (Prep. Will Nazarian, 1998)
26. Chairman Mao's Little Red Book (F.A. unknown, 1970s; F.F.A. Jeff Thomas, Chris Jones, Alan Watts, July 21, 1979)
27. Fingers of Fate (F.A. Mike Hartley, Jim Anglin, June 30, 1979; F.F.A. Alan Lester, fall 1979)
28. Sole Survivor (F.A. Kurt Smith, spring 1988)
29. Gone With the Flake (F.A. Jeff Thomas, Roger Robinson, December 15, 1974)
30. Ho Chi Minh Trail (F.A. Wayne Haack, Steve Strauch, 1969)
31. Shanghai (F.A. Bill Ramsey, Alan Watts, July 17, 1978)
32. Cartoon Deficiency (F.A. Wayne Wallace, Ken Casper, 1989)
33. Let's Face It (F.A. T.R. Mike Smelsar, 1979; F.A. lead, Tom Egan, Mike Paulson, October 1988)
34. Peking (F.A. Tom Bauman, Osa Thatcher, May 5, 1969)
34a. Chouinard's Crack (F.A. Tom Bauman, Osa Thatcher, May 5, 1969)
34b. Burma Buttress (F.A. Ben Randall, Pete Keane, September 15, 2006)
34c. Straight Outta Peking (F.A. Tyler Adams, Mark Deffenbaugh, Moira Armen, May 1, 2008)
34d. Beijing Finish (F.R.A. Gabe Coler, Richard Draves, July 1, 2008)
35. Moscow (F.A. Pat Callis, Mickey Schurr, 1965)
35a. Mongolians (F.A. Jeff Thomas, Chris Jones, October 1, 1978)
36. Breakdown in Paradise (F.A. Gary Peterson, Mike Bourquez, Lisa Chen, Jonathon Souquet, Peter Ahern, summer 1995)
37. Havana (F.A. Wayne Haack, Steve Thompson. 1975)
38. Hawk Nest (F.A. Chuck Buzzard, T.R. April 1983)
39. Project (F.A. Steve Mrazek, 2003, F.F.A. uncompleted)
40. Metamorphic Maneuvers (F.A. Mike Barbitta, October 1984)
41. I Almost Died (F.A. Avary Tichner, August 1978; F.F.A. Jeff Thomas, Ken Currens, October 28, 1978)
42. Flex (F.A. unknown, late 1970s)
43. Red Ryder (F.A. Wayne Haack, Steve Thompson, 1975)
44. Desperately Seeking Shade (F.A. Don Cossel, August 1992)

CHAPTER 10: THE MONUMENT AREA AND STAENDER RIDGE

26. A Little Dementia (F.A. Vince Gonor, Ryan Lawson, September 1998)

27. A Little Seduction (F.A. Tom Egan, spring 1990)

28. North Ridge (F.A. unknown, 1930s)

29. North Ridge Direct (F.A. unknown, 1950s)

30. Abraxas (F.A. lower pitches, Steve Strauch, Wayne Haack, 1969; F.A. complete route, Steve Strauch, Danny Gates, 1969; F.F.A. fourth pitch, Wayne Arrington, Ken Currens, 1975; F.F.A. second pitch, Mark Cartier, Mark Jonas, 1981; F.F.A. third pitch, Thomas Emde, Ryan Lawson, spring 2001

30a. Tombstone Wall (F.A. Steve Strauch, Danny Gates, 1969; F.F.A. Wayne Arrington, Ken Currens, 1975)

31. Lounger (F.A. Steve Strauch, Wayne Haack, 1969; R.B. Sean Moore, winter 2000)

32. Bagpiping in the Buff (F.A. Ben Zimmerman, Don Cossel, August 2000)

33. Approaching the Twilight (F.A. Don Cossel, Ben Zimmerman, August 2000)

34. Snow Bunny (F.A. Sean Moore, winter 2000)

35. Praying Mantel (F.A. Sean Moore, winter 2000)

36. Moore, Please? (F.A. Sean Moore, winter 2000)

37. Sands of Time (F.A. first two pitches, Todd Rentchler, partner, fall 1977; F.A. entire route, solo, Todd Rentchler, fall 1977)

38. Project (Prep. Tom Egan, 1989)

39. Southeast Face (F.A. Ted Davis, Willy Zeigler, June 1966)

40. Osa Thatcher's Needle (F.A. Bob Martin, Eugene Dod, 1961)

41. Bird Dung Chimney (F.A. unknown, 1970s)

42. Deception Crack (F.A. Bruce Burling, Frank Jager, 1970; F.F.A. Jeff Thomas, Ted Johnson, June 4, 1977)

43. Brain Salad Surgery (F.A. Jeff Thomas, March 28, 1976)

44. Street Walker (F.A. Jeff Thomas, Cindy Jones, December 7, 1974)

45. Juniper Gully (F.A. Dean Caldwell, Byron Babcock, 1960)

46. Liberty Bell Chimney (F.A. Jack Janacek, J. Harrower, 1954)

47. The Ear (F.A. Tom Rogers, 1969)

47a. Ear Variation (F.A. unknown, 1970s)

48. The Product (F.A. aid seam, Tom Bauman, Bob Ashworth, March 24, 1969; F.F.A. entire route, Tom Egan, 1990)

49. Project (Prep. Jeff Frizzell, 1990)

50. Jamboree (F.A. unknown, 1970s)

51. Rib Traverse (F.A. unknown, 1950s)

52. Here and Never Found (F.A. Ryan Lawson, October 2000)

53. Is This Love? (F.A. Ryan Lawson, October 2000; B.R. Matt Canham, 2002)

54. Nice Guys Finish Last (F.A. Ryan Lawson, October 2000)

55. Instant Replay (F.A. Tom Rogers, Steve Wilson, 1969)

56. Parking Lot Crack (F.A. free solo, Bob Bauman, mid-1960s)

57. Anti-Reflective (Prep. Tom Egan, Jeff Frizzell, 1990; F.A. Marco Fedrizzi, Greg Lyon, May 1999)

58. Munchkin Land (F.A. unknown, 1960s)

59. Lollypop League (F.A. unknown, 1960s; R.B. John Hercher, fall 1993)

60. Project–Orange Planet (Prep. Tom Egan, 1990)

61. Out of Control (F.A. Jeff Thomas, Mike Smelsar, May 14, 1977; F.F.A. Paul Landrum, Ken Currens, 1978)

62. Free Spirit (F.A. Jeff Thomas, Scott Hansen, April 28, 1974)

63. Scoop Route (F.A. Vivian Staender, Gil Staender, 1955)

64. Midnight Rider (F.A unknown; F.F.A. Jeff Thomas, Mike Smelsar, May 14, 1977)

65. North Side (F.A. Dave Pearson, Ross Petrie, 1946)

66. D.A.R. Crack (F.A. Tom Rogers, John Sanborn, Dennis Johnson, April 25, 1970; F.F.A. Jeff Thomas, Scott Hansen, April 28, 1974)

67. Sunjammer (F.A. T.R. Del Young, Mead Hargis, summer 1971; F.F.A. Del Young 1972)

68. Chasing Blue Sky (F.A. Dave Boltz, Jeff Alzner, August 14, 1999)

69. South Face (F.A. unknown, 1970s)

70. Chopper (F.A. T.R. Del Young, Dave Jensen, summer 1971; F.A. lead, Del Young, 1972)

71. Nightshade Intolerance (F.A. Dave Cain, Thane Stumbaugh, Tony Quartararo, Jeff Cain, April 8, 1995)

72. Popper (F.A. John Hercher, Trent Hering, fall 1993)

73. Slopper (F.A. Craig Benesch, 1980)

74. North Ramp (F.A. unknown 1950s)

74a. North Ramp Variation (F.A. unknown 1950s)

74b. Silly Crack (F.R.A. free solo, Alan Watts, 1980)

75. Easy Street (F.A. unknown, 1960s)

76. Thrasher (F.A. Jeff Thomas, Scott Hansen, April 28, 1974)

77. Northeast Spur (F.R.A. Brian Holcomb, Frank Rodriquez, 1972)

78. Limestone Chimney (F.A. Vivian Staender, Gil Staender, 1955)

78a. Limestone Variation (F.A. unknown, 1960s)

79. Juniper Snag (F.A. Jim Ramsey, Clinton DeShazer, 1961)

80. East Chimney (F.A. Bruce Hahn, Jim Ramsey, 1963)

81. Skid Row (F.A. Jeff Thomas, Charly Brown, November 3, 1974)

82. Lost Fox (F.A. Steve Lyford, Bob Johnson, 1973)

83. Bump and Grind (F.A. Ray Smutek, Iain Lynn, 1969; F.F.A. unknown, early 1970s)

84. Deliverance (F.A. T.R. Tom Rogers, Dean Shostrum, October 31,1970)

85. Direct Northwest Crack (F.A. Jim Ramsey, Jerry Ramsey, 1958)

86. Lieback Face (F.A. Miles Paul, Dorothy Paul, 1970)

87. Prune Face (F.A. Don Cossel, 1989)

88. Lower West Chimney (F.A. Vivian Staender, Gil Staender, 1956)

89. South Buttress (F.A. Vivian Staender, Gil Staender, 1956)

90. Peanuts (F.A. unknown, 1970s)

91. Defecation Crack (F.A unknown, 1970s)

91a. Nut Case (F.A. unknown, 1970s)

92. East Side Chimney (F.A. unknown, 1960s)

93. Desiderata (F.A. unknown, 1960s; F.F.A. Jeff Thomas, Jim Eliot, March 6, 1974)

94. North Chimney (F.R.A. Dave Pearson, Ross Petrie, 1946)

95. Northwest Corner (F.A. Jim Ramsey, Clinton DeShazer, 1961)

95a. West Ledges (F.A. unknown, 1960s)

96. Falling Rock Zone (F.A. unknown, 1970s)

97. Smut (F.A. Dave Jensen, 1960; F.F.A. Alan Watts, January 4, 1981)

98. Affliction (F.A. unknown, 1970s)

99. Milwaukee's Best (Tyler Adams, Jake Hector, October 2006)

100. North Ledge (F.A. unknown, 1950s)

101. South Bowl (F.A. Jim Ramsey, Ken Bierly, 1964)

102. Rotten Crack (F.A. Vivian Staender, Gil Staender, 1956; F.F.A. Kim Schmitz, mid-1960s)

103. Friction Arête (F.A. Jim Rixon, Kim Schmitz, 1965)

104. Orange Peel (F.A. unknown, early 1970s)

105. Lemon Peel (F.A. unknown, early 1970s)

106. Brown Cow (F.A. unknown, 1960s)

107. Cow Pie (F.A. unknown, 1960s)

108. The Long Walk (F.A. Tyler Adams, Jake Hector, Nick Dolecek, February 23, 2006)

CHAPTER 11:
THE MARSUPIAL CRAGS AND SURROUNDING AREAS

1. Ryan's Arête (F.A. Ryan Lawson, Will Darin, Synne Chadwick, October 1997)

1a. Ryan's Direct (Prep. Ryan Lawson, March 1998; F.A. T.R., Alan Watts, 1999; F.A. lead, unknown, early 2000s)

1b. Project (Prep. Ryan Lawson, March 1998)

2. Heatstroke (F.A. Eric Freden, Charles Arnett, June 1986)

3. Through Being Cool (F.A. Bill Soule, 1994)

4. Cool Air (F.A. Bill Soule, 1994)

5. South Gully (F.A. unknown, 1960s)

6. Suck My Kiss (F.A. Ryan Lawson, Thomas Emde, March 1999)

7. Thin Air (F.A. first pitch, unknown, 1960s; F.F.A. first pitch, Larry and Susan Kemp, August 1971; F.A. second pitch, Eric Freden, Paul Underwood, May 1987; F.A. third pitch, Brad Englund, solo, September 30, 1995)

7a. Changing Lanes (F.R.A. Mark Deffenbaugh, 2003)

8. Here Today, Gone Tomorrow (F.A. Tom Heins, mid-1990s; B.R. Ryan Lawson, 1999)

9. Buffalo Power (F.A. Ryan Lawson, June 1999)

9a. Chipmunk Power (F.A. Thomas Emde, 2000)

10. Catty Corner (F.A. Doug Phillips, Bob Johnson, 1974)

11. Crazies (F.A. Ed Beacham, 1972; F.F.A. unknown, 1970s)

12. Round Here (F.A. John Hercher, Trent Hering, fall 1993)

13. Cool Man Luke (F.A. Pat Luke, Marilyn Geninatti, September 2006)

14. Round There (F.A. Gary Peterson, Kevin Kofford, summer 1995)

15. Desert Solitaire (F.A. Jeff Thomas, Keith Edwards, Dean Fry, November 25, 1972)

16. Round River (F.A. Alan Amos, 1972; R.B. first pitch, Ryan Lawson, 1999)

16a. Round River Direct (F.A. Jeff Thomas, October 26, 1974; R.B. Ryan Lawson, October 1999)

17. Virgin Arête (F.A. Ryan Lawson, February 1998)

18. The Knob (F.A. Ryan Lawson, free solo, November 1999)

19. Hero of the Day (F.A. Ryan Lawson, free solo, November 1999)

20. Exercise in Futility (F.A. Ryan Lawson, free solo, November 1999)

21. Exit of Humanity (F.A. Ryan Lawson, Holly Beck, November 1999)

22. Keep the Faith (F.A. Ryan Lawson, November 1999)

23. I'm Your Life (F.A. Ryan Lawson, Phil Cromwell, September 1997)

24. To Live is to Die (F.A. Ryan Lawson, November 1999)

25. King of Pain (F.A. Ryan Lawson, November 1999)

26. Knuckle-Draggers Anonymous (F.A. Vince Gonor, Ryan Lawson, March 1998)

27. Project (Prep. Ryan Lawson, summer 1999)

28. The Optimist (F.A. Steve Heim, Jim Nieland, 1967; F.F.A. Beth Rodden, October 2004)

28a. The Great Roof (F.A. Steve Heim, Jim Nieland, 1967)

29. Project (Prep. Ryan Lawson, summer 1999)

30. Pouches (F.A. Bill Soule, 1994)

31. Pin Bender (F.A. Dean Fry, Russ Bunker, February 17, 1973)

32. Nice Beak (F.A. Wayne Wallace, mid-1990s)

33. Project (Prep. Jeff Frizzell, 1990)

34. Perry Masonry (F.A. Wayne Wallace, mid-1990s)

35. West Face (F.A. unknown, 1960s)

36. Smash the Silence (Prep. Ryan Lawson, 1999; F.A. Thomas Emde, 2000)

37. West Gully (F.A. Ted Davis, Jon Marshall, 1963; F.F.A. Alan Watts, free solo, 1981)

37a. West Gully Variation (F.A. Jeff Thomas, Guy Keene, November 2, 1974)

38. Death of a Raven (F.A. Shannon Thalman, Danielle Thalman, Jim Ablao, June 22, 2007)

39. Barred Reality (F.A. Ryan Lawson, Alan Watts, September 26, 1999)

40. South Buttress (F.R.A. Alan Watts, free solo, 1981)

40a. South Buttress original start (F.A. Bruce Watson, Brian Watson, Charles Cunningham, 1970)

41. Walking on Broken Glass (F.A. Ron Vickrey, Bill Soule, 1996)

42. Short Sharp Shock (F.A. Bill Soule, Jay Wells, 1996)

43. Under the Gun (F.A. Bill Soule, Ron Vickrey, 1996)

44. The Cave Route (F.A. first two pitches, Jim and Jerry Ramsey, 1960; F.A. to summit, Ted Davis, Jon Marshall, 1963; R.B. first pitch, unknown, 1990s)

45. North Face Traverse (F.A. unknown, 1960s)

45a. Tail Direct (F.R.A. Alan Watts, free solo, 1981)

46. Living Blindly (F.A. the *Tail* via the *Opossum,* Ted Davis, Don Chattin, 1963; F.A. entire route, Ryan Lawson, October 1999)

46a. Blind Opossum (F.A. unknown, 1960s; R.B. Ryan Lawson, October 1999)

47. Diagonal Crack (F.A. Jim Ramsey, Jerry Ramsey, 1960)

48. Dogfight Crack (F.A. Jeff Thomas, Doug Phillips, November 16, 1974)

49. Mini Half Dome (F.A. unknown, 1960s)

50. Spankies Quest for the Nectar Hole (F.A. T.R. Ryan Lawson, September 1997; F.F.A. Thomas Emde, summer 1999)

51. Tuff Shit (F.A. Thomas Emde, Ryan Lawson, March 1999)

52. My Name is Mud (F.A.) Ryan Lawson, Holly Beck, November 1999)

53. Xenophobe (F.A. Ryan Lawson, November 1999

54. The Wormhole (F.A. unknown, 1960s)

55. Kid-Packed Mini-Van from Hell (F.A. Tom Egan, Ryan Lawson, Thomas Emde, Michael Richter, November 1999)

56. Undying Spite (F.A. Ryan Lawson, June 1999)

57. Lusty Lady (F.A. Ryan Lawson, Holly Beck, October 1999)

57a. Carla the Stripper (F.A. Ryan Lawson, Thomas Emde, March 1999)

58. Blacklisted (F.A. Ryan Lawson, Alan Watts, September 1999)

59. Truth Assassin (F.A. Ryan Lawson, July 3, 1999)

60. Project (Prep. unknown, 2000)

61. Project (Prep. Ryan Lawson, 2000)

62. Climb Like A Bomb (Prep. Adam Grosowsky, fall 1999; F.A. Michael Stöger, September 20, 2006)

63. Project (Prep. Ryan Lawson, 2000; F.A. Michael Stöger, 2006)

64. Project (Prep. Adam Grosowsky, fall 1999)

65. Project (Prep. Adam Grosowsky, fall 1999)

66. Project (Prep. Adam Grosowsky, fall 1999)

67. Jacobs-Strain Line (Prep. Adam Grosowsky, fall 1999; F.F.A. David Jacobs-Strain, 2000)

68. Project (Prep. Adam Grosowsky, 2000)

69. Rampage (F.A. Ryan Lawson, 1999; F.F.A. David Jacob-Strain, 2000)

70. Marsupial Madness (F.A. Thomas Emde, Ryan Lawson, March 1999)

71. Edge of the World (F.A. Ryan Lawson, Thomas Emde, March 1999)

72. The Marsupials Traverse (F.A. Ryan Lawson, 2000)

73. Loose Hookers (F.A Tyler Adams, Brad Markle, June 25, 2005)

74. Delirium Tremens (F.A. Dave Jensen, 1970; F.F.A. Del Young, summer 1972)

75. Blurred Vision (F.A. Tom Egan, Jeff Frizzell, January 1989)

76. South Side (F.A. Clark Shelk, spring 1994)

77. Airstream (F.A. Clark Shelk, spring 1994)

78. North Wall (F.A. Kim Schmitz, Alan Amos, Jon Marshall, 1963; F.F.A. Alan Lester, Alan Watts, January 30, 1982)

79. North Ledges Traverse (F.A. Kim Schmitz, Alan Amos, Jon Marshall, 1963)

80. South Face (F.A. Eugene Dod, Gerald Bjorkman, 1964; F.F.A. unknown, 1980s)

81. Southwest Side (F.A. Jim Ramsey, Jerry Ramsey, 1961)

82. Challenger's Lost Pinnacle (F.A. Brian Holcomb, Greg Parsons, 1981)

82a. Challenger's Lost Pinnacle finish (F.A. Thomas Emde, Pete Keane, late 1990s)

83. Project (to low point, Ryan Lawson, 1999)

84. Solstice Slab (F.A. Eric Freden, Brian Baird, June 1983)

85. And Justice For All (F.A. Ryan Lawson, 2000)

86. Catfight Cracks (F.A. first pitch, Tom Rogers, Jack Barrar, September 26, 1970; F.A. entire route, Dean Fry, Jeff Thomas, September 30, 1972)

87. Bolts Anonymous (F.A. Greg [last name unknown], 1990s)

88. Deffenbaugh Flake (F.A. Mark Deffenbaugh, 2007)

89. C.L. Concerto (F.A. Dean Fry, Jack Barrar, September 13-14, 1972)

90. Santiam Highway Ledges (F.A. Bill Cummins, Jon Marshall, Jim Nieland, 1969; F.F.A. Jeff Thomas, Brian Holcomb, October 5, 1984)

91. The Scab (F.A. to highpoint, Vince Gonor, May 1999)

92. What? (F.A. Ryan Lawson, Brian Nelson, March 1998)

93. Where? (F.A. Ryan Lawson, Brian Nelson, March 1998)

94. Vombatus Ursinus (F.A. Ryan Lawson, Ryan Kerner, December 1998; F.F.A. Alan Watts, Ryan Lawson, fall 1999)

95. Green Gully (F.A. Jon Marshall, Carol Anderson, September 1967)

96. Birds in a Rut (F.A. Ryan Lawson, Darin Chadwick, February 1998)

96a. Birds in a Rut Variation (F.A. Tyler Adams, Josh Lagallo, 2007)

96b. Solo on the Scale (F.A. Ryan Lawson, free solo, February 1998)

97. Project–To Go Beyond (Prep. Ryan Lawson, February 1998)

98. Endless Weekend (F.A. Ryan Lawson, Brian Nelson, March 1998)

99. Whitecloud (F.A. Tom Rogers, Jack Barrar, April 10, 1971; F.F.A. Tom Rogers, Wayne Arrington, March 1972)

100. The Thumb (F.A. Ted Davis, Bill Cummins, Sue Davis, Willy Zeigler, 1964)

101. Project (Prep. John Rich, 1990s)

102. Wombat Chimney (F.A. Tyler Adams, Mark Deffenbaugh, 2007)

103. Lost Hardware Route (F.A. unknown, 1960s; F.F.A. Tom Rogers, Jack Barrar, M. Youngblood, John Sanborn, 1970)

104. Over the Hill (F.A. Jeff Thomas, Bill Thomas, Brian Holcomb, May 22, 1983)

105. The Far Side (F.A. Jeff Thomas, Brian Holcomb, September 6, 1984)

106. Disappearing Tower (F.A. unknown, 1960s)

107. Pocket Hold Route (F.A. unknown, 1960s)

108. Devil in Disguise (F.A. unknown, 1970s; F.F.A Thomas Emde, Ryan Lawson, fall 2000)

109. Cavity Search (F.A. Bill Soule, 1992)

110. Put Me in the Zoo (F.A. Bill Soule, 1992)

111. Covert Operations (F.A. Don Cossel, Grant Bailey, February 2001)

112. Ticks are for Kids (F.A. Don Cossel, Trevor Hostettler, February 2001)

113. Don's Dream (F.A. Don Cossel, February 2001)

114. North Side (F.A. Geodetic Survey Team, 1940s)

115. Spiral (F.A. Johnny Bissell, summer 1935)

115a. Direct Variation (F.A. Jim Ramsey, Bruce Hahn, 1963)

116. South Spiral (F.A. unknown, 1960s)

117. South Face (F.A. John Ohrenschall, C. Richards, 1957)

118. North Face (F.A. Dave Jensen, Jim Benham, 1963)

119. Pale Face (F.A. Brad Englund, solo, November 14, 1995)

120. South Buttress (F.A. Brad Englund, T.R. November 14, 1995)

121. Papoose, Southeast Ridge (F.A. Bruce Hahn, Jim Ramsey, 1962)

122. Little Big Horn (F.A. unknown, 1960s)

123. Little Finger (F.A. unknown, 1960s)

124. Index Finger (F.A. unknown, 1960s)

125. Tilted Slab (F.A. E. J. Zimmerman, Charlie Zimmerman, 1952)

126. Tilted Mud (F.A. Brad England, solo, June 26, 1995)

127. South Chimney (F.A. Ross Petrie, Dave Wagstaff, Bill Van Atta, March 1949)

128. North Chimney (F.A. Jeff Thomas, Brian Holcomb, May 1983)

CHAPTER 12:
BASALT RIMROCK

1. Lost in Montana (F.A. David Tvedt, Dee Tvedt, July 1994)

2. Laid-Back Screaming (F.A. David Tvedt, August 1994)

3. Soft Asylum (F.A. Jeff Frizzell, September 2, 1991)

4. Flicker Flash (F.A. free solo, Alan Watts, 1984)

5. Flash in the Pan (F.A. T.R. Alan Watts, 1984)

6. Lightning (F.A. T.R. Alan Watts, 1984)

7. Rambo Roof (F.A. T.R. Brooke Sandahl, spring 1986)

8. Project (Prep. Jeff Frizzell, fall 1991)

9. Greenhouse (F.A. Alan Watts, free solo, summer 1991)

10. Jersey Shore (F.R.A. Alan Watts, free solo, summer 1991)

10a. Rossi's Variation (F.R.A. Alan Watts, free solo, summer 1991)

11. Lean Cuisine (F.R.A. Alan Watts, summer 1991)

12. Little Wonder (F.R.A. Alan Watts, free solo, summer 1991)

13. Insulation Arête (F.A. Sam Elmore, David Sowerby, fall 2005)

14. Dave's Dihedral (F.A. David Sowerby, spring 2006)

15. Thumper (F.A. Wayne Arrington, mid-1970s)

16. Block Head (F.A. Wayne Arrington, mid-1970s)

17. Meat Grinder (F.A. Wayne Arrington, mid-1970s)

18. Llamas on the Lam (F.A. David Tvedt, Dee Tvedt, August 24, 1994)

19. Double Time (F.A. Wayne Arrington, mid-1970s)

20. Devil's Delight (F.A. Wayne Arrington, mid-1970s)

21. Swan Song (F.A Alan Watts, T.R. summer 1991)

22. Big Bad Wolf (F.A Alan Watts, T.R. summer 1991)

23. Microcosm (F.A. Dave Boltz, Jeff Alzner, September 1999; F.F.A. Ben Moon; September 26, 1999)

24. Jiminy Cricket (F.A. Wayne Arrington, mid-1970s)

25. Phantom (F.A. Wayne Arrington, mid-1970s)

26. A Little Twisted (F.A. David Tvedt, May 1994)

27. Handyman (F.A. Wayne Arrington, mid-1970s)

28. Run Spot Run (F.A. unknown, late-1990s)

29. Sweet Spot (F.A Alan Watts, T.R. summer 1991)

30. Pumpkin Patch (F.A. Alan Watts, free solo, summer 1991)

31. Jurassic Park (F.R.A. Keenan Tvedt, May 1994; B.R. unknown, mid-1990s)

32. Winnie the Pooh (F.R.A. Keenan Tvedt, May 1994)

33. Who Pudding (F.A. Alan Watts, free solo, summer 1991)

33a. Who Hash (F.A. Alan Watts, free solo, summer 1991)

34. Moni's Line (F.A. unknown, 1990s)

34a. It's All About Me (F.A. unknown, 1990s)

34b. Imra (F.A. unknown, 1990s)

35. Playing With Fire (F.A. Wayne Arrington, mid-1970s)

36. Burn Baby Burn (F.A. Wayne Arrington, mid-1970s)

37. Firestarter (F.A. Alan Watts, summer 1991)

38. Lifeguard (F.A. Wayne Arrington, mid-1970s)

39. Runaway Bunny (F.A. Alan Watts, T.R. 1984, F.A. lead, Michael Stöger, 2007)

40. If I Ran the Circus (F.A. unknown, 1970s)

41. Woman in the Meadow (F.A. Chip Brejc, Jeff Frizzell, July 1991)

42. Shredder Girl (F.A. Michael Stöger, 2005)

43. The Heathen (Prep. Jeff Frizzell, July 1991; F.F.A. Mark Huth, June 22, 1996)

44. Made in the Rain (F.A. Rio Rose, September 2002)

45. Shiva (F.A. Jeff Frizzell, July 1991; F.F.A. Mark Huth, May 22, 2000)

46. The Limbo (F.A. Bill Soule, 1993)

47. Dat Be Up Da Butt, Bob (F.A. Greg McRoberts, Drew McRoberts, May 1993)

48. Hang it Loose (F.A. Wayne Arrington, mid-1970s)

49. Lamoidian Power Dance (F.A. David Tvedt, August 3, 1994)

50. Morning Dew (F.A. Megan Tvedt, May 1994, B.R. unknown, mid-1990s)

51. Metamorphic Dawning (F.A. David Tvedt, May 24, 1994)

51a. Ledges (F.A. David Tvedt, Dee Tvedt, T.R. 1994)

52. Sidewinder (F.A. David Tvedt, November 28, 1999)

53. Jungle Fever (F.A. Jeff Frizzell, July 1991)

54. Torrid Zone (F.A. Jeff Frizzell, July 1991)

55. Havana Smack (F.A. Jeff Frizzell, July 1991, F.F.A. Mark Huth, September 6, 1993)

55a. Drill, Sarah, Drill (F.A. Michael Stöger, summer 2008)

56. Flower Power (F.A. Aaron Lish, 1997)

57. The Four Nymphs (F.A. Chip Brejc, Jeff Frizzell, July 1991)

58. Sidewalk Café (F.A. Chip Brejc, Jeff Frizzell, July 1991)

59. Spring Break (F.A. unknown, 1970s)

60. Flunked Out (F.A. unknown, 1970s)

61. Cram Session (F.A. unknown, 1970s)

61a Cram Variant (F.A. unknown, 2001)

62. Fist Fight (F.A. unknown, 1970s)

63. Frat Jerks (F.A. unknown, 1970s)

64. Bonfire (F.A. unknown, 1970s)

65. Passing Grade (F.A. unknown, 1970s)

66. Puppet Master (F.A. Alan Watts, T.R. summer 1991)

67. Pop Quiz (F.A. Ted Johnson, Catherine Freer, early 1980s)

68. Fight Song (F.A. unknown, 1970s)

68a. Sorority Girl (F.A. Michael Stöger, summer 2008)

69. Embryonic (F.A. Jeff Frizzell, Susan Price, September 1, 1991)

70. Drilling Zona (F.A. Jeff Frizzell, August 5, 1991)

70a. Project (Prep. Jeff Frizzell, summer 1991)

71. Class Dismissed (F.A. Alan Lester, 1983)

72. First Aid (F.A. Mike Volk, 1984)

73. Cardiac Fib (F.A. Chuck Buzzard, 1983)

74. Cardiac Kid (F.A. unknown, 1970s)

75. Gridlocked (F.A. unknown, 1960s; F.F.A. T.R. Ryan Lawson, June 1999; F.F.A. lead, Alan Watts, Tom Egan, October 10, 1999)

76. The Living End (F.A. unknown, 1970s)

77. Kindergarten Crack (F.A. unknown, 1970s)

78. Cheat Sheet (F.A. Chuck Buzzard, fall 1984)

79. The Fire Within (F.A. K.C. Baum, August 7, 1994)

80. School's Out (F.A. unknown, 1970s)

81. Chalkboard (F.A. Don Cossel, Ron Hampton, May 19, 1995)

82. Prom Night (F.A. unknown, 1970s)

83. Doorknob People (F.A. unknown, 1970s)

83a. Slam Dance (F.A. unknown, 1970s)

84. Rage (F.A. unknown, 1970s)

85. Dunce Cap (F.A. unknown, 1970s)

86. Boys Visit Charm School (F.A. Don Cossel, Tim Goodfellow, May 12, 1995)

87. Bad Manners (F.A. unknown, 1970s)

88. Panic Seizure (F.A. Alan Watts, summer 1985)

89. Little Black Sambo (F.A. unknown, 1970s)

90. Global Motion (F.R.A. Alan Watts, free solo, summer 1985)

91. Homecoming Queen (F.A. unknown, 1970s)

92. Silly Boy (F.A. Alan Lester, 1983)

93. Heart Throb (F.A. unknown, 1970s)

93a. Dancing Hearts (F.A. unknown, 1970s)

94. Dead Week (F.A. unknown, 1970s)

95. Theseus (F.A. Del Young, 1971)

96. Little Bo Peep (F.R.A. Alan Watts, T.R. summer 1991)

97. Deep Sleep (F.A. unknown, 1970s)

98. The Virgin Slayer (F.A. unknown, 1970s)

99. Labyrinth (F.A. unknown, 1970s)

100. Minotaur (F.A. Del Young, 1971)

101. Big Man on Campus (F.A. unknown, 1970s)

102. Astro Bunny (F.R.A. Alan Watts, T.R. summer 1991)

103. Block Party (F.R.A. Alan Watts, T.R. summer 1991)

104. Splash (F.R.A. Alan Watts, T.R. 1991)

105. Avant Garde (F.A. Alan Watts, T.R. 1991)

106. Graduation Day (F.R.A. Troy Longstroths, Don Cossel, 1995)

CHAPTER 13: THE LOWER GORGE

1. The Lonesome Crowded West (F.A. Mark Deffenbaugh, Chris Garner, May 11, 2004)

2. Edgewise (F.A. Bill Soule, 1993)

3. Little Orphan Jammies (F.A. Chuck Buzzard, Jerry Radant, January 1984)

4. Squeal and Peel (F.A. Chuck Buzzard, July 1984; F.F.A. Alan Watts, Mike Puddy, August 7, 1984)

6. Cretin's Retreat (F.A. to old anchor, Stu Stuller, Pete Pollard, 1981; F.A. entire route, Chuck Buzzard, 1983)

7. Oriface (F.A. Chuck Buzzard, Jerry Radant, January 1984)

8. The Ferret's Dead (F.A. Chuck Buzzard, John Rich, April 1984)

9. Cox Rocks (F.A. Wayne Arrington, Clay Cox 1974)

9. Three Fingered Hack (F.A. Tom Blust, Doug Phillips, 1981)

10. Hack Attack (F.A. T.R. Chuck Buzzard, 1985; F.F.A. uncompleted)

11. Vulture Crest (F.A. unknown, 1980s)

12. Terrorbonne (F.A. Chuck Buzzard, Jeff Turner, 1984)

13. Physical Abuse (F.A. Wayne Arrington, 1974)

14. Byrne's Revenge (F.A. Chuck Buzzard, fall 1985)

15. Mad Man (F.A. Wayne Arrington, Bob Ashworth, April 1973)

16. Wildfire (F.A. Paul Landrum, Ken Currens, March 1975)

17. La Vie Dansante (F.A. Chuck Buzzard, fall 1985)

18. Crime Wave (F.A. Alan Lester, 1983)

19. Gruff (F.A. Ken Currens, Paul Landrum, March 1975)

20. Rim Job (F.A. Jim Davis, Chris Grover, 1979)

21. Iron Cross (F.A. Alan Watts, Mike Puddy, October 6, 1983)

22. Neutral Zone (F.A. Alan Watts, Mike Puddy, October 5, 1983)

23. Organ Grinder (F.A. Jeff Thomas, Paul Fry, August 1975)

24. Badfinger (F.A. Todd Rentchler, Terry Schulz, June 1975)

25. Soft Touch (F.A. Alan Watts, Kent Benesch, October 28, 1983)

26. On the Road (F.A. Chris Grover, Jim Davis, 1980)

27. Edge of the Road (F.A. T.R. Alan Watts, March 31, 1984)

28. Titus (F.A. Wayne Arrington, Jack Barrar 1973)

29. Split Decision (F.A. Alan Watts, April 2, 1984)

30. Pure Palm (F.A. Alan Watts, April 2, 1984)
31. Cornercopia (F.A. Steve Byrne, Sean Olmstead, 1983)
32. The Caning (F.A. John Rich, spring 1997)
33. Teachers in Space (F.A. John Rich, 1986)
34. Bold Line (F.A. Chuck Buzzard, Graeme Aimeer, June 1983)
34a. Passover (F.A. Chuck Buzzard, June 1983)
35. Resuscitation (F.A. John Rich, October 1988)
36. Project (F.A. on aid, John Rich, 1988; F.F.A. uncompleted)
37. White Trash (F.A. John Rich, September, 1988)
37a. White Trash finish (F.A. John Rich, winter 1997)
38. Lion of Judah (F.A. T.R. Chuck Buzzard, August 1984; F.A. lead, John Rich, 1989)
38a. Judah Direct (F.A. T.R. Alan Watts, August 19, 1984; F.A. lead, unknown, 1990s)
39. Cry of the Poor (F.A. Chuck Buzzard, March 1984)
40. Just Say Yes (F.A. direct line, T.R. Alan Watts, September 15, 1984; F.A. regular route, John Rich, October 1988)
41. Out of Darkness (F.A. Chuck Buzzard, Pete Pollard, May 1984)
42. Try to Be Hip (F.A. John Rich, October 1988)
43. Jessie's Line (F.A. Chuck Buzzard, Alan Watts, June 1984)
44. Come to the Quiet (F.A. Chuck Buzzard, Jerry Radant, 1982)
45. On Eagles Wings (F.A. T.R. Chuck Buzzard, 1984; F.F.A. Alan Watts, Mike Puddy, August 13, 1984)
46. Seam of Dreams (F.A Chuck Buzzard, Steve Byrne, July 1984)
47. Flutter By (F.A. Chuck Buzzard, August 1984)
48. Send Your Clone (F.A. Chuck Buzzard, Steve Byrne, August 1983)
49. Boulderdash (F.A Chuck Buzzard, August 1983)
50. Project (F.A. T.R. Mark Deffenbaugh, September 2004)
51. Crossroads (F.A. Mark Deffenbaugh, September 2004)
52. Prometheus (F.A. Ken Currens, Paul Landrum, March 1975)
53. Northern Lights (F.A. Alan Watts, October 1, 1983; R.B. John Rich, 1988)
54. Last Chance (F.A. Chris Grover, Jim Davis, 1980)
55. Strike Force (F.A. Alan Watts, October 5, 1983)
56. Silent Holocaust (F.A. Chuck Buzzard, September 1983; F.F.A. Alan Watts, September 27, 1983)
57. Mid-Life Celebration (F.A. John Rich, Paul Marshall, November 7, 1999)
58. Diminishing Returns (F.A. Chuck Buzzard, October 1983)
59. Spiritual Warfare (F.A. Chuck Buzzard, Jerry Radant, October 1983)
60. The Pearl (F.A. Chuck Buzzard, Jerry Radant, October 1983)
61. Nuclear (F.A. John Rich, October 1987)
62. Full Court Press (F.A. John Rich, July 1988)
63. Baby Fit (F.A. John Rich, Mike Puddy, June 1988)
64. Pet Semetery (F.A. Ted Stahl, Brett Yost, 2003)
65. Bat Flake (F.A. Sean Olmstead, Steve Byrne, 1982)
66. Satan's Awaiting (F.A. Steve Byrne, Sean Olmstead, 1983)

67. Rising Star (F.A. Kent Benesch, Alan Watts, October 18, 1980)
68. White Dwarf (F.A. Alan Watts, Chris Grover, October 1, 1983)
69. Night Shift (F.A. Alan Watts, September 27, 1983)
70. Ground Zero (F.A. Alan Watts, May 1, 1982)
71. Quasar (F.A. Alan Watts, Alan Lester, October 11, 1980)
72. Erogenous Zone (F.A. Kent Benesch, Alan Watts, May 1, 1982)
73. Battle of the Bulge (F.A. Jeff Thomas, Del Young, Talbot Bielefeldt, February 1976)
74. Blood Clot (F.A. Jeff Thomas, Jack Callahan, January 1975)
75. Crack-a-no-go (F.A. T.R. Chris Jones, Bill Soule, 1978; F.F.A. T.R. Alan Watts, March 18, 1980; F.F.A. lead, Alan Watts, June 28, 1981)
76. Cruel Sister (F.A. Mike Seeley, Wayne Arrington, October 1974)
77. Child Abuse (F.A. T.R. Alan Watts, November 1, 1981; F.A. lead, Jeff Frizzell, Tom Egan, December 1988)
78. Taxtor (F.A. Wayne Arrington, Jack Barrar 1973)
79. Southern Cross (F.A. Pat Carr, Craig Benesch, 1983)
80. Harvest (F.A. Chuck Buzzard, Steve Mrazek, June 1984)
81. Grim Tales (F.A. Chuck Buzzard, Jerry Radant, August 1984)
82. Patent Leather Pump (F.A. Chuck Buzzard, June 1984)
83. Old and In the Way (F.A Chuck Buzzard, Jerry Radant, Jeff Frank, June 1984)
84. Father Mercy (F.A. Chuck Buzzard, Jeff Frank, July 1984)
85. Conversion Excursion (F.A. Chuck Buzzard, Jeff Turner, August 1984)
86. Bean Time (F.A. Chuck Buzzard, Jerry Radant, August 1984)
87. Lava Tube (F.A. Wayne Arrington, 1974)
88. Brain Death (F.A. Chuck Buzzard, T.R. August 8, 1984; F.F.A. Alan Watts, Mike Puddy, August 8, 1984)
89. On the Spot (F.A. Wayne Arrington, 1974)
90. Wasted Words (F.A. Wayne Arrington, 1974)
91. Lost Souls (F.A. Wayne Arrington, 1974)
92. Religious Fervor (F.A. Wayne Arrington, 1974)
93. Sitting Duck (F.A. Wayne Arrington, 1974)
94. Greasy Spoon (F.A. Ralph Moore, 1976)
95. Dire Wolf (F.A. Wayne Arrington, 1974)
96. Delicatessen (F.A. Tim Carpenter, Doug Phillips, 1976)
97. Fast Food Junky (F.A. Ralph Moore, 1976)
98. Phallic Symbol (F.A. Wayne Arrington, summer 1991)
99. Chimney of Ghouls (F.A. Wayne Arrington, 1974)
100. Old Trouble's Number Seven (F.A. Steve Mrazek, Chuck Buzzard, September 1984)
101. Pink Roadgrader (F.A. Chuck Buzzard, Steve Mrazek, September 1984)
102. Kneegobee (F.A. Chuck Buzzard, Steve Mrazek, September 1984)
103. Jenga (F.A. Wayne Arrington, 1974)
104. Left Wing (F.A. Mark Deffenbaugh, May 2004)
105. Last Days (F.A Chuck Buzzard, March 1984)
106. Levitate (F.A. Mark Deffenbaugh, Tyler Kamm, May 2004)

107. Turning Point (F.A. Chuck Buzzard, Eve Dearborn, March 1983)

108. St. Paddee's Day (F.A. Chuck Buzzard, March 1984)

109. Lethal Dose (F.A. Alan Watts, Sean Olmstead, September 30, 1983)

110. Mantra (F.A. Paul Landrum, John Zeneroski, March 1975)

111. Tantra (F.A. T.R. Mark Deffenbaugh, 2004)

112. Cry of the Gerbil (F.A. John Rich, 1986)

113. Dark Star (F.A. Alan Watts, Bill Ramsey, July 14, 1981)

114. Neutron Star (F.A. Alan Watts, November 1, 1981)

115. Jonny and the Melonheads (F.A. Alan Watts, July 20, 1984)

116. Morning Star (F.A. Paul Landrum, Ken Currens, March 1975)

117. Daytime Drama (F.A. Bill Soule, John Rich, 1993)

118. Night Crossing (F.A. Alan Watts, April 3, 1984)

119. Freon (F.A. Jeff Thomas, May 1974)

120. Whispers (F.A. Wayne Arrington, 1974)

121. Tree Route (F.A. Wayne Arrington, 1974)

122. Hand Jive (F.A. Wayne Arrington, 1974)

123. Herky Jerky (F.A. Wayne Arrington, December 1973)

124. Judas (F.A Chuck Buzzard, 1984)

125. Big Chimney (F.A. Wayne Arrington, 1974)

126. Masquerade (F.A. Alan Watts, Brooke Sandahl, May 8, 1984)

127. Bush Doctor (F.A. Brooke Sandahl, Alan Watts, April 13, 1984)

128. Razor Boy (F.A. Brooke Sandahl, Alan Watts, April 3, 1984)

129. Little Weenie (F.A. unknown, 1980s)

130. Runt's Grunt (F.A. unknown, 1980s)

131. Sawed Off Runt (F.A. unknown, 1980s)

132. Pipsqueak (F.A. unknown, 1980s)

133. Little Squirt (F.A. unknown, 1980s)

134. Dwarf's Delight (F.A. unknown, 1980s)

135. Short Man's Complex (F.A. unknown, 1980s)

136. Stunted Growth (F.A. unknown, 1980s)

137. Napoleon Complex (F.A. T.R. Alan Watts, August 1991; F.A. lead, unknown, 1990s)

138. Short Stuff (F.A. T.R. Alan Watts, August 1991; F.A. lead, unknown, 1990s)

139. Punk Kid (F.A. T.R. Alan Watts, August 1991)

140. Emmaus (F.A. unknown, 1970s)

141. Zealot (F.A. Chuck Buzzard, 1985)

142. Midnight Creeper (F.A. Jeff Thomas, Cindy Jones, March 1976)

142a. Jeepers Creepers (F.A. Jeff Thomas, Doug Phillips, mid-1970s)

143. Across the Water (F.A. Jeff Thomas, Bob Grundy, 1974)

144. Margo's Madness (F.A. Chuck Buzzard, Jerry Radant, January 1984)

145. Fool's Pleasure (F.A. Chuck Buzzard, Jeff Turner, November 1983)

146. Llama Momma (F.A. Chuck Buzzard, Jeff Turner, December 1984)

147. Baby Walks (F.A. first pitch, Chuck Buzzard, March 1982; F.A. entire route, Jerry Radant, Chuck Buzzard, January 1984)

148. Windfall (F.A. Chuck Buzzard, Jerry Radant, March 1984)

149. Hard Attack (F.A. Chuck Buzzard, March 1984)

150. The Sheepgate (F.A. unknown, 1980s)

151. Wave of Mutilation (F.A. Jim Davis, John Rich, May 1997)

152. Mister Reach (F.A. John Rich, Chuck Buzzard, 1985)

153. Bridge of Sighs (F.A. Chuck Buzzard, January 1984)

154. Genocide (F.A. Chuck Buzzard, November 1983)

155. Left Gnarly Crack (F.A. T.R. Ryan Lawson, June 1999)

156. Right Gnarly Crack (F.A. T.R. Ryan Lawson, June 1999)

157. Swallowed (F.A. Ryan Lawson, June 1998)

158. Dink (F.R.A. Alan Watts, free solo, 1991)

159. Quickie (F.A. Ryan Lawson, June 1998)

160. My Friend of Misery (F.A. lower part, Ryan Lawson, June 1998; F.A. finish, uncompleted)

161. Independence Day (F.A. Ryan Lawson, Brian Nelson, July 4, 1998)

162. Lost and Found (F.A. unknown, 1980s)

163. Huckleberry Hound (F.A. unknown, 1980s)

164. Gagged and Bound (F.A. unknown, 1980s)

165. Lube Me Up, Scotty (F.A. Ryan Lawson, June 1998)

166. Into White (F.A. free solo, Chuck Buzzard, November 1983)

167. Strawberry Blonde (F.A. Steve Mrazek, September 1985)

168. Demander Cody (F.A. Chuck Buzzard, Jerry Radant, March 1982)

169. Mines of Moria (F.A. Wayne Arrington, 1975)

170. Cody's Corner (F.A. Chuck Buzzard, Jerry Radant, March 1982)

171. McKenzie's Way (F.A. Chuck Buzzard, Jerry Radant, April 1984)

172. Killer Jism (F.A. Steve Mrazek, Chuck Buzzard, August 1985)

173. Ugly as Sin (F.A. Chuck Buzzard, Jerry Radant, 1984)

174. Hand Job (F.A. Wayne Arrington, Tom Bauman, 1975)

175. Original Sin (F.A. Jeff Thomas, March 1976)

176. Blitzkrieg (F.A. Jeff Thomas, Bob Grundy, May 1974)

177. Blitzen (F.A. Alan Watts, summer 1991)

178. Crunch Time (F.A. Alan Watts, summer 1991)

179. Exiled Man (F.A. Alan Watts, summer 1991)

180. Brother's Child (F.A. Chuck Buzzard, December 1984)

181. Chimney Sweep (F.A. Wayne Arrington, 1974)

182. Master Loony (F.A. Chuck Buzzard, Jerry Radant, December 1984)

183. Loony Tunes (F.A. Chuck Buzzard, 1985)

184. Tuned Out (F.A. Wayne Arrington, 1974)

185. Stuffed Turkey (F..A. Wayne Arrington, 1974)

186. Off Tempo (F.A. Wayne Arrington, 1974)

187. Banana Split (F.A. Wayne Arrington, 1974)

188. Chimney Fire (F.A. Wayne Arrington, 1974)

189. Lucky Guy (F.A. Alan Watts, summer 1991)

190. Common Criminal (F.A. Wayne Arrington, 1974)

191. Banned for Life (F.A. Alan Watts, summer 1991)

192. Shackles and Chains (F.A. Wayne Arrington, 1974)

193. Sleeping Dog (F.A. Wayne Arrington, 1974)

194. Slasher (F.A. unknown, 1980s)

CHAPTER 14:
THE UPPER GORGE

22. Bangstick (F.A. Jeff Frizzell, March 26, 1992)
23. Shark Infested Waters (F.A. Tom Egan, October 1, 1989)
24. The Big Kill (F.A. Jeff Frizzell, March 14, 1992)
25. Screams and Whispers (F.A. Jeff Frizzell, December 15, 1991)
26. Brazilian Skies (F.A. Tom Egan, July 1989)
27. Red Lily Q (F.A. Jeff Frizzell, March 1992; F.F.A. unknown)
28. Persuasion (F.A. Tom Egan, June 1989)
29. Atlas Shrugged (F.A. Jeff Frizzell, Ted Stahl, 2002)
30. Slay the Dragon (F.A. Tom Egan, May 1989)
31. Rainbow's End (F.A. Tom Egan, May 1989)
32. Almost Something (F.A. Tom Egan, September 1989)
33. Empty-Headed Hound (F.A. Jeff Frizzell, Jim Hayes, spring 1999)
34. Dig Dig (F.A. Jeff Frizzell, Jim Hayes, spring 1999)
35. The Seep (F.A. Jeff Frizzell, February 17, 1992)
36. Formula One (F.A. Jeff Frizzell, Paul Marshall, spring 1999)
37. Racer X (F.A. Jeff Frizzell, Paul Marshall, November 5, 2000)
38. Sprint Car (F.A. Jeff Frizzell, Jim Hayes, spring 1999)
39. Talladega (F.A. Jeff Frizzell, spring 1999)
40. Black Orpheus (F.A. Jeff Frizzell, Paul Marshall, summer 1999)
41. Calliope (F.A. Jeff Frizzell, Tom Egan, October 2000)
42. Drepane (F.A. Jeff Frizzell, David Kessler, October 2000)
43. Six Hits of Sunshine (F.A. Jeff Frizzell, Paul Marshall, spring 1999)
44. Milky Way (F.A. T.R. Jeff Frizzell, John McDaniel, March 1992; F.A. lead, Jeff Frizzell, Jim Hayes, spring 1999)
44a. Milky Way start (F.A. T.R. Jeff Frizzell, John McDaniel, March 1992; F.A. lead, Jeff Frizzell, Jim Hayes, spring 1999)
45. Virtual Beach (F.A. John and Cyndee McDaniel, February 1992)
46. Spellbound (F.A. Tom Egan, Mark Larisch, March 1989)
47. Playing in Traffic (F.A. Tom Egan, October 1989)
48. Octane 96 (F.A. Jeff Frizzell, spring 2002)
49. Starkist (F.A. Tyler Schlicting, spring 2002)
50. Just Do It (F.A. Tom Egan, Jeff Frizzell, April 1989)
51. Mother Superior (Prep. John McDaniel, March 1992; F.A. Jeff Frizzell, 2002)
52. The Sign of the Priest (F.A. John and Cyndee McDaniel, March 1992)
53. Hail Mary (F.A. Jeff Frizzell, spring 2002)
54. Land of the Lost (F.A. Wayne Arrington, 1975)
55. Voodoo Child (F.A. Jeff Frizzell, 2001)
56. Second Pedestal Crack (F.A. Wayne Arrington, 1975)
57. Pedal to the Metal (F.R.A. Pete Whitson, Rusty Bard, summer 2003)
58. E-Type Jag (F.A. Jeff Frizzell, November 23, 1991)
58a. E-Type in Drag (F.A. unknown, 1992)
58b. E-Type Shag (F.A. Jeff Frizzell, Ted Stahl, 2001)
59. The Fifth Dimension (F.A. T.R. Jeff Frizzell, 2001)
60. Conflicted Goddess (F.A. Jeff Frizzell, Paul Marshall, 2002)
61. The Seventh Deadly Sin (F.A. Jeff Frizzell, Paul Marshall, 2002)

62. Peruvian Skies (F.A. Jeff Frizzell, August 15, 1991)
63. Blame It On Rio (F.A. John Rich, 1990)
64. Bushwhacker (F.A. John Rich, 1990)
65. Feminazis (F.A. Jeff Frizzell, March 8, 1992)
66. Tears For Tonya (aka Shut Up and Skate) (F.A. John Rich, 1993)
67. Tomb of Love (F.A. Jeff Frizzell, February 1991)
68. Hot Lava (F.A. Jeff Frizzell, May 1989)
69. Gapers on a Tangent (F.A. Jeff Frizzell, Tom Egan, November 28, 1990)
70. Naxis (F.A. Jeff Frizzell, February 1991)
71. Unique Monique (F.A. Jeff Frizzell, Alan Watts, March 16, 1991)
72. Up Country (F.A. T.R. Jeff Frizzell, October 1990, F.A. lead, Tom Egan, November 3, 1990)
73. Groove Cat (F.A. Jeff Frizzell, 2001)
74. Natural Art (F.A. Tom Egan, 1990)
75. Get That Feeling (F.A. John Rich, Tom Egan, 1990)
76. Isengard (F.A. Wayne Arrington, 1975)
77. First Pedestal Crack (F.A. Wayne Arrington, 1975)
78. Mordor (F.A. Wayne Arrington, 1975)
79. P.W. (F.A. T.R. Roy Presswood, summer 1990)
80. Larry (F.A. Jeff Frizzell, February 13, 1992)
81. Moe (F.A. Jeff Frizzell, February 9, 1992)
82. Squeeze Play (F.A. Pete Chamus, Tedd Whitson, fall 1990)
83. Curly (F.A. Jeff Frizzell, February 1, 1992)
84. Gondor (F.A. Wayne Arrington, 1975)
85. Predator (Prep. John McDaniel, July 1991; F.F.A. T.R. unknown)
86. Shelob's Lair (F.A. Wayne Arrington, 1974)

87. Easy For Some (F.A. John and Cyndee McDaniel, July 1991)
88. Huck Fin (F.A. Jeff Frizzell, 2001)
89. Chienne No More (F.A. T.R., Jeff Frizzell, 1990; F.A. lead, John and Cyndee McDaniel, July 1991)
89a. Always a Bitch (F.A. Jeff Frizzell, 2001)
90. Integrated Imaging (F.A. Tom Egan, Jeff Frizzell, March 1989)
91. Project (F.A. T.R. Jeff Frizzell, David Potter, 2000; F.F.A. uncompleted)
92. Mojomatic (F.A. Jeff Frizzell, Tom Egan, March 1989)
93. Animation (F.A. Tom Egan, Jeff Frizzell, February 1989)
94. Celibate Wives (F.A. Jeff Frizzell, Tom Egan, February 1989)
95. Hieroglyphics (F.A. Tom Egan, Jeff Frizzell, March 1989)
96. Blind Dogs Need Bones, Too (F.A. Mark Larisch, Tom Egan, Jeff Frizzell, March 1989)
97. Dances with Dogs (F.A. Cyndee and John McDaniel, July 1991)
98. This Dog Won't Hunt (F.A. Jeff Frizzell, 2001)
99. Sink the Sub (F.A. John Fup, summer 1990)
100. Pruning the Family Tree (F.A. Jeff Frizzell, February 16, 1992)
101. L.K. and Ruby May (F.A. Jeff Frizzell, 2001)
102. Forty Acres and a Mule (F.A. Jeff Frizzell, Lisa Rust, October 2000)
103. Kid'n Play (F.A. Kari McDaniel, John McDaniel, July 1991)
104. Cranking with Kari (F.A. T.R. Jeff Frizzell, 1991; F.A. lead, John McDaniel, Kari McDaniel, July 1991)

CHAPTER 15: BOULDERING

1. The Nose (F.A. Mike Adams, spring 1979)
1a. Nosed Out (F.A. Alan Watts, 1980)
1b. By a Nose (F.A. Alan Watts, 1980)
1c. Hard Nosed (F.A. Alan Watts, 1982)
2. Loose Lucy (F.A. Kent Benesch, 1982)
3. Black Dike (F.A. Alan Watts, 1982)
4. Kent's Big Day (F.A. Kent Benesch, 1981)
5. Take Me to the River (F.A. Alan Watts, 1980)
6. Trail Walking (F.A. unknown)
7. Oblong Lunge (F.A. Chris Jones, summer 1979)
8. Leach Lunge (F.A. Marcus Leach, summer 1979)
9. Oregon Trail (F.R.A. Chris Jones, summer 1979)
10. Thin Excuse (F.A. Alan Watts, 1980)
11. Original Roof (F.R.A. Mike Adams, spring 1979)
12. Adams' Roof (F.R.A. Mike Adams, spring 1979)
12a. Adams' Problem (F.A. Mike Adams, spring 1978)
13. Ballad of a Thin Man (F.A. Chris Jones, summer 1979)
13a. Leap of Faith (F.A. Alan Watts, 1982)
14. Roof Boulder Traverse (F.A. Alan Watts, 1982)
15. The Great Gazoo (F.A. Alan Watts, 1980)
16. Stone Age (F.A. Chris Jones, summer 1979)
17. Mr. Slate (F.A. Chris Jones, summer 1979)
18. Dino (F.A. Chris Jones, summer 1979)
19. Circus Lunge (F.A. Mike Adams, spring 1979)
20. Three Rings (F.A. Mike Adams, spring 1979)
21. Big Top (F.A. Mike Adams, spring 1979)
22. Dinosaur Mantel (F.A. Chris Jones, summer 1979)
22a. Dinosaur Bypass (F.A. Chris Jones, summer 1979)
23. Mantel Piece (F.A. Chris Jones, 1979)
24. Center Mantel (F.A. Chris Jones, 1979)
25. Original Mantel (F.A. Mike Adams, spring 1979)
26. Mantel Block Lip Traverse (F.A Alan Watts, 1982)
27. Buffalo Practice Rock (F.A. Dillon Bruzzano, 1998)
28. Pubic Direct Start (F.A. Brooke Sandahl, spring 1986)
29. River Face Crack (F.A. unknown)
30. Right Slab (F.A. unknown)
31. Left Slab (F.A. unknown)
32. Leaning Edge (F.A. unknown)
33. K+B Hand Traverse (F.A. unknown)
34. K+B Crack (F.A. unknown)
34a. (F.A. Chris Jones, summer 1979)
34b. (F.A. Alan Watts, summer 1979)
35. Sick Little Seam (F.A. Alan Watts, 1981)
36. Puke-a-lot-Wall Traverse (F.A. Alan Watts, 1981)
36a. Crux Bypass (F.A. Alan Watts, 1980)
37. Right Exit (F.A. Chris Jones, summer 1979)
38. Original Exit (F.A. unknown)
39. Jones Problem (F.A. Chris Jones, summer 1979)
39a. Keeping Up With the Joneses (F.A. Alan Watts, 1984)
40. Left Exit (F.A. Chris Jones, 1979)
40a. (F.A. Alan Watts, 1982)
40b. (F.A. Chris Jones, 1983)
41. Underdog (F.A. Alan Watts, 1982)
41a. Underdog Escape (F.A. Alan Watts, 1982)
42. Under Fire (F.A. Alan Watts, 1985)
43. Cop Out (F.A. unknown)
44. Drill Team (F.A. unknown)
45. First Timer (F.A. unknown)

46. Practice Slab (F.A. unknown)

46a. Slab Escape (F.A. unknown)

47. Lizard Problem (F.A. Chris Jones, summer 1979)

48. Faking It (F.A. unknown)

49. Making It (F.A. unknown)

50. Pocket Crack (F.A. unknown)

51. Practice Makes Perfect (F.A. Alan Watts, 1982)

52. Perfect Stranger (F.A. Alan Watts, 1982)

53. The Girdle Traverse (F.A. Michael Stöger, 2005)

54. King Tut (F.A. Chris Jones, summer 1979)

55. Pocket Hold Route (F.A. Chris Jones, summer 1979)

55a. (F.A. Alan Watts, 1983)

56. Cursed (F.A. Alan Watts, 1983)

56a. (F.A. Alan Watts, 1982)

57. Kid's in Action (F.A. unknown)

58. I Want My Mummy (F.A. Alan Watts, 1980)

58a. Mummy Variant (F.A. Alan Watts, 1980)

59. Where Boneheads Dare (Kent Benesch, 1982)

60. Where Boneheads Slam (F.A. Alan Watts, 1985)

61. Slack Jaw Traverse (F.A. Brooke Sandahl, 1985)

62. Lysergic Roof (F.A. Mel Johnson, 1980)

63. Just Say No (F.A. Alan Watts, 1980)

64. Heavenly Blue (F.A. Alan Watts, 1980

65. Morning Glory Wall Traverse (F.A. Alan Watts, 1982)

66. Roof Bypass (F.A. Chris Jones, summer 1979)

67. Tator Tots Direct (F.A. Chris Jones, summer 1979)

67a. Jones Route (F.A. Chris Jones, summer 1979)

67b. Original Line (Alan Watts, summer 1979)

68. Total Eclipse (F.A. Alan Watts, 1982)

68a. Sunshine Traverse (F.A. Alan Watts, 1980)

68b. Last Waltz Traverse (F.A. Alan Watts, 1982)

68c. Moonshine Traverse (F.A. Alan Watts, 1980)

69. Right Pockets (F.A. Alan Watts, 1984)

70. Center Pockets (F.A. Alan Watts, 1982)

70a. Center Right (F.A. Alan Watts, 1982)

71. Original Pockets (F.A. Chris Jones, summer 1979)

72. Hand Traverse (F.A. unknown)

72a. Traverse Variant (F.A. unknown)

72b. (F.A. Alan Watts, 1984)

73. Nasty Seam (F.A. Alan Watts, 1983)

74. Smokin' (F.A. Marcus Leach, 1979)

75. Molten Fingers (F.A. Marcus Leach, 1979)

76. Big Al's Arête (F.A Alan Watts, 1982)

77. Leach Reach (F.A. Marcus Leach, 1979)

77a. Leach Variant (F.A. Marcus Leach, 1979)

78. Go Fetch (F.A. Chris Jones, summer 1979)

79. Phi Slamma Grandma (F.A. Chris Jones, summer 1979)

80. The Overhanging Flake (F.A. Bill Ramsey, 1978)

80a. (F.A. Chris Jones, summer 1979)

81. Penny Pincher (F.A. Alan Watts, 1983)

82. Scar Tissue (F.A. Chris Jones, summer 1979)

82a. (F.A. Chris Jones, summer 1979)

83. Scarred for Life (F.A. Chris Jones, summer 1979)

83a. Nameless Variant (F.A. Alan Watts, 1982)

84. Little Friend (F.A. Alan Watts, 1982)

85. Toes of the Fisherman start (F.A. Chris Jones, summer 1979)

86. Testament Slab Traverse (F.A. unknown)

87. Combination Blocks Traverse (F.A. Alan Watts, 1982)

87a. Round Trip (F.A. Alan Watts, 1983)

87b. Extension (F.A. Alan Watts, 1982)

88. Butt-Scraping Traverse (F.A. Alan Watts, 1985)

88a. Around the Block (F.A. Alan Watts, 1985)

89. Private Trust start (F.A. Alan Watts, 1983)

90. Night All Day (F.A. Alan Watts, 1983)

91. Blue Sea Glass (F.A. Alan Watts, 1985)

92. Speck of Dust (F.A. Alan Watts, 1985)

93. Phoenix Problem (F.A. unknown)

94. The Undercling (F.A. unknown)

95. Ape Shit (F.A. Bill Ramsey, 1980)

96. Me and My Monkey (F.A. unknown)

96a. My Monkey and I (F.A. Alan Watts, 1980)

96b. My Monkey and Me (F.A. Alan Watts, 1980)

97. Spider Monkey (F.A. Alan Watts, 1980)

97a. Spider Variant (F.A. Alan Watts, 1980)

98. Monkey in the Middle (F.A. Bill Ramsey, 1980)

99. Monkey See, Monkey Do (F.A. Alan Watts, 1980)

100. Barrel of Monkeys (F.A. Alan Watts, 1980)

101. Monkey Lip Traverse (F.A. Michael Stöger, 2000s)

102. Jungle Gym (F.A. Alan Watts, 1980)

103. Red Boulder (F.A. Alan Watts, 1980)

104. Logan's Problem (F.A. Logan Carr, early 2000s)

105. Easy's Left Traverse (F.A Michael Stöger, 2007)

106. Easy's Right Traverse (F.A. Michael Stöger, 2007)

107. The Jug Route (F.R.A. Mike Adams, spring 1978)

107a. The Begin Down Under Problem (F.A. Chris Jones, summer 1979)

107b. (F.A. Chris Jones, summer 1979)

107c. (F.A. Chris Jones, summer 1979)

107d. (F.A. undone)

108. Red Clot (F.A. Mike Adams, spring 1979)

108a. (F.A. Chris Jones, summer 1979)

108b. (F.A. Chris Jones, summer 1979)

108c. (F.A. Chris Jones, summer 1979)

108d. (F.A. Chris Jones, summer 1979)

109. Red Herring (F.A. Mike Adams, spring 1979)

110. Red Eye (F.A. Mike Adams, spring 1979)

111. Red Clot Lip Traverse (F.A. Chris Jones, summer 1979)

112. Red Backside (F.A. Mike Adams, spring 1979)

112a. (F.A. Mike Adams, spring 1979)

113. Simple Simon (F.A. Mike Adams, spring 1979)

114. Blob Job (F.A. Mike Adams, spring 1979)

115. Fat Slob (F.A. Mike Adams, spring 1979)

116. Blobular (F.A. Mike Adams, spring 1979)

117. The Blob Traverse (F.A. Mike Adams, spring 1979)

118. Donini Traverse (F.A. Jim Donini, 1980)

119. Double-Dog Dare (F.A. Mike Adams, spring 1979)

120. Quick Tick (F.A. Mike Adams, spring 1979)

121. Red Spike (F.A. Mike Adams, 1978)

122. Crimson Tide (F.A. Alan Watts, 1981)

123. Better Dead than Red (F.A. Alan Watts, 1981)

124. Red Headed Stepchild (F.A. Mike Adams, spring 1979)

125. Money to Burn (F.A. unknown)

126. Fireplace Problem (F.A. unknown)

126a. Fire and Rain (F.A. unknown)

127. Light My Fire (F.A. unknown)

127a. (F.A. unknown)

127b. (F.A. Chris Jones, summer 1979)

128. Hot Spot (F.A. unknown)

129. Jones Traverse (F.A. Chris Jones, summer 1979)

130. Jones Mantel (F.A. Chris Jones, summer 1979)

131. The Leg Swing Traverse (F.A. Chris Jones, summer 1979)

132. The Begin Down Under Prow (F.A. Chris Jones, summer 1979)

133. Fire Nation (F.A. unknown)

134. Pioneer Traverse (F.A. unknown)

135. Native Son (F.A. unknown)

136. Old Timer (F.A. unknown)

137. Thomas No-Hands (F.A. Jeff Thomas, summer 1979)

138. River Rock Slab (F.A. unknown)

138a. (F.A. Chris Jones, summer 1979)

139. Lucky Charms (F.A. Chris Jones, summer 1979)

140. Magically Delicious (F.A. Chris Jones, summer 1979)

141. Adit Slab (F.A. Alan Watts, 1981)

142. Subtract It (F.A. Alan Watts, 1981)

143. Drift Mine (F.A. Alan Watts, 1981)

144. Adit Up (F.A. unknown)

145. Barnacle Bill (F.A. unknown)

146. Pacific Ocean Wall (F.A. unknown)

147. Boogie Board (F.A. Chris Jones, summer 1979)

148. Seaside Ocean (F.A. Chris Jones, summer 1979)

149. Ebby's (F.A. Chris Jones, summer 1979)

150. Salt Water Taffy (F.A. Chris Jones, summer 1979)

151. Underhanded (F.A. Chris Jones, summer 1979)

152. Mike's Arête (F.A. Mike Adams, spring 1979)

153. Wild Man (F.A. Mike Adams, spring 1979)

154. Addams Family (F.A. Mike Adams, spring 1979)

155. Adams Apple (F.A. Mike Adams, spring 1979)

156. Alley Traverse (F.A. unknown)

156a. Alley Cat Traverse (F.A. unknown)

157. Alley Cat (F.A. unknown)

158. Indiana Jones (F.A. unknown)

159. Jonestown (F.A. through crux, Chris Jones, summer 1979; F.A. entire line, unknown)

160. Maple Slam (F.A. unknown)

161. Red Licorice (F.A. unknown)

162. Jonesing (F.A. Mike Adams, spring 1979)

163. Too Much Trouble (F.A. Chris Jones, summer 1979)

164. Pet Sounds (F.A. unknown)

165. The Wall (F.A. unknown)

166. Sticky Fingers (F.A. Chris Jones, summer 1979)

167. Abbey Road (F.A. Chris Jones, summer 1979)

168. Back in Black (F.A. Chris Jones, summer 1979)

169. Classic Column (F.A. Mike Adams, spring 1979)

170. Little Fella (F.A. Chris Jones, summer 1979)

171. Volk's Slab (F.A. Mike Volk, 1983)

172. Black Dog (F.A. unknown)

173. Sneeze Machine (F.A. Chris Jones, summer 1979)

174. Fella, Not a Wella (F.A. unknown)

175. South Corner Overhang (F.A. Chris Jones, summer 1979)

176. Preparation H (F.A. Chris Jones, summer 1979)

177. Right Butt Cheek (F.A. Chris Jones, summer 1979)

178. Emerald Face (F.A. Mike Adams, spring 1979)

178a. Emerald Edge (F.A. unknown)

179. Sapphire Wall (F.A. unknown)

179a. Sapphire Escape (F.A. Mike Adams, spring 1979)

180. Diamond Face (F.A. Mike Adams, spring 1979)

181. Jones' Jump (F.A. Chris Jones, summer 1979)

182. Gem Traverse (F.A. Chris Jones, summer 1979)

183. Yellow Brick Road (F.A. Alan Watts, 1982)

184. Delirium Traverse (F.A. unknown)

185. Burning Eyes Red (F.A. Alan Watts, 1982)

186. Sun Cottage (F.A. Alan Watts, 1982)

187. Bury the Egg (F.A. Alan Watts, 1982)

188. J-Bru (F.A. Alan Watts, 1982)

189. Delirium Jam (F.A. Mike Adams, spring 1979)

190. One Piece Truck (F.A. Alan Watts, 1982)

191. Backside Slab (F.A. Mike Volk, 1983)

192. Chimney Arête (F.A. unknown)

193. Sweet Home Alabama (F.A. Alan Watts, 1982)

194. Black Betty (F.A. unknown)

195. Whipping Post (F.A. Alan Watts, 1982)

196. Free Bird (F.A. Alan Watts, 1982)

197. Ramblin Man (F.A. Alan Watts, 1982)

198. Dixie Chicken (F.A. unknown)

199. Right Jugs (F.A. unknown)

200. Left Jugs (F.A. unknown)

201. The Apple Farm (F.A. Alan Watts, 1982)

202. One Humid Day (F.A. Alan Watts, 1982)

203. Bobby Eat Peaches (F.A. Alan Watts, 1982)

204. My Gravy's No Good (F.A. Alan Watts, 1982)

205. Choss Time (F.A. Alan Watts, 1982)

206. The Whale's Head (F.A. Chris Jones, summer 1979)

206a. (F.A. Chris Jones, summer 1979)

207. The Heathen Traverse (F.A. Michael Stöger, 2005)

208. Northstar (F.A. unknown)

209. Point Blank (F.A. unknown)

210. Point Pleasant (F.A. unknown)

211. The Sappy Traverse (F.A. Rio Rose, 2002)

212. The Coffin Problem (F.A. Rio Rose, 2002)

212a. Coffin Bypass (F.A. Rio Rose, 2002)

213. Rose Wall (F.A. Rio Rose, 2002)

213a. Rose Traverse (F.A. Rio Rose, 2002)

214. Feeling Sappy (F.A. Rio Rose, 2002)

215. Jizz Sap (F.A. Rio Rose, 2002)

216. A Pirate's Life For Me (F.A. Rio Rose, 2002)

217. Argh! (F.A. Rio Rose, 2002)

218. Pirate Traverse (F.A. Michael Stöger, 2006)

219. Basalt of the Earth (F.A. Rio Rose, 2002)

220. Basalt and Pepper (F.A. unknown)

221. Center Wall (F.A. Michael Stöger, 2006)

222. Basalt Arête (F.A. Rio Rose, 2002)

223. Left Wall (F.A. unknown)

224. Basalt Traverse (F.A. Michael Stöger, 2006)

225. Jughead (F.A. Jeff Frizzell, 1992)

226. Black Sheep (F.A. Jeff Frizzell, 1992)

227. Frizzell's Line (F.A. Jeff Frizzell, 1992)

228. Buckets of Rain (F.A. Jeff Frizzell, 1992)

229. Moonbeams (F.A. unknown)

230. To Be or Not to Bolt (F.A. Jeff Frizzell, 1992)

231. Off the Hook (F.A. unknown)

232. The Offset (F.A. Jeff Frizzell, 1992)

233. Ovaltine (F.A. Jeff Frizzell, 1992)

233a. Oval Direct (F.A. unknown)

234. Left Scoop (F.A. unknown)

235. Center Scoop (F.A. unknown)

236. Bivy Seam (F.A. unknown)

237. Right Scoop (F.A. unknown)

238. Bivy Wall Traverse (F.A. unknown)

239. One Hit Wonder (F.A. unknown)

240. Two to Tango (F.A. unknown)

241. Three-peat (F.A. unknown)

242. Final Four (F.A. unknown)

243. Five and Dime (F.A. unknown)

243a. Alternate Ending (F.A. unknown)

244. Six Feet Under (F.A. unknown)

245. Seven Dwarfs (F.A. unknown)

246. Eight Mile (F.A. unknown)

247. Revolution 9 (F.A. unknown)

247a. Nine Millimeter (F.A. unknown)

248. Ten Second Rule (F.A. unknown)

249. Eleventh Hour (F.A. unknown)

250. Twelve Angry Men (F.A. unknown)

251. Friday the 13th (F.A. Michael Stöger, 2007)

252. Fearless Fourteen (F.A. unknown)

252a. Fearless Variation (F.A. unknown)

253. Fifteen Minutes of Fame (F.A. unknown)

254. Sweet Sixteen (F.A. unknown)

255. She Was Just Seventeen (F.A. unknown)

256. The Stöger Traverse (F.A. Michael Stöger, 2006)

256a. Cliff Notes (F.A. unknown)

257. Waterfall Traverse (F.A. Michael Stöger, 2007)

258. Clear Cut (F.A. unknown)

259. Tree Hugger (F.A. unknown)

260. Skewer Problem (F.A. unknown)

261. Treebeard (F.A. unknown)

262. WTF? (F.A. Greg Garretson, 2007)

263. Sage Walk (F.A. Greg Garretson, 2007)

INDEX

ABOUT THE AUTHOR

Alan Watts grew up in Madras, Oregon, and started climbing at Smith Rock in 1975. Over two decades, he pioneered hundreds of first ascents, including some of the most difficult routes in the country. The style of climbing he developed at Smith Rock during the 1980s helped change the direction of the sport in the United States.

After graduating from the University of Oregon in 1987, he co-founded Entre Prises USA the following year. He wrote his first edition of this book in 1992 and received his master's degree from Portland State University in 2002. He lives in Bend, Oregon, with his wife and two children.

ACCESS: IT'S EVERYONE'S CONCERN

The Access Fund is a national nonprofit climbers' organization working to keep climbing areas open and conserve the climbing environment. Need help with a climbing related issue? Call us and please consider these principles when climbing.

- **ASPIRE TO CLIMB WITHOUT LEAVING A TRACE:** Especially in environmentally sensitive areas like caves. Chalk can be a significant impact. Pick up litter and leave trees and plants intact.
- **MAINTAIN A LOW PROFILE:** Minimize noise and yelling at the crag.
- **DISPOSE OF HUMAN WASTE PROPERLY:** Use toilets whenever possible. If toilets are not available, dig a "cat hole" at least six inches deep and 200 feet from any water, trails, campsites or the base of climbs. Always pack out toilet paper. Use a "poop tube" on big wall routes.
- **USE EXISTING TRAILS:** Cutting switchbacks causes erosion. When walking off-trail, tread lightly, especially in the desert on cryptogamic soils.
- **BE DISCRETE WITH FIXED ANCHORS:** Bolts are controversial and are not a convenience. Avoid placing unless they are absolutely necessary. Camouflage all anchors and remove unsightly slings from rappel stations.
- **RESPECT THE RULES:** Speak up when other climbers do not. Expect restrictions in designated wilderness areas, rock art sites and caves. Power drills are illegal in wilderness and all national parks.
- **PARK AND CAMP IN DESIGNATED AREAS:** Some climbing areas require a permit for overnight camping.
- **RESPECT PRIVATE PROPERTY:** Be courteous to landowners.
- **JOIN THE ACCESS FUND:** To become a member, make a tax-deductible donation of $35.

P.O. Box 17010
Boulder, CO 80308
303.545.6772

ACCESS FUND
your climbing future
www.accessfund.org